CAPITAL INVESTMENT & FINANCING: A PRACTICAL GUIDE TO FINANCIAL EVALUATION

CAPITAL INVESTMENT & FINANCING: A PRACTICAL GUIDE TO FINANCIAL EVALUATION

Christopher Agar

ELSEVIER
BUTTERWORTH
HEINEMANN

AMSTERDAM • BOSTON • HEIDELBERG • LONDON • NEW YORK • OXFORD
PARIS • SAN DIEGO • SAN FRANCISCO • SINGAPORE • SYDNEY • TOKYO

Elsevier Butterworth-Heinemann
Linacre House, Jordan Hill, Oxford OX2 8DP
30 Corporate Drive, Burlington, MA 01803

First published 2005

British Library Cataloguing in Publication Data
A catalogue record for this book is available from the British Library

Library of Congress Cataloguing in Publication Data
A catalogue record for this book is available from the Library of Congress

ISBN 0 7506 6532 7

For information on all Elsevier Butterworth-Heinemann publications visit our website at http://books.elsevier.com

Printed and bound in Great Britain

In memory of Carrie

CONTENTS

LIST OF EQUATIONS, EXAMPLES AND EXHIBITS

Equations

Chapter 1

Chapter 2

Chapter 3

Chapter 4

Appendix A

Appendix B1

Appendix B2

Examples

Chapter 1

Chapter 2

Chapter 3

Chapter 4

Appendix C

Example

Exhibits

Chapter 1

Exhibit

Chapter 4

Exhibit

Appendix C

Exhibit

PREFACE

This book discusses practical ways of carrying out a financial evaluation when making corporate capital investment, financing and financial risk management decisions that involve questions such as:

- What is the intrinsic value of a tangible asset, business, or company? What financial risks are associated with an investment, and how can these be identified and controlled? What should the purchase price and form of consideration be?
- What type of funding should be raised? What alternative forms of finance are possible? How are financial instruments priced? How will the risk for the financier affect the terms of any financing offer and agreement?
- How do the providers of debt, equity and other finance evaluate their investment, and what returns do they require? How can capital, and its associated risks, be managed by a company so as to maximise returns for its owners (shareholders)?

The practical application of established corporate finance theories and techniques is discussed in the context of capital investment (Chapter 1) and financing (raising and managing capital, so as to maximise returns and minimise risk for capital providers)(Chapters 2 to 4). These chapters are non-technical, written with the aim of guiding the reader through the subject matter fairly quickly (the Futures examples in Chapter 4 being an exception). More quantitative analysis is covered in technical Appendices that deal with traditional financial ratio analysis (A), techniques to price and value equity, bonds and derivatives or related instruments and investments (Forwards, Options, Real Options, Convertible Bonds)(B1 to B5), and lease finance (C). Over 100 Excel™ based examples are provided (with workings shown), and a detailed case study involving a fictional company is used to illustrate some of the techniques discussed (Appendices D1 to D6).

Only traditional theories about pricing the Cost of Equity and Options are discussed in any detail. Basic mathematics is involved, and the discussion goes no further than is needed in order to understand the background to a theory or technique. The book does not discuss (1) subjects involving more advanced mathematics, (2) subjects that are more relevant for financial institutions compared to a corporate, and (3) current market conditions or market evidence for the theories discussed.

All the methods and techniques are universal, although the examples given are UK focused (i.e. £ cash flows, UK financing instruments, risk for a UK based investor, and UK tax and accounting). Capital instruments and derivatives are based on UK markets; these will have comparables in other areas and be priced in the same way, although market conventions may differ.

I would like to thank Mike Cash and his colleagues at Butterworth-Heinemann for their patience and support.

Structure of *Capital Investment & Financing*

AREA	GENERAL TOPIC	SUBJECT	CHAPTER	APPENDICES *Technical*	APPENDICES *Case Study*
INVESTMENT					
Evaluation	Valuation	Discounted Cash Flows (DCF)	1	**A, B1**	**D4**
		Multiples			
		Real Options		**B4 - 5**	
	Structuring	Evaluating economic benefits		**B1**	**D1, D5**
FINANCING					
Evaluation	Funding	Loans	2	**A**	**D2**
		Straight Bonds		**B2**	
		Convertible Bonds		**B5**	
		Equity IPOs & Rights Issues			**D3**
		Warrants		**B5**	
	Financing	Leasing		**C**	
Implementation		Loan agreements			
Management	Long Term Capital	Debt refinancing	3		
		Dividends and Share Buybacks			
		Equity restructuring			
	Short Term Capital	Traditional Working Capital management			**D2**
		Trade Receivables Securitisations			
		Money Market Instruments			
	Financial Risk	Interest Rate Risk	4	**B3 - 5**	**D6**
		Currency Risk		**B4 - 5**	

Technical Appendices

A Financial Ratios
B1 Corporate DCF Valuation
B2 Straight Bond Pricing
B3 Forward Pricing
B4 Basic Option Pricing
B5 Option Pricing Applications
C Leasing

Case Study

D1 Management Buyout
D2 Bank lending review
D3 Initial Public Offering (IPO)
D4 Valuation
D5 Acquisition
D6 Short Term Interest Rate Futures hedging

The following subjects (that either involve fairly advanced mathematics or are not wholly relevant for a corporate borrower) are not discussed:

- Volatility and correlation measurement
- 'Value At Risk' and other risk models
- Portfolio / Investment management
- Derivatives not wholly relevant for a borrower (credit derivatives, stock index futures, asset swaps etc.)
- 'Exotic' options pricing
- Advanced derivative mathematics
- Credit risk measurement and modeling
- Interest rate models
- Option-embedded bonds (other than Convertibles)
- Insurance and operating risk
- Trading strategies
- Valuation of Intangible Assets

CAPITAL INVESTMENT & FINANCING

A Practical Guide to Financial Evaluation

1 CAPITAL INVESTMENT

INTRODUCTION

The Financial Evaluation of Capital Investment Decisions

A corporate investor should undertake a financial evaluation when deciding whether to invest in tangible assets (capital expenditure on plant, machinery, equipment and other fixed assets required to generate revenues and grow the business 'organically') or other businesses (acquisitions). The investor needs to ensure that it pays no more than a fair value to purchase the investment (and acquire ownership of economic benefits to be derived from the investment) and that financial gains for its owners (shareholders) are maximised.

The fair, or intrinsic, value of an asset, project or business can be determined by estimating the current value of expected future cash flows (net cash flows arising over the investment holding period and any sale proceeds), taking into account the risk that actual cash flows, in terms of amount and timing, differ to those initially expected at the date of valuation (risk, in this context, is traditionally defined as the variation, or volatility, of cash flows around the expected level). The investor's shareholders will require a higher return (in the form of income and a capital gain) if their capital is invested in assets and businesses with greater risk. Before committing capital, the investor should estimate the investment's intrinsic value, based on a reasonable forecast of future cash flows (taking into account the most likely scenarios) and an acceptable method of capturing relevant risk. Economic gains will arise for shareholders if the intrinsic value of the investment exceeds the cost of investment.

Financial evaluation is one part of the investment process, and contributes to the overall objective of managing risk (identified from 'Due Diligence' and other analysis) and maximising financial returns for the investor, based on a set of assumptions and expectations at the date of the investment transaction.

Chapter Contents

This chapter discusses financial evaluation in the context of investment decisions, with a focus on investment valuation (mainly Discounted Cash Flow and 'Real Options' approaches), structuring and evaluation techniques. Technical issues and practical examples can be found in the Appendices (A, B1, B4, B5, D1, D4 and D5).

CAPITAL EXPENDITURE ON TANGIBLE ASSETS

Investment Rationale

Capital provided to a company, and any equity generated internally (i.e. accumulated profits), should only be invested in assets if value is created for shareholders, when the value of economic benefits arising from the assets exceeds the cost of acquiring those benefits. Since capital is a limited resource, it should be allocated to those assets that maximise the value created (shareholders would invest elsewhere if a higher return, for the same level of risk, was available).

Estimating Value

The intrinsic value of an asset should be estimated using cash flows (receipts and payments are recognised as and when received or incurred) rather than profit (which reflects local accounting treatment and the normal policy of matching costs to revenues, and may involve estimation – for example, the amount of capital expenditure charged to profit via depreciation would partly reflect the investor's own estimate of the asset's expected economic life). Over the investment holding period, cash inflows from revenues and any sale proceeds should exceed cash outflows (including tax payments) by a sufficient amount to justify the initial expenditure (and any subsequent repairs and maintenance, or modification or enhancement, costs).

The relevant cash flows to be assessed are the total incremental, net after-tax cash flows that the investor expects to receive as a result of the expenditure. The evaluation should compare the investor's total net cash flows with and without the new investment; any change in cash flows arising on existing investments, as a result of the new investment, should be taken into account.

Cash flows should be stated in economically equivalent amounts at the date of valuation ('discounted' to their 'Present Value'). The decision to invest should only be taken if the asset or project has a positive 'Net Present Value' (NPV): the present value of all future net cash flows exceeds the cost of investment.

Discounting and NPV analysis are discussed in more detail in 'Discounting and Present Values' in Appendix B1 (an alternative measure, the Internal Rate of Return, is also discussed – 'Payback', which shows the number of years it takes to recover the cost of the investment from its cash flows, will not be discussed further, since it fails to capture the true economic value of an investment).

ACQUISITIONS – AN OVERVIEW

Introduction

Investment Rationale

In general, an investment in a separate business may allow the investor to:

- implement its growth strategy quicker and cheaper: revenue and cash flow growth via the acquisition of a controlling, majority shareholding in an existing business ('target') may be preferred to organic growth, or the building of the business from scratch[1];
- implement its growth strategy in stages: the acquisition of a minority shareholding may give the investor the option to expand by gaining full control when conditions are optimal (conversely, the investor can abandon the investment at a lower cost than for a majority acquisition, if it fails);
- share risks and resources with a co-investor via a Joint Venture: two or more parties may contribute assets, liabilities, services and other resources to a new venture, each taking an equity or partnership interest and sharing the risks and rewards proportionately, where, for example,
  - a one-off project is too large to undertake alone, or
  - access to each party's skills, resources and know-how is essential for the business;
- generate superior financial returns arising on an eventual sale (private equity investors or 'financial investors').

Structure of Investment

An interest in a business may, in general, be acquired by (1) subscribing for new shares, (2) purchasing existing shares, or (3) purchasing the underlying business and assets (consideration is paid to the investee company in the case of (1) and (3), and to an existing shareholder in the case of (2)). The choice will largely depend on tax, legal and accounting issues, the requirements of the investee company and its shareholders, and the structure that maximises economic benefits for the acquirer's shareholders.

1 The acquisition may be via 'Horizontal Integration' (where the target operates in the same business as the acquirer), 'Diversification' (the target operates in a different business), or 'Vertical Integration' (the target provides inputs to - a supplier - or receives output from the acquirer), with the aim of improving the acquirer's competitive advantage.

The degree of influence that the investor obtains over the financing and operating policies of the investee company will normally determine how it recognises the investment in its own financial statements. If a controlling shareholding is acquired, the acquirer should be able to consolidate the results, assets and liabilities of the target in full (before deducting the 'Minority Interest' in respect of any remaining target shareholders).

Financial Evaluation

The intrinsic value of the investment to the investor will reflect its assessment of the amount and timing of the investment cash flows and its perception of the associated risks. The investor will not want to pay more than this intrinsic value; it will also wish to minimise the risk that unexpected future expenditure will be required to maintain the value of the investment. Above all, the investor will want to ensure its shareholders benefit from the acquisition and that their returns are maximised (see Bruner (2004 p.36-51, p.108-113) for a discussion on various studies of acquisition returns). The acquisition of a majority shareholding will normally require payment of a 'control premium over and above the current market value per share for a minority holding in the target, effectively increasing the wealth of the target's selling shareholders at the expense of the acquirer's shareholders.

The Acquisition Process

All Companies

The transaction process for a majority acquisition is likely to involve the key stages shown in **Exhibit 1.1** (and action to be taken by the acquirer). Financial evaluation is just one part of the process (see ❸ and ❹).

Exhibit 1.1 Transaction Process for Majority Acquisition – Key Stages

❶ Identification of target:

- ensure the best strategic 'fit' (sector, stage in industry 'life-cycle', extent of geographic and product overlap, opportunity for market expansion, competitive position);
- assess the opportunity for future cost savings and other 'synergies';
- determine the post-acquisition integration issues (cultural fit, reorganisation costs, internal and financial control risks).

❷ Due diligence (using public information):

- assess management's track record and ability;
- identify the key business and operational risks.

❸ Valuation and pricing:
- analyse the historic financial statements;
- prepare financial forecasts under different scenarios;
- estimate the intrinsic value to the acquirer;
- determine the acquisition pricing range.

❹ Consideration, financing, structuring and impact analysis:
- determine the financial impact of cash and non-cash consideration;
- consider the ability to raise equity and debt finance;
- compare an acquisition of shares vs. the underlying business and assets;
- assess the impact on the financial statements;
- evaluate opportunities to minimise tax (arising from the acquisition and in the future).

❺ Formal offer:
- approach the target;
- agree to proceed (a non-binding 'Memorandum of Understanding', or 'Heads of Agreement', may be signed to acknowledge the key terms and the process to be followed).

❻ Further due diligence (using the target's internal information):
- agree procedures for inspecting documentation and management information (the target will usually require a confidentiality agreement to be signed);
- assess the extent of legal, tax, accounting, financial, operational, regulatory and other risks by holding discussions with management and analysing relevant management information and agreements / contracts.

❼ Reassessment following completion of due diligence:
- quantify risks and possible future liabilities, and adjust the offer price and/or provide for such uncertainties in the sale and purchase agreement.

❽ Negotiation of the sale and purchase agreement and formal completion:
- the consideration and terms of offer;
- the obligations of the acquirer and target;
- warranties and representations given to the acquirer concerning uncertainties unresolved from due diligence;
- conditions precedent required to be satisfied before formal completion;
- transfer of consideration and title to shares on completion.

Quoted or Public Companies

In addition, the acquirer must comply with any regulations or laws concerning the protection of shareholders. These are likely to include rules to prevent shareholders from being mistreated or misled, and rules to avoid the creation of a 'false market' in quoted shares (share trading based on rumour, misleading information, or private information). If the target of a majority acquisition (of voting equity shares) is a listed or unlisted public company (or, in some cases, a private company), resident in the UK, Channel Islands or the Isle of Man, the acquirer should comply with 'The City Code on Takeovers and Mergers' (issued by The Panel on Takeovers and Mergers); if the acquirer has shares listed on the London Stock Exchange, it would also need to comply with the Listing Rules (issued by the Financial Services Authority), which require notification and shareholder approval, depending on the size of the transaction.

Financial Due Diligence

The acquirer should determine (1) whether the target financial forecasts and valuation need to be adjusted due to new information obtained from the target's operating and financing agreements (for example, additional uncertainties or risks may only become apparent from a review of such arrangements), (2) whether there are additional costs not provided for in the financial statements that might arise from the target's past action or inaction (i.e. new liabilities), and (3) whether the operating and financing arrangements will be materially affected by a change of control of the target. Legal issues would need to be considered (beyond the scope of this book), such as litigation or a breach of company law, employee and management issues, health and safety, and environmental liabilities (see Collins and Murphy (1997)).

Some of the main financial issues to be addressed are shown in **Exhibit 1.2** (terms relating to debt agreements are discussed in Chapter 2):

Exhibit 1.2 Financial Due Diligence – Key Questions

❶ Share capital and financing arrangements

- What is the fully diluted equity capital after any existing rights of acquisition, subscription and conversion (of 'non-equity', such as preference shares) have been taken into account? What impact does an offer for ordinary shares have on such rights? *The acquirer needs to consider possible dilution of its shareholding, changes in existing shareholdings, and the rights of any investors to be bought out.*

- What agreement is in place between shareholders under a Shareholders' Agreement?

- What are the reasons for any change in equity capital over the last few years, and has there been full compliance with company law provisions regarding the giving of financial assistance for the acquisition of own shares and the purchase and redemption of capital?

- How will any target inter-company balances owed to or by the vendor be discharged on completion of the acquisition?

- What impact does the acquisition have on the terms of existing debt agreements? Is there a change of control clause likely to trigger a 'cross default'? *The acquirer needs to know the extent of any required re-financing on acquisition and whether a breach of agreement will arise.*

- To what extent can existing and future assets be used to secure additional debt finance? Do loan agreements contain 'negative pledge' clauses? *The acquirer may need to refinance existing loans if the agreements do not permit further security over assets to be given.*

- Have third parties or group companies provided guarantees for the target's debt? *Loan terms may need amendment if existing guarantors have a right to end their commitment.*

- What is the risk that debt facilities will have to be repaid early? Is a potential 'event of default' likely in the next 12 months?

❷ Financial statements, assets and liabilities

- Have the accounts been prepared in accordance with the relevant accounting standards?

- What adjustments are required to bring the target's accounting policies in line with the acquirer's?

- Are there any proposed changes to existing accounting standards that might materially impact the target in the future?

- Are any assets subject to existing charges or other encumbrances?

- Are assets legally owned (and fully insured)? What are the terms of any leases, and is there a change of control impact?

- Will the book value of any assets (fixed assets, trade debtors and stock) need to be reduced to their recoverable or realisable value?

- Have adequate provisions been made, and have all contingent liabilities been disclosed, for pensions, warranties, litigation, etc.?

- What exposure does the target have to off-balance sheet arrangements or associate and joint venture investments?

❸ Taxation

- Does the target have unused losses or other forms of tax relief that the acquirer will be able to gain access to?

- Are any previous tax computations subject to dispute, and what is the maximum liability arising?

- What impact does the departure of the target from the vendor's tax group have?

- Could any previous transactions be caught by anti-avoidance provisions?

❹ Risk management policies

- How exposed is the company to interest rate and currency risks, and what policy is adopted with respect to minimising, hedging or controlling such risks?

- How exposed is the company to operational risks?

❺ Adequacy of internal accounting systems

- What procedures and systems are in place for:
  - preventing and detecting the occurrence of fraudulent activities;
  - ensuring all revenues and costs are captured and recorded in the management information system;
  - reconciling external information to management information, and management information to the financial accounting records;
  - investigating actual vs. budgeted performance differences;
  - efficiently managing Working Capital (credit control policies, stock control systems, and cash flow forecasting);
  - controlling and authorising the level of capital expenditure?

Financial Evaluation

Corporate Investors

Mergers & Acquisitions

Shareholders of two companies may benefit from the commercial and financial advantages of combining their respective businesses together within a single corporate entity, where both businesses are under common control (a merger). Alternatively, shareholders of one company may benefit if that company obtains control of another company (majority acquisition) or acquires a shareholding that gives limited influence (minority acquisition); in both cases, the shareholders of the investee company may also benefit – in the case of majority acquisitions, where the acquirer should be prepared to pay a control premium, shareholders of the target company will benefit at the expense of the acquirer's shareholders.

Financial evaluation would focus on (1) establishing the intrinsic value of the investment to the acquirer, (2) determining the offer price, (3) evaluating how best to structure the investment so as to maximise benefits and minimise costs and risks, and (4) assessing future financing and investment requirements within the investee.

Joint Ventures

Joint Venture (JV) partners need to consider additional factors, including:

- the desired accounting and tax treatment;
- procedures for approving JV investments and other strategic decisions;
- procedures for operational management;
- a process for quantifying and meeting periodic funding requirements (i.e. preparation and approval of budgets and forecasts);
- the method of extracting profits;
- the provision of services from the JV partners to the JV entity;
- the extent of recourse to the JV partners for third party debt funding (guarantees and indemnities);
- protection for minority shareholders and a mechanism for resolving disputes and disagreements;
- exit arrangements, such as pre-emption rights (a selling shareholder must first offer its shares to other shareholders), 'piggy back' arrangements (an offer to one shareholder must also be made to another shareholder), and other agreements.

Financial Investors

The benefits for a financial investor, such as a private equity investor or venture capital provider, principally derive from investment income over a short to medium term holding period and a significant capital gain on exit (from a sale of its shareholding via a private trade sale or flotation). The longer term strategic benefits available to a corporate investor (rapid growth and synergies for a controlling acquisition, or the ability to step up an initial presence in a new market, in the case of a minority holding) would be less relevant.

Early stage companies, unable to service significant debt levels, can look to financial investors for equity and non-equity finance (which may have features linked to equity). Short term bank lending might still be possible, subject to extra security and proportional equity contributions being available. The increased risk for a start-up normally requires financing over several stages and a greater total financial return (as measured by the Internal Rate of Return, or 'IRR'). Staged financing grants the capital provider the option to expand or terminate the investment as and when performance or risk changes.

A financial investor would rely on a significant capital gain on exit, since income returns during the holding period would be less than its target return. By estimating the 'Equity Value' (see below) at the exit date, the investor can calculate the required holding on exit to achieve sufficient proceeds to generate the target return. Typically, the financial investor would evaluate and structure its investment by:

(1) preparing financial forecasts over the investment holding period in order to estimate (a) the amount of required funding and (b) the likely value of the business at the proposed exit date;

(2) estimating the maximum debt that the company can support, and establishing the maximum funding that other investors are prepared to provide and their desired shareholdings;

(3) assuming an initial investment (the remaining funding from 1(a) after deducting third party funding from (2)) in the form of equity and non-equity, and determining the resulting shareholding (based on valuations at each date);

(4) forecasting expected cash flows from the investment (income, redemption of non-equity, and equity proceeds on an exit);

(5) restructuring its investment so that the expected IRR of its investment cash flows is at the required level (non-equity may have to carry rights to convert into equity in order to obtain the target IRR);

(6) agreeing terms that encourage management to maximise profits, cash flows and the final exit value (rewarding) and minimise risk and the threat of bankruptcy (penalising).

➡ For an example of this approach, see Appendix D1.

CORPORATE VALUATION

Introduction

The fair value of a business can be estimated by:

- discounting all expected future net cash flows to their economically equivalent amounts (present values) at the valuation date, and aggregating them ('Discounted Cash Flow' or 'DCF' valuation);
- applying a multiple to a current accounting measure.

A business is a collection of net assets (including intangible assets), financed by the providers of capital: ordinary shareholders ('equity providers'), preference shareholders and other non-equity investors, and debt holders (bank lenders, bondholders, asset financiers / lessors, and holders of other interest-bearing securities). The value of the whole business (the 'Enterprise Value') represents the sum of individual value components (the fair value of each type of capital).

The Enterprise Value is estimated using cash flows and accounting measures that relate to the underlying business, net of any related tax (i.e. non-financing). The Equity Value, available for the equity providers, can be calculated by deducting from the Enterprise Value the market values of debt and non-equity capital instruments. Any surplus cash, that could be used to repay debt and non-equity without affecting operating or business cash flows, can be deducted from gross debt or added to the Equity Value. Similarly, other non-operating assets (which would not be reflected in the business cash flows or accounting measures used for the valuation) can be added in, at market value:

Market value of corporate bonds, bank loans, overdrafts	x	1.1
Leases (capitalised value)(discussed in Appendix C)	x	
Other interest bearing debt	x	
Less: surplus cash	(x)	
'Net debt'	x	
Preference shares and other non-equity capital	x	
Equity Value	x	
Enterprise Value	x	

Cash flows and accounting measures used in valuations include (see **Exhibit 1.3**):

- DCF valuation: 'Free Cash Flows to the Firm' ('FCF') (occasionally referred to hereafter as just 'Free Cash Flows') and 'Free Cash Flows to Equity' ('FCE');
- Multiples valuation: revenues, 'EBITDA' (Earnings Before Interest, Tax, Depreciation and Amortisation), 'EBIT' (Earnings Before Interest and Tax),

Profits attributable to ordinary shareholders (to give Earnings Per Share, or 'EPS'), Operating Capital (or 'Invested Capital'), and Equity Book Value.

Exhibit 1.3 Accounting Measures used in Valuations

£m

Profit & Loss

	1 Year
Revenues	**52.00**
Cost of sales (70% of revenues)	(36.40)
Gross Profit	15.60
Selling, General & Admin Expenses	(2.84)
'EBITDA'	**12.76**
Depreciation	(2.36)
'EBIT' (20% of revenues)	10.40
Interest Income (5% x average cash balance)	0.07
Interest Expense (7.25% x opening loan)	(0.44)
Profit Before Tax	10.04
Tax at 30% (see note)	(3.01)
Profit After Tax	7.03
Dividends on preference shares (10%)	(0.45)
Profit attributable to ordinary shareholders	**6.58**
Dividends on ordinary shares (20% payout)	(1.32)
Retained Profit	5.26

Cash Flow

	Year
EBITDA	12.76
Working capital investment	(0.10)
Fixed capital expenditures ('Capex')	(2.60)
less: tax on non-financial items	(3.12)
Free Cash Flows to the Firm ('FCF')	**6.94**
Net interest paid (after tax)	(0.25)
Repayment of debt principal	(2.00)
Dividends on preference shares	(0.45)
Free Cash Flows to Equity holders ('FCE')	4.24
Dividends on ordinary shares	(1.32)
Net cash flow	2.92

Balance Sheet

	Opening	*Closing*
Fixed assets (cost)	30.00	32.60
Accumulated depreciation	(2.00)	(4.36)
Tangible Fixed Assets	28.00	28.24
Stocks / inventories	0.50	0.70
Trade debtors / receivables	2.50	3.00
Gross current assets	3.00	3.70
Trade Creditors	(0.50)	(1.10)
Gross working capital	2.50	2.60
Invested Capital	**30.50**	**30.84**
Bank loan	6.00	4.00
Cash	0.00	2.92
Net Debt	6.00	1.08
Preference Share Capital	4.50	4.50
Debt & Non-equity	10.50	5.58
Ordinary Share Capital (£1)	18.00	18.00
Profit and Loss Account	2.00	7.26
Equity book value	20.00	25.26
Financial Capital	**30.50**	**30.84**

Note on tax:

Profit before tax	10.04
add back: depreciation	2.36
less: tax deductions for capex	(2.36)
Taxable profits	10.04
Tax at 30%	3.01
add back: net interest expense tax relief	0.11
Tax on non-financial items	3.12

FCF can be reconciled to another valuation measure, NOPAT. This represents Operating Profits less taxes paid thereon (= EBIT x (1 – tax rate) in this example). Since depreciation and non-finance taxes have already been deducted, to reconcile to FCF, Net New Investment is deducted (Working Capital investment + (capex – depreciation)):

Net Operating Profits After Tax ('NOPAT')	7.28
less: Net New Investment	(0.34)
Free Cash Flows to the Firm	6.94

To simplify matters (so that taxes paid on non-financing cash flows are simply EBIT x tax rate), it has been assumed that capex eligible for tax relief equals the annual depreciation charge ('tax depreciation'); this will not be the case in practice if tax relief is 'accelerated' – based on a reducing balance method, rather than the conventional straight line method for depreciation – as is currently the case, for example, in the UK.

Discounted Cash Flow Valuation

Enterprise Value

Discounting

As noted above, the DCF Enterprise Value is the intrinsic value to be shared between all providers of capital, being the aggregate of all future after-tax Free Cash Flows to the Firm, discounted to their Present Values (PV). Discounting reduces each cash flow by a 'discount factor' (cash flow x $[1 \div (1 + r)^n]$, where r is the effective discount rate for each period, and n the number of periods from the date of valuation to the date the relevant cash flow arises). This procedure recognises that a cash flow at time t + 1 is equivalent to a cash flow at time t (the PV), 'compounded' forward to t + 1 by the required rate of return (i.e. discounting is the opposite of compounding).

Example 1.1 Discounting

£m	Forecast Year 1	2	3	4	5
Required rate of return	9.89%	9.89%	9.89%	9.89%	9.89%
Discount factor	$\frac{1}{(1+9.89\%)^1}$ = 0.9100	$\frac{1}{(1+9.89\%)^2}$ = 0.8281	$\frac{1}{(1+9.89\%)^3}$ = 0.7536	$\frac{1}{(1+9.89\%)^4}$ = 0.6857	$\frac{1}{(1+9.89\%)^5}$ = 0.6240
	x	x	x	x	x
Free Cash Flows	3.68	3.86	4.05	4.25	4.47
	=	=	=	=	=
PV of Free Cash Flows	3.34	3.20	3.05	2.92	2.79

Equivalent cash flows at each date (PV plus required return)

	Time 0					
1	3.34	+ 9.89% = **3.68**				
2	3.20	+ 9.89% = 3.51	+ 9.89% = **3.86**			
3	3.05	+ 9.89% = 3.36	+ 9.89% = 3.69	+ 9.89% = **4.05**		
4	2.92	+ 9.89% = 3.21	+ 9.89% = 3.52	+ 9.89% = 3.87	+ 9.89% = **4.25**	
5	2.79	+ 9.89% = 3.06	+ 9.89% = 3.37	+ 9.89% = 3.70	+ 9.89% = 4.07	+ 9.89% = **4.47**
Total PV	15.30					

⇨ For further discussion on present values and discounting, see Appendix B1 (pages to 157 to 165).

The Discount Rate

The rate used to discount Free Cash Flows to the Firm should represent the average risk-adjusted return currently required by the providers of capital, weighted according to their respective market values (the 'Weighted Average Cost of Capital' or 'WACC'). The required return represents the 'opportunity cost' or rate of return that would be available on other investments of similar risk. If an investment is free of any risk, expected future cash flows would be received with certainty and the rate of return (risk free rate) would only compensate an investor for having funds tied up for the period. If an investment is risky, a risk premium must be added.

The adjustment for risk in the discount rate should reflect the uncertainty associated with the cash flows being valued. The WACC can be seen as a risk free rate plus a blended risk premium (the risk free rate would be equivalent to the return that could be obtained from an investment in government securities, where repayment of capital and interest is, in most cases, considered certain). In practice, the WACC is calculated by multiplying the rate of return required for each type of capital by its percentage contribution to total capital (using market values) and aggregating each weighted component.

Example 1.2 WACC

	Market Values		Required Rate of Return %	
	£m	%	Actual	Weighted
Short term debt and overdrafts	50	6.3	5.0[1]	0.3
Medium term debt	75	9.4	5.5[1]	0.5
Preference share capital	35	4.3	8.5	0.4
Ordinary share capital (equity)	640	80.0	11.0	8.8
Enterprise Value	800	100.0		WACC = 10.0

[1] The tax deductibility of interest payments is taken into account by reducing the required return by (1 – tax rate); the above rates are post-tax.

The required rate of return will depend on each capital provider's perception of the 'business risk' associated with the company's operating cash flows (how stable, predictable and volatile they are) and the 'financial risk' associated with the company's chosen financing policy (the uncertainty associated with interest, dividends and capital repayments). The rate of return for debt and non-equity is easier to estimate than the rate of return required by equity providers (the 'Cost of Equity'), which can be estimated using the Capital Asset Pricing Model.

Financial risk is greatest for shareholders, who rank behind debt and non-equity providers on insolvency due to failure of the company to meet its financial obligations: if a company cannot pay its debts, then shareholders lose the lot. Furthermore, whilst a borrower has a contractual commitment to pay periodic interest to debt holders, dividends need not be paid. Consequently, shareholders require a greater return than other capital providers for the extra risk.

As stated above, the discount rate should reflect the risk, as perceived by the investor, associated with the cash flows being valued. For example, if an acquirer is valuing a target that operates in another business sector with significantly different business risk, then using its own WACC could result in the target being under- or over-valued (the acquirer's WACC being more than or less than, respectively, the target's).

➡ For further discussion on the WACC and the Capital Asset Pricing Model ('CAPM'), see Appendix B1 (pages 166 to 177).

The Forecast Period

The DCF Enterprise Value is estimated by discounting cash flows arising over a forecast period, based on an explicit forecast of revenues, operating profits, capital investments, and other factors that determine value ('Value Drivers'). At the end of this period, the business will have a value ('Terminal Value' or 'Continuing Value'), based on cash flows expected over the 'Terminal Period'. The Enterprise Value, therefore, comprises two components: the PV of cash flows arising over the forecast period and the PV of the Terminal Value.

A full set of financial statements should be prepared for each year of the forecast period, since, although cash flows are being valued, the capital structure should be reviewed to ensure the assumptions underlying the WACC calculation are valid (detailed, integrated financial statements are also useful when evaluating the impact of acquiring another company).

The following factors should be considered when forecasting:

- **Value drivers** — The main factors that affect Free Cash Flows to the Firm and Enterprise Value are:
  - revenue size and growth rates;
  - operating profit and EBITDA margins;
  - investment in working capital and capital expenditure;
  - tax rates;
  - the WACC; and
  - the length of period during which new capital invested generates 'economic profits' (discussed in Appendix B1).

- **Revenues** — Revenues can be estimated by assuming:
  - a share of the expected accessible market ('top-down');
  - unit sales and prices (building revenues 'bottom-up'); or
  - current revenues (adjusted for abnormal conditions) grow at stated annual rates.

  The estimation method will depend, in part, on the type and maturity of the business, the level of competition and the volatility of prices.

- **Operating profits and costs** — Assumed gross and operating profit margins can be used to determine cost of sales and other operating costs. Alternatively, costs can be analysed by type. Some costs will vary directly with sales (e.g. direct cost of sales, sales commissions, royalties), while others will be fixed (e.g. head office costs, R&D).

For early stage, high growth businesses the fixed cost base is likely to be fairly high, since upfront costs will be needed to support rapid future sales growth (e.g. product development costs, marketing, advertising). For more mature companies, costs can be based on assumed growth rates (fixed costs) and a percentage of revenues (variable costs). The 'operating leverage' (the sensitivity of operating profits to changes in revenues) can indicate the extent to which operating costs are fixed. A more accurate estimate of the fixed vs. variable cost relationship may be obtained by using 'linear regression' and other statistical techniques.

- Capital investment — The amount of capital expenditure and ongoing running or replacement costs for fixed assets needs to be estimated for the given level of forecast sales. High level estimates can be made by assuming capital expenditure varies with revenues or is at a level that results in year end fixed assets being an assumed multiple of revenues (fixed asset turnover ratio). Working Capital investment each period (the change in Working Capital) will depend on the assumptions made about trade credit offered to customers or by suppliers and stock / inventory levels (and can also be assumed to vary with revenues).

- Tax rates — The availability of tax losses and deductions for capital expenditure may defer payment of tax for a number of years. The effective tax rate to be applied to operating profits for the Free Cash Flow calculation will not be the same as the statutory rate during these years.

The Terminal Value

Although the ability to accurately forecast cash flows beyond a period of, say, 3 or 4 years is questionable, cash flow estimates need to be made for each year until, ideally, a 'steady state' is achieved (a 10 year forecast would be typical). At this point, when the business is fairly mature, growth rates and business ratios should be steady, and reasonable assumptions can be made for the Terminal period.

The forecast period may represent several stages of an industry life-cycle, characterised by (a) low sales, significant new business development costs (capital expenditures, marketing costs, etc.), tax losses and negative Free Cash Flows (development stage), (b) rapid sales growth, significant Working Capital investment, an increasing proportion of variable operating costs, and a move towards positive Free Cash Flows (growth stage), and, finally, (c) efforts to protect existing sales from competitive threats (increased marketing, R&D, and capital investment) and to expand via acquisitions (maturity stage).

The Terminal Value ('TV') will partly depend on operating performance in the final forecast year, and can be estimated by valuing a sustainable Free Cash Flow (perpetuity method) or measure of operating profit (multiple method) at the start of the terminal period, as follows:

- determine a sustainable Free Cash Flow for the first year in the Terminal Period (year 11, say), and calculate the present value in perpetuity, either with or without annual growth ('g'):

$$TV_{\text{end of yr10}} = \text{Year 11 Free Cash Flows} \div (\text{WACC} - g) \qquad \textbf{1.2}$$

- apply a valuation multiple to earnings or cash flows (for example, EBITDA multiples) – any growth would be factored into the choice of multiple and size:

$$TV_{\text{end of yr10}} = \text{Year 10 EBITDA} \times \text{EBITDA multiple} \qquad \textbf{1.3}$$

Both these approaches give an estimate of the Enterprise Value at the end of the forecast period, which can then be discounted back to the present value at the valuation date (the perpetuity method is preferred).

A significant proportion of the Enterprise Value may be due to the Terminal Value, particularly if there are negative Free Cash Flows during the early years of the forecast period. It is important, therefore, to ensure that Terminal Value assumptions are realistic and consistent with the expected competitive environment for a relatively mature business. Superior rates of return on capital may be possible during a high growth stage if a company has a competitive advantage, and this should attract new competitors. As price competition, excess capacity and product innovations reduce revenue growth rates and operating margins, so the returns on new capital invested should, in theory, reduce to a long term sustainable, equilibrium level (at or just above the WACC). By maturity, the value of the business should be enhanced by adopting a strategy of increasing operating cash flows from existing assets (by improving operational efficiencies, for example), increasing the market's expectations about future cash flow growth and rates of return, and minimising the WACC (by reducing risk, for example).

By the final year of the forecast period, the rates of return and growth should be at fairly sustainable levels:

- the Terminal Period Free Cash Flow perpetuity growth rate should not exceed the expected growth rate in the economy;
- the marginal return on new capital invested should be realistic, given that the business should be fairly mature by this stage and competition should have driven marginal returns down to sustainable levels.

➡ For further discussion on Terminal Values and rates of return, see Appendix B1 (pages 195 to 203).

Impact of Financing

Shareholders benefit from the effective tax saving that arises from the tax deductibility of debt interest. One method of capturing this effect is to reduce the Cost of Debt component in the WACC by the marginal tax rate (as in **Example 1.2**) when discounting Free Cash Flows to the Firm and estimating the Enterprise Value.

As the proportion of debt in the capital structure increases (higher leverage), the WACC should reduce as cheaper debt replaces more expensive equity: although the Cost of Equity increases due to the extra financial risk, the weighted Cost of Equity decreases by more than the increase in the weighted Cost of Debt. However, at some level of financial risk the WACC will increase as debt becomes more costly (the financial strain increases the required return for debt holders): the increase in the weighted Cost of Debt will exceed the decrease in the weighted Cost of Equity.

This suggests there may be some optimal leverage at which a company's WACC will be minimised and its Enterprise Value maximised (due to the lower discount rate). Capital investment can be financed in a manner that ensures the capital structure adjusts to, and remains at, this optimal level (to accelerate the transition, dividend payments or stock repurchases could be financed with debt or new equity). Hence the debt and equity mix assumed in the WACC estimate would normally be the long term target leverage for the company being valued (using market values rather than book values, which depend on accounting treatment and hence may vary), assuming new finance is raised at the optimal mix.

If a constant discount rate is being used, there is an implicit assumption that all components of the WACC, including the capital structure, are constant or change in a manner that leaves the WACC the same. For a private company, a constant capital structure implies a constant net debt / Enterprise Value ratio at each period end (this is illustrated in **Example 1.3** – since leverage determines the WACC, which determines the Enterprise Value, the calculation of net debt is circular).

Where projects are initially financed with high levels of debt or equity, then a constant capital structure assumption can be relaxed. In leveraged finance projects, for example, debt may be paid off in a manner that maximises the IRR for the equity investor; Free Cash Flows will be dedicated to debt service, and the capital structure may change quickly. In this case, the WACC would change as the capital structure and financial risk varied.

The WACC may also vary as the business matures. The level of business risk (as reflected in the asset 'beta' for a CAPM-derived Cost of Equity) should reduce as a company matures and growth rates reduce to sustainable levels. Financial risk should decrease as Free Cash Flows grow and debt is reduced to more manageable levels.

However, the overall impact of varying the WACC may be fairly immaterial, particularly if a large part of the Enterprise Value is derived from the Terminal Value, which would normally be calculated using a constant WACC. Using a constant WACC may be acceptable, therefore.

⇨ For further discussion on the capital structure, see Appendix B1 (pages 178 to 183).

Other Issues

- **Real v nominal cash flows** — Cash flows can be 'deflated' to real cash flows (divide each relevant annual cash flow by 1 + forecast inflation rate) and discounted back at a real discount rate[1]. In general,
  - Free Cash Flows and the discount rate should be either both nominal or both real;
  - a real WACC requires substitution of a real risk free rate in the WACC formula;
  - the Terminal Value, calculated using the perpetuity method, should be based on nominal Free Cash Flows, a nominal growth rate (which may be calculated using assumed real growth and inflation rates), and a nominal discount rate.

[1] The real rate can be estimated as follows:

$$\text{Real rate \%} = \left(\frac{1 + \text{nominal rate \%}}{1 + \text{inflation rate \%}} \right) - 1 \qquad \mathbf{1.4}$$

- **Mid year discounting** — It can be assumed that cash flows are received evenly throughout the year, rather than on the last day. In this case, the discount rates would be calculated using periods 0.5, 1.5, 2.5, etc., since, on average, cash flows will be received mid-year.

Equity Value

Estimating the Equity Value from the Enterprise Value

As already stated, the DCF Equity Value can be estimated by subtracting from the Enterprise Value the current market value of all debt and non-equity:

PV of forecast period Free Cash Flows to the Firm, discounted at the WACC	x
PV of Terminal Value, discounted at the WACC	x
Enterprise Value at start of forecast period (valuation date)	x
Add: market value of non-operating assets	x
Less: market value of gross debt (less: surplus cash and deposits) and non-equity	(x)
Equity Value	x

Estimating the Equity Value from Free Cash Flows to Equity

The DCF Equity Value can also be estimated by discounting Free Cash Flows to Equity at the 'geared' Cost of Equity (adjusted to reflect the level of financial risk).

Example 1.3 DCF Equity Value

The following 5 year cash flow forecast produces an Equity Value of £51.61m, either by discounting Free Cash Flows to the Firm at a 9.89% WACC or by discounting Free Cash Flows to Equity at a 11.10% geared Cost of Equity, calculating using the CAPM (both cash flows are assumed to grow at 4.0% in perpetuity during the Terminal Period):

£m		Forecast Year 1	2	3	4	5
Cash Flows						
EBITDA		11.41	11.98	12.58	13.21	13.87
less: capital expenditures		(5.25)	(5.51)	(5.79)	(6.08)	(6.38)
less: increase in working capital		(0.13)	(0.13)	(0.14)	(0.14)	(0.15)
less: taxes paid (excluding financing)		(2.36)	(2.48)	(2.60)	(2.73)	(2.87)
Free Cash Flows to the Firm (FCF)		**3.68**	**3.86**	**4.05**	**4.25**	**4.47**
Debt cash flows (after tax relief on interest - see below)		(0.11)	(0.12)	(0.14)	(0.15)	(0.16)
Free Cash Flows to Equity (FCE)		**3.56**	**3.73**	**3.92**	**4.11**	**4.30**
FCF discounted at 9.89% WACC						
Free Cash Flows to the Firm		3.68	3.86	4.05	4.25	4.47
Terminal Value [= 4.47 x (1 + 4%) / (9.89% - 4%)]						78.9
Discount Factor (post-tax WACC 9.89%)		0.9100	0.8281	0.7536	0.6857	0.6240
PV of cash flows today (total = Enterprise Value)	**64.51**	3.34	3.20	3.05	2.92	52.00
less: market value of debt at valuation date	(12.90)					
Equity Value	**51.61**					
FCE discounted at 11.10% geared Cost of Equity						
Equity Cash Flows		3.56	3.73	3.92	4.11	4.30
Terminal Value [= 4.30 x (1 + 4%) / (11.10% - 4%)]						63.09
Discount factor (11.10% geared cost of equity)		0.9001	0.8102	0.7293	0.6565	0.5909
PV of Equity Cash Flows (total = Equity Value)	**51.61**	3.21	3.03	2.86	2.70	39.83

Notes:

1. The above Free Cash Flows to the Firm and discount rates come from **Example B1.18** in Appendix B1 (Valuation Methods **I** and **II**). The Terminal Values are higher than in that example since they are based on a growing cash flow received in perpetuity, rather than the year 5 Invested Capital or Book Value of Equity, as in **Example B1.18**.
2. Debt has been set at a level that ensures the debt / Enterprise Value ratio (leverage ratio based on market values, where the book value of debt is assumed to be the market value) is a constant 20%. The Enterprise Value needs to be calculated as at each period:

£m	Forecast Year 0	1	2	3	4	5
Constant Leverage calculation						
Enterprise Value at year end (at 9.89% WACC)	64.51	67.22[1]	70.01	72.88	75.83	78.87
Debt ratio	20%	20%	20%	20%	20%	20%
Debt balance (constant market value proportion)	12.90	13.44	14.00	14.58	15.17	15.77

1 'Ex-div' value = (Value + Cash Flows) next year / (1+ WACC) = (70.01 + 3.86) / (1 + 9.89%) = 67.22

	Forecast Year				
	1	2	3	4	5
Debt funding / (principal repayments)	0.54	0.56	0.57	0.59	0.61
Interest at 7.25% x opening balance	(0.94)	(0.97)	(1.02)	(1.06)	(1.10)
Pre-tax capital cash flows to debt holders	(0.39)	(0.42)	(0.44)	(0.47)	(0.49)
Tax relief on interest	0.28	0.29	0.30	0.32	0.33
Debt servicing (post-tax)	(0.11)	(0.12)	(0.14)	(0.15)	(0.16)

3. The pre-tax Cost of Debt is 7.25% constant, and the tax rate is 30%. See **Example B1.15** in Appendix B1 for the WACC calculation.

The DCF Equity Value per share is the 'stand-alone' intrinsic value for a minority holding of quoted shares (some of the CAPM inputs, for the Cost of Equity estimate, relate to quoted prices that reflect a small holding of shares that give no influence or control over the company's policies). If the company is private, a 'non-marketability' or 'illiquidity' discount should be applied, as the shares will not be freely tradable and the lack of any liquid market will involve higher disposal costs and a lower sale price than for equivalent quoted shares. The size of the discount will vary (see Damodaran (2002 p.677 - 681) and Bruner (2004 p.462 - 465) for further discussion and market evidence for discounts). As discussed below in 'Acquisition Structuring & Evaluation', when assessing the intrinsic value of a company for a takeover, additional value arising from having control needs to be added in as well.

For other valuation methods, see Appendix B1 (pages 187 to 194).

Estimating the Equity Value using the Dividend Discount Model

A small shareholding may also be valued by discounting dividends. A shareholder's expected return (the Cost of Equity) can be used to value a stream of constant or growing dividend receipts received in perpetuity:

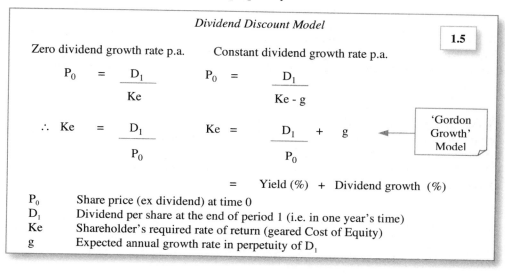

Dividend Discount Model

1.5

Zero dividend growth rate p.a.

$$P_0 = \frac{D_1}{Ke}$$

$$\therefore \; Ke = \frac{D_1}{P_0}$$

Constant dividend growth rate p.a.

$$P_0 = \frac{D_1}{Ke - g}$$

$$Ke = \frac{D_1}{P_0} + g$$

← 'Gordon Growth' Model

= Yield (%) + Dividend growth (%)

P_0 Share price (ex dividend) at time 0
D_1 Dividend per share at the end of period 1 (i.e. in one year's time)
Ke Shareholder's required rate of return (geared Cost of Equity)
g Expected annual growth rate in perpetuity of D_1

Alternatively, a cash flow forecast can be prepared and dividends discounted at the geared Cost of Equity (a dividend 'payout' ratio would need to be assumed). The valuations based on Free Cash Flows to Equity and dividends will be the same when (a) the dividend paid equals the Free Cash Flow to Equity each year (i.e. full payout), or (b) the dividend paid is less than the Free Cash Flow to Equity but the amount retained is reinvested to produce a return equal to the geared Cost of Equity (the reinvested dividends do not create any value for the shareholders).

Example 1.4 Dividend vs. Free Cash Flow to Equity Valuation

Using **Example 1.3**, if 50% of positive Free Cash Flows to Equity are paid out annually as a dividend, then, provided a return equal to the geared Cost of Equity is achieved on the reinvested equity, a similar Equity Value will result as when valuing the Free Cash Flows to Equity (i.e. assuming a 100% dividend payout):

		Forecast Year				
£m	**0**	**1**	**2**	**3**	**4**	**5**
PV of Equity Cash Flows	**51.61**	3.21	3.03	2.86	2.70	39.83
Free Cash Flows to Equity (FCE)		3.56	3.73	3.92	4.11	4.30
Dividends paid (50% payout ratio)		(1.78)	(1.87)	(1.96)	(2.05)	(2.15)
Equity cash flows reinvested at 11.10% required return		1.78	1.87	1.96	2.05	2.15
Return on opening equity investment			0.20	0.43	0.69	1.00
Equity investment		1.78	3.85	6.23	8.97	12.12
Dividends		1.78	1.87	1.96	2.05	2.15
Dividend Terminal Value [= 2.15 x (1 + 4%) / (11.10% - 4%)]						31.55
Discount factor (11.10% geared cost of equity)		0.9001	0.8102	0.7293	0.6565	0.5909
PV of dividends and reinvested equity	**25.804**	1.60	1.51	1.43	1.35	19.91
	50.0%					
Reinvested FCE over yrs 1 - 5						12.12
Reinvested FCE Terminal Value [= 50.0% x 4.30 x (1 + 4%) / (11.10% - 4%)]						31.55
Discount factor (11.10% geared cost of equity)		0.9001	0.8102	0.7293	0.6565	0.5909
PV of dividends and reinvested equity	**25.804**	0.00	0.00	0.00	0.00	25.80
	50.0%					
Total	**51.61**					

If the return on reinvested equity was less than the required return (11.1%), shareholders would have been worse off compared to a full payout (this is one reason why surplus cash is often returned to shareholders as a special dividend or via a repurchase, or 'buyback', of shares).

Valuing dividends directly using the Dividend Discount Model places too much emphasis on the dividend payout ratio, and can be distorted by special dividends and stock repurchases. Using Free Cash Flows to Equity may be preferred, although debt cash flows need to be explicitly modelled, compared to a valuation using Free Cash Flows to the Firm.

International Valuation

There are a number of issues to consider when valuing companies or businesses operating in foreign countries:

- Inflation & Exchange Rates — Which cash flows should be discounted and at what rate? Forecast foreign currency cash flows (nominal or real, adjusted for expected future local inflation) can be:
  - discounted at the foreign currency discount rate, and the PV translated into the home currency using the current 'spot' exchange rate; or
  - translated into home currency cash flows at the expected future spot exchange rates and then discounted at the home currency discount rate.

  In either case, nominal and real cash flows should be discounted using nominal and real discount rates, respectively. Possible approaches include the following:

1.6

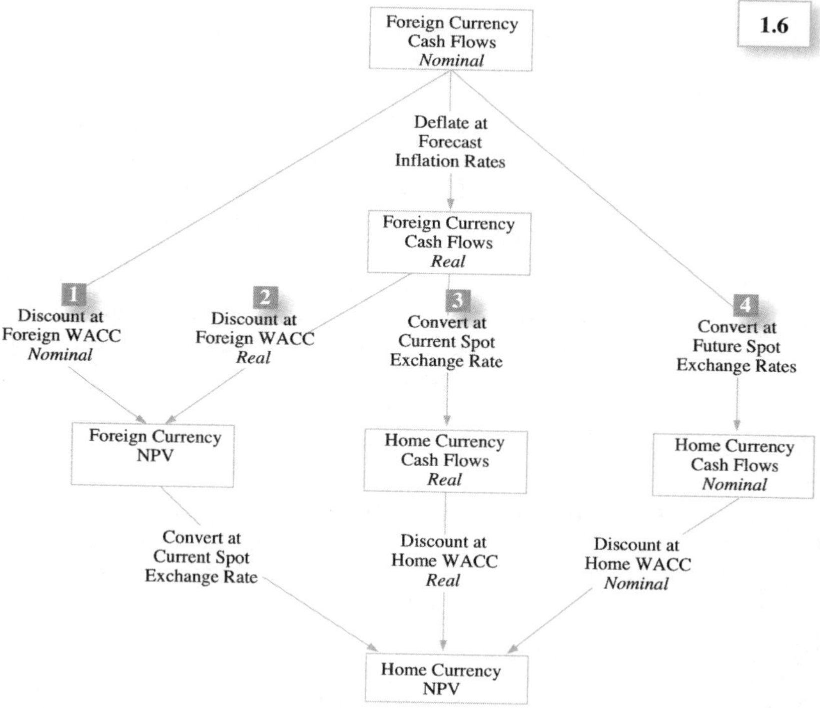

In **Example 1.5**, the same home currency PV is obtained, using the above four approaches, due to perfect parity conditions, where:

- the inflation differential determines the interest rate differential (the 'Fisher Effect'):

$$\frac{(1 + R_F)}{(1 + R_H)} = \frac{(1 + I_F)}{(1 + I_H)}$$

- the interest rate differential determines the change in the expected spot exchange rate ('International Fisher Effect'):

$$\frac{E_t}{E_{t-1}} = \frac{(1 + R_F)}{(1 + R_H)}$$

- the change in the spot exchange rate determines the risk premium differential (home and foreign based investors have the same perception of risk for the project and all other foreign risk can be diversified away):

$$\frac{P_F}{P_H} = \frac{E_t}{E_{t-1}}$$

Given these relationships, the real WACCs will be identical:

$$\frac{(1 + \text{nominal WACC}_F)}{(1 + I_F)} - 1 = \frac{(1 + \text{nominal WACC}_H)}{(1 + I_H)} - 1$$

where
- R_F R_H - Foreign and Home risk free rates at time t
- I_F I_H - Foreign and Home inflation rates at time t
- E_t E_{t-1} - Exchange rate at time t and t-1
- P_F P_H - Foreign and Home risk premium at time t

Forecast exchange rates can be estimated using analysts' consensus rates or forward exchange rates implied from the derivatives markets; if no such information is available, then it may be appropriate to assume parity conditions, where exchange rates move in line with inflation differentials.

Example1.5 International DCF Valuation with Parity conditions

	Assumptions		Forecast Year 0	1	2	3	4	5
HOME	Risk free rate	Assumed	5.00%	5.00%	5.00%	5.00%	5.00%	5.00%
	Inflation rate	Assumed	2.00%	2.00%	2.00%	2.00%	2.00%	2.00%
	Real risk free rate		2.94%	2.94%	2.94%	2.94%	2.94%	2.94%
	Risk premium		4.77%	4.74%	4.72%	4.70%	4.70%	4.70%
	Nominal WACC		9.77%	9.74%	9.72%	9.70%	9.70%	9.70%
	Real WACC (see **1.4**)		7.61%	7.59%	7.57%	7.55%	7.55%	7.55%

Assumptions		0	1	2	3	4	5
			Forecast Year				
FOREIGN							
Risk free rate		10.15%	10.66%	11.18%	11.69%	11.69%	11.69%
Inflation rate	Assumed	7.00%	7.50%	8.00%	8.50%	8.50%	8.50%
Real risk free rate		2.94%	2.94%	2.94%	2.94%	2.94%	2.94%
Risk premium	Assumed	5.00%	5.00%	5.00%	5.00%	5.00%	5.00%
Nominal WACC		15.15%	15.66%	16.18%	16.69%	16.69%	16.69%
Real WACC (see **1.4**)		7.61%	7.59%	7.57%	7.55%	7.55%	7.55%
Exchange rates (1.0 = home currency)		125.0 = 1.0	131.74	139.49	148.38	157.83	167.89
Nominal foreign currency cash flows	Assumed		500.0	800.0	1,245.0	1,710.0	2,120.0
Using foreign WACC							
Nominal foreign discount factor			0.8646	0.7442 (1)	0.6378	0.5465	0.4684
PV of nominal foreign currency cash flows		3,749.2	432.3	595.4	794.0	934.6	992.9
Translated at spot rate	1 **PV =**	**30.0**					
Inflation index (compounded)		*1.000*	*1.075*	*1.161* (2)	*1.260*	*1.367*	*1.483*
Real foreign currency cash flows (nominal / index)			465.1	689.1	988.3	1,251.1	1,429.6
Real foreign discount factor			0.9294	0.8640	0.8034	0.7470	0.6945
PV of real foreign currency cash flows		3,749.2	432.3	595.4	794.0	934.6	992.9
Translated at spot rate	2 **PV =**	**30.0**					
Using home WACC							
Nominal foreign currency cash flows ÷ forecast exchange rates			3.8	5.7	8.4	10.8	12.6
Nominal home discount factor			0.9112	0.8305	0.7570	0.6901	0.6291
	4 **PV =**	**30.0**	3.5	4.8	6.4	7.5	7.9
Real foreign currency cash flows ÷ spot exchange rate (125=1)			3.7	5.5	7.9	10.0	11.4
Real home discount factor			0.9294	0.8640	0.8034	0.7470	0.6945
	3 **PV =**	**30.0**	3.5	4.8	6.4	7.5	7.9

Workings for year 2:

(1) 1/((1 / 0.8646) x (1 + 16.18%)) = 0.7442

(2) 1.075 x (1+8.00%) = 1.161

- **Discount rate** — For a discussion on the discount rate to use for international investments, see Appendix B1 (pages 184 to 186).

- **Tax** — How should differences in tax rates be dealt with? Foreign currency Free Cash Flows should be net of local taxes. Where additional taxes are imposed on dividend remittances (withholding taxes), which cannot be recovered by the parent under the relevant tax provisions, then these should be taken into account.

- **Remittability of cash flows** — Should all foreign cash flows be valued or only those that are remittable to the UK? Where remittance of cash flows (via dividends, loan repayments, royalties, etc.) is subject to exchange control or other local government regulations, then only those cash flows that can be remitted should be valued.

- **Other political risks** — How should the risk of war, political disturbance or expropriation of assets be dealt with? Ideally, the cash flows should be adjusted to reflect these uncertainties, but, in practice, a risk premium may be added to the discount rate.

Valuing Real Options

Introduction

An investment decision is based on a set of assumptions made at the date of appraisal. Market conditions and other circumstances at a later date may not support these initial assumptions, and an investment initially considered unattractive may appear to be justified at a later date (and vice versa). Where a company acquires the right to alter, in response to changing future circumstances, the operations or scale of investment, at a known cost, then a 'Real Option' is said to exist. These options might allow the company to benefit from the right to participate in any unexpected improvement in market conditions (for example, by increasing the scale of operations) or the right to protect (hedge) against any unexpected deterioration (for example, by contracting or abandoning the project). Action would be taken if conditions at the future date made exercising the option commercially sensible; if no economic benefit would arise, no action would be taken and the Real Option would lapse.

The uncertainty of future cash flows can be modelled in a DCF framework, using sensitivity and scenario analysis, with probabilities assigned to each possible outcome in order to arrive at a single expected cash flow in each period. The resulting valuation would be based on expectations of future 'states', but would take no account of the investor's flexibility to change the nature of the investment and project if those future states did not arise. A Real Options approach values this flexibility using option pricing techniques developed in the financial options market.

Option valuation

Terminology

An option holder has the right (without an obligation) to buy ('Call' Option) or sell ('Put' Option) an asset at a certain price ('exercise' or 'strike' price) at some future specified date ('exercise date') before such a right expires ('expiry date'). The exercise date may be at any specified time before expiry ('American' option) or on expiry ('European' option). The price paid to acquire the option ('option premium') is the option's fair value.

Option Profit

A Call option should be exercised when the asset value at the exercise date exceeds the exercise price (pay-off on immediate sale = asset value – (exercise price + premium)), otherwise no action should be taken (maximum loss = premium). The reverse holds for a Put option (i.e. exercise when the asset can be sold at an exercise price higher than the true asset value).

Option Value

At any point in time, an option will have a value comprising two elements: (1) the value if exercised immediately: the difference between the asset value at that date ('S') and the exercise price ('X') (the 'Intrinsic Value', being max{0, S – X} for a Call Option and max {0, X – S} for a Put Option); and (2) the extra value (in present value terms) if exercised at a later date (the 'Time Value'), based on the probability of the asset value increasing (for a Call option) or decreasing (Put option) to above or below, respectively, the exercise price at the future date:

Option Premium (Value) = Intrinsic Value + Time Value

If an option has Intrinsic Value (an 'in-the-money' option) it may be beneficial to wait and exercise at a later date due to its Time Value. If an option has no Intrinsic Value ('out-of-the-money') it may still have some Time Value if there is some probability of the option going in-the-money at a future date; this probability will be greater the more volatile the asset value and the longer the time to exercise.

The option value should, therefore, depend, in part, on the current asset value and the exercise price (for the Intrinsic Value) and the volatility of the asset value and the time to exercise (for the Time Value). These factors can be built into financial models to predict future asset values. Option pricing models, generally:

- assume the behaviour of asset prices over time is governed by some probability distribution;
- forecast a range of possible asset prices at the future exercise dates, based on this distribution and an assumed degree of price volatility;
- isolate those asset prices at the exercise date where it would be optimal to exercise the option (i.e. where there is Intrinsic Value and no Time Value); and
- discount to present value the expected payoffs on exercise at those asset prices (weighted by the probability of occurrence).

➡ For further discussion on the two main pricing models for equity options (the Binomial Option Pricing Model and the Black-Scholes Model), see Appendix B4.

Factors Affecting Option Value

Option prices are determined by factors relating to the underlying asset (current price, volatility of the asset returns and the level of asset income), as well as the time to the expiry of the option and the risk free rate. For example, a Call option will increase in value due to the following factors (using the Black-Scholes model):

Pricing input	*Requirement for increase in Call option value*
• Asset value and exercise price	*The asset value increases above the exercise price.* The Intrinsic Value component of the option value increases as the asset value increases relative to the exercise price.
• Time to exercise date	*The time to exercise date increases.* Time Value increases to a maximum when the Intrinsic Value is zero (when the asset value is less than or equal to - 'at-the-money' - the exercise price). As time to exercise increases, so there are more opportunities for the option to become in-the-money at the exercise date; conversely, the Time Value reduces as the exercise date approaches.
• Volatility	*Volatility increases.* The higher the volatility, the greater the probability that the option will become in-the-money on exercise.
• Risk free rate	*The risk free rate increases.* The expected growth rate in the underlying asset value increase as rates increase.
• Dividends	*Dividends reduce or are not paid.* Dividends reduce the asset value (due to the cash outlay), reducing the Intrinsic Value.

Types of Real Option

Examples of Real Option investment decisions include the following (real and financial option types are shown):

- invest in a new plant that produces output with a significantly volatile sales price: if the investor could defer the investment until a future date at a fixed price (for example, by leasing the plant with an option to purchase it), it could monitor market conditions during the life of the option and decide whether or not to invest at the optimal time prior to expiry (Deferral / Call option);
- invest in a new plant with the option to invest again at a later date to increase the scale of production: the expansion would only be carried out if prices at the future date made it economically worthwhile (Expansion / Call option);
- invest in a new venture with the option to invest further in stages at subsequent dates: each investment phase creates an option to invest at a later date (Growth / Compound option - a series of Call options);
- cut back the scale of production in response to unexpected deteriorating market conditions: this represents a Put option, with an exercise price equivalent to the future costs avoided (Contraction / Put option);
- sell a plant for a known sum at some future date, when the project is aborted (Abandon / Put option).

➡ For further discussion on Real Option pricing, see Appendix B5.

Valuation Using Multiples

Introduction

A 'Trading Multiple' expresses a company's quoted share price as a multiple of some accounting or cash flow measure (see **Exhibit 1.4**), reflecting market conditions at that time and the fundamental performance of the company. A 'Transaction Multiple' would reflect the price paid by an acquirer to purchase a minority or majority holding of quoted or unquoted shares; any control premium (majority) or illiquidity discount (unquoted) would be reflected in the multiple.

The market's current implied valuation of a private company can be estimated using multiples for comparable quoted companies of similar risk. An average multiple, based on a sample of 'proxy' companies, adjusted for differences in business and financial risk (i.e. the same line of business, growth prospects, size and leverage), will give a 'relative' valuation of the private company. The resulting valuation should be adjusted to reflect the size of holding being valued (add the value of control - discussed in the next section - to a trading multiple valuation or remove a control premium from a transaction multiple valuation, as appropriate) and to ensure the multiple is for a private company (apply an illiquidity discount for quoted trading or transaction multiple valuations).

Exhibit 1.4 Main valuation multiples

Multiples	Period	Value
Price / Earnings Per Share (EPS) (P/E)	Last financial year / last four quarters, or next year.	Equity
Price / Equity Book Value per share (Price-to-Book)	Latest balance sheet.	Equity
Value / revenues	Last financial year / last four quarters, or next year.	Enterprise
Value / EBITDA	Last financial year / last four quarters, or next year.	Enterprise
Value / Free Cash Flow (Price-to-Cash Flow)	Last financial year / last four quarters, or next year.	Enterprise

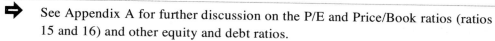

➡ See Appendix A for further discussion on the P/E and Price/Book ratios (ratios 15 and 16) and other equity and debt ratios.

General points to consider when using multiples for valuation purposes:

- multiples indicate relative valuation (compared to the sample of comparable companies) and not intrinsic valuation (DCF valuation);
- the riskiness associated with the financial measure is assumed to stay constant;

- the accounting measure may be negative (e.g. revenues for start-ups, cyclical businesses or distressed companies may be the only positive non-balance sheet measure);
- adjustments to the accounting measure may be needed to bring the target company's accounting policies in line with the acquirer's, and to ensure they are sustainable and 'normalised' (to remove the impact of one-off, non-recurring events);
- adjustments to earnings will be required to remove differences in leverage (which affects financial risk) and growth (see Arzac (2005 p. 71 – 76)).

The P/E Multiple

A Trading P/E for each proxy company can be calculated by dividing its share price (or an average price for a recent period, if there is short term market volatility) by the most recent actual EPS (to give a 'trailing' P/E) or the analysts' consensus expected EPS for the next period (to give a 'leading' P/E). The average sample P/E (after weighting each company accordingly) would then be applied to the EPS of the company being valued for the same accounting period. The resulting Equity Value per share would represent the estimated fair price for a minority holding of quoted shares, to which a discount for illiquidity would be applied for a private company; this private minority shareholding value would be increased to reflect the additional value of control when estimating the fair value of a private majority shareholding. Transaction P/E's for the acquisition of quoted majority shareholdings will reflect the actual premium paid over the minority market price - the control premium - which may reflect the value of control *and* any additional value from synergies (hence they should be used with caution for fair value estimation).

The sample of proxy companies can only provide a useful P/E for valuation if market prices are fair, risk and growth characteristics are similar, and underlying earnings are sustainable and comparable (and based on similar accounting policies). Operating profits are affected by business risks and growth factors (industry type, scale of operations, stage in life cycle, product and geographic diversification, cyclical factors, etc.); net profits are also affected by financial risk (leverage), due to interest and other finance charges. A relatively low P/E may indicate high risk and/or low growth expectations; conversely, a relatively high P/E could indicate that current earnings, when valued in perpetuity, account for a small part of the share price (the difference representing earnings growth expectations).

The EBITDA Multiple

If leverage varies across a sample of proxy companies, the use of EBITDA multiples avoids the need to adjust P/E ratios for financial risk, since the accounting measure is before interest costs. As for any multiple based on non-cash flow accounting measures that depend on accounting policy, adjustments may have to be made when making comparisons.

ACQUISITION STRUCTURING & EVALUATION

Introduction

If an investor obtains effective control over the financing and operating policies of another business (a takeover), it can control access to the underlying economic benefits (via dividends and other cash flow remittances) and ensure the business is optimally managed. Control would be achieved by acquiring a majority of the shareholder voting rights, leaving any remaining minority interest with little or no influence (under acquisition accounting, the acquirer would normally have to consolidate the results of the acquired business with its own, when preparing financial statements). A merger arises if two businesses are combined but neither set of shareholders controls the other (there is a genuine mutual sharing of the risks and rewards of the combined businesses).

In a majority acquisition, the acquirer would hope to create additional value, over and above the target's existing 'stand-alone' intrinsic value (or market price if quoted), due to (1) its control over the target's financing and investment decisions and (2) additional net cash inflows, and/or a reduction in the WACC, due to the business combination (synergies). The maximum purchase price will be the value to the acquirer (stand-alone value acquired plus the additional value of control and synergies). The acquirer's shareholders will benefit if the value to the acquirer exceeds the purchase price (value received exceeds value given); the target shareholders/vendors will benefit if the purchase price exceeds the stand-alone value (or the value to the vendor if different).

Purchase Price

Value to the Acquirer

Preliminary Strategic Review

The target's current business performance and growth prospects should be assessed in the context of the whole market (share of market, market demand growth trends, customer characteristics, differentiation vs. standardisation of product, risk of product substitutes and technological obsolescence, etc.) and the competition (price vs. quality, strengths and weaknesses of main competitors vs. the target, cost advantages, etc.).

The target's exposure to economic and political factors affecting all companies (market risk) and to factors that are unique to it and its sector (specific risk) should be evaluated.

Valuation

The acquirer should analyse the past performance of the target and prepare financial forecasts based on publicly available information and its own assessment of future revenue growth, margins, capital investment and resulting Free Cash Flows. The valuation will comprise three elements:

(1) *Stand-alone intrinsic value*: this can be estimated using a DCF valuation, or a weighted average of a DCF and multiples-based valuation, based on the existing business.

(2) *Value of control*: the acquirer may be able to generate additional value from its ability to control the investment and financing decisions of the target, by restructuring existing investments, businesses and assets (for example, by selling non-core businesses or surplus non-operating assets) and improving the management of debt and equity capital (as discussed in Chapter 3).

(3) *Synergies*: the business combination may create value due to:

- a reduction in costs, for example due to:
  - operating efficiencies arising from the sharing of techniques or capabilities;
  - 'economies of scale' due to an increase in the size of production (where fixed costs are spread over a greater number of units of output, reducing unit costs);
  - the elimination of duplicating functions;
  - lower input costs due to an increase in the acquirer's negotiating power with suppliers;
  - lower tax payments due to more efficient tax planning;
- an increase in revenues, for example due to 'economies of scope', where the target's unique capabilities can be used by the acquirer to enter new but related product lines; and
- a decrease in risk, reducing the WACC and increasing the value of the businesses when combined over and above the aggregated values as separate stand-alone businesses (this may arise, for example, from a decrease in earnings or cash flow volatility reducing the Cost of Equity - if estimated using the CAPM, this would be indicated by a lower asset beta - and, possibly, the Cost of Debt).

If there are 'embedded' real options that are created as a result of the acquisition of the target (such as the ability to expand into a new market or product line), then these can be evaluated using a Real Options approach.

Value to the Target Shareholders

The target shareholders would expect to receive an offer price equivalent to their estimate of the current stand-alone fair value plus a premium for the additional value of control that the acquirer would hope to realise. If the target is quoted and market conditions are poor, an offer may be rejected if the target shareholders consider the market price to be undervalued (market price being less than the true fair or intrinsic value, based on a DCF valuation, for example). If the target is private, the acquirer and target shareholders are likely to have different estimates for the target's stand-alone intrinsic value (due to different expectations of growth, assessment of risk and illiquidity discount estimates). The acquirer and target shareholders may also have different estimates for the control premium (see Bruner (2004 p.465-471) for further discussion on control premiums).

Economic Gains

As noted above, the excess of the value to the acquirer over the purchase price represents the economic gains for the acquirer and its shareholders. Payment of a control premium will create value for the target shareholders that are selling (over and above the market price for a minority holding).

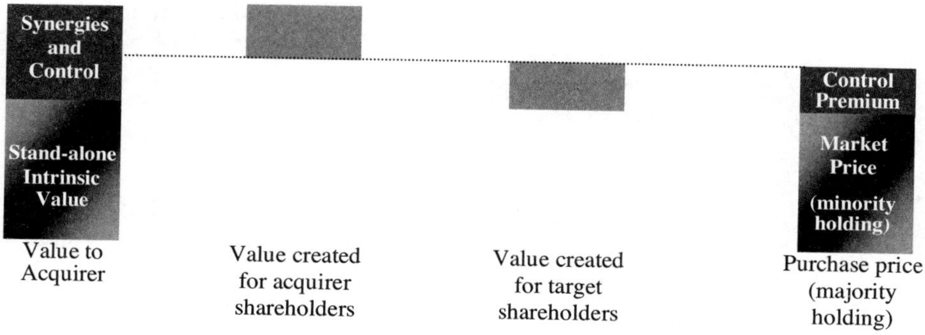

For simplicity, it is assumed that the target's stand-alone intrinsic value for the acquirer equals the market price (and that the market price is a fair value to the target shareholders).

If the target is quoted, its share price may increase on announcement of an offer at a premium, as investors purchase shares in the expectation of being bought out at the higher offer price (a small discount will remain due to the risk that the offer may not be implemented). If the acquirer is quoted, its share price should also increase, in theory, to reflect the economic gains to its shareholders, but may decrease if the market considers the offer price too high (i.e. synergies and other benefits for the acquirer do not justify the size of the premium implied in the offer price).

If the target is private, the vendors' required sale price will be based on their assessment of the fair value for the holding being acquired (the stand-alone intrinsic value can be estimated using a DCF and multiples approach, taking a suitable average of the two, and a control premium added in). The acquirer would focus on a DCF valuation to estimate the value of the acquisition to it, and ensure the NPV was maximised (the offer price would need to be supported by current market multiples to ensure it was relatively attractive).

Purchase Consideration

Issues for the Acquirer and Vendor

For both private and quoted acquisitions, the choice of consideration would depend on the needs and restrictions of the acquirer and vendors.

Exhibit 1.5 Purchase Consideration - Issues

Consideration	*Acquirer*	*Target shareholder*
• Cash	- ability to raise and service new debt; - ability to raise cash via rights issue or other means, and likely cost; - balance sheet impact.	- likely to crystallise tax charge; - may need cash to reinvest elsewhere.
• Equity	- dilution of existing shareholdings; - EPS dilution due to new shares being issued; - stock exchange and legal requirements for share issues.	- may be able to defer any tax until a sale of the new shares; - exposure to acquirer equity risk; - acquirer shares need to be marketable.
• Debt & Non-equity instruments	- existing shareholders only diluted on conversion (if applicable); - balance sheet impact (non-equity may be treated as 'debt' for gearing purposes).	- tax deferral until redemption of debt or preference shares may be possible; - lower risk than pure equity, but participation in equity upside may be possible.

Economic Gains

Unquoted / Private

- All Cash

In theory, the economic gains for the acquirer's shareholders will equal the acquisition Net Present Value. If the acquirer needs to raise new funds to finance the purchase price, then:

- if new equity is raised, the economic gains will have to be shared with any new shareholders if existing shareholders do not take up their rights, and EPS will be diluted due to the new shares in issue;
- if debt finance is used, financial risk for existing shareholders may increase significantly (unless the acquirer or target have stable cash flows that can support the debt), which would increase their required rate of return and reduce the acquirer's intrinsic or market value.

- All Shares

The target's shareholders will want to ensure their share of the combined value (acquirer DCF Equity Value + target purchase cost + NPV gain), when the transaction is completed (min T%), is not less than the purchase cost in shares. Their likely minimum 'Exchange Ratio' (ER_{min}) - the number of new acquirer shares issued (A_{NS}) for each target share acquired (T_S) - will be the ratio that ensures the intrinsic value of their shareholding equals the purchase cost (T_S x Purchase Price in shares*). The following must be satisfied (A_{ES} = existing Acquirer shares):

$$\text{Shareholding (min T\%)} = \frac{T_S \text{ x Purchase Price*}}{\text{Combined Value}} = \frac{ER_{min} \text{ x } T_S}{A_{ES} + ER_{min} \text{ x } T_S} \qquad \boxed{1.7}$$

$$ER_{min} = \frac{\boxed{\dfrac{\text{min T\%}}{1 - \text{min T\%}} \text{ x } A_{ES}}}{T_S} = \frac{A_{ES} \text{ x Purchase Price*}}{\underset{\text{(= Acquirer Value + NPV)}}{\text{Combined Value} - \text{Purchase Cost}}}$$

(A_{NS} → boxed expression)

The acquirer's shareholders will want to ensure their share of the combined value (min A%) is not less than their current value. The following must be satisfied:

$$\text{Shareholding (min A\%)} = \frac{A_{ES} \text{ x Acquirer Price}}{\text{Combined Value}} = \frac{A_{ES}}{A_{ES} + ER_{max} \text{ x } T_S} \qquad \boxed{1.8}$$

$$ER_{max} = \frac{\boxed{\dfrac{1 - \text{min A\%}}{\text{min A\%}} \text{ x } A_{ES}}}{T_S} = \frac{\overset{\text{Combined Value} - \text{Acquirer Value}}{\text{(= Purchase Cost* + NPV)}}}{T_S \text{ x Acquirer Price}}$$

(A_{NS} → boxed expression)

The NPV benefit accrues 100% to the acquirer shareholders at ER_{min} and 100% to the target shareholders at ER_{max}. Both sets of shareholders will share the NPV if the Exchange Ratio falls between the maximum and minimum. If a zero NPV is assumed, then the minimum and maximum reduce to: Purchase Price / Acquirer Price.

- Cash and Shares

The Exchange Ratio is calculated as above, but after stripping out the cash component (the purchase price and cost, where indicated * above, are multiplied by the % of the offer in shares).

Example 1.6 Exchange Ratios and NPV sharing (unquoted / private)

'Acquirer' is to offer £42.00 a share for 80% of 'Target' for £67.2m total cost (plus £0.8m transaction costs), payable 100% cash, 100% shares (Exchange Ratio = 2.1), or a mix of 71.4% shares / 28.6% cash (Exchange Ratio = 1.5). The total NPV is £8m.

	Acquirer	Target	
Holding	100%	100%	80%
Shares outstanding	12.50 m	2.00 m	1.60 m
DCF Equity Value per share	£20.00	£35.00	
Stand-alone Equity Value (private / no control)	£250.0 m	£70.0 m	£56.0 m
Control Value + Synergies (35.7% of stand-alone value)			£20.0 m
Value to acquirer			£76.0 m
Purchase price			£42.00 per share
Purchase cost			£67.2 m
Transaction costs			£0.8 m
Acquisition cost			£68.0 m
Control Value and Synergies			£20.0 m
less: premium paid over stand-alone Equity Value (£67.2m - £56.0m)			(£11.2m)
less: transaction costs			(£0.8m)
NPV gains			£8.0 m

100% cash consideration

	Merged	*Holding*	*Value*	*NPV*
Existing Acquirer Shareholders	12.50 m	100.0%	258.0	8.0
Acquirer shares issued to Target shareholders	-	-	-	-
	12.50 m	100.0%	258.0	8.0
Combined value (= £250.0m + £76.0m)	326.0			
less: cash element of offer + transaction costs	(68.0)			
Post-acquisition value	258.0			
Post-acquisition share price	£ 20.64			

100% shares consideration

	Merged	*Holding*	*Value*	*NPV*
Existing Acquirer Shareholders	12.50 m	78.8%	256.3	6.3
Acquirer shares issued to Target shareholders	3.36 m	21.2%	68.9	1.7
	15.86 m	100.0%	325.2	8.0
Combined value (= £250.0m + £76.0m)	326.0	Offer	67.2	
less: cash element of offer + transaction costs	(0.8)	NPV	1.7	
Post-acquisition value	325.2		68.9	
Post-acquisition share price	£ 20.50			

Exchange Ratios:

Exchange Ratio = offer price in shares (£42.00) / acquirer's share price (£20.00) = **2.100**
2.1 x 1.60m shares = 3.36m shares

or = new Acquirer shares (3.36m) / old Target shares (1.60m)
where new shares = Acquirer shares (12.50m) x Y% / (1-Y%)
and Y = Share Consideration (£67.2m) / (Acquirer Value (£250.0m) + Share Consideration)

		Merged	*Holding*	*Value*	*NPV*
MIN = (12.5m x £42.00) / (£250.0m + £8.0m NPV) =	**2.035**				
Existing Acquirer Shareholders		12.50 m	79.3%	258.0	8.0
Acquirer shares issued to Target shareholders		3.26 m	20.7%	67.2	0.0
		15.76 m	100.0%	325.2	8.0
Post-acquisition share price		£ 20.64	Offer	67.2	
			NPV	0.0	
				67.2	
MAX = (£67.2m + £8.0 NPV) / (1.6m x £20.0) =	**2.350**				
Existing Acquirer Shareholders		12.50 m	76.9%	250.0	0.0
Acquirer shares issued to Target shareholders		3.76 m	23.1%	75.2	8.0
		16.26 m	100.0%	325.2	8.0
Post-acquisition share price		£ 20.00	Offer	67.2	
			NPV	8.0	
				75.2	

Cash + Shares

71.4% shares : 28.6% cash	*Merged*	*Holding*	*Value*	*NPV*
Existing Acquirer Shareholders	12.50 m	83.9%	256.7	6.7
Acquirer shares issued to Target shareholders	2.40 m	16.1%	49.3	1.3
	14.90 m	100.0%	306.0	8.0
Combined value (= £250.0m + £76.0m)	326.0			
less cash element of offer (=£67.2m x 28.6%) + transaction costs	(20.0)	Cash	19.2	
Post-acquisition value	306.0	Shares	49.3	
Post-acquisition share price	£ 20.54		68.5	
		Offer	67.2	
		NPV	1.3	
			68.5	

	Per share
Cash	£ 12.00
Shares	£ 30.81
Total	£ 42.81
NPV share	-£ 0.81
Offer price	£ 42.00

Exchange Ratios

Exchange Ratio = offer price in shares (£42.00 x 71.4%) / acquirer's share price (£20.00) = **1.5**
1.50 x 1.60m shares = 2.40m shares

or = new Acquirer shares (2.4m) / old Target shares (1.6m)
where new shares = Acquirer shares (12.5m) x Y% / (1-Y%)
and Y = Share Consideration (£67.2m x 71.4%) /
(Acquirer Value (£250.0m) + Share Consideration)

	Merged	*Holding*	*Value*	*NPV*
MIN = (12.5m x £42.00x 71.4%) / (£250.0m + £8.0m NPV) =	**1.453**			
Existing Acquirer Shareholders	12.50 m	84.3%	258.0	8.0
Acquirer shares issued to Target shareholders	2.32 m	15.7%	48.0	0.0
	14.82 m	100.0%	306.0	8.0
Post-acquisition share price	£ 20.64			
		Cash	19.2	
		Shares	48.0	
			67.2	
		Offer	67.2	
		NPV	0.0	
			67.2	
MAX = (£67.2m x 71.4% + £8.0 NPV) / (1.6m x £20.0) =	**1.750**			
Existing Acquirer Shareholders	12.50 m	81.7%	250.0	0.0
Acquirer shares issued to Target shareholders	2.80 m	18.3%	56.0	8.0
	15.30 m	100.0%	306.0	8.0
Post-acquisition share price	£ 20.00			
		Cash	19.2	
		Shares	56.0	
			75.2	
		Offer	67.2	
		NPV	8.0	
			75.2	

- Non-equity

Since no ordinary shares are being issued, the analysis is similar as for an all cash offer. The Equity Value of the acquirer would increase by the fair value of the target being acquired less the non-equity issued.

- Deferred Consideration

Part of the consideration may be deferred and become payable at a future date, contingent on certain conditions being met. This should reduce the risk of overpayment if some of the acquirer's key assumptions underlying the valuation of the target turn out to be invalid. An 'Earn-Out' would normally involve an upfront cash payment on completion and a deferred element linked to the achievement of specified profits or cash flows over the next 2 or 3 years. The acquirer would need to be satisfied that the type of financial measure used reflected actual operating performance, rather than any accounting or cash flow manipulation, or any tax effects (a pre-tax profit would be a common measure).

Quoted

The acquirer will focus on the impact on EPS (if considered an important measure for shareholders) if finance is raised, the dilution of EPS and existing shareholdings if shares are issued, the impact on key risk and return measures (return on equity, debt servicing, etc.) and the ability to raise finance. An increase in the post-acquisition EPS may not represent genuine value creation if shares are issued. The combined EPS can be increased if the target has a lower P/E ratio than the acquirer. There may be an illusory benefit to shareholders ('bootstrapping'), caused by the percentage increase in earnings exceeding the percentage increase in the number of issued shares. The true economic gain (NPV) needs to be determined.

Example 1.7 EPS 'Bootstrapping' (quoted)

It is assumed that 'Acquirer' and 'Target' from **Example 1.6** are both quoted; all other details remain the same (quoted share prices are equal to the DCF equity value per share, and hence a 20% control premium is being paid), except the consideration will be 100% shares. The £20m of synergies and control value comprise (1) a break-even, zero NPV component, equal to the sum of the control premium and transaction costs (£12.0m = £11.2m + £0.8m), and (2) an NPV component (£8.0m). Assuming transaction costs can be capitalised (and are included as part of the 'goodwill' calculation – cost of acquisition less fair value of net assets acquired), the increase in EPS before any charge for goodwill (which may be considered a key measure) will comprise a zero NPV component ('bootstrapping' component) and a positive NPV component. In this example, it is assumed that a constant cash flow in respect of synergies and the value of control is received in perpetuity (£2.0m per year in perpetuity, giving a present value of £20.0m assuming a 10% Cost of Capital). If control value and synergies are included, then EPS will increase by £0.11 due to the bootstrapping effect and by £0.05 due to genuine positive NPV (to a final £0.83 per share).

£m, unless otherwise stated

	Acquirer	Target	*being acquired*
Holding	100%	100%	80%
Shares outstanding	12.50 m	2.00 m	1.60 m
Share price	£20.00	£35.00	
Market value	£250.0 m	£70.0 m	£56.0 m
EPS (excl. goodwill amortisation)	£0.67 per share	£1.75 per share	
P/E	x 30.00	x 20.00	
Headline earnings (excl. goodwill amortisation)	£8.3 m	£3.5 m	£2.8 m
Cost of capital	10%	10%	

Market value of shares acquired	56.0	£35.00 per share
Control premium 20%	11.2	£7.00 per share
Offer value - 100% shares consideration	67.2	£42.00 per share
Acquisition costs 1.2% of offer value	0.8	
Total cost for acquirer	68.0	
Market value of shares acquired	56.0	£35.00 per share
Synergies + Control Value	20.0	£12.50 per share
Value to acquirer	76.0	£47.50 per share
Economic benefits	*8.0*	

		NPV	*Received annually in perpetuity p.a.*
Being:	Synergies + Control Value	20.0	2.0
	less: control premium and acquisition costs	(12.0)	(1.2)
		8.0	0.8

	Earnings	Shares (Acquirer)	Value	NPV	EPS	Value per share	P/E
	£m	m	£m	£m	£	£	
Acquirer	8.33	12.50	250.0		0.67	20.00	x 30.00
Target (% acquired)	2.80	3.36	56.0		0.83	16.67	x 20.00
Transaction costs			(0.8)			-0.24	
Combined value (ignoring synergies)	11.13	15.86	305.2	(12.0)	0.70	19.24	x 27.41
Combined value (breakeven synergies)	12.33	15.86	317.2	0.0	0.78	20.00	x 25.72
Combined value (all synergies)	13.13	15.86	325.2	8.0	0.83	20.50	x 24.76

	Holding	*Value*	
Existing Acquirer shareholders	78.8%	256.3	
Target shareholders (80%)	21.2%	68.9	(see **Example 1.6** for 100% share offer)
	100.0%	325.2	

	EPS		*Earnings % change*	
Acquirer	0.67	= 8.33 / 12.50m shares		
Bootstrapping effect	0.03			
Combined - no synergies	0.70	= 11.13 / 15.86m shares	33.6%	= 8.33 to 11.13
Bootstrapping effect	0.08			
Combined - breakeven / zero NPV synergies	0.78	= 12.33 / 15.86m shares	48.0%	= 8.33 to 12.33
Increase due to genuine economic benefits	0.05			
Combined - all synergies	0.83	= 13.13 / 15.86m shares	57.6%	= 8.33 to 13.13
Increase in shares			26.9%	= 12.50m to 15.86m

Note: transaction costs have been capitalised (hence will form part of the goodwill calculation)

It is assumed there will be no change to the acquirer's P/E due to an increase in perceived risk for its shareholders. If part of the consideration was in the form of cash funded from debt sources, then the shareholders' required rate of return may increase (reducing P/E below the combined P/E).

If shares are offered, minimum and maximum Exchange Ratios can be stated in the same way as for a private acquisition, but with the value being the market capitalisation (or P/E x EPS – see Bruner (2004 p.590-607)). Exchange Ratios will change as the share price of the acquirer and target change following the announcement of the transaction; a 'Collar' attempts to protect the target's shareholders from a change in the acquirer's share price over a specified period around the acquisition date by adjusting the Exchange Ratio or providing compensation in some other way.

➡ For an example of acquisition structuring, see Appendix D5.

2 CAPITAL RAISING

INTRODUCTION

Chapter Contents

Capital investments need to be financed in a manner that (1) reduces the overall cost of capital, (2) ensures operating cash flows and asset realisations are reasonably well matched to financing cash flows, and (3) minimises the volatility of post-financing cash flows. These issues are covered elsewhere (see Chapter 1 and Appendix B1 for a discussion on capital structure, Chapter 3 for long term capital management, and Chapter 4 for financial risk management). This chapter discusses the main features, benefits and risks of long-term debt (loans and bonds), equity and alternative forms of asset finance, and issues to consider when making the financing decision.

Debt

A borrower needs to ensure that (1) the cost of debt finance is minimised, given its own risk status ('Credit Rating'), (2) the contractual obligations contained in the debt agreement are reasonable and the best available (and can be met without any restrictions being imposed on the underlying business and other existing financing arrangements), and (3) it retains maximum flexibility for future financing requirements.

A borrower should be aware of the risks that a lender will consider when pricing the debt. Like equity, the fair value of debt is the present value of future cash flows discounted at a risk-adjusted rate of return (a risk-free rate plus a risk premium). Much of the risk will relate to the borrower's ability to finance the debt ('Credit' or 'Default' risk); holders of quoted bonds traded on the capital markets will face additional risks associated with bond price volatility. A discussion on how credit risk is quantified and incorporated into a risk premium is beyond the scope of this book; this chapter highlights the issues a lender will consider when assessing the level of risk and the means by which these risks are addressed in the loan agreement. Appendix B2 discusses bond pricing and price volatility (Convertible Bonds are discussed in Appendix B5), and Appendix C discusses the evaluation of lease finance.

Equity

The section on equity discusses funding by way of a flotation ('Initial Public Offering')(an example is given in Appendix D3), a rights issue or the issue of warrants. The valuation of equity and related options is discussed in Appendices B1 and B4, respectively.

DEBT

Introduction

Features of Debt Finance

Debt finance allows a company to raise funds at a lower cost than equity (both pre- and post-tax), and have more flexibility when managing the pool of capital (debt can be repaid, refinanced, restructured or 'synthetically' altered using derivatives, for example). Furthermore, it can enhance the return on equity via the leverage affect (see ratio 13 in Appendix A).

In some cases, significant debt funding can be made available relatively quickly. For example, a publicly quoted bond issue can usually be implemented quicker than an equity rights issue. Where a bank relationship has been established, and the bank has more confidence in the ability of management and their assessment of the business prospects, then further debt funding can be put in place relatively speedily (in practice, for significant debt funding, relationships will be established with a 'core' of banks).

The terms of a debt funding agreement may require the borrower to provide significant commitments by way of security, representations, warranties and covenants (financial and otherwise), depending on the balance between the return for the lender and its perception of the risk involved. The owners of the business (i.e. shareholders) will, effectively, have less control due to these financing commitments.

Alternative Forms of Finance

Leasing

If an asset is leased for the whole, or substantially the whole, of its economic life, effectively it is being debt financed: the asset purchase price is repaid over time plus interest (the rental charge), similar to repayments on a loan used to purchase the asset, although legal ownership has not transferred (leases can have end-of-term options that allow for the transfer of title to the lessee). There may be occasions when, providing the asset is suitable for leasing, it is cheaper, on an after-tax basis, to lease rather than purchase the asset. If the asset has already been purchased, then it can be sold and leased back, effectively using the asset to provide debt funding.

➡ For a discussion on lease evaluation, see Appendix C.

Project Finance

The financing of a new plant, facility or other infrastructure (such as a power plant or toll bridge), may involve Project Financing techniques. Financing is needed to construct the asset and to allow it to operate (working capital), and a mixture of financing instruments will be used (possibly including lease finance) in a manner that minimises the risk for debt providers and equity providers, and maximises the equity return.

In general, the following characteristics are likely to be present:

- the project is being initiated by one or more 'sponsors' (usually shareholders or partners, depending on the choice of legal entity established to own and manage the asset), on the basis of preliminary technical, financial and marketing studies;
- once constructed and fully operational, stable and predictable cash flows should permit a large proportion of the construction costs to be debt financed (the leverage ratio is often as high as 75% - 80%), with debt servicing tailored to the expected cash flows (based on agreed financial forecasts);
- given the significant debt levels, sponsors, acting as joint venture partners, are likely to require an off-balance sheet accounting treatment and to ensure that there is 'limited recourse' to them in case the project fails (lenders may only have rights of recourse to sponsors until construction is complete, thereafter having to rely on the project cash flows);
- debt providers will try to maximise their risk protection ('credit enhancement') from security, guarantees, warranties, covenants, insurance and other commitments (which may involve local government support), and by obtaining comfort that the expected cash flows are reasonably certain (from feasibility studies and third party long term commitments to purchase the asset's output);
- a large number of other contracts and agreements will be put in place in order to allocate risk to those parties in the project willing to accept it and who are more able to manage it (for example, due to their technological expertise or knowledge about the market).

In these cases, where the project is a specific 'ring-fenced' investment, the capital structure will change and this will be factored into the periodic valuations.

'Non-equity' and Hybrid debt instruments

A debt agreement can be structured in a way that introduces an element of equity risk, in exchange for a higher return. The degree of equity risk would depend on the rights and obligations of both parties with respect to annual distributions - rights to receive an agreed return not dependant on the borrower's profits or assets (debt) versus rights to receive dividends, dependent on the profits or assets (equity) – and the repayment of capital (equity holders only have a right to repayment from surplus assets arising on a winding-up).

'Non-equity' instruments (such as redeemable preference shares) may have similar income and capital repayment provisions as pure debt, with the exception that (1) dividends need not be paid if profits are insufficient (debt interest must be paid), and (2) debt would rank ahead on any winding up (non-equity would rank ahead of equity). Preference share dividends may be at a fixed rate and/or be linked to the profits available for ordinary shareholders ('participating'); if there are insufficient profits, then preference dividends may be carried forward to a future period when profits are available ('cumulative').

Financial risk will depend on the nature of the company's contractual obligations with respect to non-equity (whether or not it will have to transfer economic benefits to the holder); leverage and 'fixed charge' coverage ratios should include non-equity where there is a likelihood of such cash outflows having to be paid.

Rights to convert a bond or non-equity into the issuer's or a third party's shares (a 'Convertible' and 'Exchangeable' bond, respectively) give the holder the opportunity to benefit from any equity 'upside' (if converted) whilst being protected on the 'downside' by the usual rights of a debt holder or lender (rights to repayment of capital, if the 'option' to convert is ignored). On conversion, this downside protection would be lost as the instrument would be pure equity. Convertible bonds are discussed below and in Appendix B5.

Rights to subscribe for equity at favourable rates can be given in the form of 'warrants', 'attached' to a debt instrument. On exercise, the holder would pay the agreed subscription price to the company, receive title to the agreed number of shares and hope to have a positive pay-off (the value of the shares after exercise being more than the warrant subscription cost). Unlike a Convertible, the debt would remain as a separate instrument.

Loans

Loan Characteristics

Overview

A loan agreement may be with a single lender (a 'bilateral' loan) or a group of lenders (a 'syndicated' loan), where the amount required is in excess of the amount a single lender is prepared to advance (alternatively, a number of separate bilateral agreements could be entered into with different banks). In a syndicated facility, the loan would be arranged and managed by one or two agent banks on behalf of the whole banking syndicate.

Funds are provided on the date the agreement starts, or on specified dates during a pre-defined 'draw down' period, and repaid during the loan term ('amortising' loan) or at the end of the loan ('bullet repayment' on 'maturity'), although the borrower will normally be given the right to repay, or 'prepay', the loan early. A loan would normally be a 'Term' loan (where funds are drawn down once by the borrower soon after agreement is signed and repaid in an agreed manner over the term) or a 'Revolving Credit Facility' (the bank agrees to provide funds over the loan term, and the borrower has the option as to how much to draw down or repay each interest period). Interest would be payable at the end of each specified interest period (normally, monthly, quarterly or semi-annually), based on a fixed or variable ('floating') rate set at the start of each interest period, applied to the balance of the loan outstanding ('principal') at that date.

The loan agreement will require the borrower to do or refrain from doing certain acts, financial or otherwise ('covenants'), to promise that certain information given to the lender is materially true ('warranty'), and to provide indemnities or guarantees to limit any loss suffered. Failure to comply with the loan agreement obligations may trigger an 'Event of Default' (such as a failure to make a payment), which, unless rectified, will usually 'accelerate' repayment of the loan and terminate the loan agreement. In a 'secured' loan, the lender would be entitled to seek recovery (via insolvency proceedings) from any assets of the borrower 'charged' (either a single asset under a 'fixed charge' or a collection of assets or, effectively, the whole business, in a 'floating charge'), mortgaged or collateralised in their favour, or from any third party who has guaranteed the borrower's obligations (the guarantor would then seek to recover off the borrower, effectively 'stepping into the shoes' of the lender). An unsecured lender, unless they have certain agreed 'priority rights' over other creditors, would rank alongside general creditors in any insolvency proceedings.

Arranging the Loan Facility

Before negotiation of the loan agreement starts, the borrower needs to know the terms and conditions required by the lender. Although not normally legally binding, a 'Term Sheet' would summarise the terms of the loan offer. In a syndicated facility, a bank or banks ('arrangers') would negotiate (via a chosen 'arranging agent' if there is more than one arranger) the financial, commercial and significant legal terms of the loan with the borrower, and incorporate them in the Term Sheet. The borrower would then sign a 'Mandate Letter' (which would be legally binding, unless stated otherwise), giving authority to the bank to arrange the facility in accordance with the terms. After signing, the borrower becomes responsible for meeting all arrangement costs and fees (including the lenders' legal costs), and hence it should be confident that no further negotiation of the key terms will take place during preparation of the facility agreement (so as to minimise legal costs).

The Arranger would (1) agree to provide all of the funds on the agreed terms, whether or not syndication is successful ('Fully Committed'), (2) agree to provide part of the funds on the agreed terms and the remainder on whatever terms are acceptable to syndicate banks ('Partially Committed'), or (3) agree to do its best to find banks prepared to lend on the best possible terms, failing which the Mandate would be cancelled ('Best Efforts').

The arranger would then invite banks to participate, usually on the basis of an Information Memorandum that contained details about the borrower and its business prospects. These will include the 'Lead Manager', 'Manager' and other 'Participating Banks', ranked according to the amount of funds they are willing to commit. Where the loan is being 'underwritten' (an agreement to lend any shortfall which cannot be raised from other lenders), then some of these banks will be 'Underwriting Banks'.

Once the loan facility has been signed, the borrower would be permitted to draw down on the funds under the terms of the agreement, which would stipulate a period by which all funds must be drawn down and what conditions must be satisfied for each draw-down ('availability tests').

The 'Facility Agent', or 'Administrative Agent', would manage the loan cash flows on a daily basis on behalf of the syndicate (for example, distributing interest from the borrower to the relevant banks, according to their share in the facility). A 'Managing Agent' would negotiate any issues with the lender concerning the loan agreement during the loan term (such as potential events of default or other credit issues).

Purpose of Loan

Bank debt may be used to finance the cost of new assets, to re-finance existing capital, or to increase leverage in the capital structure. The purpose of the loan should be matched to the type of debt; for example, an overdraft, or short term revolving facility, would normally finance working capital, whereas a longer-term loan would finance fixed capital expenditure or acquisitions. Existing debt may need to be refinanced if a lower loan rate is available, following an improvement in market conditions (a decrease in the risk free rate) or the borrower's credit status (a decrease in the Credit Risk Premium – the excess of the rate of borrowing over the risk free rate).

The ability to service the loan will partly depend on the purpose, since a risk of default may be increased unless it can be shown that, as a result of the bank loan, (1) future operating cash flows available to service debt costs will increase, (2) financing cash flows are more predictable and stable, and (3) the risk profile of total debt is improved.

Term

The term, or maturity, of the loan will depend on the ability of the borrower to service the debt, the security provided to the lender, and other risks for the lender. The lender's exposure ('Exposure At Risk') will depend on the amount of principal outstanding throughout the loan term, its assessment of the probability of the borrower defaulting, and the estimated amount recoverable. It will be more concerned with the average life of the loan (the average loan balance, time-weighted) rather than the actual loan term (illustrated in **Example 2.1**).

A loan to finance new assets should have a term similar to the useful economic life of the assets. A short term loan would, therefore, be used to finance short term assets (as discussed above, an overdraft can be used to finance working capital, which fluctuates due to seasonal and other factors). A medium term (5-7 years) or long term loan would normally be used to finance fixed assets – as would equity – where the investment is being made to generate long term sustainable operating cash flows.

Principal Repayment

The principal may be repaid on one date or a number of dates (by instalments or 'amortised').

Example 2.1 Loan repayment profiles

A 5 year 7% (nominal) fixed rate £10m loan, where interest is paid quarterly in arrears (interest is calculated on a daily basis, assuming the loan starts on 1 June), could be repaid as follows:

- In full at maturity ('Bullet' repayment)

Year	*Principal*	*Interest*	*Total*	*Av balance*
1		(0.70)	(0.70)	10.00
2		(0.70)	(0.70)	10.00
3		(0.70)	(0.70)	10.00
4		(0.70)	(0.70)	10.00
5	(10.00)	(0.70)	(10.70)	10.00
	(10.00)	(3.50)	(13.50)	5.00 years

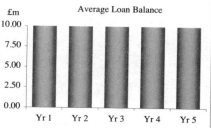

The lender is at risk for the full amount of the loan for 5 years, making it the most risky.

- Part repaid during term (quarterly) and significant proportion at maturity ('Balloon')

Year	Principal	Interest	Total	Av balance
1	(1.00)	(0.67)	(1.67)	9.63
2	(1.00)	(0.60)	(1.60)	8.63
3	(1.00)	(0.53)	(1.53)	7.63
4	(1.00)	(0.47)	(1.47)	6.63
5	(6.00)	(0.39)	(6.39)	5.63
	(10.00)	(2.67)	(12.67)	3.81 years

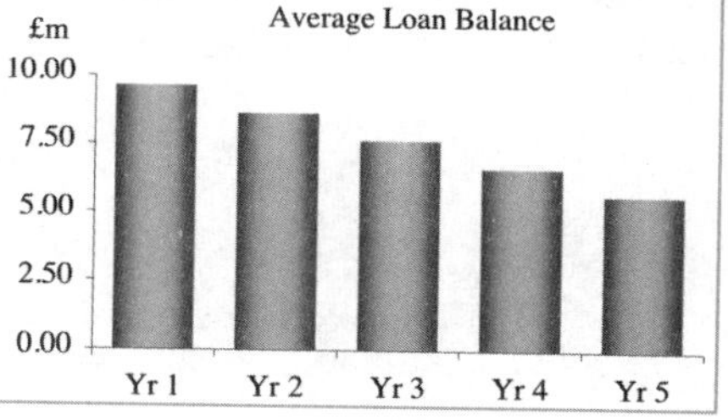

50% of the loan is being amortised in equal quarterly instalments, with the remaining 50% being paid on maturity. This structure may allow the borrow to match the loan servicing to expected cash flows from a project, asset or other investment.

- Equal annual payment of principal and interest

Year	Principal	Interest	Total	Av balance
1	(1.73)	(0.66)	(2.39)	9.36
2	(1.86)	(0.53)	(2.39)	7.58
3	(1.99)	(0.40)	(2.39)	5.68
4	(2.13)	(0.25)	(2.39)	3.63
5	(2.29)	(0.10)	(2.39)	1.44
	(10.00)	(1.94)	(11.94)	2.77 years

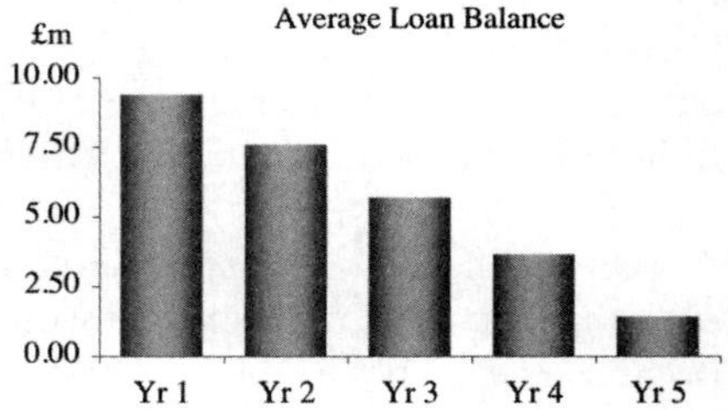

This structure is fairly common for unsecured small business bank loans or consumer repayment mortgages. A fixed payment comprising a capital and interest element is calculated using the annuity formula in Appendix B1 (see **B1.4**):

$$= £10\text{m} \times \frac{7\%}{\left\{1 - \frac{1}{\left[1 + 7.00\% / 4\right]^{20}}\right\}}$$

= £2.39m Using Excel Function: PMT(0.07/4, 20, -10) x 4

- Equal annual payment of principal

Year	Principal	Interest	Total	Av balance
1	(2.00)	(0.65)	(2.65)	9.25
2	(2.00)	(0.51)	(2.51)	7.25
3	(2.00)	(0.37)	(2.37)	5.25
4	(2.00)	(0.23)	(2.23)	3.25
5	(2.00)	(0.09)	(2.09)	1.25
	(10.00)	(1.84)	(11.84)	2.63 years

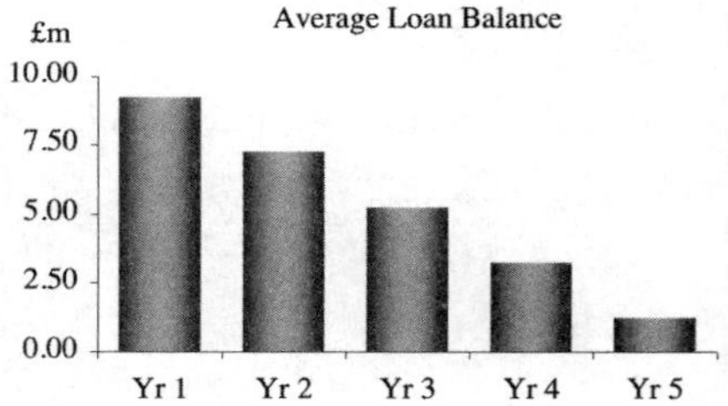

The principal repayments may be structured in any number of ways, which may be required if the loan is to be serviced from cash flows from a specific project or asset, so that total debt servicing costs can be matched to the underlying cash flows. In leveraged leasing, for example, debt structuring is determined by the after-tax lease cash flows profile, in order to maximise the returns for equity investors.

Interest Rate

The interest rate will be based on an agreed margin ('applicable margin') over the cost to the lender of funding the loan for the relevant interest period (typically 1, 3, or 6 months), and, possibly, a further margin to comply with capital adequacy rules set by the relevant banking regulator.

The pre-margin rate may be fixed throughout the loan term, and could be based on the 'swap rate' for the relevant loan term (the rate offered by banks under an interest rate swap, where the banks agree to pay or receive a fixed rate in exchange for a floating rate – these are discussed in Chapter 4). Alternatively, the pre-margin rate may be reset at the start of each interest period, based on a reference rate relevant for that period (floating rate). For sterling loans this would typically be the rate at which banks lend funds to each other (the London Inter-Bank Offered Rate, LIBOR), fixed at the start of the interest period by reference to the length of that period (e.g. 3 month LIBOR, 6 month LIBOR, etc.).

The applicable margin would compensate the lender for management costs and other overheads, for borrower credit risk and likely loan losses, and for maturity risk (longer term loans being more risky than shorter ones). The margin may be fixed or may vary over the loan term as the borrower's perceived credit risk changes.

Fees

In addition to the applicable margin, the lender will seek to charge certain fees. A syndicated loan might include any of the following (a bilateral facility is likely to have a simple Facility fee, similar to the Arrangement fee below):

Fee / Payee	*Paid for ….*	*Size*	*When paid*
Arrangement / Arrangers	arranging the facility	% of facility	On signing
Underwriting / Underwriters	guaranteeing funds	% of amount underwritten	On signing
Management / Lead and Co- Managers	managing the loan	% of facility	On signing
Participation / Non-Manager banks	participating in the syndicate	% of facility	On signing
Commitment / all lenders	committing to provide amounts so far undrawn	% of undrawn amount	Periodically
Agency / Facility Agent	servicing the loan	Flat £ amount	Annually

Lender's Evaluation

The Lender's Return

The loan must yield a risk-adjusted rate of return greater than the lender's hurdle rate (usually its own cost of capital). Although lenders have developed their own methods of calculating the yield, the risk-adjusted return is often shown as an after-tax profit divided by a measure of the amount of loan at risk. The Risk Adjusted Return On Capital ('RAROC') is a traditional measure that shows the return as the expected net profit (after losses and tax) over a one year period divided by the loan value at risk:

RAROC **2.1**

$$\text{RAROC} = \frac{(\text{Loan rate} - \text{Cost of funds}) + \text{Fees} - \text{Expected losses} - \text{Operating costs}}{\text{Loan x - D x } \Delta r / (1+R)}$$

where D the Macaulay Duration (see **B2.10** in Appendix B2)
Δr the expected change in the credit risk premium over the next year (often estimated from ratings information relevant to a bond issuer with the same credit rating or implied rating as the borrower)
R the yield on similar rated bonds (Δr / (1+R) is the present value of the expected change in the premium after one year).

Example 2.2 Risk Adjusted Return for lender

A 5 year £10m 7.0% fixed rate loan is repayable in full on maturity, with interest paid annually in arrears. The lender's cost of funds is 6.35%, annual fees are 0.15%, the expected losses 0.2%, and the marginal tax rate 30%. The adjusted net income is £42,000 (= £10m x [(7.0% - 6.35%) + 0.15% - 0.2%] x (1 – 30%)). Assuming, for simplicity, that the yield on equivalent 5 year bonds (7%) for borrowers of similar credit standing is expected to change by 1% over the next year, the amount of loan at risk would be £410,465 (= £10m x 4.39 x 0.00935 [= Δr / (1+R) = 0.01 / 1.07], where 4.39 is the Macaulay duration, calculated below). If the resulting 10.2% RAROC (= £42,000 / £410,465), exceeded the bank's post-tax hurdle rate, the loan would have an acceptable return (using this measure).

Year	Cash Flows	PV at 7.0%	x year
1	0.70	0.65	0.65
2	0.70	0.61	1.22
3	0.70	0.57	1.71
4	0.70	0.54	2.14
5	10.70	7.63	38.14
	13.50	10.00	43.88
		divided by value	/ 10.00
		= Macaulay duration	*4.39 years*

This is a very simplistic example, and banks have developed much more sophisticated methods of assessing the loan at risk (see Saunders and Allen (2002)).

The Lender's Risks

The risk that the lender will not receive the expected loan cash flows can be analysed as follows:

- Default — The borrower may be unable to pay the principal and interest at the scheduled dates. The probability of default will depend on the borrower's business and financial risk associated with its operating and financing strategies and policies, as well as overall economic and market conditions, which may vary over the loan term.

- Recovery — The expected recovery from exercising any security rights on a default will depend on the credit risk of any guarantor, the market value risk of any asset provided as security (the uncertainty of the realisable value), and the legal risk associated with enforcing the security.

- Interest rate — Interest rates may change over the loan term, increasing the effective cost for the lender where the funding for the loan is on a different interest basis and any increased interest costs cannot be passed on to the borrower:
  - if a floating rate loan (bank asset) is funded with fixed rate debt (liability), the lender's net interest income will increase as rates rise and decrease as rates fall (in practice, as rates fall, the lender could re-finance the fixed rate debt with floating rate debt, or enter into an interest rate swap);
  - if a fixed rate loan is funded with floating rate debt, net interest income decreases as rates rise and increases as rates fall (in practice, as rates fall, the borrower would try to refinance its debt at a lower fixed rate).

- Reinvest-ment — The option to prepay a fixed rate loan is likely to be exercised by a borrower if refunding can be at a lower rate. This leads to reinvestment risk for the lender, since it may have to reinvest the loan principal at a return well below the yield on the loan without prepayment.

- Currency /Inflation — Interest and principal repayments on foreign currency loans may have to be translated into the lender's home currency at unfavourable exchange rates (this risk can be reduced using currency derivatives, discussed in Chapter 4). Inflation will reduce the lender's real return, unless factored into the pricing.

Credit Risk Assessment

The lender needs comfort that the borrower can meet its debt servicing obligations from cash flows arising on operating activities, and from the sale of assets, if a default occurs. The lender will not achieve its required yield if loan payments are delayed and not made as scheduled in the loan agreement (i.e. the realised return will be less than the initial promised return). The probability of default can be assessed using credit risk modelling techniques (beyond the scope of this book). More traditional methods focus on actual and forecast profitability, cash flow, liquidity and security measures (see Appendix A for debt ratios).

The lender may consider the following factors:

- Industry risk — Default risk may increase if operating cash flows are sensitive to cyclical, seasonal, market and industry specific factors (technological change, regulatory risks, falling market demand, rivalry amongst competitors).

- Economic and political risks — Inflation and currency risk may increase if the loan is cross-border. Default risk will increase due to political actions (for example, strikes, nationalisation and expropriation of assets) and banking regulations (for example, restrictions on cross border interest payments).

- Competitive position — Default risk will partly depend on the borrower's market share and growth trends, the nature and diversification of its revenues (and the reliance on a single product or key customers), and its cost structure and advantages (i.e. factors that determine the uncertainty associated with future operating cash flows).

- Management — Lenders will focus on management's financial and investment decision-making abilities and policies (including its attitude to risk, financial control and performance evaluation).

The lender's financial evaluation of the borrower will focus on profitability, liquidity and security ratios, for both a going concern and insolvency situation. The relevance of each measure will depend on the type of business and the nature of the loan (particularly whether it is short term or medium/long term funding). The ratio analysis would attempt to indicate:

- the ability of the business to fund growth internally from profits;
- the availability of net cash flows to service debt interest and principal;
- the degree of balance sheet 'strain' (including the claims of other creditors);
- the availability of high quality assets as security;
- the amount of the debt likely to be recovered on a default (insolvency).

The key financial measures will include:

- Operating profits — The operating profit, or earnings before interest and tax (EBIT), provides a quick indication of a company's capacity to borrow. Lenders will require a minimum interest coverage ratio (EBIT divided by interest expense), based on past loan performance and default probabilities. Using this coverage ratio, a suitable interest rate, and the prospective borrower's actual level of EBIT, the maximum debt capacity can be estimated.

- Cash flows — Cash flows available for debt servicing are the pre-financing Free Cash Flow to the Firm (ignoring discretionary cash flows).

- Financial strain — The probability of default arising from greater leverage will depend on the quality of earnings and debt servicing cash flows and the availability of assets that can be disposed of.

- Security — Debt holders have a prior claim on the company's assets over equity providers, and can usually take action against the borrower to recover outstanding amounts (i.e. start insolvency proceedings). The quality of the assets – the extent to which their value can be maintained and realised – can thus indicate the likely recovery.

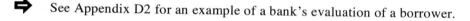

⇨ See Appendix D2 for an example of a bank's evaluation of a borrower.

Credit Risk Management

Having estimated the level of risk for a potential loan, the lender will take steps to reduce its maximum exposure and loss on any default during the proposed loan term. These protection measures will include third party guarantees, security arrangements and loan agreement clauses, designed to reduce risk (guarantees), maximise recovery (security), prevent the borrower from significantly increasing its current risk profile and allow the lender to terminate the loan (loan obligations).

- Priority & Security

An inter-creditor agreement may give preferred rights to one class of debt ('senior' debt) over another ('subordinated' or 'junior' debt). Cash flows and available net funds on liquidation may be required to service or repay senior debt before subordinated debt. The lender can be given priority over all unsecured creditors by being granted a charge over assets. In the UK, these would include the following:

- Fixed Charge: a 'legal' charge over specific, identified assets owned by the borrower (normally property or other fixed assets) that prevents the borrower from selling or otherwise dealing with the asset without the consent of the chargeholder (the lender);

- Floating charge — an 'equitable' charge over the borrower's general pool, or 'fund', of assets, including current assets (the borrower is able to deal in those assets without the consent of the charge holder, until a default arises).

- Guarantees

  A legally binding guarantee, covering the full amount outstanding, effectively allows the lender to swap the credit risk of the borrower for that of the guarantor. The margin on the loan should, therefore, partly reflect the guarantor credit risk.

- Rights of transfer

  Syndicated loan agreements typically allow participants to 'assign' their benefits and rights arising from the loan to a third party. In effect, this allows them to sell their economic interest in the loan, if they are no longer prepared to accept the credit risk, for example (although they still retain any remaining obligations under the loan agreement). A transfer by way of 'novation' would involve the new lender entering into a new agreement directly with the borrower.

- Conditions precedent, covenants, undertakings and representations

  The borrower will be required to confirm certain matters (representations) and to promise that certain events will or will not take place, where it can control them, both before (Conditions Precedent) and after (covenants and undertakings) the loan is drawn down. If any of these terms are breached, the loan could be terminated and all amounts outstanding would be repayable immediately, subject to certain allowed exceptions ('carve-outs'). Where the borrower has other debt agreements that contain 'cross default' clauses – an automatic event of default caused by a default in another debt agreement – then the resulting acceleration of all loans could result in insolvency. Hence, the borrower should be permitted time to rectify any potential or actual default or consult with the lender.

  Conditions precedent might require the following:

  - certain information to be delivered to the lender before a draw down (for example, signed security documentation);
  - pre-agreed capital changes to be put in place (for example, confirmation that equity contribution will be made);
  - availability tests to be satisfied (these would relate to the achievement of specific operating measures or targets);
  - the lender being satisfied as to certain matters (for example, that no new matters have arisen out of its due diligence findings, or that the latest business plan or management accounts are satisfactory).

At all times, or at certain specified times during the loan term, the lender will want assurances (representations) that there are no matters affecting the legal validity and enforceability of the borrower's obligations under the loan, for example:

- it is legally empowered to borrow and service the debt, either under its own constitution or according to other laws or regulations;
- no default has arisen, or is likely to arise in the near future, on other borrowings;
- all consents have been obtained.

The lender may also need assurances relating to information about the borrower that it has relied upon in making the decision to provide the loan (for example, that the financial statements are audited, or that there is no litigation existing likely to result in material new liabilities).

As to covenants and undertakings, the lender's main objective would be to ensure that future debt risk measures (adequate liquid resources to meet ongoing debt interest and principal costs, and sufficient quality and quantify of assets to enable repayment of debt on insolvency - including no dilution of the lender's share of those assets) are in line with its expectations at the time the loan is entered into. Any deviation from the initial financial forecasts, increase in the riskiness of the operating cash flows (by, for example, the borrower diversifying into high risk areas), or increase in the legal risks associated with the loan (which might restrict proceedings to formally recover the loan on default), should not be permitted unless the lender has formally consented.

Financial covenants require a borrower to conduct its financial affairs within prescribed limits. They allow the lender to be warned of a possible deterioration in credit standing, and would normally lead to negotiation rather than an automatic event of default; the borrower would notify the lender of a potential breach of a covenant, and steps would be taken to avoid an actual or 'technical' default (breach of financial covenant due to factors other than a worsening of the financial position), or to restructure the debt. A 'grace period' of several days would normally be given by the bank to allow the borrower to rectify any event of default.

Typical financial covenants would include the following:

Debt-to-equity	Maximum Debt ÷ Equity ratio
Cash Flow	Minimum Operating Cashflow
Interest coverage	Minimum EBIT ÷ interest payable
Debt service coverage	Minimum Operating Cash flow (or EBITDA) ÷ Debt principal and interest payable

Debt-to-cash flow	Maximum debt balance ÷ Operating Cash flow
Tangible Net Worth	Minimum net tangible assets
Liquidity measures	Minimum current assets ÷ current liabilities

Other covenants and undertakings would typically include the following:

- Borrowings restriction — No new borrowings are permitted other than those specifically allowed (for example, finance leases or working capital facilities up to a certain size).

- No asset disposals — No disposal of assets is permitted other than in the normal course of business or those specifically exempted (for example, up to a certain amount in aggregate). This prevents a material reduction in assets (e.g. a sale of assets followed by a special dividend to shareholders) or replacement of assets (such as assets being replaced with less marketable assets or those with higher risk).

- Negative pledge — No new security over assets can be created, other than those arising in the ordinary course of business, or those specifically exempted (for example, security up to a level not exceeding a certain percentage of the borrower's tangible net assets). This prevents dilution of an existing lender's rights on exercise of any security (i.e. its share of the pool of assets available on a default is not reduced due to new rights being created, or some party being given higher priority), and preserves equal treatment for existing unsecured lenders.

- Dividends — Distributions to shareholders can only be made if, for example, specific financial covenants are not breached at the date of the distribution (usually cash flow coverage ratios). This maintains cash flow for debt servicing.

- Information to be provided — Audited financial statements, periodic unaudited management accounts, and business plans must be provided by certain dates.

- Notifications — The borrower must notify the lender of the occurrence of certain events, usually an event of default or a potential event of default.

Default

On receiving notification from the borrower of the occurrence of an event of default, the lender would have the right to demand immediate repayment, but may waive this right if the default is a technical one of little substance. Amounts outstanding after a demand for repayment is issued would normally attract a penalty interest rate ('default interest').

Default would typically arise on the occurrence of any of the following (assuming any grace period allowed to remedy the potential default had expired):

- failure to make a payment
- breach of financial covenant
- misleading or incorrect representations or warranties
- failure to comply with other provisions of the loan agreement
- a cross default arising on other borrowings over a specified amount
- commencement of insolvency proceedings or arrangement with other creditors
- change of control of the borrower or specified subsidiaries
- an event occurs which is likely to have a 'material adverse effect' on the ability of the borrower to perform its obligations (for example, the loss of a licence allowing the borrower the conduct its business)

Lenders should have become aware of a potential default arising from deteriorating financial performance at a fairly early stage (if the financial covenants are adequate). If a default is likely, a lender will investigate whether or not exercising its rights to seek full repayment via the commencement of insolvency proceedings is preferred to a restructuring of the debt whilst avoiding formal insolvency.

Borrower's Evaluation

Borrower's Concerns

The borrower will wish to ensure that:

- the lender has a sound understanding of the borrower's business and strategy, so as to avoid any unnecessary concern or risk perception;
- its negotiation position at the time of arranging the loan is as strong as possible (i.e. its credit standing is strong and there is no apparent urgency in raising the loan finance);
- negotiation of the loan agreement starts only when all commercial terms have been agreed and proceeds as quickly as possible, so as to minimise legal costs and other fees;
- the number of lenders in a syndicated facility does not hinder management of the loan (delays and disputes are avoided);

- the lender is able to comply with its obligations.

The borrower will need to be satisfied that, as regards the loan agreement:

- the scheduled debt servicing profile is fairly well matched to the expected future operating cash flows;
- the commercial terms are the best available, and the 'all-in' annual cost of the loan (including fees) competitive;
- the loan agreement contains fairly standard terms that are consistent with those for other existing borrowings, thus reducing the need to monitor compliance across all debt agreements;
- no terms are drafted in a vague manner, such that there is imprecision about the definition of financial measures, the timing of any financial covenants or other undertakings, what constitutes a default, and what is required on the occurrence of a default or potential default;
- financial covenants are expected to be adequately covered, based on current financial forecasts;
- the terms are as flexible as possible and
    - do not restrict the borrower from carrying on its operating activities in the normal manner;
    - give the borrower time to rectify a technical or potential default (either to rectify the cause or to negotiate with the lenders);
    - allow the borrower to prepay the loan (to lock in to lower borrowing costs, following a change in market conditions); and
    - do not prevent growth investment (for example, via mergers and acquisitions).

Borrowing Cost Evaluation

The borrower should schedule out all expected cash flows arising under the loan agreement (expected draw downs, fees, interest and principal repayments) and determine the resulting all-in pre-tax borrowing cost (the IRR of the cash flows). Tax should then be calculated to determine the post-tax effective cost.

The impact of the loan on financial forecasts, existing covenants and debt and equity measures would also need to be considered to determine incremental costs to the borrower.

Corporate Bonds

Bond Characteristics

Main Features

A 'straight' bond is a debt instrument with a stated 'par', nominal, or face value (normally £100 in the UK, and $1,000 in the US, depending on the type of bond) that entitles the holder to receive a fixed 'coupon' (an annual percentage of the face value, 'coupon rate') every 'coupon period' (semi-annual or annual) until maturity, when the bond is redeemed (usually at face value), 2 – 30 years after issue. There are other types of bonds, however, that have different coupon and redemption features, and may grant certain options to the issuer and/or bondholders ('option-embedded' bonds).

Issuers and Investors

Bonds are issued in the 'Primary' capital markets by national and local governments and their agencies, supranational bodies (such as the World Bank), and companies. National government (Sovereign) bonds include 'Gilts' (UK) and 'Treasuries' (US – 'Treasury Notes' have maturities of between 2 and 10 years; 'Treasury Bonds' have maturities over 10 years, up to 30 years). 'Treasury Bills' are US/UK government securities with maturities of up to one year, issued on a discount basis in the Money Market (see Chapter 3).

Bondholders would include institutional investors (pension funds, life assurance and insurance companies, building societies, and banks) and specialist funds (such as managers of hedge and money market funds), each of whom will have a preference for short, medium or long term maturities, depending on the investment objective and their attitude to risk.

Repayment

If interest rates have fallen since the issue date, the issuer may wish to refinance the old bond with a new issue at a lower cost. Most bond agreements, therefore, would give the issuer a right, without an obligation, to redeem the bonds prior to maturity at specific dates and prices ('Callable' bonds). The issuer may have an obligation to pay off part of the bond principal over time ('sinking fund' provision), with the balance redeemed in the normal manner at maturity (similar to the 'balloon' structure for loans).

Security & Priority

The obligations of the issuer are usually contained in a bond 'Indenture', or trust deed, between the issuing company and the trustee representing the bondholders. This would contain details of security to be provided in the form of a floating charge over the issuer's entire pool of assets (such as for a 'Debenture' in the UK), a fixed charge over a specific, identified tangible asset (or a 'Pledge' or 'Lien' over such an asset, such as a 'Mortgage Bond' or 'Equipment-Trust Bond' in the US), or a lien over financial securities owned by the issuer (such as a 'Collateral Trust' bond in the US), or a combination of these. If different bond issues have security over the same asset, there may be an agreement giving some of the relevant secured bondholders a prior claim over the asset (or such priority rights may be provided for in law).

If the risk of the issuer defaulting is relatively low, security may not be required due to the issuer's high credit quality (these are 'Debentures' in the US), in which case bondholders rank alongside other unsecured creditors. Priority rights may, however, be given to senior bondholders, who would then rank ahead of subordinated bondholders (who would then normally rank alongside general unsecured creditors).

Pricing

The fair price of a bond (quoted as a percentage of par) is the present value of its future cash flows (coupons plus redemption amount) discounted at the current Yield to Maturity ('YTM'). The bond trading price will fluctuate as the yield required in the market changes, and this will affect how the bondholder receives the return:

- if a bond is purchased at a price above par (at a premium), the coupon rate will exceed the YTM but a capital loss will arise if held to maturity (to offset the excess coupon income);
- if a bond is purchased at below par (at a discount), the coupon rate will be less than the YTM and a capital gain will arise if held to maturity (to ensure the 'promised' yield at the purchase date is achieved);
- if a bond is purchased at par, the coupon rate will equal the YTM (a bond would normally be issued at a coupon rate that ensured the issue price was at or just below par).

The yield on a corporate bond will comprise the yield on a risk-free bond of similar currency and maturity (the yield on a government bond) plus a risk premium ('spread') to reflect the specific risks of the issuer. For quoted bonds, the bond market price (in the 'Secondary' capital markets) would fluctuate as the risk free rate changed (as the general level of interest rates changed), the risk characteristics of the issuer changed, or the overall demand for fixed income securities changed (supply / demand factors).

➡ For further discussion on straight bond pricing (and the sensitivity of bond prices to changes in yields), see Appendix B2.

Types of Bonds

There are a number of types of bonds other than straight, fixed rate bonds that have different coupon, redemption and conversion features:

Coupon features	
Floating Rate Floating Rate Notes ('FRN')	A coupon is initially set for the first period at a fixed spread over some reference rate (such as LIBOR), and reset at the start of each subsequent coupon period at the prevailing rate (similar to a floating rate loan). There are a variety of FRNs, including 'capped' FRNs (coupon rates are subject to a maximum rate), 'inverse floaters' (coupon rates move in opposite direction to changes in the reference rate), or 'range notes' (the coupon rate is set only if the reference rate is within a stated range, otherwise no coupon is paid).
Index-linked	Coupons (and the redemption value) are adjusted in line with inflation to ensure the real yield is maintained.
Zero Coupon	No coupon is paid, and the required yield is obtained solely from a capital gain (the purchase price is significantly below the redemption amount).
Low coupon 'Deep Discount' / 'Original Issue Discount'	The coupon rate is well below the required yield, with the deficit provided by way of a capital gain on redemption (the purchase price is below the redemption amount, usually at a discount of at least 15%).
High coupon 'High Yield Debt'	The required yield (measured as a spread over the yield on government bonds) is relatively high due to the poor credit quality of the issuer.
Other coupon features	'Participating Bond': the bondholder is entitled to a share of the profits above the coupon rate. 'Dual Coupon': the coupon rate changes after a specified period. 'Pay-in-kind': the bond issuer has an option to pay interest in kind by issuing new similar bonds to the bondholder in lieu of cash.

	Redemption and Conversion features
Perpetual	A coupon is paid in perpetuity and the bond is never redeemed.
Dual currency	The bondholder has the right to receive the redemption value in one of two possible currencies at an exchange rate fixed at issue.
Equity Clawback	The issuer has the right to redeem part of the bonds at a premium with the proceeds of any equity rights issue.
Convertibles	A fixed rate coupon is paid until maturity as for a straight bond, however the bondholder has the option to convert the bond into the issuer's shares (or another company's shares in the case of 'Exchangeable' bonds) at specified dates and at a specified conversion price or Conversion Ratio (number of share received for each bond). Convertibles are discussed below.

Bondholder's Evaluation

Default Risk

A bond issuer can arrange for a rating agency (such as Standard and Poor's or Moody's) to have a bond issue rated, based on an assessment of the issuer's ability to pay the bond cash flows as and when promised. The rating agency would carry out a detailed analysis of the issuing company's current and future cash flows and overall financial performance in relation to its industry sector; it would focus on operating cash flow generation, existing debt service obligations, the quality and stability of the asset base, the ability to realise funds quickly (liquidity), capital expenditure requirements, and industry specific risk (using financial ratio analysis). The rating assigned would reflect the default risk and hence the required yield at issue (Standard & Poor's and Moody's rating categories can be found on their web sites: www.standardandpoors.com and www.moodys.com).

A default would usually arise when a scheduled bond cash flow is missed or delayed, a compromise is offered to bondholders (the issuer offers to replace the bonds with a security which carries a reduced financial burden for the issuer, such as a lower coupon rate) or insolvency proceedings commence.

Other Risks

A bondholder faces the following additional risks:

- Market / interest rate risk: the bond market price fluctuates in response to yield changes - this is a risk only if the investor wishes to sell before maturity, since the bond price may fall below the redemption value (the yield expected on purchase would not be realised).

- Liquidity risk: the bond cannot be sold at its fair value due to an illiquid market (as shown by a high 'Bid-Offer' spread – the difference between a bond dealer's sale and purchase price).

- Reinvestment risk: deposit and investment rates fall such that coupons cannot be reinvested at the yield to maturity expected at the purchase date (there is an implicit assumption when calculating the expected yield, as for any IRR calculation, that cash receipts during the investment holding period can be reinvested at this yield).

- Call risk: the issuer has a call option entitling it to redeem the bonds early (prepay), leading to reinvestment risk and an uncertain cash flow profile (Callable bonds are worth less than non-Callable bonds due to this extra risk).

Borrower's Evaluation

The main benefits for a bond issuer are as follows:

- Diversification: a borrower may prefer a mix of debt funding sources, rather than rely on bank loans;

- Longer maturity: a borrower may prefer the longer maturities available with bonds compared to bank loans (to allow a better match to the investments being financed);

- Speed of issue: an issue can be arranged fairly quickly to take advantage of market conditions.

Convertible Bonds

Terminology

The holder of a Convertible bond is entitled to swap the bond for shares in the issuing company (an 'Exchangeable' would involve swapping into shares in a company other than the issuer), effectively redeeming the bond for shares rather than cash. This conversion option is exercisable at a specific date or in a predetermined period, at a specific price ('Conversion Price'). Whilst no cash is paid on conversion, the cost to the holder is the foregone value of the bond if held to redemption as a straight bond.

The fixed number of shares received for each bond ('Conversion Ratio') is set at the date of the bond issue (although the terms of the issue may allow the ratio to be adjusted for certain events, such as anti-dilution protection):

$$\text{Conversion ratio} = \frac{\text{Bond Face Value}}{\text{Share Price at issue date} \times (1+ \text{Conversion Premium \% at issue date})}$$

(The denominator is marked 'Conversion Price'.)

The Conversion Premium at any date after issue will depend on market appetite, on the expected share price growth and volatility, and on the dividends paid on the underlying shares relative to the Convertible bond coupon rate. The Conversion Price represents the minimum share price to ensure that the market value of the shares received for each bond on conversion ('Conversion Value' or 'Parity Value'= Conversion Ratio x Share Price on conversion) equals the opportunity cost of the bond as a straight bond held to redemption. If the actual share price increases above the Conversion Price, then the bond is worth more if swapped into shares.

The fair price of the Convertible will equal the fair price of the bond ignoring conversion ('Investment Value') plus a premium to reflect the value of the option to convert. The value of the conversion option means the bond issuer can reduce the bond coupon to below the rate for an equivalent non-Convertible bond (since the possible capital gain on conversion compensates). At low share prices, the conversion option is unattractive and the Convertible fair value will be set, largely, by the bond Investment Value (the bondholder is protected, since the Convertible price should never fall below the value as a straight bond). As the share price increases, so conversion becomes attractive and investors will be prepared to pay a premium over and above the Investment Value. The Convertible price will exceed the Conversion Value if the expected share price growth makes delaying conversion attractive and the bond has a yield advantage over the shares (coupon yield exceeds dividend yield).

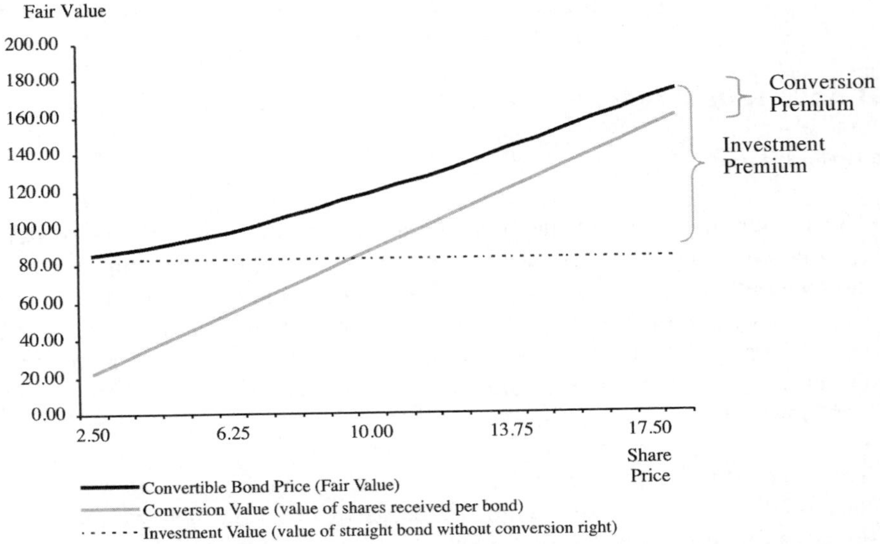

Convertible issuers are usually given rights to Call the bonds at set dates and prices. The issuer can 'force' conversion by serving notice of an intention to Call the bonds, at a time when the cost of repurchasing the bonds (Call price) is less than their Conversion Value: Convertible holders, willing to hold the equity, would immediately convert and receive the higher value shares. This avoids any cash outlay for the issuer on redemption, and effectively makes the Convertible a form of deferred equity.

Convertible Bond Pricing

At high share prices, the Convertible price will be driven by those factors affecting the share price (earnings growth, dividend yield), since the bond will effectively be trading as equity.

At low share prices, however, straight bond valuation factors (general level of interest rates, issuer credit risk, maturity, yield characteristics, call features, etc.) dominate (although credit risk will partly be determined by business risk factors such as earnings).

Over time, for a given range of possible share prices, the Convertible will be trading at prices that reflect the equity and/or debt components:

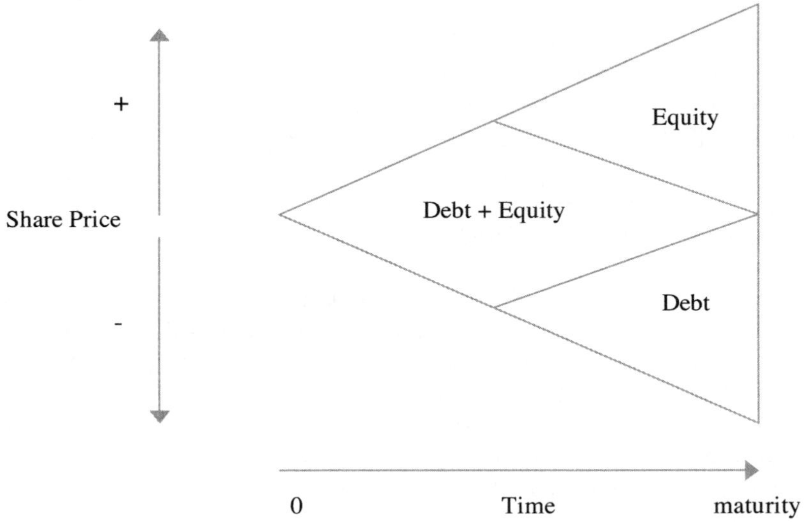

Since a Convertible has an 'embedded' option to convert to equity, the Convertible may be valued as straight debt plus an equity option.

➡ For a discussion on Convertible Bond pricing using Binomial Trees, see Appendix B5.

EQUITY

Introduction

Generally, an equity investment would enable a shareholder (1) to receive an income return in the form of dividends paid out of post-tax profits (if distributable profits were available, and if the company decided to pay a dividend), (2) to receive a repayment of the investment on the winding up of the company, limited to any surplus funds from the sale of assets after settlement of all other prior claims (liabilities and non-equity), and (3) to vote at a shareholders' meeting.

Initial Public Offerings ('IPO')

Characteristics

The shares of a company may be admitted for official listing on a recognised stock exchange, provided the company satisfies the relevant listing conditions. New investors in a flotation or IPO would subscribe for shares ('Primary Offering'), allowing the issuer to raise funds, and / or purchase existing shares off shareholders who want to sell ('Secondary Offering').

The method by which shares are offered to new investors and the offering structure will depend on the stock exchange concerned, the size of the local market, the size of the offer, the type of investor being sought, the preferred pricing procedure (such as an auction, a fixed price offer, or a 'bookbuilding' method), and whether or not funds need to be guaranteed (underwritten).

Advantages and Disadvantages

A flotation would enable a company to raise funds, to use its shares as consideration when acquiring other companies, to raise its public profile (and increase brand awareness), to provide an exit route for shareholders, and to provide incentives for its employees and management via share options. The upfront and ongoing financial costs, the stock exchange's requirements, the change in management style (particularly exposure to corporate governance practices), and the threat of an unwelcome takeover, are some of the disadvantages.

Issues to Consider

Market

If an issuer satisfies all the conditions for listing on its local exchange ('Listing Criteria'), it will still want to ensure that its stock will be fairly priced in the market;

as a minimum, the relevant market needs to be sufficiently liquid, with active trading in all shares and sectors. If the size of the offer is relatively large compared to the issuer's local market, or there is unlikely to be sufficient local demand, the issuer would need to broaden the market by accessing international demand.

A 'Dual Listing', where the issuer lists on the local market and on a recognised, liquid foreign market, may improve pricing and share performance, and raise the company's profile, but will impose additional stock exchange obligations. To avoid these, the issuer could arrange for 'Depositary Receipts' to be traded on the foreign market; these are certificates of title in respect of shares in the issuer, held in custody by a 'Depositary Bank', which acts as agent in paying any dividends on the underlying shares to the foreign investors (paid in the foreign currency). 'American Depositary Receipts' are traded in the US, 'Global Depositary Receipts' in Europe, principally London and Luxembourg (see Geddes (2003) for further discussion). There is always a risk, however, that foreign share ownership will be transferred to local investors, due to significant local demand, relative to foreign demand (this could be caused by a restricted local offer size) ('Flowback').

Economic and political factors may lead to pronounced market volatility or a prolonged downturn. A float may need to be postponed until the timing is right and market sentiment recovers, but even then there may be little demand for the new stock: if the market perceives the issuer's cash flows to be extremely volatile, unpredictable and uncertain, with little opportunity for long term sustainable growth, appetite is likely to be poor.

Offer

The offer may be at a stated price to all investors ('Offer for Sale') or selected long term investors ('Placing'), or be by way of an auction or 'Tender' (where the price is set according to bids received). The nature of the offer document ('Listing Particulars'), the underwriting arrangements and the size of issue costs will vary.

The issuer will usually carry out pre-float marketing, aimed at target long-term institutional investors. This may be combined with a 'Bookbuilding' pricing procedure, where the issuer's investment bank(s), which is managing the float process ('Global Co-Ordinator' and/or 'Lead Manager'), (1) receives from institutional investors bids for blocks of shares at stated prices over the Manager's given price range, (2) determines the optimal 'Bookbuild Price', and (3) allocates the shares at its discretion ('Institutional Offer'). The remaining non-institutional float shares ('Retail Offer') would be priced at the level of, or at small discount to, the Bookbuild price ('Retail Price'). The Lead Manager will have established the likely valuation range beforehand, having carried out its own valuation, taking into account market conditions, trading multiples for other comparable quoted companies, and relative float prices on other new issues.

Price Stabilisation

Due to insufficient demand and/or the actions of hedge funds and speculators exploiting short-term price movements immediately post-float, the share price may fall or be highly volatile. A controlled price stabilisation programme, for a limited period (subject to Stock Exchange rules), may help to prevent this. It could be achieved by the Lead Manager stimulating market demand by actively trading in the shares. The procedure would involve the following:

- the Lead Manager would allocate extra shares over and above those included in the primary offering: it would 'sell short' (shares that it does not legally own), at the float price, a number of shares that the issuer does not intend to issue (usually up to 15% extra), usually by borrowing shares from an existing non-selling shareholder under a 'stock lending' agreement;
- the short position would be 'covered' (i.e. the shares would be returned to the stock lender at the end of the agreed period, usually no more than 30 days) by (1) the Lead Manager purchasing stock in the market, if the trading price falls below the float price (giving a profit), or (2) at the Lead Manager's request, the company issuing additional shares to the Lead Manager at the float price.

The Lead Manager's right to force the company to issue it new shares at a fixed price ((2) above) would be an option - an 'Over-Allotment' or 'Greenshoe' option – granted to it by the issuer at the time of the float, so as to ensure price stabilisation can occur without the Lead Manager suffering any loss. Without a guaranteed maximum repurchase price, the Lead Manager would suffer a loss if it had to cover its short position by buying in the market at a price above the short sale price (offer price). The company would effectively be insuring against a price fall. If the price actually rose, the Greenshoe would be exercised and the company would receive more funds; existing shareholders would be diluted, unless they had a right to subscribe for new shares to preserve their percentage shareholding.

⇨ See Appendix D3 for an example of an IPO.

Rights Issues

A company may need additional equity finance, in which case it could offer its existing shareholders additional shares, to be subscribed for in cash in proportion to their shareholdings ('Rights Issue'). To encourage shareholders to increase their holdings, the shares may be offered at a discount to the existing price (subject to any legal restrictions). Shareholders who do not wish to participate can sell their 'rights' (the theoretical profit if the additional shares were subscribed for and immediately sold, being the difference between the diluted share price after the rights – the 'Theoretical Ex-Rights Price' – and the rights offer price). If priced fair, the value of a holding pre- and post-rights should be the same if the shares are subscribed for or the rights sold.

A rights issue can be seen as an issue of shares at full price plus a 'bonus issue' of free shares.

Example 2.3 Rights Issue

A company valued at £300m intends to raise £45m via a 1 for 6 rights issue at a 10% discount to the current £3.00 share price. The equity value should increase by the cash injected into the company (new value £345m), but the rights discount means the post-rights share price will be diluted to £2.96. The £45m will, effectively, be raised by issuing 15m shares at the £3.00 price and 1.67m bonus shares.

Assumptions	
Current share price	£3.00
Shares in issue	100.0 m
Cash to be raised	£45.0 m
Rights discount	10.0%

Impact for all shareholders

	Shares #	*Price*	*Value*
At present	100.00 m	£3.00	£300.0 m
Rights issue (1 for 6)	16.67 m	£2.70	£45.0 m
Post-rights issue	116.67 m	£2.96 *	£345.0 m

* Theoretical Ex-Rights Price

Payoff on rights = dilution factor x (£3.00 - £2.70) = £0.26

where dilution factor = $1 / (1 + \gamma) = 1 / (1 + (16.67 / 100.00)) = 0.8571$

Or shown as:

	Shares #	*Price*	*Value*
At present	100.00 m	£3.00	£300.0 m
Issue at full price	15.00 m	£3.00	£45.0 m
	115.00 m	£3.00	£345.0 m
Bonus issue (1 for 9 rights shares)	1.67 m		
	116.67 m	£2.96	£345.0 m

The dilution factor is now $1 / (1 + \gamma^*) = 1 / (1 + (1.67 / 115.00)) = 0.9857$

Impact for a shareholder with 6 shares:

	Shares #	*Price*	*Value*
Pre - rights issue	6	£3.00	£18.00
Take up rights			
Cost of rights	1	-£2.70	-£2.70
Post - rights issue	7	£2.96	£20.70
			£18.00
Change invalue			£0.00
Sell rights			
Sale of rights (not shares)	1	£0.26	£0.26
Post - rights issue	6	£2.96	£17.74
			£18.00
Change invalue			£0.00

Warrants

A Warrant is a right to subscribe for new shares to be issued (cash is paid to the issuing company), whereas an Option is a right to buy or sell shares already issued (cash is paid to or received from third parties). The option pricing models discussed in Appendix B4 (the Binomial Model and Black-Scholes model) can be used to determine the fair value of an option or a warrant (providing an adjustment is made for the dilution effect on the share price, caused by the issue of new shares).

The rights issue in **Example B2.3** can be analysed in terms of a warrant, exercisable at the rights issue price. At the date of the rights issue, the value of each right is the value of an equivalent warrant:

$$\text{'Warrant' value at exercise} = \left(\begin{matrix}\text{Price}\\ \text{Dilution}\end{matrix} \times \begin{matrix}\text{Pre-rights}\\ \text{Share price}\end{matrix} \right) - \begin{matrix}\text{Rights}\\ \text{Price}\end{matrix}$$

$$= (0.9857 \times £3.00) = £2.96 - £2.70 = £0.26$$

$$\text{'Warrant' value at exercise} = \begin{matrix}\text{Share}\\ \text{Dilution}\end{matrix} \times \left(\begin{matrix}\text{Pre-rights}\\ \text{Share price}\end{matrix} - \begin{matrix}\text{Rights}\\ \text{Price}\end{matrix} \right)$$

$$= 0.8571 \times (£3.00 - £2.70) = £0.26$$

Since warrants have already been issued, but not exercised, they will have a value that needs to be added to the current share price (assuming no value has already been factored in - this follows the approach suggested by Galai and Schneller (1978), see Hull (2003 p.249)):

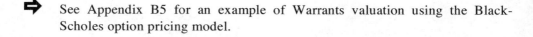

$$\text{Warrant value at exercise} = \frac{1}{(1+\gamma)} \times \text{MAX}\left(\frac{V}{N} - \text{Exercise price} \right)$$

where V is the equity value (inclusive of a value for the warrants) and N is the existing number of shares.

⇨ See Appendix B5 for an example of Warrants valuation using the Black-Scholes option pricing model.

3 CAPITAL MANAGEMENT

INTRODUCTION

Chapter Contents

When considering how to finance capital investments (see Chapter 1 and Appendix B1), a company needs to be aware of available funding and financing sources (see Chapter 2 and Appendices B2 and C), what proportion of each should be raised, and how the capital should be managed so as to maintain value for shareholders. This Chapter discusses management of long-term debt and equity (debt management using Derivatives is discussed in Chapter 4) and short-term working capital (cash management is limited to a discussion on short-term Money Market investment opportunities).

Long Term Capital

The proportion of debt and equity in the capital structure has implications for the Cost of Capital and hence the intrinsic value of a company (see Appendix B1). At some level, increasing the proportion of low cost (after-tax) debt will have a detrimental effect due to the increased financial risk and threat of bankruptcy. The traditional theory of capital structure states that there is some optimal debt and equity mix (minimum Cost of Capital, maximum intrinsic value). It is debatable, however, whether companies are rewarded for adopting a financing policy that aims for a target, optimal capital structure (and even whether such a policy is adopted). Debt may be preferred to equity since (1) it is cheaper and less risky (the 'Pecking Order' theory mentioned in Appendix B1), (2) it imposes discipline on the investment process by forcing companies to pay out surplus Free Cash Flows that might otherwise be invested in projects that generate inadequate returns (Jensen (1986)), and (3) it signals to the market that the company is confident of the level of future Free Cash Flows (Ross (1977)). Furthermore, an equity issue may lead to a market perception that the company believes the share price is overvalued (conversely, a share buyback might indicate a belief that the share price is undervalued) or that the equity will simply be used to pay off debt ((Myers (1977)), thereby increasing the required return. This chapter focuses on practical issues concerning long term capital management.

Short Term Capital

The present value of operating cash flows will be affected by the terms of credit offered (customers) and accepted (suppliers), and the management of gross working capital (i.e. ensuring customers comply with terms offered, and maximising the benefits of credit given by suppliers). Amounts due from third parties may be sold or 'securitised', and may be accounted for as a sale rather than an asset-backed loan.

LONG TERM CAPITAL MANAGEMENT

Debt

Borrower's Objectives

In general, a borrower would wish to ensure that, in respect of existing debt:

- financial forecasts, based on the most likely operating scenarios, indicate that (1) debt cash flows are fully covered by and reasonably matched to (correlated with) operating cash flows (this partly depends on where the company is in its 'life-cycle' – high growth vs. mature – and how predictable and stable its operating cash flows are), and (2) no breach will arise in respect of financial covenants;
- the after-tax Cost of Debt is minimised by (1) maintaining debt at optimal levels (see Appendix B1 for a discussion on the capital structure and its effect on the Cost of Capital), (2) refinancing at lower rates, if interest rates and/or the borrower's credit risk fall, (3) using interest rate risk derivatives to reduce the effective cost (discussed in Chapter 4), and (4) ensuring maximum tax relief is available;
- the debt servicing 'profile' (interest payment frequency and principal amortisation structure and maturity) is appropriate, given the nature of the assets being financed (the average life of debt is matched to the expected economic lives of assets – or, preferably, their respective 'Duration' measures are matched (see Appendix B2)) and the volatility of operating cash flows: 'core' debt matched to the long term asset base (and serviced from 'normalised', sustainable operating cash flows) and a fluctuating element matched to short term investments (too much short term debt, however, will expose the borrower to the risk of refinancing - 'rolling over' existing debt - when market conditions are unfavourable);
- interest rate and currency risks implicit in the debt are measured and managed (for example, the mix of fixed and floating rate interest needs to take account of the sensitivity of operating cash flows to changes in the interest rates) (discussed in Chapter 4).

In respect of new debt, the borrower will want to ensure that:

- it will be able to raise debt finance as and when required, when markets conditions are favourable, and when its negotiating position is strong;
- the terms of new debt are favourable and will not reduce flexibility when making future financing decisions;
- there is no potential for conflict with existing debt facilities;
- good relations are maintained with the new debt providers at all times.

Issues to Consider

Loans

It may be preferable to raise further debt from existing debt providers, if, for example, the size of an existing facility can be increased at little extra cost (in terms of the interest cost and financial covenants), compared to negotiating a new facility with a new lender (assuming the credit risk of the borrower has not changed – if its negotiating position has improved due to a lower default risk, then the borrower would seek to exert maximum pressure on existing lenders to offer the best terms on the new debt).

Bonds

If yields are falling, a bond's trading price (excluding accrued interest) may increase above its face value (coupon rate exceeds yield). If a borrower was permitted to redeem the bonds early, it could refinance them at a lower coupon rate by issuing new bonds at par, priced at the lower required yield (coupon rate equals yield).

Example 3.1 Bond Refinancing

On 24 June 2004 a company refinances its existing 6% 7 Sept 2014 bonds (issued just under 5 years ago at a yield of 6%) since yields have fallen to 5.0%. It raises sufficient funds to repay the bonds (£111.88m, inclusive of refinance costs and accrued interest) by issuing bonds at par and reducing its annual coupon costs by approximately 7% (assuming the terms are identical). (In practice, the tax effects of the refinancing would have to be considered.)

		Old debt	*New debt*
Issue date		7 September 1999	24 June 2004
Last coupon date		7 March 2004	-
Next coupon date		7 September 2004	7 September 2004
Maturity date		7 September 2014	7 September 2014
Nominal value		£100	£100
Coupon		6.00%	5.00%
Coupon periods per year		2	2
Valuation date		24 June 2004	24 June 2004
Yield at issue date		6.00%	5.00%
Yield at valuation date		5.00%	5.00%
Price (incl. accrued interest)		109.69	100.00
Bonds in issue		1,000,000	1,118,787
Market value		£109.69m	£111.88m
Repurchase costs	2.00%	£2.19m	
Buyback cost		£111.88m	
Annual coupon cost		£60,000	£55,939

As well as buying back the bonds on the market, the borrower could exercise any call option, granted to it at the time of the bond issue, to repurchase the bonds according to a schedule of fixed prices for a given set of call dates. The borrower would not call the bonds until the trading price had exceeded the call price by some margin (to provide for the costs of refinancing).

Equity

Distributions

Dividends

The proportion of annual profits distributed will depend on a number of factors:

- company law provisions that restrict the dividend to the maximum distributable profits, so as to protect creditors;
- internal restrictions contained in financing agreements: loan and bond agreements are likely to contain dividend related covenants;
- the amount of fixed and working capital investment needed to achieve expected future profits;
- the advantages of financing capital investment from internal (reinvesting profits) as opposed to external (new debt and equity) sources, and the availability of these sources;
- shareholders' preference for receiving a greater part of their required return from dividend income rather than capital gain (from growth in equity value due to the reinvestment of profits in value creating investments): this could be due to tax reasons, a fear that growth will not be achieved, or a need for an income; and
- for a quoted company, the likely impact on the share price of a dividend announcement (increase or a cut): how to meet current market expectations, how to convey positive information about future prospects, and how to manage expectations of future dividend levels.

Share Buybacks

If a company cannot invest its fixed capital in projects that earn the shareholders' required rate of return, then it should consider ceasing such investments and returning surplus cash to shareholders, to allow them to earn their return elsewhere. Cash could be returned as a 'special' dividend or as consideration for the company repurchasing some of the shares (a share 'buyback' or 'stock repurchase'), usually over time as part of a repurchase programme. For tax purposes, the buyback may be treated as a part repayment of capital plus a distribution, whereas the special dividend would be a distribution. Both the tax treatment and the level of distributable profits will need to be considered.

The buyback mechanism will depend on local stock exchange and company law provisions, tax issues and the preferred method of pricing (whether shares are acquired in the open market or via an off-market offer or auction, for example).

A share buyback can also:

- enable a company to gradually adjust its capital structure to its preferred level by increasing leverage: the book value of equity decreases as shares are repurchased and cancelled, and net debt increases as surplus cash is reduced (gross debt will increase if the buyback is financed with new debt);
- signal to the market (1) the company's belief that the share price is undervalued or (2) the company's optimism about the level of future cash flows, if the buyback is financed with debt (see Grullon and Ikenberry (2003));
- increase the Earnings Per Share on the remaining shares in issue after the buyback: this may be an illusory benefit - similar to the bootstrapping effect for mergers and acquisitions discussed in Chapter 1 **Example 1.7** – that arises simply because the percentage reduction in profits from the cost of financing the buyback is less than the percentage reduction in the number of shares (the share price would only increase if it was driven solely by the P/E multiple and the P/E did not reduce).

Example 3.2 Share Buyback Impact

A quoted company is to commence a share buyback programme in order distribute to shareholders some of its surplus cash. The company is unable to achieve sufficient rates of return on invested capital: the expected post-tax return on capital over the next three years (6.9% - 7.3%) is less than the Cost of Capital (9%); the expected post-tax return on equity (7.5% - 7.9%) is less than the geared Cost of Equity (10-11%).

A buyback has been chosen in preference to increasing the current dividend levels (60% of post-tax profits are currently paid out as dividends). The company intends, as soon as possible, to purchase 'on-market' 10% of its issued shares at the current 47p share price (cost of buyback = £23.5m). Further repurchases will take place at later dates, depending on the success of the programme and whether or not the company is able to find suitable investment opportunities for the remaining surplus cash.

The company expects the buyback to have the following incremental impact over the next 3 years (compared to the position without any buyback):

- Earnings Per Share (EPS) to increase by approximately 7.5% p.a.;
- leverage (book values) to increase 4% up to a maximum of 21% (using forecast future market values, based on a Dividend Discount Model approach – see **1.5** in Chapter 1 - the leverage is expected to increase to a maximum of 33%);
- return on equity to increase marginally.

The company expects a marginal increase in the year 1 dividend per share and shareholders' required rate of return; the P / E ratio, based on a dividend discount model, is expected to reduce slightly over the next 3 years. Shareholder wealth (the buyback proceeds, with interest earned at the shareholders' required rate of return, plus the value of the remaining shares) is expected to increase £4.5m immediately (ignoring the tax effect of the buyback).

The highlights are as follows (figures are in £m unless stated otherwise):

Valuation Measures	
Share price	47p
Shares in issue	500.0m
Market Capitalisation	£235.0m
Latest EPS	6.4p
Trailing P/E x	7.3 x
Trailing EBITDA x	4.1 x
Price-to-Book x	0.5 x
Leverage (book value)	16.7%

Cost of Capital	
Risk Free Rate	5.5%
Ungeared / asset beta	0.90
Equity Risk Premium	4.5%
Debt Risk Premium	0.85%
Ungeared Cost of Equity	9.6%
Geared Cost of Equity	10.6%
Post-tax Cost of Debt (t = 30%)	4.4%
Leverage (mkt cap)	27.7%
WACC	8.9%

Capital (book value)	
Cash	85.0
Debt	175.0
Net Debt	90.0
BV Equity	450.0
Book value of capital	*540.0*

Buyback details	
Shares repurchased	50.0m
Percentage of shares acquired	10%
Repurchase price premium	0.0%
Repurchase cost	£23.5m
Repurchase P/E	7.3 x
Breakeven PE	22.5 x

Immediate impact (before and after buyback)	*Before*	*After*
Pre-tax Cost of Debt	6.4%	6.4%
Geared Cost of Equity	10.6%	10.9%
Dividend per Share - end year 1	4.08p	4.28p
Long term growth rate (g)	2.0%	2.0%
Share price = D1 / (K - g)	47p	48p
Shares in issue	500.0m	450.0m
P / E	7.3 x	7.5 x
Market Capitalisation	£235.0m	£216.0m
Cash from buyback	-	£23.5m
Wealth (before tax effect)	*£235.0m*	*£239.5m*

Forecast highlights (ignoring buyback)	*Year 1*	*Year 2*	*Year 3*
NOPAT	37.4	39.2	41.2
Profits After Tax	33.7	35.7	37.7
Dividends	20.4	21.7	23.0
Equity Capital (BV)	463.3	477.3	492.0
Net Debt	90.0	90.0	90.0
Post-tax ROE	7.5%	7.7%	7.9%
Post-tax ROIC	6.9%	7.1%	7.3%

Impact Analysis

Forecast year		1	2	3
Shares in issue				
Pre-buyback		500m	500m	500m
Post-buyback	❶	450m	450m	450m
EPS				
Pre-buyback		6.74p	7.13p	7.55p
Post-buyback		7.23p	7.67p	8.12p
Change		+ 0.50p	+ 0.53p	+ 0.57p
Change		7.4%	7.5%	7.6%
Breakeven increase in cost of debt	❷	+ 1.82%	+ 1.96%	+ 2.10%
Return on Equity				
Pre-buyback		7.5%	7.7%	7.9%
Post-buyback		7.6%	7.8%	8.1%
Change		+ 0.1%	+ 0.1%	+ 0.1%
Dividend payout ratio				
Pre-buyback	❸	60.5%	60.8%	61.1%
Post-buyback		59.1%	59.5%	59.8%
Change		-1.4%	-1.3%	-1.3%
Estimated P/E (trailing)	❹			
Pre-buyback		7.6 x	7.6 x	7.7 x
Post-buyback		7.0 x	7.2 x	7.3 x
Change		-0.5 x	-0.4 x	-0.4 x

		Forecast year	1	2	3
Shareholder value at year end					
Pre-buyback	Value of shares		£255m	£270m	£290m
Post-buyback	Value of shares		£230m	£248m	£266m
	Buyback cash	❺	£26m	£28m	£31m
	Total value		£255m	£276m	£296m
Change			£0m	£6m	£6m
Geared Cost of Equity					
Pre-buyback			10.6%	10.5%	10.4%
Post-buyback			11.0%	10.9%	10.8%
Change		❻	*+ 0.4%*	*+ 0.4%*	*+ 0.3%*
Cost of debt (after-tax)					
Pre-buyback			4.4%	4.4%	4.4%
Post-buyback			4.4%	4.4%	4.4%
Change			-	-	-
Leverage (net debt / capital) - market value					
Pre-buyback			26.1%	25.0%	23.7%
Post-buyback			33.1%	31.4%	29.9%
Change			*+ 7.0%*	*+ 6.4%*	*+ 6.3%*
Cost of Capital					
Pre-buyback			9.0%	9.0%	9.0%
Post-buyback			8.8%	8.8%	8.9%
Change			*-0.2%*	*-0.1%*	*-0.1%*

Notes

❶ 10% of shares are repurchased immediately; the impact of future buybacks is not shown.

❷ This shows the minimum increase in the cost of existing debt, in response to extra financial risk due to higher leverage, above which EPS would reduce. In the example, it has been assumed that the Cost of Debt will not increase due to the slight increase in leveage.

❸ Equity cash flows are paid out in full as dividends (Free Cash Flows less post-tax debt servicing). The above payout ratio is the dividend as a percentage of profits after tax.

❹ The trailing P/E is the estimated share price at each year end divided by EPS for that year. Theoretical share prices have been calculated based on the expected dividend for the next year, growing in perpetuity at a nominal 2% growth rate per annum (discounted at the geared Cost of Equity).

❺ It is assumed that shareholders can reinvest the buyback cash at their required rate of return (9.6% ungeared Cost of Equity).

❻ The geared Cost of Equity (estimated using the CAPM – see Appendix B1) increases due to leverage.

	PRE BUYBACK			POST BUYBACK		
Forecast year	1	2	3	1	2	3
Cash flow / P&L extract						
EBITDA *	80.0	84.0	88.2			
Capex and working capital change	(40.0)	(41.9)	(44.0)			
Tax (ignoring financing) *	(16.0)	(16.8)	(17.7)			
Free Cash Flow	24.0	25.2	26.5	24.0	25.2	26.5
Interest payable (net of tax relief)	(7.8)	(7.8)	(7.8)	(7.8)	(7.8)	(7.8)
Interest received (net of tax)	4.1	4.2	4.3	3.0	3.1	3.1
Sale of short term investments				23.5		
Share buyback (at start of year)				(23.5)		
Dividends	(20.4)	(21.7)	(23.0)	(19.2)	(20.5)	(21.9)
Net cash flow	**0.0**	**0.0**	**0.0**	**0.0**	**0.0**	**0.0**
add back: capex, dividends, buyback, funding	60.3	63.6	67.1	59.2	62.5	65.9
Depreciation charge *	(26.6)	(28.0)	(29.4)	(26.6)	(28.0)	(29.4)
Profit after tax	**33.7**	**35.7**	**37.7**	**32.6**	**34.5**	**36.5**
Net Operating Profits After Taxes (NOPAT) *	37.4	39.2	41.2	37.4	39.2	41.2
Balance Sheet extracts						
Surplus cash (short term investments)	85.0	85.0	85.0	61.5	61.5	61.5
Debt	175.0	175.0	175.0	175.0	175.0	175.0
Net debt	90.0	90.0	90.0	113.5	113.5	113.5
Equity	463.3	477.3	492.0	439.8	453.8	468.5
Capital	553.3	567.3	582.0	553.3	567.3	582.0
Net Operating Assets	553.3	567.3	582.0	553.3	567.3	582.0
Shares in issue	500.0m	500.0m	500.0m	450.0m	450.0m	450.0m
Cost of Capital						
Risk Free Rate	5.5%	5.5%	5.5%	5.5%	5.5%	5.5%
Equity Risk Premium	4.5%	4.5%	4.5%	4.5%	4.5%	4.5%
Ungeared beta	0.90	0.90	0.90	0.90	0.90	0.90
Geared beta (with tax)	1.12	1.11	1.10	1.21	1.19	1.17
Geared Cost of Equity	10.6%	10.5%	10.4%	11.0%	10.9%	10.8%
Pre-tax Cost of Debt	6.4%	6.4%	6.4%	6.4%	6.4%	6.4%
After tax Cost of Debt	4.4%	4.4%	4.4%	4.4%	4.4%	4.4%
Leverage (net debt / mkt value capital) - end year	26.1%	25.0%	23.7%	33.1%	31.4%	29.9%
WACC	**9.0%**	**9.0%**	**9.0%**	**8.8%**	**8.8%**	**8.9%**
Valuation						
EPS	6.74p	7.13p	7.55p	7.23p	7.67p	8.12p
Dividend per share	4.08p	4.34p	4.61p	4.28p	4.56p	4.86p
Dividend payout ratio	60.5%	60.8%	61.1%	59.1%	59.5%	59.8%
Dividend growth rate	6.0%	6.4%	6.3%	0.0%	6.6%	6.5%
Share price (dividend discount model)	51p	54p	58p	51p	55p	59p
Share price growth	8.5%	5.9%	7.4%	8.5%	7.8%	7.3%
Market Value of equity at year end [1]	£255m	£270m	£290m	£230m	£248m	£266m
Market:Book ratio	0.6 x	0.6 x	0.6 x	0.5 x	0.5 x	0.6 x
Enterprise value / EBITDA multiple	5.4 x	5.3 x	5.3 x	5.1 x	5.0 x	5.0 x
P:E Multiple	7.6 x	7.6 x	7.7 x	7.0 x	7.2 x	7.3 x
Earnings yield	13.2%	13.2%	13.0%	14.2%	13.9%	13.8%

[1] = Next year dividend / (Geared Cost of Equity - 2% growth)

EPS should increase, following a buyback, so long as the percentage reduction in profits is less than the percentage reduction in the number of shares. Profits will reduce due to the cost of financing the buyback. In this example, the buyback has been financed from surplus cash; if financed with new debt, then the break-even buyback price (assuming no change in the Cost of Debt), above which EPS will reduce, can be calculated as the current EPS divided by the after-tax Cost of Debt (144.4p in the example, giving a break-even P/E purchase price of 22.5):

Latest EPS	6.4p
Post-tax cost of debt	4.4%
Break-even price	144.4p
Premium to current	207.2%

$$\text{Break-even purchase price} = \frac{\text{EPS}}{\text{Post-tax cost of debt}}$$

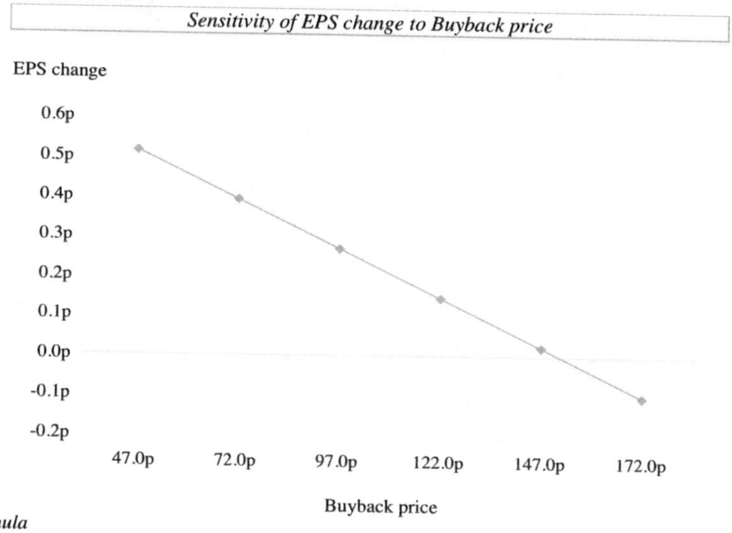

Break even formula

For the Earnings per Share to be the same before and after the buyback:

$$\text{Current EPS} = \frac{\text{Current net profits} - (\text{After-tax cost of debt} \times \text{Shares repurchased} \times \text{Buyback price})}{\text{Current shares} - \text{Shares repurchased}}$$

$$\text{Buyback price} = \frac{\text{Current net profits} - \text{Current EPS} \times (\text{Current shares} - \text{Shares repurchased})}{\text{After tax cost of debt} \times \text{Shares repurchased}}$$

$$= \frac{\text{Current EPS} \times \text{Shares repurchased}}{\text{After tax cost of debt} \times \text{Shares repurchased}}$$

$$= \frac{\text{Current EPS}}{\text{After tax cost of debt}}$$

$$\text{Break even Buyback P/E} = \frac{1}{\text{After tax cost of debt}}$$

$$\text{Break even im plied earnings yield} = \text{After tax cost of debt}$$

Equity Restructuring

The directors of a quoted company may feel that the share price does not fully reflect the aggregate fair value of each component business. They may perceive a discount to the 'sum of the parts' valuation implicit in the share price, or an insufficient 'rating' of certain high growth businesses in the group. Unlocking shareholder value may be possible by making underlying businesses more transparent (via separate financial reporting) and/or by allowing direct ownership in those businesses (to increase the valuation of the business as a stand-alone compared to its implicit value within the group). Examples of equity restructuring include the following:

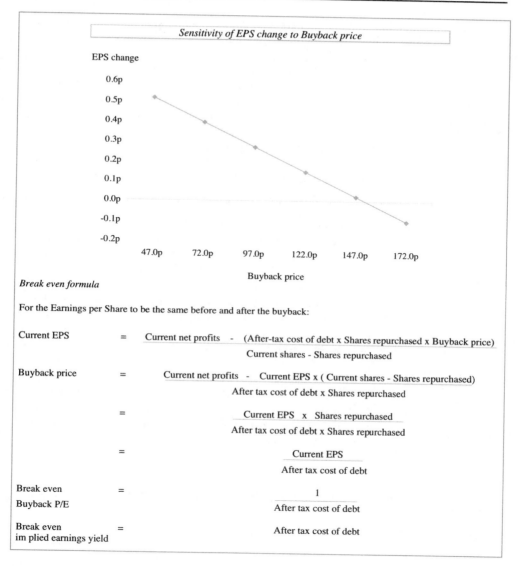

- Demerger	One or more divisions are transferred out of a single company into new separate subsidiaries.
- Spin-off	Existing shareholders acquire a direct shareholding in a subsidiary with no cash cost (transferred as a dividend in specie), resulting in the business being a new stand-alone entity, unaffected by the performance of its former parent.
- Carve - out	New shareholders acquire a holding (usually a minority interest) in a subsidiary or a division, either following a direct sale by the parent or following a subscription for new shares, possibly on a flotation.
- Tracking stock (or 'Targeted' stock)	A new class of share is issued that provides a return linked to the operating performance of a business unit. This could allow a high growth business to be rated separately from the other businesses in the group, and hence attract a wider or different type of investor (a 'growth' investor interested in undervalued earnings growth potential, as indicated by a relatively low price/earnings ratio). This may have some of the effects of a merger but without the legal separation of the businesses (and related costs).
- Bonus issues / stock splits	Additional shares are issued to existing shareholders in proportion to their holdings for no cash consideration, diluting the fair value per share, without changing the wealth of shareholders. This enables a company to reduce its share price to a level that might attract more buyers.

SHORT TERM CAPITAL MANAGEMENT

Working Capital

Introduction

'Gross Working Capital' represents investment in short term operating assets (stock and trade debtors), not financed by short-term operating liabilities (trade creditors). 'Net Working Capital' adds in operating cash balances that are essential to the daily operating needs of the business and are not surplus funds that could be used to repay debt (included in Net Debt). This section is concerned with Gross Working Capital, principally its management and effect on operating cash flows.

Operating Cycle

An increase in Working Capital represents (1) current year net operating profits received as cash next year or thereafter (net profit on credit, increasing net trade debtors), (2) prior year net operating costs paid for this year (settlement of opening balances), and (3) stock purchased and paid for this year but unsold at the year end (see Appendix D2 ❸ for a simple illustration of a cycle over one period) where a bank lender is carrying out a financial review of a customer). An increase in Working Capital will require financing

The amount of financing due to (1) above will depend on the Operating Cycle. For example, a manufacturing company, which purchases materials and processes them into finished stock for sale, might have the following (simplified) cycle: (A) materials are ordered and delivered (and, in some cases, paid for), (B) the material is used to manufacture goods, and operating costs are accrued (some goods will be unfinished Work-In-Progress at the year end), (C) purchased materials, manufacturing overheads and other operating costs are paid for (some of these may be paid when incurred or remain unpaid at the year end in accordance with suppliers' credit terms), (D) finished goods are sold for cash and on credit, and (E) credit sales are paid for. Financing will be required due to the cash flow timing differences: the length of time it takes to process and sell stock, during which costs have been incurred and paid for - (A) to (D) - plus the length of time it takes to receive cash from stock sold on credit - (D) to (E) - less the credit period given by suppliers.

If sales are rapidly increasing, then Working Capital needs to grow at a manageable rate to ensure the peak funding requirement can be financed out of sales receipts and timing differences are minimal and constant. If the Operating Cycle increases, then additional financing will be required. The sensitivity of monthly operating profits to seasonal demand patterns will also have an effect (the example in Appendix D2 illustrates this).

Working Capital Policies

Credit management aims to:

- accelerate and maximise customer collections (subject to terms remaining competitive) by:
  - invoicing without delay after delivery;
  - encouraging early settlement via cash discounts (subject to an evaluation of the cash discount cost / early receipt benefit);
  - negotiating settlement of outstanding amounts;
  - minimising the exposure to customer defaults via an up-front credit review;
- delay supplier payments by:
  - taking the maximum credit offered;
  - negotiating for special extended credit terms;

- hold optimal stock balances by:
  - planning raw material purchases and Work-in-Progress in line with production and sales forecasts;
  - increasing the accuracy of forecasts;
  - ensuring suppliers are reliable and can deliver when required.

Trade Receivables Securitisation

Introduction

Securitisation is the sale by an 'Originator' of financial assets (such as trade debtors or receivables) to a third party (usually a 'Special Purpose Vehicle', 'SPV', set up for the transaction, owned by Investors and financed by the issue of debt securities). The financial assets would need to meet certain eligibility criteria and generate identifiable and relatively predictable cash flows that can be used to provide security for and service the debt.

The arrangement may be a single sale or a facility that gives the Investors an option to purchase further financial assets over an agreed term. In such a rolling facility, any cash flows received by the SPV from the financial assets (income and capital, where amounts are collected by the Originator as agent for the SPV), in excess of amounts required to service its debt and pay all fees and expenses, could be used to purchase more assets.

Accounting Treatment

If the transaction is recognised under local accounting provisions as a genuine arm's length sale, the financial asset will be removed from the balance sheet. Sale recognition will reflect the commercial substance of the arrangement and the sharing of risks between the Originator and the SPV. For example, if the SPV's return does not depend on any risks associated with the financial assets (such as the risk of a customer defaulting in a trade receivables securitisation), but only depends on risk associated with the Originator (i.e. default risk), then the transaction is, in effect, a secured loan. In this case, the financial asset should remain on the balance sheet and a loan would be recorded.

The financial assets may be sold at a discount to their market value, reflecting a provision to cover potential future losses and to meet the SPV's financing costs. In this case, the non-returnable discounted sale price would represent the genuine sale component (treatment of the discount component would vary – in the UK, part of it, relating to the loss provision, would remain on the balance sheet as part of the non-securitised financial assets, recoverable from the SPV only if the provision is not required).

Trade Receivables

A large pool of trade debtors can be securitised to reduce Working Capital levels. If the facility is a rolling programme, then the reduction will last the length of the facility (usually short to medium term). The Originator would sell the qualifying trade debtor balances to the SPV in return for the discounted sale price ('Net Investment'). The transaction would need to be treated as a true sale.

On day one, the Originator would receive the Net Investment funding in respect of the qualifying debtors outstanding at that date (part of the outstanding amounts being held back and allocated to the reserve element of the purchase price). Having assigned the customer contracts to the SPV, the Originator continues, on behalf of the SPV, to seek repayment from the outstanding trade debtors. Collections received and transferred to the SPV would be used to purchase new invoiced amounts on those contracts.

The eligibility criteria cover a range of requirements to ensure the qualifying trade debtors pool maintains a high quality, is well diversified and not too exposed to trade debtor default risk (for example, for the day one sale, invoices unpaid for a certain number of days would be non-qualifying). This should ensure that the best possible rating is given to the SPV's securities (usually short term rated debt securities, such as Commercial Paper).

The Originator would hope to benefit from converting the debtor balances into cash at a cost of financing that is lower than a straight unsecured loan. Some financial ratios may appear to have improved, given that assets have been taken off-balance sheet.

Example 3.3 Trade Receivables / Debtors Securitisation

A company is to securitise its trade debtors via a 5 year rolling facility. All of its customer contracts meet the initial conditions required by the Investors, however of the total £440m due from these customers only some £295m can be included in the programme (the balance relate to aged, disputed, foreign currency and other debts not meeting the qualifying conditions). The Investors, acting via an SPV (in the form of a Trust), have agreed to purchase £222.5m of the qualifying trade debtors balance at their book value, but will retain some of the purchase price as a provision for potential losses arising (£10.5m) and for financing costs for the first month (£12.5m) (£22.5m total 'Reserves'). The Investors will finance the £200m discounted sale price ('Net Investment') by issuing short term highly rated Commercial Paper.

At the end of the first month, collections from customers received by the Originator as agent for the Trust and identified as relating to the qualifying debtor balances that have been purchased to date by the Trust (£145.2m), will be transferred to the Trust. These collections will be allocated as follows:

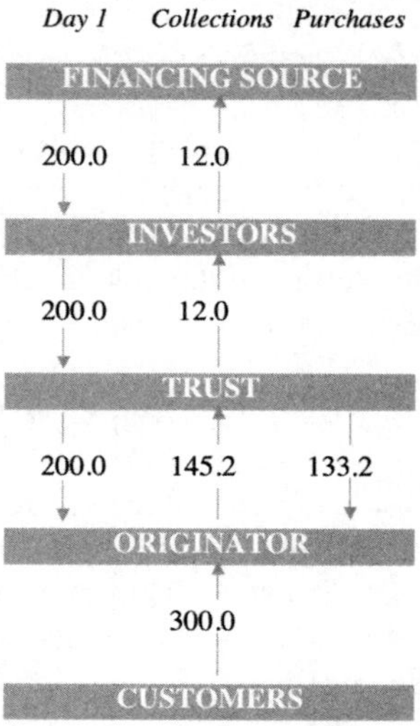

(1) £12m will be paid to the Investors to finance the £200m Commercial Paper;

(2) £2.7m will be payable to the Originator since it relates to collections on debts provided for by way of the £10.5m provision in the reserves (this represents the deferred part of the initial £222.5m purchase price that is now being paid, since a provision is no longer required); and

(3) the £130.5m balance will be paid to the Originator as payment for new debtor balances arising on amounts invoiced (£152.7m) less a £22.2m increase in required reserves (£12m for the following month's financing cost, £2.7m to increase the general provision, and £7.5m as a specific provision for debtor balances purchased that are now thought to be non-recoverable).

Hence, a total amount of £133.2m will be paid back to the Originator, as shown in the diagram above. The Investors' share of the total qualifying trade debtors' pool will increase from the £222.5m purchased on day 1 to £230m, the increase representing the excess of the invoiced amounts purchased (£152.7m) over the amounts collected (£145.2m). In practice, the only cash transfers will be the payment from the Originator of the £12.0m financing cost. The original £200m will only be increased if the facility size is increased. Detailed entries for the day 1 and first month are shown below (this would be replicated across all future months over the 5 year facility term).

		Start Month 1	*Invoiced on credit*	*Collections*	*End Month 1*	
Opening trade debtors		440.0		(300.0)	140.0	
Invoiced in month			280.0		280.0	
less: non-qualifying		(145.0)	(75.0)	107.5	(112.5)	
Closing qualifying trade debtors		295.0	205.0	(192.5)	307.5	
less: Originator's share		(72.5)	(52.3)	47.3	(77.5)	
Investors' share		222.5	152.7	(145.2)	230.0	
Loss reserve (financing costs)		(12.0)	(12.0)	12.0	(12.0)	
Investors' share net of financing costs		210.5	140.7	(133.2)	218.0	
Loss reserve (general provision)		(10.5)	(2.7)	2.7	(10.5)	
Net Investment before defaults		200.0	138.1	(130.5)	207.5	
Cumulative defaults (specific provisions)		0.0	(7.5)	-	(7.5)	
Net Investment		200.0	130.5	(130.5)	200.0	
Opening Reserves		0.0			22.5	
Collections allocated to reserves		0.0			(14.7)	
Specific provision required for new defaults		0.0			(7.5)	
Movement on reserves		22.5			22.2	
Required reserves (based on assumed % provisions)		22.5			22.5	
Facility size		200.0			200.0	
Reserves		22.5			22.5	
Cumulative defaults		0.0			7.5	
Investors' share	*75.4%*	222.5			230.0	*74.8%*
Originator's share	*24.6%*	72.5			77.5	*25.2%*
Qualifying trade debtors pool	*100.0%*	295.0			307.5	*100.0%*

Short Term Instruments – the Money Market

Introduction

The Money Market provides a source of short-term (maturities up to one year) finance (such as Commercial Paper), as well as investment opportunities (deposits and short term government securities ('Bills')).

Yields and Discounts

The fair value of a money market instrument at any 'Settlement' date (i.e. the purchase price), is the amount received or paid on maturity ('Future Value'), discounted back at the Yield to Maturity (see Appendix B2):

$$\text{Purchase Price (Present Value)} = \frac{\text{Future Value}}{\left(1 + \text{Yield} \times \frac{D_p}{\text{Year}}\right)}$$

where

- Yield - required yield at purchase date (expressed as a Simple rate)
- D_p - number of days from purchase date to maturity
- Year - 365 or 360 days, depending on the daycount for the instrument (£ instruments are 365, while US$ and many other non-£ instruments are 360)

Yield to maturity (Simple rate)[1] **3.1**

$$\text{Yield } \% = \left(\frac{\text{Future Value}}{\text{Purchase Price}} - 1\right) \times \frac{\text{Year}}{D_p}$$

1 The Effective return can be calculated from **B2.2** in Appendix B2 based on this Nominal / Simple return, or as follows:

$$\text{Effective yield } \% = \left(\frac{\text{Future Value}}{\text{Purchase Price}}\right)^{\frac{\text{Year}}{D_p}} - 1$$

The realised yield if the instrument is sold before maturity is calculated as follows:

$$\text{Yield } \% = \left(\frac{\text{Sale Price}}{\text{Purchase Price}} - 1\right) \times \frac{\text{Year}}{\text{Days held}}$$

3.2

Realised Yield (simple rate)

$$\text{Yield }\% = \left(\frac{1 + Y_p \times \frac{D_p}{\text{Year}}}{1 + Y_s \times \frac{D_s}{\text{Year}}} - 1 \right) \times \frac{\text{Year}}{(D_p - D_s)}$$

(i.e. days held)

where Y_p, Y_s - Yield at the date of purchase and sale, respectively

D_p, D_s - Number of days from the date of purchase and sale to maturity, respectively

The Future Value will depend on the type of money market instrument:

- Yield quoted

If the Future Value represents the face value plus a coupon based on a Simple rate from the original issue date to the maturity date (since no interim coupons are received for reinvestment), then the yield above would be the Simple rate of interest:

$$\text{Future Value} = \text{Face Value} + \text{Coupon}$$

$$\text{Purchase Price} = \frac{\text{Face Value} + \text{Coupon}}{\left(1 + \text{Yield} \times \frac{D_p}{\text{Year}}\right)}$$

$$\text{Yield \% (simple)} = \left(\frac{\text{Face Value} + \text{Coupon}}{\text{Purchase Price}} - 1\right) \times \frac{\text{Year}}{D_p}$$

where $\text{Coupon} = \text{Face Value} \times \text{Coupon Rate} \times \frac{D_i}{\text{Year}}$

D_i - Days from issue to maturity (i.e. the coupon period)

D_p - Days from purchase to maturity

If Purchase Price = Face Value

$\therefore$ Coupon rate = Yield (as for deposits)

Example 3.4 Yield Calculation - Certificate of Deposit

A Certificate of Deposit (see below for definition), with a face value of £1m, is issued with a 3.5% coupon rate, payable on maturity in 91 days. If the original purchaser decided to sell the CD when there were 30 days left to maturity and yields had decreased from the 3.50% at issue (the coupon rate would have equalled the yield at the issued date) to 3.40%, an effective return of 3.54% could be achieved.

Future Value	$= £\ 1{,}000{,}000 \times (1 + 3.50\% \times 91 / 365)$ $= £\ 1{,}008{,}726$	Purchase Price	$= \dfrac{£1{,}008{,}726.03}{1 + 3.40\% \times 30 / 365}$ $= £\ 1{,}005{,}915$
Yield	$= \left(\dfrac{£\ 1{,}005{,}915}{£1{,}000{,}000} - 1\right) \times \dfrac{365}{(91 - 30)}$ $= 3.54\%$		

- Discount quoted

A discount security pays no coupon, but has an effective rolled up rate of interest ('discount') in the difference between the Future Value and the purchase price:

$$\text{Future Value} = \text{Face Value}$$

$$\text{Purchase Price} = \frac{\text{Face Value}}{\left(1 + \text{Yield} \times \dfrac{D_p}{\text{Year}}\right)} = \text{Face Value} - \text{Discount}$$

where

$$\text{Discount} = \text{Face Value} \times \text{Discount Rate} \times \frac{D_p}{\text{Year}}$$

D_p - Number of days from settlement to maturity

$$\therefore \quad \text{Purchase Price} = \text{Face Value} \times \left(1 - \text{Discount Rate} \times \frac{D_p}{\text{Year}}\right)$$

Using the above expression for the Purchase Price (and after re-arranging):

$$\text{Yield} = \frac{\text{Discount}}{\text{Purchase Price}} \times \frac{\text{Year}}{D_p}$$

$$= \frac{\text{Face Value} \times \left(\text{Discount Rate} \times \dfrac{D_p}{\text{Year}}\right)}{\left(\dfrac{\text{Face Value}}{1 + \text{Yield} \times \dfrac{D_p}{\text{Year}}}\right)} \times \frac{\text{Year}}{D_p}$$

$$= \text{Discount Rate} \times \left(1 + \text{Yield} \times \frac{D_p}{\text{Year}}\right)$$

$$\text{Discount rate} = \frac{\text{Yield}}{\left(1 + \text{Yield} \times \dfrac{D_p}{\text{Year}}\right)} \qquad \text{Yield} = \frac{\text{Discount Rate}}{\left(1 - \text{Discount Rate} \times \dfrac{D_p}{\text{Year}}\right)} \qquad \mathbf{3.3}$$

Short Term Investments

A company that intends to invest surplus cash for a period of up to one year has a number of options, including:

- *Time deposits* (Yield quoted). These are overnight, 'call' (on demand, usually subject to 2 days notice) and 'term' deposits (1 month, 3 months, etc.) placed with banks, with interest referenced to LIBOR.
- *Certificate of Deposit* ('CD')(Yield quoted). A CD represents title to a deposit placed with a financial institution for a stated maturity at a specified rate, issued in minimum denominations, depending on the currency. A fixed or floating rate of interest is paid, usually on maturity (unless the term is more than one year). CDs are normally tradable ('negotiable') on the 'Secondary market', and hence can be sold in the money market at any time before maturity at a price that depends on the required Yield to Maturity on the sale date; on maturity, the current title holder receives the maturity proceeds (the face value paid by the original purchaser in the 'Primary' market, plus any interest).
- *Treasury bills* (Discount quoted). These are short-term government securities (issued at a discount and redeemed at par), issued regularly throughout the year, in stated denominations, and normally repayable in 91 days. A Repurchase Agreement ('Repo') is an agreement where one party sells government securities to another, with a commitment to repurchase them at a later date (a 'Reverse Repo' is an agreement to buy them and then sell them back).

Short Term Borrowings

Sources of short term financing would include the following:

- *Bank overdrafts.* These are unsecured, short term, on demand bank facilities, linked to a current account (with minimal documentation).
- *Commercial Paper* ('CP')(Discount quoted). CP instruments are short term unsecured debt securities (promissory notes) issued - at a discount to their face value - by highly rated borrowers (corporates, banks, and other financial institutions). The average size and maturity of a CP 'programme' varies, depending, partly, on the currency and issue location (Sterling CP is typically under 30 days).
- *Bills of Exchange.* A commercial Bill of Exchange is an order, issued by a 'drawer' to a 'drawee' (the addressee), to pay on demand ('Sight Draft') or at a future date ('Term Draft') a stated amount to the payee (the drawer or to the bearer - Bills are transferable, hence the drawer can transfer title to the Bill to another party, as consideration for the settlement of some other debt, for example). When the drawee 'accepts' the bill it becomes the 'Acceptor'. Bills are used for short term trade finance (usually 91 days), issued by an exporter to an importer.

4 FINANCIAL RISK MANAGEMENT

INTRODUCTION

Chapter Contents

Capital should be allocated so as to maximise value for the providers of that capital (Enterprise Value) (see Chapter 1 and Appendices A and B1 for investment appraisal techniques, and Chapter 2 and Appendices B2 and C for funding and financing sources). The obligations to capital providers (contractual or otherwise) need to be managed so as to maintain the Enterprise Value (see Chapter 3 and Appendix B1 for a discussion on capital management issues).

This chapter introduces techniques to manage the exposure of financing cash flows to changes in certain market prices (interest rates and exchange rates), using derivative instruments (Forwards, Futures, Swaps and Options). Commodity risks and other market uncertainties affecting operating cash flows are not discussed, although the concepts underlying the use of derivatives will be the same. Basic pricing of derivative instruments is discussed in Appendices B3 and B4.

Risk Management

Risk is traditionally viewed as the uncertainty associated with future cash flows, prices or returns, expressed as some volatility measure (variance). This includes favourable and unfavourable movements in response to changes in interest rates and exchange rates: downside protection measures (i.e. hedging) may, therefore, limit upside benefits.

Subject to this qualification, a corporate will benefit if it can manage its risk in a way that maximises its Enterprise Value by increasing Free Cash Flows (decreasing the exposure of Free Cash Flows to interest rate and currency changes, for example) and reducing the Cost of Capital (decreasing the after-tax Cost of Debt and decreasing the level of risk that a shareholder cannot avoid and which is, therefore, relevant according to the CAPM – discussed in Appendix B1). If the relevant risk is passed on to a third party via a hedging transaction, a benefit will arise if the cost of transferring it is less than the cost of bearing it (Stultz (2003a p.45)).

Risk management can be aimed at reducing volatility to acceptable levels (upside and downside), or may be used solely to eliminate the risk of financial distress (downside cases only)(Stulz (2003b)).

INTEREST RATE RISK

Measuring Interest Rate Risk

To estimate the exposure to interest rate risk, a corporate borrower could:

- determine the sensitivity of operating and financing cash flows to changes in interest rates and whether a change in one offsets the other, thereby reducing the volatility of net cash flows and, possibly, the need for further funding (which may have to be more debt, thus increasing financial risk): if operating cash flows are sensitive to rate changes (via an indirect effect on revenues, for example), fixed-rate debt finance will increase net cash flow volatility (leverage effect), and floating rate debt would be preferred (with an interest rate structure that ensures a decrease in operating cash flows is offset by a decrease in finance costs, i.e. inversely related to interest rates);
- analyse the mix of existing fixed and floating rate debt to determine whether the overall Cost of Debt is partly protected against rising interest rates (fixed rate debt) and exposed to falling interest rates (floating rate debt);
- determine the exposure to a change in interest rates over the interim period before negotiations are due to start on a new debt facility (or when short term debt is due to be rolled over);
- estimate the impact on the Enterprise Value due to a change of interest rates over a forecast period, based on the sensitivity of Free Cash Flows, non-operating rate-sensitive assets, interest-bearing liabilities and the Cost of Capital to such changes (rate changes expected by the market will already be factored into the market's pricing of a quoted company, but the company should still need to carry out its own estimates, given that its expectation of future Free Cash Flows may differ due to the market's inefficiency).

A financial institution would measure interest rate risk using traditional measures that compare the value of its interest rate sensitive assets and liabilities over specific periods ('Maturity Gap') or in general ('Duration Gap'), as well as more dynamic measures that estimate the potential loss arising from a change in interest rates or yields ('Value At Risk')(see Stulz (2003a), Penza and Bansal (2001), Choudhry (2001)).

Some of a financial institution's assets will be stated at market value in the balance sheet ('Marked to Market'), and any loss in value will affect earnings and equity capital (and regulatory capital).

Managing Interest Rate Risk with Derivatives

Introduction

A borrower may want to protect against interest rates having increased by the time it enters into a new debt facility, or wish to change the interest rate characteristics of existing debt. Derivative contracts can be used by a borrower to:

- fix a rate ('Forward Rate') for a period ('Forward Period') starting at some time in the future ('Forward Delivery Date'), by either agreeing a rate today ('Forward Rate Agreement') or buying an option (with no obligation) to agree a rate at some future date ('Interest Rate Option');
- protect against a rise in interest rates from today until the Forward Delivery Date by selling Interest Rate Futures and buying them back at, or as close as possible to, the Delivery Date (using 'Short Term Interest Rate Futures' or long term 'Bond Futures', depending, in part, on the length of time until the Delivery Date);
- 'Swap' a floating rate into a fixed rate (and vice versa) or into another floating rate;
- 'Cap' a floating rate, restricting the financing cost to a maximum rate.

Derivatives Pricing

Derivatives are normally priced on the basis that the fair price for the purchase or sale of an asset in the future ('Forward Price') can be determined using principles of arbitrage elimination (preventing risk free profit making) and replicating cash flows (similar cash flows with identical risk should have the same current price), based on current 'Spot' prices (current market prices and rates that apply for periods starting today). The main principles of Forward Pricing are discussed in Appendix B3 (B3.1 and B3.2).

Where a derivative has an 'embedded' option, or is a pure option, then option pricing principles must be used. Basic option pricing models are discussed in Appendix B4.

Interest Rate Derivatives

Forward Interest Rate Contracts

Definition

The buyer of a Forward Rate Agreement ('FRA') is able to fix a rate of interest for a future period commencing at a future date.

An FRA involves:

- a buyer agreeing with a seller[1] on a 'Trade Date' or 'Dealing Date' to pay the seller at a future date (Forward Date, Delivery Date or 'Settlement Date')
- a specified fixed rate of interest ('Contract Rate') on a notional principal sum (i.e. no amounts are lent or borrowed),
- in respect of a period ('Contract Period') starting on the Forward Date,
- in return for the seller paying a floating 'Reference Rate' or 'Settlement Rate', being the actual market rate (Spot Rate) available at the start of that period[2].

However:

- rather than exchange principals and interest cash flows at the end of the Contract Period (when the Reference Rate would normally be paid, such as interest on a cash deposit), payment is made upfront on the Settlement Date (to eliminate any counterparty credit risk); and
- rather than actually exchange cash flows, only the difference (the 'Settlement Amount') is paid.

1 The counterparty is normally a financial institution in the 'Over-The-Counter' market, rather than a 'Clearing House' in a trade on an exchange.

2 The rate is fixed on the Settlement Date for UK £ FRAs (two business days before the Settlement Date for US $ and other FRAs).

The buyer and seller are effectively agreeing to lend each other the principal for the Contract Period, with the buyer paying the fixed FRA rate and the seller paying the floating Reference Rate.

The Settlement Amount is, therefore, the present value of the difference between the two cash flows that would normally arise at the end of the Contract Period:

FRA Settlement Amount **4.1**

$$\text{Settlement Amount} = \frac{\text{Principal} \times \left(r - \text{FRA Rate}\right) \times p}{(1 + r \times p)}$$

where p - Days in Contract Period ÷ days in year (365 or 360 for US$)
r - Reference rate (such as LIBOR)

Seller pays buyer if reference rate (e.g. LIBOR) exceeds FRA rate

Buyer pays seller if reference rate (e.g. LIBOR) is less than FRA rate

Example 4.1 FRA hedging

The next interest period for a borrower's £100m loan (a floating rate loan based on 3 month £ LIBOR plus a fixed margin) commences on 19 April. The borrower believes interest rates are likely to rise, and, to lock into current rates, enters into an FRA fixed on 19 January (spot date) at 5.92613% for settlement on 19 April (this would be termed a '3 x 6' FRA, since there are three months from the spot date – two business days after the dealing date – to the settlement date, and six months from the spot date to the maturity date). Actual rates on the settlement date are 6.50%, but the borrower will receive the Settlement amount, reducing the effective borrowing cost to the agreed contract rate.

Principal		£100m
FRA type	3 x	6
Contract rate		5.92613%
Contract period (mths)		3 months
Contract period (days)		91 days
Days in year		365
Interest period in years (P)		0.2493 years
Reference rate (3 month LIBOR for 19 April settlement)		6.50000%

$$\text{Settlement Amount} = \frac{\text{Principal} \times (\text{Reference rate} - \text{Contract rate}) \times P}{1 + (\text{reference rate} \times P)}$$

$$= \frac{£100\text{m} \times (6.50000\% - 5.92613\%) \times 0.2493 \text{ years}}{1 + (6.50000\% \times 0.2493 \text{ years})}$$

$$= \mathbf{£140{,}794}$$

☞ The seller (bank) will pay the buyer £140,794 on 19 April

➡ See Appendix B3 (**Example B3.4** in B3.3).

Pricing

An FRA Contract Rate will be based on the Forward Rate on the settlement date, implied from current Spot Rates. Given current Spot Rates from today until the settlement date and from today until the end of the Forward Period (maturity date), it is possible to fix a borrowing or deposit rate for the Forward Period today.

Hedging

Hedging with FRAs allows:

- an FRA buyer to protect against rising interest rates (a borrower could effectively swap a floating rate for a fixed rate);
- an FRA seller to protect against falling interest rates.

A borrower buys an FRA if interest rates are expected to rise

A lender sells an FRA if interest rates are expected to fall

Interest Rate Futures

Short Term Interest Rate Futures

Definition

The buyer of a Short Term Interest Rate future, as for an FRA, is able to fix a rate of interest for a future period commencing at a future date.

A Short Term Interest Rate futures transaction involves:

- a buyer agreeing to deliver at a Forward Date ('Delivery Date') a fixed rate of interest on a notional principal sum in respect of a short term tradable money market instrument (such as 3 month Euro or Sterling, or 90 day Eurodollar deposits);
- the agreement is subject to standardised contract terms (with fixed trading units, Forward Periods and Delivery Dates), transacted with the relevant Exchange clearing house via a broker (the clearing house acts as a central counter party and guarantees payment);
- futures prices change daily in response to changes in market prices of the underlying instrument (subject to a minimum daily price change, or 'Tick Size', with an equivalent 'Tick Value' for each contract);
- upfront and daily cash deposits with the clearing house ('Initial' and 'Variation' margins) are required (via the broker) to cover potential losses arising from daily price changes – contracts are 'Marked to Market' and effectively settled on a daily basis;
- a position can be closed out before a Delivery Date by entering into an opposite position (for a buyer, selling a future and vice versa)('lifting' the hedge).

Pricing

Futures are priced on the same basis as for Forwards (to eliminate arbitrage opportunities):

Interest Rate Futures

4.2

Futures Price = 100 - annualised Forward Interest Rate

where the Forward Rate is implied from current Spot Rates, subject to some adjustment for 'Convexity' (discussed at the end of **Example 4.3**) and the cash flow impact of the 'margining' procedure. For example, the 3 month Sterling Interest Rate Future is based on an implied 3 month LIBOR.

As the Delivery Date approaches (start of Forward Period), so the rate implied from the futures price (100 – futures price) will converge to the Spot Rate on that date.

⇨ See Appendix B3 (section B3.2) for Forward Rates.

Example 4.2 Forward Rates for futures periods

The 3 month Sterling futures contract traded on LIFFE is delivered (i.e. expiry date) four days a year, on the third Wednesday in March, June, September and December. If 3 and 6 month LIBOR on 17 June are 3.65% and 3.667%, respectively, then the implied Forward Rate for the 3 months starting on 17 September (the third Wednesday during the September futures delivery month) would be 3.65% (the same as Spot Rates).

			From	*To*	*Period*
LIBOR on 17 June	3 month	3.650%	17 June	17 September	92 days
	6 month	3.667%	17 June	17 December	183 days
Forward rate	3 month	3.650%	17 September	17 December	91 days

$$\text{Forward rate} = \left\{ \left(\frac{(1 + 3.667\% \times 183 / 365)}{(1 + 3.650\% \times 92 / 365)} \right) - 1 \right\} \times 365 / 91 = 3.650\%$$

If rates were expected to increase, then 6 month LIBOR would be higher and the Forward Rate would be higher than the Spot Rate:

			From	*To*	*Period*
LIBOR on 17 June	3 month	3.650%	17 June	17 September	92 days
	6 month	3.692%	17 June	17 December	183 days
Forward rate	3 month	3.700%	17 September	17 December	91 days

$$\text{Forward rate} = \left\{ \left(\frac{(1 + 3.692\% \times 183 / 365)}{(1 + 3.650\% \times 92 / 365)} \right) - 1 \right\} \times 365 / 91 = 3.700\%$$

Margin arrangements are set by each exchange, but would normally involve the following:

- an ‘Initial’ margin is deposited with the broker on the deal date as collateral (the amount would normally be based on an estimated worst-case one day change in the relevant futures price, repayable on delivery);
- daily gains and losses arising from changes in futures prices are paid to or from the margin account via ‘Variation’ margins (i.e. cash settlement occurs daily at the start of the next business day, such that the total profit or loss over the whole futures life is collected or paid out daily).

Hedging

Introduction

Selling interest rate futures 'short' would allow a borrower to protect against rising interest rates, since as rates increase, the futures price falls: a profit on the short sale would offset the increase in rates. The borrower can fix a borrowing rate at the rate implied in the futures price at the deal date.

> *A borrower sells IR futures if interest rates are expected to rise*

Conversely, buying interest rate futures ('going long') would allow a lender to protect against falling interest rates (the profit on closing out the futures position at a higher price – caused by a fall in market rates – offsets the lower income on the investment). Again, the lender can fix a lending rate at the rate implied in the futures price at the deal date (less the bid-offer spread – the difference between the London interbank borrowing and lending rates):

> *A lender buys IR futures if interest rates are expected to fall*

Hedging is made complicated by the following:

① the loan or deposit being hedged may differ to the cash market instrument underlying the futures contract:

(i) the interest period and equivalent futures Forward Periods may not be common: the interest period may start on a date other than the futures Delivery Date, and/or the interest period may differ to the length of the Forward Period for the futures contract or the length of the interest period of the cash instrument underlying the futures contract;

(ii) the currency and interest rate basis may differ;

② the number of contracts to be hedged will depend on the relative sensitivities of the values of the underlying hedged loan/deposit and futures contract to changes in interest rates.

Basic Hedging

One Interest Period

A borrower can lock in to the rate implied in the futures price, assuming, to simplify the hedge, that ① and ② above do not apply.

Example 4.3 Short Term £ Interest Rate Futures: Loan interest period = Forward Period

On 17 June, 3 and 6 month LIBOR are 3.65% and 3.692%, respectively, and the 3 month £ Short Term Interest Rate futures price for September delivery (expiry 17 September) is 96.30. A borrower could lock in at the implied 3.70% 3 month rate on that date (100 – 96.30) for the next 3 month (91 day) interest period on a £100m floating rate loan (interest paid quarterly, based on 3 month LIBOR), starting on 17 September (see **Example 4.2**). The borrower would short sell September futures at 96.30 and purchase them just before the interest period started (i.e. just before the Delivery Date). The net financing cost would be as follows:

Net financing cost = Interest paid – (profit on futures + interest on margin)

Interest paid	Interest paid on underlying loan at the end of the interest period
Futures profit	Tick change x Tick Value x number of contracts
Tick change	(Change in futures price x 100) ticks
Tick value	£500,000 standardised contract size x 0.01/100 x ¼ where ¼ is the Forward Period in years (exactly 0.25 years) = £12.50
Contracts	The standard number of contracts to be hedged is calculated as the face value of the liability (£100m) divided by the contract size (£0.5m) = 200. It will be shown later that this is not the optimal number.
Margin interest	Since the variation margin is paid or collected as and when futures prices change, interest can be earned from the date of receipt (the day following the change in futures prices) up to the date the interest is paid on the underlying loan. In this simple example, it is assumed that rates unexpectedly change just before the Delivery Date (i.e. the futures price changes at the last moment, so margin interest need only be considered from the Delivery Date to the end of the interest period).

If 3 month LIBOR on 17 September was 1 basis point higher than expected (3.71%, decreasing the futures price to 96.29), then the net financing cost would be 3.6999% (if rates decrease, the rate is 3.7001%). This compares to a fixed 3.70% FRA rate.

17 June	92 days	17 September	91 days	17 December
Spot date		Delivery + Start of Interest Period	0.2493 years	End of Interest Period

	17 September			17 December
Expected on 17 June				
Futures Price	96.30			
3mth LIBOR		3.70% p.a. over 91 days		
Loan interest		= £100.0m x (3.70% + 0.0% margin) x 91 / 365 =		(£922,466)
Rates increase on 17 September				
Futures Price	96.29			
3mth LIBOR		3.71% p.a. over 91 days		
Loan Interest		= £100.0m x (3.71% + 0.0% margin) x 91 / 365 =		(£924,959)
FRA settlement sum	£2,470 ❶	+ interest income = £2,470 x 3.71% x 91 / 365 =		£2,493
Net cost with FRA			**3.7000%**	**(£922,466)**
Futures profit / (loss)	£2,500 ❷	+ interest income = £2,500 x 3.71% x 91 / 365 =		£2,523
Net cost withFutures			**3.6999%**	**(£922,436)**
Difference	**(£30)**			**(£30)** ❸

Notes

❶ £2,470 = $\frac{£100\text{m} \times (3.71\% - 3.70\%) \times 0.2493 \text{ years}}{1 + (3.71\% \times 0.2493 \text{ years})}$

❷ £2,500 = (96.30 - 96.29) x 100 x 200.0000 contracts x £12.50

❸

		17 September		17 December
FRA	£100.00m x (3.71% - 3.70%) x 0.2493 years =			£2,493
	Discounted back to allow for interest earned =	£2,470		
Futures	£100.00m x (3.71% - 3.70%) x 0.2500 years =	£2,500	+ interest	£2,523
Difference		**(£30)**		**(£30)**

The correct number of contracts to equate the two in this scenario (for a small rate change) is calculated as follows:

Contracts = 200 x 0.988145 = 197.629

The adjustment factor (or 'Hedge Ratio') is calculated as follows:

$$\text{Hedge ratio} = \frac{T_I}{T_F} \times \frac{1}{\left(1 + r_F \times \frac{d_I}{365}\right)} \qquad \textbf{4.3}$$

T_I, T_F Length of interest period and futures period (in years), respectively.

r_F The Forward Rate on the trade date for the period from Delivery Date.

d_I The length of interest period in days.

$$\text{Hedge ratio} = \frac{91/365 \text{ years}}{0.25 \text{ years}} \times \frac{1}{(1 + 3.70\% \times 91/365 \text{ years})}$$

Profit on futures contract = 197.629 x £12.50 x 1 tick = £2,470 (= FRA sum)

Assumptions

1. A fractional number of contracts can be traded: in practice, the nearest whole number of contracts would be chosen: trading in 198 contracts would reduce the difference between the FRA and futures hedges from £30 in the up and down state scenarios using 200 contracts, to £5.

2. The September futures price changes immediately before the hedge is lifted (Delivery Date), so that margin cash flows and related interest income / expense can be ignored: in practice, the market's expected Spot Rate for 17 September (as reflected in the futures price) would adjust as the Delivery Date / lifting date approached.

   Had rates unexpectedly changed just after the 17 June trade date (assuming Spot Rates and futures rates change by the same amount), the resulting additional interest income and expense on the futures profit and loss received when prices changed – i.e. over the period 17 June to 17 September – would have increased the above £5 difference to £28. The correct number of contracts to hedge would be calculated by 'tailing' the hedge by discounting the above 197.629 contracts over the period to the start of the Forward Period at the current Spot Rate:

$$\text{Contracts} = 197.629 \times \frac{1}{\left(1 + r_M \times \frac{d_D}{365}\right)}$$

4.4

r_M The assumed rate from the date of receipt of the margin to the Delivery Date (spot 3 month LIBOR at the date of trade, just before the rates increase).

d_D The number of days from the date of receipt of the margin to the Delivery Date.

Contracts = 197.629 x 1 / (1 + 3.65% 3mth LIBOR x 92 / 365) = 195.827

or = 200 x T_I / T_F x 1 / (1 + 3.692% 6mth LIBOR x 183/365) = 195.827

Futures profit = 195.827 x £12.50 x 1 tick = £2,448 x (1 + 3.65% x 92/365) = £2,470

The position for a 1 Basis point increase / decrease using 195.827 contracts would be as follows:

17 June	*92 days*	17 September	*91 days*	17 December
Spot date		Delivery + Start of Interest Period		

	17 September		17 December
Rates increase on 17 June			
Futures Price	96.29		
3mth LIBOR		3.71% p.a. over 91 days	
Loan Interest		= £100.0m x (3.71% + 0.0% margin) x 91 / 365 =	(£924,959)
Futures profit / (loss)	£2,470 ❶	= £2,470 x 3.71% x 91 / 365 =	£2,493
Net cost withFutures		**3.7000%**	**(£922,466)**
Rates decrease on 17 June			
Futures Price	96.31		
3mth LIBOR		3.69% p.a. over 91 days	
Loan Interest		= £100.0m x (3.69% + 0.0% margin) x 91 / 365 =	(£919,973)
Futures profit / (loss)	(£2,470) ❷	= - £2,470 x 3.69% x 91 / 365 =	(£2,493)
Net cost withFutures		**3.7000%**	**(£922,466)**

Notes

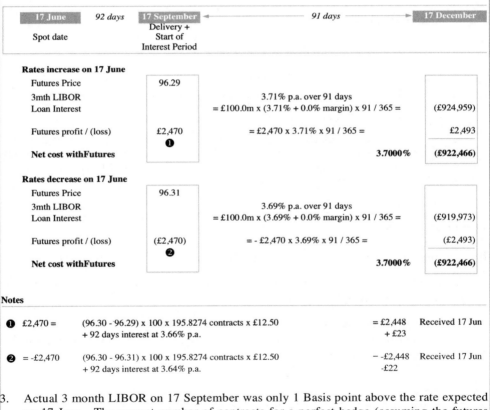

❶	£2,470 =	(96.30 - 96.29) x 100 x 195.8274 contracts x £12.50 + 92 days interest at 3.66% p.a.	= £2,448 + £23	Received 17 Jun
❷	= -£2,470	(96.30 - 96.31) x 100 x 195.8274 contracts x £12.50 + 92 days interest at 3.64% p.a.	– -£2,448 -£22	Received 17 Jun

3. Actual 3 month LIBOR on 17 September was only 1 Basis point above the rate expected on 17 June. The correct number of contracts for a perfect hedge (assuming the futures price changes just before delivery) for a given range of spot LIBOR on 17 September is as follows:

3mth LIBOR 17 Sep	Contracts Traded	*Value on 17 Sep*		*Change*		Contracts Optimal
		FRA	*Futures*	*FRA*	*Futures*	
3.65%	197.629	(12,353.3)	(12,351.8)	2,471.0	2,470.4	197.653
3.66%	197.629	(9,882.4)	(9,881.4)	2,470.9	2,470.4	197.649
3.67%	197.629	(7,411.6)	(7,411.1)	2,470.8	2,470.4	197.644
3.68%	197.629	(4,941.0)	(4,940.7)	2,470.7	2,470.4	197.639
3.69%	197.629	(2,470.4)	(2,470.4)	2,470.5	2,470.4	197.634
3.70%	197.629	**(0.0)**	**0.0**	**2,470.4**	**2,470.4**	197.629
3.71%	197.629	2,470.3	2,470.4	2,470.3	2,470.4	197.624
3.72%	197.629	4,940.5	4,940.7	2,470.2	2,470.4	197.619
3.73%	197.629	7,410.5	7,411.1	2,470.1	2,470.4	197.614
3.74%	197.629	9,880.5	9,881.4	2,469.9	2,470.4	197.609
3.75%	197.629	12,350.3	12,351.8	2,469.8	2,470.4	197.605

The above 197.629 fractional traded contracts is calculated assuming that interest over the Forward Period could be earned at the rate expected on 17 June (3.70%). The optimal number of contracts simply uses the actual 3 month LIBOR rates shown in the Hedge Ratio equation **4.3**. It can also be calculated by adjusting the Hedge Ratio in **4.3** by the ratio of the FRA value to the Futures value for the above 17 Sept 3 month LIBOR:

$$\text{Hedge ratio} = \frac{T_I}{T_F} \times \frac{1}{\left(1 + \frac{r_F \times d_I}{365}\right)} \times \frac{V_{FRA}}{V_{Futures}} \qquad \textbf{4.5}$$

where V_{FRA} - Value of FRA for given 3 month LIBOR 17 Sept

$V_{Futures}$ - Value of Futures position for given 3 month LIBOR 17 Sept

(see **4.3** for other symbols)

Whilst the Futures position changes by a constant amount for each Basis point change in spot 3 month LIBOR on 17 September, the FRA sum changes by a varying amount (this is due to Convexity). Hedging with 197.629 futures contracts (i.e. 198), therefore, would be preferred to hedging with an FRA only if rates increase.

Two Interest Periods

If the borrower wants to hedge two consecutive 3 month interest periods, it can:

- trade in the two relevant delivery months and lift the hedges at the start of each interest period ('Strip' hedge); or
- trade in the first relevant delivery month, lift the hedge at the start of the first interest period and simultaneously trade in the second delivery month, and lift the second hedge at the start of the second interest period ('Stack' or 'Rolling' hedge)

Example 4.4 Short Term Interest Rate Futures – Strip and Stack hedges – Identical periods

On 17 June, the borrower from **Example 4.3** wants to lock in at the Forward Rates for the next two interest periods on the £100m floating rate loan (3 month LIBOR), being Wednesday17 September to 17 December, and Wednesday 17 December to 17 March, the following year. As in **Example 4.3**, 3 and 6 month LIBOR on 17 June are 3.650% and 3.692%, respectively. The September and December futures prices are 96.30 and 96.28, respectively. The borrower believes rates will increase, and hence will need to sell futures contracts.

It will be assumed that:

1. no interest income or expense will arise on the futures profit or loss from the date the position is closed (the start of each interest period) to the date the loan interest is paid (at the end of each interest period); as discussed above, in practice, the profit or loss is settled as and when futures prices change (due to the margining process), hence any interest income and expense (or opportunity cost) up to the end of the interest period should be taken into account;
2. the cash instrument underlying the futures contract has the same price sensitivity as the instrument being hedged (i.e. both are based on 3 month LIBOR), and the rate implied from the futures price exactly equals the Forward Rate;
3. the length of the loan interest period and futures Forward period are both the same (other than a small difference due to the futures period being exactly ¼ of a year).

These simplifying assumptions mean that 200 contracts will be sold (£100m ÷ £500,000 standard size). The hedge could be achieved by:

- Selling 200 September and 200 December futures on 17 June, and lifting the hedges just before the respective Delivery Dates (17 September and 17 December) (Strip), or
- Selling 2 x 200 September futures on 17 June, lifting the hedge just before the September Delivery Date (17 September) and immediately selling 200 December futures (hedge lifted on the 17 December Delivery Date) (Stack).

The Strip hedge might be used where December futures were considered to be 'liquid' (i.e. trading was sufficient to make the implied rate a fair estimate of the forward price, due to a lower bid-offer spread). If, on 17 June, they were not liquid, then selling double the required number of September contracts, buying them back and then selling the required number of December contracts would allow the December futures to be used when they were considered liquid (nearer dated futures are usually more liquid).

The net borrowing rate should be the same if rates change the same for all maturities (i.e. a 'Parallel shift' in the yield curve). Assume the following scenario for actual (Spot) and Forward Rates at the relevant dates (trade date and start of each interest period):

Actual interest in 1st period		**£929,945**	£100m x 3.73% x 91 / 365		
			From	*To*	
LIBOR on 17 September	3 month	3.730%	17 September	17 December	91 days
	6 month	3.757%	17 September	17 March	182 days
Forward rate	3 month	3.750%	17 December	17 March	91 days

Actual interest in 2nd period		**£939,918**	£100m x 3.77% x 91 / 365		
			From	*To*	
LIBOR on 17 December	3 month	3.770%	17 December	17 March	91 days
	6 month	3.798%	17 December	17 June	183 days
Forward rate	3 month	3.790%	17 March	17 June	92 days

Strip hedge: On 17 June the borrower sells 200 September contracts (96.30 price – 3.70% implied rate) and 200 December contracts (96.28 price – 3.72% implied rate). The contracts would be lifted on 17 September and 17 December. If 3 LIBOR on these dates was actually 3.73% and 3.77%, respectively, (giving futures prices on delivery of 96.27 and 96.23), the borrower will have benefited from the hedge, since it will have an effective financing cost equivalent to the rates it fixed when the futures were sold:

Sept futures		
Position closed on	Wednesday	17 September
Futures price on 17 June	96.30	3.700%
Futures price on 17 September	96.27	3.730%
Tick movement	3 ticks	
Profit	£7,500	200 contracts x £12.50 tick size x 3 ticks
Actual interest in 1st period	£929,945	£100m x 3.73% x 91 / 365
Net cost	**£922,445**	**3.70%**

Dec futures		
Position closed on	Wednesday	17 December
Futures price on 17 June	96.28	3.72%
Futures price on 17 December	96.23	3.77%
Tick movement	5 ticks	
Profit	£12,500	200 contracts x £12.50 tick size x 5 ticks
Actual interest in 2nd period	£939,918	£100m x 3.77% x 91 / 365
Net cost	**£927,418**	**3.72%**

Stack hedge: On 17 June the borrower sells 400 September contracts (96.30 price – 3.70% implied rate). The contracts would be bought back on 17 September, and immediately 200 December contracts would be sold at their 17 September price of 96.25 (equivalent to the 3.75% Forward Rate at that date) and bought back on 17 December at the 96.23 price.

Sept futures		
Position closed on	Wednesday	17 September
Futures price on 17 June	96.30	3.700%
Futures price on 17 September	96.27	3.73%
Tick movement	3 ticks	
Profit	£15,000	400 contracts x £12.50 tick size x 3 ticks
less: December contracts allocated	-£7,500	
Actual interest in period	£929,945	£100m x 3.73% x 91 / 365
Net cost	**£922,445**	**3.70%**

Dec futures		
Position closed on	Wednesday	17 December
Futures price on 17 September	96.25	3.75%
Futures price on 17 December	96.23	3.77%
Tick movement	2 ticks	
Profit	£5,000	200 contracts x £12.50 tick size x 2 ticks
Allocated from September	£7,500	
Actual interest in period	£939,918	£100m x 3.77% x 91 / 365
Net cost	**£927,418**	**3.72%**

In this example, the net financing cost is the same for both strategies because the unexpected increase in 3 month LIBOR on 17 September (from the 3.70% expected on 17 June - reflected in the 96.30 futures price – to 3.73% spot) increased the expected LIBOR for 17 December by exactly the same amount (from the 3.72% expected on 17 June to 3.75% expected on 17 September).

Spot Date		Forward Date				
			17 June	*17 September*	*17 December*	*17 March*
17 June		Expected	3.650%	3.700%	3.720%	
3mth LIBOR	3.650%	vs spot		0.050%	0.070%	
6mth LIBOR	3.692%	vs prior date				
17 September		Expected		3.730%	3.750%	
3mth LIBOR	3.730%	vs spot			0.020%	
6mth LIBOR	3.757%	vs prior date		0.030%	0.030%	
17 December		Expected			3.770%	3.790%
3mth LIBOR	3.770%	vs spot				0.020%
6mth LIBOR	3.798%	vs prior date			0.020%	

Actual and expected rates at each date

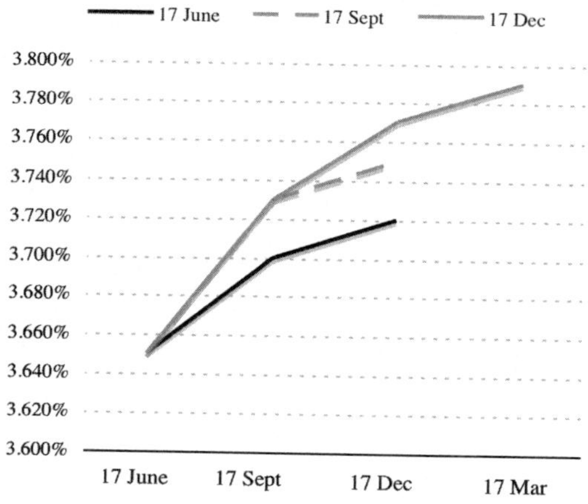

The yield curve has shifted in a parallel manner to reflect a similar increase in the expected future rates for all maturities (the difference between the Forward Rate for a period and the current 3 month spot is called the 'Basis', which is discussed further below). If the December futures price on 17 September was less than 96.25, then the yield curve would have steepened, and the strip hedge would be preferred, as shown below (if the price was more than 96.25, then the curve would have flattened, and a stack hedge would be preferred).

Yield Curve steepens

Spot Date		Forward Date				
			17 June	*17 September*	*17 December*	*17 March*
17 June		Expected	3.650%	3.700%	3.720%	
3mth LIBOR	3.650%	vs spot		0.050%	0.070%	
6mth LIBOR	3.692%	vs prior date				
17 September		Expected		3.730%	3.850%	
3mth LIBOR	3.730%	vs spot			0.120%	
6mth LIBOR	3.808%	vs prior date		0.030%	0.130%	
17 December		Expected			4.020%	4.170%
3mth LIBOR	4.020%	vs spot				0.150%
6mth LIBOR	4.116%	vs prior date			0.170%	

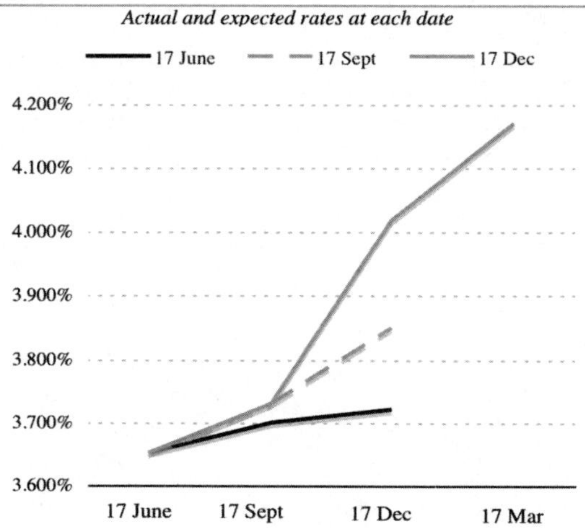

Strip

Dec futures		
Position closed on	Wednesday	17 December
Futures price on 17 June	96.28	3.72%
Futures price on 17 December	95.98	4.02%
Tick movement	30 ticks	
Profit	£75,000	200 contracts x £12.50 tick size x 30 ticks
Actual interest in 2nd period	£1,002,247	£100m x 4.02% x 91 / 365
Net cost	**£927,247**	**3.72%**

Stack

Dec futures		
Position closed on	Wednesday	17 December
Futures price on 17 September	96.15	3.85%
Futures price on 17 December	95.98	4.02%
Tick movement	17 ticks	
Profit	£42,500	200 contracts x £12.50 tick size x 17 ticks
Allocated from September	£7,500	
Actual interest in period	£1,002,247	£100m x 4.02% x 91 / 365
Net cost	**£952,247**	**3.82%**

More Complicated Hedging

Price Sensitivities

In **Example 4.4** the simplifying assumptions meant the number of contracts could be calculated using a Hedge Ratio of 1.0:

$$\text{Contracts} = \frac{\text{Value of liability being hedged (£)}}{\text{Standard contract size (£)}} \times \text{'Hedge Ratio'} \qquad \textbf{4.6}$$

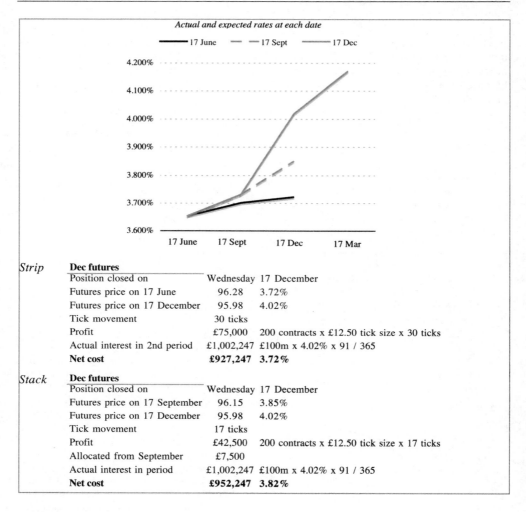

It has been assumed so far that the Sterling LIBOR referenced floating rate interest payments are being hedged with LIFFE Sterling short term (LIBOR) interest rate futures. The liability being hedged and the futures contract both have the same price sensitivity in response to interest rate changes (other than the Convexity effect noted in **Example 4.3**). In many cases, there will not exist a futures contract with an identical underlying instrument (3 month LIBOR in the examples above), and a futures contract with a different instrument will have to be chosen ('Cross Hedge').

The Hedge Ratio needs to incorporate an adjustment to account for the relative sensitivity of each instrument's value to a change in rates (similar to the adjustment **4.5** in **Example 4.3**). The relative price sensitivity can be measured by determining:

- the beta coefficient: this is similar to the beta used in the 'CAPM' Cost of Equity estimate (i.e. the product of the correlation coefficient and ratio of standard deviations, or volatilities), calculated by regressing the spot price against the futures price:

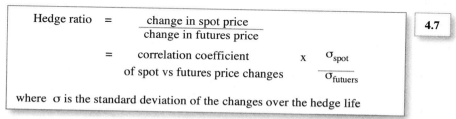

$$\text{Hedge ratio} = \frac{\text{change in spot price}}{\text{change in futures price}} \quad \textbf{4.7}$$

$$= \text{correlation coefficient of spot vs futures price changes} \times \frac{\sigma_{spot}}{\sigma_{futuers}}$$

where σ is the standard deviation of the changes over the hedge life

- the ratio of their respective 'Price Value of a Basis Point', or 'PVBP', measures (the bond price's sensitivity to interest rates):

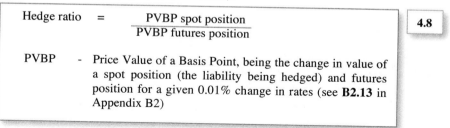

$$\text{Hedge ratio} = \frac{\text{PVBP spot position}}{\text{PVBP futures position}} \quad \textbf{4.8}$$

PVBP - Price Value of a Basis Point, being the change in value of a spot position (the liability being hedged) and futures position for a given 0.01% change in rates (see **B2.13** in Appendix B2)

If the rates underlying the liability being hedged and the futures contract are zero coupon rates (such as LIBOR), where Duration equals maturity, the Hedge Ratio using **4.7** would simply be the maturity ratios:

$$\text{Hedge ratio} = \frac{\text{Maturity of liability being hedged}}{\text{Maturity of futures contract}} \quad \textbf{4.9}$$

If a 6 month interest period was being hedged, for example, using the 3 month Sterling futures, then the hedge ratio would be 2 (= 0.5 years / 0.25 years or {actual days in the 6 month period / 365} years / 0.25 years, if not on a 30 / 360 basis).

(Note: Hedge ratio equations **4.7** to **4.9** would need to be adjusted to 'tail the hedge', as discussed in **Example 4.3** at **4.3** and **4.4**).

Basis Risk

The difference between the 3 month Spot Rate and implied 3 month Forward Rate at any date is termed the 'Basis', often shown as the difference in equivalent futures prices ((100 - Spot Rate) – (100 - implied Forward Rate)). Basis will converge to zero by the Delivery Date, usually from a negative (a positive Basis would arise, for example, where 6 month rates were less than 3 month rates, as for a negative sloping yield curve). The locked-in net borrowing rate would be the rate implied in the futures price at the trade date. If a borrower has to lift the hedge before the Delivery Date (i.e. the interest period starts before the Delivery Date), the actual net financing cost as at the lifting date (Spot Rate at that date less profit on futures position) can be estimated by assuming Basis converges in some manner. The expected locked-in rate would then be:

$$\text{Expected financing rate \% at trade date} = \frac{100 - (\text{Futures price} + \text{Expected Basis})}{100}$$

where

$$\text{Basis} = (100 - \text{Spot Rate \%} \times 100) - \text{Futures Price}$$

$$\text{Expected Basis} = \text{Basis at trade date} \times \frac{d_{LD}}{d_{TD}}$$

d_{LD}, d_{TD} - Days from relevant date (Lifting Date) and Trade Date to Delivery Date, respectively.

Assuming Basis converges to zero in a linear manner by the Delivery Date, hence:

$$\text{Expected financing rate \% at trade date} = \text{Spot Rate} - (\text{Spot Rate} - \text{Forward rate}) \times \frac{(d_{TD} - d_{LD})}{d_{TD}}$$

Example 4.5 Basis risk – Linearly Interpolated Expected Rates

September Sterling futures are sold on 4 August at 96.30, when 3 month LIBOR is 3.6%. Assuming Forward Rates are identical to futures-implied rates – see **4.1** – this gives a 3.7% Forward Rate for the 3 month period commencing 17 September. (This suggests, for example, an effective rate of 3.500% for the 44 day period to the 17 September Delivery Date, and 3.645% for the 135 day period to the end of the 91 day Forward Period: = ((1 + 3.645% x 135/365) / (1 + 3.500% x 44/365) - 1) x 365/91) .)

The actual Basis on 4 August is 0.1 (= ((100 – 3.6) – 96.30)). Assume the hedge is to be lifted on 23 August (25 days before delivery), when the underlying loan interest period commences. As at the trade date, the Basis expected on 23 August is 0.0568 (= 0.1 x 25 days / 44 days) and the expected net financing rate would be (= ((100 – (96.30 + 0.0568)) /100 = 3.643%). This rate represents the linearly interpolated 3 month LIBOR between the trade date (actual 3.6%) and Delivery Date (expected 3.7%) (= 3.6% - (3.6% - 3.7%) x (44 – 25) /44).

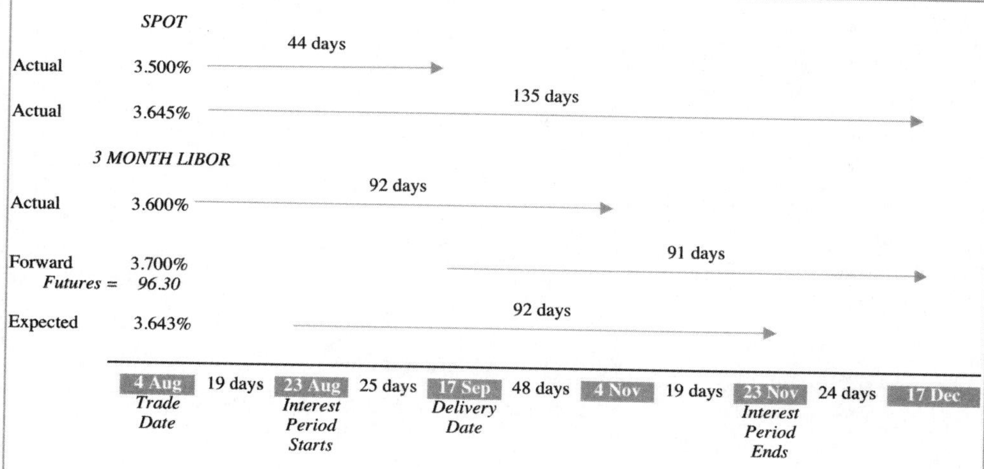

If actual Basis on the lifting date is less than the expected Basis, then the net borrowing rate will be higher than the expected rate. If it is assumed that rates for longer maturities (over 3 months) unexpectedly decrease by approximately 2 Basis points just before the lifting date, but short term rates are unchanged, then the Forward Rate for 17 September will reduce. If the Forward Rate reduces to 3.68%, a loss will arise as the futures price increases.

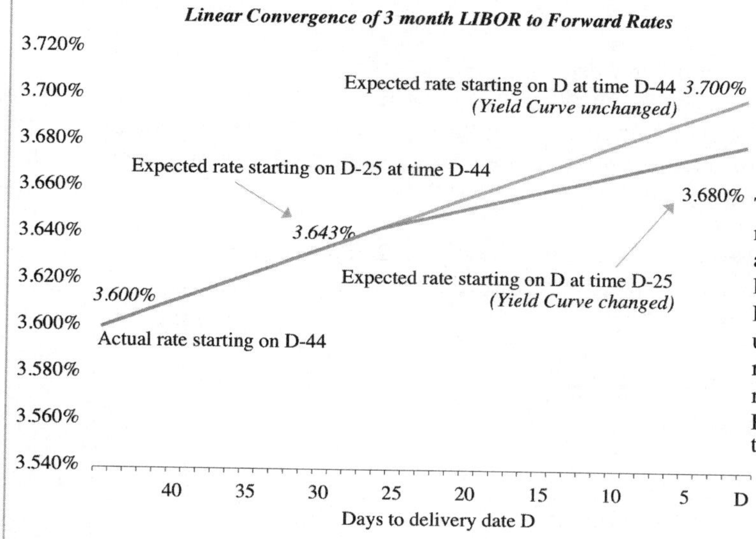

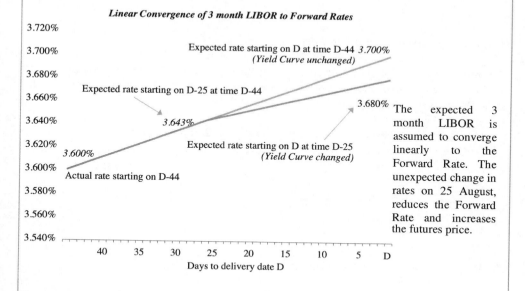

The expected 3 month LIBOR is assumed to converge linearly to the Forward Rate. The unexpected change in rates on 25 August, reduces the Forward Rate and increases the futures price.

Actual Basis will be less than expected ((100 – 3.643) – 96.32 = 0.0368 versus 0.0568).

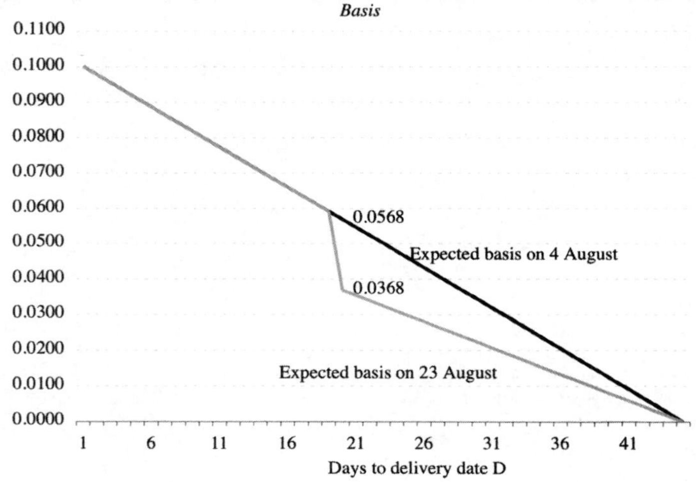

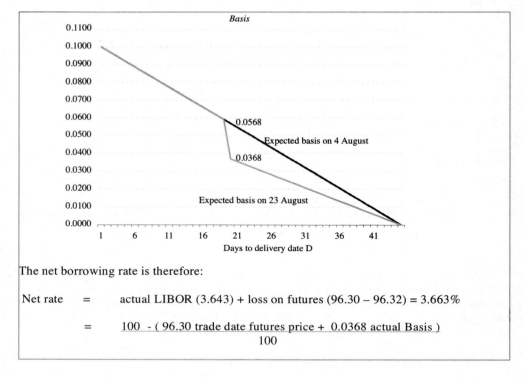

The net borrowing rate is therefore:

Net rate = actual LIBOR (3.643) + loss on futures (96.30 – 96.32) = 3.663%

$$= \frac{100 - (96.30 \text{ trade date futures price} + 0.0368 \text{ actual Basis})}{100}$$

Hedging with Non-Overlapping Periods

The interest period may not coincide with futures periods, and hence a borrower may not be able to lock in at the Forward Rate. For example, the interest period may 'straddle' two Forward Periods:

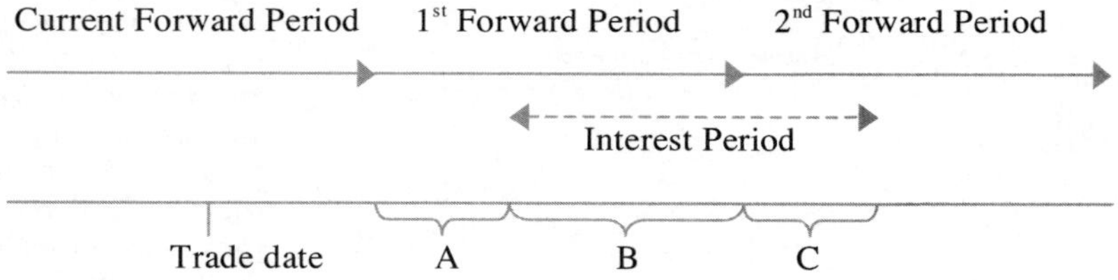

The borrower has a number of options.

a. Sell futures contracts for the first period, lift the hedge just before delivery, and remain exposed for period 'A'.

b. Sell futures contracts for the second period, lift the hedge before delivery at the start of the interest period, and be exposed to Basis risk at the start of period 'B'. If Basis is assumed to converge to zero at the Delivery Date in a linear fashion, then the target borrowing rate can be estimated using linear interpolation. The actual effective borrowing rate (3 month LIBOR at the start of the interest period less the profit on the futures position closed out on that date) will only be the same if the Basis on the closeout date is the same as the above expected Basis.

c. Estimate an effective financing rate by interpolating between the rates implied from today's futures prices for the two futures Delivery Dates, and targeting this rate by using an interpolative hedge (first period contracts = period B / period (B + C) x (loan / contract size), second period contracts = period C / period (B + C) x (loan / contract size)).

See Appendix D6 for a detailed example of this type of hedge, plus a Basis risk hedge (and Fitzgerald (1993) for further discussion).

Long Term Interest Rate Futures (Bond Futures)

Definition

Bond Futures operate as follows:

- a buyer agrees to take physical delivery of a government bond, selected by a seller from a list of eligible bonds published by the relevant futures Exchange;
- delivery occurs at a Forward Delivery Date, normally any business day, selected by the seller, *during* a delivery month (usually March, June, September and December);
- the settlement price ('Invoice Amount') is the Forward Price of the eligible bond, using a standardised 'notional' yield set by the relevant futures Exchange, plus interest accrued at the Delivery Date;
- like Short Term Interest Rate Futures,
    - o the agreement is subject to standardised contract terms, and transacted via a Clearing House;
    - o upfront ('Initial') and daily ('Variation') margins are required;
    - o the hedge can be lifted before Delivery Date by entering into an opposite position.

The Underlying Bond

Eligible Bonds

The relevant Exchange (such as LIFFE) publishes the list of government bonds that are eligible for physical delivery for each delivery month. A number of bonds are needed to ensure the futures price is based on a sufficiently liquid underlying instrument (a single bond is unlikely to be sufficient). Although each bond will have a different market value, a 'Conversion Factor' or 'Price Factor' is required to ensure that each bond has equivalent economic value (i.e. the same Yield to Maturity).

Invoice Amount

For a LIFFE contract (as for other bond futures), the price payable by the party with a long position to the short seller, as consideration for the eligible bond that the seller has chosen to deliver, is as follows:

4.10

Invoice Amount

Invoice Amount = (Futures Price at Settlement date x Price Factor) + Accrued interest at Settlement date

where:

Price Factor -	The 'Clean' fair price of the eligible bond on the first delivery date, calculated using a fixed yield specified by the Exchange, divided by the face value of the eligible bond. The June 2004 LIFFE eligible bonds, for example, have a stated yield of 6.0% p.a. The Price Factor will be more than or less than 1, if the eligible bond coupon is more than or less than the notional yield, respectively.
Futures Price	The Forward Price of a bond is the Clean price as at the Delivery Date, calculated to ensure no profit or loss would arise from arbitrage activities that replicate the cash flows and seek to achieve risk free profits (see Appendix B3 (B3.5)). Assuming there was only one eligible bond in the list, the futures price would be the Forward Price of the bond divided by the Price Factor. However, - since there are a number of possible government bonds ('gilts') that could be delivered, the futures price is based on the market's expectation of which bond short sellers will choose to deliver, assuming all sellers will choose the 'Cheapest To Deliver' eligible bond; and - since the seller has an option to choose which bond can be delivered and at what date to deliver it, futures prices, in practice, will incorporate a value to reflect these 'embedded' options.
Accrued interest	The actual interest accrued on the bond in the market as at the settlement date, to which any buyer would be entitled.

These will now be discussed in more detail, using the June 2004 LIFFE contract, details of which are as follows (source: www.liffe.com):

Exhibit 4.1 LIFFE June 2004 Long Gilt Contract

Contract size	£100,000 nominal value per 'lot'
Notional coupon/yield	6% of £100 face value
Minimum price change	0.01 (tick value £10)
Delivery day	A seller may give a Delivery Notice to the Clearing House on any business day (Delivery Day) during a period from two business days before the first day of a delivery month (March, June, September, December) to two business days before the last business day of the month, for settlement two business days later.
Eligible bonds	The List of Eligible Gilts published by LIFFE include the following requirements: - a maturity of 8¾ - 13 years, inclusive, from the first day of the delivery month; - a fixed coupon payable semi-annually in arrears (in Sterling), with principal repayable in full on maturity (in Sterling); - no rights of conversion or early redemption.

June 2004 Eligibles		Price Factor
Coupon	*Maturity*	
8.00%	27 Sep 2013	1.1410760
5.00%	7 Sep 2014	0.9240793
4.75%	7 Sep 2015	0.8986086
8.00%	7 Dec 2015	1.1646196

	An Eligible Gilt must be selected by the seller from the List of Eligible Gilts for physical delivery.
Price Factor	The price (÷ 100) of an Eligible Gilt as at the first day of the delivery month, assuming a Yield to Maturity of 6.0% (from March 2004), less accrued interest on that day ('Initial Accrued', being the 'Daily Accrued' amount x number of days up to first delivery day).
Invoice Amount	(1000 x 'EDSP' x Price Factor) + Initial Accrued + (Daily Accrued x number of days from and including the first day in the delivery month up to and including the Settlement Day). 'EDSP' is the settlement futures price (the Exchange Delivery Settlement Price as at the date the Seller gives notice of an intention to deliver).

Price Factor

The formula for the Price Factor can be found on www.liffe.com. The 8.0% 27 September 2013 bond shown on the list in **Exhibit 4.1** can also be calculated as follows (see **Example B2.9** in Appendix B2 for pricing a bond part-way through its coupon period):

Example 4.6 Calculating the Price Factor: 8.0% 27 September 2013 Gilt

Bond information

NV	Nominal value (total)	£100,000	Maturity date	27 September 2013	9.329 yrs
P	Face value	£100			*Days in period*
C	Coupon rate	8.00%	Last coupon date	27 March 2004	
r	Notional yield	6.00%	Settlement date	31 May 2004	65
m	No. of interest payments each year	2	Delivery date	01 June 2004	1
mn	Future coupons excl. next coupon	18	Next coupon date	27 September 2004	118
			Current coupon period		184 days
			Daily coupon	£100 x (8.00% / 2) / 184	£ 0.02174

Clean price calculation

Bond price $= \text{Coupon} \times \left\{ \frac{1}{r/m} \times \left[1 - \frac{1}{(1 + r/m)^{mn}} \right] \right\} + \frac{\text{Nominal value}}{(1 + r/m)^{mn}}$

Price at next coupon period (27 Sep: 118 days from Settlement) $= 4.00 \times \left\{ \frac{1}{0.0300} \times \left[1 - \frac{1}{(1 + 0.0300)\text{^}18} \right] \right\} + \frac{100}{(1 + 0.0300)\text{^}18}$

	=	55.01		+ 58.74
	=	113.75	+ 4.00 coupon received on that date	
Price at next coupon date (27 Sep)	=	117.75		
Price on Delivery date (1 Jun)	=	115.54238	= 117.75 x 1 / (1 + 3.00% x 118 days / 184 days)	
Less: accrued interest on delivery date		-0.02174	= 0.021739 daily coupon x 1 day	
less: accrued interest at Settlement		-1.41304	= 0.021739 x 65 days	
Clean price on Settlement	=	114.10760		
Price factor	**=**	**1.1410760**		

Bond Forward Price

A party with a short futures position is required to physically deliver a bond. It could purchase the bond in the market just before delivery and receipt of the Invoice Amount (borrowing for a single day), or it could purchase the bond at the time it sold the bond futures, borrowing for the period to delivery and receiving any income on the underlying bond.

The Forward Price is the fair 'clean' price at the Delivery Date, calculated to ensure no arbitrage profit or loss would arise from a transaction, based on current market prices and Spot Rates, that enables delivery of the bond at the required date (see Appendix B3 sections B3.1 and B3.5), such as the following:

Day 0	- Take out a loan
	- Use the borrowings to buy an eligible bond
Day 1 - X	- Pay loan interest
	- Receive bond coupons
Day X	- Sell the bond at the market price
	- Use the proceeds to repay the loan plus accrued interest

The only unknown on Day 0 is the bond market price on Day X. For there to be no profit or loss from this transaction, the fair price agreed on Day 0 for delivery of the bond on Day X, payable on Day X, would have to be as follows:

4.11

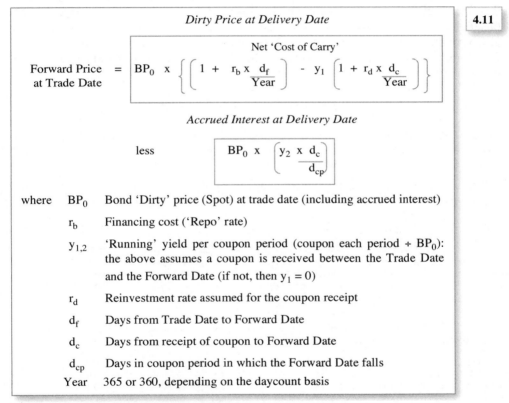

Dirty Price at Delivery Date

Net 'Cost of Carry'

$$\text{Forward Price at Trade Date} = BP_0 \times \left\{ \left(1 + r_b \times \frac{d_f}{\text{Year}}\right) - y_1 \left(1 + r_d \times \frac{d_c}{\text{Year}}\right) \right\}$$

Accrued Interest at Delivery Date

$$\text{less} \quad BP_0 \times \left(y_2 \times \frac{d_c}{d_{cp}} \right)$$

where

BP_0	Bond 'Dirty' price (Spot) at trade date (including accrued interest)
r_b	Financing cost ('Repo' rate)
$y_{1,2}$	'Running' yield per coupon period (coupon each period ÷ BP_0): the above assumes a coupon is received between the Trade Date and the Forward Date (if not, then $y_1 = 0$)
r_d	Reinvestment rate assumed for the coupon receipt
d_f	Days from Trade Date to Forward Date
d_c	Days from receipt of coupon to Forward Date
d_{cp}	Days in coupon period in which the Forward Date falls
Year	365 or 360, depending on the daycount basis

➡ See Appendix B3 (**Example B3.6** in B3.5).

As already stated in **4.10**, if there was only one bond that could be delivered on a certain delivery date, the Futures Price should equal the Forward Price of that bond divided by its Price Factor.

Cheapest To Deliver Bond ('CTD')

On delivery, the party with the short position will have the following cash flows (ignoring margin cash flows):

Receive Invoice Amount (= FP x PF + AI_d)	x
Buy bond in market (= BP_d + AI_d)	(x)
Net cash flow	x

FP	Settlement Futures Price
PF	Price Factor for CTD
BP_d	CTD clean price at delivery
AI_d	Accrued interest on delivery

During the delivery month, the CTD will be the eligible bond that maximises the above net cash flow, or CTD = Max [FP x PF - BP_d]. Prior to the delivery month, the CTD is likely to be the bond which has the highest implied 'Repo' rate (giving the highest Forward Price per **4.11**). The Bond's duration (see Appendix B2) can also provide some guidance: if yields are falling below the 6% notional coupon, then short duration bonds are likely to be the CTD, whereas bonds with higher duration will be favoured if yields are higher (Kolb (2003 p.167)).

Example 4.7 Determining the Cheapest-To-Deliver (CTD) bond

The June 2004 LIFFE futures price on 19 January 2004 was 108.67. The 8.0% 27 September 2013 bond was the CTD at that date, based on the quoted bond prices and yields (obtained from the Debt Management Office, www.dmo.gov.uk - see next page):

- Highest implied Repo rate: assuming the Delivery Date is on the last business day in June (30 June), then, on 19 January (163 days earlier), the implied Repo rates were as follows:

	Trading date (19 January 2004)					
June 2004 Eligibles	Bond Price (clean)	Bond Price (dirty)	Bond Yield	Futures Price	Price Factor	FP x PF
		BPo		FP	PF	*A*
8.00% 27 Sep 2013	125.44	127.97	4.698558%	108.67	1.1410760	124.00
5.00% 7 Sep 2014	102.21	104.06	4.732345%	108.67	0.9240793	100.42
4.75% 7 Sep 2015	100.01	101.52	4.748436%	108.67	0.8986086	97.65
8.00% 7 Dec 2015	129.41	130.37	4.733948%	108.67	1.1646196	126.56

Coupons have been reinvested at the 6 month Repo on 19 January. In practice, Forward Rates would be used.

	End of delivery month (30 June 2004)									
June 2004 Eligibles	Last coupon	Next coupon	Coupon Period	Days Accrued	Coupon received	Repo rate	Interest on Coupon	AId 30 June	Total Receipts	REPO
					B		*C*	*D*	*=A+B+C+D*	
8.00% 27 Sep 2013	27 Mar	27 Sep	184	95	4.00	4.0133%	0.0418	2.07	130.11	**3.7452%**
5.00% 7 Sep 2014	7 Mar	7 Sep	184	115	2.50	4.0133%	0.0316	1.56	104.51	0.9671%
4.75% 7 Sep 2015	7 Mar	7 Sep	184	115	2.38	4.0133%	0.0300	1.48	101.54	0.0385%
8.00% 7 Dec 2015	7 June	7 Dec	183	23	4.00	4.0133%	0.0101	0.50	131.07	1.2029%

The implied Repo rate for the CTD bond is calculated as follows:

Expected receipt at end		Interim Cash Flows		Cash paid at start
Futures Price x Price Factor 19 Jan	Accrued interest 30 June	Coupon received	Interest on reinvested coupon	Dirty price 19 Jan

$$\frac{124.00 + 2.07 + \left(4.00 + 0.0418\right) - 127.97}{127.97} \times \frac{365 \text{ days}}{163 \text{ days}}$$

= 3.7452%

The dirty price for the 8.0% 27 September 2013 bond, as quoted by the Debt Management Office, was 127.967473 at a yield of 4.698558%. The Dirty price using the bond formulae discussed in Appendix B2 is 127.951144, calculated as follows:

$$\text{Bond price} = \text{Coupon} \times \left\{ \frac{1}{r/m} \times \left[1 - \frac{1}{(1 + r/m)^{mn}} \right] \right\} + \frac{\text{Nominal value}}{(1 + r/m)^{mn}}$$

Price at next coupon date in 68 days

$$= £4.00 \times \left\{ \frac{1}{0.0235} \times \left[1 - \frac{1}{(1 + 0.0235)^{\wedge}19} \right] \right\} + \frac{£100}{(1 + 0.0235)^{\wedge}19}$$

$$= £60.74 + £64.33$$

Price on 27 March 2004 = £125.07

Discounted back over 68 days

$$= \frac{\left[£125.07 + £4.00 \text{ coupon received on that date} \right]}{(1 + 4.70\% / 2)^{\wedge} (68 / 182)}$$

Price on 19 January 2004 = 127.951144

Last coupon date	27 September 2003	0 days
Trade date	19 January 2004	114 days
1st coupon date	27 March 2004	68 days
1st coupon period		182.0 days

with 29 days in February

Or using Microsoft Excel™ functions:

PRICE (19 January 2004 , 27 September 2013 , 8.00% coupon, 4.70% yield , £100 , 2 coupons p.a., 1)	125.445649
PRICE (27 September 2003 , 27 March 2004 , 19 January 2004 , 8.0% coupon, £100 , 2 coupons p.a., 1)	2.505495
Dirty Spot Bond Price at Trade Date	127.951144

Accrued interest above	£4.0 coupon / 182 day coupon period = 0.021978 daily coupon x 114 days	2.505495
add: 1 day		0.021978
		2.527473
Clean price (rounded)		125.440000
Dirty price		127.967473

In this example, the dirty price of 127.951144 has been used

- Lowest modified duration (yields are below the 6.0% notional coupon):

June 2004 Eligibles	Bond Yield	Modified Duration
8.00% 27 Sep 2013	4.698558%	**6.95**
5.00% 7 Sep 2014	4.732345%	8.07
4.75% 7 Sep 2015	4.748436%	8.71
8.00% 7 Dec 2015	4.733948%	8.16

see Excel™ calculation

6.95 = MDURATION (19 Jan 04 , 27 Sep 13, 8.00% , 4.698558% ,2 coupons,1)

Forward Prices, Futures Prices and Basis

The theoretical futures price is the Forward Price of the CTD bond ÷ Price Factor.

Example 4.8 Estimating the Theoretical Futures Price

The Theoretical Futures Price as at 19 January for the 8.0% 2013 CTD bond from **Example 4.7**, with delivery on the last day of the delivery period (30 June), and a 6mth Repo rate of 4.0133% (source: the British Bankers' Association www.bba.org.uk) is calculated as follows (using the formula **4.11**):

Dirty Bond Price; 'Carry costs'; Coupon yield; 'Carry return'

$$127.95 \times \left\{ \underbrace{\left(1 + 4.0133\% \times \frac{163 \text{ days}}{365 \text{ days}}\right)}_{\text{'Carry costs'}} - \underbrace{3.13\% \left(1 + 4.0133\% \times \frac{95 \text{ days}}{365 \text{ days}}\right)}_{\text{'Carry return'}} \right\}$$

= £126.2026 less accrued interest of £2.0652 at 30 June

Forward Price	Price Factor	Futures Price
= £124.1374	1.1410760	**108.79**

vs 108.67 actual

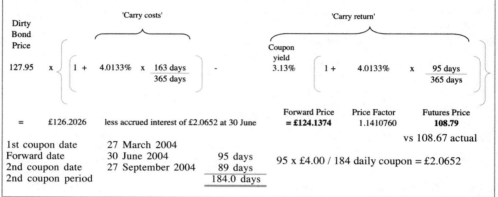

1st coupon date	27 March 2004		
Forward date	30 June 2004	95 days	95 x £4.00 / 184 daily coupon = £2.0652
2nd coupon date	27 September 2004	89 days	
2nd coupon period		184.0 days	

On any date prior to the delivery month, the theoretical futures price based on the CTD bond is likely to be different to the actual futures price, since the seller can choose to deliver:

① on any date during the delivery month, and

② any of the other deliverable bonds if conditions change by the date of delivery (the CTD bond may changed over time as yields fluctuate)

These Put options will usually mean the actual futures price is less than the theoretical futures price and the actual Repo rate is more than the implied Repo rate (Dubofsky & Miller (2003 p.244)): from **Examples 4.7** and **4.8**, the actual futures price (108.67) is less than the theoretical futures price for the CTD (108.79), and the actual Repo rate (4.0133%) is more than the implied rate (3.7452%).

The difference between the actual futures price ('AFP") and the theoretical futures price ('TFP') is the 'Net Basis'. The difference between the actual futures price and the futures price implied from the CTD bond clean price (Spot price) and its Price Factor is the 'Gross Basis':

$$\begin{aligned}
\text{Gross Basis} &= \frac{\text{Spot price (clean)}}{\text{Price Factor}} - \text{AFP} \\
&= \left(\frac{\text{Spot price (clean)}}{\text{Price Factor}} - \text{TFP}\right) + \left(\text{TFP - AFP}\right) \\
&= \left(\frac{\text{Spot price (clean)} - \text{Forward price (clean)}}{\text{Price Factor}}\right) + \left(\text{TFP - AFP}\right) \\
&= \text{Carry Basis} + \text{Net Basis}
\end{aligned} \qquad \textbf{4.12}$$

Example 4.9 Basis

Using the CTD bond from **Examples 4.7** and **4.8**, gross Basis can be analysed as follows:

$$\text{Gross Basis} = \frac{125.45 \text{ clean CTD price}}{1.1410760 \text{ Price Factor}} - 108.67 \text{ AFP}$$

$$= \frac{125.45 - 124.14}{1.1410760} + 108.79 - 108.67$$

$$= 1.15 \text{ Carry Basis} + 0.12 \text{ Net Basis}$$

Converges to zero as delivery approaches (Carry Basis); *Depends on value of seller's options ① and ② above* (Net Basis)

where $125.45 - 124.14 = S_{clean} - F_{clean} = (S_{dirty} - F_{dirty}) - (AI_0 - AI_d)$

$S_{dirty} - F_{dirty} = S_{dirty} \times (1 - \text{Net Cost of Carry})$ from **4.11**

S, F - CTD bond price, today (Spot) and on delivery (Forward)

AI_0, AI_d - Accrued interest at spot date (trade) and forward date (Delivery)

The Carry Basis can be shown, therefore, as follows:

Carry cost	= 127.9511 x 4.0133% x 163 / 365	-2.2932
Carry return	= 4.00 x (1 + 4.0133% x 95 / 365)	4.0418
Dirty Spot price (127.9511) - Dirty Forward price (126.2026)		1.7486
Accrued int. change = 2.5055 - 2.0652		-0.4403
		1.3083
Carry basis	/ Price Factor =	1.15

If yields and Repo Rates are the same at each date prior to delivery, Carry Basis reduces linearly as the assumed 30 June Delivery Date approaches, as follows:

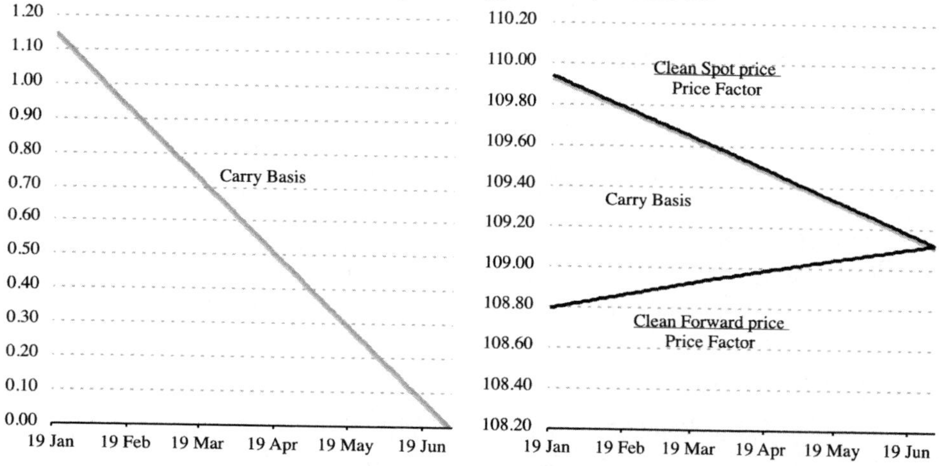

In practice, the Repo rate used would be the relevant rate for the period from each date to delivery. If yields and Repo rates change before delivery, Carry will change. If long term bond yields increase more than the short term Repo rates (steeper yield curve), then, at some level, Carry will increase (and decrease if the yield curve flattens out): as yields increase, the fall in the bond price reduces the Cost of Carry (partly offset by the increase in the Repo rates), the Carry return increases as Repo rates increase.

Hedging

Introduction

Bond futures prices move inversely with required yields and interest rates (like short term interest rate futures). A corporate borrower, wishing to hedge against an increase in required rates by the time it enters into some future borrowing commitment, would short sell bond futures: if rates increased and futures prices decreased, the hedge could be lifted before the delivery month, and the futures profit would offset the increase in borrowing costs. As well as selecting the appropriate futures contract, the hedger would need to determine the optimal number of contracts.

Hedge Ratio

The borrower would like the change in the value of the liability being hedged (the present value of the additional borrowing costs arising from a rise in required yields or interest rates) to be exactly offset by the change in value of the futures position:

$$\text{Change in value of hedged security} + \text{Change in value of futures position} = 0$$

or

$$\Delta_{HS} \times N_{HS} + \Delta_F \times N_F \times \text{Contracts} = 0$$

where Δ_{HS} - the change in price per nominal value of the hedged security (N_{HS})
Δ_F - the change in futures price per nominal value of contract (N_F)

4.13

$$\text{Contracts} = \frac{N_{HS}}{N_F} \times \frac{\Delta_{HS}}{\Delta_F}$$

$$= \frac{\text{Value of hedged security}}{\text{Face value of futures contract}} \times \text{'Hedge Ratio'}$$

The Hedge Ratio reflects the sensitivity of the price of the hedged security (Δ_{HS}) to a given change in yields relative to the sensitivity of the price of the futures contract to the change in yields (Δ_F). This can be related to the change in value of CTD bond underlying the futures contract (Δ_{CTD}):

$$\text{Hedge Ratio} = \frac{\Delta_{HS}}{\Delta_F} = \frac{\Delta_{HS}}{\Delta_{CTD}} \times \frac{\Delta_{CTD}}{\Delta_F}$$

The relative price sensitivities can be estimated as follows:

- Modified Duration

Modified Duration (see **B2.11** in Appendix B2) is a reasonable estimate of price sensitivity provided yield changes are very small (Convexity can be ignored). The Duration of the CTD bond can be used to estimate the Duration of the futures contract (adjusting by the Price Factor):

4.14

$$\text{Hedge Ratio} = \frac{\left(\text{Price}_{HS} \times \dfrac{M_{HS}}{(1 + \text{yield}_{HS}\text{ before change})} \times \text{Yield change}_{HS}\right)}{\left(\dfrac{\text{Price}_{CTD} \times \dfrac{M_{CTD}}{(1 + \text{yield}_{CTD}\text{ before change})} \times \text{Yield change}_{CTD}}{\text{Price Factor}}\right)}$$

where Price_{HS} Value of the liability being hedged (or asset)

Price_{CTD} Dirty price of CTD bond

M_{HS}, M_{CTD} Macaulay Duration (based on Dirty prices) of the Hedged Security and the CTD bond

In the discussion that follows, it is assumed that yields change by the same amount: a 0.1% change in the CTD bond yield, for example, would result in a similar change in the yield of the hedged security (at all maturities). If a corporate borrower is hedging a new bond issue, this implies that the government-corporate bond yield spread is constant at all maturities for a given change in yields (the shift in the yield curve is parallel for both). A statistical regression of historic yields would indicate the true yield relationship (see Dubofsky and Miller (2003 p.245)). Assuming the yield changes are the same, therefore:

$$\text{Hedge Ratio} = \left(\frac{\text{Price}_{HS} \times \text{Modified Duration}_{HS}}{\text{Price}_{CTD} \times \text{Modified Duration}_{CTD}}\right) \times \text{Price Factor}$$

$$= \frac{\text{PVBP}_{HS}}{\text{PVBP}_{CTD}} \times \text{Price Factor}$$

where PVBP - Price Value of a Basis Point (change in value for 0.01% yield change)

Example 4.10 Bond Futures Hedge Ratio - Duration

A company needs to raise £100m in order to finance a capital investment, and intends to issue a 12 year 6.0% (semi-annual coupon) corporate bond, priced at par with a promised Yield to Maturity of 6.0% (the rate required by the market, based on comparable bonds, with similar maturity and credit risk, issued at today's date, 19 January 2004). One million £100 bonds will be issued on 30 June 2004 to raise the required £100m (issue costs have been ignored). The company wants to hedge against yields increasing by the time it issues the bond. An increase in the required yield at the date of issue will reduce the total proceeds, if a 6.0% coupon is to be set: this will be considered the opportunity cost to be hedged (following the approach used by Fitzgerald (1993)). The borrower decides to short sell June 2004 bond futures. The Cheapest-To-Deliver (CTD) bond is estimated to be the 8.0% 2013 Bond (see **Example 4.7**). Market rates on 19 January were as follows

CTD bond yield (%)	4.6986
CTD bond price (dirty)	127.9511
Repo rate (6 months) (%)	4.0133
June Futures price	108.67
Hedged bond yield (%)	6.0000

The Theoretical Futures Price is 108.79, assuming delivery takes place on the last delivery day, 30 June (see **Example 4.8**). Hence Basis is calculated as follows (see **4.12** and **Example 4.9**):

	Clean / PF	*Clean*	*Acc Int.*	*Total*
CTD spot price 19 Jan		125.45	2.5055	127.9511
Net cost of carry, 19 Jan to 30 Jun				(1.7486)
CTD forward price 19 Jan	108.79	124.14	2.0652	126.2026
Futures price 19 Jan	108.67	124.00 ← CTD forward price implied from futures price ('futures cash equivalent')		

CTD spot price 19 Jan / Price Factor (1.1410760)	109.94
Actual futures price 19 Jan	108.67
Gross basis	1.27
being: Carry basis = (125.45 - 124.14) / 1.1410760	1.15 ← Clean spot price - Theoretical Futures Price
Net basis = (124.14 - 124.00) / 1.1410760	0.12 ← Theoretical Futures Price - Actual Futures Price
	1.27

The standard number of contracts is 1,000 (£100m value of liability being hedged ÷ £100,000 face value of each contract). The hedge ratio will depend on when the hedge is to be lifted. If margin cash flows are ignored (i.e. changes in futures prices before the date of lifting can be ignored) and yield changes before the date the bonds are issued are ignored (i.e. the yield at the date the bonds are issued – the date the hedge is lifted – determines the change in value), then the duration at the date of lifting should be used (Hull (2003 p.116)). It is assumed that the bonds are issued on the Delivery Date, 30 June. The fair prices of the hedged bond and CTD bond as at the lifting date (30 June) are calculated assuming yields are unchanged from 19 Jan, and their respective durations are determined.

	Hedged bond	*CTD Bond*	
Bond details			
Face value	£100	£100	
Coupon (semi-annual)	6.00%	8.00%	
Maturity	19 Jan 2016	27 Sep 2013	
Price Factor		1.1410760	
Fair prices at 30 June 2004			
Valuation date	30 Jun 2004	30 Jun 2004	
Last Coupon Date	-	27 Mar 2004	
Next Coupon Date	30 Dec 2004	27 Sep 2004	
Maturity	30 Jun 2016	27 Sep 2013	
Maturity in years	12.008 yrs	9.249 yrs	
Yield To Maturity	6.0000%	4.6986%	
Clean Price	100.0000	124.5093	See ❶ in **Example**
Accrued Interest	-	2.0652	**B3.6** in App. B3.
Dirty Price	100.0000	126.5745	
Modified Duration (years) - dirty price	8.4678	6.7297	
PVBP	0.084678	0.085180	

Hedge ratio = (100.0000 x 8.4678) / ({126.5745 x 6.7297} / 1.1410760) = 1.1343

Contracts = 1,000 x 1.1343 = 1,134

On delivery, the actual futures price converges to the CTD spot price (clean). The 30 June CTD yield was 5.104% (0.4055% higher than at 19 Jan) giving a clean bond price of 121.11, and an equivalent futures price of 106.14 (=121.11 ÷ Price Factor)(the actual price for the last trading day was 106.08). Assuming the required yield on the hedged bond increased by 0.4055% as well, then actual prices at the date of lifting are as follows:

	Hedged bond	*CTD Bond*
Fair prices at 30 June 2004		
Valuation date	30 Jun 2004	30 Jun 2004
Last Coupon Date	-	27 Mar 2004
Next Coupon Date	30 Dec 2004	27 Sep 2004
Maturity	30 Jun 2016	27 Sep 2013
Maturity in years	12.008 yrs	9.249 yrs
Yield To Maturity	6.4055%	5.1040%
Clean Price	96.6405	121.1149
Accrued Interest	-	2.0652
Dirty Price	96.6405	123.1801

Hedged bond loss in value	= 1m bonds x (96.64 – 100.0)	- £3,360,000
Futures profit	= 259 ticks (= 108.67-106.08) x £10 tick size x 1,134 contracts	£2,937,060
Net loss		422,940
% Hedge effectiveness		87%

The actual relative price sensitivity was 1.1440 rather than the 1.1343 predicted by duration.

An alternative method (Rendleman (2002 p.341)) would be to use the forward CTD price implied from the 19 Jan futures price (this assumes zero Net Basis):

Forward CTD	=	108.67 futures price on 19 Jan x 1.141076 Price Factor
	=	124.0007 (vs 124.5093 above) + 2.0652 accrued interest on delivery
	=	126.0659 dirty price
Implied yield	=	4.7584% (vs 4.4986% above)
Duration	=	6.7223
Hedge ratio	=	(100.0000 x 8.4678) / ({126.0659 x 6.7223} / 1.1410760) = 1.1402
Contracts	=	1,140

This would increase the hedge effectiveness to 88%.

- Calculating fair prices for an assumed yield change ('Perturbation')

Duration can only predict price changes for very small yield changes (0.01%), depending on the degree of Convexity. It failed to predict the actual relative price volatilities in the above example, and hence the hedge was relatively poor. An alternative method would be to estimate the change in price of the hedged security and the futures contract as a result of an assumed yield change.

The fair value of the hedged security can be calculated for given yield changes. The fair value of the futures price can be estimated from the bond forward pricing equation **4.11**.

Example 4.11 Bond Futures Hedge Ratio – Forward pricing

Two scenarios are shown for the hedge in **Example B4.10**: the hedge being lifted on delivery (30 June) and on 19 May (in both scenarios, these dates will be the date the hedged bond is issued). The hedge will be based on an assumed increase of 0.30% in the corporate bond yield, CTD yield and Repo Rates as at the lifting date (compared to 19 Jan – margin cash flows are ignored, for simplicity).

♦ *Hedge lifting and bond issue date = delivery (30 June)* ♦

Expected prices on 30 June (Net Basis is ignored on delivery):

	Yields / Rates unchanged		*Yields / Rates increase*	
	Hedged bond	*Forward CTD*	*Hedged bond*	*Forward CTD*
Fair prices at 30 June 2004				
Valuation date	30 Jun 2004	30 Jun 2004		
Last Coupon Date	-	27 Mar 2004		
Next Coupon Date	30 Dec 2004	27 Sep 2004		
Maturity	30 Jun 2016	27 Sep 2013		
Maturity in years	12.008 yrs	9.249 yrs		
Yield To Maturity	6.0000%	4.6986%	6.3000%	4.9986%
Clean Price	100.0000	124.5093	97.5002	121.9864
Accrued Interest	-	2.0652	-	2.0652
Dirty Price	100.0000	126.5745	97.5002	124.0516

Implied from actual futures price	*Fair prices on 19 Jan 2004*	Forward price converges to CTD bond price on delivery (see ❷ **Example B3.6** in App. B3 for bond fair price on 30 June with assumed 0.30% yield increase).	*Fair prices on 30 June 2004*
Forward Price on 30 June 2004	124.0007		121.9864
Price Factor	1.1410760		1.1410760
Actual / Theoretical Futures Price	108.67		106.90

The correct number of contracts for a perfect hedge if yields increase 0.30% (assuming (1) actual futures prices equal theoretical futures prices at the date of lifting, (2) fractional contracts can be traded) is 1,412.43 (see **Example 4.11 (a)** below). (In practice, the hedger would monitor the position and renew the hedge – close out the old hedge and short sell an adjusted number of contracts – as yields or market expectations changed.)

Actual yields increased 0.4055%. Using 1,412 contracts, the actual hedge position (with actual futures prices) is as follows:

Hedged bond loss in value	= 1m bonds x (96.64 – 100.0)	- £3,360,000
Futures profit	= 259 ticks (= 108.67-106.08 actual) x £10 tick size x 1,412 contracts	£3,657,080
Net (loss) / gain		£297,080
% Hedge effectiveness		109%

♦ *Hedge lifting and bond issue date = before delivery (19 May)* ♦

The same approach as above can be used, calculating expected prices at 19 May, assuming yields and rates increase 0.30% on or before that date (the Forward Price will now be the CTD bond price at 19 May adjusted for the Cost of Carry):

	Yields / Rates unchanged		*Yields / Rates increase*	
	Hedged bond	*Forward CTD*	*Hedged bond*	*Forward CTD*
Fair prices on 19 May 2004				
Valuation date	19 May 2004	30 Jun 2004		
Last Coupon Date	-	27 Mar 2004		
Next Coupon Date	19 Nov 2004	27 Sep 2004		
Maturity	19 May 2016	27 Sep 2013		
Maturity in years	12.008 yrs	9.249 yrs		
Yield To Maturity	6.0000%	4.7089%	6.3000%	5.0088%
Clean Price	100.0000	124.4216	97.5002	121.9016
Accrued Interest	-	2.0652	-	2.0652
Dirty Price	100.0000	126.4869	97.5002	123.9668
	Implied from actual Futures Price. Forward Price using Repo rates = 124.1374	*Fair prices on 19 Jan 2004*		*Fair prices at 19 May 2004*
Forward Price on 30 June 2004		124.0007	See ❸ in **Example B3.6** in App.B3.	121.9016
Price Factor		1.1410760		1.1410760
Actual / Theoretical Futures Price		108.67		106.83

The Forward price on 19 May is calculated in **Example B3.6** in Appendix B3.

The correct number of contracts for a perfect hedge if yields increase 0.30% (assuming (1) actual futures prices equal theoretical futures prices at the date of lifting, (2) fractional contracts can be traded) is 1,358.70 (see **Example 4.11 (b)**). The CTD bond yield on 19 May was actually 5.1482%, 0.4496% higher than at 19 Jan. Assuming the hedged bond yield increased the same amount, the 19 May issue price for the 6.0% corporate bond would fall to 96.28. The actual futures price on 19 May was 105.69. The hedging result is as follows:

Hedged bond loss in value	= 1m bonds x (96.28 – 100.0)	- £3,720,000
Futures profit =	298 ticks (= 108.67-105.69 actual) x £10 tick size x 1,359 contracts	£4,049,820
Net (loss) / gain		£329,820
% Hedge effectiveness		109%

***Example 4.11 (a)** – Hedge held to delivery with assumed 0.30% increase in yields. Fractional contracts / Fair Prices / Perfect Hedge*

Price Sensitivity	£97.50 6% Bond Price with 6.30% yield - £100 6% Bond Price with 6% yield / 30 Jun Fwd Price at 30 Jun (106.90 x 1.1410760) - 30 Jun Fwd Price at 19 Jan (108.67 x 1.1410760)	=	(£2.5000) / (£2.0197)	= 1.237805
Contracts	Standard Number of Contracts 1,000 x Price Factor 1.141076 x Price Sensitivity 1.237805			= 1412.43
Tick change	Theoretical 30 Jun Fut. Price on 30 Jun with 4.9986% CTD yield (106.90) - Actual Jun Fut. Price on 19 Jan (108.67)			= 1.77
Futures Profit	= 1.77 tick change x 100 = 177 ticks x 10.00 tick size x 1,412.43 contracts			£2,500,000
Bond Cost	(£97.50 6% Bond Price with 6.30% yield - £100 6% Bond Price with 6% yield) x £100m Bond issue size / £100 face value			(£2,500,000)

***Example 4.11 (b)** – Hedge lifted on 19 May with assumed 0.30% increase in yields. Fractional contracts / Fair Prices / Perfect Hedge*

Price Sensitivity	£97.50 6% Bond Price with 6.30% yield - £100 6% Bond Price with 6% yield / 30 Jun Fwd Price at 19 May (106.83 x 1.1410760) - 30 Jun Fwd Price at 19 Jan (108.67 x 1.1410760)	=	(£2.5000) / (£2.0996)	= 1.190714
Contracts	Standard Number of Contracts 1,000 x Price Factor 1.141076 x Price Sensitivity 1.190714			= 1358.70
Tick change	Theoretical 30 Jun Fut. Price on 19 May with 4.9986% CTD yield (106.83) - Actual Jun Fut. Price on 19 Jan (108.67)			= 1.84
Futures Profit	= 1.84 tick change x 100 = 184 ticks x 10.00 tick size x 1,358.70 contracts			£2,500,000
Bond Cost	(£97.50 6% Bond Price with 6.30% yield - £100 6% Bond Price with 6% yield) x £100m Bond issue size / £100 face value			(£2,500,000)

Notes

- Prices for the bond being hedged and futures prices have been rounded to two decimal places.
- The Forward Price on 19 January is implied from the actual futures price (108.67 x 1.141076 = 124.00 vs the forward price calculated from Repo rates, 124.1374).

An alternative approach (Fitzgerald (1993 p.202)) would be to:

① estimate the CTD clean bond price at the date of lifting (19 May) by linear interpolation between the actual price on 19 Jan (125.45) and the price implied for the assumed 30 June Delivery Date from the 19 Jan futures price (124.007): the interpolated price is 124.37;

= Price on 19 May = 125.45 + (124.00 - 125.45) x 121 [19 Jan - 19 May] / 163 [19 Jan - 30 Jun]

② calculate the implied yield for this interpolated price, and calculate the adjusted bond price if this yield increases by an assumed amount (0.30% in this example): the implied yield is 4.7431%:

Fair prices on 19 May 2004	*CTD Bond*	*CTD Bond*
Valuation date	19 May 2004	
Last Coupon Date	27 Mar 2004	
Next Coupon Date	27 Sep 2004	
Maturity	27 Sep 2013	
Maturity in years	9.364 yrs	
Yield To Maturity	4.7431%	5.0431%
Clean Price	124.3700	121.8290
Accrued Interest	1.1522	1.1522
Dirty Price	125.5222	122.9812

Yield based on assumed 124.37 clean price on 19 May, plus 0.30%

③ estimate the theoretical futures price based on this new price, using the Forward Price formula **4.11** (with Repo rates 0.30% higher), and hence calculate the hedge ratio:

Fair prices at 19 May 2004		
Dirty Bond Price		122.9812
Carry Cost	= £122.98 x 4.3133% x 42 / 365	0.6104
Carry Return	n/a	0.0000
Dirty Forward Price		*123.5916*
less: accrued interest		-2.0652
Forward price		***121.5263***

Predicted futures price
= 121.5263 / 1.141076
= 106.50

Contracts = 1,000 x $\frac{\text{(100.00 – 97.50) Hedged bond price change}}{\text{(108.67 – 106.50) Futures price change}}$ x 1.141076 = 1,315

Hedge result = - £3,720,000 + 298 ticks x £10 x 1,315 = 198,700 (105%)

Interest Rate Swaps

Definition

In an Interest Rate Swap ('IRS'), two parties agree[1] on a 'Trade Date' to:

- pay each other, at the end of each interest period over the term ('Tenor'), interest on a principal amount[2],
- at a fixed or floating rate[3] applicable for the interest period,
- payable in the same currency as the principal, at the end of the interest period[4].

[1] Contract terms are normally standardised, with the first interest period starting on the 'Value Date', normally two business days after the Trade Date.

[2] This amount is a 'notional' principal: no exchange of principals usually takes place.

[3] Bid-Offer swap rates are quoted in terms of the fixed rate a bank is prepared to pay (the lower Bid rate) or receive (the higher Offer rate). The swap buyer would normally be considered to be the party that pays the fixed rate.

[4] Usually, one party pays the other the interest differential; unlike an FRA, the settlement sum is paid on the last day of each interest period (or the next business day).

In general, a borrower would use an IRS to transform:

- a fixed rate loan into a floating rate loan ('Fixed-to-Floating'), by agreeing to pay the counterparty a floating rate (for example, 3 or 6 month LIBOR) in return for receiving a fixed rate (the net interest cost is the floating rate plus the fixed rate differential);
- a floating rate loan (for example, 3 or 6 month LIBOR plus a margin) into a fixed rate ('Floating-to-Fixed' or a 'Reverse' swap) by paying a fixed rate in return for a floating rate (the net interest cost is the fixed rate plus the margin on the floating rate loan);
- a reference rate on a floating rate loan ('Basis' swap) by, for example, agreeing to pay 3 month LIBOR in exchange for 6 month LIBOR (on different dates).

Example 4.12 Standard swaps ('Plain Vanilla')

A borrower pays a nominal 6.75% fixed rate on a £100m loan (1.688% paid quarterly). It could refinance the loan at a floating rate (3 month LIBOR) plus a 2.0% margin; however a Fixed-to-Floating swap would be cheaper: a fixed 5.10% would be received from the counterparty (1.275% per quarter), in return for 3 month LIBOR. The net financing cost would be 3 month LIBOR + 1.65% (= 6.75% - 5.10%).

A borrower pays a nominal 2.0% above 3 month LIBOR on a £100m loan. It could refinance the loan at a fixed rate of 8.0%; however a Floating-to-Fixed swap would be cheaper: 3 month LIBOR would be received from the counterparty, in return for a fixed 5.35% (1.338% per quarter). The net financing cost would be 7.35% (= 5.35% + 2.0%).

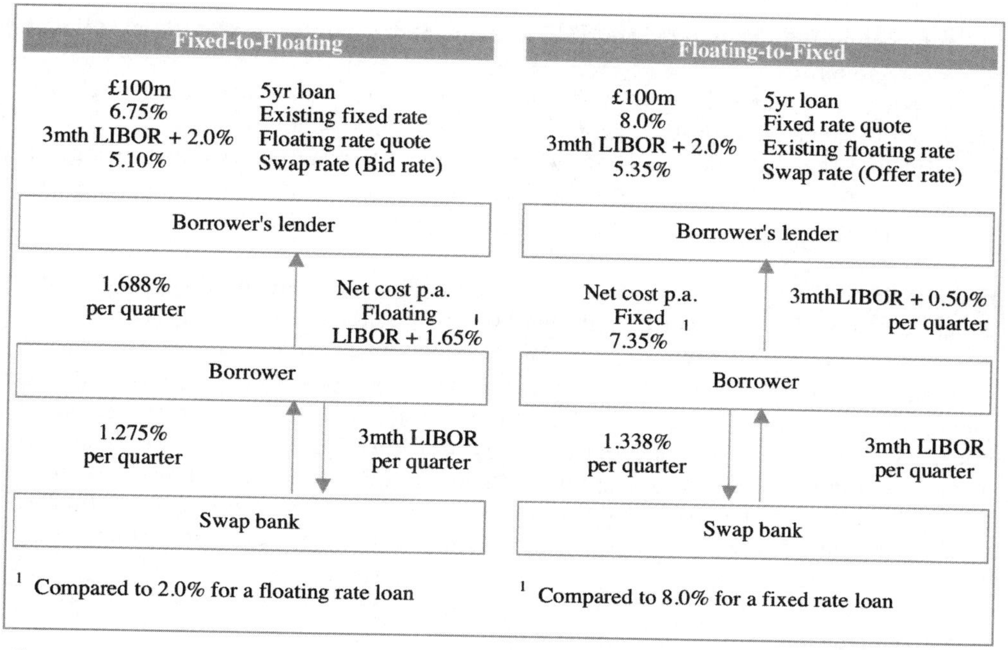

Swaps can be classified according to the agreed terms:

- the notional principal may increase ('Accreting'), decrease ('Amortising'), or fluctuate ('Roller-Coaster') over the Tenor;
- the fixed interest rate may change over time, be rolled up and paid on maturity, or be structured in some other manner;
- the floating rate may be based on the reference rate at the end of the interest period ('Swap-in-Arrears') rather than at the start, as is usually the case;
- the first interest period may start at some point in the future after the Trade Date ('Forward');
- one party may be given an option ('Swaption') to enter into an IRS starting at some point in the future;
- one party may have the right to terminate the swap early ('Callable' swap) or to extend it beyond its stated maturity ('Extendable').

Effective termination can be achieved by entering into an equal and opposite swap, so that cash flows on the second swap exactly offset those of the first (alternatively, both parties could specify termination provisions in the contract).

Pricing

The swap fixed rate can be calculated so that, at the start of the swap, the present value of the floating rate cash flows equals the present value of the fixed rate cash flows (i.e. zero value). This involves:

- forecasting future floating rates (i.e. Forward Rates) for each interest period over the swap term;
- discounting the resulting forecast floating rate cash flows and fixed rate cash flows (using an assumed starting fixed rate) at Spot discount rates;
- adjusting the assumed fixed rate in an iterative manner (for example, using the Microsoft Excel™ goal seek function) to ensure the difference between the present value of the fixed and floating rate cash flows is zero.

Forward Rates and Spot discount rates can be estimated from current market rates, depending on the availability of market information, the reliability of that information, and the length of the swap. Since markets are priced to prevent arbitrage (in theory), there is a relationship between Spot Rates[1], Forward Rates, yields on government bonds priced at par ('Par rates'), and other risk-free swap rates. **Example B2.11** in Appendix B2 illustrates how Spot Rates can be estimated using a technique called 'Bootstrapping'; Appendix B3 (section B3.4) discusses how Forward Rates can be estimated from Spot Rates. Alternatively, quoted futures prices can be used to derive implied Forward Rates, from which Spot discount rates can be calculated.

In practice, estimating rates is more complicated:

- market rates and implied rates may not be directly observable for a relevant swap interest period (in which case, interpolation techniques will need to be applied (see Martin (2001 p.219) and Flavell (2002 p.14) for further discussion);
- market rates may not be considered reliable due to illiquidity (for example, futures prices with Delivery Dates well into the future may not represent fair value);
- a combination of different market rates, linear interpolation and 'smoothing' techniques, to produced a 'blended' Forward Rate curve, may be needed (see Flavell (2002 p.58)).

The present value of each swap cash flow stream will change over time if the actual future Spot Rates differ to the initial Forward Rates.

Example 4.13 Basic Interest Rate Swap pricing

A borrower, paying a floating rate (6 month LIBOR plus 2%) on a 5 year £10m loan (principal repaid on maturity), would like to convert to a fixed rate (it expects interest rates to increase by more than the market expects). It believes a lower rate will be achieved by entering into a Swap, compared to refinancing the existing loan. Using the Forward Rates derived in Appendix B3 (B3.4), the 5 year Swap Rate (fixed rate) for a Floating-to-Fixed swap, based on a £10m notional principal and 6 month LIBOR, would be 5.56%.

[1] The effective yield from an investment that pays out a single cash flow on maturity, such as a 3 or 6 month deposit paying interest at 3 or 6 month LIBOR, respectively, or a Zero Coupon bond (see **B1.1** in Appendix B1).

				FLOATING		FIXED	
Year	Zero Rate	Discount Factors	Forward Rates	Interest received	Present Value	Interest paid	Present Value
	(ii)	(ii)			(iii)		(iv)
0.50	5.0000%	0.975610	5.0000%	250,000	243,902	(278,000)	(271,220)
1.00	5.1500%	0.950423	5.3001%	265,005	251,867	(278,000)	(264,218)
1.50	5.2540%	0.925156	5.4622%	273,108	252,667	(278,000)	(257,193)
2.00	5.3259%	0.900213	5.5417%	277,085	249,436	(278,000)	(250,259)
2.50	5.3881%	0.875535	5.6371%	281,854	246,773	(278,000)	(243,399)
3.00	5.4403%	0.851267	5.7018%	285,088	242,686	(278,000)	(236,652)
3.50	5.4824%	0.827538	5.7348%	286,740	237,288	(278,000)	(230,056)
4.00	5.5195%	0.804296	5.7794%	288,970	232,418	(278,000)	(223,594)
4.50	5.5515%	0.781599	5.8079%	290,395	226,973	(278,000)	(217,285)
5.00	5.5783%	0.759498	5.8198%	290,988	221,005	(278,000)	(211,141)
		£10.0m			**2,405,016**		**(2,405,016)**
		5.5600%					

Notes:

(i) For simplicity, it is assumed that each period is exactly 0.5 years.

(ii) See Example B3.5 in Appendix B3 for derivation.

(iii) For time 0.5, for example: interest = £10.0m x 5.0000% floating rate (Forward Rate) x 1/2 year x discount factor 0.975610 = £243,902 present value.

(iv) For time 0.5, for example: interest = £10.0m x 5.5600% Swap Rate x 1/2 year x discount factor 0.975610 = -£271,220 present value.

At the start of the Swap, the borrower is expecting to pay 6 month LIBOR (the Forward Rates) plus 2% margin on the loan plus the Swap fixed rate cash flows, and receive the Swap floating rate cash flows (the Forward Rates). The net financing cost represents the Swap fixed rate plus the 2% margin (£378,000 = (5.56% + 2%) x 0.5 x £10m)(the margin that the bank would apply to the fixed rate for default risk has been ignored, for simplicity).

If, after 1 year, the market believes 6 month LIBOR at future dates will be higher than originally expected at time 0 (i.e. the Forward Rate curve is steeper), then Swap rates would need to increase (to ensure a zero NPV at the start of any new Swaps). Since the borrower continues to pay the contracted net interest cost of £378,000, it will have benefited. The present value of this benefit is £88,240, as shown below.

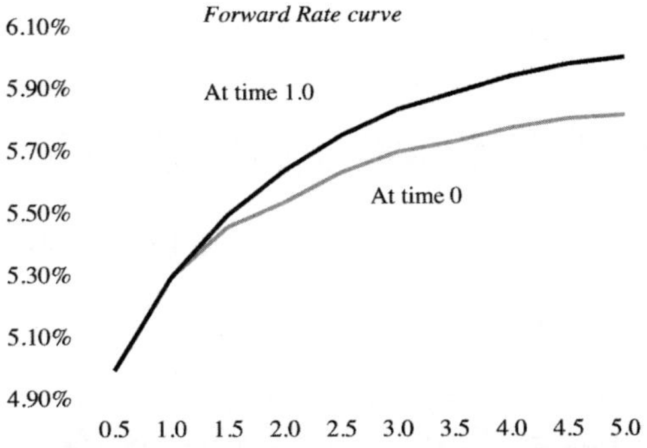

	EXPECTED AT TIME 0			EXPECTED AT TIME 1.0							
	SWAP	LOAN	NET	SWAP						LOAN	NET
Year	Net Swap Cash Flows	LIBOR + 2.0% margin	Net Loan Cash Flows	Zero Rate	Discount factor	Forward Rates	Interest received	Interest paid	Net Swap Cash Flows	LIBOR + 2.0% margin	Net loan cost
0.50	(28,000)	(350,000)	(378,000)								
1.00	(12,995)	(365,005)	(378,000)								
1.50	(4,892)	(373,108)	(378,000)	5.50%	0.973236	5.50%	275,000	(278,000)	(3,000)	(375,000)	(378,000)
2.00	(915)	(377,085)	(378,000)	5.57%	0.946534	5.64%	282,099	(278,000)	4,099	(382,099)	(378,000)
2.50	3,854	(381,854)	(378,000)	5.63%	0.920059	5.76%	287,760	(278,000)	9,760	(387,760)	(378,000)
3.00	7,088	(385,088)	(378,000)	5.68%	0.893960	5.84%	291,942	(278,000)	13,942	(391,942)	(378,000)
3.50	8,740	(386,740)	(378,000)	5.73%	0.868378	5.89%	294,599	(278,000)	16,599	(394,599)	(378,000)
4.00	10,970	(388,970)	(378,000)	5.76%	0.843306	5.95%	297,300	(278,000)	19,300	(397,300)	(378,000)
4.50	12,395	(390,395)	(378,000)	5.79%	0.818806	5.98%	299,226	(278,000)	21,226	(399,226)	(378,000)
5.00	12,988	(390,988)	(378,000)	5.82%	0.794930	6.01%	300,350	(278,000)	22,350	(400,350)	(378,000)
	0 PV at time 0								**88,240** PV at time 1.0		

The borrower has benefited from locking in rates at 5.56%. The fixed rate payer (the borrower) benefits if interest rates unexpectedly increase and loses out if rates unexpectedly decrease (and vice versa for a fixed rate receiver). This is similar to a party with a short position in a series of futures contracts (where an unexpected increase in rates increases the value of the short position due to the decrease in the futures price).

The fixed and floating rate cash flows can be likened to bond and money market cash flows, respectively (hence they are likely to have similar daycount conventions).

Hedging

An Interest Rate Swap allows a borrower to:

- convert an existing or new floating rate liability to a fixed rate, for example to:
  - ☞ hedge against rising interest rates;
  - ☞ improve the match of debt cash flows to operating cash flows; or
  - ☞ exploit a comparative advantage it has in the floating rate market.
- convert an existing or new fixed rate liability to a floating rate, for example to
  - ☞ take advantage of falling interest rates;
  - ☞ improve the match of debt cash flows to operating cash flows; or
  - ☞ exploit a comparative advantage it has in the fixed rate market; or
  - ☞ enable a fixed rate bond to be issued with the required coupon features (from institutional investors, for example), but financed at a floating rate (this could allow a borrower to diversify its funding sources away from bank debt);

Interest Rate Options

Options on Interest Rate Futures ('Futures Options')

Definition

A Futures Option can be a Call or a Put:

- a Call Option on an interest rate futures contract (Call Futures Option) gives the holder (having paid a premium) the right to purchase a futures contract (a long position) at any time before expiry (i.e. an American Option) at a stated futures price (Exercise Price); a Put Option gives the right to sell (or short) a futures contract;
- in both cases, the Option holder receives a cash sum equivalent to the difference between the Exercise Price (X) and the futures price (F) at the date of exercise (F – X for a Call, and X – F for a Put).

Having exercised the option, the futures contract can then be closed out or held until delivery.

Pricing

Futures Options can be priced using Binomial Trees; if the Option is exercisable on expiry only, it can be valued using an adjusted version of the Black-Scholes Model (see Appendix B5).

Hedging

Since futures prices increase as rates decrease (and vice versa), the buyer of a Call Futures Option would expect the futures price to increase above the exercise price (similar to a Call Option on equity) as interest rates decrease. Therefore, a borrower, to protect against interest rates increasing, could buy a Put Futures Option: as rates increase, the futures price would fall below the exercise price, and, on exercise, the put holder could receive a payoff equivalent to the difference between the exercise price and the futures price at that date.

Options on Interest Rate Swaps ('Swaptions')

Definition

In a Swaption, one party:

- pays an upfront non-returnable sum (option 'Premium'),
- as consideration for the right (with no obligation) to enter into an Interest Rate Swap during the period to (American option) – or at (European option) – an expiry date,
- and either pay ('Call Swaption' or 'Pay Fixed Swaption') or receive ('Put Swaption' or 'Receive Fixed Swaption') an agreed fixed Swap rate in exchange for a floating rate.

Pricing

Swaptions can be priced using the adjusted Black-Scholes model used for Futures Options (see Appendix B5), or a model based on a binomial interest rate tree (see Buetow and Fabozzi (2001)).

Hedging

If a borrower is to enter into a Floating-to-Fixed Interest Rate Swap at some point in the future, it could purchase a Call Swaption to protect against Swap rates increasing over the interim period: if Swap rates increase above the Swaption Exercise Price, the borrower would exercise the Call and lock into the lower Swaption rate.

Caps, Floors and Collars (Portfolios of Options)

In a Cap, for each relevant interest period over the term, a seller agrees to pay a buyer the excess of a market rate over an agreed 'strike' rate (with interest, based on a notional principal, being paid at the end of each interest period), in return for the buyer paying an upfront non-returnable premium.

A cap (a series of maximum rates, or 'Caplets') protects a buyer / borrower from a rise in interest rates: the effective interest cost would not exceed a stated amount, since the excess of the loan floating reference rate over the Cap would be recovered from the Cap seller. Effectively, an insurance premium is being paid to fix a rate: the Cap buyer has acquired a series of Call Options on interest rates (exercised automatically if rates rise above the Cap rate).

A Floor is similar to a cap but protects the buyer (such as a lender or depositor) from a fall in interest rates: a minimum interest rate can be guaranteed for a stated period. Hence a floor is similar to the purchase of a series of Put options.

A Collar is a combination of a Cap and a Floor.

CURRENCY RISK

Nature of Currency Risk

The value of a company's assets, liabilities and cash flows may be sensitive to changes in the rate of exchange between its reporting currency and foreign currencies. This sensitivity can be reflected in a change in, or uncertainty about, (1) the competitiveness of the business as a whole and the volatility of its operating cash flows ('Strategic' or 'Economic' exposure), (2) the value of transactions involving foreign currency denominated contracted monies ('Transaction' exposure), and (3) the value of assets and liabilities as reported in the balance sheet, where such items need to be restated at current exchange rates ('Translation' exposure).

This section is concerned with managing Transaction exposure (i.e. the impact on known cash flows), rather than broader strategic decisions about where to sell, buy (i.e. exporting and importing) and manufacture, and how to protect against foreign competition (Economic exposure), or how best to manage balance sheet values (Translation exposure).

Managing Currency Risk with Derivatives

Forward Currency Contracts

Definition

In a Currency contract, two parties agree on a Trade Date to:

- exchange one unit of a 'Base' (or 'Fixed') currency for a variable number of units of another 'Terms' (or 'Variable') currency,
- at an exchange rate, fixed on a date ('Value Date'), usually two business days after the trade date ('Spot exchange contract' with a 'Spot Value date') or later (a 'Forward exchange contract' with a 'Forward Value date' – if the Forward Value Date is within one month of the Spot Value Date, the agreement would be a 'Short Date' contract, otherwise a 'Forward Outright').

The date of exchange or settlement (Value Date) must be a business day: if the Value Date is not a working day (weekends and public holidays) in either of the currency market centres (for example, London and New York), then the next working / business day is deemed to be the Value Date (there are a number of exceptions, depending on which currencies are being traded).

Spot Exchange Rates

Exchange rates are quoted in terms of the number of units of a Variable currency that a dealer is prepared to buy ('Bid rate') or sell ('Offer rate') for one unit of a Fixed currency. If the Fixed currency is the foreign currency, the quote is 'Direct' (for example, £0.61 to the US dollar, being the mid price of a direct quote from a UK bank of 'US$ (*Fixed*):£ 0.6091 – 0.6109'); if the Fixed currency is the domestic currency, the quote is 'Indirect' (i.e. the reciprocal – for example, US$1.64 to the pound, being the mid price of an indirect quote from a UK bank of '£ (*Fixed*):US$ 1.6369 – 1.6418'). The type of quote depends on the currency and the type and location of the market. Most currencies are quoted in terms of the US dollar, and a 'Cross Rate' between two non-US currencies can be determined from their respective US dollar exchange rates.

Example 4.14 Cross Exchange Rates

If both rates are Indirect quotes, the Bid and Offer Variable rate (NZ$) is divided by the Offer and Bid Fixed rate (A$).	If the Variable currency is Indirect (Euro) but the Fixed currency direct (£), the Bid and Offer Variable currency quotes are multiplied by the Bid and Offer Fixed currency quotes.

Indirect / indirect				Indirect / direct			
		Bank buys	Bank sells			Bank buys	Bank sells
Fixed Variable				*Fixed Variable*			
		US$1 for	US$1 for			1 US$ for	1 US$ for
US$ / NZ$	NZ$	1.7111 -	21	US$ / Euro	Euro	0.8418 -	28
	mid	1.7116			mid	0.8423	
		US$1 for	US$1 for			1 £ for	1 £ for
US$ / A$	A$	1.5160 -	70	£ / US$	US$	1.6409 -	19
	mid	1.5165			mid	1.6414	
A$ / NZ$		1.7111	1.7121	£ / Euro		0.8418	0.8428
		÷	÷			×	×
		1.5170 ↺	1.5160			1.6409	1.6419
		Bank buys	Bank sells			Bank buys	Bank sells
		1 A$ for	1 A$ for			1 £ for	1 £ for
	NZ$	1.1279	1.1294		Euro	1.3813	1.3838
	mid	1.1287			mid	1.3826	
Dealer rounding in its favour		Rounded down	Rounded up			Rounded down	Rounded up

Forward Exchange Rates

Forward Exchange Rates are derived from Spot Exchange Rates, adjusting for the interest rate differential for the two currencies over the Forward Period. This assumes that interest rates expressed in the same currency, assuming similar risk, are equal ('Interest Rate Parity'), on the basis that arbitrage from replicating the cash flows is eliminated.

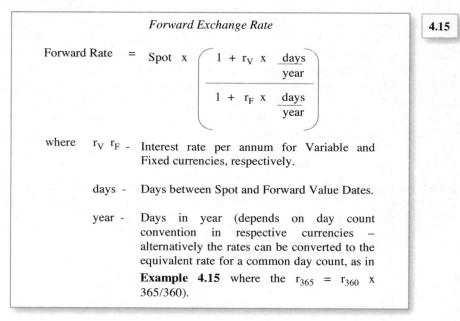

Forward Exchange Rate **4.15**

$$\text{Forward Rate} = \text{Spot} \times \left(\frac{1 + r_V \times \frac{\text{days}}{\text{year}}}{1 + r_F \times \frac{\text{days}}{\text{year}}} \right)$$

where r_V r_F - Interest rate per annum for Variable and Fixed currencies, respectively.

days - Days between Spot and Forward Value Dates.

year - Days in year (depends on day count convention in respective currencies – alternatively the rates can be converted to the equivalent rate for a common day count, as in **Example 4.15** where the $r_{365} = r_{360} \times 365/360$).

If one unit of the Fixed currency can be exchanged for more units of the Variable currency at the Forward date compared to the Spot date (r_F is less than r_V), the Fixed currency is said to be at a premium and the Variable currency at a discount); if the Fixed currency can be exchanged for fewer units of the Variable currency (r_F is greater than r_V), the Fixed currency is at a discount (the Variable currency is at a premium), as in **Example 4.15** (the Forward US$/J Yen rate is at a discount, since US interest rates are higher than Japanese interest rates).

Example 4.15 Forward Exchange Rates

If Spot Rates on 24 June are US$ / JP¥ 107.0650, and 3 month US$ borrowing and JP¥ lending rates are 1.5625% and 0.05125%, respectively, the implied Forward Rate for 13 September delivery (81 days away) would be US$ / JP¥ 106.7072. This can be calculated as the rate which eliminates any profit from borrowing in US$ (at the Dollar rate of interest), using the proceeds to buy and deposit JP¥ (at the Yen rate of interest), and using the deposit proceeds to buy enough US$ to repay the borrowings.

Assumptions

Base currency	US$
Variable currency	JP¥
Principal	JP¥ 100,000,000
Forward period	81 days
Year	365 days
Dealing date	22 June
Spot date	24 June
Forward date	13 September

	US$	*JP¥*
Spot rates at 24 June	0.0093 =1 JPY	107.0650 =1 US$
3 month rate at 24 June	1.5625% 365 days	0.05125% 365 days
Forward rates for 13 Sep	0.0094 =1 JPY	106.7072 =1 US$

	Spot date	*Forward date*
	JP¥	JP¥
Buy JP¥100m at US$ / JP¥ 107.0650	100,000,000	
Deposit	(100,000,000)	
Deposit + 81 days interest at 0.05125%		100,011,373
Exchange JP¥ for US$		(100,011,373)
Net Cash Flows	*0*	*0*
	US$	US$
Borrow JP¥100m at US$ / JP¥ 107.0650	934,012	
Pay US$ for JP¥	(934,012)	
Receive US$ from JP¥		937,251
Borrowings + 81 days interest at 1.5625%		(937,251)
Net Cash Flows	*0*	*0*

The Forward ¥ is at a premium relative to the US$, and the US$ at a discount relative to the ¥ ($1 buys less ¥: 106.7072 vs. 107.065 at the Spot date). Premium = ¥0.3578, Discount = $0.000031 (=1/106.7072–1/107.065)

☞ Forward rate (JP¥ 100,011,373 / US$ 937,251) . 106.7072 =1 US$

$$\text{Forward rate} = \text{Spot} \times \text{Rate differential}$$

$$= 107.0650 = 1\text{ US\$} \times \left(\frac{1 + 0.05125\% \times 81/365}{1 + 1.5625\% \times 81/365} \right)$$

$$= 106.7072 = 1\text{ US\$}$$

where Forward / Spot rates Difference = Interest rates (at PV) Difference

$$\frac{106.7072 - 107.0650}{107.0650} = \frac{(0.05125\% - 1.5625\%) \times 81/365}{1 + 1.5625\% \times 81/365}$$

$$-0.334214\% = -0.334214\%$$

Hedging

If a company is expecting to pay or receive foreign currency at a known date in the future, it can lock in at today's Forward Exchange Rate to hedge against exchange rates having increased or decreased, respectively, by the time the cash is paid or received. If paying foreign currency (for example, interest on a foreign currency denominated loan or foreign currency capital expenditure) it would purchase the currency forward (pay the domestic currency in exchange for the foreign currency); an expected foreign currency receipt (income from a foreign currency asset or foreign currency revenues, for example) would require a forward sale of the foreign currency (pay foreign currency in exchange for domestic currency). In both cases, the amount and timing of the foreign currency cash flow would need to be certain (since a forward contract is a binding agreement).

In practice, transactions with known amounts and dates could be aggregated together and an overall exchange rate exposure could be determined (by measuring the impact, in the domestic currency cash flows, from various assumed exchange rate changes or scenarios). A series of Forwards could then be arranged.

Given that Forward Exchange rates can be derived from borrowing and lending transactions, hedging could also be achieved using such transactions.

Currency Futures

Currency Futures are like Interest Rate Futures, but priced on an underlying foreign exchange rate. The seller of a futures contract is required to physically deliver, on expiry, the nominal value of the Variable / Terms foreign currency for the given contract, in exchange for receiving the nominal value in the Fixed / Base currency times the futures settlement price. Therefore, a party wishing to buy the Variable currency on the expiry date would be able to fix an equivalent Forward Rate by buying the Currency Future.

Currency Swaps

Definition

In a Currency Swap, two parties agree to:

- pay each other[1], at the end of each interest period over the term, interest on a principal amount[2] stated *in different currencies*,
- at a fixed or floating rate applicable for the interest period and the currency,
- payable in the same currency as the principal, at the end of the interest period.

[1] Both parties pay the interest without any 'set-off' as in an Interest Rate Swap.

[2] The principal amounts are exchange on maturity, and often at commencement.

A basic Plain Vanilla currency swap would involve:

- exchanging a fixed rate in one currency for a floating rate in another ('Fixed-to-Floating' or 'Currency Coupon Swap'); or
- exchanging a floating rate in one currency for a floating rate in another ('Floating/Floating' or 'Cross Currency Basis Swap'); or
- exchanging a fixed rate in one currency for a fixed rate in another ('Fixed/Fixed').

Pricing

Currency swaps can be priced using the same method used for interest rate swaps, however the interest and principal cash flows need to be converted into a common currency. For example, to value a Floating-to-Fixed / Cross Currency Swap a procedure similar to that shown in **Example 4.13** can be used, but with two sets of discount rates:

	Floating Rate Currency	Fixed Rate Currency
Principal	Floating rate principal amount.	Translate the floating rate principal to the fixed rate currency at the Spot Exchange Rates at the valuation date.
Forward Interest Rates	Estimate the Forward Interest Rates for each interest period.	Assume a Fixed Interest Rate (as a first trial run).
Cash Flows	Calculate the floating rate cash flows using the Forward Interest Rates, based on the floating rate principal.	Calculate the fixed rate cash flows using the assumed fixed rate, based on the translated floating rate principal.
Discount Rates	Estimate Zero Coupon discount rates for the floating rate currency.	Estimate Zero Coupon discount rates for the fixed rate currency.
Present Values	Calculate the present value of the cash flows, and convert the total into the fixed rate currency at the Spot Exchange Rate at the valuation date.	Calculate the sum of the present value of the cash flows. Adjust the above assumed Fixed Interest Rate so that the two present values are identical (using Microsoft Excel™'s goal seek function, for example).

Example 4.16 Basic Cross Currency Swap Pricing

A company with a 5 year £10m floating rate debt wishes to swap its cash flows into a fixed US$ rate. The floating rate cash flows based on the forecast £ Forward Interest Rates (see **Example 4.13**), discounted at the Zero Coupon discount rates, have a present value, translated into US$ at the current 1.8 exchange rate, of $4.31m.

For the fixed rate US$ cash flows, based on the US$ equivalent of the £10m principal ($18m), to have the same present value, the fixed rate must be 5.6487%.

	FLOATING					FIXED				
Year	Zero rate	Discount factors	Forward rate	Interest received	Present Value	Zero rate	Discount factors	Forward rate	Interest paid	Present Value
				£	£				$	$
0.50	5.00%	0.975610	5.00%	250,000	243,902	5.75%	0.972043	5.75%	508,386	494,173
1.00	5.15%	0.950423	5.30%	265,005	251,867	5.90%	0.943486	6.05%	508,386	479,655
1.50	5.25%	0.925156	5.46%	273,108	252,667	6.01%	0.915045	6.22%	508,386	465,197
2.00	5.33%	0.900213	5.54%	277,085	249,436	6.08%	0.887119	6.30%	508,386	450,999
2.50	5.39%	0.875535	5.64%	281,854	246,773	6.14%	0.859646	6.39%	508,386	437,032
3.00	5.44%	0.851267	5.70%	285,088	242,686	6.19%	0.832762	6.46%	508,386	423,365
3.50	5.48%	0.827538	5.73%	286,740	237,288	6.24%	0.806589	6.49%	508,386	410,059
4.00	5.52%	0.804296	5.78%	288,970	232,418	6.27%	0.781069	6.53%	508,386	397,085
4.50	5.55%	0.781599	5.81%	290,395	226,973	6.31%	0.756252	6.56%	508,386	384,468
5.00	5.58%	0.759498	5.82%	290,988	221,005	6.33%	0.732181	6.58%	508,386	372,231
Principal	£10.0m	= $18.00m			£2,405,016	5.6487% x 0.5 x $18m				
£/US$ rate	1.8				@ 1.80					
Swap rate	**5.6487%**				**$4,314,263**	$508,386 x US$ DF_t				**$4,314,263**

(See Flavell (2002 Ch. 6) for more advanced pricing.)

Currency Options

Definition

In a currency option contract a buyer acquires the right (without any obligation) to buy (Call option) or sell (Put option) a specified amount of foreign currency on a stated future date (Exercise Date) at an agreed rate of exchange (Exercise Price), paying an upfront non-returnable 'premium' as consideration.

Whilst a Forward Currency contract locks a buyer into an exchange rate at the agreement date, a Currency Option contract does not: the buyer can let the option lapse if exchange rates do not turn out to be favourable.

Hedging

The buyer of a Currency Call option has the right to buy a foreign currency at a specified exchange rate. If the option is exercised, the buyer would pay the domestic currency in return for receiving the foreign currency, which it could use to meet its obligations to pay foreign currency amounts. If a borrower is to pay foreign currency loan payments on scheduled dates, it can insure against any adverse change in the exchange rates during the loan term by buying, in advance, a series of Currency Call Options that have exercise dates similar to the interest and principal payment dates. Effectively, an insurance premium is being paid to have a guaranteed exchange rate (if the option is exercised), whilst retaining the ability to benefit from any favourable exchange rate movements.

APPENDIX A

FINANCIAL RATIOS

A FINANCIAL RATIOS

EQUITY RATIOS

Operating profitability

	Ratio	Formula	Description
1.	Revenue growth	$\frac{\text{Revenue change}_{t-1 \rightarrow t}}{\text{Revenue}_{t-1}}$	Real sales growth (volume), excluding the effects of price inflation, can also be calculated.
2.	Gross profit margin	$\frac{\text{Gross profit}}{\text{Revenues}}$	Indicates the mark-up on the cost of sales, and the ability of the company to pass on its direct costs to customers
3.	EBITDA[1] margin [1]Earnings Before Interest Tax, Depreciation & Amortisation	$\frac{\text{EBITDA}}{\text{Revenues}}$	Represents the pre-tax operating cash flow margin, assuming (1) zero Fixed and Working capital investment, and (2) EBITDA excludes profits or losses from non-trading and other activities that are not included in revenues. Note: Free Cash Flows to the Firm = EBITDA (assuming (2)) less capital investment, taxes on non-financial activities and other non-cash items.
4.	Operating profit margin	$\frac{\text{EBIT}}{\text{Revenues}}$	Adjusts the EBITDA margin to take account of capital investment (except working capital) allocated to the period via the depreciation and amortisation charge (both varying according to the chosen accounting policy and method).
5.	Operating leverage	$\frac{\text{\% change in EBI}}{\text{\% change in revenues}}$	Indicates the sensitivity of operating profits to changes in revenues, which partly depends on the ratio of variable operating costs (sensitive to revenues) to fixed operating costs (insensitive to revenues in the short term).

Investment / cash flows

	Ratio	Formula	Description
6.	Re-investment rate	$\frac{\text{Capital expenditure + change in working capital}}{\text{EBITDA less taxes paid thereon}}$	Shows the proportion of EBITDA, net of tax, reinvested in the business. The Reinvestment Rate can also be shown as Net Capital Expenditure (Capital expenditure – Depreciation) and change in working capital divided by EBIT less taxes on non-financial items (or Net Operating Profits After Taxes , 'NOPAT') as used in Appendix B1.

7.	'Capex' ratio	$\frac{\text{Capital expenditure}}{\text{Revenues}}$	A general indication of capital intensity, and the degree to which revenues depend on fixed capital investment.
8.	Working capital investment ratio	$\frac{\text{Increase in gross working capital}}{\text{Revenues}}$	The increase in gross working capital equals the increase in stock / inventories and trade debtors less the increase in trade creditors between two balance sheet dates. If the terms of trade and stock holding policy remain the same, one would expect the ratio to be fairly constant. Working capital investment is discussed in Chapter 3 and the example in Appendix D2.
9.	Replacement capex	$\frac{\text{Capital expenditure}}{\text{Depreciation}}$	If capex exceeds depreciation, there is some indication that capital investment is for growth rather than replacement or maintenance purposes (however, the ratio depends on the accounting policy adopted for depreciation and the age of plant and equipment).
10.	Quality of profits	$\frac{\text{EBITDA – increase in working capital}}{\text{EBITDA}}$	Adjusts EBITDA for working capital investment, to improve the operating cash flow measure in ratio 3 above.

Operating returns

11.	Pre-tax Return on Invested Capital ($ROIC_{av}$)	$\frac{\text{Operating Profits}}{\text{Operating Capital (start of period)}}$	The operating profit (EBIT in the absence of non-operating items) represents the profit from which a charge is deducted for the providers of the operating capital. Hence this shows the return available for capital providers.
	See ❷ in Appendix D2 for an example.	(The average capital may also be used).	Operating capital (or 'Invested Capital' or 'Capital Employed') is the sum of operating fixed assets (i.e. excluding 'lazy' capital, such as head-office property that generates no revenue) and gross working capital (stock, or inventories, plus operating / trade debtors less operating / trade creditors). If there were no other assets or liabilities, this would be equivalent to the financial capital (debt, equity and non-equity). Using Net Operating Profits After Taxes (NOPAT) in the numerator would give a post-tax return.

The return on capital can be decomposed into the operating profit margin (amount of operating profit per unit currency of sales) and the asset turnover (amount of sales per unit currency of operating capital), providing the same profit and capital measures are used.

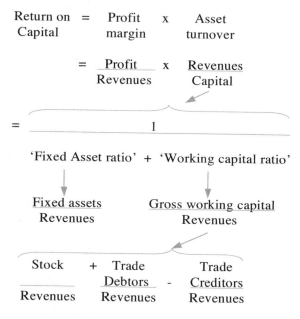

$$\text{Return on Capital} = \text{Profit margin} \times \text{Asset turnover}$$

$$= \frac{\text{Profit}}{\text{Revenues}} \times \frac{\text{Revenues}}{\text{Capital}}$$

$$= \frac{1}{\text{‘Fixed Asset ratio’} + \text{‘Working capital ratio’}}$$

$$\text{‘Fixed Asset ratio’} = \frac{\text{Fixed assets}}{\text{Revenues}} \qquad \text{‘Working capital ratio’} = \frac{\text{Gross working capital}}{\text{Revenues}}$$

$$\frac{\text{Gross working capital}}{\text{Revenues}} = \frac{\text{Stock}}{\text{Revenues}} + \frac{\text{Trade Debtors}}{\text{Revenues}} - \frac{\text{Trade Creditors}}{\text{Revenues}}$$

12. Asset turnover	$\frac{\text{Revenues}}{\text{Operating Capital (start of period)}}$	The asset turnover ratio is the inverse of the sum of the fixed asset ratio and the working capital ratio (as shown above). Operating Capital is all capital that contributes to revenues in the period. A low fixed asset ratio (fixed assets / revenues), relative to comparable companies in the same sector, may indicate efficiency but may also be a reflection of the depreciation policy and age of the assets. Capital intensive industries will have relatively high ratios, as will industries where there is spare capacity (i.e. some fixed assets are not generating sales).

The working capital ratio depends on the level of non-cash sales and purchases (determined by the type of business and the credit terms applicable to the company) and the ability to collect overdue amounts from customers and obtain maximum credit from suppliers (customer defaults will require bad debt write-offs, and general provisions may be required). It represents the amount of cash being tied up in the working capital cycle in order to generate one unit currency of revenues. If relatively high for the sector, this may indicate, amongst other things, inefficient stock control, poor credit policies and a low quality customer base.

Multiplying the stock ratio (stock / revenues (or cost of goods sold)) by the number of days in the year gives an estimate of the length of time before stock is sold (stock holding period – stock divided by average daily revenues). An increase could indicate that stock is becoming obsolete and may require a write-off. The inverse of the stock ratio (the 'stock turn') indicates the number of times the stock balance is 'turned over' in the year.

The debtors' collection period (or 'Days Sales Outstanding') and creditors' payment period can be estimated by multiplying the trade debtors ratio (trade debtors / revenue) and trade creditors ratio (trade creditors / revenue) by 365. An increase in the former will often indicate poor credit management, whilst an increase in the latter is desired so long as the relationship with suppliers is not damaged.

Equity returns and relative pricing

13. Return on Equity (ROE)	$\frac{\text{Profit attributable to Ordinary Shareholders}}{\text{Ordinary Shareholders' funds}}$	This shows the return to shareholders (either before or after tax) based on the book value of equity (dividing the return by the price-to-book ratio (No.16) gives a market value based return). Where debt is introduced, then financial leverage can increase returns to equity holders:

A1.1

$$ROE = \frac{P}{E}$$

$$= \frac{P}{E} + \frac{i(1-t)}{E} - \frac{i(1-t)}{E}$$

$$= \frac{P + i(1-t)}{E + D} \times \frac{E+D}{E} - \frac{i(1-t)}{E}$$

$$= \frac{P + i(1-t)}{E + D} \times \left(1 + \frac{D}{E}\right) - \frac{i(1-t)}{E}$$

$$= ROA + \frac{D}{E} \times ROA - \frac{D}{D} \times \frac{i(1-t)}{E}$$

$$= ROA + \frac{D}{E}\left(ROA - \frac{i(1-t)}{D}\right)$$

(See Damodaran (2002 p.286))

where
- P - Profits after tax
- E,D - Book Value of Equity and Debt
- i(1-t) - Debt interest after tax (x (1 – effective tax rate))
- ROA - Post-tax return on assets if assets = Invested Capital = D + E.

This indicates the relationship between the post-tax ROE and post-tax ROIC (using the above definitions) due to gearing (D/E).

➡ For an example see ❻ in Appendix D4.

14. Earnings Per Share (EPS)	$\frac{\text{Profit attributable to ordinary Shareholders}}{\text{Ordinary shares}}$	EPS can be before or after goodwill amortisation. The ratio is used for the Price/Earnings Ratio and as a measure of earnings growth.
15. Price/ Earnings ratio (P/E)	$\frac{\text{Share Price}}{\text{EPS}}$	A relatively high ratio indicates that the market is expecting growth in earnings. Assuming the fair value for each share can be estimated by discounting Dividends Per Share (EPS x the 'Payout' ratio) in perpetuity, then the excess of the market price over this no-growth perpetuity fair price represents expectations of future growth. In theory, the share price should change in response to unexpected EPS changes (which have not already been incorporated into the price).

P/Es will vary to reflect differences in business risk (sensitivity of operating profits to economic and industry sector factors), financial risk (sensitivity of net profits to choice of financing mix), and the amount of EPS actually being paid out in dividends (payout ratio) as opposed to being reinvested in fixed and working capital (retention ratio).

A1.2

$$P/E = \frac{\text{Share Price}}{\text{EPS}^{1}}$$

EPS paid out + *EPS retained*

$$\frac{1}{P/E} = \frac{\text{Ord. Dividend per share}}{\text{Share Price}} + \frac{\text{EPS}^{1} \times \text{Retention Ratio}}{\text{Share Price}}$$

$$= \text{Dividend yield} + \text{Earnings yield} \times \text{Retention ratio}$$

[1] Assumes no change in number of ordinary shares outstanding

The 'sustainable growth' model assumes that operating profits, dividends and assets all grow at a constant rate in perpetuity, and that the ROE and dividend payout ratio are both constant. If it is also assumed that (a) the company is financed entirely with equity, (b) new capital investment is funded entirely from retained profits, and (c) the proportion of retained profits reinvested in capital each year (reinvestment rate) is constant, then the invested capital (book value of equity in this case) will grow at a rate equivalent to the ROE multiplied by the proportion of net profits retained for reinvestment. Using the Dividend Discount Model (see **1.5** in Chapter 1), and this relationship, the P/E, the ROE and the growth rates can be linked:

A1.3

Constant growth (100% equity financed)

$$\text{Share Price} = \frac{D_1}{K_u - g}$$

$$= \frac{EPS\,(1 - r)}{K_u - g}$$

$$P / E = \frac{1 - r}{K_u - g}$$

$$= \frac{1 - (g / ROE^1)}{K_u - g}$$

$$= \frac{ROE - g}{ROE\,(K_u - g)}$$

where
- D_1 Dividend in 1 year's time
- K_u Required rate of return (ungeared cost of equity)
- g Sustainable dividend growth rate (equal to EPS growth rate, since a constant payout ratio is assumed)
- EPS Earnings per share
- r Retention ratio = (Net profits – dividends) / Net profits = 1 – dividend payout %
- ROE Return on Equity = Net profits per share / BV
- BV Book value of equity per share (growth in book value of equity being equal to g, due to constant growth assumption)

[1] If the ROE, Retention Ratio, and growth rates are constant:

$$BV_{closing} = BV_{opening} + \text{net profits} \times r$$

$$= BV_{opening} + (ROE \times BV_{opening}) \times r$$

$$= BV_{opening} \times (1 + ROE \times r)$$

$$1 + g = 1 + ROE \times r$$

$$g = ROE \times r$$

$$r = g / ROE$$

Maximum growth rate of Invested Capital without requiring new equity funding (Sustainable Growth Rate)

In the case of constant growth and self-financing (i.e. new investments are funded from operating cash flows), the ROE will be constant if the dividend payout ratio is at a level which equates the dividend growth rate to the sustainable growth rate (ROE x (1 – payout ratio)). Where the payout ratio is at a different level, the ROE will increase or decrease, such that ROE x (1-payout ratio) converges to the dividend growth rate over time.

16. Price-to-Book Ratio — $\frac{\text{Market Value}}{\text{Book Value of equity}}$ — The price-to-book ratio (current share price / book value of equity per share) is linked to the P/E as follows:

A1.4

$$\text{EPS} = \frac{\text{Net profits}}{\text{Shares}}$$

$$= \frac{\text{Net profits}}{\text{BV}} \times \frac{\text{BV}}{\text{Shares}}$$

$$= \text{ROE} \times \text{BV per share}$$

$$\frac{\text{Price}}{\text{EPS}} = \frac{\text{Price}}{\text{ROE} \times \text{BV per share}}$$

$$\text{P/E} = \frac{1}{\text{ROE}} \times \text{Price-to-book ratio}$$

$$\frac{\text{P/ E}}{\left(\frac{1}{\text{ROE}}\right)} = \text{Price-to-book ratio}$$

where BV = Book Value of Equity

If the net profit growth and dividend payout ratios are constant, then, using the above constant growth formula and the P/E ratio from **A1.3** for a 100% equity financed company:

$$\frac{\left(\frac{\text{ROE} - g}{\text{ROE}\,(K_u - g)}\right)}{\frac{1}{\text{ROE}}} = \text{Price-to-book ratio}$$

$$\frac{\text{ROE} - g}{K_u - g} = \text{Price-to-book ratio}$$

Example A1 Constant growth formula

In the following 5 year forecast, the payout ratio of a debt free company with constant growth (no external funding is required), has been set at a level which equates dividend growth to the long term sustainable level (hence the Return on Equity is constant):

£m	Forecast Year 1	2	3	4	5
Profit & Loss					
Revenues	52.00	54.08	56.24	58.49	60.83
EBIT	7.80	8.11	8.44	8.77	9.12
Tax	(2.34)	(2.43)	(2.53)	(2.63)	(2.74)
Post-tax profits	5.46	5.68	5.91	6.14	6.39
Ordinary dividends	(4.24)	(4.41)	(4.59)	(4.77)	(4.96)
Retained profits	1.22	1.27	1.32	1.37	1.43
Cash Flow					
EBITDA less tax paid on operating profits	7.82	8.14	8.46	8.80	9.15
Capital expenditures	(2.60)	(2.70)	(2.81)	(2.92)	(3.04)
Increase in working capital	(0.10)	(0.10)	(0.11)	(0.11)	(0.12)
Free Cash Flows	5.12	5.33	5.54	5.76	5.99
Dividends	(4.24)	(4.41)	(4.59)	(4.77)	(4.96)
Equity funding	0.00	0.00	0.00	0.00	0.00
Net cash flows	0.88	0.92	0.96	0.99	1.03
Opening cash	0.00	0.88	1.80	2.76	3.75
Closing cash	0.88	1.80	2.76	3.75	4.79
Balance Sheet					
Operating fixed assets					
At cost	32.60	35.30	38.12	41.04	44.08
Accumulated depreciation	(4.36)	(6.82)	(9.38)	(12.04)	(14.80)
Fixed Assets	28.24	28.48	28.74	29.00	29.28
Operating working captal	2.60	2.70	2.81	2.92	3.04
Operating capital	30.84	31.19	31.55	31.93	32.32
Gross bank debt	0.00	0.00	0.00	0.00	0.00
less: cash	0.88	1.80	2.76	3.75	4.79
Net Debt / (Cash balances)	(0.88)	(1.80)	(2.76)	(3.75)	(4.79)
Ordinary shares # £0.25 each	*2.0 m*	*2.0 m*	*2.0 m*	*2.0 m*	*2.0 m*
Nominal value	0.50	0.50	0.50	0.50	0.50
Share premium	28.83	28.83	28.83	28.83	28.83
Share capital	29.33	29.33	29.33	29.33	29.33
Reserves	2.39	3.66	4.98	6.35	7.78
Equity	31.72	32.99	34.31	35.68	37.11
Financial capital	30.84	31.19	31.55	31.93	32.32
Growth, retention rates and ROE					
Net profit growth	4.00%	4.00%	4.00%	4.00%	4.00%
Dividend growth rate	4.00%	4.00%	4.00%	4.00%	4.00%
Assumed retention rate	22.34%	22.34%	22.34%	22.34%	22.34%
Return on Equity	17.90%	17.90%	17.90%	17.90%	17.90%
Sustainable growth (ROE x retention)	**4.00%**	**4.00%**	**4.00%**	**4.00%**	**4.00%**
Book Value of equity growth rate	**4.00%**	**4.00%**	**4.00%**	**4.00%**	**4.00%**

The equity value calculated using the sustainable ROE and growth rates gives the same result as discounting dividends at the cost of equity:

£m		Forecast Year 1	2	3	4	5
Equity value - sustainable growth model						
ROE - Sustainable growth rate (g)		13.90%	13.90%	13.90%	13.90%	13.90%
x opening book value of equity =		4.24	4.41	4.59	4.77	4.96
PV at cost of equity	17.21	3.85	3.63	3.43	3.24	3.06
Year 6 : ROE - g						13.90%
Year 6 : Ku - g						6.15%
Price : Book Multiple (=(ROE - g)/(Ku - g))						x 2.3
x year 5 book value of equity						83.9
PV of terminal value	51.73					
Equity Value	**68.94**					
Equity value - dividend discount model						
Shareholders' required rate of return ('Ku')		10.15%	10.15%	10.15%	10.15%	10.15%
Discount rate = 1 / { (1 + Ku)^year }		0.9079	0.8242	0.7482	0.6793	0.6167
Dividends		4.24	4.41	4.59	4.77	4.96
PV of dividends	17.21	3.85	3.63	3.43	3.24	3.06
Dividend growth rate (g)						4.00%
Year 6 dividend (= D_6)						5.16
Perpetuity value = D_6 / (Ku - g)						83.88
PV of perpetuity (x yr 5 disc. factor)	51.73					
Equity Value	**68.94**					

17. Dividend cover

$$\frac{\text{Profits attributable to ordinary shareholders}}{\text{Annual dividends}}$$

This shows the number of times the dividend can be paid out of available profits, and can be related to the P:E ratio, earnings and dividend yield:

A1.5

$$\text{Dividend Cover} = \frac{\text{EPS}}{\text{DPS}}$$

$$= \frac{\text{EPS / share price}}{\text{DPS / share price}}$$

$$= \frac{\text{Earnings Yield}}{\text{Dividend Yield}}$$

$$= \frac{\left(\dfrac{1}{\text{P / E}}\right)}{\text{Dividend yield}}$$

DEBT RATIOS

18. Interest coverage	EBIT / Gross interest expense	Indicates the ability of the borrower to pay interest out of sustainable operating profits (where EBIT has been adjusted to remove non-recurring items). The 'fixed charge coverage' ratio would include all committed debt and non-equity financing costs in the numerator (debt interest, fixed preference share coupons, leasing finance costs).
	EBITDA / Gross interest expense	EBITDA is here being used as a proxy for operating cash flow to show a 'cash flow coverage ratio'. EBITDA could be reduced by gross new investments in capex and working capital. Discretionary cash flow (non-essential capex, for example) may be excluded.
19. Debt servicing	EBITDA / Debt principal repayments + gross interest expense	Net operating Free Cash Flow should also be used to indicate how many times debt maturing in the next year (plus total interest) can be paid out of cash flows.
	Gross debt outstanding / EBITDA	Indicates how many years of current annual EBITDA are needed to pay off outstanding debt.
	Free Cash Flow / Gross debt	The inverse shows how long it would take to pay off debt from pre-financing cash flows (capital investment may be excluded from the numerator, to show a measure based on 'Funds Flow').
20. Liquidity	Current assets / Current liabilities	The 'current ratio' indicates the amount of current liabilities that could be paid off in the short term from the realisation of current assets (including cash). The minimum acceptable ratio varies with the length of the production cycle and the time taken to convert stock into cash, and hence depends on the industry sector. A high ratio (over 1.5) may indicate stock obsolescence or poor credit management (as indicated by high stock and trade debtors) or a policy of accumulating cash rather than reinvesting it.

	Liquid current assets / Current liabilities	The 'quick ratio' restricts current assets to those that are immediately saleable, and hence usually excludes stock.
	Liquid current assets / Daily operating cash expenses	The 'defensive interval measure' is an estimate of how long liquid current assets (cash and deposits, and recoverable debtors) could fund average daily cash expenses.
21. Financial strain	Gross debt / Book value of capital	The 'leverage' ratio indicates the proportion of debt in the capital structure. Market values can be used to remove the effects of different accounting treatment. Cash is often deducted off gross debt in the numerator and denominator. Debt should include short and long term debt plus the capitalised value of finance leases.
	Gross debt / Book value of equity	'Gearing' is another form of showing the leverage ratio (assuming there is no non-equity), since leverage = gearing ratio / (1 + gearing ratio).
	Gross debt / Total assets	This shows the proportion of assets being debt financed. When the market value of assets is used, this gives some indication of the likelihood of bankruptcy. When the market value of assets falls below the market value of total liabilities, then financial risk has increased considerably.
	Liquidation value / Gross debt	The liquidation value (the market value of the assets on a liquidation or 'forced-sale' value) may exceed both gross debt and total liabilities, in which case full recovery should be achieved (ignoring liquidation costs and taxes) unless there are significant secured lenders or 'preferential' creditors who have first claim on the assets.

➡ For an example of Debt ratios see ❹ in Appendix D2.

APPENDIX B

PRICING TECHNIQUES

B1 CORPORATE DCF VALUATION

DISCOUNTING AND PRESENT VALUES

Introduction

Future cash flows can be restated ('Discounted') to economically equivalent amounts at the date of valuation ('Present Values', 'PV'), in order to determine whether the expected value to be derived from a capital investment (the aggregate PV of all future expected cash flows) exceeds the upfront cost of investment. If the PV exceeds the cost - a positive 'Net Present Value' ('NPV') - the investment should be undertaken, since the wealth of the investor should, in theory, increase by the NPV.

Present Value Formulae

An investor should be indifferent between receiving £A today and £A plus £a 'n' years later, where £a is the required compensation for giving up the right to consume £A today in return for consuming it after 'n' years and for facing the risk that £A may not be repaid in full. The £a return will be in the form of an income 'yield' (r_1 x £A) plus a capital gain (r_2 x £A), to give a combined return (r x £A), where r is the 'effective' rate (see **B2.2** in Appendix B2).

At the end of the 'n' year period, therefore, the investor receives an equivalent 'Future Value' ('FV') as follows:

$$\text{FV (cash flow at time n)} = A(1+r)^n \qquad \textbf{B1.1}$$

If the Future Value at time n is known, the equivalent amount the investor should be prepared to receive today (i.e. the PV of the Future Value) can be calculated:

$$PV = A = FV\left(\frac{1}{(1+r)^n}\right) \qquad \textbf{B1.2}$$

← 'Simple' Discount Factor

Example B1.1 PV of single cash flow received at the end of n years

The PV of £1.00 received at the end of 3 years, discounted at an effective rate of 8.0%, is £0.79 (= £1.00 x the simple discount factor 0.7938)

PV of cash flow received at end of year n $= £1.00 \times \dfrac{1}{(1+r)^n}$

$= £1.00 \times \dfrac{1}{(1+0.08)^\wedge 3}$

$= £0.79$

C	Cash Flow received at period 'n'	£1
r	Discount rate p.a.	8.00%
n	Time in years	3

The aggregate PV of a series of constant ('annuity') cash flows ('C') received at the end of periods 1, 2, 3, ...n (the equivalent of FV) is as follows:

$$PV = \frac{C}{(1+r)^1} + \frac{C}{(1+r)^2} + \frac{C}{(1+r)^3} + \ldots + \frac{C}{(1+r)^n}$$

Which simplifies to (see Brealey and Myers (2003 p.39)):

$$PV = C\left\{\frac{1}{r}\left(1 - \frac{1}{(1+r)^n}\right)\right\} \quad \textbf{B1.3}$$

← 'Cumulative' Discount Factor (no growth)

Example B1.2 PV of constant cash flow received each time period for n years

The PV of £1.00 received at the end of each year for 3 years, discounted at an effective rate of 8.0%, is £2.58 (= £1.00 x the cumulative discount factor 2.58):

PV of constant cash flow received annually for n years

$$= £1.00 \times \frac{1}{r} \times \left(1 - \frac{1}{(1+r)^n}\right)$$

$$= £1.00 \times \frac{1}{0.08} \times \left(1 - \frac{1}{(1+0.08)^{\wedge}3}\right)$$

$$= £2.58$$

C	Cash Flow received at the end of each year	£1
r	Discount rate p.a.	8.00%
n	Time in years	3

The annuity (for example, loan interest and principal payments) required (C) to give a return (r) based on a amount (for example, loan principal) at time 0 (PV), can be calculated from equation **B1.3**:

$$\text{Annuity } C = PV\left(\frac{r}{1 - \frac{1}{(1+r)^n}}\right) \quad \textbf{B1.4}$$

The aggregate PV of a series of constant cash flows ('C') received each period in perpetuity is as follows (n = infinity, hence the term $1/(1+r)^n$ approaches zero, so equation **B1.3** can be simplified):

$$\text{Perpetuity } PV = \frac{C}{r} \quad \textbf{B1.5}$$

The PV if the cash flow in equation **B1.5** grows annually in perpetuity at a rate 'g' (cash flow at the end of year 1 = C(1+g)) is as follows (see Brealey and Myers (2003 p.38)):

$$\text{Growing perpetuity PV} = \frac{C\,(1+g)}{r-g} \qquad \textbf{B1.6}$$

The aggregate PV of a series of cash flows, growing at a constant rate ('g') from an initial amount ('C'), received at the end of periods 1, 2, 3, ...n, is as follows:

$$PV = C \times \frac{(1+g)^1}{(1+r)^1} + C \times \frac{(1+g)^2}{(1+r)^2} + C \times \frac{(1+g)^3}{(1+r)^3} + \ldots + C \times \frac{(1+g)^n}{(1+r)^n}$$

Which simplifies to (from equations **B1.2** and **B1.6**):

$$PV = \underbrace{\frac{C(1+g)}{r-g}}_{\text{PV Perpetuity B1.6}} - \underbrace{\frac{C(1+g)^n\,(1+g)}{r-g}\left(\frac{1}{(1+r)^n}\right)}_{\text{PV Perpetuity 'Terminal Value' (at year n discounted back)}} = C\underbrace{\left(\frac{1+g}{r-g}\right)\left(1 - \frac{(1+g)^n}{(1+r)^n}\right)}_{\text{'Cumulative' Discount Factor (with growth)}} \qquad \textbf{B1.7}$$

Example B1.3 PV of growing cash flow received each time period for n years

The PV of £1.00 growing in each year at a rate of 3.0% and received at the end of each year for 3 years, discounted at an effective rate of 8.0%, is £2.73 (= £1.00 x 1.03 x the cumulative discount factor with growth 2.6512):

PV of growing cash flow received annually for n years

$$= £1.00 \times \frac{(1+0.03)}{r-g} \times \left(1 - \frac{(1+g)^n}{(1+r)^n}\right)$$

$$= £1.00 \times \frac{1.03}{0.08-0.03} \times \left(1 - \frac{(1+0.03)^{\wedge}3}{(1+0.08)^{\wedge}3}\right)$$

$$= £2.73$$

C	Cash Flow received at	£1
r	Discount rate p.a.	8.00%
n	Time in years	3
g	Growth rate p.a.	3.00%

The aggregate PV of a series of cash flows, growing at a constant rate g_1 from an initial amount ('C'), received at the end of periods 1, 2, 3, ...n (equation **B1.7**) and increasing thereafter from period n at a constant rate g_2 in perpetuity (equation **B1.6** with the valuation as at the end of year n, based on an initial cash flow $C(1+g1)^n$ being discounted back n years to time 0), is as follows:

$$PV = C\left(\frac{1+g1}{r-g1}\right)\left(1 - \frac{(1+g1)^n}{(1+r)^n}\right) + \frac{C\,(1+g1)^n\,(1+g2)}{r-g2}\left(\frac{1}{(1+r)^n}\right) \qquad \textbf{B1.8}$$

This formula shows the PV from cash flows growing at two different rates, where the change from one rate to the other occurs immediately at the end of year n. It may be more appropriate to assume that g1 changes to g2 over a transition period of several time periods ('tp'), before growing at g2 in perpetuity from year n + tp (this is probably best handled by explicitly modelling this stage in a spreadsheet).

Discounting and Investment Appraisal

NPV and the Internal Rate of Return (IRR)

As stated above, projects that provide a positive NPV should be accepted. The project's implicit (i.e. internal) rate of return (IRR) is the discount rate that yields an NPV of zero; subject to certain limitations associated with the IRR (discussed below), the investment should be accepted if the IRR exceeds the investor's required rate of return (or 'hurdle' rate).

Example B1.4 NPV and IRR

An investment with a fair value (PV) of £46.3m (10% discount rate) costs £35.0m to acquire, giving an NPV of £11.3m. The present value break-even discount rate (IRR) is 15.99%, greater than the required rate of 10%. The project should be accepted.

NPV for investment costing £35m

	Year					
£m	**0**	**1**	**2**	**3**	**4**	**5**
Relevant cash flows from project	(35.0)	(13.0)	(3.0)	18.0	28.0	45.0
Discount factor using 10.00% rate		0.9091	0.8264	0.7513	0.6830	0.6209
Present Value of cash flows		(11.8)	(2.5)	13.5	19.1	27.9
Total PV	46.3					
NPV	11.3					
NPV profitability	32.3%					

IRR for investment costing £35m

	Year					
£m	**0**	**1**	**2**	**3**	**4**	**5**
Relevant cash flows from project	(35.0)	(13.0)	(3.0)	18.0	28.0	45.0
Discount factor using 15.99% rate		0.8621	0.7433	0.6408	0.5525	0.4763
Present Value of cash flows		(11.2)	(2.2)	11.5	15.5	21.4
Total PV	35.0					
NPV	0.0					

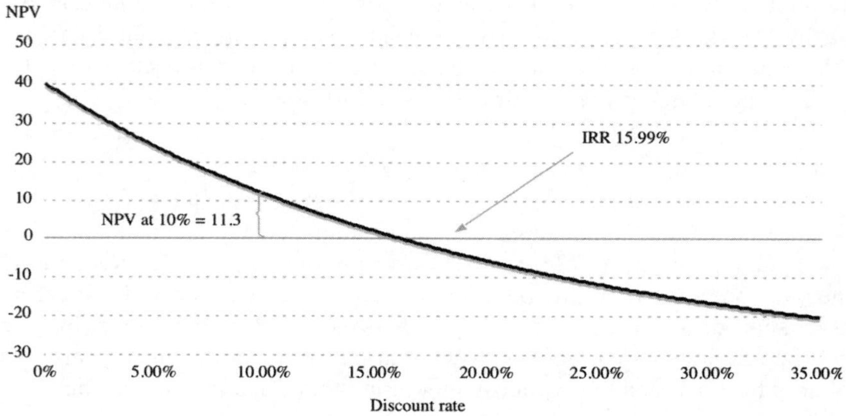

The IRR can also be viewed as a rate of interest charged on the Net Cash Invested ('NCI'), which reduces this NCI to zero at the end of the project (this method is often used for leases and loan evaluation). Similarly, when interest is accumulated at the required rate, the NPV is the amount of cash that could be extracted at time 0 to give a zero NCI at the end of the project.

Example B1.5 Alternative calculation of NPV and IRR

£m				Year		
	Now	1	2	3	4	5
Relevant cash flows from project	(35.0)	(13.0)	(3.0)	18.0	28.0	45.0
Interest on cash balances at 15.99%		(5.6)	(8.6)	(10.4)	(9.2)	(6.2)
Cash balances	(35.0)	(53.6)	(65.2)	(57.6)	(38.8)	**(0.0**
Relevant cash flows from project	(35.0)	(13.0)	(3.0)	18.0	28.0	45.0
Interest on cash balances at 10.00%		(4.6)	(6.4)	(7.3)	(6.3)	(4.1)
NPV extracted	(11.3)					
Cash balances	(46.3)	(63.9)	(73.3)	(62.6)	(40.9)	**0.0**

The IRR will either be a pre- or post-tax rate, depending on whether the interest is taxed:

Example B1.6 Pre- and post-tax IRR

If it is assumed that the project cash flows in Example **B1.5** have already been taxed, then the pre-tax equivalent IRR would be 22.84% (= 15.99% / (1 – t) where, in this example, t is a 30% marginal tax rate and tax is paid at the same time as the relevant cash flow):

£m					Year		
	Excel IRR	Now	1	2	3	4	5
Relevant cash flows from project	15.99%	(35.0)	(13.0)	(3.0)	18.0	28.0	45.0
Interest on cash balances at 22.84%			(8.0)	(12.2)	(14.9)	(13.2)	(8.9)
Tax on interest at 30%			2.4	3.7	4.5	3.9	2.7
Cash balances		(35.0)	(53.6)	(65.2)	(57.6)	(38.8)	(0.0)

Problems with the IRR

There are a number of problems associated with using an IRR:

- It ignores the size of project and amount of value created.

  Investment decisions should be based on the absolute size of a project's NPV rather than whether the IRR exceeds the required rate (i.e. value created rather than yield 'spread'). A small project with a high IRR may seem more attractive than a large project with a lower IRR, even though the latter may have a higher NPV and create more wealth for the investor.

- There may be more than one IRR.

If there is more than one change in sign of the cash flows, then multiple IRRs may result.

Example B1.7 Multiple IRR

The following project cash flows, although extreme, have the same NPV as in **Example B1.4** (discounting at 10%) but have two IRRs at 3.09% and 110.75%:

			Year			
£m	**0**	**1**	**2**	**3**	**4**	**5**
Relevant cash flows from project	(35.0)	45.0	55.0	30.0	20.0	(122.8)
Discount factor using 10.00% rate		0.9091	0.8264	0.7513	0.6830	0.6209
Present Value of cash flows		40.9	45.5	22.5	13.7	(76.3)
Total PV	46.3					
NPV	11.3					

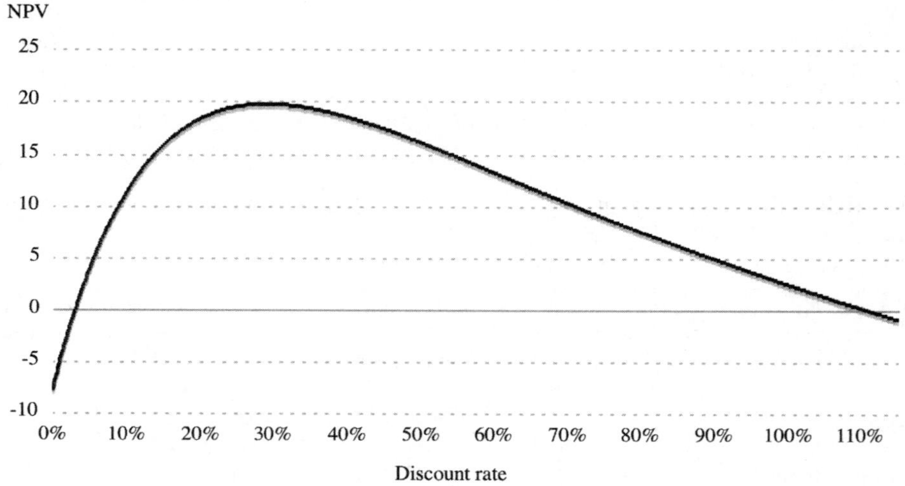

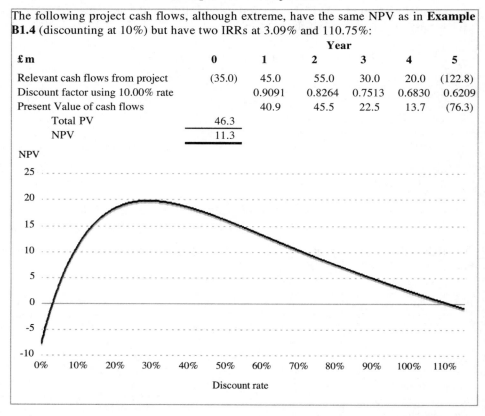

One solution would be to eliminate interim negative cash flows by compounding forward positive cash flows at the required rate to their Future Values, starting with later cash flows ('Sinking Fund Method'). This ensures there is only one change of cash flow sign (see Herbst (2002)).

Example B1.8 Adjusting cash flow to eliminate multiple IRRs – Sinking Fund

The project cash flows from **Example B1.7** can be adjusted as follows:

			Year			
£m	**0**	**1**	**2**	**3**	**4**	**5**
Relevant cash flows from project	(35.0)	45.0	55.0	30.0	20.0	(122.8)
FV of 20.0 at 10.0% at yr 5					(20.0)	22.0
FV of 30.0 at 10.0% at yr 5				(30.0)		36.3
FV of 48.5 at 10.0% at yr 5			(48.5)			64.5
Adjusted cash flows: IRR = 41.70%	(35.0)	45.0	6.5	0.0	0.0	0.0
Discount rate	10.00%					

In **Example B1.8** the negative cash flow is eliminated with the compounded, future value of the immediately preceding positive cash flows ('last-in first-out'). A more conservative approach would be to compound forward the earliest cash flows ('first-in first-out')('Initial Investment Method'):

Example B1.9 Adjusting cash flow to eliminate multiple IRRs – Initial Investment

The project cash flows from **Example B1.7** can be adjusted as follows:

£m			Year			
	0	**1**	**2**	**3**	**4**	**5**
Relevant cash flows from project	(35.0)	45.0	55.0	30.0	20.0	(122.8)
FV of 45.0 at 10.0% at yr 5		(45.0)				65.9
FV of 55.0 at 10.0% at yr 5			(42.8)			57.0
Adjusted cash flows: IRR = 20.55%	(35.0)	0.0	12.2	30.0	20.0	0.0
Discount rate	10.00%					

- Reinvestment rates

When the IRR is used, there is an assumption that surplus cumulative cash flows can be reinvested at the IRR, which might not always be the case.

Example B1.10 IRR and reinvestment rates

Using **Examples B1.4** and **B1.5**, a similar IRR could be achieved from the following cash flows:

£m	*Excel IRR*	**Now**	**1**	**2**	**3**	**4**	**5**
Relevant cash flows from project	15.99%	(35.0)	30.0	25.0	(25.0)	(10.0)	25.4
Interest on cash balances at 15.99%			(5.6)	(1.7)	2.0	(1.6)	(3.5)
Cash balances		(35.0)	(10.6)	12.7	(10.3)	(21.9)	0.0

It is implicitly being assumed that the positive £12.7m cash balance at the end of year 2 will earn a rate of return equal to the 15.99% IRR. If surplus funds can only be reinvested at a lower reinvestment rate or, say, the Cost of Capital (10%), then the effective IRR would be lower (this approach will be used when discussing leases):

£m			Year			
	0	**1**	**2**	**3**	**4**	**5**
Relevant cash flows from project	(35.0)	30.0	25.0	(25.0)	(10.0)	25.4
Interest on -ve cash bals at 15.05%		(5.3)	(1.5)	0.0	(1.6)	(3.3)
Interest on +ve cash bals at 10.00%		0.0	0.0	1.3	0.0	0.0
Cash balances	(35.0)	(10.3)	13.2	(10.5)	(22.1)	(0.0)
Finance rate	15.05%					
Reinvestment rate	10.00%					

NPV and Accounting Return (ROIC)

Although the accounting rate of return (profit ÷ book value of investment) is an inadequate measure to use for an investment decision (since it depends on the chosen accounting policy and ignores cash flows and their timing), it can be linked to the NPV under certain conditions. For a single investment made at time 0, the NPV will equal the PV of future 'Economic Profits', defined as the excess rate of return, or 'spread' (the accounting rate of return less the required rate of return – the discount rate) multiplied by the depreciated book value of the investment at the start of each period.

For a collection of investments (i.e. a business), the accounting rate of return in each period (the average post-tax Return On Invested Capital, $ROIC_{av}$) is the Net Operating Profit After Taxes ('NOPAT') divided by the book value of the 'Invested Capital' at the start of each period. NOPAT is equal to the Free Cash Flow being discounted for the DCF valuation with 'Net New Investment' added back (capital investment in excess of depreciation). For a single investment, where an initial capital investment is made, NOPAT is simply the Free Cash Flow less depreciation charge.

Economic profits can also be shown as the excess of NOPAT over the required return (in £). (Economic Profit, as defined here, is also known as Economic Value Added, or EVA^{TM}, a registered trademark of the consultancy firm Stern Stewart.)

Example B1.11 NPV and Return On Invested Capital

The PV of the project cash flows from **Example B1.4**, discounted at 10%, produce an NPV of £9.3m (see **Example B1.4** for discount factors). This is equal to the PV of future economic profits.

				Forecast Year		
£m	**0**	**1**	**2**	**3**	**4**	**5**
NOPAT	0.0	(20.0)	(10.0)	11.0	21.0	38.0
add back: Depreciation	0.0	7.0	7.0	7.0	7.0	7.0
less: Gross New Investment	(35.0)					
Project Cash Flows (post-tax)	(35.0)	(13.0)	(3.0)	18.0	28.0	45.0
Opening Invested Capital ('IC')	0.0	35.0	28.0	21.0	14.0	7.0
Gross New Investment	35.0	0.0	0.0	0.0	0.0	0.0
Depreciation	0.0	(7.0)	(7.0)	(7.0)	(7.0)	(7.0)
Closing Invested Capital ('IC')	35.0	28.0	21.0	14.0	7.0	0.0
$ROIC_{av}$ = NOPAT / Opening IC		-57.1%	-35.7%	52.4%	150.0%	542.9%
Discount Rate		10.0%	10.0%	10.0%	10.0%	10.0%
Excess return		-67.14%	-45.71%	42.38%	140.00%	532.86%
Economic Profit (=Excess Return x Opening IC)		(23.5)	(12.8)	8.9	19.6	37.3
PV Economic Profit	**11.3**	(21.4)	(10.6)	6.7	13.4	23.2

This is a simple example that assumes the project has no value at the end of the 5 year period (any 'salvage' value would be added to the final year project cash flows). An average ROIC can be calculated as the average NOPAT divided by the average capital over the whole period: (total NOPAT £40 ÷ 5) ÷ (£35 ÷ 2) = 45.7%.

If the investment is depreciated over a longer period (10 years), an adjustment would be required to reflect the invested capital remaining at the end of the project:

£m	Forecast Year					
	0	1	2	3	4	5
NOPAT	0.0	(16.5)	(6.5)	14.5	24.5	41.5
add back: Depreciation	0.0	3.5	3.5	3.5	3.5	3.5
less: Gross New Investment	(35.0)					
Project Cash Flows (post-tax)	(35.0)	(13.0)	(3.0)	18.0	28.0	45.0
Opening Invested Capital ('IC')	0.0	35.0	31.5	28.0	24.5	21.0
Gross New Investment	35.0	0.0	0.0	0.0	0.0	0.0
Depreciation	0.0	(3.5)	(3.5)	(3.5)	(3.5)	(3.5)
Closing Invested Capital ('IC')	35.0	31.5	28.0	24.5	21.0	17.5
$ROIC_{av}$ = NOPAT / Opening IC		-47.1%	-20.6%	51.8%	100.0%	197.6%
Discount Rate		10.0%	10.0%	10.0%	10.0%	10.0%
Excess return		-57.14%	-30.63%	41.79%	90.00%	187.62%
Economic Profit (=Excess Return x Opening IC)		(20.0)	(9.7)	11.7	22.1	39.4
PV Economic Profit	**22.2**	(18.2)	(8.0)	8.8	15.1	24.5
less: PV of Invested Capital at time 5	(10.9)					
Enterprise Value at time 0	**11.3**					

If the investment is depreciated over a shorter period (3 years), then economic profits during years when there was no depreciation would simply be NOPAT:

£m	Forecast Year					
	0	1	2	3	4	5
NOPAT	0.0	(24.7)	(14.7)	6.3	28.0	45.0
add back: Depreciation	0.0	11.7	11.7	11.7	0.0	0.0
less: Gross New Investment	(35.0)					
Project Cash Flows (post-tax)	(35.0)	(13.0)	(3.0)	18.0	28.0	45.0
Opening Invested Capital ('IC')	0.0	35.0	23.3	11.7	0.0	0.0
Gross New Investment	35.0	0.0	0.0	0.0	0.0	0.0
Depreciation	0.0	(11.7)	(11.7)	(11.7)	0.0	0.0
Closing Invested Capital ('IC')	35.0	23.3	11.7	0.0	0.0	0.0
$ROIC_{av}$ = NOPAT / Opening IC		-70.5%	-62.9%	54.3%		
Discount Rate		10.0%	10.0%	10.0%		
Excess return		-80.48%	-72.86%	44.29%		
Economic Profit (=Excess Return x Opening IC)		(28.2)	(17.0)	5.2	28.0	45.0
PV Economic Profit	**11.3**	(25.6)	(14.0)	3.9	19.1	27.9

The 3 year depreciation case shows the alternative presentation of economic profits as NOPAT less a 'charge' for the capital (= required rate of return x opening Invested Capital), which is zero for years 4 and 5.

In practice, depreciation adjustments would be required to ensure the capital investment is depreciated over its 5 year useful economic life.

Economic profits and accounting rates of return will be discussed later in the context of valuing companies as a whole (i.e. a collection of investments or projects).

THE COST OF CAPITAL

The Discount Rate for Domestic Investment

Introduction

The intrinsic value of a company (Enterprise Value) is the present value of its future net operating cash flows (the post-tax operating Free Cash Flows to the Firm), discounted at a rate of return required by the providers of capital (the Weighted Average Cost of Capital, WACC). This section discusses how to estimate the WACC.

The Shareholders' Required Rate of Return (Cost of Equity)

Components of Return

The actual return for equity investors over a single period comprises an income return (cash inflow assumed to arise at the end of the period ÷ market price at start of the period) and a capital gain / loss (change in market price over the period divided by the market price at the start of the period). For an ordinary share, this would be as follows:

B1.9

Shareholders' Rate of Return

$$\text{Return over single period \%} = \frac{D_1}{MV_0} + \frac{MV_1 - MV_0}{MV_0}$$

$$= \text{Dividend Yield} + \text{Capital Gain}$$

where D_1 - dividend per share received at time 1
$MV_{0,1}$ - market values (ex- div share price) at t_0, t_1

The return for the next period, expected at the start of that period, would depend on the investors' expectations about the size of the cash inflow for that period and the market price of the investment at the end of the period. Assuming market prices reflect fair values, based on discounting future expected cash flows, then market prices would change over the period due to a change in expectations about future cash flows (which would take account of the cash inflow just paid, and expected at the start of the period), a change in the discount rate, and the time effect (future cash flows discounted over a shorter period). If expectations and the discount rate are the same, the expected rate will be the same as for the actual rate in the prior period.

Example B1.12 Equity Return Components

Equity investors expect the following cash flows over the next 5 years, plus a cash flow in perpetuity based on the year 5 cash flow, growing at a constant 4% p.a. (see **B1.6** for the perpetuity PV equation). The fair value at each time period is based on future cash flows discounted at a constant 11.10% discount rate (the rate required for this type of investment, that an investor could obtain elsewhere). The return from the cash inflow and capital gain is shown as follows:

£m	Forecast Year					
	0	1	2	3	4	5
Discount factor (11.10% discount rate)		0.9001	0.8102	0.7293	0.6565	0.5909
Cash inflows		3.56	3.73	3.92	4.11	4.30
Perpetuity Value [= 4.30 x (1 + 4%) / (11.10% - 4%)]						63.09
PV of Cash Flows	**51.61**	3.21	3.03	2.86	2.70	39.83
PV of Perpetuity at each period end	37.28	41.42	46.01	51.12	56.79	63.09
PV of future forecast cash flows at each period end	14.33	12.35	9.99	7.18	3.87	
Fair Value at each period end	**51.61**	**53.77**	**56.00**	**58.30**	**60.67**	**63.09**
Income yield = cash inflow / starting fair value		6.90%	6.95%	6.99%	7.04%	7.10%
Capital gain = change in fair value / starting fair value		4.19%	4.15%	4.10%	4.05%	4.00%
Actual return = expected return		11.10%	11.10%	11.10%	11.10%	11.10%

Components of Discount Rate

If an expected future cash flow is certain to be received on the expected date, the return is said to be free of any risk. A risky asset is one whose cash flows (and hence income and capital return) are uncertain as to amount and timing. The required rate of return in equation **B1.1** and the 11.10% rate in **Example B1.12** both include a premium to reflect the investors' perception of the uncertainty that the future expected cash flows will be achieved:

$$\text{Required rate} = \text{Risk Free Rate} + \text{Risk Premium}$$

If expected cash flows can be adjusted so that the adjusted cash flows are certain to arise ('certainty equivalent') – the probability of their occurrence is 1.0 – then a risk free rate can be used (this approach will be discussed later when considering option pricing).

Example B1.13 Certainty Equivalents

Assuming a risk-free rate of 4.75%, the PV in **Example B1.12** can be replicated by adjusting the cash flows to their certainty equivalents and discounting at the risk free rate (11.10% = 4.75% + risk premium).

£m				Forecast Year		
	0	1	2	3	4	5
Discount factor (4.75% discount rate)		0.9547	0.9114	0.8700	0.8306	0.7929
Cash inflows		3.56	3.73	3.92	4.11	4.30
Adjustment factor to remove risk (0.1052615441)		0.1053	0.1053	0.1053	0.1053	0.1053
Certainty equivalent cash flows		0.37	0.39	0.41	0.43	0.45
Perpetuity Value [= 0.45 x (1 + 4%) / (4.75% - 4%)]						62.83
PV of Cash Flows	**51.61**	0.36	0.36	0.36	0.36	50.18

This assumes that the risk for each cash flow and period is exactly the same; in practice, the uncertainty and risk of each cash flow would increase the more distant the cash flow (i.e. the above factors would decrease with time). For the PVs to be the same, the adjustment factor for each period would be $(1+\text{risk free rate})^t / (1+\text{risk free rate} + \text{premium})^t$.

Given the difficulty in capturing all the risk in the cash flows - to allow the risk premium in the discount rate to be ignored – it is easier to use a risk-adjusted discount rate.

Risk-Free Rate

The main risks that affect the certainty of an investment or security cash flows include market risk (uncertainty of cash flows due to economic or market factors), default risk (uncertainty of cash flows due to a failure of the issuer of the security), and reinvestment risk (uncertainty of return due to the need to reinvest interim security cash flows - dividends, coupons, interest – at the IRR at the date of purchase) (see **Example B1.10** and Appendix B2 for further discussion on reinvestment risk). A risk-free security should exhibit none of these uncertainties.

Equity Risk

Debt and non-equity holders (bank lenders, bondholders, preference shareholders, for example) rank ahead of ordinary shareholders for annual distributions (interest on capital) and rights to repayment of capital on insolvency, since they have a contractual relationship with the company. A shareholder faces a risk of not receiving a dividend (the company is not legally obliged to pay one) and not receiving a return of its capital in part (the value of its shareholding may decline) or in full (if the company is unable to pay its debts as and when they fall due, formal insolvency proceedings may commence, and there may not be any surplus of net assets available for ordinary shareholders after settlement of all debts and prior claims).

The ability of a company to pay interest and capital to debt providers (credit risk), will partly depend on the stability and predictability of its operating cash flows (after-tax), which are, in turn, affected by the business risk faced by the company, that is, risk that affects all companies in every sector due to wider market factors (market risk), all companies in the relevant sector, and only that particular company.

The greater the debt servicing obligations, the greater the 'financial risk' for shareholders that dividends will be threatened and, in the worst case scenario, that bankruptcy will follow. If residual cash flows available for equity investors and earnings are highly volatile and uncertain, then shareholders will require a greater rate of return.

Reducing Risk by Diversification

Assuming a company's ordinary shareholders hold shares in other companies, then they should be able to eliminate certain risks by diversification (under Portfolio Theory). If risk can be eliminated, then no return should be expected for that risk.

Under Portfolio Theory, it is assumed that the volatility of a portfolio's aggregate returns can be reduced by increasing the number of stocks in that portfolio. By combining stocks whose rates of return change to different degrees (and in the opposite direction, if the returns are 'negatively correlated') in response to certain factors, the total portfolio may be less risky than the sum of the risks of its constituent stocks. As the number of stocks increase, so the aggregate portfolio risk should decrease, as the risks unique to each stock ('specific' or 'unsystematic' risks) are reduced and eventually eliminated.

At the extreme, if a shareholder's portfolio contained every stock in the whole market (with the same value weighting as in the 'market portfolio' – such as the relevant stock exchange index covering all shares), then the portfolio risk would equal the market risk. The relevant risk for an individual stock would be its sensitivity to the market risk, since all other risk would have been eliminated.

Estimating the Cost of Equity using 'CAPM'

Using Portfolio Theory, the Capital Asset Pricing Model ('CAPM') states that the required return for a given stock (Cost of Equity) equals a risk free rate plus an Equity Risk Premium for market risk, adjusted by a factor ('Beta') to reflect the sensitivity of that stock's returns to total market risk:

$$\text{Cost of Equity (CAPM)} = \text{Risk Free Rate} + \left(\text{Market Equity Risk Premium} \times \text{Equity Beta}\right) \qquad \textbf{B1.10}$$

Risk Free Rate: A risk-free rate would usually be represented by the yield to maturity on a government bond of similar currency and maturity (or 'Duration' – see Appendix B2) as the security cash flows being valued.

If the bond is a long-dated, coupon-paying bond, then it may be argued that expected returns are partly dependent on market factors (market risk due to inflation eroding real returns, and reinvestment risk eroding nominal returns) and the maturity (a higher return may be required – 'liquidity premium' – for longer dated bonds). Some bonds may have systematic risk, therefore. A 'Zero-Coupon', 'Index-Linked' bond would be free of such risk. However, in spite of the possibility of there being some risk, a coupon-paying bond with 10 or 20 years remaining to maturity can be used.

Market Equity Risk Premium ('ERP')

The current ERP required by shareholders is usually estimated by (1) taking an average of past, observable excess returns (periodic equity returns - income and capital - over and above the risk free returns), on the assumption that this long term average will apply to future years (historic or 'ex-post' ERP), and /or (2) calculating a premium from current market prices and expectations (implied or 'ex-ante' ERP).

- Historic ERP

The Historic ERP is an average ERP ('arithmetic' or 'geometric'[1]) over some time interval (enough years to provide a statistically valid long term average) of periodic (usually monthly) equity market returns (based on a representative stock market index[2]) in excess of a risk free rate (yield on government bond or bill). Estimates, therefore, vary considerably, depending on the chosen parameters.

Estimates of UK, US and other country historic ERPs can be obtained from Ibbotson Associates (www.ibbotson.com) and Dimson et al (2002). The latter estimate the historic UK ERP over 1900-2000 to be between 4.4% - 6.5% depending on whether an arithmetic or geometric mean, or long term government bond or bill, is used (compared to 5.0% - 7.7% for the US). The arithmetic average, using bond yields, is 5.6% for the UK and 7.0% for the US.

[1] The arithmetic average of year end cash flows (= $(x_1 + x_2 + x_3 + \dots + x_n) \div n$) is higher than the geometric average, or compound average growth rate (= $(x_n \div x_1)^{1/(n-1)} - 1$). For DCF valuation purposes, Brealey and Myers (2003 p.157), Dimson et al (2002 p. 194), Ibbotson Associates (www.ibbotson.com), and Copeland et al (2000 p.220) provide arguments in favour of the arithmetic mean as a forward looking measure (see Ogier et al (2004)).

[2] The index needs to represent the market value weighted total returns (dividends are usually assumed to be reinvested, and an adjustment is made accordingly).

- Implied ERP

If the market value of the whole stock market (represented by the market index) equals the present value of all future expected dividends, discounted at the market's required rate of return (market Cost of Equity = risk free rate + ERP), then an implied ERP can be determined if all other inputs are known or assumed (market index, dividend yields and growth rates, government bond yield).

To determine the required return, a forecast of future dividends could be prepared, based on current dividends (market index x market dividend yield) growing over the next few years at the analysts' consensus EPS growth rate, and thereafter at an assumed long term rate in perpetuity, adjusting for any changes in expected dividend payout ratios. If real growth rates are used, then the resulting discount rate would be real, and current inflation would need to be added in to determine the nominal return (= (1 + real return)(1 + inflation) -1).

Another approach is to estimate the required market return as the sum of the dividend yield expected for the next period and the long term dividend growth rate (the Gordon Growth Model – see **1.5** in Chapter 1). Based on this approach, Dimson et al (2002) estimate an implied UK ERP of 3.7% (arithmetic) and 2.4% (geometric) (5.4% and 4.1%, respectively, for the US).

All examples here are based on an estimated UK ERP of 4.5%, being the average of the Dimson arithmetic historic and implied ERP (rounded).

Equity Beta

The equity beta measures the sensitivity of a stock's return relative to changes in the market return (statistically shown as the correlation coefficient of the stock return and market return multiplied by their relative standard deviations).

B1.11

$$\text{Equity beta} = \text{Correlation Coefficient of stock vs market returns} \times \frac{\sigma_{stock}}{\sigma_{market}}$$

$$= \frac{\text{Covariance}}{\sigma^2_{market}}$$

where σ is the standard deviation and σ^2 the variance

Equity betas can be observed by regressing stock returns against market returns, where the beta is the slope of the regression line. A simple example is given below (based on monthly returns).

Example B1.14 Estimating the Equity Beta by Regression

A share's monthly returns (capital gain, ignoring dividends) are regressed against the market return. The low correlation coefficient (0.34), leads to a fairly low beta and relatively low risk security. In practice, the length of period would be longer, typically 60 months.

Month	Stock price £	Market Index	Stock return	Market return
1	30.75	179.63		
2	28.00	181.19	-8.94%	0.87%
3	27.75	180.66	-0.89%	-0.29%
4	27.50	179.83	-0.90%	-0.46%
5	26.38	189.55	-4.07%	5.41%
6	26.00	191.85	-1.44%	1.21%
7	28.25	190.92	8.65%	-0.48%
8	26.00	188.63	-7.96%	-1.20%
9	25.75	182.08	-0.96%	-3.47%
10	25.50	189.82	-0.97%	4.25%
11	28.50	202.17	11.76%	6.51%
12	29.25	211.28	2.63%	4.51%

Standard deviation of Stock returns (s_s)		0.0620405
Variance of stock		0.38%
Standard deviation of Market returns (s_m)		0.0316843
Variance of market		0.10%
Relative volatility (s_s / s_m)		1.95808
Correlation coefficient of returns	x	0.3401308
Equity beta		**0.67**

The total stock return variance can be split into its systematic (market) and non-systematic (specific) risk components:

$$\text{Stock risk } (\sigma_s) = \text{Specific risk} + \text{Market risk} \qquad \textbf{B1.12}$$

$$\therefore \quad \text{Stock risk } (\sigma_s)^2 = \text{Specific risk}^2 + \beta^2 \text{ x Market risk } (\sigma_{mr})^2$$

In **Example B1.14**, total stock risk$(\sigma_s)^2$ = 0.38%, β^2 x Market risk $(\sigma_{mr})^2$ = 0.04, hence specific risk (variance) is 0.34% accounting for almost 90% of the stock's variance. The CAPM assumes this high specific risk component can be eliminated by diversification.

Equity betas are available from consultancies, such as Bloomberg and, in the USA, Ibbotson Associates.

Companies with high equity betas tend to have high business risk and/or high financial risk, such as:

- non-diversified businesses with revenues, earnings and cash flows that are highly sensitive to economic factors;
- highly geared, capital intensive businesses that have a large proportion of fixed operating costs (increasing the volatility of operating and net cash flows);
- early stage or start-up ventures.

Equity betas fluctuate over time as the company matures and its capital structure changes. There is some evidence that equity betas (derived from regression) tend towards a mean level of 1.0. An adjustment is often made to the equity beta to reflect this 'mean reverting' trend (Bloomberg adjust the 'raw' beta observed from regression as follows: 0.67 x raw equity β + 0.33 x market β 1.0)(see Ogier et al (2004 p.54)).

Estimating the Cost of Equity for a Private Company

An equity beta cannot be observed for a private company, and hence it needs to be estimated, typically by taking the average beta for a sample of quoted 'proxy' companies with similar risk characteristics (betas can also be estimated by applying statistical regression techniques to the private company's earnings – see Damodaran (2002 p.196) for further discussion).

Choosing companies in the same sector should reduce any business risk differences to a minimum. However, since the capital structure, and hence financial risk, is likely to differ within the same sector, an adjustment needs to be made to strip out ('de-gear') the effects of financial risk from the observed equity beta, in order to arrive at an equivalent equity beta for an all equity financed company (an 'ungeared' or 'assets' beta) that only reflects business risk. The actual capital structure of the private company can then be used to 're-gear' the ungeared beta to ensure the correct level of financial risk is incorporated.

The re-gearing procedure assumes that the company's ungeared beta (all equity-financed) would be exactly the same as the sum of its equity and debt betas, weighted according to their market value ratios, if it chose to finance the same operations with some debt. The tax deductibility of debt interest would need to be taken into account.

One way of re-gearing the ungeared beta is to multiply it by 1 + D*/E as shown in **B1.13** below (see Brealey and Myers (2003 p.227), Damodaran (2001 p.204), and **Example B1.15** below).

B1.13

$$\beta_u = \beta_g \left(\frac{E}{E + D^*}\right) + \beta_d \left(\frac{D^*}{E + D^*}\right)$$

$$\therefore \quad \beta_g = \beta_u \left(\frac{E + D^*}{E}\right) - \beta_d \left(\frac{D^*}{E}\right)$$

Which simplifies to:

$$\beta_g = \beta_u + \frac{D^*}{E} \left(\beta_u - \beta_d\right)$$

$$\text{or} \quad \beta_g = \beta_u \left(1 + \frac{D^*}{E}\right) - \left(\beta_d \times \frac{D^*}{E}\right)$$

Assuming β_d is zero[1]:

$$\beta_g = \beta_u \left(1 + \frac{D^*}{E}\right)$$

Used to 're-gear' the average de-geared sample equity beta with the private co's D*/E.

$$\therefore \quad \beta_u = \frac{\beta_g}{\left(1 + \frac{D^*}{E}\right)}$$

Used to 'de-gear' each equity beta in sample with proxy company's D*/E ratio.

Where β_u, β_g, β_d - ungeared equity, geared equity and debt betas
E - market value of equity
D* - market value of debt: there are two options*:

1. D* = D(1-t), where t is the tax rate (after Hamada (1972): see Damodaran (2001 p.204) and Copeland et al (2000 p.309)).
2. D* = D (after Harris and Pringle (1985): see Brealey and Myers (2003 p.535) and Arzac (2005 p.48) for further discussion on D* ignoring this tax adjustment).

[1] Debt will have a beta of greater than zero if it has market risk (the cost of debt is sensitive to changes in market returns); a zero debt beta implicitly assumes that shareholders bear all the market risk.

As stated above, each equity beta in the sample is de-geared using each company's gearing ratio (using market values). The sample average de-geared beta is then re-geared as follows: βg = quoted company sample average βu x (1 + D*/E), where D*/E is the debt-to-equity ratio for the private company (often multiplied by (1 – tax rate) as discussed in **B1.13**). Since a private company's equity market value is the DCF equity value being calculated, the market value gearing ratio can be estimated using an iterative process: assume a market value gearing ratio, and adjust this so it equals the ratio of debt to the DCF calculated equity value.

Issues to consider when using CAPM

The following factors should be taken into account when using the CAPM:

- **Beta estimation**: Beta estimates for a quoted stock depend on the return interval (daily, weekly, monthly, etc.) and the measurement period (1yr, 5yrs, 10yrs, etc). Estimates for private companies depend on the sample of comparable companies and what adjustments are made for gearing differences.

- **Validity of assumptions**:
  - A security's risk is given by the variance of its returns – Investors may be more concerned with downside risk or the risk of portfolio returns moving out of line with a specific target index.
  - Diversifiable risk is irrelevant – Investors may not be as diversified as portfolio theory envisages (particular for small private companies).
  - Investors share the same perception of risk – Investors may not focus on the same risk attributes of a given stock

- **Explanatory power**: Stock returns may be explained by additional non-CAPM factors:
  - Fama and French (1992) provide US evidence of a relatively poor relationship between a stock's return and its beta: returns are higher for companies with low market capitalisations and low Price-to-Book ('P/B') ratios (market value of equity ÷ book value of equity: see ratio 16 in Appendix A), suggesting a higher risk premium than given by their betas (partly due to greater default risk and illiquidity). They recommend adding a 'size premium' to compensate for the relatively low market values and P/B ratios (see Arzac (2005 p. 16, 51 and 55 – 58)).
  - Ross (1976) proposed an Arbitrage Pricing Theory model ('APTM'). Unlike the CAPM, which has one risk factor (sensitivity to the market portfolio), the APTM includes a number of factors (GDP growth, inflation, investor confidence, the term structure of interest rates, etc.) that, it is argued, help to explain a stock's return.

The Required Rate of Return for Debt (Cost of Debt)

Debt and non-equity finance includes straight debt (such as loans, bonds, commercial paper, overdrafts and other interest-bearing liabilities), capitalised finance leases (and the capitalised value of off-balance sheet operating leases), preferred stock and debt-equity 'hybrid' instruments (such as convertibles).

The Cost of Debt and Non-Equity is the marginal return currently expected by the providers of that capital (i.e. based on current risk factors). The Cost of Debt, therefore, is the market required rate of return[1]: the yield for equivalent maturity government bonds (the risk free rate) plus a premium for the borrower's risk of default and other risks. If quoted debt securities are priced at par, the yield and Cost of Debt would equal the coupon rate. For bank loans and overdrafts, the effective cost will be the current required floating or fixed rate, unless the redemption amount is at a premium or discount to the nominal value of the debt (the IRR would need to be used). For private companies, the marginal medium to long term Cost of Debt could be estimated by assuming a given credit rating for the company and determining the implied Cost of Debt from quoted bond yields on similar rated debt.

Since interest costs are tax deductible (unlike dividends), the Cost of Debt should be calculated on an after-tax basis, typically calculated as the pre-tax Cost of Debt x (1 – marginal tax rate).

Total Required Rate of Return for All Providers of Capital (Cost of Capital)

Definition

The Cost of Capital is the average after-tax required rate of return for all providers of capital (the Weighted Average Cost of Capital, 'WACC'), comprising a nominal risk free rate (real risk free rate + inflation premium) and a blended premium to reflect equity, debt and non-equity risk.

Estimation

Assuming a company is financed with equity and debt, the WACC equation can be shown as follows (extra weighted terms would be required for each additional type of capital):

1 The implicit rate (IRR) - based on the current market value of the debt instrument - of cash flows to maturity, or an earlier date if there are rights of prepayment or early redemption.

B1.14

Post tax WACC = Geared Cost of Equity[1] x $\frac{E}{D+E}$[2] + Post-tax Cost of debt x $\frac{D}{D+E}$[2]

1. Estimated using the CAPM
2. D = market value of net debt (gross debt less surplus cash balances), E = market value of equity; D / D + E = long term target leverage ratio.

Example B1.15 Estimating the Cost of Capital using CAPM

A private company finances its capital investments so as to maintain a 20% leverage ratio. Given its likely credit rating, it could obtain new long term debt funding at a margin of 2.5% over the 4.75% risk free rate (the current yield to maturity for 10 year government bonds), giving an after-tax cost of debt of 5.08%. Based on a sample of quoted companies operating in the same sector, an asset beta of 1.20 is estimated (a beta consultancy would probably be used in practice to estimate the assets beta – the following illustrates the de-gearing procedure discussed in **B1.13**), and a WACC of 9.89% is estimated:

Proxy Company	Net Debt Mkt Value	Equity Mkt Value	Observed Equity beta	Gearing	Tax rate	Adj. gearing	Assets β	
	D	E	βg	D / E	t	D(1-t)/E	βg / (D / E)	βg / (D(1-t)/E)
	£m	£m	*Adj. regressed*	%	%	%		
A	50	312	1.32	16.0	30	11.2	1.13	1.18
B	62	278	1.31	22.3	30	15.6	1.07	1.13
C	110	349	1.43	31.5	30	22.1	1.09	1.17
D	44	302	1.34	14.6	30	10.2	1.17	1.22
E	43	244	1.37	17.6	30	12.3	1.16	1.22
F	45	389	1.41	11.6	30	8.1	1.26	1.30
Totals	*354*	*1,874*						
			Simple average	18.93		Simple average	1.15	1.20
			Weighted av (=354 / 1,874)	18.89		Median	1.15	**1.20**

The WACC is calculated as follows:

Pre-tax = 10.33% (i.e. t = 0%)

9.89%

80% x

Geared Cost of Equity

11.095%

=

4.75% + 1.41 x 4.5%

Risk Free Rate	Equity Beta	Equity Risk Premium
4.75%	1.41	4.5%

1.41 = 1.2 x { 1 + (20.0 / 80.0) x (1 - 30.0%) }

Asset Beta	D / D+E	Tax rate
1.20	20.0%	30%

20% x

After-tax Cost of Debt

5.075%

=

7.25% x (1 - 30%)

Cost of Debt	Tax rate
7.25%	30%

7.25% = 4.75% + 2.5%

RiskFree Rate	Debt Risk Premium
4.75%	2.5%

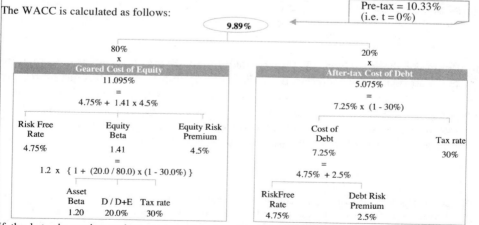

If the beta de-gearing and re-gearing procedure ignored tax (using the median 1.15 asset beta and ignoring the tax adjustment in the equity beta), WACC would be lower (9.68% - D*=D in **B1.13**).

Capital Structure and the Cost of Capital

Optimal Leverage

The Cost of Debt is cheaper than the Cost of Equity due to lower risk and the tax deductibility of interest: debt holders rank ahead of shareholders and may have security under contractual arrangements; interest is tax deductible for the borrower (dividends are not usually tax deductible, since they represent a distribution of after-tax profits). The traditional 'Trade-Off' theory states that whilst an increase in leverage will increase the weighting of 'cheaper' debt and decrease the weighting of more expensive equity, reducing the WACC, at some level an increase in the risk of bankruptcy ('Financial Distress') and other possible hidden costs will increase the WACC. Under this theory, there may be an optimal leverage (or range) at which the WACC will be minimised and the Enterprise Value maximised[1].

If the Debt Risk Premium in **Example B1.15** increases as shown below, the actual optimal capital structure is 22% (20% used).

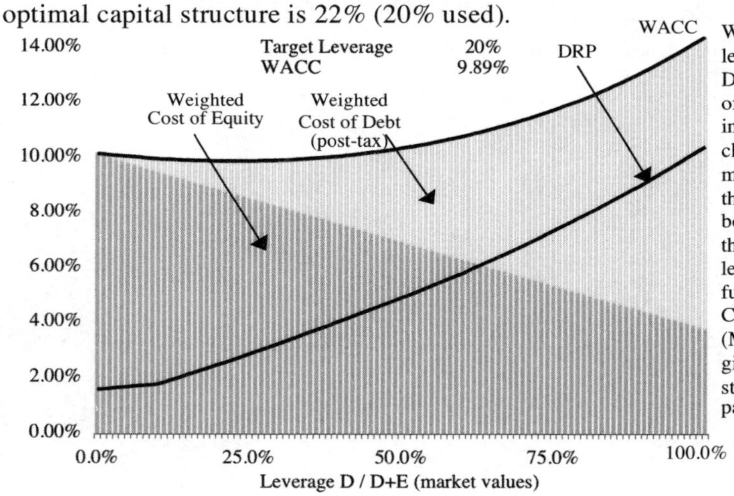

WACC increases above 22% leverage since the increasing Debt Risk Premium ('DRP') offsets any benefit from increasing the weighting of cheaper debt relative to the more expensive equity (under the CAPM, the Cost of Equity, before weighting, increases as the geared beta increases with leverage). This is discussed further below when reviewing Corporate Valuation methods (Method **VI**). Appendix D4 gives an example of the target structure change over time, as part of a valuation.

B1.15

An alternative theory ('Pecking Order Theory') states that companies do not raise debt and equity finance to move towards some optimal capital structure, but only raise external finance for capital investment projects (with positive NPVs), where there are insufficient internal cash flows (post-tax operating cash flows less steady or growing dividend payments), and then choose funding in order of least risk (debt is preferred to equity)(for further discussion see Myers (2003)).

1 The incremental tax effect for an investor providing debt rather than equity has been ignored: if more of the return is provided via income rather than a capital gain, there may be less opportunity for deferring personal tax (a gain would need to be realised before it was taxed) and a higher marginal tax rate may be suffered (if income is taxed at a higher marginal rate than capital gains).

Modigliani & Miller ('MM')

MM (1958, 1963) believed that, ignoring tax, the market value and WACC of two companies with identical Free Cash Flows and business risk would be the same, whatever their capital structure and financing policy. The WACC of the geared company would equal the ungeared Cost of Equity of the ungeared company. The Cost of Equity for a debt-financed company would be related to the Cost of Equity of a debt-free, otherwise identical, company as follows:

$$\text{Geared Cost of Equity} = \text{Ungeared Cost of Equity} + \left(\text{Ungeared Cost of Equity} - \text{Cost of Debt}\right) \times D/E \qquad \textbf{B1.16}$$

$$K_g = K_u + (K_u - K_d)\ D/E$$

where - Market Value ('MV') of geared co. $(D+E_g)$ = MV of ungeared co. (E_u)

- $WACC_{geared} = WACC_{ungeared}\ (=K_u) = K_g \times E/D+E + K_d \times D/D+E$
- K_d is the pre-tax Cost of Debt, *which MM assumed to be the risk free rate*

Taking into account tax, the market value of the geared company should exceed the market value of the ungeared company by an amount equal to the 'tax shield' (the present value of the tax deductibility of debt interest payments). The Cost of Capital will now be different.

$$\text{Geared Cost of Equity} = \text{Ungeared Cost of Equity} + \left(\text{Ungeared Cost of Equity} - \text{Cost of Debt}\right) \times D/E \times (1-t) \qquad \textbf{B1.17}$$

$$K_g = K_u + (K_u - K_d)\ D(1\text{-}t)/E$$

where - MV of geared co. $(D+E_g)$ = MV of ungeared co. (E_u) + $D \times t$

- $WACC_{geared} = WACC_{ungeared}\ (= K_u) \times$ MV of geared co. /MV of ungeared co.
- $D \times t$ = Market Value of Debt x tax rate

The MM equation **B1.17** is based on the theory that the intrinsic value of a business (Enterprise Value), based on a constant Free Cash Flow (FCF) received in perpetuity, can be broken down into two components:

- the PV of FCF (after taxes on non-financing items) discounted at the WACC for an all equity-financed company (ungeared cost of equity, K_u) = FCF / K_u;
- the PV of the tax savings on interest on any debt used to finance an otherwise identical business, discounted at the pre-tax cost of debt = $(D \times t \times K_d) / K_d$ = $D \times t$ (where D = market value of debt, K_d = pre-tax cost of debt, t = tax rate).

This leads to the equation for WACC and the cost of equity (see **B1.18**).

B1.18

$$\text{Enterprise Value } (D+E) = \frac{FCF}{WACC_g}$$

$$\frac{FCF}{WACC_g} = \frac{FCF}{K_u} + \frac{D\,K_d\,t}{K_d}$$

= D/D+E x D+E
= D

$$= \frac{FCF}{K_u} + L\left(\frac{FCF}{WACC_g}\right)\left(\frac{K_d\,t}{K_d}\right)$$

$$WACC_g = K_u \times \left(1 - Lt\right)$$

$$\text{Since } WACC_g = K_g(1-L) + K_d(1-t)\,L$$

$$\therefore \quad K_g = K_u + (K_u - K_d)\,\frac{D}{E}(1-t) \qquad \text{where } D/E = L/(1-L)$$

Where:

FCF	-	Free Cash Flows to the Firm
$WACC_g$	-	Cost of Capital for geared company
K_u, K_g	-	Cost of Equity for ungeared company and geared company, respectively
K_d, t	-	Pre-tax Cost of Debt and tax rate, respectively
L	-	Leverage ratio = D / (D + E)
D, E	-	Market value of debt and equity, respectively

MM assumed the Cost of Debt was the risk free rate, hence K_d = Risk free rate in their equations.

Example B1.16 MM WACC

If the debt risk premium in **Example B1.15** is zero (since the MM K_d = risk free rate), then the 9.89% WACC is reduced to 9.54% (by 2.5% x (1 – 30%) x 20%) under the MM WACC formula:

$WACC_{MM}$ = (4.75% + 1.41 x 4.5%) (1 - 20%) + (4.75% + 0%)(1 – 30%) (20%) = 9.54%

Or using the the equations from **B1.18**:

$WACC_{MM}$ = 10.15% x (1 - 20% x 30%) = 9.54%

K_g = 10.15% + (10.15% - 4.75%) (20% / 80%) (1 - 30%) = 11.10%

where 10.15% = ungeared cost of equity (= 4.75% + 1.20 asset beta x 4.5%)

The MM WACC can also be obtained by assuming the debt risk premium is not zero and by assuming the debt beta equals the debt risk premium divided by the equity risk premium (2.5% / 4.5% = 0.5556). The geared equity beta can be calculated using the asset beta formula in **B1.13**:

$$\beta_g = \beta_u \left(\frac{E + D(1\text{-}t)}{E} \right) - \beta d \left(\frac{D\,(1\text{-}t)}{E} \right)$$

$$= \beta_u \left(1 + \frac{L(1 - t)}{1 - L} \right) - \beta d \left(\frac{L\,(1 - t)}{1 - L} \right)$$

$$= 1.20 \left(1 + \frac{20\% \times 70\%}{1 - 20\%} \right) - 0.5556 \left(\frac{20\% \times 70\%}{1 - 20\%} \right)$$

$$= 1.41 - 0.0972$$

$$\beta_g = 1.3128$$

$$WACC_{MM} = (4.75\% + 1.3128 \times 4.5\%)(1\text{-}20\%) + (4.75\% + 2.5\%)(1-30\%)\,(20\%) = 9.54\%$$

Estimating the Tax Impact from the WACC Formula

The WACC formula shown in **Example B1.15** can be re-arranged in terms of the ungeared cost of equity as follows:

- if equity beta calculated using D(1-t)/E:

$$WACC = K_u\ (1 - tL) + P_d\,(1 - t)L$$ **B1.19**

where K_u - Ungeared cost of equity

P_d - Debt Risk Premium (pre-tax cost of debt – risk free rate)

L - Leverage (D/D+E)

t - Tax rate

when $P_d = 0$ $WACC = K_u\ (1 - tL)$ (per MM equation **B1.18**)

$$= K_u - K_u\,tL$$

- if equity beta calculated using D/E:

$$\text{WACC} = K_u - RtL + P_d(1-t)L \qquad \textbf{B1.20}$$

where R - Risk Free Rate (see **B1.17** for other symbols)

when $P_d = 0$ $\text{WACC} = K_u - RtL$

Example B1.17 Re-stating WACC in terms of Ungeared Cost of Equity

The WACC in **Example B1.15** can be restated in terms of the ungeared cost of equity (to isolate debt and tax) using equations **B1.19** (when the asset beta is re-geared using D(1-t)/E as in Example B1.15) and **B1.20** (when the alternative method of re-gearing using D/E is used – note that the 10.22% WACC in this case is not the same as the 9.68% referred to in Example B1.15, since the 1.20 asset beta is used):

			Beta re-geared using	
			D(1-t)/E	D/E
Cost of debt				
Risk free rate		R	4.75%	"
Debt risk premium		P_d	2.50%	"
Pre-tax cost of debt	= 4.75% + 2.50%	Kd	7.25%	"
Tax rate		t	30.00%	"
Post-tax cost of debt	= 7.25% x (1 - 30.00%)	Kdt	5.08%	"
Debt ratio		L	20.00%	"
Weighted rate			***1.015%***	***1.015%***
Cost of equity				
Risk free rate		R	4.75%	"
Equity risk premium		ERP	4.50%	"
Ungeared, assets beta		βa	1.20	"
Ungeared cost equity	= 4.75% + 1.20 x 4.50%	Ku	10.15%	"
Geared equity beta	= 1.20 x (1+ [20% / 80%] x (1- 30.0%))	βe	1.41	
Geared equity beta	= 1.20 x (1+ [20% / 80%])	βe		1.50
Geared Cost of Equity	= 4.75% + 1.41 x 4.50%, 4.75% + 1.50 x 4.50%	Kg	11.10%	11.50%
Equity ratio		1 - L	80.00%	"
Weighted rate			***8.876%***	***9.200%***
WACC	= 1.015% + 8.876%, 1.015% + 9.200%		**9.89%**	**10.22%**

WACC	**B1.19**	= 10.15% x (1 - 6.00%) + 0.35%		**9.89%**	
	B1.20	= 10.15% - (4.75% x 6.00%) + 0.35%			**10.22%**
tL		= 30.00% x 20.00%	6.00%		
Pd(1-t)L		= 2.50% x (1 - 30.00%) x 20.00%	0.35%		

Note: WACC – Pd(1-t)L = 9.89% - 0.35% = 9.54%, the MM WACC in **Example B1.16.**

For completeness (i.e. of questionable use), the WACC formula can also be shown in terms of the risk free rate:

- if equity beta calculated using D(1-t)/E:

		WACC = $R^* + \beta_g^* \times ERP$		**B1.21**
Where	R^* =	$R(1 - Lt)$		
	B_g^* =	$\beta_u(1 - Lt) + \beta_d L(1 - t)$		
	β_d =	Debt beta (debt risk premium / equity risk premium)		
See **Example B1.17** for key to symbols.				

(In **Example B1.17**: 4.75% x 0.94 + (1.20 x 0.94 + 0.35% / 4.5%) x 4.5% = 9.89%)

- if equity beta calculated using D/E:

		WACC = $R^* + \beta_g^{**} \times ERP$		**B1.22**
Where	R^* =	$R(1 - Lt)$		
	B_g^{**} =	$\beta_u + \beta_d L(1 - t)$		
	β_d =	Debt beta (debt risk premium / equity risk premium)		
See **Example B1.17** for key to symbols.				

(In **Example B1.17**: 4.75% x 0.94 + (1.20 + 0.35% / 4.5%) x 4.5% = 10.22%)

Adjusted Present Value ('APV')

The re-statement of the WACC formula allows the PV of Free Cash Flows (i.e. the Enterprise Value) to be broken down into an ungeared component and a tax component (this is discussed further in Method **VI** under the section 'DCF Valuation Methods'). The APV (Myers (1974)) is based on MM's work, and estimates the value of the tax shield. Free Cash Flows to the Firm are discounted at the ungeared Cost of Equity, and the tax saved on interest costs discounted at the pre-tax Cost of Debt to reflect the associated risk (replacing the risk free rate assumed in the MM formula)(this is discussed in Method **VII** below).

The Discount Rate for International Investment

Overseas Risks

Risks in an Overseas Country

The risks of an overseas project or company may be significantly different to those of a company operating in the equivalent domestic sector. The overseas company's cash flows will be sensitive to local factors (economic, political, regulatory, etc.) and worldwide influences (global interest rates, exchange rates, oil prices, etc.), making the returns from an investment in that company, perhaps, more uncertain and volatile that the returns from an equivalent investment at home.

Economic and political risks are usually greater in emerging markets, where:
- unexpected tax or currency regulations can reduce profitability;
- exchange rate instabilities can increase the costs of sales;
- the risk of expropriation of assets may be high;
- financing opportunities may be restricted by local State Bank regulations;
- war, or other internal conflicts, affect business performance;
- debt funding may only be possible using a 'hard' foreign currency, which will increase the local currency interest cost when that currency is reducing in value;
- the risk free rate of return (adjusting for any exchange rate differences) may be high due to high sovereign risk (risk of default by government on its bonds).

Additional Risks for Overseas Investors

Investors located outside the overseas country may suffer additional risks, such as:
- exchange rate fluctuations, reducing the real value of any dividend remittances;
- local regulations restricting the remittance of dividends abroad;
- additional tax on dividends paid abroad (withholding tax).

Capturing Overseas Risk in the CAPM

Introduction

Using the CAPM, a shareholder located in country F, with a diversified portfolio of domestic investments, would required a return on a new domestic investment equivalent to the 'local' CAPM-derived cost of equity: local risk free rate + beta based on local market x local Equity Risk Premium (ERP). A shareholder located in country H, making the same investment in country F, may have a diversified portfolio of investments located in country H and/or other countries (and could have a worldwide portfolio). The shareholder in H would need to determine how to incorporate the relevant risk into the cash flows or discount rate.

Where the uncertainty of the foreign investment's cash flows can be quantified with reasonable certainty (by specifying the probability of certain events occurring), then risk can be accounted for in the cash flows by reducing them to account for the uncertainty. In many cases, the risk cannot be quantified in this way, and a country risk premium needs to be added to the discount rate.

In addition to adding a premium for country F, the investor in country H would need to consider (1) which market to use for the CAPM factors (whether the risk free rate, beta and ERP should be based on country H, country F or, if investments were held worldwide, a global market, and whether these are reliable indicators of risk), (2) how the returns on the foreign investment varied with the returns on its other investments, and (3) how to avoid any duplication of risk (for example, ensuring a country risk premium was not partly duplicated in that country's ERP). There are various approaches to calculating the CAPM-derived cost of equity for a foreign investment, based on these issues.

Global CAPM

The Global CAPM assumes investors hold diversified portfolios of worldwide investments and that all country markets are integrated into one global market. Investors are assumed to be able to reduce risk by sector diversification (as in the domestic CAPM) and geographic diversification (foreign investment returns vary, not only with the foreign market index, but also some global market index). Capital markets are assumed to be integrated and not segregated, such that investors can invest anywhere in the world without restriction (it also assumes that a global market can be identified). CAPM inputs would be calculated with reference to the world market (which could be based on a recognized world index), on the assumption that investors hold a scaled down version of the world market and only non-diversifiable world market risk is relevant:

Risk Free Rate	A global risk free rate should be free of any inflation premium and be relevant for the currency of the cash flows being valued. A global real risk free rate can be converted into a nominal rate for the currency of the cash flows by adjusting for inflation, assuming parity conditions hold (see **1.4** and **Example 1.5** in Chapter 1). The real risk free rate for an efficient, liquid market in the developed world (such as the UK or US) could be used as a proxy.
Equity Risk Premium	A global ERP represents the excess of returns on the global portfolio (as shown by a worldwide index such as the MSCI index) over the global risk free rate. In practice, this could be estimated using the average ERP for developed countries (Dimson et al (2002) estimate the arithmetic average historic ERP over 1900-2000 (using bonds) for 16 countries to be 5.6%).

Beta The global equity beta represents the sensitivity of the returns on the foreign investment to the returns on the global market portfolio. The beta could be estimated by regressing the foreign investment returns against the world market index (or indirectly by multiplying the local beta - foreign investment regressed against the foreign market - by the 'foreign market beta' - foreign market returns regressed against world market returns). Alternatively, a beta could be estimated by multiplying the beta for a comparable proxy company in a mature liquid market (such as the UK or US) by the beta for that market (vs. the world market - this could be obtained from a consultancy such as Bloomberg).

Country Risk Premium 'CRP' Foreign risks that cannot be factored into the cash flows can be adjusted for by adding in a country risk premium, estimated by using the 'yield spread' between the yield on the foreign government bonds (adjusting to remove the effects of currency differences) and the yield on a default-risk free bond, such as a US bond, of similar maturity. Consultancies, such as Pricewaterhouse Coopers, provide estimates of CRPs.

Home and Foreign Hybrid CAPM

If international diversification does not apply, or markets are not considered to be integrated (as may be the case for emerging markets), then the CAPM inputs could be based on the overseas country's market (the 'local' foreign market F discussed in the introduction to this section), adjusted, if required, for 'home' factors (the investor's market H).

Risk Free Rate The foreign risk free rate could be based on the yield on the overseas country's government bonds. Where local yields are not available or are untrustworthy (due to an illiquid local market, for example), the government bond yield in the home market or another liquid market could be used and a country risk premium added.

Equity Risk Premium The foreign ERP might not be reliable where the local market is illiquid, or is dominated by a few stocks. A UK or US premium could be used as a proxy and a premium for additional local equity market risk added in.

Beta Betas could be based on local, foreign comparable betas (measured against the foreign market) where estimates would be reliable (sufficient historical data and a liquid market); alternatively, the beta could be obtained by regressing returns on proxy companies (or the industry sector) in the home market against the foreign market.

See Pereiro (2002) and Bruner (2004) for further discussion.

DCF VALUATION METHODS

Valuation Approaches

Although estimating the Equity Value by discounting Free Cash Flows at the WACC, and deducting net debt, is the simplest approach, there are other methods of reaching the same value.

A DCF Value can be calculated using a number of approaches that either estimate the Enterprise Value (**I** – **III** below) - from which the market value of net debt and other non-equity existing at the valuation date is deducted – or the Equity Value directly (**IV** – **V**):

I discount post-tax Free Cash Flows to the Firm at the post-tax WACC (this is usually the preferred method); or

II discount pre-tax 'Capital Cash Flows' (gross cash flows paid to all capital providers, both principal and interest) at the pre-tax WACC; or

III discount post-tax 'Economic Profits' (Net Operating Profits After Tax, 'NOPAT', less a charge for the required rate of return for all providers of capital) at the post tax WACC, and add the value of Invested Capital at the date of valuation; or

IV discount Free Cash Flows to Equity at the geared Cost of Equity (if all net cash flows, after debt and other non-equity financing and all taxes, are paid out as dividends to ordinary shareholders, this is equivalent to the dividend discount model); or

V discount 'Residual Income' (Profits After Tax – as stated in the Profit & Loss Account, before dividends to ordinary shareholders – less a charge for the required rate of return for ordinary shareholders) at the geared Cost of Equity, and add the book value of equity at the date of valuation.

Two other methods show the 'tax shield' from debt finance:

VI discount Free Cash Flows to the Firm and the tax cash flows on debt interest, both at the ungeared Cost of Equity (this gives the same result as in methods **I** – **V,** since it simply re-states the WACC formula (see **B1.19** above));

VII discount Free Cash Flows to the Firm at the ungeared Cost of Equity and the tax cash flows on debt interest at the pre-tax Cost of Debt (the Adjusted Present Value)– it will not give the same result as in methods **I** – **V** (as discussed below).

In summary: **B1.23**

	Cash flows	Pre / post tax	Discount rate	Value
I	Free Cash Flows to the Firm	Post-tax	Post-tax WACC	Enterprise
II	Capital Cash Flows	Pre-tax	Pre-tax WACC	Enterprise
III	Economic Profits + Existing Invested Capital	Post-tax n / a	Post-tax WACC n / a	Enterprise
IV	Free Cash Flows to Equity	Post-tax	Geared Cost of Equity	Equity
V	Residual Income + Existing Book Value of Equity	Post-tax n / a	Geared Cost of Equity n / a	Equity
VI	Free Cash Flows to the Firm + Tax cash flows on debt interest	Post-tax Tax	Ungeared Cost of Equity (K_u) Ungeared Cost of Equity (K_u)	Enterprise
VII	Free Cash Flows to the Firm + Tax cash flows on debt interest	Post-tax Tax	Ungeared Cost of Equity (K_u) Pre-tax Cost of Debt	Enterprise

Where there are non-operating, surplus net assets (properties owned but not used by the business to generate Free Cash Flows, for example), then these should be added to the Enterprise Value.

An example will be used to illustrate how the above methods calculate the same values. A five year forecast has been chosen for presentation purposes; in practice, the forecast would usually be ten years. It is assumed that the Enterprise Value of the company at the end of the forecast period (Terminal Value) is the value of its Invested Capital at that date (Terminal Value formulae are discussed later):

Example B1.18 DCF Valuation Methods

A company is expected to generate cash flows for 5 years, distribute this cash in full to shareholders, and have a value at the end of year 5 equal to the book value of its Invested Capital. The WACC is estimated to be 9.89% (from **Example B1.15**). Highlights from the financial forecasts for the next five years are as follows:

£m	Forecast Year 1	2	3	4	5
Profit & Loss					
Revenues	52.50	55.13	57.88	60.78	63.81
EBITDA	11.41	11.98	12.58	13.21	13.87
Depreciation	(3.54)	(3.71)	(3.90)	(4.10)	(4.30)
EBIT	**7.88**	**8.27**	**8.68**	**9.12**	**9.57**
Interest	(0.59)	(0.59)	(0.60)	(0.60)	(0.60)
Pre-tax profits	**7.29**	**7.67**	**8.08**	**8.52**	**8.98**
Tax	(2.19)	(2.30)	(2.43)	(2.56)	(2.69)
Post-tax profits	**5.10**	**5.37**	**5.66**	**5.96**	**6.28**
Ordinary dividends	(3.33)	(3.48)	(3.64)	(3.80)	(3.97)
Retained profits	**1.77**	**1.89**	**2.02**	**2.16**	**2.31**
Cash Flows					
EBITDA	11.41	11.98	12.58	13.21	13.87
less: capital expenditures	(5.25)	(5.51)	(5.79)	(6.08)	(6.38)
less: increase in working capital	(0.13)	(0.13)	(0.14)	(0.14)	(0.15)
less: taxes paid (excluding financing)	(2.36)	(2.48)	(2.60)	(2.73)	(2.87)
Free Cash Flows to the Firm	**3.68**	**3.86**	**4.05**	**4.25**	**4.47**
Debt cash flows (after tax relief on interest)	(0.34)	(0.38)	(0.41)	(0.45)	(0.50)
Dividends paid to ordinary shareholders	(3.33)	(3.48)	(3.64)	(3.80)	(3.97)
Net cash flows	**0.00**	**0.00**	**0.00**	**0.00**	**0.00**
Balance Sheet					
Fixed assets	29.71	31.51	33.40	35.38	37.46
Gross working capital	2.63	2.76	2.89	3.04	3.19
Invested Capital	**32.34**	**34.27**	**36.29**	**38.42**	**40.65**
Gross debt (nil cash)	8.20	8.24	8.25	8.21	8.13
Ordinary Share Capital	29.05	29.05	29.05	29.05	29.05
Reserves	(4.91)	(3.02)	(1.00)	1.16	3.47
Equity	***24.13***	***26.02***	***28.05***	***30.21***	***32.52***
Financial Capital	**32.34**	**34.27**	**36.29**	**38.42**	**40.65**
Note: after-tax debt cash flows					
Debt	8.20	8.24	8.25	8.21	8.13
Debt funding / (principal repayments)	0.07	0.04	0.00	(0.04)	(0.08)
Interest at 7.25% x opening balance	(0.59)	(0.59)	(0.60)	(0.60)	(0.60)
Pre-tax capital cash flows to debt holders	(0.52)	(0.56)	(0.59)	(0.63)	(0.68)
Tax relief on interest	0.18	0.18	0.18	0.18	0.18
Debt servicing (post-tax)	(0.34)	(0.38)	(0.41)	(0.45)	(0.50)
Free Cash Flows to Equity (paid out as dividends)	3.33	3.48	3.64	3.80	3.97

Note: tax has been simplified so that non-finance related tax is simply the tax rate applied to operating profits (i.e. tax relief on capital expenditure is given on depreciation, and deferred tax is ignored).

Method I

£m	0	1	2	3	4	5
				Forecast Year		
Post-tax Free Cash Flows at post-tax WACC						
Free Cash Flows to the Firm		3.68	3.86	4.05	4.25	4.47
Terminal Value						40.65
Discount Factor (9.89% post-tax WACC)		0.9100	0.8281	0.7536	0.6857	0.6240
PV of cash flows today	**40.67**	3.34	3.20	3.05	2.92	28.15
less: market value of debt at valuation date	(8.13)					
Equity Value	**32.53**					

Since a constant WACC is being used, it is being assumed that the capital structure (market value of net debt / (market value of net debt plus equity value, i.e. the Enterprise Value)) is constant. The debt balance each year has been set accordingly:

£m	0	1	2	3	4	5
				Forecast Year		
Enterprise Value at each year end (at 9.89% WACC)	40.67	41.01[1]	41.21	41.23	41.06	40.65
Debt ratio	20%	20%	20%	20%	20%	20%
Required debt balance (constant % Ent Value)	8.13	8.20	8.24	8.25	8.21	8.13

[1] 'Ex-div' value = (Value + Cash Flows) next year / (1+ WACC) = (41.21 + 3.86) / (1 + 9.89%) = 41.01

If, for example, the debt principal is paid off over the 5 years in equal annual instalments, then the capital structure will not be constant. The resulting WACC and Cost of Equity would be as follows:

£m	0	1	2	3	4	5
				Forecast Year		
Post-tax Free Cash Flows at post-tax WACC						
Free Cash Flows to the Firm		3.68	3.86	4.05	4.25	4.47
Terminal Value						40.65
Discount Factor (9.89% post-tax WACC)		0.9100	0.8277	0.7525	0.6838	0.6210
PV of cash flows today	**40.52**	3.34	3.19	3.05	2.91	28.02
less: market value of debt at valuation date	(8.13)					
Equity Value	**32.38**					
Enterprise Value at each year end (at 9.89% WACC)	40.67	41.01	41.21	41.23	41.06	40.65
Debt ratio	20.00%	15.86%	11.84%	7.89%	3.96%	0.00%
Calculation of WACC						
Post-tax Cost of Debt		5.08%	5.08%	5.08%	5.08%	5.08%
Leverage (at start of year)		20.00%	15.86%	11.84%	7.89%	3.96%
Weighted post-tax Cost of Debt		1.02%	0.81%	0.60%	0.40%	0.20%
Ungeared Cost of Equity		10.15%	10.15%	10.15%	10.15%	10.15%
Equity beta		1.41	1.36	1.31	1.27	1.23
Geared Cost of Equity		11.10%	10.86%	10.66%	10.47%	10.31%
Weighted geared Cost of Equity		8.88%	9.14%	9.40%	9.65%	9.90%
WACC (at start of year)		**9.89%**	**9.94%**	**10.00%**	**10.05%**	**10.10%**

Method **II**

£m	0	1	2	3	4	5
		Forecast Year				
Pre-tax Capital Cash Flows at pre-tax WACC						
Equity Cash Flows		3.33	3.48	3.64	3.80	3.97
Pre-tax debt servicing		0.52	0.56	0.59	0.63	0.68
Terminal Value						40.65
Capital cash flows (Free CF to Firm plus tax on interest)		3.85	4.04	4.23	4.43	45.30
Discount factor (10.33% pre-tax WACC)		0.9064	0.8216	0.7447	0.6750	0.6118
PV of pre-tax capital cash flows	**40.67**	3.49	3.32	3.15	2.99	27.71
less: debt	(8.13)					
Equity Value	**32.53**					

Method **III**

This method was discussed briefly in the first section of this Appendix (see **Example B1.11**), and will be discussed later in the context of Terminal Values (as mentioned Economic Profit is also known as EVA™, a registered trademark of the consultancy firm, Stern Steward & Co.).

£m	0	1	2	3	4	5
		Forecast Year				
Economic Profits						
Net Operating Profits After Taxes (NOPAT)		5.51	5.79	6.08	6.38	6.70
less: Net New Investment		(1.84)	(1.93)	(2.03)	(2.13)	(2.23)
Free Cash Flows to the Firm		*3.68*	*3.86*	*4.05*	*4.25*	*4.47*
Invested Capital (IC)	30.50	32.34	34.27	36.29	38.42	40.65
Post-tax Return on Opening IC (ROIC = NOPAT / IC)		18.1%	17.9%	17.7%	17.6%	17.4%
Post-tax WACC		9.89%	9.89%	9.89%	9.89%	9.89%
Economic Profit = Opening IC x (ROIC - WACC)		2.50	2.59	2.69	2.79	2.90
= NOPAT - Opening IC x WACC						
Discount Factor (9.89% post-tax WACC)		0.9100	0.8281	0.7536	0.6857	0.6240
PV of Economic Profits	10.17	2.27	2.14	2.03	1.91	1.81
add: IC at valuation date	30.50					
Enterprise Value	**40.67**					
less: debt	(8.13)					
Equity Value	**32.53**					

See ❹ in Appendix D4 for a more detailed example.

Notes
1. NOPAT = Operating Profits (EBIT) less taxes paid (excluding financing)
2. Net New Investment = capital expenditures less depreciation ('growth' capex) + increase in working capital

Method **IV**

£m	0	1	2	3	4	5
		Forecast Year				
Discounting Free Cash Flows to Equity						
Equity Cash Flows		3.33	3.48	3.64	3.80	3.97
Terminal Value (equity)						32.52
Discount factor (11.10% geared cost of equity)		0.9001	0.8102	0.7293	0.6565	0.5909
PV of Equity Cash Flows	**32.53**	3.00	2.82	2.65	2.50	21.56

Method **V**

This method is similar to Method **III**, but is concerned with accounting measures relating to equity (see ratio 13 and **Example A1** in Appendix A for ROE analysis, and Fernandez (2002 p.282) – referred to there as 'Economic Profit' - for further discussion):

£m	Forecast Year 0	1	2	3	4	5
Residual Income						
Profits After Tax (PAT)		5.10	5.37	5.66	5.96	6.28
Retention Ratio (1 - Payout Ratio)		34.7%	35.2%	35.7%	36.3%	36.8%
Retained Profits = Change in Book Value of Equity		1.77	1.89	2.02	2.16	2.31
Book Value of Equity (BVe)	22.37	24.13	26.02	28.05	30.21	32.52
PAT = Equity Cash Flows / Payout Ratio		5.10	5.37	5.66	5.96	6.28
Post-tax Return on Opening BVe (ROE = PAT / BVe)		22.8%	22.3%	21.7%	21.3%	20.8%
Required return (geared cost of equity Ke)		11.10%	11.10%	11.10%	11.10%	11.10%
Residual Income = Opening BVe x (ROE - Ke)		2.62	2.69	2.77	2.85	2.93
Discount factor (11.10% geared cost of equity)		0.9001	0.8102	0.7293	0.6565	0.5909
PV of Residual Income	10.17	2.36	2.18	2.02	1.87	1.73
add: BVe at valuation date	22.37					
Equity Value	**32.53**					

£24.13m BVe at end year 1 less £1.77m retained profit for year (allowing for a rounding difference).

Method **VI**

The equation in **B1.19** can be used to determine the tax savings available to an equity financed company if it introduced debt at a constant ratio to its Enterprise Value (L). Since the WACC has been re-stated in terms of an ungeared cost of equity component (K_u), this simply allows the following (see **B1.19** for symbol key):

$$\text{PV Free Cash Flows to the Firm @ WACC} = \text{PV Free Cash Flows to the Firm @}K_u + \text{PV of tax savings @}K_u$$

where

$$\text{Tax Savings} = \text{Debt} \times \left[Ku\,t - Pd\,(1-t) \right]$$

$$\text{Debt} = \text{Enterprise Value at start of each period} \times L$$

Note:

$$\text{WACC} = K_u\,(1 - tL) + P_d\,(1-t)L \quad \text{per } \mathbf{B1.19}$$

$$= K_u - L\left[Ku\,t - Pd\,(1-t) \right]$$

$$\text{where } L = \text{Debt / Enterprise Value}$$

The WACC (using the CAPM with the beta geared with D(1-t)/E) will reduce as the debt ratio increases from one level (L) to the next (H), so long as $\Delta\% < K_u\{ t / (1-t) \}$

$$\text{where } \Delta = \frac{\text{Leverage}_H \times \text{debt premium}_H - \text{Leverage}_L \times \text{debt premium}_L}{\text{Leverage}_H - \text{Leverage}_L}$$

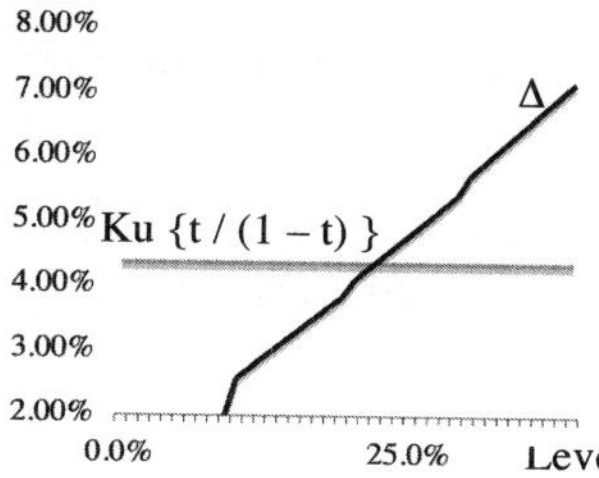

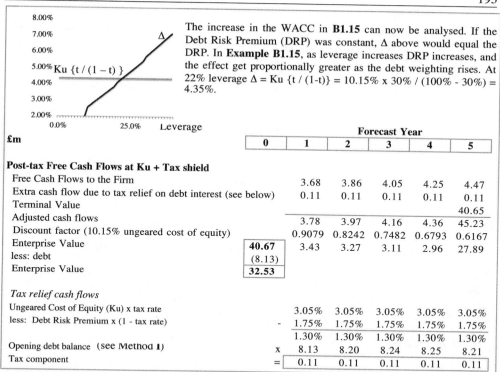

The increase in the WACC in **B1.15** can now be analysed. If the Debt Risk Premium (DRP) was constant, Δ above would equal the DRP. In **Example B1.15**, as leverage increases DRP increases, and the effect get proportionally greater as the debt weighting rises. At 22% leverage Δ = Ku {t / (1-t)} = 10.15% x 30% / (100% - 30%) = 4.35%.

£m		Forecast Year 0	1	2	3	4	5
Post-tax Free Cash Flows at Ku + Tax shield							
Free Cash Flows to the Firm			3.68	3.86	4.05	4.25	4.47
Extra cash flow due to tax relief on debt interest (see below)			0.11	0.11	0.11	0.11	0.11
Terminal Value							40.65
Adjusted cash flows			3.78	3.97	4.16	4.36	45.23
Discount factor (10.15% ungeared cost of equity)			0.9079	0.8242	0.7482	0.6793	0.6167
Enterprise Value		**40.67**	3.43	3.27	3.11	2.96	27.89
less: debt		(8.13)					
Enterprise Value		**32.53**					
Tax relief cash flows							
Ungeared Cost of Equity (Ku) x tax rate			3.05%	3.05%	3.05%	3.05%	3.05%
less: Debt Risk Premium x (1 - tax rate)	-		1.75%	1.75%	1.75%	1.75%	1.75%
			1.30%	1.30%	1.30%	1.30%	1.30%
Opening debt balance (see Method I)	x		8.13	8.20	8.24	8.25	8.21
Tax component	=		0.11	0.11	0.11	0.11	0.11

Method **VII**

£m	Forecast Year 0	1	2	3	4	5
Adjusted Present Value						
Free Cash Flows to the Firm (FCFF)		3.68	3.86	4.05	4.25	4.47
Terminal Value						40.65
Discount factor (10.15% ungeared cost of equity)		0.9079	0.8242	0.7482	0.6793	0.6167
PV of FCFF at 10.15% ungeared cost of equity	40.26	3.34	3.18	3.03	2.89	27.83
Tax on debt interest		0.18	0.18	0.18	0.18	0.18
Discount factor at 7.25% pre-tax cost of debt		0.9324	0.8694	0.8106	0.7558	0.7047
Tax shield = PV at 7.25% pre-tax cost of debt	0.73	0.16	0.16	0.15	0.14	0.13
APV	**40.99**	3.50	3.34	3.18	3.03	27.95

The debt will not be a constant 20% of the Enterprise Value at each period (as was the case in Method **I**), and will not depend on the market risk of the company (hence the pre-tax cost of debt is used as the discount rate (Arzac (2005))). The APV is not the same as the Enterprise Value as calculated under Methods **I** – **VI**:

£m	Forecast Year 0	1	2	3	4	5
PV of free cash flows at 10.15% Ku at each date	40.26	40.68	40.95	41.05	40.96	40.65
Tax shield at each time period	0.73	0.60	0.47	0.32	0.17	0.00
Enterprise Value	**40.99**	**41.28**	**41.41**	**41.37**	**41.13**	**40.65**
Debt	8.13	8.20	8.24	8.25	8.21	8.13
Leverage (L)	19.84%	19.87%	19.90%	19.93%	19.97%	

The APV can be shown in terms of Method **I,** discounting Free Cash Flows to the Firm at a WACC. In this case, the WACC is calculated assuming a debt beta equal to the debt risk premium divided by the equity risk premium (= 2.5% / 4.5% = 0.5556) and the geared equity beta calculated from the equation in **B1.13** (see **Example B1.16**), but replacing the marginal tax rate (30%) with the tax shield rate (PV of tax shield / Enterprise Value at each date):

$$\beta_g = \beta_u \left(1 + \frac{L(1-t)}{1-L}\right) - \beta_d \left(\frac{L(1-t)}{1-L}\right)$$

£m	Forecast Year 0	1	2	3	4	5
Enterprise Value	40.99	41.28	41.41	41.37	41.13	40.65
Debt	8.13	8.20	8.24	8.25	8.21	8.13
Leverage (L)	19.84%	19.87%	19.90%	19.93%	19.97%	
Tax shield / debt	8.94%	7.35%	5.68%	3.91%	2.03%	
Θ = L / (1 - L) (i.e. D / E) x (1 - tax shield %)	22.54%	22.98%	23.44%	23.92%	24.44%	
β_u	1.20	1.20	1.20	1.20	1.20	
βdebt	0.56	0.56	0.56	0.56	0.56	
βg = βu x (1 + Θ) - βdebt x Θ	1.35	1.35	1.35	1.35	1.36	
Kg = Rf + βg x ERP	10.80%	10.82%	10.83%	10.84%	10.86%	
Pre-tax cost of debt x (1 - actual tax rate)	5.08%	5.08%	5.08%	5.08%	5.08%	
WACC (using changing L)	9.67%	9.68%	9.68%	9.69%	9.70%	
Discount factor		0.9119	0.8314	0.758	0.691	0.6299
Free Cash Flows to the Firm		3.68	3.86	4.05	4.25	4.47
Terminal Value						40.7
Present Value	**40.99**	3.35	3.21	3.07	2.94	28.42

Workings for year 2 discount factor:

Tax shield / debt	7.35%	= 0.60 / 8.20
Θ = L / (1 - L) (i.e. D / E) x (1 - tax shield %)	22.98%	= 19.87% /(1 - 19.87%) x (1 - 7.3%)
βequity = βasset x (1 + Θ) - βdebt x Θ	1.35	= 1.20 x (1 + 22.98%) - 0.56 x 22.98%
Kg = Rf + βequity x ERP	10.82%	= 4.75% + 1.35 x 4.50%
WACC (using changing L)	9.68%	= 5.08% x 19.87% + 10.82% x (1 - 19.87%)
Discount factor	0.8314	=1 / ((1 / 0.9119) x (1 + 9.68%))

To equate this to the £40.67m Enterprise Value calculated in Method **I**, a constant 11.1% debt ratio would have to be maintained:

£m	Forecast Year 0	1	2	3	4	5
PV of free cash flows at 10.15% Ku at each date	40.26	40.68	40.95	41.05	40.96	40.65
Tax shield at each time period	0.40	0.33	0.26	0.18	0.09	0.00
APV	**40.67**	41.01	41.20	41.23	41.05	40.65
Leverage	11.04%	11.04%	11.04%	11.04%	11.04%	11.04%
Required debt	4.49	4.53	4.55	4.55	4.53	4.49
Interest		0.33	0.33	0.33	0.33	0.33
Tax on interest		0.10	0.10	0.10	0.10	0.10
PV at each year end at 7.25% pre-tax cost of debt	0.40	0.33	0.26	0.18	0.09	0.00

Terminal Values

Introduction

This section discusses techniques to estimate the Enterprise Value at the end of the 'n' year forecast period (the 'Terminal Value' or 'Continuing Value'). Since forecasting revenue growth rates, margins and capital investment rates on an annual basis during the terminal period (n+1, n+2 ...) is not practical, the Terminal Value (TV) is normally estimated by assuming Free Cash Flows for the first terminal year n+1 are received in perpetuity (usually growing annually). In **Example B1.18**, the TV was equal to the final forecast year Invested Capital, since the business terminated at that date (in practice, a liquidation, or break-up, value would be used, re-stating assets to their realisable values). However, a similar TV would result if Free Cash Flows were generated in perpetuity beyond that date but no economic profit arose (see Method **III**). Before considering TV formulae, Economic Profits will be discussed further.

Economic Profits, Accounting Rates of Return and Reinvestment Rates

As already stated, a rate of return on all capital ($ROIC_{av}$) in excess of the cost of that capital (WACC) will generate Economic Profits (see **Example B1.11** and **Example B1.18**, Method **III**), or EVA™ (see Stewart (1991) for a detailed discussion of EVA, including its use for performance measurement – Stern Stewart & Co. propose a number of accounting adjustments, which will not be discussed here):

B1.24

$$\text{Economic Profits} = \text{Net Operating Profits} - \text{Charge for Capital}$$

$$= \text{NOPAT} - \left(\text{WACC} \times \text{Capital}\right)$$

$$= \left(\text{ROIC}_{av} - \text{WACC}\right) \times \text{Capital}$$

where	NOPAT	Net Operating Profits After Taxes paid
	Capital	Opening Invested Capital (operating Fixed Assets and gross working capital)
	$ROIC_{av}$	NOPAT ÷ Capital
and	Free Cash Flows	NOPAT - NNI or NOPAT x (1 – RR)
	NNI	Net New Investment = Capital Expenditures in excess of the depreciation charge + Working Capital Investment
	RR	Reinvestment Rate = NNI / NOPAT

Since, for any given capital investment plan, the Invested Capital at any date partly depends on accounting policies (for example, depreciation, as illustrated in **Example B1.11**), assessing true value creation is more problematic. However, the sum of all Economic Profits over the life of the company, in present value terms, represents Enterprise Value over and above the current Invested Capital.

As noted in **B1.24**, Free Cash Flows to the Firm represent the proportion of NOPAT retained: Free Cash Flows = NOPAT x (1 – Reinvestment Rate) (if any two of these three components are assumed, the third can be calculated). Invested Capital (as defined above) will increase each year by the amount of these profits reinvested (change in Invested Capital = Net New Investment), equivalent to NOPAT x Reinvestment Rate. The Net New Investment each period should produce additional NOPAT, to give a return (the marginal, or incremental, Return On Invested Capital '$ROIC_m$') that, over period t to t+1, can be shown by one measure as the increase in $NOPAT_{t+1}$ divided by the Net New $Investment_t$ (because it is assumed that cash flows arise at each year end, the Net New Investment is assumed to occur at the start of the year, with the additional NOPAT being received at the end of that year and thereafter in perpetuity – NOPAT growth after t+1 is assumed to arise due to further investment). This allows $ROIC_m$ to be expressed in terms of NOPAT growth:

$$\text{Marginal Return } (ROIC_m) = \frac{\text{Increase in } NOPAT_{t \rightarrow t+1}}{\text{Net New Investment}_t} = \frac{NOPAT_{t+1} - NOPAT_t}{NOPAT_t \text{ x } RR_t} = \frac{g_{t+1}}{RR_t} \qquad \textbf{B1.25}$$

where g is the NOPAT growth rate and RR the Reinvestment Rate. Using this measure of the marginal return (1) assumes that NOPAT growth is due to Net New Investment in each period (no growth is due to other capital previously invested), and (2) depends on the depreciation policy adopted. (See Damodaran (2001 p.695, 814) and Copeland et al (2000 p.269) for further discussion.)

From **B1.25**

$$\text{Reinvestment Rate} = \frac{g}{ROIC_m} \qquad \textbf{B1.26}$$

In general, a company would want to ensure that new capital invested each year earns a marginal return ($ROIC_m$) - and the remaining, previously invested capital continues to earn a rate of return - above that required by the providers of the capital (WACC)(the average return on all capital, $ROIC_{av}$, will, over time, reduce to the marginal return, as measured using **B1.25**). Future cash flows relating to capital expenditure incurred in a given year t need to earn an IRR (if reliable) in excess of the WACC to make that investment worthwhile (value created in year t = NPV); future cash flows from prior capital expenditures (i.e. existing assets at the start of year t) also need to be considered (additional value will be created if expectations about future cash flows relating to these earlier investments change – see **B1.9** and the related discussion).

The Cash Flow Return On Investment ('CFROI'), developed by the Boston Consulting Group, is an IRR measure for existing assets (measured in real terms, ignoring inflation, and compared to the real WACC). The IRR is based on (1) an initial investment at any date t ('Gross Investment', being operating assets with accumulated depreciation added back), (2) constant cash flows over the expected life of the assets ('Gross Cash Flows' [the current year NOPAT with depreciation and other non-cash items added back] or EBITDA less taxes on non-financial items) and (3) a Terminal Value based on the salvage value of the assets at the end of the period. All of these inputs (1)-(3) are expressed in real terms (i.e. the currency value at date t). (See Madden (1998) for further discussion.)

Implications for Terminal Values

The final year n Free Cash Flows, on which the TV largely depends, should be based on (1) rates of return that are economically justifiable (competitive forces should drive down rates of return towards sustainable levels, possibly at or just above the WACC) and (2) margins and reinvestment rates that reflect the company's relatively mature stage. Whilst the n year forecast can be extended until such a 'steady state' arises, it is possible to use a 'two-stage' formula (valuing cash flows over an interim terminal period, during which cash flows converge to a steady state, and valuing cash flows in perpetuity thereafter).

Terminal Value Formulae

Although there are other methods of estimating the TV (such as using P/E, EBITDA or cash flow multiples, or the break-up or liquidation value), the following discussion focuses on valuing cash flows in perpetuity. Year n is the final forecast year (usually year 10), and n+1 is the first terminal year. In the examples given, year n is year 5 from **Example B1.18**.

Year n + 1 Free Cash Flows to the Firm (FCF) in perpetuity

1. *Year n FCF with no growth* **B1.27**

$$FCF_{n+1} = FCF_n$$

(This assumes a decrease in FCF in real terms if a nominal WACC is used – Arzac (2005 p.82)).

$$TV = \frac{FCF_{n+1}}{WACC}$$

2. *Year n FCF with constant growth* **B1.28**

$$FCF_{n+1} = FCF_n \times g^*$$

$$TV = \frac{FCF_{n+1}}{WACC - g}$$

The growth rate, g*, may or may not be the same as the perpetuity growth rate 'g' – the adjustment g* is simply an adjustment to FCF_n to set up the sustainable cash flow. The marginal return ($ROIC_m$) will remain constant, although the Invested Capital will increase at a decreasing rate, reducing the average return (ROICav), eventually down to $ROIC_m$.

3. *Marginal return set to an assumed rate as from year n+1*

Free Cash Flows for year n+1 can be calculated using NOPAT for year n and assuming a growth rate and marginal rate of return (to generate the Reinvestment Rate from equation **B1.26**). This Free Cash Flow can then be valued using the TV Formula No.2:

$$FCF_{n+1} = NOPAT_{n+1} \times \left(1 - \text{Reinvestment Rate}\right)$$

$$TV = \frac{NOPAT_{n+1} \times \left(1 - g \div ROIC_m\right)}{WACC - g} \qquad \textbf{B1.29}$$

Arzac (2005 p.18) states that g and $ROIC_m$ must be in real terms, to strip out the inflation effect on NOPAT. This adjustment is not shown in **Example B1.19**.

If $ROIC_m$ is set to equal WACC, then:

$$TV = \frac{NOPAT_{n+1}}{WACC}$$

and

$$\begin{aligned} NOPAT_{n+1} &= NOPAT_n + g \times NOPAT_n \\ &= NOPAT_n + NNI_n \times ROIC_{m\ n+1} \\ &= NOPAT_n + NNI_n \times WACC \end{aligned}$$

Example B1.19 Terminal Value – Constant Marginal Return on Capital

In **Example B1.18**, the Terminal Value would be £68.98m if the marginal return was set to equal the 9.89% WACC from the first year of the terminal period (see page 202):

NOPAT	=	£6.7m + £2.23m x 9.89% = £6.92m
Reinvestment Rate	=	3.5% / 9.89% = 35.4%
Free Cash Flows	=	£6.92m x (1 – 35.4%) = £4.47
TV	=	£4.47 / (9.89% - 3.5%) = £69.98m
TV also	=	$NOPAT_{n+1}$ (£6.92m) / WACC (9.89%) = £69.98m

4. *Average return set to equal an assumed rate as from year n+1*

The Free Cash Flow is calculated to ensure the average Return on Invested Capital ($ROIC_{av}$) is at the assumed level. The TV formula is the same as for 2. above, however in this case the perpetuity growth formula 'g' is not the same as the year n+1 growth rate. Calculating FCF_{n+1} involves the following:

$$NOPAT_{n+1} = \text{Invested Capital}_n \times ROIC_{av}$$

$$\text{Net New Investment} = \text{Invested Capital}_n \times g$$

$$FCF_{n+1} = \text{Invested Capital}_n \times (ROIC_{av} - \text{perpetuity 'g'})$$

$$TV = \text{Invested Capital}_n \times (ROIC_{av} - g) / (WACC - g)$$

By setting $ROIC_{av}$ = WACC, there would be zero economic profit in the terminal period and the TV at the end of the forecast period would simply be the amount of Invested Capital at the end of that period. It may be more appropriate to assume that some value will be added for the first G years of the TV period, and the TV at end year n + G would be the Invested Capital at that date.

Two Stage growth

5. *Year n FCF with constant growth*

If year n+1 Free Cash Flows grow at g_1% for N years, and g_2% thereafter in perpetuity, they should be multiplied by the following factor to calculate the present value (see equation **B1.8**):

$$\frac{1}{WACC - g} \times \left[1 - \frac{(1 + g_1)^{(N+1)}}{(1 + WACC)^{(N+1)}}\right] + \frac{(1 + g_1)^N (1 + g_2)}{(WACC - g_2)(1 + WACC)^{(N+1)}}$$

Example B1.20 Terminal Value - Two Stages - Assumed growth rates

If in **Example B1.18**, the final forecast year Free Cash Flow to the Firm (£4.47m) grows at 6.0% to £4.74m in year 6 and 6.0% p.a. for a further 5 years, growing 3.5% in perpetuity (from the start of year 7 in the terminal period), the terminal value at the end of year 5 would be £82m, being £4.74 x the discount factor 17.3052, calculated as follows:

$$\frac{1}{9.89\% - 6\%} \times \left[1 - \frac{(1 + 6\%)\text{^}6}{(1 + 9.89\%)\text{^}6}\right] + \frac{(1 + 6\%)\text{^}5 \times (1 + 3.5\%)}{(9.89\% - 3.5\%) \times (1 + 9.89\%)\text{^}6}$$

$$= 25.70 \times \left[0.1945\right] + 12.31$$

$$= 17.3052$$

6. *Marginal return moves towards a target rate over a transition period*

Rather than setting the marginal Return on Invested Capital ($ROIC_m$) to an assumed rate immediately (formula 3), the year n marginal rate can gradually be reduced over an N year transition period. This could, for example, be used to reduce marginal returns (linearly) down to the WACC such that after N terminal years, new Net Investment (NI) creates no economic profit (returns on existing capital may continue to create economic profit). This reduction can be achieved by changing the growth rates of NOPAT and/or the reinvestment rates. The TV is the sum of the PV at end year n of Free Cash Flows over the interim period and Free Cash Flows in the first year after the interim period in perpetuity.

Example B1.21 Terminal Value - Two Stages – Reducing Marginal Return on Capital

If in **Example B1.18** the 15.0% year 5 (year n) marginal return ($ROIC_m$)(year 5 NOPAT increase £0.32m / year 5 Net New Investment £2.13m) is reduced linearly over the first 6 years (N) of the terminal period, so that from year 7 it equals the 9.89% WACC (this produces an abnormal cash flow for the first year in the terminal period), the terminal value at the end of year 5 would be £72.61 (perpetuity growth rate 3.5%)(see page 203).

$$NOPAT_{n+1} = NOPAT_n + NI_n \times R_1 \times (1 + d))$$

$$\text{Reinvestment rate} = g_1 / (R_1 \times (1 + d)^2)$$

where:

- NI_n = Net Investment in year n (capex–depreciation + working capital change)
- R_1 = starting $ROIC_m$ rate (i.e. year n marginal return on new capital)
- g_1 = assumed long term growth rate of NOPAT
- d = annual reduction in rate (= $(R_2 / R_1)^{[1/(N+1)]} - 1$) where:
  - R_2 = target marginal rate of return
  - N = period of reduction

PV cash flows TV yrs 1 - 6	$NOPAT_{n+1} \times \frac{1}{WACC - g_1} \times \left[1 - \frac{(1+g_1)^N}{(1+WACC)^N}\right]$	33.15
less	$NI_{n+1} \times \frac{1}{WACC - g_2} \times \left[1 - \frac{(1+g_2)^N}{(1+WACC)^N}\right]$	(10.06)
		23.09
PV cash flows	$NOPAT_{n+1+N} = NOPAT_{n+1} \times (1 + g_1)^N$	8.62
TV yr 7 on less	$NI_{n+1+N} = NI_{n+1} \times (1 + g_2)^{(N-1)} \times (1 + g_1)$	(3.05)
	Free Cash $Flow_{n+1+N}$	5.57
	$\times 1/(WACC - g_1) \times 1/(1 + WACC)^N$	49.51
Terminal Value		**72.61**

where

$NOPAT_{n+1}$	=	$NOPAT_n + NI_n \times R_1 \times (1 + d)$	$NOPAT_{n+1}$	7.02
	where	NOPATn = 6.70, NIn = 2.23		
WACC		Assumed		9.89%
$NOPAT_{n+1}$growth		Assumed	g_1	3.5%
Period		Assumed	N	6 years
NI_{n+1}	=	$NOPAT_{n+1} \times g_1 / \{R_1 \times (1 + d)^2\}$	NI_{n+1}	1.84
NI_{n+1}growt	=	$(1 + g_1)/(1 + d) - 1$	g_2	9.85%
	where	d = linear reduction factor $(R_2 / R_1)^{[1/(N+1)]} - 1$	d	-5.78%
		R_1 = starting rate	R_1	15.00%
		R_2 = target rate	R_2	9.89%

7. *Average return moves towards a target rate over transition period*

The average Return on Invested Capital ($ROIC_{av}$) is reduced over N years to a target level and remains fixed in perpertuity. If $ROIC_{av}$ is reduced to the WACC level, then no economic profits will be generated thereafter. A similar two stage approach is used as for method 6, however the calculations are simpler:

$$NOPAT_{n+1} = IC_n + R_1 \times (1 + d)$$

$$\text{Reinvestment rate} = IC_n \times g_1$$

where:

IC_n = Invested Capital at end year n
R_1 = starting $ROIC_{av}$ rate (i.e. $ROIC_{av}$ for year n)
g_1 = assumed long term growth rate of NOPAT
d = annual reduction in rate ($= (R_2 / R_1)^{[1/(N+1)]} - 1$) where:
- R_2 = target average rate of return
- N = period of reduction

Example B1.22 Terminal Value - Two Stages – Reducing Average Return on Capital

If in **Example B1.18** the 17.44% year 5 average return ($ROIC_{av}$) reduced linearly so that it equals the WACC from year 7 onwards, the Terminal Value would be much lower (£47.48m = year 5 Invested Capital £40.65m + PV of Economic Profits over years 1 – 6 in Terminal Period £6.83m), since no Economic Profits would arise after this date:

PV cash flows TV yrs 1 - 6		$NOPAT_{n+1} \times \frac{1}{WACC - g_1} \times \left(1 - \frac{(1+g_1)^N}{(1+WACC)^N}\right)$	25.83
	less	$NI_{n+1} \times \frac{1}{WACC - g2} \times \left(1 - \frac{(1+g_2)^N}{(1+WACC)^N}\right)$	(6.72)
			19.11
PV cash flows TV yr 7 on		$NOPAT_{n+1+N} = NOPAT_{n+1} \times (1+g_1)^N$	4.94
	less	$NI_{n+1+N} = NI_{n+1} \times (1+g_2)^N$	(1.75)
		Free Cash $Flow_{n+1+N}$	3.19
		$\times 1/(WACC - g_2) \times 1/(1+WACC)^N$	28.38
Terminal Value			**47.48**

where:

$NOPAT_{n+1}$	=	$IC_n \times R_1 \times (1 + d)$	(where ICn = 40.65)	$NOPAT_{n+1}$	6.54
WACC		Assumed			9.89%
$NOPAT_{n+1g}$	=	$(1 + g_2) \times (1 + d) - 1$		g_1	-4.6%
	where	NI_{n+1} growth is assumed		g_2	3.50%
		d = linear reduction factor	$(R_2 / R_1)^{(N+1)} - 1$	d	-7.78%
		R_1 = starting rate		R_1	17.44%
		R_2 = target rate		R_2	9.89%
Period		Assumed		N	6 years
NI_{n+1}	=	$IC_n \times g_2$		NI_{n+1}	1.42

Example B1.19 (cont.)

Marginal return on new capital ($ROIC_m$) reduces to WACC immediately.

This shows the first 10 years of the Terminal Period, where Year n is year 5 from **Example B1.18**.

	Year n (*Year 5 Example B1.18*)	1	2	3	4	5	6	7	8	9	10
		First 10 years of Terminal Period: years n + ...									
Free Cash Flows											
EBITDA less operating taxes paid	11.00	11.39	11.78	12.20	12.62	13.07	13.52	14.00	14.49	14.99	15.52
Capital invested (= depreciation)	(4.30)	(4.46)	(4.62)	(4.78)	(4.95)	(5.12)	(5.30)	(5.49)	(5.68)	(5.88)	(6.08)
NOPAT	6.70	6.92	7.16	7.41	7.67	7.94	8.22	8.51	8.81	9.11	9.43
Net new capital invested	(2.23)	(2.45)	(2.53)	(2.62)	(2.72)	(2.81)	(2.91)	(3.01)	(3.12)	(3.23)	(3.34)
Free Cash Flows	4.47	4.47	4.63	4.79	4.96	5.13	5.31	5.50	5.69	5.89	6.10
Discount factor		0.9100	0.8281	0.7536	0.6857	0.6240	0.5678	0.5167	0.4702	0.4279	0.3894
	31.54	4.07	3.83	3.61	3.40	3.20	3.02	2.84	2.68	2.52	2.37
Invested Capital											
Opening operating capital	38.42	40.65	43.10	45.64	48.26	50.98	53.79	56.69	59.71	62.82	66.05
Net new capital	2.23	2.45	2.53	2.62	2.72	2.81	2.91	3.01	3.12	3.23	3.34
Closing operating capital	40.65	43.10	45.64	48.26	50.98	53.79	56.69	59.71	62.82	66.05	69.38
Reinvestment rate	33.3%	35.4%	35.4%	35.4%	35.4%	35.4%	35.4%	35.4%	35.4%	35.4%	35.4%
Growth rates											
New replacement capital invested (=depreciation)	--	3.8%	3.5%	3.5%	3.5%	3.5%	3.5%	3.5%	3.5%	3.5%	3.5%
Total new capital invested	--	5.8%	3.5%	3.5%	3.5%	3.5%	3.5%	3.5%	3.5%	3.5%	3.5%
Operating capital	5.8%	6.0%	5.9%	5.7%	5.6%	5.5%	5.4%	5.3%	5.2%	5.1%	5.1%
NOPAT	--	3.3%	3.5%	3.5%	3.5%	3.5%	3.5%	3.5%	3.5%	3.5%	3.5%
Free Cash Flows	--	0.1%	3.5%	3.5%	3.5%	3.5%	3.5%	3.5%	3.5%	3.5%	3.5%
Returns											
Average return for year 10	17.44%	17.44%	17.44%	17.44%	17.44%	17.44%	17.44%	17.44%	17.44%	17.44%	17.44%
weighted contribution	*16.61%*	*16.48%*	*15.55%*	*14.68%*	*13.88%*	*13.14%*	*12.46%*	*11.82%*	*11.22%*	*10.67%*	*10.15%*
Marginal return for new investment in previous year (ROICm)	15.00%	9.89%	9.89%	9.89%	9.89%	9.89%	9.89%	9.89%	9.89%	9.89%	9.89%
weighted contribution	*0.83%*	*0.54%*	*0.56%*	*0.55%*	*0.54%*	*0.53%*	*0.52%*	*0.51%*	*0.50%*	*0.49%*	*0.48%*
Average return for other new investments to date	--	--	9.89%	9.89%	9.89%	9.89%	9.89%	9.89%	9.89%	9.89%	9.89%
weighted contribution	--	--	*0.51%*	*1.01%*	*1.48%*	*1.91%*	*2.31%*	*2.68%*	*3.03%*	*3.35%*	*3.65%*
Total average return on all capital (ROICav)	**17.44%**	**17.03%**	**16.62%**	**16.25%**	**15.90%**	**15.58%**	**15.28%**	**15.01%**	**14.75%**	**14.51%**	**14.28%**
Economic profit											
Economic profit for year 1	17.91	2.90	2.90	2.90	2.90	2.90	2.90	2.90	2.90	2.90	2.90
Economic profit for new investment in year	(0.00)	0.00	(0.00)	(0.00)	(0.00)	(0.00)	(0.00)	(0.00)	(0.00)	(0.00)	(0.00)
Economic profit for other new investments	(0.00)	0.00	(0.00)	(0.00)	(0.00)	(0.00)	(0.00)	(0.00)	(0.00)	(0.00)	(0.00)
PV of econonomic profit TVyr 1 - 10	17.91	2.64	2.40	2.19	1.99	1.81	1.65	1.50	1.36	1.24	1.13
PV of economic profit after yr 10	11.42										
Year 1 opening capital	40.65										
	69.98										

Value in perpetuity

PV of cash flows during terminal years 1 - 10 above	31.54
TV at end yr 10 (=FCF $_{10}$ x (1+g) / (WACC - g) x yr 10 disc fact.)	38.44
	69.98

Free Cash Flow TV = TV at end yr 10 (=FCF $_{10}$ x (1+g) / (WACC - g) = 6.10 x 1.035/ (9.89% - 3.50%) =	98.71
Opening Inv. Capita = Invested Capital at end year 10	(69.38)
Terminal economic profits	29.32
or shown as:	
Year 11 ec. profit = IC $_{10}$ x (ROICav for yr 11 - WACC) / WACC = 69.38 x (14.07% - 9.89%) / 9.89% =	29.32
Growth thereafter = NI $_{11}$ x (ROIC m for yr11 - WACC) / { WACC x (WACC - g) } = 3.45 x (9.89% - 9.89%) / { 9.89% x (9.89% - 3.50%) }	(0.0)
Terminal economic profits	29.32

Assumptions

Growth = g	3.50%
WACC	9.89%

also equal to NOPAT yr11 / WACC = £6.92m / 9.89%

PV of Terminal economic profits x year 10 discount factor 0.3894 = **11.42**

Example B1.21 (cont.)

Marginal return on new capital ($ROIC_m$) reduces to WACC over 6 years.

This shows the first 10 years of the Terminal Period, where Year n is year 5 from **Example B1.18**.

	Year n	First 10 years of Terminal Period: years n + ... 1	2	3	4	5	6	7	8	9	10
	Year 5 Example B1.18										
Free Cash Flows											
EBITDA less operating taxes paid	11.00	11.52	11.92	12.34	12.77	13.22	13.68	14.16	14.66	15.17	15.70
Capital invested (= depreciation)	(4.30)	(4.50)	(4.66)	(4.82)	(4.99)	(5.17)	(5.35)	(5.53)	(5.73)	(5.93)	(6.14)
NOPAT	6.70	7.02	7.26	7.52	7.78	8.05	8.33	8.62	8.93	9.24	9.56
Net new capital invested	(2.23)	(1.84)	(2.03)	(2.22)	(2.44)	(2.68)	(2.95)	(3.05)	(3.16)	(3.27)	(3.38)
Free Cash Flows	4.47	5.17	5.24	5.29	5.34	5.37	5.38	5.57	5.77	5.97	6.18
Discount factor		0.9100	0.8281	0.7536	0.6857	0.6240	0.5678	0.5167	0.4702	0.4279	0.3894
	33.65	4.71	4.34	3.99	3.66	3.35	3.06	2.88	2.71	2.55	2.41
Invested Capital											
Opening operating capital	38.42	40.65	42.50	44.52	46.75	49.19	51.87	54.82	57.87	61.03	64.30
Net new capital	2.23	1.84	2.03	2.22	2.44	2.68	2.95	3.05	3.16	3.27	3.38
Closing operating capital	40.65	42.50	44.52	46.75	49.19	51.87	54.82	57.87	61.03	64.30	67.69
Reinvestment rate	33.3%	26.3%	27.9%	29.6%	31.4%	33.3%	35.4%	35.4%	35.4%	35.4%	35.4%
Growth rates											
New replacement capital invested (=depreciation)	--	4.7%	3.5%	3.5%	3.5%	3.5%	3.5%	3.5%	3.5%	3.5%	3.5%
Total new capital invested	--	-2.9%	5.3%	5.4%	5.5%	5.6%	5.7%	3.5%	3.5%	3.5%	3.5%
Operating capital	5.8%	4.5%	4.8%	5.0%	5.2%	5.5%	5.7%	5.6%	5.5%	5.4%	5.3%
NOPAT	--	4.7%	3.5%	3.5%	3.5%	3.5%	3.5%	3.5%	3.5%	3.5%	3.5%
Free Cash Flows	--	15.8%	1.2%	1.0%	0.8%	0.6%	0.3%	3.5%	3.5%	3.5%	3.5%
Returns											
Average return for year 10	17.44%	17.44%	17.44%	17.44%	17.44%	17.44%	17.44%	17.44%	17.44%	17.44%	17.44%
weighted contribution	*16.61%*	*16.48%*	*15.77%*	*15.05%*	*14.33%*	*13.62%*	*12.92%*	*12.22%*	*11.58%*	*10.98%*	*10.42%*
Marginal return for new investment in previous year (ROICm)	15.00%	14.14%	13.32%	12.55%	11.82%	11.14%	10.50%	9.89%	9.89%	9.89%	9.89%
weighted contribution	*0.83%*	*0.78%*	*0.58%*	*0.57%*	*0.56%*	*0.55%*	*0.54%*	*0.53%*	*0.52%*	*0.51%*	*0.50%*
Average return for other new investments to date	--	--	14.14%	13.77%	13.36%	12.95%	12.54%	12.13%	11.73%	11.44%	11.22%
weighted contribution	--	--	*0.74%*	*1.26%*	*1.74%*	*2.19%*	*2.60%*	*2.98%*	*3.32%*	*3.65%*	*3.95%*
Total average return on all capital (ROICav)	**17.44%**	**17.26%**	**17.09%**	**16.88%**	**16.64%**	**16.37%**	**16.06%**	**15.73%**	**15.42%**	**15.14%**	**14.87%**
Economic profit											
Economic profit for year 1	18.49	3.00	3.00	3.00	3.00	3.00	3.00	3.00	3.00	3.00	3.00
Economic profit for new investment in year	0.15	0.00	0.06	0.05	0.04	0.03	0.02	(0.00)	(0.00)	0.00	(0.00)
Economic profit for other new investments	0.71	0.00	0.00	0.06	0.12	0.16	0.19	0.21	0.21	0.21	0.21
PV of econonomic profit TVyr 1 - 10	19.35	2.73	2.53	2.35	2.16	1.99	1.82	1.65	1.51	1.37	1.25
PV of economic profit after yr 10	12.61										
Year 1 opening capital	40.65										
	72.61										

Free Cash Flow TV	= TV at end yr 10 (=FCF $_{10}$ x (1+g) / (WACC - g)	
	= 6.18 x 1.035/ (9.89% - 3.50%) =	100.06
Opening Inv. Capita	= Invested Capital at end year 10	(67.69)
Terminal economic profits		32.37
or shown as:		
Year 11 ec. profit	= IC $_{10}$ x (ROICav for yr 11 - WACC) / WACC	
	= 67.69 x (14.62% - 9.89%) / 9.89% =	32.37
Growth thereafter	= NI $_{11}$ x (ROIC m for yr11 - WACC) / { WACC x (WACC - g) }	
	= 3.50 x (9.89% - 9.89%) / { 9.89% x (9.89% - 3.50%) }	(0.0)
Terminal economic profits		32.37

Value in perpetuity

PV of cash flows during terminal years 1 - 10 above	33.65
TV at end yr 10 (=FCF $_{10}$ x (1+g) / (WACC - g) x yr 10 disc fact.)	38.96
	72.61

Assumptions

Growth = g	3.50%
WACC	9.89%

PV of Terminal economic profits x year 10 discount factor 0.3894 = **12.61**

B2 STRAIGHT BOND PRICING

INTRODUCTION TO INTEREST RATES

Simple and Compound Interest

Simple Rates

If interest is received only once at the end of a deposit term (on maturity), there would be no opportunity to earn interest on any interest received during that term (interest on interest). For a one year deposit, the actual, 'Effective' rate of interest earned would be the quoted, 'Simple' (or 'Nominal') rate per annum.

Example B2.1 Simple interest, paid annually

£100m placed on deposit at 5.0% p.a.
for 1 year (no interim interest)

	Today	1 year *365 days*
Principal	(100.00)	100.00
Interest received on Principal		5.00
Future Value		105.00

Quoted, nominal rate 5.00% per year

Actual return = { Future Value (£105.00m) / Principal (£100.00m) }^(365/365) - 1
= 5.00% for 365 days

A quoted simple annual rate assumes interest is paid once on maturity after 1 year. The interest paid on a period shorter than one year is calculated as follows:

Simple Interest and Future Value (1 year)

B2.1

$$\text{Interest} = P \times r \times \frac{t}{Y}$$

$$\text{Future Value} = P + \text{Interest}$$

$$= P \times \left(1 + r \times \frac{t}{Y}\right)$$

where
- P Principal repaid in t days
- r Simple ('Nominal') interest rate (%) for 1 year
- Y Year in days (some securities / countries use 360 days – see **B2.7** – 365 will be used in this Appendix)
- t Number of days after which interest is received (see **B2.7** for 30 day month restriction for some securities)

If interest is paid during the year, the actual interest earned over the 1 year would be higher than the Simple rate due to the compounding effect of receiving interest on interest (the equivalent Effective rate earned over the whole period would be higher than the Simple rate).

Example B2.2 Simple interest, paid semi-annually

£100m placed on deposit at 5.0% p.a. for 1 year (interest paid half yearly). Note: it is assumed that interest is paid exactly half way through the year (182.5 days) – this would not be the case in practice, but an equal interest period is shown to simplify matters.

	Today	1/2 year *182.5 days*		1 year *365 days*
Principal	(100.00)			100.00
Interest received on Principal		2.50	See ❶	
Reinvested interest		(2.50)		2.50
Interest on Interest			See ❷	0.06
Interest received on Principal				2.50
Future Value				105.06

❶ Interest = £100.0m x (5.00% x 182.5 / 365)
❷ Interest on interest = £2.5m x (5.00% x 182.5 / 365)

Quoted, nominal rate 5.00% per year
Actual return = { Future Value (£105.06m) / Principal (£100.00m) }^(365/365) - 1
= 5.06% for 365 days

The effective rate of interest is 5.06%, compared to the quoted nominal rate of 5.0%.

Compound Rates

If the above period is split into two periods of length t_1 and t_2, and interest at the same Simple rate is earned in each period, then interest for the second period t_2 will be based on a deposit equal to the principal plus interest for the first period.

The deposit after t_1 is:

$$\text{Deposit at } t_1 = P \times \left(1 + r \times t_1 / 365\right)$$

The future value, or deposit, at t_2 will be:

$$\text{Deposit at } t_2 = P \times \left(1 + r \times t_1 / 365\right) \times \left(1 + r \times t_2 / 365\right)$$

If both periods are the same ($t_1 = t_2$), then the effective interest rate is:

$$\text{Interest } R\% = \left(1 + r \times t_1 / 365\right)^2 - 1$$

Comparing Rates

One Year – Same Frequency

A Simple (Nominal) rate can be converted into a (higher) Compound (Effective) rate for the same period if the two future values are equated. An investment ('P') paying interest once at the end of the year at a rate of R%, will have a future value of P (1 + R). For this to be equivalent to an investment paying interest twice a year at a Simple rate of r%, then:

$$P\left(1 + R\right) = P \times \left(1 + \frac{r}{2}\right)^2$$

B2.2

Simple ↔ Compound
(same interest frequency)

Simple rate r → Compound rate R:

$$R = \left(1 + \frac{r}{m}\right)^m - 1$$

∴ Compound rate R → Simple rate r:

$$r = \left\{\left(1 + R\right)^{1/m} - 1\right\} \times m$$

where
- m - Number of interest periods a year
- r - Simple (Nominal) rate, compounded m times
- R - Compound (Effective) rate

If the number of compounding periods per year increases, so that each time period reduces to a small time step of length δt, then the Effective rate will increase.

Example B2.3 Nominal → Effective: various compounding frequencies

Assuming, rather unrealistically, that interest is paid at every time period from annually to each minute over 365 days, then the effective annual rates would be as follows:

Period	Fraction of year	Periods a year	Nominal	Effective
Annual	1	1	**5.000000%**	5.000000%
Semi-annual	0.5	2	5.000000%	5.062500%
Quarterly	0.25	4	5.000000%	❶ 5.094534%
Monthly	0.0833333	12	5.000000%	5.116190%
Weekly	0.0192308	52	5.000000%	5.124584%
Daily	0.0027397	365	5.000000%	5.126750%
Hourly	0.0001142	8,760	5.000000%	5.127095%
Every minute	0.0000019	525,600	5.000000%	5.127109%

Input

❶ 5.094534% = (1 + 5.0000% / 4)^4 - 1

The Nominal 5.0% minute rate is approximately equivalent to a 'continuously compounded' rate (r^*), implying an exponential growth:

Effective rate = constant 2.7182818285 (= e) $^{5.0\%}$ - 1 = 5.127109%

Nominal rate = ln (1 + 5.127109%) where ln is the natural logarithm

Compounding a rate of 5.0% continuously, therefore, is the same as compounding a rate 5.12719% once a year. Since r^* is continuously compounded, the rate over any period δt is equal to $r^*\delta t$.

Exponentials and natural logarithms are related to each other as follows:

B2.3

$e^{\ln(a)} = a$	$\ln(e^a) = a$
$e^0 = 1$	$\ln(1) = 0$
$e^a e^b = e^{a+b}$	$\ln(ab) = \ln(a) + \ln(b)$
$(e^a)^y = e^{ab}$	$\ln(a)^b = b \ln(a)$
$e^{-a} = 1/e^a$	$\ln(a) - \ln(b) = \ln(a/b)$

The Effective rate for various compounding frequencies can be converted into an equivalent Nominal rate p.a.

Example B2.4 Effective → Nominal: various compounding frequencies

Period	Fraction of year	Periods a year	Nominal	Effective
Annual	1	1	5.000000%	**5.000000%**
Semi-annual	0.5	2	4.939015%	5.000000%
Quarterly	0.25	4	❷4.908894%	5.000000%
Monthly	0.0833333	12	4.888949%	5.000000%
Weekly	0.0192308	52	4.881306%	5.000000%
Daily	0.0027397	365	4.879343%	5.000000%
Hourly	0.0001142	8,760	4.879030%	5.000000%
Every minute	0.0000019	525,600	4.879017%	5.000000%

Input

❷ 4.908894% = ((1 + 5.0000%)^(1 / 4) - 1) x 4

The Nominal rate with interest paid m times a year can be converted to an equivalent Nominal rate with interest paid N times a year (same Effective rate):

B2.4

Simple → Simple
(different interest frequency)

Simple interest rate from simple interest rate:

$$r_N = \left\{ \left(1 + \frac{r}{m} \right)^{m/N} - 1 \right\} \times N$$

where r - Simple (Nominal) rate for interest paid m times p.a.
r_N - Nominal rate for interest paid N times p.a.

Example B2.5 Nominal → Nominal: different frequencies p.a.

A 5% nominal rate for quarterly interest payments is equivalent (i.e. same effective rate) to the following nominal rates for other interest periods:

Periods a year	Nominal	Periods a year	Nominal	Effective
4	**5.000000%**	1	5.094534%	5.094534%
4	5.000000%	2	❸ 5.031250%	❹ 5.094534%
4	5.000000%	4	5.000000%	5.094534%
4	5.000000%	12	4.979310%	5.094534%

Input

❸ 5.031250% = { (1 + 5.0000% / 4)^(4 / 2) - 1 } x 2
❹ 5.094534% = (1 + 5.0313% / 2)^2 - 1

Given a Nominal rate (r) with compounding m times a year, the equivalent continuously compounded rate (r*) can be calculated as follows:

Simple rate → Continuous Rate **B2.5**

$$r^* = \ln(1 + R)$$

$$= \ln\left(1 + \frac{r}{m}\right)^m$$

$$= m \ln\left(1 + \frac{r}{m}\right)$$

(see **B2.2** for symbols)

Example B2.6 Comparing Nominal, Effective and Continuous rates

Periods a year	Nominal	Continuous	Effective
1	5.127109%	5.000000%	5.127109%
2	5.063024%	5.000000%	5.127109%
4	❺ 5.031380%	❻ 5.000000%	5.127109%
12	5.010431%	5.000000%	5.127109%
52	5.002404%	5.000000%	5.127109%
365	5.000342%	5.000000%	5.127109%
8,760	5.000014%	5.000000%	5.127109%
525,600	5.000000%	5.000000%	5.127109%

Input

❺ 5.031380% = ((1 + 5.127109%)^(1 / 4) - 1) x 4
❻ 5.000000% = 4 x LN (1 + 5.031380% / 4)
5.000000% = LN(1 + 5.127109%)

Compounding Over More Than One Year

If there is compounding over more than one year, the future value is:

B2.6

Future Value (several years compounding)

$$\text{Future Value} = P\left(1+\frac{r}{m}\right)^{mT} = P\left(1+R\right)^{T}$$

were T = Number of years to maturity, P = Principal
(see **B2.2** for other symbols)

Daycount Convention

The calculation of yields and accrued interest on securities varies according to which daycount convention is used. In the simple interest rate formula **B2.1** 't' was assumed to be the number of days in the interest period and 365 the number of days in the year. The convention varies from security to security:

B2.7

Basis	*Month*	*Year*	*Example*
ACT/ACT	Actual days	365 or 366	US Treasury bonds (semi-annual coupons) UK Gilts (semi-annual coupons) UK Corporate bonds (semi-annual coupons)
ACT/365	Actual days	Fixed 365	UK Money market
ACT / 360	Actual days	Fixed 360	US Treasury bills, US Money market
30 / 360	30 days	Fixed 360	US Corporate bonds (semi-annual coupons)

ACT = Actual

Example B2.7 – Daycount conversions

An annual simple rate of 3.5% from 26 May 2004 to 6 August 2004 (2004 being a Leap year), can be converted into the other day count bases as follows:

Interest period Wednesday 26 May 2004 Start date (included)
to Friday 06 August 2004 End date (Settlement date - ignored)

	*Days **	*Year*	*Conversion*	
ACT / ACT	72	366	$\left(3.50\% \times \frac{72}{365}\right) \times \frac{366}{72}$	= 3.510%
ACT / 365	72	365	3.50%	= 3.500%
ACT / 360	72	360	$\left(3.50\% \times \frac{72}{365}\right) \times \frac{360}{72}$	= 3.452%
30 / 360	70	360	$\left(3.50\% \times \frac{72}{365}\right) \times \frac{360}{70}$	= 3.551%

** Days*

	ACT basis	*30 basis*
May	6	5
June	30	30
July	31	30
August	5	5
Total in period	72	*70*

The 30/360 basis requires the following adjustments to the start date day of month (D_1) and/or the end date day of month (D_2):

- If D1 = 28, 29, or 31 change D1 to 30
- If D1 *and* D2 = 28, 29, or 31 change both to 30

In all other cases, each month has a maximum of 30 days

STRAIGHT (OPTION-FREE) BOND PRICING

Bond Prices

Introduction

The fair value of a bond is the present value of its future cash flows (coupons and redemption amount) discounted at the 'Yield to Maturity' or 'Gross Redemption Yield' (the Internal Rate of Return, IRR, for a given market price).

The amount and timing of the cash flows is uncertain if (1) the coupon rate or date varies (if reset periodically according to a reference rate), (2) the redemption amount or date can be changed (if the issuer or holder have options allowing early repayment or conversion), or (3) there is a risk that the issuer will default on its obligations. The degree of uncertainty will be reflected in the yield (for example, the greater the risk of default, the larger the yield differential, or 'spread', compared to the yield on a bond without any default risk, such as a government bond).

A bond's fair value is inversely related to its yield, since the present value of its cash flows decreases as the discount rate (yield) increases.

Valuation at the Start of a Coupon Period

If coupons are paid annually, the fair price at the start of an interest, or coupon, period ('Clean Price') will be as follows:

Fair price of bond – valuation at start of coupon period (1 year)

B2.8

$$\text{Price} = \frac{c}{(1+r)^1} + \frac{c}{(1+r)^2} + \ldots\ldots + \frac{c+P}{(1+r)^n}$$

$$= c\,\frac{1}{r}\left(1 - \frac{1}{(1+r)^n}\right) + P\left(\frac{1}{(1+r)^n}\right)$$

$$= c \times \text{CDF}^{1\ldots n} + P \times \text{SDF}^n$$

where

c	Equal annual coupon, starting in 1 year (c% x £par value)
P	Redemption amount (principal)
r	Yield to Maturity (IRR) % per annum
n	Number of complete years until maturity
CDF, SDF	Cumulative and Simple Discount Factors (see **B1.3**, **B1.2**)

If coupons are paid more than once during the year, each coupon equals the annual coupon divided by the number of coupon periods, which, together with the redemption amount, would be discounted at the nominal Yield to Maturity:

B2.9

Fair price of bond - valuation at start of a coupon period (< 1 year)

$$\text{Price} = \frac{c/m}{(1+r/m)^1} + \frac{c/m}{(1+r/m)^2} + \ldots + \frac{c/m + P}{(1+r/m)^{nm}} \quad \text{(i)}$$

$$= c/m \; \frac{1}{r/m}\left(1 - \frac{1}{(1+r/m)^{nm}}\right) + P\left(\frac{1}{(1+r/m)^{nm}}\right) \quad \text{(ii)}$$

where c — Equal annual coupon (coupon % x bond face value)
m — Number of *equal length* coupon periods per year (hence n x m is the number of time periods)

Example B2.8 Bond pricing example – valuation on coupon date

Settlement date (valuation date)		08 March 2004
Next coupon date		07 September 2004
Maturity date	10.507 yrs	07 September 2014
Nominal value		£100
Coupon rate		5.00%
Yield to maturity		4.66%
No. of interest payments each year		2

This bond is a Gilt - the 5% Treasury 2014, with a 'clean' price of £102.81 on Mon 8 March 2004, yielding 4.658397%, per the UK Debt Management Office (HM Treasury's agency). Gilts are quoted for next day settlement.

The valuation using Excel™'s bond pricing function is shown below.

Date	*Time period*	*c / m*	*P*	*PV at 4.66%*
08 Mar 2004	0			
07 Sep 2004	1	2.50		2.44
07 Mar 2005	2	2.50		2.39
07 Sep 2005	3	2.50		2.33
07 Mar 2006	4	2.50		2.28
07 Sep 2006	5	2.50		2.23
07 Mar 2007	6	2.50		2.18
07 Sep 2007	7	2.50		2.13
07 Mar 2008	8	2.50		2.08
07 Sep 2008	9	2.50		2.03
07 Mar 2009	10	2.50		1.99
07 Sep 2009	11	2.50		1.94
07 Mar 2010	12	2.50		1.90
07 Sep 2010	13	2.50		1.85
07 Mar 2011	14	2.50		1.81
07 Sep 2011	15	2.50		1.77
07 Mar 2012	16	2.50		1.73
07 Sep 2012	17	2.50		1.69
07 Mar 2013	18	2.50		1.65
07 Sep 2013	19	2.50		1.61
07 Mar 2014	20	2.50		1.58
07 Sep 2014	21	2.50	100.00	63.20
		52.50	**100.00**	**102.81**

$$\text{Coupon} \times \left\{\frac{1}{r/m} \times \left(1 - \frac{1}{(1+r/m)^{mn}}\right)\right\} + \frac{\text{Nominal value}}{(1+r/m)^{mn}}$$

$$= £2.50 \times \left\{\frac{1}{0.0233} \times \left(1 - \frac{1}{(1+0.0233)\verb|^|21}\right)\right\} + \frac{£100}{(1+0.0233)\verb|^|21}$$

$$= £41.15 + £61.66$$

$$= \mathbf{£102.81}$$

Using Excel functions	
PRICE(08 March 04 , 07 September 14 , 5.00% , 4.66% , £100 , 2 payments p.a. , 1)	£102.81
ACCRINT(08 March 04 , 07 September 04 , 08 March 04, 5.00% , £100 , 2 paymen	£0.00
Dirty price	**£102.81**

Valuation During a Coupon Period

Daily interest is accrued on a bond up until the date the coupon is paid, so that, if a bond is purchased during a coupon period, the purchase price ('Dirty Price') includes accrued interest from the last coupon date to the day before the purchase or 'settlement' date (inclusive): accrued interest = coupon p.a. x days accrued / days in coupon period (if the 'actual / actual' convention is used, as is the case for accrued interest on UK bonds and some US bonds – otherwise, the days in the year are used).

Example B2.9 Bond pricing example – valuation during coupon period

The settlement date for the bond in **Example B2.8** is now 24 June 2004 rather than 8 March 2004; the yield has increased 0.432% to 5.0904%. The settlement date is 109 days since the last coupon date, and falls in a 184 coupon period. The fair price can be calculated from the previous coupon date or the next coupon date.

1. From previous coupon date

   The dirty price is the fair value as if calculated as at the start of the coupon period, based on the new yield, compounded forward over the accrual period:

$$PV = \text{Bond Price at last coupon date} \times (1 + r/m)^{s}$$

$$\text{where } s = \frac{\text{number of days from last coupon date until settlement date}}{\text{days in coupon period}}$$

$$\begin{aligned}\text{Price} &= \text{Price at last coupon date with 5.09\% yield} \times (1 + \text{yield}/2)^{(109/184)}\\ &= £99.27 \ (\textbf{Example B2.8} \text{ with } 5.0904\%) \times (1 + 5.0904\%/2)^{(109/184)}\\ &= £100.76 \text{ dirty price less } £1.48 \text{ accrued interest } (£2.50 \times 109/184)\\ &= £99.28 \text{ clean price (actual clean price for 5\% Treasury 2014 Gilt)}\end{aligned}$$

The dirty price can be calculated as at the settlement date using the same spreadsheet approach as above, but the first time period is 75 days away (75 /184 time periods away or 0.40761 time periods) - this assumes an actual / actual daycount basis is used for the accrued interest:

Date	*Time period*	*c / m*	*P*	*PV at 5.09%*
24 Jun 2004	0			
07 Sep 2004	0.40761	2.50		2.47
07 Mar 2005	1.40761	2.50		2.41
07 Sep 2005	2.40761	2.50		2.35
07 Mar 2006	3.40761	2.50		2.29
07 Sep 2006	4.40761	2.50		2.24
07 Mar 2007	5.40761	2.50		2.18
07 Sep 2007	6.40761	2.50		2.13
07 Mar 2008	7.40761	2.50		2.08
07 Sep 2008	8.40761	2.50		2.02
07 Mar 2009	9.40761	2.50		1.97
07 Sep 2009	10.4076	2.50		1.92
07 Mar 2010	11.4076	2.50		1.88
07 Sep 2010	12.4076	2.50		1.83
07 Mar 2011	13.4076	2.50		1.78
07 Sep 2011	14.4076	2.50		1.74
07 Mar 2012	15.4076	2.50		1.70
07 Sep 2012	16.4076	2.50		1.66
07 Mar 2013	17.4076	2.50		1.61
07 Sep 2013	18.4076	2.50		1.57
07 Mar 2014	19.4076	2.50		1.53
07 Sep 2014	20.4076	2.50	100.00	61.37
		52.50	**100.00**	**100.76**

The valuation using Excel™'s bond pricing function is shown below.

Using Excel functions	
PRICE(24 June 04 , 07 September 14 , 5.00% , 5.09% , £100 , 2 payments p.a. , 1)	£99.28
ACCRINT(07 March 04 , 07 September 04 , 24 June 04, 5.00% , £100 , 2 payments	£1.48
Dirty price	**£100.76**

2. From next coupon date

The fair value of the bond (dirty price) is the sum of the fair value calculated as at the end of the coupon period (this time with 20 coupons left) and the coupon receipt on that date, discounted back at the yield to the settlement date (the accrued interest will be the same as above).

	Next coupon allocation		
	Pre-settlement	Post-settlement	Coup period
Actual days	109 days	75 days	184.0 days
Share	59.2391%	40.7609%	100.0000%
Coupon	£1.4810	£1.0190	£2.5000

Bond price $= \text{Coupon} \times \left\{ \frac{1}{r/m} \times \left(1 - \frac{1}{(1 + r/m)^{mn}} \right) \right\} + \frac{\text{Nominal value}}{(1 + r/m)^{mn}}$

Price at next coupo[n] in 75 days $= £2.50 \times \left\{ \frac{1}{0.0255} \times \left(1 - \frac{1}{(1 + 0.0255)\text{^}20} \right) \right\} + \frac{£100}{(1 + 0.0255)\text{^}20}$

$= £38.81 + £60.49$

Discounted back over 75 days $= \frac{[\,£99.30 + £2.50 \text{ coupon received on that date}\,]}{(1+ 5.09\% / 2)\ \text{^}\ (75 / 184)}$

Dirty price = **£100.76**

Bond Yields

Type of Yield

An income yield, such as the 'Nominal Yield' (annual coupon ÷ bond par value) or the 'Current Yield' (annual coupon ÷ current market price), does not provide a true measure of the expected yield over the investment holding period. The Yield to Maturity ('YTM') for an annual coupon-paying bond is the periodic IRR of the bond if held to maturity (as at any date): the discount rate which makes the present value of the coupons and redemption amount equal to the current (dirty) price of the bond. A quoted YTM for a semi-annual coupon-paying bond would be the periodic IRR (i.e. for each 6 month period) multiplied by the number of coupon periods (i.e. a Simple / Nominal rate, being the market convention). For example, the 4.66% quoted YTM in **Example B2.8** is 2 x the IRR per period (2.33%); the true effective yield is 4.71% ($= (1 + 2.33\%)^2 - 1$).

The Effective annual yield 'Y' for a semi-annual coupon paying bond, with a quoted simple annual Yield to Maturity of '$y_{semi\text{-}annual}$', can be calculated from the Nominal / Effective rate formulas given in **B2.2** (where $y_{semi\text{-}annual}$ = 2 x IRR per 6 month period). In order to compare bonds with a different number of coupons per year, the effective annual yields need to be calculated.

Yield Components

The 'Total Return' is the effective yield from compounding forward all coupons (to include interest on coupons), at an assumed reinvestment rate, to the maturity date, adding the redemption or sale price, and comparing this to the purchase price (Fabozzi (2000)): Total Return = (Future Value ÷ Purchase price) $^{1/\text{periods}}$ – 1. The income and capital gain components can then be determined.

Example B2.10 Impact of reinvestment of coupons

Using the bond from **Example B2.9**:

Present Value of c

$$PV = c/m \; \frac{1}{r/m} \left(1 - \frac{1}{(1 + r/m)^n}\right)$$

Future Value of c

$$FV = PV\ (1 + r/m)^n$$

$$= c/m \; \frac{1}{r/m} \left[(1 + r/m)^n - 1\right]$$

$$= \frac{5.00/2\ [(1 + 0.05094/2)^{21} - 1)]}{(0.050904 / 2)}$$

$$= 68.29$$

Date	Time period	Coupons	Future Value of coupons
			Compounded 5.09% (simple rate)
24 Jun 2004	0		
07 Sep 2004	0.40761	2.50	2.50
07 Mar 2005	1.40761	2.50	5.06
07 Sep 2005	2.40761	2.50	7.69
07 Mar 2006	3.40761	2.50	10.39
07 Sep 2006	4.40761	2.50	13.15
07 Mar 2007	5.40761	2.50	15.99
07 Sep 2007	6.40761	2.50	18.89
07 Mar 2008	7.40761	2.50	21.88
07 Sep 2008	8.40761	2.50	24.93
07 Mar 2009	9.40761	2.50	28.07
07 Sep 2009	10.4076	2.50	31.28
07 Mar 2010	11.4076	2.50	34.58
07 Sep 2010	12.4076	2.50	37.96
07 Mar 2011	13.4076	2.50	41.42
07 Sep 2011	14.4076	2.50	44.98
07 Mar 2012	15.4076	2.50	48.62
07 Sep 2012	16.4076	2.50	52.36
07 Mar 2013	17.4076	2.50	56.19
07 Sep 2013	18.4076	2.50	60.12
07 Mar 2014	19.4076	2.50	64.15
07 Sep 2014	20.4076	2.50	68.29
		52.50	

The yield of 5.09% can be shown in terms of the yield from the reinvestment of coupons and receipt of the redemption sum:

Future Value = Future Value of Coupons (£68.29) + Redemption Amount (£100.0		168.29
Yield	2 x { [(68.29 + 100.00) / 100.76)] ^(1 / 20.4076) -1 }	5.09%

The effective yield can be broken down into its components:

Coupons		52.50	3.96%
Interest on coupons	=Future value of coupons (£68.29) - Coupons (£52.50)	15.79	1.19%
Capital gain / (loss)	= Price (£100.76) - Redemption value (£100.00)	(0.76)	-0.06%
		67.53	5.09%
Dirty price		100.76	
Future value		*168.29*	

Reinvestment Risk and Spot / Zero Coupon Rates

The Yield to Maturity at the date of a bond purchase will only become realised if the bond is held to maturity and the coupon receipts can be reinvested at this yield. Interest on coupon receipts increases with maturity and/or the size of the coupon, hence there will be more reinvestment risk (the risk that deposit or investment rates fall). A reinvestment rate different to the Yield to Maturity can be assumed, to give a lower effective rate (see **Example B1.10** in Appendix B1).

An investor who wants to eliminate any reinvestment risk can purchase a 'Zero Coupon' bond, where all of the yield is derived from a capital gain (the redemption amount being in excess of the purchase price). A Zero Coupon bond pays a single cash flow on maturity, equal to the purchase price compounded at the yield (see **B1.1** in Appendix B1): purchase price x $(1 + \text{Zero Coupon yield})^{\text{periods to maturity}}$.

The Zero Coupon bond's yield does not depend on interest rates for future periods between the purchase date and maturity date: no coupons are received and hence there is no requirement for the reinvestment rates at the start of each future coupon period to equal the Yield to Maturity on purchase (an implicit assumption of any IRR calculation).

A coupon bond can be seen as a package of Zero Coupon bonds, with maturities corresponding to the coupon payment dates (from 1 to n) and the maturity values being equal to the coupons (plus the coupon bond redemption amount for the Zero Coupon bond with the longest maturity). Since identical cash flows with identical risks should have the same value, the aggregate fair value of the 'n' Zero Coupon bonds should equal the fair value of the 'n' coupon bond. By 'stripping' an existing coupon bond into 'n' Zero Coupon bonds, an arbitrageur could exploit any price differences unless the aggregate prices of all n Zero Coupon bonds equalled the price of the coupon bond (similarly, Zero Coupon bonds, with identical cash flows as the coupon bond, when aggregated, could be 'reconstituted' and sold as a single coupon bond).

The fair price of a Zero Coupon bond, maturing in t years, is the redemption amount discounted using a simple discount factor (see **B1.2** in Appendix B1), with the discount rate equal to the 'Zero Coupon rate'. In order to value the coupon bond cash flows, so as to eliminate any arbitrage opportunities, each cash flow over 1 to n coupon periods should be discounted at the Zero Coupon rate, relevant for each period.

Unfortunately, reliable, liquid Zero Coupon rates are not directly observable in the market for the majority of maturities, and so a theoretical set of rates needs to be constructed ('Zero Coupon Curve' or 'Spot Rate Curve'), from which discount rates, used to value the bond cash flows, can be calculated. If a Zero Coupon rate is available for the first period, then future spot rates can be estimated fairly crudely using a procedure called 'bootstrapping': the observed market price of a coupon paying bond which matures in two periods will equal the first coupon discounted at the first period Zero Coupon rate (known) plus the second coupon and redemption amount discounted at the second period Zero Coupon rate (unknown, but calculated). The Zero Coupon rates derived for periods one and two can then be used to value a coupon bond that matures in three periods, and the third period Zero Coupon rate can be determined. This process continues until 'n' Zero Coupon rates are estimated to value the coupon bond.

Zero Coupon rates (current spot rates) are related to Forward Rates, as is discussed in Appendix B3. Hence they can be determined from a combination of instruments, whose prices are liquid and arbitrage-free. If the estimated Zero Coupon rates are risk-free (i.e. are derived from risk-free instruments), then a risk premium should be added to each period's Zero Coupon rate ('Static Spread'), to determine risk-adjusted discount rates. In the example below, risk has been ignored.

Example B2.11 Valuing a bond with Zero Coupon discount factors

A 5 year 6.00% semi-annual coupon-paying bond (risk free) is to be valued using Zero Coupon rates. The observed yield on a 6 month Treasury bill (5.00%) is used to estimate Zero Coupon rates for period 2 to 10 (years 1.0 to 5.0), based on market prices for nine recently issued ('On-The-Run') coupon-paying government bonds with maturities of 1, 1.5, ... 5 years. These bonds are currently priced at par, so their yields are 'Par Yields', equal to their coupon rates. The fair price of the 6.0% bond is 101.90, giving a Yield To Maturity (YTM) of 5.6%.

Year	Par yield (nominal)	Zero Rate	Zero Disc Factor	Bond Cash Flows	Present Value
0.5	5.000%	5.0000%	0.975610	3.00	2.93
1.0	5.148%	5.1500%	0.950423	3.00	2.85
1.5	5.250%	5.2540%	0.925156	3.00	2.78
2.0	5.320%	5.3259%	0.900213	3.00	2.70
2.5	5.380%	5.3881%	0.875535	3.00	2.63
3.0	5.430%	5.4403%	0.851267	3.00	2.55
3.5	5.470%	5.4824%	0.827538	3.00	2.48
4.0	5.505%	5.5195%	0.804296	3.00	2.41
4.5	5.535%	5.5515%	0.781599	3.00	2.34
5.0	5.560%	5.5783%	0.759498	103.00	78.23
				Price =	**101.90**

See Appendix B3 (B3.4) for derivation of the Zero and Forward Rates.

Bond Price Volatility

Factors Affecting Bond Prices

Bond prices fluctuate in response to changes in the required yield (due to changes in the market yield of comparable bonds or changes in the credit quality of the issuer), or the time to maturity. As market yields (discount rates) increase, so bond prices decrease (and vice versa). The percentage change in bond prices will not be the same for all bonds, and the relationship will be convex rather than linear (the percentage increase in price tends to be more than the decrease, unless yield changes are extremely small). The relationship between yields and maturities for a bond of similar credit risk is shown by the 'Yield Curve'. If market yields change by the same amount (say by 0.01% or 1 'basis point') for all maturities, the Yield Curve shifts in a parallel manner ('Net Interest Risk'). However, yield changes may vary depending on the coupon size ('Basis Risk') and maturity ('Yield Curve Risk').

Where a larger proportion of the present value of a bond's cash flows (i.e. its price) is due to cash flows in later years, then a change in yield will have a greater impact on the price. Bond price volatility increases (steeper price / yield curve) the lower the coupon rate (since more of the present value is represented in the final year redemption amount), and/or the longer the maturity (assuming the required yield does not equal the coupon rate - when the bond would sell at par until maturity - then the bond price will increases or decrease to the redemption amount).

Example B2.12 Bond price volatility: coupon and maturity effect

The bond from **Example B2.9** and **B2.10** can be restructured to have a lower coupon and higher redemption sum, but have the same yield:

				5.0% semi-annual coupon			2.0% semi-annual coupon		
Date	**Time period**	**Days in period**	**Time in years**	**Coupons**	**Principal**	**PV at 5.09%**	**Coupons**	**Principal**	**PV at 5.09%**
24 Jun 2004	0								
07 Sep 2004	0.40761	75	0.21	2.50		2.47	1.00		0.99
07 Mar 2005	1.40761	181	0.70	2.50		2.41	1.00		0.97
07 Sep 2005	2.40761	184	1.21	2.50		2.35	1.00		0.94
07 Mar 2006	3.40761	181	1.70	2.50		2.29	1.00		0.92
07 Sep 2006	4.40761	184	2.21	2.50		2.24	1.00		0.90
07 Mar 2007	5.40761	181	2.70	2.50		2.18	1.00		0.87
07 Sep 2007	6.40761	184	3.21	2.50		2.13	1.00		0.85
07 Mar 2008	7.40761	181	3.70	2.50		2.08	1.00		0.83
07 Sep 2008	8.40761	184	4.21	2.50		2.02	1.00		0.81
07 Mar 2009	9.40761	181	4.70	2.50		1.97	1.00		0.79
07 Sep 2009	10.4076	184	5.21	2.50		1.92	1.00		0.77
07 Mar 2010	11.4076	181	5.70	2.50		1.88	1.00		0.75
07 Sep 2010	12.4076	184	6.21	2.50		1.83	1.00		0.73
07 Mar 2011	13.4076	181	6.70	2.50		1.78	1.00		0.71
07 Sep 2011	14.4076	184	7.21	2.50		1.74	1.00		0.70
07 Mar 2012	15.4076	181	7.70	2.50		1.70	1.00		0.68
07 Sep 2012	16.4076	184	8.21	2.50		1.66	1.00		0.66
07 Mar 2013	17.4076	181	8.70	2.50		1.61	1.00		0.65
07 Sep 2013	18.4076	184	9.21	2.50		1.57	1.00		0.63
07 Mar 2014	19.4076	181	9.70	2.50		1.53	1.00		0.61
07 Sep 2014	20.4076	184	10.21	2.50	100.00	61.37	1.00	140.97	85.01
				52.50	**100.00**	**100.76**	**21.00**	**140.97**	**100.76**

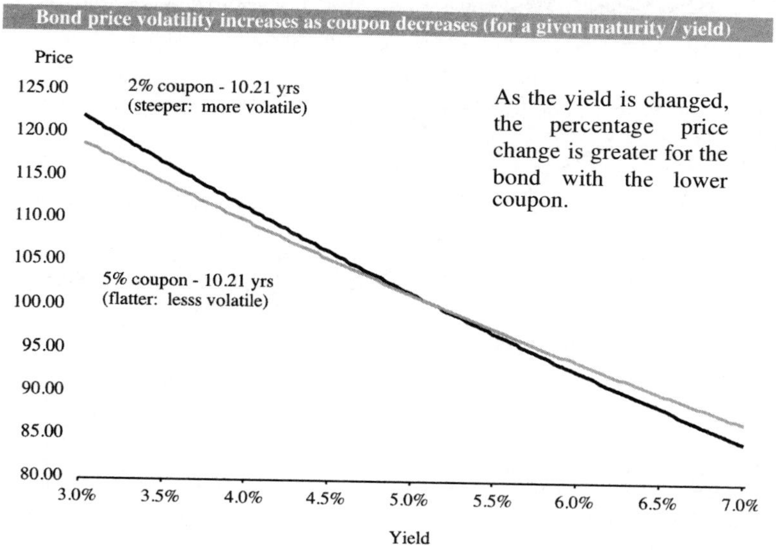

As the yield is changed, the percentage price change is greater for the bond with the lower coupon.

If the maturity of the 5% bond is extended by 5 years, and the redemption amount adjusted so as to yield the same 5.09%, the maturity effect can be shown:

Date	Time period	Days in period	Time in years	5% coupon, 10.21yrs Coupons	Principal	PV at 5.09%	5% coupon, 15.21yrs Coupons	Principal	PV at 5.09%
24 Jun 2004	0								
07 Sep 2004	0.40761	75	0.21	2.50		2.47	2.50		2.47
07 Mar 2005	1.40761	181	0.70	2.50		2.41	2.50		2.41
07 Sep 2005	2.40761	184	1.21	2.50		2.35	2.50		2.35
07 Mar 2006	3.40761	181	1.70	2.50		2.29	2.50		2.29
07 Sep 2006	4.40761	184	2.21	2.50		2.24	2.50		2.24
07 Mar 2007	5.40761	181	2.70	2.50		2.18	2.50		2.18
07 Sep 2007	6.40761	184	3.21	2.50		2.13	2.50		2.13
07 Mar 2008	7.40761	181	3.70	2.50		2.08	2.50		2.08
07 Sep 2008	8.40761	184	4.21	2.50		2.02	2.50		2.02
07 Mar 2009	9.40761	181	4.70	2.50		1.97	2.50		1.97
07 Sep 2009	10.4076	184	5.21	2.50		1.92	2.50		1.92
07 Mar 2010	11.4076	181	5.70	2.50		1.88	2.50		1.88
07 Sep 2010	12.4076	184	6.21	2.50		1.83	2.50		1.83
07 Mar 2011	13.4076	181	6.70	2.50		1.78	2.50		1.78
07 Sep 2011	14.4076	184	7.21	2.50		1.74	2.50		1.74
07 Mar 2012	15.4076	181	7.70	2.50		1.70	2.50		1.70
07 Sep 2012	16.4076	184	8.21	2.50		1.66	2.50		1.66
07 Mar 2013	17.4076	181	8.70	2.50		1.61	2.50		1.61
07 Sep 2013	18.4076	184	9.21	2.50		1.57	2.50		1.57
07 Mar 2014	19.4076	181	9.70	2.50		1.53	2.50		1.53
07 Sep 2014	20.4076	184	10.21	2.50	100.00	61.37	2.50		1.50
07 Mar 2015	21.4076	181	10.85				2.50		1.46
07 Sep 2015	22.4076	184	11.36				2.50		1.42
07 Mar 2016	23.4076	181	11.86				2.50		1.39
07 Sep 2016	24.4076	184	12.38				2.50		1.35
07 Mar 2017	25.4076	181	12.88				2.50		1.32
07 Sep 2017	26.4076	184	13.39				2.50		1.29
07 Mar 2018	27.4076	181	13.89				2.50		1.26
07 Sep 2018	28.4076	184	14.40				2.50		1.22
07 Mar 2019	29.4076	181	14.91				2.50		1.19
07 Sep 2019	30.4076	184	15.42				2.50	100.51	47.97
				52.50	**100.00**	**100.76**	**77.50**	**100.51**	**100.76**

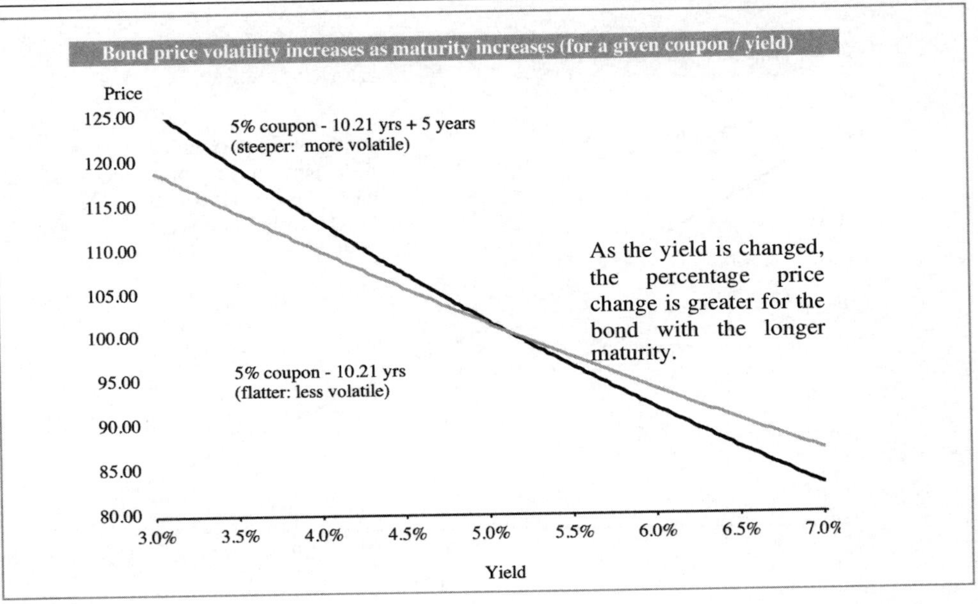

Duration

The 'Macaulay' Duration (introduced by Frederick Macaulay in 1938) is a measure of the average time it takes to receive the present value of a bond's future cash flows. In terms of the bond pricing equation, it can be shown as follows:

B2.10

Macaulay Duration

$$D = \frac{\left(\frac{C}{(1+r/m)}\right) \times t_1 + \left(\frac{C}{(1+r/m)^2}\right) \times t_2 + \ldots + \left(\frac{C+P}{(1+r/m)^n}\right) \times t_3}{\text{Price}}$$

Where $t_1 \ldots t_n$ are the time periods (see **B2.8** and **B2.9** for key to other symbols).

The Macaulay Duration is calculated by multiplying the present value of each period's cash flows, as a percentage of the total present value (i.e. price), by the time period (the Duration will be per time period, so will need to be annualised by multiplying by the number of coupon periods per year, if the time period is the coupon period). The Macaulay Duration increases as a greater proportion of the present value of the bond cash flows is received in later years. It can never exceed the maturity period (for a Zero Coupon bond, where only one cash flow is received on maturity, then Duration equals maturity).

Example B2.13 Macaulay Duration

Using the three bond structures in **Example B2.12**:

Date	Time period	Days on period	Time in years	5% coupon 2014 PV%	5% coupon 2014 x time (yrs)	2% coupon 2014 PV%	2% coupon 2014 x time (yrs)	5% coupon 2019 PV%	5% coupon 2019 x time (yrs)
24 Jun 2004	0								
07 Sep 2004	0.40761	75	0.21	2.46%	0.005	0.98%	0.002	2.46%	0.005
07 Mar 2005	1.40761	181	0.70	2.39%	0.017	0.96%	0.007	2.39%	0.017
07 Sep 2005	2.40761	184	1.21	2.34%	0.028	0.93%	0.011	2.34%	0.028
07 Mar 2006	3.40761	181	1.70	2.28%	0.039	0.91%	0.015	2.28%	0.039
07 Sep 2006	4.40761	184	2.21	2.22%	0.049	0.89%	0.020	2.22%	0.049
07 Mar 2007	5.40761	181	2.70	2.17%	0.059	0.87%	0.023	2.17%	0.059
07 Sep 2007	6.40761	184	3.21	2.11%	0.068	0.84%	0.027	2.11%	0.068
07 Mar 2008	7.40761	182	3.70	2.06%	0.076	0.82%	0.031	2.06%	0.076
07 Sep 2008	8.40761	184	4.21	2.01%	0.085	0.80%	0.034	2.01%	0.085
07 Mar 2009	9.40761	181	4.70	1.96%	0.092	0.78%	0.037	1.96%	0.092
07 Sep 2009	10.4076	184	5.21	1.91%	0.099	0.76%	0.040	1.91%	0.099
07 Mar 2010	11.4076	181	5.70	1.86%	0.106	0.75%	0.042	1.86%	0.106
07 Sep 2010	12.4076	184	6.21	1.82%	0.113	0.73%	0.045	1.82%	0.113
07 Mar 2011	13.4076	181	6.70	1.77%	0.119	0.71%	0.048	1.77%	0.119
07 Sep 2011	14.4076	184	7.21	1.73%	0.125	0.69%	0.050	1.73%	0.125
07 Mar 2012	15.4076	182	7.71	1.68%	0.130	0.67%	0.052	1.68%	0.130
07 Sep 2012	16.4076	184	8.21	1.64%	0.135	0.66%	0.054	1.64%	0.135
07 Mar 2013	17.4076	181	8.71	1.60%	0.139	0.64%	0.056	1.60%	0.139
07 Sep 2013	18.4076	184	9.21	1.56%	0.144	0.62%	0.058	1.56%	0.144
07 Mar 2014	19.4076	181	9.71	1.52%	0.148	0.61%	0.059	1.52%	0.148
07 Sep 2014	20.4076	184	10.21	60.91%	6.219	84.36%	8.614	1.49%	0.152
07 Mar 2015	21.4076	181	10.71					1.45%	0.155
07 Sep 2015	22.4076	184	11.21					1.41%	0.158
07 Mar 2016	23.4076	182	11.71					1.38%	0.161
07 Sep 2016	24.4076	184	12.21					1.34%	0.164
07 Mar 2017	25.4076	181	12.71					1.31%	0.167
07 Sep 2017	26.4076	184	13.21					1.28%	0.169
07 Mar 2018	27.4076	181	13.71					1.25%	0.171
07 Sep 2018	28.4076	184	14.21					1.21%	0.173
07 Mar 2019	29.4076	181	14.71					1.18%	0.174
07 Sep 2019	30.4076	184	15.21					47.61%	7.243
				100.00%	7.99	100.00%	9.32	100.00%	10.66

The weighted average time to receive the present value of the cash flows increases, therefore, from 7.99 years to 9.32 years as the coupon is cut from 5% to 2%, and from 7.99 years to 10.66 years as the maturity is increased.

The Macaulay Duration can also be calculated using the relevant Microsoft Excel™ spreadsheet function, providing the redemption value is par. The 5% 2014 Bond's Macaulay Duration shown above (7.99 years) can be calculated as: DURATION (24 June 2004 , 7 September 2014, 5.00%, 5.09%, 2).

The 'Modified' Duration is the 'first derivative' of the bond pricing equation, and shows the change in the price for a given (very small) change in the yield (Duration is the slope of the line at a tangent to the price / yield curve). It can be shown as follows (see Choudhry (2003 p,160, 173)):

Modified Duration

B2.11

$$\text{Modified Duration} = \frac{-\text{ Macaulay Duration in years}}{1 + (\text{yield} \div \text{coupons per year})}$$

The 5% 2014 Bond's Modified Duration (see **Example B2.13**) is - 7.79 (= - 7.99 Macaulay Duration ÷ (1 + (5.09% ÷ 2)), also calculated using the relevant Excel™ function: MDURATION (24 June 2004 , 7 September 2014, 5.00%, 5.09%, 2).

A more accurate measure of price sensitivity can be derived by recalculating the bond prices for a given percentage increase and decrease in the yield (Fabozzi and Mann (2001 p.266)):

Effective / Approximate Duration **B2.12**

$$\text{Effective Duration} = \frac{\text{Av change in price\%}}{\text{Change in yield \%}} = \frac{-(P_u + P_d)/2P_0}{\Delta Y}$$

where P_0 current bond price
P_u, P_d bond prices for +/- change in yield
ΔY change in yield

Example B2.14 Effective Duration

Taking the above 5% 2014 Bond from **Examples B2.9** and **B2.13**, the Duration can be calculated by analysing the price around the current 5.09% yield for a given 0.01% increase and decrease in the yield (prices are not rounded to 2 decimal places, to ensure the answer matches the Excel™ result):

Yield	*Dirty Price*	
5.08%	100.8393	
5.09%	100.7608	Duration = - [(100.6823 – 100.8393) / 100.7608] / (2 x 0.01%) = 7.79
5.10%	100.6823	

The change in bond price due to its Duration is as follows:

Price change due to Duration **B2.13**

$$\text{Price change}_{\text{Duration}} = -\ \text{Modified Duration} \times \text{Price} \times \text{Yield change}$$

Where the yield change is 1 basis point (0.01%), this expression is called the 'Price Value of a Basis Point' ('PVBP') or 'Basis Value Point'.

Convexity

Since Duration is the tangent of the price / yield curve at the current yield, for very small yield changes it gives a reasonable approximation of the resulting price change. For larger yield changes, however, it will not account for the Convexity of the price / yield curve (i.e. the rate at which Duration – measured at a point on the curve – changes as yields change). Two bonds may have the same Duration, but one may have a more convex price/yield curve making the Duration estimate more inaccurate:

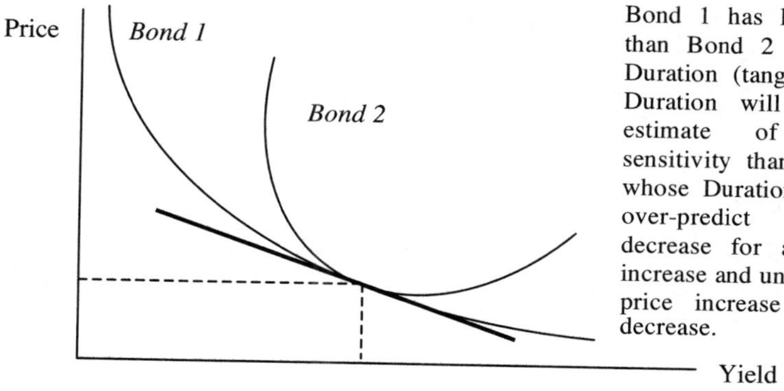

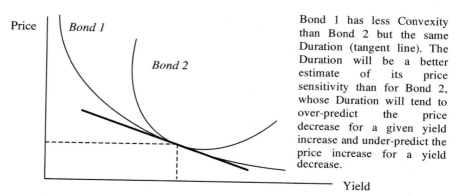

Bond 1 has less Convexity than Bond 2 but the same Duration (tangent line). The Duration will be a better estimate of its price sensitivity than for Bond 2, whose Duration will tend to over-predict the price decrease for a given yield increase and under-predict the price increase for a yield decrease.

Convexity will always be positive for option-free bonds, since the price will always increase at an increasing rate and decrease at a decreasing rate for a yield decrease and increase, respectively.

Like Duration, Convexity can be calculated by time-weighting the present value of the bond cash flows, with each period time-weighted again by t+1 and the total divided by $(1+r/m)^2$. The Convexity per period is then divided by m^2 for the Convexity per annum, where m is the number of coupon periods per year. Convexity can also be approximated using the following expression (Fabozzi and Mann (2001 p.291)):

Effective / Approximate Convexity **B2.14**

$$\text{Effective Convexity} = \frac{(P_u + P_d - 2P_0) / P_0}{(\Delta Y)^2}$$

where

- P_0 current bond price
- P_u, P_d bond prices for +/- change in yield
- ΔY change in yield

The change in bond price due to its Convexity can be shown as:

Price change due to Convexity **B2.15**

$$\text{Change in price}_{\text{Convexity}} = \frac{\text{Convexity}}{2} \times \text{Price} \times \text{Yield change}^2$$

The total expected price change for a given yield change can be obtained from **B2.13** and **B2.15**.

Example B2.15 Convexity – coupon and maturity effect

Using the 5% 2014 bond from **Examples B2.9** and **B2.13**, and multiplying the weighted present value percentages:

		5% coupon 2014			2% coupon 2014			5% coupon 2019		
Date	**Time period**	PV%	x time period	x (time period + 1)	PV%	x time period	x (time period + 1)	PV%	x time period	x (time period + 1)
24 Jun 2004	0									
07 Sep 2004	0.40761	2.46%	0.010	0.014	0.98%	0.004	0.006	2.46%	0.010	0.014
07 Mar 2005	1.40761	2.39%	0.042	0.081	0.96%	0.007	0.032	2.39%	0.042	0.081
07 Sep 2005	2.40761	2.34%	0.070	0.192	0.93%	0.011	0.077	2.34%	0.070	0.192
07 Mar 2006	3.40761	2.28%	0.097	0.342	0.91%	0.015	0.137	2.28%	0.097	0.342
07 Sep 2006	4.40761	2.22%	0.122	0.529	0.89%	0.020	0.212	2.22%	0.122	0.529
07 Mar 2007	5.40761	2.17%	0.146	0.750	0.87%	0.023	0.300	2.17%	0.146	0.750
07 Sep 2007	6.40761	2.11%	0.169	1.002	0.84%	0.027	0.401	2.11%	0.169	1.002
07 Mar 2008	7.40761	2.06%	0.191	1.283	0.82%	0.031	0.513	2.06%	0.191	1.283
07 Sep 2008	8.40761	2.01%	0.211	1.589	0.80%	0.034	0.635	2.01%	0.211	1.589
07 Mar 2009	9.40761	1.96%	0.230	1.918	0.78%	0.037	0.767	1.96%	0.230	1.918
07 Sep 2009	10.4076	1.91%	0.249	2.268	0.76%	0.040	0.907	1.91%	0.249	2.268
07 Mar 2010	11.4076	1.86%	0.266	2.636	0.75%	0.042	1.055	1.86%	0.266	2.636
07 Sep 2010	12.4076	1.82%	0.282	3.022	0.73%	0.045	1.209	1.82%	0.282	3.022
07 Mar 2011	13.4076	1.77%	0.297	3.422	0.71%	0.048	1.369	1.77%	0.297	3.422
07 Sep 2011	14.4076	1.73%	0.311	3.835	0.69%	0.050	1.534	1.73%	0.311	3.835
07 Mar 2012	15.4076	1.68%	0.325	4.258	0.67%	0.052	1.703	1.68%	0.325	4.258
07 Sep 2012	16.4076	1.64%	0.337	4.692	0.66%	0.054	1.877	1.64%	0.337	4.692
07 Mar 2013	17.4076	1.60%	0.349	5.133	0.64%	0.056	2.053	1.60%	0.349	5.133
07 Sep 2013	18.4076	1.56%	0.360	5.581	0.62%	0.058	2.232	1.56%	0.360	5.581
07 Mar 2014	19.4076	1.52%	0.370	6.034	0.61%	0.059	2.413	1.52%	0.370	6.034
07 Sep 2014	20.4076	60.91%	15.548	266.095	84.36%	8.614	368.565	1.49%	0.379	6.490
07 Mar 2015	21.4076							1.45%	0.388	6.949
07 Sep 2015	22.4076							1.41%	0.396	7.410
07 Mar 2016	23.4076							1.38%	0.403	7.871
07 Sep 2016	24.4076							1.34%	0.410	8.331
07 Mar 2017	25.4076							1.31%	0.416	8.790
07 Sep 2017	26.4076							1.28%	0.422	9.247
07 Mar 2018	27.4076							1.25%	0.427	9.700
07 Sep 2018	28.4076							1.21%	0.432	10.150
07 Mar 2019	29.4076							1.18%	0.436	10.595
07 Sep 2019	30.4076							47.61%	18.107	454.658
		100.00%		314.67	100.00%		388.00	100.00%		588.77

5% coupon 2014	Convexity = 314.67 / { (1 + 5.09/2)^2 / (2^2)	74.81
2% coupon 2014	Convexity = 388.00 / { (1 + 5.09/2)^2 / (2^2)	92.24
5% coupon 2019	Convexity = 588.77 / { (1 + 5.09/2)^2 / (2^2)	139.98

Alternative methods for estimating Convexity: 5% 2014 bond

Change in price / yield change for yield change

Yield Δ 0.01%	Dirty Price	Price Δ / Yield Δ	(PΔ/YΔ)Δ / Price
5.08%	100.8393		
5.09%	100.7608	-785.3587	74.81
5.10%	100.6823	-784.6049	

(see Tuckman (2002 p.102))

Effective Convexity (see **B2.14**)

Yield Δ 1%	Dirty Price
4.09%	109.0011
5.09%	100.7608
6.09%	93.2751

$$\frac{(93.2751 + 109.0011 - 2 \times 100.7608) / 100.7608}{(1\%)^2} = 74.89$$

Assuming yields increase by 1% to 6.09%, the 5% coupon 2014 bond's price would fall from 100.76 to 93.28, or 7.48. From **B2.13** and **B2.15** the expected price change is:

Price change = Price x Yield Change (Modified Duration + Convexity/2 x Yield change)
= 100.76 x 0.01 x (- 7.79 + 74.81 / 2 x 0.01)
= 1.008 x 7.416
= 7.48

B3 FORWARD PRICING

B3.1 FORWARD PRICES

'Cash and Carry' Arbitrage

In order to hold an asset for sale at a future date ('Forward Date'), an arbitrageur could purchase and take possession of the asset:

1. on the Forward Date at an unknown future market price (future 'Spot' price); or
2. on the Forward Date at today's 'Forward Price'; or
3. today at today's Spot price, holding the asset until the Forward Date.

A potential profit might arise if the arbitrageur sold the asset at the Forward Price and simultaneously purchased the asset with borrowings ('Cash and Carry' arbitrage). A fair Forward Price would be calculated to eliminate any such profit: the net cash flows from a combination of transaction 2 (in reverse) and 3 would have to be zero.

Time	*Transaction 2 (reverse)*		*Transaction 3*
0	- Sell the asset forward		- Borrow and purchase the asset today at current Spot rates
0-D			- Receive any income from asset
D	- Receive Forward Price	→	- Pay off the loan principal and interest with the Forward Price proceeds
D	- Deliver asset at Forward Date	←	- Deliver asset

Example B3.1 Forward Price - 'Cash and Carry'

An asset with a Spot price of £100m and an income yield of 3.0% (nominal rate – received on 5 February and on the Forward Date) would have a Forward Price in 91 days of approximately £100.5m, assuming borrowing costs were 5.0% p.a. This Forward Price is calculated so that, at each period, net cash flows are zero:

Spot Value Date	19 January
Income date	5 February
Forward / Delivery Date	19 April
Time to Delivery Date	91 days
Year	365 days
Spot Price	£100m
Financing cost (3 month LIBOR)	5.000%
Reinvestment rate	5.000%
Income yield (nominal)	3.000%

The reinvestment rate is assumed to be the same as the borrowing rate. In practice, this is unlikely to be the case due to the 'spread' between a bank's Bid and Offer rates. This assumption is relaxed later.

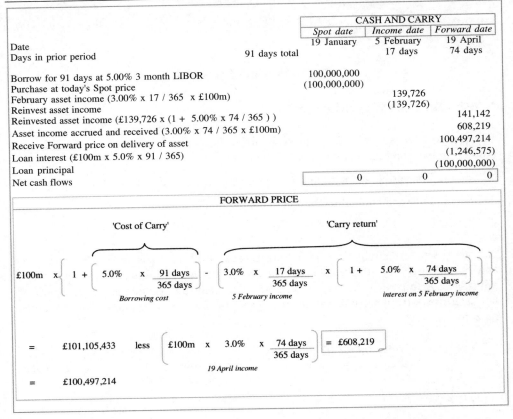

		CASH AND CARRY		
		Spot date	*Income date*	*Forward date*
Date		19 January	5 February	19 April
Days in prior period	91 days total		17 days	74 days
Borrow for 91 days at 5.00% 3 month LIBOR		100,000,000		
Purchase at today's Spot price		(100,000,000)		
February asset income (3.00% x 17 / 365 x £100m)			139,726	
Reinvest asset income			(139,726)	
Reinvested asset income (£139,726 x (1 + 5.00% x 74 / 365))				141,142
Asset income accrued and received (3.00% x 74 / 365 x £100m)				608,219
Receive Forward price on delivery of asset				100,497,214
Loan interest (£100m x 5.0% x 91 / 365)				(1,246,575)
Loan principal				(100,000,000)
Net cash flows		0	0	0

FORWARD PRICE

$$\text{£100m} \times \left\{ 1 + \underbrace{\left[5.0\% \times \frac{91 \text{ days}}{365 \text{ days}} \right]}_{\text{Borrowing cost}}^{\text{'Cost of Carry'}} - \overbrace{\underbrace{\left[3.0\% \times \frac{17 \text{ days}}{365 \text{ days}} \right]}_{\text{5 February income}} \times \underbrace{\left[1 + 5.0\% \times \frac{74 \text{ days}}{365 \text{ days}} \right]}_{\text{interest on 5 February income}}}^{\text{'Carry return'}} \right\}$$

$$= \text{£101,105,433} \quad \text{less} \quad \underbrace{\left[\text{£100m} \times 3.0\% \times \frac{74 \text{ days}}{365 \text{ days}} \right]}_{\text{19 April income}} = \text{£608,219}$$

$$= \text{£100,497,214}$$

The Forward Price is the current Spot price compounded forward by the net financing costs ('Net Cost of Carry') over the period to the Forward Delivery date. The general formula is as follows:

B3.1

Forward Price (discrete) – interim income

$$\text{Forward Price at Trade Date} = S_0 \times \left\{ \left(1 + r_b \times \frac{d_f}{\text{Year}} \right) - y_1 \left(1 + r_d \times \frac{d_c}{\text{Year}} \right) \right\}$$

$$\text{less} \quad S_0 \times y_2$$

where

S_0	Spot Price
r_b	Financing cost
y_1	Interim income yield for period = Y x $(d_f - d_c)$ / year
y_2	Final income yield for period = Y x d_c / year
Y	Income yield p.a. (nominal rate)(annual income ÷ S_0)
r_d	Reinvestment rate
d_f	Days from Spot Date to Forward Date
d_c	Days from interim income receipt to Forward Date

If the asset only pays income on the Forward Date (i.e. reinvestment can be ignored), the Forward Price formula reduces to:

Forward Price (discrete) – no interim income **B3.2**

$$\text{Forward Price} = S_0 \times \left(1 + (r_b - Y) \times \frac{d_f}{\text{Year}} \right)$$

where
S_0 Spot Price
r_b Financing cost
Y Income yield p.a. (nominal rate) ($Y \times d_f / \text{Year} = y_1 + y_2$ in **B3.1**)
d_f Days from Spot Date to Forward Date
Year 365 or 360, depending on the daycount basis

Where continuous compounding is assumed, the above Forward Price is as follows:

Forward Price (continuous) – no interim income **B3.3**

$$\text{Forward Price} = S_0 \times e^{(r_b^* - Y^*)(d_f / \text{Year})}$$

where r_b^*, Y^* continuously compounded equivalent rates of r_b and Y from **B3.2**.

Since the current Spot price already incorporates expected future increases in the asset value (since valuation is based on expected future cash flows), it is effectively the present value of the Forward Price plus any cash received on that date, discounted at the financing rate. For **Example B3.1**:

Forward price ('ex-div')	£100,497,214
Plus 'dividend' (£141,142 + £608,219)	£749,362
Cum-div' price	£101,246,575
Discount factor = 1 / (1 + 5.00% x 91 / 365)	0.987687728
Present Value	£100,000,000

The Forward Price will change as the time to delivery decreases, and will converge to the future Spot Price on the Forward / Delivery Date. There are several theories as to whether Forward Prices prior to delivery are below ('Normal Backwardation'), above ('Contango') or equal to ('Unbiased Expectations Hypothesis') the market's expectation of the future Spot Price (see Dubofsky and Miller (2003 p.98)).

The Financing Cost in **B3.1-B3.2** is the effective borrowing cost available in a 'Repurchase Agreement' ('Repo'), where an asset (usually a government security) is sold to a third party at the current Spot Price (receive principal) with an agreement to repurchase it on the forward Delivery Date at the Forward Price plus any accrued income (pay principal plus 'interest'). From the third party's point of view, the effective rate in this transaction ('Repo' rate) is the annualised return from paying the Spot price today and receiving the Forward Price and the compounded value of the asset income (future value) on the Delivery Date:

REPO RATE

$$\frac{£100{,}497{,}214 + \left(£141{,}142 + £608{,}219\right) - £100{,}000{,}000}{£100{,}000{,}000} \times \frac{365 \text{ days}}{91 \text{ days}}$$

$= 5.00\%$

If a party could actually borrow for less than this rate (i.e. the rate implied from Forward Prices), then it would make an arbitrage profit (ignoring transaction costs).

It was assumed in **Example B3.1** that the borrowing and lending / reinvesting rates were the same. If the reinvestment rate was 4.875% rather than 5.0%, for example, then the Forward Price would be marginally higher due to the lower Carry Return (£100,497,249).

'Reverse Cash and Carry' Arbitrage

A 'Reverse Cash and Carry' arbitrage could involve the following:

Time	*Transaction 2*	*Transaction 3 (reverse)*
0	- Buy the asset forward	- Sell the asset short under an asset lending agreement and deposit the cash proceeds.
0 - D		- Pay the asset lender any income on the asset.
0 - D		- Receive deposit interest
D	- Pay the Forward Price, and hand back the delivered asset to the asset lender to cover the short position	- Receive deposit balance

Example B3.2 Forward Pricing - 'Reverse Cash and Carry'

The cash flows, Forward Price and 'Reverse' Repo rate for **Example B3.1**, if a lower deposit rate (4.875%) is assumed, are as follows:

		REVERSE CASH AND CARRY		
		Spot date	*Income date*	*Forward date*
Date		19 January	5 February	19 April
Days in prior period	91 days total		17 days	74 days
Sell the asset short at today's Spot price		100,000,000		
Deposit for 91 days at 4.875% deposit rate		(100,000,000)		
Borrow for 74 days at 5.00% 3 month LIBOR			139,726	
Pay asset lender February asset income at 3.00% x (17 / 365) x £100m			(139,726)	
Repay asset income loan (£139,726 x (1 + 5.00% x 74 / 365))				(141,142)
Pay asset lender April asset income at 3.00% x (74 / 365) x £100m				(608,219)
Deposit interest (£100m x 4.875% x 91 / 365)				1,215,411
Deposit principal				100,000,000
Pay Forward price				(100,466,049)
Net cash flows		0	0	0

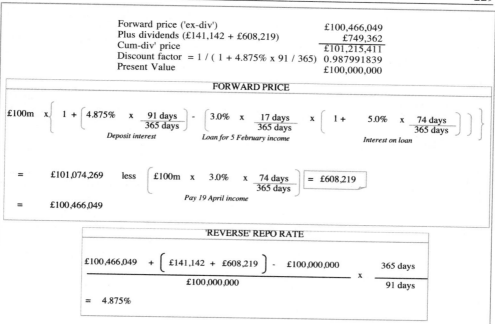

Forward price ('ex-div')		£100,466,049
Plus dividends (£141,142 + £608,219)		£749,362
Cum-div' price		£101,215,411
Discount factor	= 1 / (1 + 4.875% x 91 / 365)	0.987991839
Present Value		£100,000,000

FORWARD PRICE

$$\pounds 100\text{m} \times \left\{ 1 + \underbrace{\left(4.875\% \times \frac{91 \text{ days}}{365 \text{ days}} \right)}_{\text{Deposit interest}} - \underbrace{\left(3.0\% \times \frac{17 \text{ days}}{365 \text{ days}} \right)}_{\text{Loan for 5 February income}} \times \left(1 + \underbrace{5.0\% \times \frac{74 \text{ days}}{365 \text{ days}}}_{\text{Interest on loan}} \right) \right\}$$

$$= \pounds 101{,}074{,}269 \text{ less } \underbrace{\left(\pounds 100\text{m} \times 3.0\% \times \frac{74 \text{ days}}{365 \text{ days}} \right)}_{\text{Pay 19 April income}} = \pounds 608{,}219$$

$$= \pounds 100{,}466{,}049$$

'REVERSE' REPO RATE

$$\frac{\pounds 100{,}466{,}049 + \left(\pounds 141{,}142 + \pounds 608{,}219 \right) - \pounds 100{,}000{,}000}{\pounds 100{,}000{,}000} \times \frac{365 \text{ days}}{91 \text{ days}}$$

$$= 4.875\%$$

With a Repo rate of 5.0% and reverse Repo rate of 4.875%, the Forward Price now has a no-arbitrage range of £100,466,049 (lending) to £100,497,249 (borrowing).

B3.2

FORWARD INTEREST RATES

Identical cash flows (with the same risk) should have identical fair values (assuming investors have the same risk preference). Cash flows from a security or derivative can, therefore, be valued by considering replicating cash flows and eliminating any opportunity to make a risk free profit by exploiting price mismatching. A borrowing rate for the Forward Period starting on a Forward Date can be estimated by borrowing for the long period and lending or depositing the borrowed funds for the short period (the loan principal and interest paid at the end of the Forward Period implies an effective rate for the cash received at the start of the Forward Period). Similarly, lending long and borrowing short will give an implied lending rate for the Forward Period.

Example B3.3 Locking in a borrowing and deposit rate

			Deposit LIBID Bid	Borrow LIBOR Offer
Principal	£100m	Spot rates on 19 January		
Forward Period	91 days			
Days in year	365			
Spot Date	19 January			
Forward Date	19 April	3 month LIBOR 19 January	4.875%	5.000%
Maturity Date	19 July	6 month LIBOR 19 January	5.375%	5.500%

'LIBID' and 'LIBOR' are the London Interbank Bid and Offered Rates, respectively.

		Spot date	Forward date	Maturity date
Date		19 January	19 April	19 July
Days in prior period			91 days	91 days
Fixing a borrowing rate				
Borrow (£100m / (1 + 4.875% x 91 / 365))		98,799,184		
Deposit		(98,799,184)		
Deposit + 3 months interest at 4.875%			100,000,000	
Borrowings + 6 months interest at 5.50%				(101,508,718)
Forward rate (£101.51m / £100.00m x 365 / 91)	**6.051%**	0	100,000,000	(101,508,718)
Fixing a deposit rate				
Borrow (£100m / (1 + 5.00% x 91 / 365))		98,768,773		
Deposit		(98,768,773)		
Borrowings + 3 months interest at 5.00%			(100,000,000)	
Deposit + 6 months interest at 5.375%				101,415,911
Forward rate (£101.42m / £100.00m x 365 / 91)	**5.679%**	0	(100,000,000)	101,415,911
Difference due to bid-offer spread	0.372%			

$$\text{Difference} = \frac{365}{91} \times \left(\frac{1+5.500\% \times 182/365}{1+4.875\% \times 91/365} - \frac{1+5.375\% \times 182/365}{1+5.000\% \times 91/365} \right) = 0.372\%$$

$$\text{or} \quad \frac{365}{91} \times \left(\frac{1+5.500\% \times 182/365}{1+(5.000\% - \text{spread}) \times 91/365} - \frac{1+(5.500\% - \text{spread}) \times 182/365}{1+5.000\% \times 91/365} \right)$$

Summary of rates

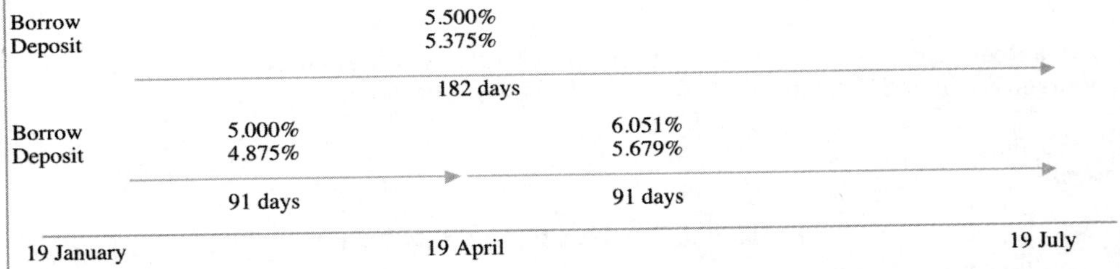

Assuming borrowing and lending is at the same rate, therefore, the implied Forward Rate is derived as follows:

- borrowing for 6 months at 19 January 6 month LIBOR (rate $S_{0.5}$) ;
- lending the funds for 3 months at 19 January 3 month LIBOR (rate $S_{0.25}$);
- rolling over the funds (compounding interest) for a further 3 months at the 19 April 3 month LIBOR (rate $F_{0.25/0.25}$)

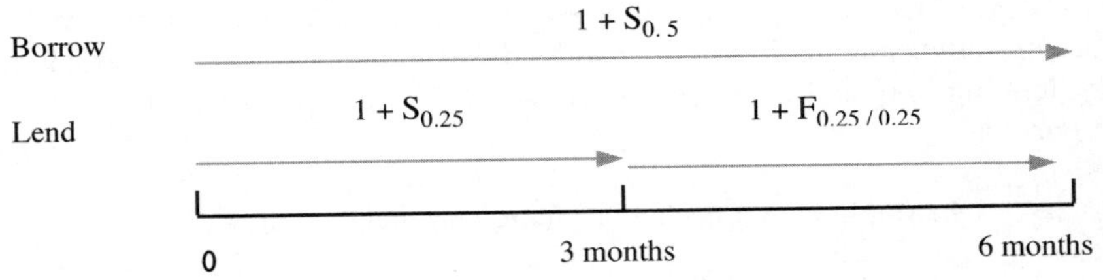

To ensure no net interest income is available: Implied Forward Rate, $F_{0.25/0.25}$

$$1 + S_{0.5} = (1 + S_{0.25})(1 + F_{0.25/0.25}) \qquad \therefore \; F_{0.25/0.25} = (1 + S_{0.5}) / (1 + S_{0.25}) - 1$$

Since the quoted Spot rates will be nominal (simple) annual rates, the implied Forward Rate in **Example B3.3** needs to be stated as an annual rate:

B3.4

Forward / Forward Rate

$$\text{Forward Rate} = \left(\frac{1 + r_L \times \dfrac{n_L}{\text{Year}}}{1 + r_S \times \dfrac{n_S}{\text{Year}}} - 1 \right) \times \frac{\text{Year}}{n_L - n_S}$$

$$= \frac{r_L \times n_L - r_S \times n_S}{n_L - n_S} \times \frac{1}{1 + r_S \times \dfrac{n_S}{\text{Year}}}$$

where r_L Spot Rate (Nominal) for longer period (with n_L actual days)
r_S Spot Rate (Nominal) for shorter period (with n_S actual days)
Year 365 or 360, depending on the daycount basis

B3.3

FORWARD INTEREST RATES AND FRAS

The seller of a Forward Rate Agreement ('FRA') is effectively agreeing to pay a floating rating and to receive a fixed FRA rate on a notional principal. To hedge the floating rate obligation, it could deposit an equivalent sum at the settlement date to earn the (unknown) floating rate being paid out, financed with borrowings at a locked-in cost (i.e. current Spot rates). On maturity, it will receive the principal plus the FRA rate and pay off the borrowings, netting to a zero cash flow.

Example B3.4 Calculating the FRA rate and Settlement Sum

Using **Example B3.3**, an FRA seller would:

1. borrow the present value of the principal (discounted back from the 19 April settlement date at the deposit rate) on 19 January for 6 months, and immediately invest the borrowed funds for 3 months;
2. reinvest the deposit on the 19 April settlement date at the then 3 month floating rate
3. use the deposit maturing on 19 July to pay off the borrowings and to pay the floating rate to the buyer, in exchange for the FRA contract rate.

The seller will wish to ensure that the cash flows at each date net off to zero. 3 and 6 month LIBOR as at 19 January are as in **Example B3.3**; the 3 month lending and borrowing rates at 19 April are unknown (referred to as Ld and Lb, respectively).

☞ The FRA Contract Rate

	Spot	Settlement	Maturity
Date	*19 January*	*19 April*	*19 July*
Days in period		*91 days*	*91 days*
Borrow and Deposit	$\frac{£100m}{(1 + 4.875\% \times 91/365)}$		
Deposit maturity		£100m	
Deposit		(£100m)	
Deposit maturity			£100m x (1 + (Ld x 91/365))
Pay LIBOR to counterparty			£100m x (Lb x 91 / 365)
Receive FRA from counterparty			£100m x (FRA% x 91 / 365)
Net cash flow before financing costs	£0	£0	£100m x (1 + (FRA% + spread) x 91 / 365)
			= *
Repay borrowings			$\frac{£100m \times (1 + 5.500\% \times 182/365)}{(1 + 4.875\% \times 91/365)}$

*for zero profit / loss, hence (after re-arranging):

$$FRA\% = \left(\frac{1+5.500\% \times 182/365}{1+(5.000\% - spread) \times 91/365} - 1 \right) \times 365 / 91 \quad \text{less: bid-offer spread}$$

Forward (ignoring spread)

$$= \left(\frac{1+5.500\% \times 182/365}{1+5.000\% \times 91/365} - 1 \right) \times 365 / 91 = \boxed{\mathbf{5.926\%}}$$

(see **B3.4**)

Note: 5.926% + 0.125% spread = 6.051% per **Example B3.3**, or:

		Spot date	*Settlement date*	*Maturity date*
Date		19 January	19 April	19 July
Days in period		0 days	91 days	91 days
Replicating the forward rate				
Borrow [1]		£98,768,773		
Invest		(£98,768,773)		
Investment maturity				£101,477,473
Repayment borrowings			(£100,000,000)	
Forward rate (£101,477,473 / £100.0m) x 365 / 91)	**5.926%**	£0	(£100,000,000)	£101,477,473

Notes

1. PV of principal - from settlement date (£100.0m / (1+5.000% x 91/365)) - borrowed at 5.000% for 91 days
   =
   PV of principal plus forward interest - from maturity date (£100.0m x (1+5.926% x 91/365) / (1+5.500% x 182/365)) - invested at 5.500% for 182 days

☞ The FRA Settlement Amount

The settlement sum will be the bank's net gain or loss on the financing side:

Deposit maturity	£100m x (1 + Lb x 91/365)
Repay borrowings £100m x (1 + FRA% x 91 / 365) =	£100m x $\left(\frac{1 + 5.500\% \times 182/365}{1 + 5.000\% \times 91/365} \right)$
Profit	£100m x (FRA - Lb) x 91/365

From the FRA buyer's point of view, the Settlement Amount, expressed in present value terms at the Settlement date (discounting back from the Maturity date at the actual LIBOR) becomes:

$$\text{Settlement Amount (at settlement date)} = \frac{\text{Principal} \times (\text{Lb} - \text{FRA}) \times \frac{\text{Forward Period}}{\text{Year}}}{1 + \text{Lb} \times \frac{\text{Forward Period}}{\text{Year}}}$$

If 3 month LIBOR on 19 April was 6.5%, then the settlement sum would arise due to the following cash flows (see **Example 4.1** in Chapter 4):

	Spot date	*Settlement date*	*Maturity date*
Date	19 January	19 April	19 July
Days in period	0 days	91 days	91 days
Replicating all cash flows (notional)			
Borrow	98,768,773		
Deposit	(98,768,773)		
Depost maturity		100,000,000	
Deposit		(100,000,000)	
Deposit + 3 months interest at 6.50%			101,620,548
Repay borrowings + 6 months interest at 5.50%			(101,477,473)
Net cash flows before exchange of interest	0	0	143,075
Pay LIBOR to FRA buyer			(1,620,548)
Receive FRA rate from FRA buyer (£100m x (1+5.926% x 91/365)			1,477,473
Net replicating cash flows (notional)	(0)	0	(0)
Settlement sum = £143,075 / (1+6.500% x 91/365)			**140,794**

B3.4

FORWARD RATES AND SPOT RATES

Forward Rates for each interest period until maturity can be implied from the relevant Spot Rates from today (t_o) until the end of each interest period (t_1, t_2, .. t_n). The Forward Rate for the first period ($t_0 - t_1$) is the Spot Rate for that period (the shorter period in **B3.4**); the Forward Rate for the second period ($t_1 - t_2$) can be implied from the Spot Rate for $t_0 - t_1$ and the Spot rate for $t_0 - t_2$ (the longer period in **B3.4**).

Risk-free and fairly priced (sufficiently liquid, as reflected in a narrow Bid-Offer spread) Spot Rates are not directly observable in the market for all maturities. One method for estimating them ('Bootstrapping') is to start with the most reliable short dated Spot Rate (the yield on a 6 month Treasury Bill, for example) and determine the Spot Rate for each subsequent period, based on the Yield to Maturity for Government bonds with corresponding maturities (if the bonds are priced at par in the market, then the Coupon rates would equal the bond's 'Par Yield').

Example B3.5 illustrates the use of Bootstrapping to estimate future Spot Rates (these are Zero Coupon Rates, since no interim cash flows are received and the effective yield does not depend on reinvestment of such income). These rates were used to price the bond in Appendix B2 (**Example B2.11**).

Example B3.5 Par Yields, Spot / Zero Coupon Rates, and Forward Rates

Assume a 6 month Treasury Bill and 1 year Government Bond (5.1481% semi-annual coupon rate) have just been issued, yielding 5.000% (Zero Coupon or Spot Rate) and 5.1481% (Par Yield) nominal, respectively. As discussed in **Example B2.11** in Appendix B2, a coupon paying bond can be considered as a package of Zero Coupon bonds.

The fair price of the bond, discounted at its Yield to Maturity, over the two equal length semi-annual time periods, is £100 par.

Equal length periods		1st 6 months	2nd 6 months
Bond price - Yield to Maturity			
Coupon at	5.1481%	2.5740	2.5740
Face value			100.0000
Cash flows		2.5740	102.5740
Rates		5.1481%	5.1481%
Discount Factors		*0.974905*	*0.950441*
		=1 / [(1 + 5.1481% / 2)^1]	*=1 / [(1 + 5.1481% / 2)^2]*
PRICE	100.0000	2.5095	97.4905

The fair price of the bond must also be the aggregate fair value of two Zero Coupon bonds. The first bond has a fair price of £2.5113 (the first coupon discounted at the known 5.000% 6 month Spot Rate); hence the second has a price of £97.4887, being the second coupon plus redemption amount, discounted at the implied 5.15% 12 month Spot Rate.

Equal length periods		1st 6 months	2nd 6 months
Bond price - Zero Coupon Rates			
Coupon		2.5740	2.5740
Face value			100.0000
Cash flows		2.5740	102.5740
Rates		5.0000%	5.1500%
Discount Factors		*0.975610*	*0.950423*
		=1 / [(1 + 5.0000% / 2)^1]	*=1 / [(1 + 5.1500% / 2)^2]*
PRICE	100.0000	2.5113	97.4887

Now assume the latest 1½ year Government Bond has also just been issued, paying a semi-annual coupon of 5.25% and priced at par. Again, the fair price can also be shown as the bond cash flows discounted at the appropriate Spot Rates (5.00% for 6 months and 5.15% for 1 year). The implied 1½ year spot rate is 5.2540%:

Price / Cash Flows per £1

Maturity	Coupon p.a.	Price	Time period 0.5	1.0	1.5
1.5	5.2500%	1.000000	0.052500 / 2	0.052500 / 2	1 + 0.052500 / 2
			$\frac{1}{(1 + 5.0000\% / 2)^1}$	$\frac{1}{(1 + 5.1500\% / 2)^2}$	$\frac{1}{(\mathbf{1 + 5.2540\% / 2})^3}$
		DF t	= *0.975610*	= *0.950423*	= *0.925156*

Spot and Forward Rates are related, as shown in **B3.4**. The Forward Rate for each period ensures that the same return is obtained from investing £1 at time 0 at the relevant Spot Rate as investing the £1 and 'rolling over' the investment each period, to earn the Forward Rate:

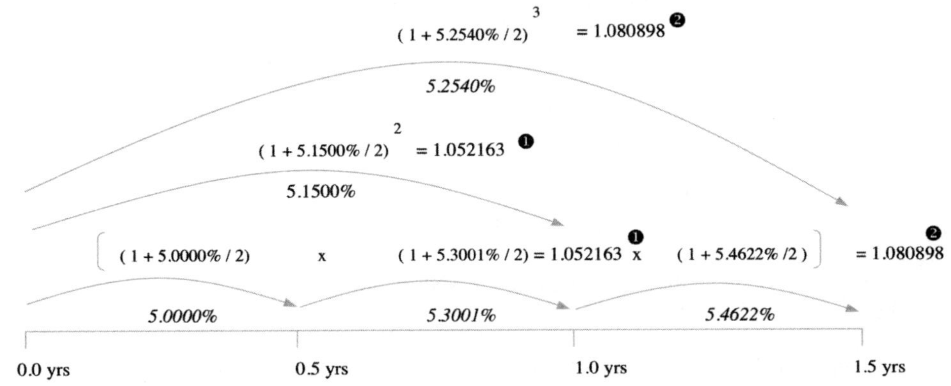

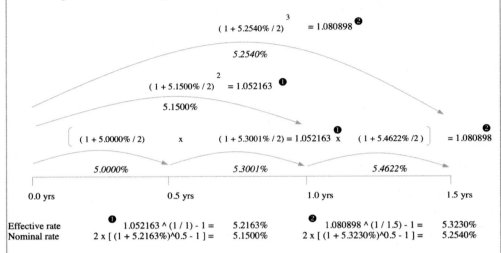

	❶		❷	
Effective rate	1.052163 ^ (1 / 1) - 1 =	5.2163%	1.080898 ^ (1 / 1.5) - 1 =	5.3230%
Nominal rate	2 x [(1 + 5.2163%)^0.5 - 1] =	5.1500%	2 x [(1 + 5.3230%)^0.5 - 1] =	5.2540%

Hence, there is a relationship between observed Par Yields and Spot Discount Factors, Spot / Zero Coupon Rates and Forward Rates:

Par Yields → Spot / Zero Coupon Discount Factors → Spot / Zero Coupon Rates
→ Forward Rates

☞ Spot / Zero Discount Factors can be calculated from Par Yields:

The Zero Coupon Discount Factor (ZDF) for the year 1.5 Spot / Zero Coupon Rate (5.2540%) can be calculated by re-arranging the 1.5 year Par bond Price / Cash Flows, shown above:

B3.5

$$ZDF_t = \frac{\underset{\textit{Par Price}}{1.0000} - \frac{Y_P}{m} \times \sum_{0}^{t-1} ZDF}{1 + \frac{Y_P}{m}}$$

m *Equal length* coupon periods p.a.
t Time period (=year x m)
Y_P Yield on the Par bond

$$0.925156 = \frac{\underset{\textit{Price}}{1} - \frac{5.2500\%}{2} \times (0.975610 + 0.950423)}{1 + \frac{5.2500\%}{2}}$$

This calculation is possible since the prior period Zero Coupon Discount Factor was first calculated using the 1.0 year Par bond; similarly Discount Factors for future period can be 'Bootstrapped' from prior year Discount Factors, based on Par Yields.

☞ Spot / Zero Discount Rates can be calculated from their Discount Factors:

The Spot Rate for the time 0 → 1.5 Spot Discount Factor (0.925156) can be calculated as follows (see **B3.5** for symbols):

$$Zt = \left(\left(\frac{1}{ZDF_t} \right)^{1/t} - 1 \right) \times m$$

B3.6

$$5.2540\% = \left(\left(\frac{1}{0.925156} \right)^{1/3} - 1 \right) \times 2$$

☞ Forward Rates can be calculated from Spot / Zero Coupon Rates or their Discount Factors (see **B3.5** for symbols):

The Forward Rate for the time 0 → 1.5 can be calculated as follows:

B3.7

$$F_{t-1 \rightarrow t} = \left\{ \frac{\left(1 + \frac{Z_t}{m}\right)^t}{\left(1 + \frac{Z_{t-1}}{m}\right)^{t-1}} - 1 \right\} \times m$$

$$5.4622\% = \left\{ \frac{\left(1 + \frac{5.2540\%}{2}\right)^3}{\left(1 + \frac{5.1500\%}{2}\right)^2} - 1 \right\} \times 2$$

And from this:

$$F_{t-1 \rightarrow t} = \left(\frac{ZDF_{t-1}}{ZDF_t} - 1 \right) \times m$$

$$5.4622\% = \left(\frac{0.950423}{0.925156} - 1 \right) \times 2$$

Using other Par bonds for years 2 – 5 produces the following set of Forward Rates:

Time Period	Year	Zero T-Bill	Par Bond Price	Par yield (nominal)	Coupon % per period	Cumulative ZDF	Zero Rate	Forward Rate
1	0.5	5.000%				0.975610	5.0000%	5.0000%
2	1.0		1.00	5.148%	2.574%	1.926033	5.1500%	5.3001%
3	1.5		1.00	5.250%	2.625%	2.851189	5.2540%	5.4622%
4	2.0		1.00	5.320%	2.660%	3.751402	5.3259%	5.5417%
5	2.5		1.00	5.380%	2.690%	4.626937	5.3881%	5.6371%
6	3.0		1.00	5.430%	2.715%	5.478204	5.4403%	5.7018%
7	3.5		1.00	5.470%	2.735%	6.305742	5.4824%	5.7348%
8	4.0		1.00	5.505%	2.753%	7.110038	5.5195%	5.7794%
9	4.5		1.00	5.535%	2.768%	7.891637	5.5515%	5.8079%
10	5.0		1.00	5.560%	2.780%	8.651135	5.5783%	5.8198%

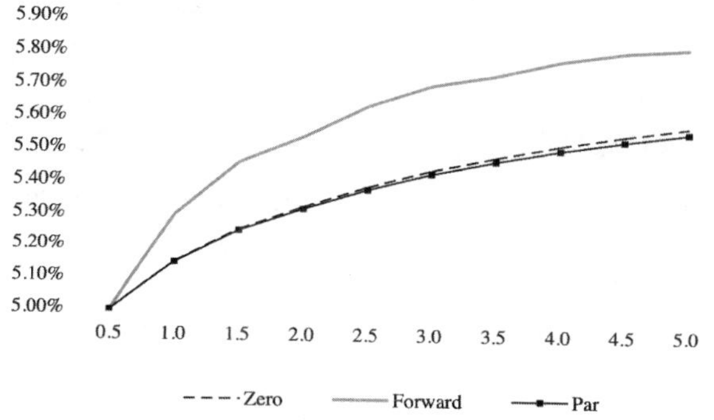

Forward Rates can also be implied from observable market prices for FRAs, Interest Rate Futures, Swaps and other instruments, and any gaps can be filled in using interpolation techniques, before the yield curve is 'smoothed' (see Flavell (2002 p.58)).

B3.5

FORWARD BOND PRICES

Today's (Trade date) fair price of a bond to be purchased at a Forward Delivery Date should ensure that no arbitrage profit is available from replicating the cash flows by borrowing and lending (Cash and Carry) at the available market Repo rates.

Example B3.6 Forward Bond Pricing and Bond Futures Prices

Forward and market information		
Trade date	Monday	19 Jan 2004
Forward delivery date	Wednesday	30 June 2004
Forward period	0.45 months	163 days
Days in year		365
6 month Repo		4.0133%
Bond information		
Face value	£100	
Coupon rate	8.00%	
Yield to maturity at trade date	4.6986%	
No. of interest payments each year	2	
Future coupons after 2nd coupon	18	
Maturity date	9.510 yrs	27 Sep 2013

This Bond is the 'CTD' Bond for the Bond Futures **Examples 4.7 – 4.11** in Chapter 4.

Coupon days and accrued interest

		Coupon days
Last coupon date	27 Sep 2003	0
Trade date	19 Jan 2004	114
1st coupon date	27 March 2004	68
1st coupon period	27 Sep 2003 to 27 Mar 2004	182
Daily coupon accrual = £100 x (8.00% / 2) / 182	→ £0.0220	
Forward date	30 June 2004	95
2nd coupon date	27 Sep 2004	89
2nd coupon period	27 March 2004 to 27 Sep 2004	184
Daily coupon accrual = £100 x (8.00% / 2) / 184	→ £0.0217	
Accrued interest at trade date	114 days x £0.0220 = £2.51	
Accrued interest at forward date	95 days x £0.0217 = £2.07	

The Forward Price will be based on the current dirty bond price and adjusted over the period to delivery for the Net Cost of Carry:

$$\underset{\substack{\textit{Dirty price}\\ \textit{19 Jan 04}}}{127.9511} \times \left\{ \left(1 + \underset{\textit{Repo rate}}{4.0133\%} \times \frac{163 \text{ days}}{365 \text{ days}} \right) - \underset{\substack{\textit{Yield}\\ \textit{(coup / price)}}}{3.13\%} \left(1 + 4.0133\% \times \frac{95 \text{ days}}{365 \text{ days}} \right) \right\}$$

Dirty price 30 Jun 04 = £126.2026

Accrued Interest £2.0652

Forward Price £124.1374

This is the Forward Price equation **4.11** from Chapter 4, also shown in **Example 4.8**.

As is shown on the following page, the yield to maturity implied from the forward bond price is not the current yield (4.6986%) but 4.7423% (Forward Bond Yield). Using Microsoft Excel$_{TM}$:

PRICE (19 January 2004 , 27 September 2013 , 8.00% coupon, 4.70% yield , £100 , 2 coupons p.a., 1)		125.4456
PRICE (27 September 2003 , 27 March 2004 , 19 January 2004 , 8.0% coupon, £100 , 2 coupons p.a., 1)		2.5055
Bond (Dirty) Price on Trade Date (Spot Price on 19 January 2004)		**127.9511**
Financing cost	£127.9511 x 4.0133% x 163 / 365	2.2932
less: coupons plus interest	£4.00 x (1 + 4.0133% x 95 / 365)	-4.0418
Dirty Forward Bond Price		126.2026
less: accrued interest in price	£0.0217 daily coupon (= £100 x (8.00% / 2) / 184) x 95 days	-2.0652
Bond (Clean) Forward Price on Delivery Date (Forward Price on 30 June 2004)		**124.1374**
YIELD (30 June 2004 , 27 September 2013 , 8.0% coupon, £124.1374 , £100 , 2 coupons p.a., 1)		4.7423%

Example B3.6 (cont.) – *Fair Price of Bond on 19 Jan and 30 June – 4.6986% Yield (no change)*

If the yield on 19 January (4.6986%) does not change, the bond's fair price on 30 June is calculated as follows:

$$4.00 \times \left\{ \frac{1}{0.0235} \times \left(1 - \frac{1}{(1+0.0235)^{\wedge}18} \right) \right\} + \frac{100}{(1+0.0235)^{\wedge}18}$$

= 124.0042 + 4.00 coupon

128.0042

$$\frac{129.0661}{(1+0.0235)^{\wedge}(68/182)} \qquad \frac{128.0042}{(1+0.0235)^{\wedge}(184/184)} \qquad \frac{128.0042}{(1+0.0235)^{\wedge}(89/184)}$$

= 125.0661 + 4.00 coupon

	19 Jan 04 Trade Date	27 Mar 04 1st coupon	30 Jun 04 Forward Date	27 Sep 04 2nd coupon date
Pd =	127.9511	129.0661	126.5745	128.0042
Acc =	(2.5055)	0.0000	(2.0652)	0.0000
Pc =	125.4456	129.0661	124.5093 ❶	128.0042

19 Jan 04 Trade Date — 68 days — 27 Mar 04 1st coupon — 95 days — 30 Jun 04 Forward Date — 89 days — 27 Sep 04 2nd coupon date — + 18 coupons — 27 Sep 13 Maturity

Pd = Dirty price
Acc = Accrued interest
Pc = Clean price

❶ See ❶ **Example 4.10** in Chapter 4.

Forward Price on 19 Jan

If an arbitrager was able to receive the above Forward Price and accrued interest (126.5745) on 30 June, a small profit (0.3720) could be made by borrowing and lending at the Repo rate on the 19 Jan trade date (4.0133%). The Forward Price will be adjusted to ensure such a profit is not possible, as shown to the right. Based on the clean correct Forward Price (126.5745 – 0.372 profit – 2.0652 accrued interest = 124.1374), the yield to maturity as at 30 June is 4.7423%.

	Trade date	1st coupon	Delivery
Date	*19 Jan 04*	*27 Mar 04*	*30 Jun 04*
Days from Trade Date		*68 days*	*163 days*
Days in prior period		*68 days*	*95 days*
Borrow 127.9511 at 4.0133% for 163 days	127.9511		
Purchase Bond	(127.9511)		
Receive 1st coupon		4.0000	
Reinvest coupon at 4.0133% for 95 days		(4.0000)	
Coupon deposit (4.00 x (1 + 4.0133% x 95 / 365 days)			4.0418
Sell bond			126.5745
Loan 127.9511 + 163 days interest at 4.0133%			(130.2444)
Net Cash Flows	0.0000	0.0000	0.3720

Required forward price of bond for nil profit	126.5745 - 0.3720 =	126.2026
less: accrued interest on bond		(2.0652)
Clean forward price		**124.1374**
Forward Yield to Maturity (based on clean Forward Price)		*4.7423%*

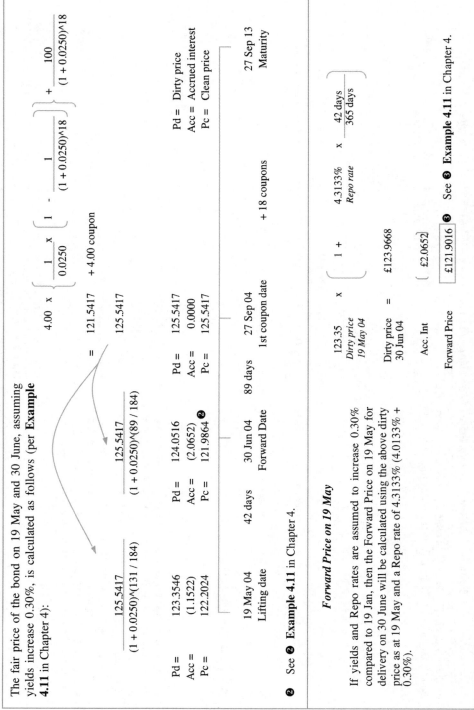

Example B3.6 (cont.) – *Fair Price of Bond on 19 May and 30 June – 4.9986% Yield (increase 0.30% compared to 19 Jan)*

The fair price of the bond on 19 May and 30 June, assuming yields increase 0.30%, is calculated as follows (per **Example 4.11** in Chapter 4):

$$4.00 \times \left\{ \frac{1}{0.0250} \times \left[1 - \frac{1}{(1+0.0250)^{\wedge}18} \right] \right\} + \frac{100}{(1+0.0250)^{\wedge}18}$$

$$= 121.5417 \quad + 4.00 \text{ coupon}$$

$$125.5417$$

$$\frac{125.5417}{(1+0.0250)^{\wedge}(131/184)} \qquad \frac{125.5417}{(1+0.0250)^{\wedge}(89/184)}$$

	19 May 04		30 Jun 04		27 Sep 04		27 Sep 13
Pd =	123.3546	Pd =	124.0516	Pd =	125.5417		
Acc =	(1.1522)	Acc =	(2.0652)	Acc =	0.0000		
Pc =	122.2024	Pc =	121.9864 ❷	Pc =	125.5417		
	19 May 04 Lifting date	42 days	30 Jun 04 Forward Date	89 days	27 Sep 04 1st coupon date	+ 18 coupons	27 Sep 13 Maturity

Pd = Dirty price
Acc = Accrued interest
Pc = Clean price

❷ See ❷ **Example 4.11** in Chapter 4.

Forward Price on 19 May

If yields and Repo rates are assumed to increase 0.30% compared to 19 Jan, then the Forward Price on 19 May for delivery on 30 June will be calculated using the above dirty price as at 19 May and a Repo rate of 4.3133% (4.0133% + 0.30%).

$$\underset{\textit{Dirty price 19 May 04}}{123.35} \times \left(1 + \underset{\textit{Repo rate}}{4.3133\%} \times \frac{42 \text{ days}}{365 \text{ days}} \right)$$

Dirty price 30 Jun 04	=	£123.9668
Acc. Int		(£2.0652)
Forward Price		£121.9016 ❸

❸ See ❸ **Example 4.11** in Chapter 4.

Example B3.6 (cont.) *Forward Price reconciliation*

The Forward Price for the above bond (the CTD bond from **Example 4.10** and **4.11** in Chapter 4) can be reconciled from 19 Jan to 19 May (with yields and rates increasing 0.30%) as follows:

FORWARD & THEORETICAL FUTURES PRICES

Date	Trade Date	Coupon date	Hedge lifted	Delivery Date
Date	19 Jan	27 Mar	19 May	30 Jun
Days in prior period		68 days	53 days	42 days
Days in coupon period	182 days	0 days	184 days	184 days
Days to delivery	163 days	95 days	42 days	

FORWARD PRICES - USING CTD BOND

Fair prices at 19 Jan 2004

		Trade Date	Coupon date	Hedge lifted	Delivery Date
Dirty Bond Price		127.9511			127.9511
Carry Cost	= 127.9511 x 4.0133% x 163 / 365				2.2932
Carry Return	= 4.00 x (1 + 4.0133% x 95 / 365)		4.000		less 4.0418
Dirty Forward Price					*126.2026*
less: accrued interest					-2.0652
Forward price					***124.1374***

Fair prices at 19 May 2004

		Trade Date	Coupon date	Hedge lifted	Delivery Date
Dirty Bond Price				123.3546	123.3546
Carry Cost	= 123.3546 x 4.3133% x 42 / 365				0.6122
Carry Return	n/a				0.0000
Dirty Forward Price					*123.9668*
less: accrued interest					-2.0652
Forward price					***121.9016***

Reconciliation of Bond Prices

	Trade Date	Coupon date	Hedge lifted
Dirty Price on 19 May at 4.9986% yield			123.3546
Dirty Price on 19 May at 4.6986% yield			125.9054
PV at 27 March = 123.3546 x 1 / [1 + (4.6986% / 2)] ^ (53 / 184)]		125.0661	
Add Coupon received		4.0000	
Dirty Price on 27 March		129.0661	
PV at 19 January 2004 = 129.0661 x 1 / [1 + (4.6986% / 2)] ^ (68 / 182)]	127.9511		

THEORETICAL FUTURES PRICES

	Fair prices at 19 Jan 2004	*Fair prices at 19 May 2004*
Forward Price on 30 June 2004	124.1374	121.9016
Price Factor	1.1410760	1.1410760
Theoretical Futures Price	108.7897	106.8304
Net Basis	0.1197	1.1404
Actual Futures Price	108.6700	105.6900

Example B3.6 (cont.) *Theoretical Futures Price reconciliation*

The change in the Theoretical Futures price (from 108.7897 on 19 Jan to 106.8304 on 19 May, assuming the CTD Bond Yield and Repo Rate increase 0.30%), multiplied by the CTD Bond Price Factor (1.141076) represents the net cash flows arising on a replicating cash and carry transaction (margin cash flows are ignored):

		Loan		CTD Bond		Futures	Cash balance
		Principal	*Interest*	*Price*	*Coupon*		
19 Jan	Sell futures at 108.7897					-	
	Borrow and buy bond	127.9511		(127.9511)			0.0000
27 Mar	Receive coupon on bond				4.0000		4.0000
19 May	Buy futures at 106.8304					-	4.0000
	Sell bond			123.3546			127.3546
30 Jun	Interest on coupon part of cash (= 4.0000 x 4.0133% x 95 / 365)				0.0418		127.3964
	Interest on bond proceeds (= 123.3546 x 4.3133% x 42 / 365)			0.6122			128.0086
	Receive Invoice Amount (= 108.7897 x 1.1410760 + 2.0652 accrued interest), deliver bond					126.2026	254.2112
	Pay Invoice Amount (= 106.8304 x 1.1410760 + 2.0652 accrued interest), receive bond					(123.9668)	130.2444
	Pay off loan (interest = 127.9511 x 4.0133% x 163 / 365)	(127.9511)	(2.2932)				0.0000
		0.0000	(2.2932)	(3.9843)	4.0418	2.2357	

Cost of carry	Loan	19 Jan to 30 June	(2.2932)
Carry return	Coupon	27 Mar to 30 June	4.0418
Sale & purchase of bond			(3.9843)
			(2.2357)

Net cash flows	£2.2357 ÷ 1.1410760 =	£1.9593
Futures price change	108.7897 – 106.8304 =	£1.9593

B4 BASIC OPTION PRICING

OVERVIEW OF PRICING APPROACH

If an option on a stock can be exercised only at some future expiry date (European option), then today's fair value for the option premium (option price) would be the present value of the difference between the stock price expected at the exercise date and the exercise price (Intrinsic Value), subject to a profit arising (the option would not be exercised if a loss arose). An option pricing model needs to predict a range of likely stock prices at the exercise date and their respective probabilities, but ignore out-of-the money stock prices.

Given a current stock price and an estimate of its volatility, if probabilities (p_i) can be assigned to a range of 'n' possible final stock prices (S_i), an estimate of the expected final stock price ($E(S_i)$) can be made (the final stock prices weighted by their respective probabilities, where the sum of all probabilities, p_1 to p_n, equals 1.0). If only those prices where the option is in-the-money are considered, then the sum of their probability weighted values will be the estimate of the in-the-money final stock price and hence the final payoff can be determined (this would be discounted back to a present value):

Ignored since out-of-the money

$$E(S_i) \text{ or } \mu = \cancel{p_1S_1 + p_2S_2} + \ldots + p_{n-1}S_{n-1} + p_nS_n = \sum_{i=1}^{n} S_i \times p(S_i)$$

The Binomial option pricing model ('BM') follows this approach, based on an incremental stock price movement over 'N' discrete time periods from the valuation date to the option expiry date, 'T' years away. Over each period (of length T / N years), the stock price is assumed to increase or decrease by fixed amounts, so that, by the expiry date, there will be a range of N + 1 prices.

By contrast, the Black-Scholes option pricing model ('BSM') assumes stock prices change continuously in accordance with some probability distribution. This model is equivalent to the BM for a European option with an infinitely large number of time steps (i.e. $N \rightarrow \infty$). Depending on the number of time steps and their length, the European option price calculated by the BM will converge to the BSM value.

The BSM is concerned with estimating the price on expiry (European options) and was not intended to be used to value an American option, where early exercise is possible. The BM, which explicitly models interim stock prices, handles both types with ease.

BINOMIAL MODEL

Replicating Portfolios and Risk-Neutral Probabilities: an Overview

If it is assumed that the current price of a stock (S_0) can either increase (true probability = p) by a factor 'u' or decrease (true probability = 1 – p) by a factor 'd', then, at the end of one period, when an option on that stock can be exercised, the option payoff will be its Intrinsic Value: the stock price less exercise price for a Call option, and vice versa for a Put option (zero if a loss arises).

This option payoff can be replicated by purchasing a number of units of the same underlying stock, part financed with debt, which exactly replicates the expected cash flows on the option at the end of the period. By taking the appropriate position in the stock (depending on whether the option is a Call or Put), the portfolio cash flows will be equal and opposite to the option cash flows, thereby eliminating any risk. The fair value of the option should, therefore, reflect the fact that only a risk free rate of return will be possible: the fair value at time 0 will equal the fair value at time 1 (the Intrinsic Value, based on the expected stock price and the certain exercise price), discounted at the risk free rate.

The expected stock price at time 1 will equal the true probability-weighted prices in the up and down states ($E(S_1) = S_0(1+u)(p) + S_0(1-d)(1-p)$), which, when discounted at the risk-adjusted rate of return (i.e. the cost of equity), equals the current stock price ($S_0 = E(S_1) \div (1 + \text{risk free rate} + \text{risk premium})$). In order to value the option payoff using the risk-free rate, an adjustment must be made to the true probabilities to ensure the up and down states are 'certainty equivalents'. The adjusted, 'risk-neutral' probabilities are calculated so that the resulting expected stock price at time 1 equals the risk-neutral true probability-weighted prices in the up and down states ($E^*(S_1) = S_0(1+u)(p^*) + S_0(1-d)(1-p^*)$), which, when discounted at the risk-free rate, also equals the current stock price ($S_0 = E^*(S_1) \div (1 + \text{risk free rate})$). The resulting probability weighted option value can then be discounted back using the risk free rate to give the same result as using the replicating portfolio approach.

Replicating Portfolios: One Period (No Dividends)

The cash flows arising from the purchase of one Call option on a stock *that pays no dividend* (at a cost of C_0 option premium) can be replicated by purchasing δ units of that stock (at a cost of δ x S_0, the current share price), part financed with debt (borrowing 'm' x S_0 for one year, paying a risk free rate of interest 'r', and repaying the debt from the sale of the stock holding). If this portfolio has an identical payoff to the Call option, then both must have the same price today (identical risk and return). If it is assumed that the share price will either increase or decrease by specified factors ('u' and 'd'), then we can calculate δ and 'm' to ensure equality of 'end-state' payoffs. A similar procedure can be used for pricing a Put option.

Example B4.1 European Call option - no dividends – Replicating Portfolio – one period

An at-the-money European Call option (current share price S_0 = exercise price = 150.00) on a volatile stock expires in one year's time, when the share price is expected to have increased by the risk-adjusted required return on equity (8.11%) to 162.16. This expected price is based on a 0.5 true probability (p) of the share price increasing to 223.77 (49.18% discrete rate of return or continuous rate of return ln (1 + 49.18%) = 40%, and a 0.5 (1-p) probability of it decreasing to 100.55 (-32.97% discrete rate or -40.0% continuous rate).

The Call has Intrinsic Value in the up-state (Call value C_u = MAX {223.77 – 150, 0} = 73.77) but none in the down-state (Call value C_d = MAX {100.55 – 150, 0} = 0). The value of the replicating portfolio in the up state (which must equal the Call value in the up state) will be the value of the share component (= δ x 223.77) less the redemption value of the loan ((m x S_0) x (1 + r)), which is the same in either state; in the down-state, the portfolio will be valued at (δ x 100.55) - ((m x S_0) x (1 + r)). The risk free rate of return is 5.13% discrete (r) or 5.00% continuous (r*).

The option price is 32.54, where m = 0.38174 and δ = 0.59869 (for the replicating portfolio approach) and the up and down factors are 1.4918 and 0.6703, respectively (for the risk-neutral approach) - the up and down factors are based on the level of volatility - standard deviation - using the method suggested by Cox, Ross and Rubinstein (1979) ('CRR'), discussed later at **B4.18**.

Assumptions

Share price	150
Exercise price	150
Volatilty σ	40.0%
Time to expiry (in yrs)	1.00
Risk free rate (continuous)	5.00%
Risk free rate (discrete) =Exp (5.00%) - 1	5.13%

Up and Down factors

				Discrete	*Continuous*
				u-1, d-1	*ln (u), ln (d)*
u	=	EXP(40.0% x SQRT 1.00)	1.4918	49.18%	40.00%
d	=	EXP(-40.0% x SQRT 1.00) = 1 / u	0.6703	-32.97%	-40.00%

Up and Down share and call prices

S_u	223.77	=	150 x 1.4918
S_d	100.55	=	150 x 0.6703
C_u	73.77	=	MAX { [150 x 1.4918 - 150], 0}
C_d	0.00	=	MAX { [150 x 0.6703 - 150], 0}

True probabilities p

Risk averse required return (Ke)	8.11%	= r* + beta (= ř x [σstock / σmarket]) x ERP	See **B1.11** in App. B1.
		= 5.13% + 0.50 x (40.0% / 30.0%) x 4.5%	
Implied true probability p	0.5000	= (1.0811 - 0.6703) / (1.4918 - 0.6703)	
Expected stock price (using p)	162.16	= 150 x 1.4918 x 0.5000 + 150 x 0.6703 x (1 - 0.5000)	
Expected stock price (using Ke)	162.16	= 150.0x (1 + 8.11%)	

Value: Call = Value: Replicating portfolio

Today

CURRENT STATE

	Call	Replicating portfolio		
	1 Share	δ Shares	Loan	Total
Stock price	150.00	(89.80)	57.26	(32.54)
Call	(32.54)			

Call C_0 = **Today's portfolio** $S_0\ (\delta\ -\ m)$

Profit: Call = Profit: Replicating portfolio

In 1 year's time

UP STATE

	Call	Replicating portfolio		
	1 Share	δ Shares	Loan	Total
Stock price	223.77	133.97	(60.20)	73.77
Call	73.77			
	C_u	$\delta \times (uS_0)$	$-\{m \times S_0\} \times (1+r)$	

DOWN STATE

	Call	Replicating portfolio		
	1 Share	δ Shares	Loan	Total
Stock price	100.55	60.20	(60.20)	0.00
Call	0.00			
	C_d	$\delta \times (dS_0)$	$-\{m \times S_0\} \times (1+r)$	

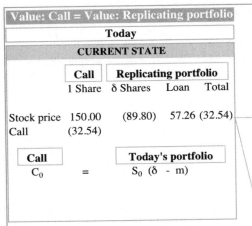

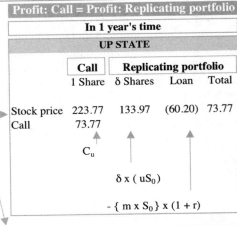

The fair price can also be shown in terms of arbitrage: the seller ('Writer') of a call option purchases 0.59869 of a share at a cost of 89.80, using the 32.54 option proceeds plus a 57.26 loan (interest at risk free rate) equivalent to 0.38174 of the current 150 price for 1 whole share. If the share price rises to 223.77, the writer will purchase (1 – 0.59869) of a share (cost 89.80) and sell the 1 share to the Call option holder for 150, and repay the loan (57.26 x 1.0513 = 60.20). If the share price falls to 100.55, the option will not be exercised, and the writer will sell the 0.59869 share for 60.2 and use this to repay the loan. In either state, there is a zero net cash flow (profit / loss) for the writer.

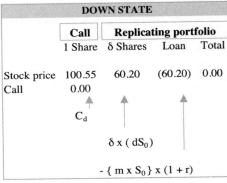

The up- and down-state values for the Call and the portfolio must have the same value:

For similar cash flows at expiry **B4.1**

$$C_u = \delta \times (uS_0) - \{m \times S_0\} \times (1+r)$$
$$C_d = \delta \times (dS_0) - \{m \times S_0\} \times (1+r)$$

$$\{m \times S_0\} \times (1+r) = \delta \times (uS_0) - C_u = \delta \times (dS_0) - C_d$$

$$\text{Hedge ratio, } \delta = \frac{C_u - C_d}{S_0 \times (u - d)}$$

$$\{m \times S_0\} \times (1+r) = \delta \times (uS_0) - C_u$$

$$= \left\{ \frac{C_u - C_d}{S_0 \times (u - d)} \right\} \times (uS_0) - C_u$$

$$mS_0 = \frac{d\,C_u - u\,C_d}{(1 + r)\,(u - d)}$$ **B4.2**

At time 0, the fair price of the Call option is the value of the replicating portfolio:

Call price $= S_0 \times (\delta - m) = = 150 \times (0.59869 - 0.38174) = 32.54$

δ	0.59869	= (73.77 - 0.0) / (150 x [1.4918 - 0.6703])
m	0.38174	= [(73.77 x 0.6703 - 0.0 x 1.4918) / ((1+5.13%) x (1.4918 - 0.6703))] / 150
Call price (replicating)	**32.54**	= 150 x (0.59869 - 0.38174)

Risk Neutral Probability Approach: One Period (No Dividends)

Since the purchase or sale of an option can be fully hedged , the fair price of the Call option (C_0) is the expected value of the Call option at the end of the period (based on weighted risk-neutral probabilities, p*), discounted at the risk free rate. Risk-neutral probabilities are adjusted true probabilities that allow the fair price to be calculated ignoring risk (fair value = risk-neutral probability weighted expected value of X discounted at the risk free rate = risk-adjusted probability weighted expected value of X discounted at the risk-adjusted rate). The replicating portfolio approach and risk-neutral approach are linked as follows:

$$C_0 = S_0\,(\delta - m)$$ **B4.3**

$$C_0 = S_0 \left(\frac{C_u - C_d}{S_0\,(u - d)} \right) - \left(\frac{dC_u - uC_d}{(1 + r)\,(u - d)} \right)$$

$$= \frac{C_u \left(\frac{(1 + r) - d}{u - d} \right) + C_d \left(\frac{u - (1 + r)}{u - d} \right)}{1 + r}$$

$$= \frac{C_u \left(p^* \right) + C_d \left(1 - p^* \right)}{1 + r}$$

Where the time to expiry is one year (T=1), and there is only one period (N=1) (so that the length of period in years is 1), the risk-neutral probabilities are as follows:

$$P^* = \frac{(1 + r - d)}{(u - d)} = \frac{e^{r^*} - d}{(u - d)}$$ **B4.4**

where r is the discrete risk free rate and r* the continuously compounded risk free rate (where $e^{r^*} = (1 + r)$ and $\ln(1 + r) = r^*$).

Example B4.2 Call option - no dividends – Risk neutral probabilities – one period

Using the example in **Example B4.1**:

p^*_{up} = (1+5.13% - 0.6703) / (1.4918 - 0.6703) = 0.4637

p^*_{down} = 1-0.4637 = 0.5363

$$\text{Call price} = \frac{0.4637 \times \text{MAX}\{[150\text{x}1.4918 - 150], 0\} + 0.5363 \times \text{MAX}\{[150\text{x}0.6703 - 150], 0\}}{1+5.13\%}$$

p*	0.4637 =	(1.0513% - 0.6703) / (1.4918 - 0.6703)
Expected stock price (using p*)	157.7 =	150 x 1.4918 x 0.4637 + 150 x 0.6703 x (1 - 0.4637)
Expected stock price (using r)	157.7 =	(150.0x (1 + 5.13%) (continous return = ln (157.7 / 150.0) = 5.0%)
Call price (risk neutral)	**32.54** =	[73.77 x 0.4637 + 0.0 x (1 - 0.4637)] / (1 + 5.13%)

The risk neutral probability weighted expected stock price provides a return equivalent to the risk free rate, since no risk premium is required as any risk from holding the option can be eliminated by hedging (replicating portfolio). By contrast, the true probability weighted expected stock price allows for a risk premium (both give a current price of 150):

		Return	Price
Risk averse pricing:	up + d(1-p) = 1 + Ke = 1 + r + (ß x ERP)	8.11%	162.2
Risk neutral pricing	up* + d(1-p*) = 1 + r	5.13%	157.7

The true probability can, therefore, be shown as (1 + ke – d)/(u – d) = 0.5 (assuming the up and down factors are consistent with the assumed volatility in the CAPM derived Ke). Although true probabilities are not needed in the option price calculation, it is possible to show that the same option price can be arrived at using the true probabilities (see MacDonald (2003 p.337)):

Expected call option value	= p C_u + (1 - p)C_d	= 0.50 x 73.77 + (1 - 0.50) x 0.00	36.89
Replicating portfolio cost	= (δ x Ke + m x r) / (δ - m)	= (0.5987 x 8.1% - 0.3817 x 5.13%) / (0.5987 - 0.3817)	13.4%
			32.54

Binomial Trees (No Dividends)

Building a Tree

A 'Binomial Tree' shows expected stock prices, Intrinsic Values and option values for each period until expiry. At the end of each stock price path (a 'node' – for example, the up and down state nodes in the above single period example), the stock price can increase or decrease, so that nodes multiply geometrically.

The up and down factors, risk neutral probabilities and risk free rates are assumed to be constant in each period. Although option prices can be calculated using the replicating portfolio method, since the portfolio mix (δ and m) needs to be recalculated at each node to reflect the option values at the next time period up and down nodes, it is easier to use the constant risk neutral probabilities.

Constructing a Binomial Tree involves the following steps:

❶ a time period T has T + 1 nodes (representing an up and down movement from the previous period's nodes), each of which show the stock price, Intrinsic Value, option value and Continuing Value (present value of expected option value at next time period);

❷ the current underlying stock price is assumed to increase by 'u' and decrease by 'd' each time period until the expiry date;

❸ at expiry, the Continuing Value is zero and the option value equals the Intrinsic Value (which equals the final state stock price at each node less the exercise price, or zero if negative);

❹ working backwards in time to the penultimate nodes, the option value for an American option will be the maximum of the Intrinsic Value at that node (predicted stock price less exercise price) and the Continuing Value, calculated as the expected value next period discounted back:

B4.5

$$\text{Continuing Value}_j = \frac{p^*(\text{Option Value}_{j+1u}) + (1-p^*)(\text{Option Value}_{j+1d})}{1 + r}$$

where

j+1u, j+1d	up and down states at next node after node j
p*	risk-neutral probability = (1 + r – d) / (u – d) (or $(e^{r*t} - d)/(u-d)$ where a continuous rate is used)
r	risk free rate of return

(for a European option, the option value will equal the Continuing Value, since early exercise is not possible);

this procedure is carried on backwards until the valuation date (the single node at the root of the Tree), where the option value represents the fair value of the option premium.

Call Options

The value of an American option at any exercise date equals the higher of the Intrinsic Value and the Continuing Value; as noted above, the value of a European option equals the Continuing Value (if the underlying stock pays no dividend, the two Call option values will be identical).

Example B4.3 American Call option - no dividends - Binomial Tree - 5 periods

Using the single period **Example B4.2**, it is now assumed that the option can be exercised at regular intervals throughout the year (every 5 periods of 0.20 years). The up and down factors (calculated using the CRR method), risk neutral probabilities and risk free rates for each period will reflect the shorter time steps. The Call option price (American and European) is now estimated at 28.16.

Model assumptions	
Share price today	150.00
ExercisePrice	150.00
Risk Free interest rate	5.00%
Volatility	40.0%
Time step (fraction of year)	1/5

Parameters		
u	1.1959	U = EXP(40.0%*SQRT (1 / 5))
d	0.8362	D = 1/1.1959
Risk-free return	1.0101	r = EXP(5%*0.2000)
Risk-neutral probability	0.4833	p* = (1.0101 - 0.8362)/(1.1959 - 0.8362)

Notation	
Share Price	S
Option value	O
Continuing value	CV
Intrinsic value	IV

See workings

0

S	150.00
O	**28.16**
CV	28.16
IV	0.00

1

S	179.38	125.43
O	45.82	12.17
CV	45.82	12.17
IV	29.38	0.00

2

S	214.52	150.00	104.88
O	72.24	22.00	3.22
CV	72.24	22.00	3.22
IV	64.52	0.00	0.00

3

S	256.54	179.38	125.43	87.71
O	109.51	38.78	6.73	0.00
CV	109.51	38.78	6.73	0.00
IV	106.54	29.38	0.00	0.00

4

S	306.79	214.52	150.00	104.88	73.34
O	158.29	66.01	14.06	0.00	0.00
CV	158.29	66.01	14.06	0.00	0.00
IV	156.79	64.52	0.00	0.00	0.00

5

S	366.89	256.54	179.38	125.43	87.71	61.33
O	**216.89**	**106.54**	**29.38**	0.00	0.00	0.00
CV	0.00	0.00	0.00	0.00	0.00	0.00
IV	216.89	106.54	29.38	0.00	0.00	0.00

Exercise Option **XXX**

	0	1	2	3	4	5
Disc Factor	1.0000	1.0101	1.0202	1.0305	1.0408	1.0513

S	$= S_{t-1} \times U$	306.79	=	256.54 x 1.1959
O	= MAX (CV, IV)	158.29	=	MAX {158.29, 156.79 }
CV	= [p*Cu + (1-p*)Cd] / (1+r)	158.29	=	[0.4833 x 216.89 + (1-0.4833) x 106.54] /1.0101
IV	= Stock Price - Exercise Price	156.79	=	306.79 - 150.00

The up and down factors were set so that the Tree 'recombines': since u = 1 / d, so ud = 1 and hence the paths ud and du from the same node meet at the same node two time periods later.

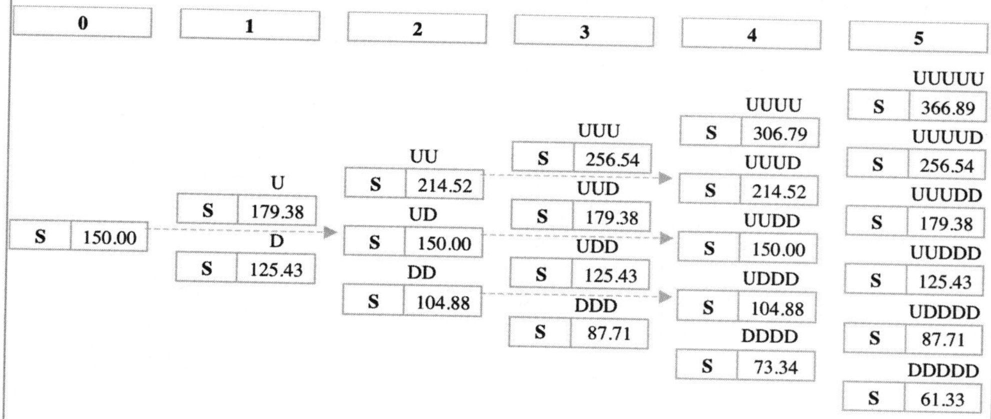

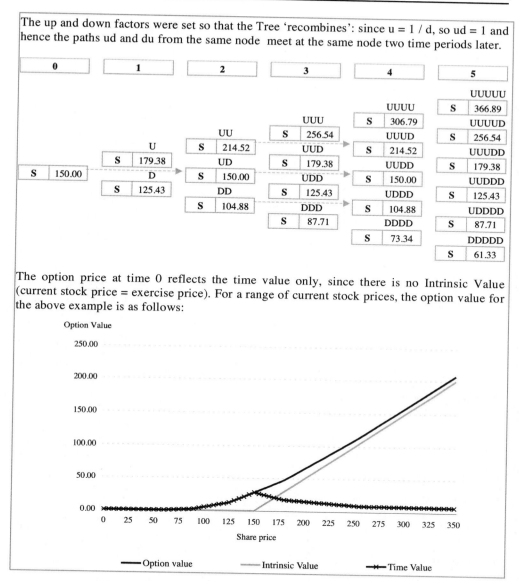

The option price at time 0 reflects the time value only, since there is no Intrinsic Value (current stock price = exercise price). For a range of current stock prices, the option value for the above example is as follows:

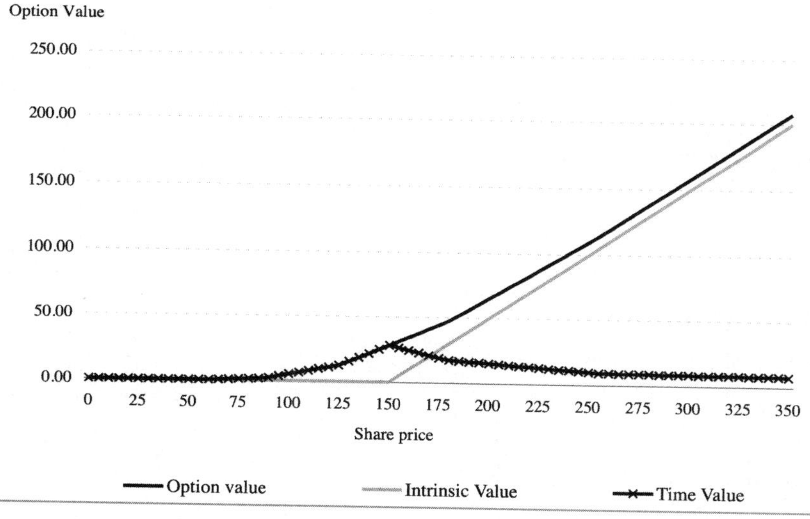

The time to expiry can be divided into any number of time steps, however it will be easier to model if the layout is adjusted. If the Tree is rotated clockwise, then:

- a share price equals the prior period share price on the same row multiplied by the 'up' factor; if there is no prior period share price on that row, it equals the prior period share price on the row above times the 'down' factor;
- the Call price is calculated as before (= $\{C_u p^* + C_d(1\text{-}p^*)\}$ / (1+ risk free rate for each period)), where C_u and C_d are the next period Call prices on the same row and row beneath, respectively.

Example B4.4 American Call option - no dividends - Binomial Tree - 12 periods

There are now 12 equal time periods in **Example B4.3** (i.e. exercise dates are every month):

	0	1	2	3	4	5	6	7	8	9	10	11	12
S	150.00	168.36	188.97	212.10	238.06	267.20	299.90	336.61	377.81	424.06	475.96	534.22	599.61
IV	0.00	18.36	38.97	62.10	88.06	117.20	149.90	186.61	227.81	274.06	325.96	384.22	449.61
TV	26.55	19.39	13.50	9.11	6.23	4.58	3.70	3.09	2.48	1.86	1.24	0.62	0.00
O	**26.55**	**37.75**	**52.46**	**71.21**	**94.29**	**121.78**	**153.61**	**189.70**	**230.29**	**275.92**	**327.21**	**384.84**	**449.61**
S		133.64	150.00	168.36	188.97	212.10	238.06	267.20	299.90	336.61	377.81	424.06	475.96
IV		0.00	0.00	18.36	38.97	62.10	88.06	117.20	149.90	186.61	227.81	274.06	325.96
TV		16.05	23.96	16.58	10.72	6.63	4.24	3.09	2.48	1.86	1.24	0.62	0.00
O		**16.05**	**23.96**	**34.94**	**49.69**	**68.73**	**92.30**	**120.29**	**152.38**	**188.47**	**229.06**	**274.68**	**325.96**
S			119.07	133.64	150.00	168.36	188.97	212.10	238.06	267.20	299.90	336.61	377.81
IV			0.00	0.00	0.00	18.36	38.97	62.10	88.06	117.20	149.90	186.61	227.81
TV			8.61	13.63	21.11	13.50	7.74	4.15	2.48	1.86	1.24	0.62	0.00
O			**8.61**	**13.63**	**21.11**	**31.86**	**46.71**	**66.24**	**90.54**	**119.06**	**151.15**	**187.23**	**227.81**
S				106.08	119.07	133.64	150.00	168.36	188.97	212.10	238.06	267.20	299.90
IV				0.00	0.00	0.00	0.00	18.36	38.97	62.10	88.06	117.20	149.90
TV				3.87	6.58	10.98	17.90	10.03	4.55	1.86	1.24	0.62	0.00
O				**3.87**	**6.58**	**10.98**	**17.90**	**28.39**	**43.52**	**63.96**	**89.30**	**117.82**	**149.90**
S					94.51	106.08	119.07	133.64	150.00	168.36	188.97	212.10	238.06
IV					0.00	0.00	0.00	0.00	0.00	18.36	38.97	62.10	88.06
TV					1.31	2.43	4.44	8.00	14.13	5.93	1.24	0.62	0.00
O					**1.31**	**2.43**	**4.44**	**8.00**	**14.13**	**24.29**	**40.21**	**62.72**	**88.06**
S						84.21	94.51	106.08	119.07	133.64	150.00	168.36	188.97
IV						0.00	0.00	0.00	0.00	0.00	0.00	18.36	38.97
TV						0.25	0.52	1.07	2.19	4.51	9.25	0.62	0.00
O						**0.25**	**0.52**	**1.07**	**2.19**	**4.51**	**9.25**	**18.98**	**38.97**
S							75.02	84.21	94.51	106.08	119.07	133.64	150.00
IV							0.00	0.00	0.00	0.00	0.00	0.00	0.00
TV							0.00	0.00	0.00	0.00	0.00	0.00	0.00
O							**0.00**	**0.00**	**0.00**	**0.00**	**0.00**	**0.00**	**0.00**
S								66.84	75.02	84.21	94.51	106.08	119.07
IV								0.00	0.00	0.00	0.00	0.00	0.00
TV								0.00	0.00	0.00	0.00	0.00	0.00
O								**0.00**	**0.00**	**0.00**	**0.00**	**0.00**	**0.00**
S									59.55	66.84	75.02	84.21	94.51
IV									0.00	0.00	0.00	0.00	0.00
TV									0.00	0.00	0.00	0.00	0.00
O									**0.00**	**0.00**	**0.00**	**0.00**	**0.00**
S										53.06	59.55	66.84	75.02
IV										0.00	0.00	0.00	0.00
TV										0.00	0.00	0.00	0.00
O										**0.00**	**0.00**	**0.00**	**0.00**
S											47.27	53.06	59.55
IV											0.00	0.00	0.00
TV											0.00	0.00	0.00
O											**0.00**	**0.00**	**0.00**
S												42.12	47.27
IV												0.00	0.00
TV												0.00	0.00
O												**0.00**	**0.00**
S													37.52
IV													0.00
TV													0.00
O													**0.00**

S Share Price
IV Intrinsic Value
TV Time Value
O Option Value

EXERCISE
(since Zero Time Value)

and +ve IV

The option value is, as before, the greater of the Intrinsic Value and the Continuing Value (not shown), the difference being the Time Value.

(Note: European option value = 26.55)

Parameters		
u	1.1224	= EXP(40.0%*SQRT(1 / 12))
d	0.8909	= 1/1.1224
r*	1.0042	= EXP(5% x (1 / 12))
p*	0.4892	= (1.0042 - 0.8909)/(1.1224 - 0.8909)

Workings for time 2

1	2	3	
168.36	188.97		= (168.36 x 1.1224)
18.36	38.97		= MAX(0, 188.97 - 150.00)
19.39	13.50		= 52.46 - 38.97
37.75	**52.46**	**71.21**	= MAX (38.97 , (71.21 x 0.4892 + 34.94 x (1 - 0.4892)) / 1.0042))
	150.00		= (168.36 x 0.8909)
	0.00		= MAX(0, 150.00 - 150.00)
	23.96		= 23.96 - 0.00
	23.96	**34.94**	= MAX (0.00 , (34.94 x 0.4892 + 13.63 x (1 - 0.4892)) / 1.0042))

Reducing each time period from 1/5 of one year to 1/12, reduces the Call option value from 28.16 (**Example B4.3**) to 26.55 (the impact of the length of time period will be discussed later).

Put Options

To calculate the price for a Put, the Intrinsic Value cell becomes MAX {X – S,0}, and all other cells remain the same.

Example B4.5 American Put option - no dividends - Binomial Tree - 12 periods

Using **Example B4.4**, but now with a Put (all other details remain the same):

	0	1	2	3	4	5	6	7	8	9	10	11	12
S	150.00	168.36	188.97	212.10	238.06	267.20	299.90	336.61	377.81	424.06	475.96	534.22	599.61
IV	0.00	0.00	0.00	0.00	0.00	0.00	0.00	0.00	0.00	0.00	0.00	0.00	0.00
TV	20.24	13.25	7.69	3.74	1.36	0.28	0.00	0.00	0.00	0.00	0.00	0.00	0.00
O	**20.24**	**13.25**	**7.69**	**3.74**	**1.36**	**0.28**	**0.00**	**0.00**	**0.00**	**0.00**	**0.00**	**0.00**	**0.00**
S		133.64	150.00	168.36	188.97	212.10	238.06	267.20	299.90	336.61	377.81	424.06	475.96
IV		16.36	0.00	0.00	0.00	0.00	0.00	0.00	0.00	0.00	0.00	0.00	0.00
TV		10.74	18.69	11.54	6.04	2.41	0.56	0.00	0.00	0.00	0.00	0.00	0.00
O		**27.09**	**18.69**	**11.54**	**6.04**	**2.41**	**0.56**	**0.00**	**0.00**	**0.00**	**0.00**	**0.00**	**0.00**
S			119.07	133.64	150.00	168.36	188.97	212.10	238.06	267.20	299.90	336.61	377.81
IV			30.93	16.36	0.00	0.00	0.00	0.00	0.00	0.00	0.00	0.00	0.00
TV			4.43	9.32	16.91	9.57	4.21	1.10	0.00	0.00	0.00	0.00	0.00
O			**35.37**	**25.68**	**16.91**	**9.57**	**4.21**	**1.10**	**0.00**	**0.00**	**0.00**	**0.00**	**0.00**
S				106.08	119.07	133.64	150.00	168.36	188.97	212.10	238.06	267.20	299.90
IV				43.92	30.93	16.36	0.00	0.00	0.00	0.00	0.00	0.00	0.00
TV				1.01	3.36	7.71	14.80	7.22	2.15	0.00	0.00	0.00	0.00
O				**44.93**	**34.29**	**24.07**	**14.80**	**7.22**	**2.15**	**0.00**	**0.00**	**0.00**	**0.00**
S					94.51	106.08	119.07	133.64	150.00	168.36	188.97	212.10	238.06
IV					55.49	43.92	30.93	16.36	0.00	0.00	0.00	0.00	0.00
TV					0.00	0.45	2.21	5.82	12.13	4.23	0.00	0.00	0.00
O					**55.49**	**44.37**	**33.14**	**22.18**	**12.13**	**4.23**	**0.00**	**0.00**	**0.00**
S						84.21	94.51	106.08	119.07	133.64	150.00	168.36	188.97
IV						65.79	55.49	43.92	30.93	16.36	0.00	0.00	0.00
TV						0.00	0.00	0.00	1.05	3.43	8.32	0.00	0.00
O						**65.79**	**55.49**	**43.92**	**31.98**	**19.79**	**8.32**	**0.00**	**0.00**
S							75.02	84.21	94.51	106.08	119.07	133.64	150.00
IV							74.98	65.79	55.49	43.92	30.93	16.36	0.00
TV							0.00	0.00	0.00	0.00	0.00	0.00	0.00
O							**74.98**	**65.79**	**55.49**	**43.92**	**30.93**	**16.36**	**0.00**
S								66.84	75.02	84.21	94.51	106.08	119.07
IV								83.16	74.98	65.79	55.49	43.92	30.93
TV								0.00	0.00	0.00	0.00	0.00	0.00
O								**83.16**	**74.98**	**65.79**	**55.49**	**43.92**	**30.93**
S									59.55	66.84	75.02	84.21	94.51
IV									90.45	83.16	74.98	65.79	55.49
TV									0.00	0.00	0.00	0.00	0.00
O									**90.45**	**83.16**	**74.98**	**65.79**	**55.49**
S										53.06	59.55	66.84	75.02
IV										96.94	90.45	83.16	74.98
TV										0.00	0.00	0.00	0.00
O										**96.94**	**90.45**	**83.16**	**74.98**
S											47.27	53.06	59.55
IV											102.73	96.94	90.45
TV											0.00	0.00	0.00
O											**102.73**	**96.94**	**90.45**
S												42.12	47.27
IV												107.88	102.73
TV												0.00	0.00
O												**107.88**	**102.73**
S													37.52
IV													112.48
TV													0.00
O													**112.48**

S Share Price
IV Intrinsic Value
TV Time Value
O Option Value

EXERCISE
(since Zero Time Value)

(Note: European option = 19.24)

Workings for time 2

1	2	3	
168.36	188.97		= (168.36 x 1.1224)
0.00	0.00		= MAX(0, 150.00 - 188.97)
13.25	7.69		= 7.69 - 0.00
13.25	**7.69**	**3.74**	= MAX (0.00 , (3.74 x 0.4892 + 11.54 x (1 - 0.4892)) / 1.0042))
	150.00		= (168.36 x 0.8909)
	0.00		= MAX(0, 150.00 - 150.00)
	18.69		= 18.69 - 0.00
	18.69	**11.54**	= MAX (0.00 , (11.54 x 0.4892 + 25.68 x (1 - 0.4892)) / 1.0042))

Early Exercise (No Dividends)

Exercising an American Option on a non-dividend paying stock before the expiry date would be optimal if the value of an early exercise (Intrinsic Value) was equal to or greater than the value of the option if exercised at some future date (i.e. zero Time Value). This may be the case for a Put Option, but will never be the case for a Call Option (ignoring dividends), where the investor plans on holding the stock until expiry. This can be proved by arbitrage theory (see Hull (2003)).

- Call Options

The optimal strategy is one where the option holder's cash at the expiry date is maximised. Comparing an exercise of a Call option at the expiry date (T) to an exercise at an earlier date (t), where the stock is sold, in both cases, at the expiry date, this would mean (using the discrete risk free rate, r):

$$\text{MAX}\ \{\ \underbrace{S_T}_{\text{Sale at expiry}} - \underbrace{X}_{\text{Purchase at expiry}} - \underbrace{P(1+r)}_{\text{Premium + financing cost}},\quad \underbrace{S_T}_{\text{Sale at expiry}} - \underbrace{X(1+r)^{\frac{T-t}{T}}}_{\text{Purchase early + financing cost}} - \underbrace{P(1+r)}_{\text{Premium + financing cost}}\ \}$$

If the stock is held to expiry, therefore, *exercising a Call option on a non-dividend paying stock is never optimal.* If the stock is not held to expiry but is sold at the time of the early exercise (payoff = Intrinsic Value at time t), then it would have been better to have sold the option rather than have exercised it, due to the additional payoff from the Time Value (Call value at time t = Intrinsic Value + Time Value).

A European Call Option on a non-dividend paying stock will have the same value as its American counterpart, since it would never be optimal to exercise the latter early (this is not the case if dividends are paid, as will be shown later).

- Put Options

Early exercise of an American Put option on a non-dividend paying stock may be optimal. Using the above analysis, cash at expiry is maximised as follows:

$$\text{MAX}\ \{\ \underbrace{X}_{\text{Sale at expiry}} - \underbrace{S_T}_{\text{Purchase at expiry}} - \underbrace{P(1+r)}_{\text{Premium + financing cost}},\quad (\underbrace{X}_{\text{Sale early}} - \underbrace{S_t}_{\text{Purchase early}})\ \underbrace{(1+r)^{\frac{T-t}{T}}}_{\text{+ Income on early payoff}} - \underbrace{P(1+r)}_{\text{Premium + financing cost}}\ \}$$

In order to exercise the Put option, the option holder must have purchased the stock. If the stock falls significantly after time t, then early exercise may not be best.

Binomial Trees (dividends)

Impact of Dividends

A dividend payment will reduce the value of the share price due to the cash outlay. When the share goes ex-div, the price drops to reflect the dividend to which a buyer is no longer entitled. This will decrease the value of a Call option and increase the value of a Put option.

Forward Stock Prices

As in the one period model, the risk-neutral probability weighted expected stock price at each period will be the expected risk-neutral price at the start of the period compounded forward by the risk free rate (the expected stock price is the 'Forward' price – see Appendix B3 for Forward pricing); this is not the same as the true expected stock price at each period, which is calculated using the true probabilities (i.e. including risk).

If the stock has gone ex-div at the relevant date, the expected risk-neutral Forward price will be reduced by the dividend. Using **Example B4.3**, if it is assumed that at time 1 a dividend of D_1 has just been paid - or is just about to be paid, so that the stock has gone ex-div – then the forward price at time 1 (F_1) will be:

$$F_1 = S_0 (1 + r)^{1/5} - D_1 \qquad \text{(r = discrete risk free rate)}$$

$$= S_0 e^{r^* \times 1/5} - D_1 \qquad \text{(r* = continuous risk free rate)}$$

If another dividend is paid at time 2 (D_2), then the forward price at time 2 will be:

$$F_2 = (S_0 (1 + r)^{1/5} - D_1) \times (1 + r)^{1/5} - D_2$$

$$= (S_0 e^{r^* \times 1/5} - D_1) \times e^{r^* \times 1/5} - D_2$$

(F_1 circled, with an arrow pointing to the bracketed term.)

Assuming a two period model (option expires at t_2), to ensure that F_1/S_0 and F_2/S_1 provide a risk free rate of return (for risk neutrality), the up and down factors are applied to the following starting share price in the Binomial model:

$$S^*_0 = \frac{F_2}{(1 + r)^{(2 \times 1/5)}}$$

$$= S_0 - \left(\frac{D_1}{(1 + r)^{1/5}} + \frac{D_2}{(1+r)^{2 \times 1/5}} \right)$$

Present value of future dividends

$$\text{or} \quad = \quad F_2 e^{-r^* \times (2 \times 1/5)}$$

$$= \quad S_0 - \left[e^{-r^* \times 1/5} D_1 + e^{-r^* \times (2 \times 1/5)} D_2 \right]$$

If a continuous dividend equivalent to a q% yield was paid over these two time periods, then:

$$F_2 \quad = \quad S_0 \, e^{(r^* - q) \times (2 \times 1/5)}$$

The continuous risk free rate is simply reduced by the dividend yield.

Modelling the Dividend Impact

Dividends can be incorporated into the BM by:

1. assuming the dividend is paid at a continuous rate q% p.a., and adjusting the risk neutral probabilities: $p^* = (e^{(r^* - q)\,t} - d) / (u - d)$; or

2. reducing the up or down stock prices by the amount of any dividend to arrive at an ex-dividend value: the next period's up and down factors would then be applied to this ex-dividend value – there are two possibilities to ensure the Tree is recombining (see Hull (2003)):

   (a) (i) at each dividend date, the share price is reduced by (1 – y%), where y% is the constant dividend yield, to give an ex-div price;

   (ii) to calculate the share price at the next period, the up and down factors are applied to this ex-div price (if there was a dividend at this date too, then the price would be reduced by (1-y%) and so on); or

   (b) (i) the £ dividends ('D') are scheduled;

   (ii) the present value of future dividends (Dpv_t) (ignoring the dividend on that date) is calculated as at each time period (where $Dpv_t = (D_{t+1} + Dpv_{t+1})$ discounted back one period by the risk free rate);

   (iii) the ex-div share price at any period, $S_t = (S_{t-1} - Dpv_{t-1})$ x 'u' (or 'd') + Dpv_t: after adjusting for the change in the present value of future dividends, a share price at any node will be the same as the share price two periods earlier after an up-down move: $S_t = (S_{t-2} - Dpv_{t-2}) + Dpv_t$ (at a node two places to the right and one down from S_t in **Examples B4.6(2)** and **B4.6(4)**).

Example B4.6 American Call / Put option - dividends - Binomial Tree - 12 periods

Using **Example B4.4**, but assuming quarterly dividends (starting at time period 1) of:

Dividend yield: 4.4% p.a. or 1.1% per quarter

Dividend £: £1.25, £1.50, £1.75, and £2.0

Model assumptions	
Share price today	150.00
ExercisePrice	150.00
Risk Free interest rate	5.00%
Volatility	40.0%
Expiry date	1.00 yrs
Time step (fraction of year)	1/12

Parameters		
u	1.1224	= EXP(40.0%*SQRT(1 / 12))
d	0.8909	= 1/1.1224
r*	1.0042	= EXP(5% x (1 / 12))
p*	0.4892	= (1.0042 - 0.8909)/(1.1224 - 0.8909)

It is assumed that the ex-div and cum-div share prices have the same volatility (this is discussed later for the Black-Scholes model).

Both cases give an American Call option value of 23.28 (the above dividend yield was set so as to ensure the prices were the same, to illustrate the effect). The American Put option values are 23.04 and 22.29. See the following pages.

Early Exercise (with dividends)

It may be optimal to exercise a Call option early if the underlying share pays dividends (see **Examples B4.6(1)** and **B4.6(2)**). On exercise, assuming the stock is held to expiry, the option holder can receive the dividend (if exercised while the stock is cum-div) and, possibly, earn more than the cost of financing the exercise price (the risk free rate). The risk is that the stock price falls below the exercise price at expiry.

A Put option on a dividend-paying stock is more likely to be exercised early, since the dividend payment reduces the stock price, pushing the option deeper in-the-money (see **Examples B4.6(3)** and **B4.6(4)**).

Example B4.6 (1) American Call option - Binomial Tree - 12 periods – 1.1% dividend yield

	0	1	2	3	4	5	6	7	8	9	10	11	12
D	-	1.86	-	-	2.60	-	-	3.64	-	-	5.09	-	-
S	150.00	166.50	186.88	209.75	232.82	261.32	293.31	325.57	365.41	410.14	455.25	510.98	573.52
IV	0.00	16.50	36.88	59.75	82.82	111.32	143.31	175.57	215.41	260.14	305.25	360.98	423.52
TV	23.28	16.86	9.89	4.36	2.99	0.84	0.00	1.24	0.62	0.00	1.24	0.62	0.00
O	**23.28**	**33.36**	**46.77**	**64.11**	**85.81**	**112.16**	**143.31**	**176.81**	**216.04**	**260.14**	**306.50**	**361.60**	**423.52**
D		1.48	-	-	2.07	-	-	2.89	-	-	4.04	-	-
S		132.16	148.34	166.50	184.81	207.43	232.82	258.43	290.06	325.57	361.37	405.61	455.25
IV		0.00	0.00	16.50	34.81	57.43	82.82	108.43	140.06	175.57	211.37	255.61	305.25
TV		13.82	20.78	14.05	9.04	3.85	0.42	1.36	0.62	0.00	1.24	0.62	0.00
O		**13.82**	**20.78**	**30.55**	**43.85**	**61.28**	**83.24**	**109.79**	**140.69**	**175.57**	**212.62**	**256.23**	**305.25**
D			-	-	1.64	-	-	2.29	-	-	3.21	-	-
S			117.75	132.16	146.70	164.66	184.81	205.14	230.25	258.43	286.85	321.96	361.37
IV			0.00	0.00	0.00	14.66	34.81	55.14	80.25	108.43	136.85	171.96	211.37
TV			7.27	11.59	18.07	12.85	5.94	3.35	0.85	0.00	1.24	0.62	0.00
O			**7.27**	**11.59**	**18.07**	**27.51**	**40.75**	**58.49**	**81.10**	**108.43**	**138.10**	**172.59**	**211.37**
D				-	1.30	-	-	1.82	-	-	2.55	-	-
S				104.91	116.45	130.70	146.70	162.84	182.77	205.14	227.70	255.57	286.85
IV				0.00	0.00	0.00	0.00	12.84	32.77	55.14	77.70	105.57	136.85
TV				3.21	5.47	9.17	15.06	11.25	4.55	0.45	1.24	0.62	0.00
O				**3.21**	**5.47**	**9.17**	**15.06**	**24.09**	**37.32**	**55.59**	**78.95**	**106.19**	**136.85**
D					1.03	-	-	1.45	-	-	2.02	-	-
S					92.44	103.75	116.45	129.26	145.08	162.84	180.75	202.87	227.70
IV					0.00	0.00	0.00	0.00	0.00	12.84	30.75	52.87	77.70
TV					1.06	1.97	3.61	6.54	11.61	7.28	2.93	0.62	0.00
O					**1.06**	**1.97**	**3.61**	**6.54**	**11.61**	**20.12**	**33.68**	**53.49**	**77.70**
D						-	-	1.15	-	-	1.60	-	-
S						82.36	92.44	102.60	115.16	129.26	143.47	161.03	180.75
IV						0.00	0.00	0.00	0.00	0.00	0.00	11.03	30.75
TV						0.20	0.41	0.84	1.73	3.55	7.30	3.94	0.00
O						**0.20**	**0.41**	**0.84**	**1.73**	**3.55**	**7.30**	**14.98**	**30.75**
D							-	0.91	-	-	1.27	-	-
S							73.37	81.44	91.41	102.60	113.89	127.83	143.47
IV							0.00	0.00	0.00	0.00	0.00	0.00	0.00
TV							0.00	0.00	0.00	0.00	0.00	0.00	0.00
O							**0.00**	**0.00**	**0.00**	**0.00**	**0.00**	**0.00**	**0.00**
D								0.72	-	-	1.01	-	-
S								64.65	72.56	81.44	90.40	101.47	113.89
IV								0.00	0.00	0.00	0.00	0.00	0.00
TV								0.00	0.00	0.00	0.00	0.00	0.00
O								**0.00**	**0.00**	**0.00**	**0.00**	**0.00**	**0.00**
D									-	-	0.80	-	-
S									57.60	64.65	71.76	80.54	90.40
IV									0.00	0.00	0.00	0.00	0.00
TV									0.00	0.00	0.00	0.00	0.00
O									**0.00**	**0.00**	**0.00**	**0.00**	**0.00**
D										-	0.64	-	-
S										51.32	56.96	63.93	71.76
IV										0.00	0.00	0.00	0.00
TV										0.00	0.00	0.00	0.00
O										**0.00**	**0.00**	**0.00**	**0.00**
D											0.51	-	-
S											45.22	50.75	56.96
IV											0.00	0.00	0.00
TV											0.00	0.00	0.00
O											**0.00**	**0.00**	**0.00**
D												-	-
S												40.29	45.22
IV												0.00	0.00
TV												0.00	0.00
O												**0.00**	**0.00**
D													-
S													35.89
IV													0.00
TV													0.00
O													**0.00**

D Dividends
S Share Price
IV Intrinsic Value
TV Time Value
O Option Value

EXERCISE
(since Zero Time Value)

Exercising early would be optimal, since the Intrinsic Value is worth more than the risk-neutral discounted Call option value at the next period.

European Call Option value = £23.17

Dividend impact

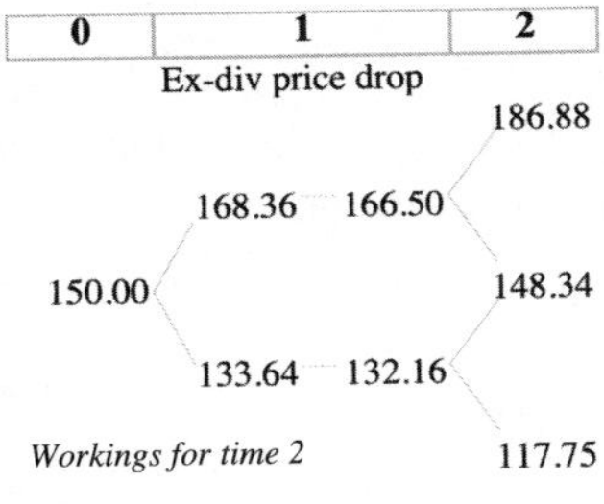

Workings for time 2

Ex-div share price (166.50) = Cum-div price (168.36) x (1 - 1.1% div yield).

1	2	3	
1.86	-		
166.50	186.88		= (166.50 x 1.1224)
16.50	36.88		= MAX(0, 186.88 - 150.00)
16.86	9.89		= 46.77 - 36.88
33.36	**46.77**	**64.11**	= MAX (36.88 , (64.11 x 0.4892 + 30.55 x (1 - 0.4892)) / 1.0042))
	-		
	148.34		= (166.50 x 0.8909)
	0.00		= MAX(0, 148.34 - 150.00)
	20.78		= 20.78 - 0.00
	20.78	**30.55**	= MAX (0.00 , (30.55 x 0.4892 + 11.59 x (1 - 0.4892)) / 1.0042))

Example B4.6 (2) American Call option - Binomial Tree - 12 periods – Known £ dividends

	0	1	2	3	4	5	6	7	8	9	10	11	12
Dpv	6.34	5.11	5.14	5.16	3.68	3.69	3.71	1.98	1.98	1.99	0.00	0.00	0.00
D	-	1.25	-	-	1.50	-	-	1.75	-	-	2.00	-	-
S	150.00	166.36	186.12	208.29	231.68	259.60	290.94	324.36	363.83	408.13	455.85	511.65	574.27
IV	0.00	16.36	36.12	58.29	81.68	109.60	140.94	174.36	213.83	258.13	305.85	361.65	424.27
TV	23.28	16.96	10.53	5.53	3.53	1.39	0.21	1.24	0.62	0.00	1.24	0.62	0.00
O	**23.28**	**33.32**	**46.65**	**63.82**	**85.21**	**110.99**	**141.15**	**175.61**	**214.45**	**258.13**	**307.09**	**362.27**	**424.27**
D		1.25	-	-	1.50	-	-	1.75	-	-	2.00	-	-
S		133.11	148.80	166.40	184.66	206.83	231.71	257.88	289.21	324.38	361.85	406.14	455.85
IV		0.00	0.00	16.40	34.66	56.83	81.71	107.88	139.21	174.38	211.85	256.14	305.85
TV		13.86	20.82	14.18	9.19	4.38	1.31	1.43	0.62	0.00	1.24	0.62	0.00
O		**13.86**	**20.82**	**30.59**	**43.85**	**61.21**	**83.02**	**109.31**	**139.84**	**174.38**	**213.09**	**256.76**	**305.85**
D			-	-	1.50	-	-	1.75	-	-	2.00	-	-
S			119.17	133.15	147.34	164.94	184.69	205.11	229.98	257.90	287.23	322.39	361.85
IV			0.00	0.00	0.00	14.94	34.69	55.11	79.98	107.90	137.23	172.39	211.85
TV			7.31	11.63	18.13	12.65	6.13	3.41	0.98	0.00	1.24	0.62	0.00
O			**7.31**	**11.63**	**18.13**	**27.59**	**40.82**	**58.52**	**80.97**	**107.90**	**138.47**	**173.01**	**211.85**
D				-	1.50	-	-	1.75	-	-	2.00	-	-
S				106.76	117.72	131.69	147.37	163.22	182.97	205.13	228.00	255.91	287.23
IV				0.00	0.00	0.00	0.00	13.22	32.97	55.13	78.00	105.91	137.23
TV				3.22	5.50	9.23	15.14	10.99	4.53	0.71	1.24	0.62	0.00
O				**3.22**	**5.50**	**9.23**	**15.14**	**24.21**	**37.50**	**55.83**	**79.24**	**106.53**	**137.23**
D					1.50	-	-	1.75	-	-	2.00	-	-
S					94.20	105.30	117.75	129.97	145.65	163.24	180.98	203.14	228.00
IV					0.00	0.00	0.00	0.00	0.00	13.24	30.98	53.14	78.00
TV					1.07	1.98	3.64	6.58	11.68	7.00	2.88	0.62	0.00
O					**1.07**	**1.98**	**3.64**	**6.58**	**11.68**	**20.24**	**33.87**	**53.76**	**78.00**
D						-	-	1.75	-	-	2.00	-	-
S						❶ 84.34	94.23	103.58	116.02	129.99	143.66	161.25	180.98
IV						0.00	0.00	0.00	0.00	0.00	0.00	11.25	30.98
TV						0.20	0.41	0.85	1.75	3.58	7.35	3.85	0.00
O						**0.20**	**0.41**	**0.85**	**1.75**	**3.58**	**7.35**	**15.09**	**30.98**
D							-	1.75	-	-	2.00	-	-
S							75.56	❷ 82.62	92.50	103.59	114.04	128.00	143.66
IV							0.00	0.00	0.00	0.00	0.00	0.00	0.00
TV							0.00	0.00	0.00	0.00	0.00	0.00	0.00
O							**0.00**	**0.00**	**0.00**	**0.00**	**0.00**	**0.00**	**0.00**
D								1.75	-	-	2.00	-	-
S								65.99	73.84	82.64	90.52	101.60	114.04
IV								0.00	0.00	0.00	0.00	0.00	0.00
TV								0.00	0.00	0.00	0.00	0.00	0.00
O								**0.00**	**0.00**	**0.00**	**0.00**	**0.00**	**0.00**
D									-	-	2.00	-	-
S									59.02	66.01	71.85	80.65	90.52
IV									0.00	0.00	0.00	0.00	0.00
TV									0.00	0.00	0.00	0.00	0.00
O									**0.00**	**0.00**	**0.00**	**0.00**	**0.00**
D										-	2.00	-	-
S										52.81	57.04	64.02	71.85
IV										0.00	0.00	0.00	0.00
TV										0.00	0.00	0.00	0.00
O										**0.00**	**0.00**	**0.00**	**0.00**
D											2.00	-	-
S											45.28	50.82	57.04
IV											0.00	0.00	0.00
TV											0.00	0.00	0.00
O											**0.00**	**0.00**	**0.00**
D												-	-
S												40.34	45.28
IV												0.00	0.00
TV												0.00	0.00
O												**0.00**	**0.00**
D													-
S													35.94
IV													0.00
TV													0.00
O													**0.00**

D Dividends
S Share Price
IV Intrinsic Value
TV Time Value
O Option Value

EXERCISE
(since Zero Time Value)

Dpv PV of dividends (discounting at risk free rate)

Exercising early at period 9 would be optimal, since the Intrinsic Value is worth more than the risk-neutral discounted Call option value at period 10 (the Intrinsic Value, since this is the expiry date).

European Call Option value = £23.27

❶❷ The Tree 'recombines' as follows, using these nodes as an example: 82.62 - 1.98 Dpv (which excludes the dividend 1.75) = 84.34 - 3.69 Dpv (allowing for a small rounding difference).

Workings for time 2

1	2	3	
5.11	5.14	5.16	
1.25	-		
166.36	186.12		= [(166.36 - 5.11) x 1.1224] + 5.14
16.36	36.12		= MAX(0, 186.12 - 150.00)
16.96	10.53		= 46.65 - 36.12
33.32	**46.65**	**63.82**	= MAX (36.12 , (63.82 x 0.4892 + 30.59 x (1 - 0.4892)) / 1.0042))
	-		
	148.80		= [(166.36 - 5.11) x 0.8909] + 5.14
	0.00		= MAX(0, 148.80 - 150.00)
	20.82		= 20.82 - 0.00
	20.82	**30.59**	= MAX (0.00 , (30.59 x 0.4892 + 11.63 x (1 - 0.4892)) / 1.0042))

Example B4.6 (3) American Put option - Binomial Tree - 12 periods – 1.1% dividend yield

	0	1	2	3	4	5	6	7	8	9	10	11	12
D	-	1.86	-	-	2.60	-	-	3.64	-	-	5.09	-	-
S	150.00	166.50	186.88	209.75	232.82	261.32	293.31	325.57	365.41	410.14	455.25	510.98	573.52
IV	0.00	0.00	0.00	0.00	0.00	0.00	0.00	0.00	0.00	0.00	0.00	0.00	0.00
TV	23.04	15.85	9.85	5.30	2.31	0.71	0.11	0.00	0.00	0.00	0.00	0.00	0.00
O	**23.04**	**15.85**	**9.85**	**5.30**	**2.31**	**0.71**	**0.11**	**0.00**	**0.00**	**0.00**	**0.00**	**0.00**	**0.00**
	D	1.48	-	-	2.07	-	-	2.89	-	-	4.04	-	-
	S	132.16	148.34	166.50	184.81	207.43	232.82	258.43	290.06	325.57	361.37	405.61	455.25
	IV	17.84	1.66	0.00	0.00	0.00	0.00	0.00	0.00	0.00	0.00	0.00	0.00
	TV	12.28	20.07	14.28	8.21	3.86	1.30	0.22	0.00	0.00	0.00	0.00	0.00
	O	**30.11**	**21.73**	**14.28**	**8.21**	**3.86**	**1.30**	**0.22**	**0.00**	**0.00**	**0.00**	**0.00**	**0.00**
		D	-	-	1.64	-	-	2.29	-	-	3.21	-	-
		S	117.75	132.16	146.70	164.66	184.81	205.14	230.25	258.43	286.85	321.96	361.37
		IV	32.25	17.84	3.30	0.00	0.00	0.00	0.00	0.00	0.00	0.00	0.00
		TV	6.14	11.20	16.91	12.45	6.35	2.34	0.44	0.00	0.00	0.00	0.00
		O	**38.39**	**29.03**	**20.21**	**12.45**	**6.35**	**2.34**	**0.44**	**0.00**	**0.00**	**0.00**	**0.00**
			D	-	1.30	-	-	1.82	-	-	2.55	-	-
			S	104.91	116.45	130.70	146.70	162.84	182.77	205.14	227.70	255.57	286.85
			IV	45.09	33.55	19.30	3.30	0.00	0.00	0.00	0.00	0.00	0.00
			TV	2.58	4.18	8.50	15.10	10.24	4.17	0.86	0.00	0.00	0.00
			O	**47.67**	**37.73**	**27.80**	**18.40**	**10.24**	**4.17**	**0.86**	**0.00**	**0.00**	**0.00**
				D	1.03	-	-	1.45	-	-	2.02	-	-
				S	92.44	103.75	116.45	129.26	145.08	162.84	180.75	202.87	227.70
				IV	57.56	46.25	33.55	20.74	4.92	0.00	0.00	0.00	0.00
				TV	0.01	1.30	3.47	5.62	11.21	7.38	1.69	0.00	0.00
				O	**57.57**	**47.55**	**37.02**	**26.37**	**16.14**	**7.38**	**1.69**	**0.00**	**0.00**
					D	-	-	1.15	-	-	1.60	-	-
					S	82.36	92.44	102.60	115.16	129.26	143.47	161.03	180.75
					IV	67.64	57.56	47.40	34.84	20.74	6.53	0.00	0.00
					TV	0.00	0.46	0.13	1.54	3.91	6.37	3.32	0.00
					O	**67.64**	**58.02**	**47.52**	**36.38**	**24.65**	**12.90**	**3.32**	**0.00**
						D	-	0.91	-	-	1.27	-	-
						S	73.37	81.44	91.41	102.60	113.89	127.83	143.47
						IV	76.63	68.56	58.59	47.40	36.11	22.17	6.53
						TV	0.19	0.00	0.00	0.51	0.00	0.00	0.00
						O	**76.81**	**68.56**	**58.59**	**47.91**	**36.11**	**22.17**	**6.53**
							D	0.72	-	-	1.01	-	-
							S	64.65	72.56	81.44	90.40	101.47	113.89
							IV	85.35	77.44	68.56	59.60	48.53	36.11
							TV	0.00	0.00	0.28	0.00	0.00	0.00
							O	**85.35**	**77.44**	**68.83**	**59.60**	**48.53**	**36.11**
								D	-	-	0.80	-	-
								S	57.60	64.65	71.76	80.54	90.40
								IV	92.40	85.35	78.24	69.46	59.60
								TV	0.00	0.09	0.00	0.00	0.00
								O	**92.40**	**85.44**	**78.24**	**69.46**	**59.60**
									D	-	0.64	-	-
									S	51.32	56.96	63.93	71.76
									IV	98.68	93.04	86.07	78.24
									TV	0.00	0.00	0.00	0.00
									O	**98.68**	**93.04**	**86.07**	**78.24**
										D	0.51	-	-
										S	45.22	50.75	56.96
										IV	104.78	99.25	93.04
										TV	0.00	0.00	0.00
										O	**104.78**	**99.25**	**93.04**
											D	-	-
											S	40.29	45.22
											IV	109.71	104.78
											TV	0.00	0.00
											O	**109.71**	**104.78**
												D	-
												S	35.89
												IV	114.11
												TV	0.00
												O	**114.11**

D Dividends
S Share Price
IV Intrinsic Value
TV Time Value
O Option Value

EXERCISE
(since Zero Time Value)

Dividend paying American Put Options are even more likely to be exercised if the ex-div share price drop pushes the option even deeper in-the-money.

European Option value = 22.38

Workings for time 2

1	2	3	
1.86	-		
166.50	186.88		= (166.50 x 1.1224)
0.00	0.00		= MAX(0, 150.00 - 186.88)
15.85	9.85		= 9.85 - 0.00
15.85	**9.85**	**5.30**	= MAX (0.00 , (5.30 x 0.4892 + 14.28 x (1 - 0.4892)) / 1.0042))
	-		
	148.34		= (166.50 x 0.8909)
	1.66		= MAX(0, 150.00 - 148.34)
	20.07		= 21.73 - 1.66
	21.73	**14.28**	= MAX (1.66 , (14.28 x 0.4892 + 29.03 x (1 - 0.4892)) / 1.0042))

Example B4.6 (4) American Put option - Binomial Tree - 12 periods – Known £ dividends

	0	1	2	3	4	5	6	7	8	9	10	11	12
Dpv	6.34	5.11	5.14	5.16	3.68	3.69	3.71	1.98	1.98	1.99	0.00	0.00	0.00
D	-	1.25	-	-	1.50	-	-	1.75	-	-	2.00	-	-
S	150.00	166.36	186.12	208.29	231.68	259.60	290.94	324.36	363.83	408.13	455.85	511.65	574.27
IV	0.00	0.00	0.00	0.00	0.00	0.00	0.00	0.00	0.00	0.00	0.00	0.00	0.00
TV	22.85	15.74	9.78	5.26	2.28	0.70	0.11	0.00	0.00	0.00	0.00	0.00	0.00
O	**22.85**	**15.74**	**9.78**	**5.26**	**2.28**	**0.70**	**0.11**	**0.00**	**0.00**	**0.00**	**0.00**	**0.00**	**0.00**
D		1.25	-	-	1.50	-	-	1.75	-	-	2.00	-	-
S		133.11	148.80	166.40	184.66	206.83	231.71	257.88	289.21	324.38	361.85	406.14	455.85
IV		16.89	1.20	0.00	0.00	0.00	0.00	0.00	0.00	0.00	0.00	0.00	0.00
TV		12.96	20.38	14.19	8.15	3.82	1.28	0.22	0.00	0.00	0.00	0.00	0.00
O		**29.85**	**21.58**	**14.19**	**8.15**	**3.82**	**1.28**	**0.22**	**0.00**	**0.00**	**0.00**	**0.00**	**0.00**
D			-	-	1.50	-	-	1.75	-	-	2.00	-	-
S			119.17	133.15	147.34	164.94	184.69	205.11	229.98	257.90	287.23	322.39	361.85
IV			30.83	16.85	2.66	0.00	0.00	0.00	0.00	0.00	0.00	0.00	0.00
TV			7.18	11.98	17.43	12.37	6.29	2.30	0.42	0.00	0.00	0.00	0.00
O			**38.01**	**28.83**	**20.09**	**12.37**	**6.29**	**2.30**	**0.42**	**0.00**	**0.00**	**0.00**	**0.00**
D				-	1.50	-	-	1.75	-	-	2.00	-	-
S				106.76	117.72	131.69	147.37	163.22	182.97	205.13	228.00	255.91	287.23
IV				43.24	32.28	18.31	2.63	0.00	0.00	0.00	0.00	0.00	0.00
TV				3.86	5.16	9.34	15.67	10.15	4.12	0.83	0.00	0.00	0.00
O				**47.11**	**37.44**	**27.65**	**18.29**	**10.15**	**4.12**	**0.83**	**0.00**	**0.00**	**0.00**
D					1.50	-	-	1.75	-	-	2.00	-	-
S					94.20	105.30	117.75	129.97	145.65	163.24	180.98	203.14	228.00
IV					55.80	44.70	32.25	20.03	4.35	0.00	0.00	0.00	0.00
TV					0.95	2.42	4.58	6.21	11.67	7.29	1.64	0.00	0.00
O					**56.75**	**47.12**	**36.83**	**26.24**	**16.02**	**7.29**	**1.64**	**0.00**	**0.00**
D						-	-	1.75	-	-	2.00	-	-
S						84.34	94.23	103.58	116.02	129.99	143.66	161.25	180.98
IV						65.66	55.77	46.42	33.98	20.01	6.34	0.00	0.00
TV						0.78	1.59	0.85	2.26	4.50	6.43	3.22	0.00
O						**66.43**	**57.36**	**47.28**	**36.24**	**24.51**	**12.76**	**3.22**	**0.00**
D							-	1.75	-	-	2.00	-	-
S							75.56	82.62	92.50	103.59	114.04	128.00	143.66
IV							74.44	67.38	57.50	46.41	35.96	22.00	6.34
TV							1.23	0.11	0.74	1.37	0.00	0.00	0.00
O							**75.67**	**67.49**	**58.23**	**47.78**	**35.96**	**22.00**	**6.34**
D								1.75	-	-	2.00	-	-
S								65.99	73.84	82.64	90.52	101.60	114.04
IV								84.01	76.16	67.36	59.48	48.40	35.96
TV								0.11	0.74	1.37	0.00	0.00	0.00
O								**84.12**	**76.90**	**68.73**	**59.48**	**48.40**	**35.96**
D									-	-	2.00	-	-
S									59.02	66.01	71.85	80.65	90.52
IV									90.98	83.99	78.15	69.35	59.48
TV									0.74	1.37	0.00	0.00	0.00
O									**91.72**	**85.36**	**78.15**	**69.35**	**59.48**
D										-	2.00	-	-
S										52.81	57.04	64.02	71.85
IV										97.19	92.96	85.98	78.15
TV										1.37	0.00	0.00	0.00
O										**98.56**	**92.96**	**85.98**	**78.15**
D											2.00	-	-
S											45.28	50.82	57.04
IV											104.72	99.18	92.96
TV											0.00	0.00	0.00
O											**104.72**	**99.18**	**92.96**
D												-	-
S												40.34	45.28
IV												109.66	104.72
TV												0.00	0.00
O												**109.66**	**104.72**
D													-
S													35.94
IV													114.06
TV													0.00
O													**114.06**

D Dividends
S Share Price
IV Intrinsic Value
TV Time Value
O Option Value

EXERCISE
(since Zero Time Value)

Dpv PV of dividends
(discounting at risk free rate)

European Option value = 22.29

Workings for time 2

1	2	3	
5.11	5.14	5.16	
1.25	-		
166.36	186.12		= [(166.36 - 5.11) x 1.1224] + 5.14
0.00	0.00		= MAX(0, 150.00 - 186.12)
15.74	9.78		= 9.78 - 0.00
15.74	**9.78**	**5.26**	= MAX (0.00 , (5.26 x 0.4892 + 14.19 x (1 - 0.4892)) / 1.0042))
	-		
	148.80		= [(166.36 - 5.11) x 0.8909] + 5.14
	1.20		= MAX(0, 150.00 - 148.80)
	20.38		= 21.58 - 1.20
	21.58	**14.19**	= MAX (1.20 , (14.19 x 0.4892 + 28.83 x (1 - 0.4892)) / 1.0042))

PROBABILITY DISTRIBUTIONS - TOWARDS BLACK-SCHOLES

Mean and variance

Under the Binomial Model, the expected price of a stock (mean) depends on the range of likely stock prices ($S_i = S_1, S_2, .., S_n$) and the probability associated with each price ($p_i = p_1, p_2, \ldots, p_n$):

$$E(S_i) \text{ (or } \mu) = \sum_{i=1}^{n} S_i \, p_i$$

The variation around this expected price (the variance σ^2 = (standard deviation $\sigma)^2$), can be expressed as follows:

$$\text{Variance } (\sigma^2) = E(S_i - \mu)^2$$

$$= E(S_i)^2 - \mu^2$$

$$= (S_1 - \mu)^2 p_1 + (S_2 - \mu)^2 p_2 + \ldots + (S_n - \mu)^2 p_n$$

$$= \sum_{i=1}^{n} (S_i - \mu)^2 p_i$$

$$= \sum S_i^2 p_i - \sum 2\mu S_i p_i + \sum \mu^2 p_i$$

$$= \sum S_i^2 p_i - 2\mu \underbrace{\sum S_i p_i}_{\mu} + \mu^2 \underbrace{\sum p_i}_{1} \quad (\mu \text{ constant})$$

In the one period case, at time T after a time interval of δt years (1 in this example) the expected stock price is as follows:

$$E(S_T) \text{ or } \mu = uS_0p + dS_0(1-p) \quad \textit{with true probability}$$
$$= S_0 \times (1 + \text{risk adjusted rate})$$

$$E^*(S_T) = uS_0p^* + dS_0(1-p^*) \quad \textit{with risk neutral probability}$$
$$= S_0 \times (1 + \text{risk free rate}) = S_0e^{r^*\delta t} \quad \text{(continuous risk free rate } r^*)$$

The variance would be as follows:

$$\text{Variance } (S^T), \sigma^2 = \sum_{i=1}^{2} S_i^2 p_i - E(S_i)^2$$

$$= \left(u^2S_0^2p + d^2 S_0^2(1-p) \right) - \left(S_0 \left[pu + (1-p)d \right] \right)^2$$

$$= S_0^2 \left(u^2p + d^2(1-p) - \left[pu + (1-p)d \right]^2 \right)$$

$$= S_0^2 \; p(1-p)(u-d)^2$$

$$= S_0^2 \; p(1-p)(\ln(u/d))^2 \quad \text{(where } \ln(u/d) = \ln(u - d))$$

In **Examples B4.1** and **B4.2**, the variance using logarithms is 3,600 (= 150^2 x 0.5 x (1 – 0.5) ln (1.4918 / 0.6703)), giving a standard deviation of 60 or 40% around the current 150 share price.

In general, taking into account the length of the period (i.e. not simply 1 year, as in the example above), the mean and variance of 1 plus the discrete rate of return, is as follows:

B4.6

Mean and variance for returns - One Period - Discrete

Expected value	=	$pu + (1-p)d = (1+r)^{\delta t} = e^{r^*\delta t}$
Variance	=	$(u-d)^2\, p\,(1-p)$
Standard deviation	=	$(u-d)\sqrt{[\,p(1-p)\,]}$

where δt	is the length of the time period as a fraction of a year
r	is the effective annually compounded rate
r^*	is the continuously compounded rate,
p	risk neutral probability (if r, r^* = risk free rate) or true probability (if r, r^* = risk adjusted rate).

Taking the natural logarithms of both sides, the continuous rate of return can be shown (this would be the case if the multi-period Tree was comprised of an infinite number of tiny time periods):

B4.7

Mean and variance for returns - One Period - Continuous

Expected return $\mu\delta t$	=	$p\ln(u) + (1-p)\ln(d) = r^*\,\delta t$ See note
Variance, $\sigma^2\,\delta t$	=	$p\,[\ln(u)]^2 + (1-p)\,[\ln(d)]^2 - [\mu\delta t]^2$
	=	$(\ln(u) - \ln(d))^2\, p\,(1-p)$
	=	$\ln(u/d)^2\, p(1-p)$
Standard deviation$\sigma\sqrt{\delta t}$	=	$\ln(u/d)\sqrt{[\,p(1-p)\,]}$

Note also = $p\ln(u/d) + \ln(d)$

The Binomial Distribution

In the 5 ('n') period Binomial Tree in **Example B4.3**, the n + 1 end-state nodes can be reached via 32 routes or paths, as follows:

PATH	*FINAL NODES*					
	0	1	2	3	4	5
10			DDDUU	DDUUU		
9			DDUDU	DUDUU		
8			DUDDU	DUUDU		
7			DDUUD	UDDUU		
6			DUUDD	UUDDU		
5		DDDDU	DUDUD	UDUDU	DUUUU	
4		DDDUD	UDDDU	DUUUD	UDUUU	
3		DDUDD	UDDUD	UDUUD	UUDUU	
2		DUDDD	UDUDD	UUDUD	UUUDU	
1	DDDDD	UDDDD	UUDDD	UUUDD	UUUUD	UUUUU

Each node can be reached via T! / (T – n!)n! paths (! is the factorial, where T! = T x (T-1) x (T-2) x ….. T-T, T the time step and n the node number, with node 0 being the lowest price). All up paths have the same probability (the true probability 'p', when pricing in risk, or the risk neutral probability p*, when ignoring risk), with down paths equal to 1 – p (up path). Each node will have the following probability:

$$P^* \text{ at node } = p^n(1-p)^{T-n}$$

The expected stock price, rate of return and standard deviation can be calculated using these probabilities. Using risk-neutral probabilities (p*):

Node 'n'	p single path	p^n	$(1-p)^{T-n}$	P(up) x P(down)	no. of paths	p* all paths	Share price Si
5 A	0.4833	0.0264	1.0000	0.0264	1	0.0264	366.89
4	0.4833	0.0546	0.5167	0.0282 B	5	0.1410	256.54
3	0.4833	0.1129	0.2669	0.0301	10	0.3014	179.38
2	0.4833	0.2336	0.1379	0.0322	10	0.3222	125.43
1	0.4833	0.4833	0.0713	0.0344	5	0.1722	87.71
0	0.4833	1.0000	0.0368	0.0368	1	0.0368	61.33
					32	1.0000	

Example of workings

A = 5! / { (5 - 4)! x 4! } = (5 x 4 x 3 x 2 x 1) / { 1 x (4 x 3 x 2 x 1) } = 5

B = (0.4833^4) x {(1 - 0.4833)^(5 - 4)} = 0.0282

The risk-neutral expected stock price at the end of year 5 (157.69) represents an effective rate of return of 5.13% per annum or a 5.0% continuous rate (=LN (1 + 5.13%)), being the risk free rate. At the end of each period, the expected prices can be calculated based on the up and down stock prices multiplied by their Binomial risk neutral probabilities (shown below – each probability has been calculated in the same manner as the year 5 probabilities shown above):

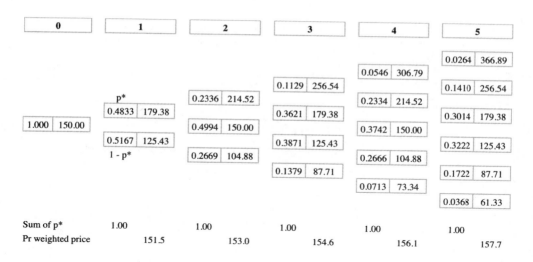

0		1		2		3		4		5	
										0.0264	366.89
								0.0546	306.79		
						0.1129	256.54			0.1410	256.54
		p*		0.2336	214.52			0.2334	214.52		
		0.4833	179.38			0.3621	179.38			0.3014	179.38
1.000	150.00			0.4994	150.00			0.3742	150.00		
		0.5167	125.43			0.3871	125.43			0.3222	125.43
		1 - p*		0.2669	104.88			0.2666	104.88		
						0.1379	87.71			0.1722	87.71
								0.0713	73.34		
										0.0368	61.33
Sum of p*		1.00		1.00		1.00		1.00		1.00	
Pr weighted price			151.5		153.0		154.6		156.1		157.7

The Forward prices (expected risk neutral prices) can be shown alongside the range of possible prices (the tree is now drawn to scale):

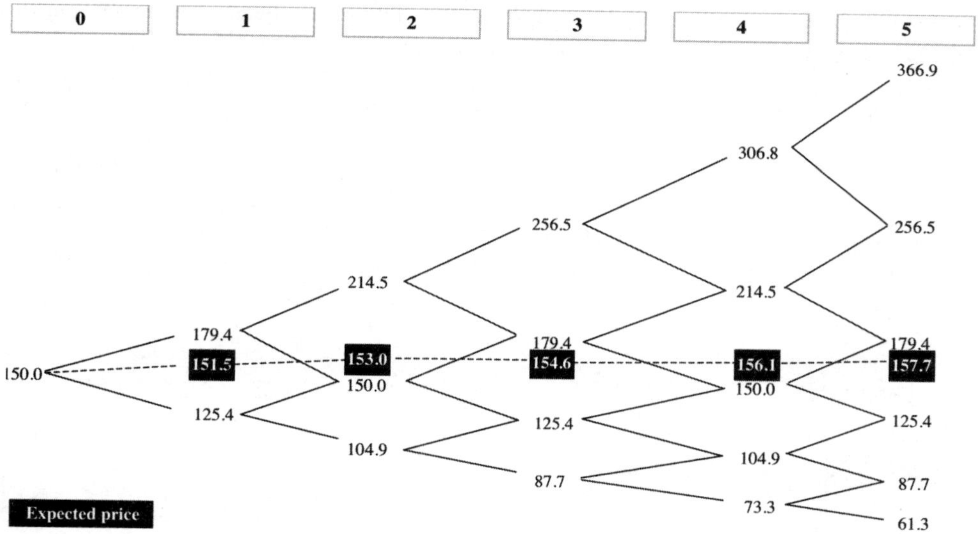

The fair value of the European Call option can be calculated (assuming the option can only be exercised at expiry) using the Binomial Probability:

Call Option value = Today's asset price (P) (Px) - PV of Exercise Price (P)

P - The sum of the probability of expected payoffs for all nodes (from time 0 – time T) where it is optimal to exercise the option (Intrinsic Value exceeds value of Call if exercised later), being:

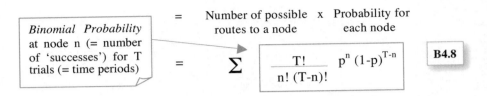

Binomial Probability at node n (= number of 'successes') for T trials (= time periods)

= Number of possible routes to a node x Probability for each node

$$= \sum \frac{T!}{n!\,(T-n)!}\; p^n\,(1-p)^{T-n}$$ **B4.8**

T Number of time periods

n Number of up nodes taken to reach the end state for the relevant node

p Probability (risk-neutral in this case i.e. p*)

Px - The discounted stock price growth factor for the end state: $u^n d^{T-n} / (1+r)^T$, where u and d are the up and down Tree factors (alternatively, the Binomial probabilities can be discounted, to give the 'Arrow-Debreu' price – see below).

Example B4.7 Pricing a Call option using the Binomial distribution

Based on the option in **Example B4.3**, the Call option should only be exercised at two nodes (the three highest nodes at period 5); the Binomial distribution can be adjusted to account for this (S_0 = stock price at time 0, X = exercise price):

Binomial probability	**Is option in the money?**	**Probability of exercise**	**State Price ('Arrow-Debreu' price)**	**Yr 5 price (S_T) / Yr 0 price (S_0)**	**PV of Expected value of S_T / S_0**
see above		**A**	**A / e^{r^*}**	$u^n \times d^{(T-n)}$ **B**	**$A \times B / e^{r^*}$**
0.0264	✓	0.0264	0.0251	2.4459	0.0614
0.1410	✓	0.1410	0.1341	1.7103	0.2294
0.3014	✓	0.3014	0.2867	1.1959	0.3429
0.3222	✖				
0.1722	✖				
0.0368	✖				
1.0000		**0.4688**			**0.6336**

$$C_0 = S_0 \times \sum_{n=a}^{T} \left\{ \left(\frac{T!}{n!\,(T-n)!}\; p^n\,(1-p)^{T-n} \right) \times \left(\frac{u^n d^{T-n}}{(1+r)^T} \right) \right\} - \frac{X}{(1+r)^T} \times \sum_{n=a}^{T} \left\{ \frac{T!}{n!\,(T-n)!}\; p^n\,(1-p)^{T-n} \right\}$$ **B4.9**

PV of expected stock price at each node, where exercising the option is optimal (probability weighted).

PV of exercise price at each node where exercising is optimal (probability weighted).

= 150 x 0.6336 - 150 / 1.0101^(5) x 0.4688
= 95.0436 - 66.8882
= **28.16** (= call price from **Example B4.3**)

The factors 0.6336 and 0.4688 can be calculated directly using the Microsoft Excel™ BINOMDIST () function. The Call price can also be calculated using the approach given by Cox, Ross and Rubinstein (1979):

B4.10

Up factor	1.1959	See **Example B4.3**
Down factor	0.8362	See **Example B4.3**
Min up moves before in-the-money (integer)	2.0000	= INT {LN [150 [X] / 150 [So] x 0.8362^5)] / LN [1.1959 / 0.8362]}
Total trials	5	Time steps
Risk neutral probability	0.4833	See **Example B4.3**
Risk free return per time step	1.0101	See **Example B4.3**
Probability of success	0.5723	= 0.4833 x (1.1959 / 1.0101)
Current share price factor	0.6336	= 1-BINOMDIST(2 , 5 , 0.5723, TRUE)
Exercise price factor	0.4688	= 1-BINOMDIST(2 , 5 , 0.4833, TRUE)
Call Price	**28.16**	= 150 x 0.6336 - 150 / 1.0101^(5) x 0.4688

TRUE' is a signal to Excel that the distribution must be cumulative (i.e. probability higher than X)

This will be used later when discussing the convergence of the Binomial to Black-Scholes model as the number of time steps in a given period is increased. To value an American option (with early exercise possibilities), a Tree would need to be constructed.

The Normal Distribution

Using all nodes for year 5 in **Example 4.3**:

- each stock price can be shown in terms of the number of standard deviations from the mean;
- the probability for each stock price can be shown in terms of the probability of being less than or equal to that stock price (the cumulative probability for each price).

Year 5 node	**0**	**1**	**2**	**3**	**4**	**5**	**Total**	
S_i	61.33	87.71	125.43	179.38	256.54	366.89		
Routes	1	5	10	10	5	1		
P	0.037	0.034	0.032	0.030	0.028	0.026		
P_i (all routes)	0.037	0.172	0.322	0.301	0.141	0.026	1.000	
$S_i \times P_i$	2.26	15.10	40.41	54.07	36.17	9.68	157.69	= Mean μ
$(Si - \mu)^2 \times P_i$	341.87	843.45	335.32	141.83	1377.68	1154.47	4194.62	= Variance σ^2
Cum pr	0.037	0.209	0.531	0.833	0.974	1.000		
$z_i = (S_i - \mu) / \sigma$	-1.49	-1.08	-0.50	0.33	1.53	3.23		
$z_i \times P_i$	-0.0547769	-0.186083	-0.1604886	0.1009528	0.2151887	0.085207	0.00	= Mean E(z)
$(z_i - E(z))^2 \times P_i$	0.08	0.20	0.08	0.03	0.33	0.28	1.00	= Variance

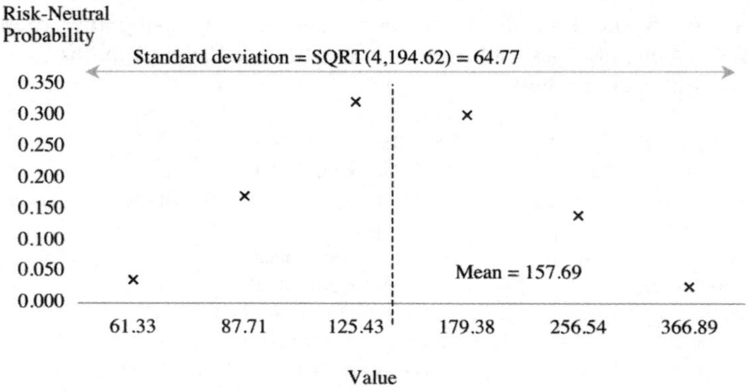

If the year is divided into 1000 time periods rather than just 5, then the same stock would have the following Binomial probability distribution, mean and standard deviation (extracts are shown for nodes 490 to 510):

BINOMIAL DISTRIBUTION - 1 YEAR = 1000 STEPS				
Trial (node)	Binomial Probability (Risk-Neutral)	Share price (S_T)	Return $S_n / S_0 - 1$	Log Return $\ln(S_n / S_0)$
.				
.				
490	0.02160	116.47	-22.35%	-25.30%
491	0.02233	119.46	-20.36%	-22.77%
492	0.02299	122.52	-18.32%	-20.24%
493	0.02358	125.66	-16.23%	-17.71%
494	0.02408	128.88	-14.08%	-15.18%
495	0.02450	132.18	-11.88%	-12.65%
496	0.02483	135.56	-9.62%	-10.12%
497	0.02506	139.04	-7.31%	-7.59%
498	0.02519	142.60	-4.93%	-5.06%
499	0.02522	146.25	-2.50%	-2.53%
500	0.02515	150.00	0.00%	0.00%
501	0.02499	153.84	2.56%	2.53%
502	0.02472	157.78	5.19%	5.06%
503	0.02436	161.83	7.88%	7.59%
504	0.02390	165.97	10.65%	10.12%
505	0.02337	170.23	13.48%	12.65%
506	0.02275	174.59	16.39%	15.18%
507	0.02206	179.06	19.37%	17.71%
508	0.02131	183.65	22.43%	20.24%
509	0.02050	188.35	25.57%	22.77%
510	0.01964	193.18	28.79%	25.30%
.				
.				
Total	*1.0000*			
Mean		*157.69*	*5.13%*	*-3.00%*
St. Dev.			*43.79%*	*40.00%*

Share price today	150.00
Risk Free interest rate	5.00%
Volatility	40.00%
Time step (fraction of year)	0.0010
Number of time periods	1000

U	1.0127	= EXP(40.0%*SQRT(0.0010))
D	0.9874	= 1/1.0127
r	1.0001	= EXP(5%*0.0010)
p*	0.4988	= (1.0001 - 0.9874)/(1.0127 - 0.9874)

The Binomial Probability is calculated using equation **B4.8**, or using the Excel™ function. For node 490:

BINOMDIST (490, 1000, 0.4988, FALSE) = 0.02160

where 0.4988 is the risk-neutral probability

Share price = $150 \times 1.0127^{490} \times 0.9874^{510}$ (allowing for rounding differences)

Mean $= \Sigma X_T p_T$

Standard Dev. $= \sqrt{\{\Sigma (X_T)^2 p_T - \text{mean}^2\}}$

where X is the share price or return (see note below)

Note: as discussed below (**B4.14**), if the log return, $\ln(S_T/S_0)$, is normally distributed, the mean (shown as 1 + return) and variance of discrete returns can be calculated from the equivalent logarithmic mean and standard deviation as follows: $E(S_T/S_0) = e^{-3.00\% + 0.5 \times 40\%^2} = 1.0513$ (where $E(\ln(S_T/S_0)) = -3.00\% = 5.00\% - 0.5 \times 40\%^2$ - see **B4.15**), $\text{Var}(S_T/S_0) = e^{2 \times -3.00\% + 40\%^2} \times (e^{40\%^2} - 1) = 19.17\%$ (i.e. $43.79\%^2$).

With an infinite number of time steps (and hence an infinite number of possible values for S_i), the Binomial Probability Distribution would approximate the 'standard normal distribution' function for a random variable S_i (with mean μ and standard deviation σ) where the random variable Z (= $(S_i - \mu)/\sigma$) has a mean of zero and a standard deviation of 1.0 based on a continuous probability distribution:

B4.11

$$f(X) = \frac{1}{(\sqrt{2\pi})\sigma} e^{-0.5\left(\frac{X-\mu}{\sigma}\right)^2}$$

$$= \frac{1}{(\sqrt{2\pi})\sigma} e^{-0.5 Z^2}$$

where
- e: constant, approximately equal to 2.71828
- π: constant, approximately equal to 3.14159
- Z: $(X - \mu)/\sigma$ with a mean of 0 and standard deviation of 1.0
- X: S_i in this case

The standard cumulative normal distribution function can be approximated as follows (as the variable X has been standardised, it is equivalent to Z): N accuracy to 4 decimal places (6 decimal place accuracy is possible if further terms are added - see Hull (2003 p.248), Chriss (1997 p.88)):

B4.12

$$N(x) = 1 - N'(x)(a_1 k + a_2 k^2 + a_3 k^3) \quad \text{for } x \ge 0$$

$$= 1 - N(-x) \quad \text{for } x < 0$$

$k = 1/[1 + 0.33267(x)]$
$a_1 = 0.4361836$
$a_2 = -0.1201676$
$a_3 = 0.9372980$

where $N'(x) = 1 - \frac{1}{(\sqrt{2\pi})\sigma} e^{-0.5x^2}$ $(\sigma = 1)$

N (x) can also be calculated using the Excel NORMSDIST(x) function.

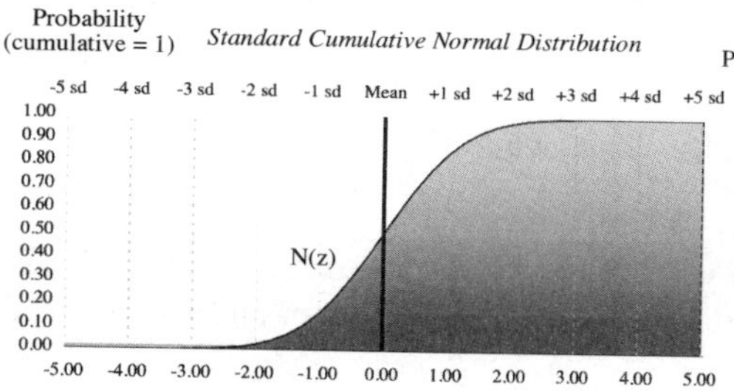

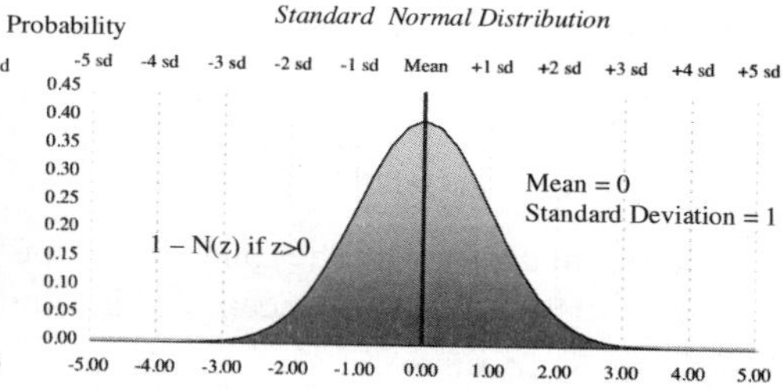

Whatever the standard deviation of a normally distributed random variable X (the width of the above curve being determined by the size of σ), X has a standard probability within a certain range from the mean (expressed as number of standard deviations from the mean):

X	1σ	1.96σ	2σ	3σ
P_X	68.3%	95.0%	96.4%	99.7%

The standard normal distribution can be used to estimate the probability of X being within a range. If the mean and standard deviation for any given random variable X are known, 'Z' can be calculated, and the probability of X being less than Z standard deviations away from the mean can, therefore, be calculated.

Example B4.8 Estimating the probability based on a Normal Distribution

The continuous rate of change in a stock price (which could be approximated by taking the logarithm of one plus the daily percentage change in prices over an annual period) is assumed to be normally distributed with an annualised mean of -3.0% and a standard deviation of 40%. The probabiliy of the stock being higher than its current 150 price in one year is 0.4701 (= 1 – NORMSDIST (0.075) where $0.075 = Z = (X - \mu) / \sigma$, and X = the logarithmic return = ln (150 / 150) = 0%, μ = -3.0%, and σ = 40%).

The Lognormal Distribution

In continuous time, it can be assumed that the rate of change in a share price comprises two components: a trend, deterministic, or 'drift' element (equal to the expected continuous rate of return μ, proportional to the time step δt, and a fluctuating, stochastic or random element (equal to the standard deviation, proportional to the square root of the time step, $\sigma\sqrt{\delta t}$, multiplied by a normally distributed random element Z):

$$S_T / S_0 - 1 = \mu\delta t + \sigma\sqrt{\delta t}Z \qquad \textit{`Geometric Brownian Motion'} \qquad \textbf{B4.13}$$
$$\therefore \; S_T = S_0 e^{\mu\delta t + \sigma\sqrt{\delta t}Z}$$

where Z is a standard normal variable with mean 0 and standard deviation 1.

If the share price follows this process, (1) the logarithm of the return ($\ln(S_T / S_0)$) will be normally distributed, and (2) the return (S_T / S_0) will be 'lognormally' distributed with the following distribution:

$$f(X) = \frac{1}{(\sqrt{2\pi})\sigma X} e^{-0.5\left(\frac{\ln X - \mu\delta t}{\sigma\sqrt{\delta t}}\right)^2} \qquad \text{where } X = S_T / S_0$$

Advanced mathematics (beyond the scope of this book) shows that if $\ln(S_T / S_0)$ is normally distributed with mean μ and standard deviation σ, the mean and variance of S_T / S_0 are as follows:

$$E(S_T / S_0) \text{ or } E(e^X) = e^{m\delta t} = e^{(\mu + 0.5\sigma^2)\delta t} \qquad \textbf{B4.14}$$

$$Var(S_T / S_0) \text{ or } Var(e^X) = s^2\delta t = e^{(2\mu + \sigma^2)\delta t}(e^{\sigma^2\delta t} - 1)$$

(See Watsham and Parramore (1997 p.157)).

Over very small time intervals, the variance of (S_T / S_0) is approximately the same as the variance of X or $\ln (S_T / S_0)$. The expected value of S_T / S_0 is shown as $E (S_T / S_0) = E (e^{\mu dt + \sigma\sqrt{dt}Z})$; however, since Z has a mean of zero $E (S_T / S_0) = E (e^X) = E (e^{\mu\delta t})$. Hence $0.5\sigma^2$ needs to be deducted (from **B4.14**)(See Stulz (2003 p.361)).

In summary:

S_T	=	$S_0 e^{(\mu - 0.5\sigma^2)\delta t + \sigma\sqrt{\delta t}\, Z}$	**B4.15**
$\ln (S_T)$	=	$\ln (S_0) + (\mu - 0.5\sigma^2)\delta t + \sigma\sqrt{\delta t}\, Z$	
$E (S_T)$	=	$S_0 e^{\mu \delta t}$	
$E (\ln (S_T))$	=	$\ln (S_0) + (\mu - 0.5\sigma^2)\delta t$	
$E (\ln (S_T / S_0))$	=	$(\mu - 0.5\sigma^2)\delta t$	
$Var (S_T)$	=	$S_0 e^{\sigma^2 \delta t}$ (if δt is very small – see **B4.14**)	
$Var (\ln (S_T / S_0))$	=	$\sigma^2 \delta t$	

Example B4.9 Simulated lognormal distribution (risk-neutral)

The share price from **Example B4.3** is assumed to have a continuously compounded expected rate of return (the risk free rate for risk-neutral pricing) of 5.0% and a standard deviation of 40%. The current price is 150 and the 1 year is divided into 1000 time steps. The share price is assumed to change from one period to the next as follows:

$$S_{t+1} = S_t e^{(\mu - 0.5\sigma^2)\delta t + \sigma\sqrt{\delta t}\, Z}$$

where
- μ - 5.00% continuously compounded expected rate of return (risk free)
- σ - 40% standard deviation
- Z - random variable, normally distributed with mean = 0 and standard deviation = 1 (which can be approximated using the Excel™ functions: NORMSINV(RAND()) (Wilmott (2000 p.924)).

Based on one simulated price run, the risk-free expected price at the end of the year is 200.61. For a European option, with an exercise price of 150, the payoff would be 50.61 with a present value of $50.61e^{5.00\%}$ = 48.14 (in practice, many more simulations would be carried out to determine an average final price and expected payoff - Cuthbertson and Nitzsche (2001 p. 463)).

Extracts from the simulation (risk neutral pricing $\mu = r$) are given below:

Time	(r - 0.5σ^2)δt		√δt		Z	√δtZ		σ		σ√δtZ	Price	ln (S_T / S_{T-1})	(S_T / S_{T-1})
	Risk-free drift									Random	S_T(risk neutral)		
0											150.00		
1	-0.0030%	+	0.0316	x	-0.5168	-0.0163	x	40%	=	-0.0065	149.02	-0.6567%	99.3454%
2	-0.0030%	+	0.0316	x	-0.7737	-0.0245	x	40%	=	-0.0098	147.56	-0.9816%	99.0232%
3	-0.0030%	+	0.0316	x	1.5201	0.0481	x	40%	=	0.0192	150.42	1.9198%	101.9383%
4	-0.0030%	+	0.0316	x	-0.5054	-0.0160	x	40%	=	-0.0064	149.46	-0.6423%	99.3597%
5	-0.0030%	+	0.0316	x	-0.4611	-0.0146	x	40%	=	-0.0058	148.59	-0.5863%	99.4154%
.													
.													
498	-0.0030%	+	0.0316	x	0.8341	0.0264	x	40%	=	0.0106	118.15	1.0520%	101.0576%
499	-0.0030%	+	0.0316	x	-1.5760	-0.0498	x	40%	=	-0.0199	115.82	-1.9965%	98.0233%
500	-0.0030%	+	0.0316	x	0.5852	0.0185	x	40%	=	0.0074	116.67	0.7373%	100.7400%
501	-0.0030%	+	0.0316	x	1.9579	0.0619	x	40%	=	0.0248	119.60	2.4736%	102.5044%
502	-0.0030%	+	0.0316	x	0.9361	0.0296	x	40%	=	0.0118	121.02	1.1810%	101.1880%
.													
.													
996	-0.0030%	+	0.0316	x	0.8701	0.0275	x	40%	=	0.0110	193.31	1.0976%	101.1037%
997	-0.0030%	+	0.0316	x	0.0254	0.0008	x	40%	=	0.0003	193.36	0.0292%	100.0292%
998	-0.0030%	+	0.0316	x	1.2697	0.0402	x	40%	=	0.0161	196.49	1.6031%	101.6160%
999	-0.0030%	+	0.0316	x	2.1902	0.0693	x	40%	=	0.0277	202.00	2.7674%	102.8060%
1000	-0.0030%	+	0.0316	x	-0.5456	-0.0173	x	40%	=	-0.0069	200.61	-0.6932%	99.3092%

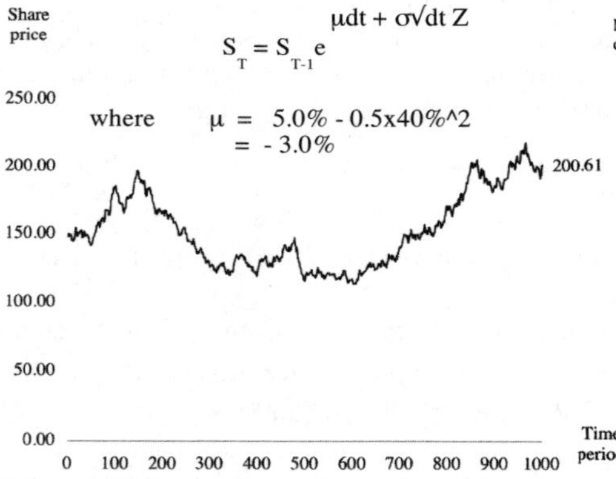

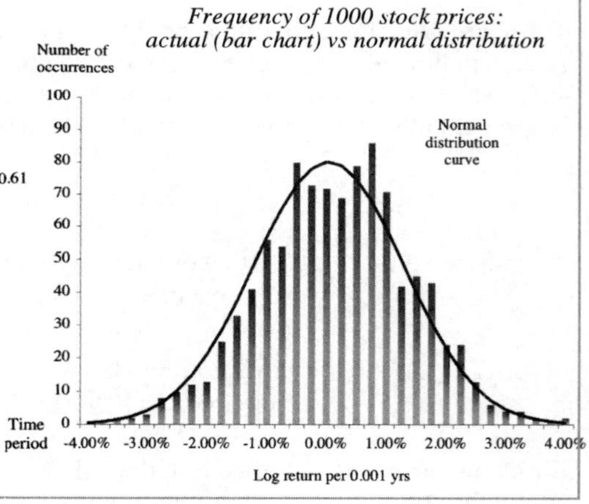

Summary

This section has given a brief overview of the probability distribution that underpins the Binomial option pricing model, discussed how that distribution approximates the normal distribution as the number of time steps becomes significantly large (i.e. the model moves towards a continuous model) and how the normal distribution can be shown for continuous rates of return (log returns). One assumption of the Black-Scholes model is that the stock price moves in accordance with the lognormal distribution.

BLACK-SCHOLES MODEL

The Black-Scholes Model (BSM) (No Dividends)

In 1973, Fischer Black and Myron Scholes developed the BSM for valuing European options on stocks (single exercise date at expiry):

Black-Scholes Model (no dividends) **B4.16**

$$\text{Call option value} = S\,N(d_1) - X e^{-rT} N(d_2)$$

$$\text{Put option value} = X e^{-rT} N(-d_2) - S\,N(-d_1)$$

S	Current stock price
X	Exercise Price
T	Time to maturity
r	Risk free rate (continuously compounded)
e	The base of natural logarithms, constant = 2.1728 …..
$X e^{-rT}$	The amount of cash needed to be invested over a period of time T at a continuously compounded interest rate r in order to receive X at maturity (i.e. it is the PV of the exercise price continuously discounted at the risk free rate).

$$d_1 = \frac{\ln(S/X) + (r + 0.5\sigma^2)T}{\sigma\sqrt{T}} = \frac{\ln(S/X) + rT}{\sigma\sqrt{T}} + 0.5\sigma\sqrt{T}$$

$$d_2 = \frac{\ln(S/X) + (r - 0.5\sigma^2)T}{\sigma\sqrt{T}} = d_1 - \sigma\sqrt{T}$$

where σ is the annualised standard deviation of logarithmic stock returns

N (x) The cumulative probability function for a standardised normal variable. N(d1) and N(d2) will be discussed later, in the context of the Binomial model.

The BSM model assumes:

- the option can only be exercised at maturity (European option);
- the stock price follows a lognormal distribution;
- the exercise price, volatility (i.e. uncertainty) and risk free rate are constant;
- there are no transaction costs, taxes, or dividends;
- there are no riskless arbitrage opportunities;
- investors can borrow or lend at the same risk free rate of interest.

Example B4.10 European Call option - BSM - no dividends

Using the same information as in **Examples B4.1-B4.3**, except this time assuming the option is a European option, the BSM valuation is as follows:

Black-Scholes - no dividends

Current share price	S	150.00
Exercise Price	X	150.00
Volatility (%)(standard deviation)	σ	40.00%
Risk Free Rate (%) (continous)	r	5.00%
Time to Expiry (years)	T	1.0000
Dividend Yield (%)	q	0.00%

d1 = (LN(150.00 / 150.00) + (5.00% + 0.5 x 40.00%^2) x 1) / (40.00% x SQRT(1)) 0.3250

d2 = (LN(150.00 / 150.00) + (5.00% - 0.5 x 40.00%^2) x 1) / (40.00% x SQRT(1))
= 0.3250 - 40.00% x SQRT(1) -0.0750

N(d1)	= NORMSDIST(0.3250)	0.6274
N(d2)	= NORMSDIST(-0.0750)	0.4701
Share price	(150.00 x N(d1))	94.11
PV of ex price	(150.00 x EXP(-5.00 x 1)) x N(d2)	67.08
Call Price		**27.03**

See **Example B4.8**: N(d2) is the probability of the option being in the money (**Example B4.8** is based on the same inputs).

N(d1) and N(d2) have been calculated using the Microsoft Excel™ function NORMSDIST, but can be calculated using the polynomial expression (**B4.12**) – see Hull (2003 p.248).

CALL OPTION VALUE

Share price			150.0000
x Normal dist factor N(d1)			0.6274
Adjusted price			94.1114
Adjust exercise price to PV	= Xe^{-rT}	= 150.00 x EXP (-5.00% x 1.00)	142.6844
x Normal dist factor N(d2)			0.4701
Adjusted price			67.0770
CALL OPTION VALUE	= 94.1114 - 67.0770		**27.03**

A Put option value would be as follows:

PUT OPTION VALUE

Adjust exercise price to PV	= Xe^{-rT}	= 150.00 x EXP (-5.00% x 1.00)	142.6844
x (1 - Normal dist factor N(d2))			0.5299
Adjusted price			75.6074
Share price			150.0000
x (1 - Normal dist factor N(d1))			0.3726
Adjusted price			55.8886
PUT OPTION VALUE	= 75.6074 - 55.8886		**19.72**

The Black-Scholes Model (BSM)(dividends)

Dividends can be incorporated into the BSM by:

1. reducing the stock price, S, by the present value of the dividends, discounted back from the ex-dividend dates at the risk free rate, or
2. assume dividends are paid continuously at a rate of q%, by replacing 'S' in the BSM model with Se^{-qT} and r (in the equations for d1 and d2) with 'r – q' as follows (Merton (1973)):

Black-Scholes / Merton Model (dividends – continuous yield) **B4.17**

$$\text{Call option value} = S\,\mathbf{e}^{-qT}\,N(d_1) - X\,e^{-rt}\,N(d_2)$$

$$\text{Put option value} = X\,e^{-rt}\,N(-d_2) - S\,\mathbf{e}^{-qT}\,N(-d_1)$$

$$d_1 = \frac{\ln(S/X) + (r - \mathbf{q} + 0.5\,\sigma^2)T}{\sigma\sqrt{T}} = \frac{\ln(S/X) + rT}{\sigma\sqrt{T}} + 0.5\sigma\sqrt{T}$$

$$d_2 = d_1 - \sigma\sqrt{T}$$

In both cases, the volatility may need to be adjusted to reflect the adjusted (ex-div) share price (if the volatility is derived from historic returns). One method is to reduce it proportionately (Hull (2003 p.253)):

$$\text{Adjusted } \sigma \text{ to be used in BSM} = \sigma \times \frac{\text{Current share price}}{\text{Current share price - PV of dividends}}$$

This assumes the dividend payments are known and hence have zero volatility ('cum-PV div' price x σ = 'ex-PV div' price x adj σ + PV of dividends x zero).

Example B4.11 European Call option - BSM - dividends

In the Binomial American Call option, where known £ dividends were paid quarterly (**Example B4.6 (2)**), the present value of future dividends at time 0 was £6.34 per share. Using method 1 this gives a European BSM Call value of 23.19 assuming no change in volatility (24.17 if volatility is adjusted). Using a continuous dividend yield of 4.32% gives the same value.

Black-Scholes - with dividends		
Current share price	S	150.00
Exercise Price	X	150.00
Volatility (%)(standard deviation)	σ	40.00%
Risk Free Rate (%) (continous)	r	5.00%
Time to Expiry (years)	T	1.0000

Discrete dividends		
Present value of dividends		6.34
Share price adjusted to 150.00 - 6.34		143.66
Volatilty adjusted to 150.00 / 143.66 x 40.0% =	41.76%	40.00%
d1 = (LN(143.66 / 150.00) + (5.00% + 0.5 x 40.00%^2) x 1) / (40.00% x SQRT(1))		0.2171
d2 = 0.2171 - 40.00% x SQRT(1)		-0.1829
N(d1)	= NORMSDIST(0.2171)	0.5859
N(d2)	= NORMSDIST(-0.1829)	0.4274
Share price (143.66) x N(d1)		84.17
PV of ex price {150.00 x EXP(-5.00 x 1) } x N(d2)		60.99
Call Price		**23.19**
Call Price with volatility adjusted		**24.17**
Continuous dividends		
Dividend yield (continous rate)		4.32%
Share price adjusted to 150.00 x EXP (4.32% x 1)		143.66
Volatilty adjusted to 150.00 / 143.66 x 40.0% =	41.76%	40.00%
d1 = (LN(150.00 / 150.00) + (5.00% - 0.00% + 0.5 x 0.00%^2) x 1) / (0.00% x SQRT(1))		0.2171
d2 = 0.0000 - 0.00% x SQRT(1)		-0.1829
N(d1)	= NORMSDIST(0.0000)	0.5859
N(d2)	= NORMSDIST(-0.1829)	0.4274
Share price (0.00) x N(d1)		84.17
PV of ex price {150.00 x EXP(-5.00 x 1) } x N(d2)		60.99
Call Price		**23.19**
Call Price with volatility adjusted		**24.17**

Early exercise

It is possible to assess, using a 'closed-form' solution like BSM, whether an American option on a dividend paying stock should be exercised early. However, there needs to be one single relevant ex-dividend date when exercise could take place, and the assessment would require the evaluation of an option on an option to exercise early, or a 'compound' option, which is beyond the scope of this book.

CONVERGENCE OF BINOMIAL AND BLACK-SCHOLES MODELS

Multi Period – No Dividends

As the number of periods in the Binomial Model increase, the Binomial factors converge to the Black-Scholes factors:

Binomial Call $= S \ (P)(Px) \ - Xe^{-rt} \ (P)$ see **4.8 – 4.10**

↓ ↓

Black-Scholes Call $= S \ N(d_1) \ - X e^{-rt} \ N(d_2)$

Example B4.12 European Call option - Convergence of Black-Scholes to Binomial

Using the 1000 step Binomial distribution (discussed earlier), and calculating the Binomial Call price using the Binomial equation (**B4.9** and **B4.10**), the price for a European Call option can be compared to the Black-Scholes price of 27.03 shown above (**Example B4.10**). Convergence to within a range of 0.01% of the Black-Scholes price arises when at least 227 time periods are used for the year. Convergence of the Binomial factors ((P)(Px) and P) to the Black Scholes equivalent factors (N(d1) and N(d2)), to four decimal places, takes longer.

EUROPEAN CALL OPTION - BINOMIAL - 1, 2,3, …, 1000 TIME PERIODS - 1 YEAR (EXTRACTS)

Time Steps in 1 year	Up	Down	1 + r*	Risk neutral p*	Min up moves	P* of success	(P) (Px)	P	Binomial Call
1	1.491825	0.670320	1.0513	0.463724	0	0.658055	0.6581	0.4637	32.54
2	1.326896	0.753638	1.0253	0.473917	1	0.613313	0.3762	0.2246	24.38
3	1.259784	0.793787	1.0168	0.478586	1	0.592949	0.6378	0.4679	28.91
4	1.221403	0.818731	1.0126	0.481403	2	0.580683	0.4421	0.2851	25.63
5	1.195884	0.836202	1.0101	0.483339	2	0.572266	0.6336	0.4688	28.16
.									
.									
9	1.142631	0.875173	1.0056	0.487546	4	0.553998	0.6308	0.4694	27.65
10	1.134839	0.881182	1.0050	0.488180	5	0.551243	0.5076	0.3482	26.46
11	1.128179	0.886384	1.0046	0.488727	5	0.548871	0.6302	0.4695	27.54
12	1.122401	0.890947	1.0042	0.489204	6	0.546800	0.5179	0.3583	26.55
13	1.117328	0.894992	1.0039	0.489626	6	0.544972	0.6298	0.4696	27.46
.									
.									
496	1.018123	0.982200	1.0001	0.498316	248	0.507296	0.6104	0.4523	27.02
497	1.018104	0.982218	1.0001	0.498318	248	0.507289	0.6275	0.4701	27.05
498	1.018086	0.982235	1.0001	0.498320	248	0.507281	0.6443	0.4879	27.02
499	1.018068	0.982253	1.0001	0.498321	249	0.507274	0.6275	0.4701	27.05
500	1.018050	0.982271	1.0001	0.498323	250	0.507267	0.6104	0.4523	27.02
.									
.									
996	1.012755	0.987405	1.0001	0.498812	497	0.505149	0.6394	0.4827	27.03
997	1.012749	0.987412	1.0001	0.498812	498	0.505146	**0.6274**	**0.4701**	27.04
998	1.012742	0.987418	1.0001	0.498813	499	0.505144	0.6154	0.4575	27.03
999	1.012736	0.987424	1.0001	0.498814	499	0.505141	**0.6274**	**0.4701**	27.04 *
1000	1.012729	0.987431	1.0001	0.498814	500	0.505139	0.6154	0.4575	27.03

* *Workings - time step 999:*

Up	= EXP(40.00% x SQRT(1 / 999))	= 1.012736	Down = 1 / U
1 + r*	= EXP(5.00% x SQRT(1 / 999))	= 1.0001	
p*	= (1.0001 - 0.9874) / (1.0127 - 0.9874)	= 0.498814	
Min moves	= INT(LN(150.0 / (150.0 x (0.9874^999)) / (LN(1.0127 / 0.9874)))	= 499	
Pr success	= 0.4988 x 1.0127 / 1.0001	= 0.505141	
(P)(Px)	= (1 - BINOMDIST(499 , 999 , 0.5051 , TRUE))	= 0.6274	
P	= (1 - BINOMDIST(499 , 999 , 0.4988 , TRUE))	= 0.4701	
Binom Call	= 0.6274 x 150.0 - 0.4701 x 142.68 (the PV of the exercise price)	= 27.04	

The Binomial Price increases and then decreases as n (the time steps) goes from even to odd and then odd to even (this effect is discussed further in Rendleman. Jr. (2002 p.93)).

EUROPEAN CALL OPTION (NO DIVIDENDS) - 1 YEAR EXPIRY - BLACK SCHOLES

Model assumptions		**Call Price**	
Current share price	150.00	d1 = (LN(150.00 / 150.00) + (5.00% + 0.5 x 40.00%^2) x 1) / (40.00% x SQRT(1))	0.3250
Exercise Price	150.00	d2 = (LN(150.00 / 150.00) + (5.00% - 0.5 x 40.00%^2) x 1) / (40.00% x SQRT(1))	-0.0750
Volatility	40.00%	N(d1) = NORMSDIST(0.3250)	0.6274
Risk Free Rate	5.00%	N(d2) = NORMSDIST(-0.0750)	0.4701
Time to Expiry (years)	1.0000		
		Share price (150.00 x N(d1)	94.11
		PV of ex price {150.00 x EXP(-5.00 x 1) } x N(d2)	67.08
		Call Price	**27.03**

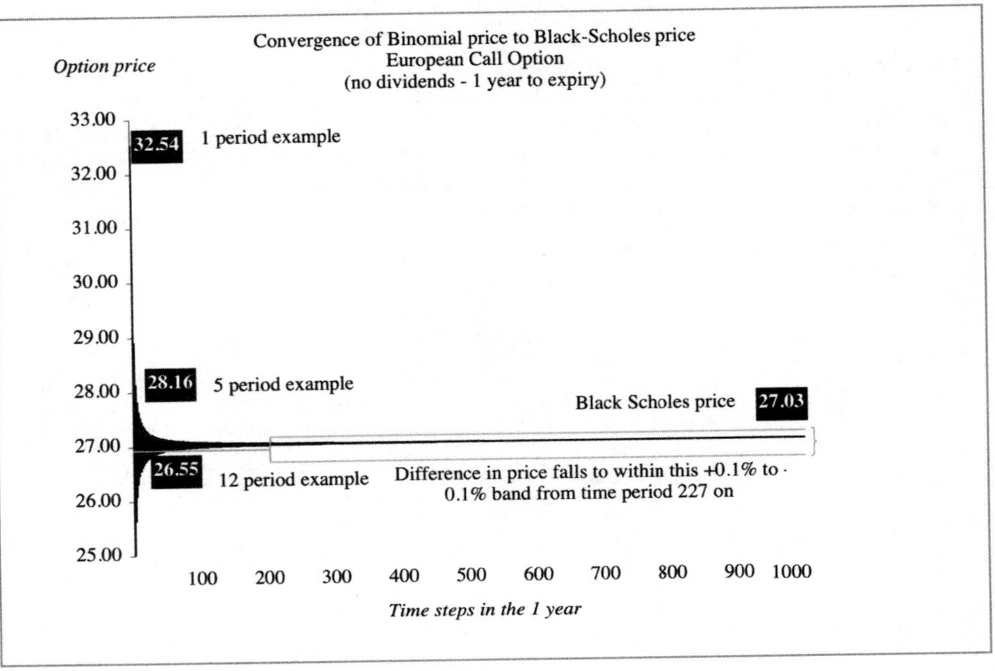

Interpreting the Black-Scholes Model

In the case of European options, the Binomial model is equivalent to a discrete time version of the Black-Scholes model. The Call price is the present value of the probability weighted positive Intrinsic Values at expiry (i.e. the sum of $S_i - X$ at expiry, with both S_i and X weighted by the Binomial probabilities).

Example B4.13 European Call option - Interpreting the BSM

For the 1000 time step case (**Example B4.12**), the sum of Binomial probabilities for all possible stock prices at the expiry date is 1.0; however, a minimum of 500 up moves is needed before the stock price reaches the 150 exercise price. Since the exercise price is constant, it can be multiplied by the sum of all probabilities where the option is in the money (0.4575 = N(d2) where convergence takes place) and discounted to present value.

As the share price is not constant, each share price, where the option is in the money, needs to be probability weighted. The aggregated probability weighted in-the-money prices can then be discounted back, and expressed as a multiple of the current stock price.

$$\text{Call option value} = S\ N(d_1) - X e^{-rt} N(d_2)$$

In terms of the Binomial model, where convergence takes place:

$$N(d_1) \approx \sum_{\text{First in-the-money trial (501)}}^{T=1000} \text{PV of Binomial Probability} \times (S_i / S_0)$$

$$N(d_2) \approx \sum_{\text{First in-the-money trial (501)}}^{T=1000} \text{Binomial Probability}$$

BINOMIAL DISTRIBUTION - 1 YEAR = 1000 STEPS

Trial (node)	Binomial Probability (Risk-Neutral)	Share price (S_T)	S_T / S_0	Binomial Probability where $S_T > X$	Probability / (1 +r) (Arrow Debreu price)	Share price factor
			a		b	a x b
.						
.						
496	0.02483	135.56				
497	0.02506	139.04				
498	0.02519	142.60				
499	0.02522	146.25				
500	0.02515	150.00				
501	0.02499	153.84	1.03	0.02499	0.02377	0.02438
502	0.02472	157.78	1.05	0.02472	0.02351	0.02473
503	0.02436	161.83	1.08	0.02436	0.02317	0.02500
504	0.02390	165.97	1.11	0.02390	0.02274	0.02516
505	0.02337	170.23	1.13	0.02337	0.02223	0.02523
.						
.						
Total	*1.0000*			*0.4575*		*0.6154*
Mean		*157.69*				
Over	*0 - 1000*	*0 - 1000*		*501 - 1000*		*501 - 1000*

This is the probability of the option being in-the-money at expiry for a 1000 time step Binomial Model (using 999 steps gives exactly the same probability as calculated in the BSM – 0.4701 per **Example B4.10**).

THE BINOMIAL MODEL REVISITED – SETTING THE PARAMETERS

Introduction

In the Binomial model, the risk-neutral probability p* is calculated so as to ensure the expected stock return over a single time step is the risk free rate: the predicted stock prices (the two up and down values) are probability weighted to determine the expected price:

$$E^*(S_T) = uS_0p^* + dS_0(1-p^*)$$

where

$$\frac{E^*(S_T)}{S_0} = (1 + r)^{\delta t} = e^{r^*\delta t}$$

If u and d are assumed, then p* can be determined (as in the examples so far); alternatively, p* can be set and u and d calculated, according to an assumed u/d relationship, volatility and probability distribution (discrete or continuous):

Discrete	*Continuous*
$(1+\mu)^{\delta t} = p^*u + (1-p^*)d = e^{r^*\delta t}$	$\mu\delta t = p^*\ln(u) + (1-p^*)\ln(d) = r^*\delta t$
$\sigma^2\delta t = (u-d)^2[p^*(1-p^*)]$	$\sigma^2\delta t = p[\ln(u)]^2 + (1-p)[\ln(d)]^2 - [\mu\delta t]^2$

See **B4.6** and **B4.7**

Cox, Ross and Rubinstein (1979)('CRR')

CRR set d = 1/u, so that ln(d) = -ln(u), hence, assuming a time step of δt and the continuous return:

$$\text{Expected return, } r^*\delta t = p^*\ln(u) + (1-p^*)(-\ln(u))$$
$$= \ln(u)(2p^* - 1)$$
$$\text{Variance, } \sigma^2 dt = p^*[\ln(u)]^2 + (1-p^*)[\ln(d)]^2 - [\mu^2\delta t^2]^{note}$$
$$= [\ln(u)]^2$$
$$\text{Standard Dev., } \sigma\sqrt{dt} = \ln(u)$$

(The term $[\mu^2\delta t^2]$ is crossed out.)

Note: in continuous time, it can be assumed that $\delta t^2 \rightarrow 0$

B4.18

Cox, Ross, Rubinstein (1979)

$$u = e^{\sigma\sqrt{\delta t}}$$
$$d = 1/u = e^{-\sigma\sqrt{\delta t}} \quad \text{where} \quad d < e^{r^*t} < u$$
$$p^* = 0.5 + \frac{0.5r^*\delta t}{\sigma}$$

This results in the upward movement being larger, relative to the downward movement, as the standard deviation increases (and, for the multi period model, in the Tree 'recombining').

Example B4.14 American/European Call option - Binomial - no dividends - 1 period - CRR

The Call price in **Example B4.1** was calculated using the CRR approach:

Assumptions	
Share price	150
Exercise price	150
Volatilty σ	40.0%
Time to expiry (in yrs)	1.00
Risk free rate (continuous)	5.00%
Risk free rate (discrete) =Exp (5.00%) - 1	5.13%

Up and Down factors			
		Discrete	*Continuous*
		u-1, d-1	*ln (u), ln (d)*
u	1.4918	49.18%	40.00%
d	0.6703	-32.97%	-40.00%

	Cox, Ross & Rubinstein (1979)		
u	1.4918	=	EXP(40.0% x SQRT 1.00)
d	0.6703	=	EXP(-40.0% x SQRT 1.00) = 1 / u
S_u	223.77	=	150 x 1.4918
S_d	100.55	=	150 x 0.6703
C_u	73.8	=	MAX { [150x1.4918 - 150], 0}
C_d	0.0	=	MAX { [150x0.6703 - 150], 0}
	Risk neutral probabilities p*		
p*	0.4637	=	(1.0513% - 0.6703) / (1.4918 - 0.6703)
Based on continous returns	0.5625	=	0.5 + 0.5 x ((5.0% x 1.00) / (40.0% x SQRT 1.00)
		=	(ln[1+5.13%] - ln [0.6703]) / (ln [1.4918] - ln [0.6703])
Expected stock price (using p*)	157.7	=	150 x 1.4918 x 0.4637 + 150 x 0.6703 x (1 - 0.4637)
Expected stock price (using r)	157.7	=	(150.0x (1 + 5.13%) (continous return = ln (157.7 / 150.0) = 5.0%)
Standard dev (s)	40.9670%	=	(1.4918 - 0.6703) x SQRT(0.4637 x (1 - 0.4637))
Standard dev (s)(log)	39.8946%	=	LN(1.4918 / 0.6703) x SQRT(0.4637 x (1 - 0.4637))
Standard dev (s)(log) when p*=0.5	40.0000%	=	LN(1.4918 / 0.6703) x SQRT(0.5 x (1 - 0.5))
Call price (risk neutral)	**32.54**	=	[73.8 x 0.46372 + 0.0 x (1 - 0.4637)] / (1 + 5.13%)

and

p* 0.4637 = (EXP(5.0% x 1.00) - EXP(-40% x SQRT 1.00)) / (EXP(40% x SQRT 1.00) - EXP(-40% x SQRT 1.00))

The volatility of the log of returns equals the assumed 40% standard deviation if the probability is 0.5. As the size of the time period tends towards zero, then this will be the case:

Discrete: $p^* = \frac{e^{r\delta t} - d}{u - d} = \frac{e^{r\delta t} - e^{-\sigma\sqrt{\delta t}}}{e^{\sigma\sqrt{dt}} - e^{-\sigma\sqrt{dt}}} \rightarrow 0.50$ as $\delta t \rightarrow 0$

Continuous $p^* = 0.5 + 0.5r\,\delta t / \sigma \rightarrow 0.50$ as $\delta t \rightarrow 0$

The discrete p* (0.4637) converges to the continuous p* (0.5625) (four decimal place accuracy) when t = 0.001 years.

Equal Probabilities

If the risk free rate is very high and the volatility low, the CRR method can give a risk neutral probability of more than 1. This would lead to the expected stock price exceeding the up state price. This can be avoided by setting the risk neutral probability to 0.5000; the up and down factors can then be calculated using the discrete or continuous mean and variance equations. Jarrow and Rudd (1983), for example, assume a log normal distribution (see Chriss (1997 p.236) and Wilmott, Howison, and Dewynne (1995 p.185) for alternative equal probability approaches):

$$\text{Expected return, } \mu\delta t = p^* \ln(u) + (1-p^*)\ln(d) = 0.5[\ln(u) + \ln(d)]$$

$$\therefore \ln(d) = 2\mu\delta t - \ln(u)$$

$$\text{Variance, } \sigma^2\delta t = [\ln(u) - \ln(d)]^2\, p^*(1-p^*) \quad \text{(see } \mathbf{B4.7}\text{)}$$

$$\sigma\sqrt{\delta t} = 0.5\,[\ln(u) - \ln(d)] \quad \text{with } p^* = 0.5$$

$$= 0.5\,[\ln(u) - \{2\mu\delta t - \ln(u)\}]$$

$$= \ln(u) - \mu\delta t$$

B4.19

Jarrow & Rudd (1983)('J&R')

$$u = e^{\mu\delta t + \sigma\sqrt{\delta t}}$$
$$d = e^{\mu\delta t - \sigma\sqrt{\delta t}}$$
$$p = 0.5$$

where μ is set to be consistent with a lognormal distribution:

$$u = e^{(r^* - 0.5\sigma^2)\delta t + \sigma\sqrt{\delta t}}$$
$$d = e^{(r^* - 0.5\sigma^2)\delta t - \sigma\sqrt{\delta t}}$$

If a continuous dividend is paid, the yield q% would be deducted from r*.

Example B4.15 American/European Call option - Binomial - no dividends - 1 period – J&R

For **Example B4.1**, the Call price would be 31.94:

Assumptions	
Share price	150
Exercise price	150
Volatilty σ	40.0%
Time to expiry (in yrs)	1.00
Risk free rate (continuous)	5.00%
Risk free rate (discrete) =Exp (5.00%) - 1	5.13%

Up and Down factors		*Discrete*	*Continuous*
		u-1, d-1	*ln (u), ln (d)*
u	1.4477	44.77%	37.00%
d	0.6505	-34.95%	-43.00%

Jarrow & Rudd			
u	1.4477	=	EXP [(5.00% - 0.5 x 40.0%^2) x 1.00 + 40.0% x SQRT 1.00]
d	0.6505	=	EXP [(5.00% - 0.5 x 40.0%^2 x 1.00) - 40.0% x SQRT 1.00]
S_u	217.16	=	150 x 1.4477
S_d	97.58	=	150 x 0.6505
C_u	67.2	=	MAX { [150 x 1.4477 - 150], 0}
C_d	0.0	=	MAX { [150 x 0.6505 - 150], 0}

Risk neutral probabilities p*		
p*	0.5000	
Expected stock price (using p*)	157.4	= 150 x 1.4477 x 0.5000 + 150 x 0.6505 x (1 - 0.5000)
Expected stock price (using r)	157.7	= (150.0x (1 + 5.13%) (continous return = ln (157.7 / 150.0) = 5.0%)
Standard dev (s)	39.8613%	= (1.4477 - 0.6505) x SQRT(0.5000 x (1 - 0.5000))
Standard dev (s)(log)	40.0000%	= (1.4477 - 0.6505) x SQRT(0.5000 x (1 - 0.5000))
Call price (risk neutral)	**31.94**	= [67.2 x 0.50000 + 0.0 x (1 - 0.5000)] / (1 + 5.13%)

OPTION PRICE SENSITIVITY

The role of the key BSM inputs in determining the option values can be illustrated for a Call option. The following measures show *the change in the option price when* (diagrams are based on the BSM **Example B4.11** – see below for equations):

❒ *the underlying asset price changes* ❸ *'Delta'*

> The delta is positive for Calls and negative for Puts (the sum of the absolute value of each equalling 1.0). The absolute value of the delta:
> - increases (decreases) as the underlying asset price increases (decreases);
> - decreases towards zero for deeply out-of-the-money options;
> - is approximately 0.5 for at-the-money options (when the underlying price equals the exercise price);
> - increases towards 1.0 for deeply in-the-money options (when the option price moves in-line with the underlying price).

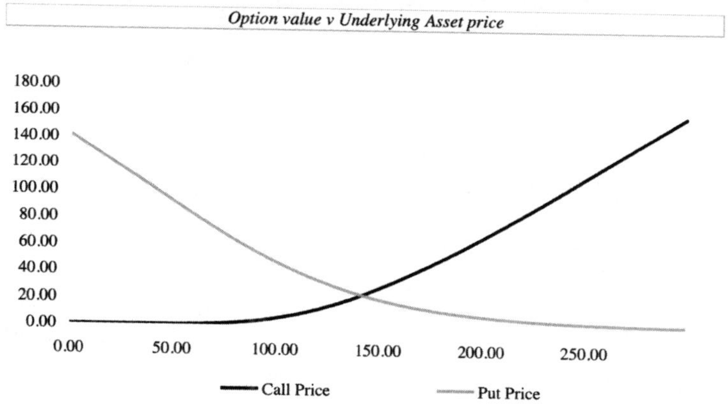

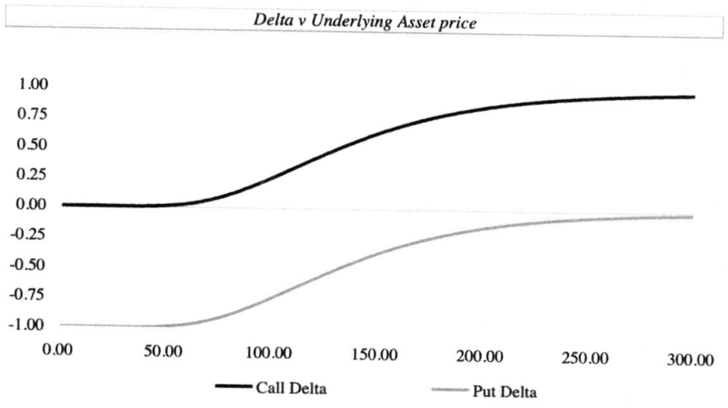

❒ *the time to expiry changes* ❸ *'Theta'*

The theta is normally negative (the option price decreasing due to 'time decay'). The absolute value of theta:
- is greatest for at-the-money options, when time value is greatest (Intrinsic Value=0);
- decreases as the option becomes either in- or out-of-the-money.

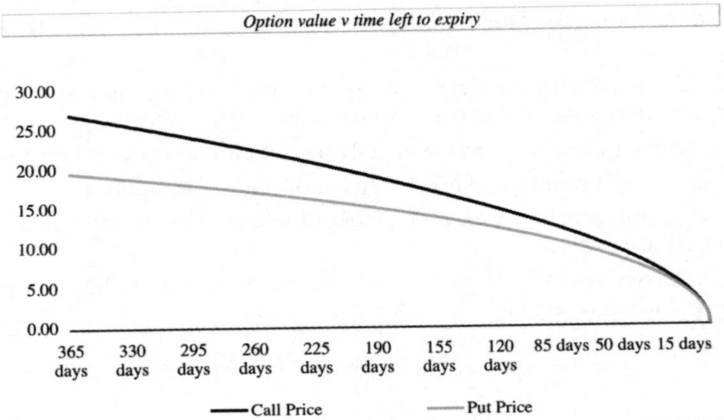

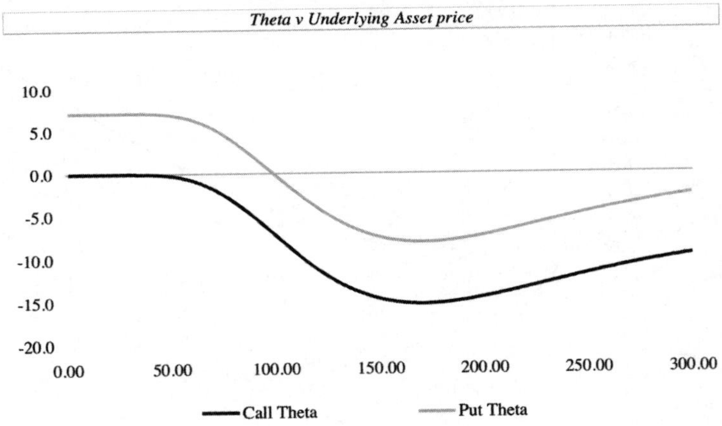

❒ *volatility changes* ❸ *'Vega'*

Vega is normally positive (option price increases with volatility). The absolute value:
- is normally greatest for at-the-money options, when time value is greatest (i.e. for a given time to expiry, the price increases as volatility increases and there is more change of the option becoming in-the-money at expiry);
- decreases as the option becomes either in- or out-of-the-money

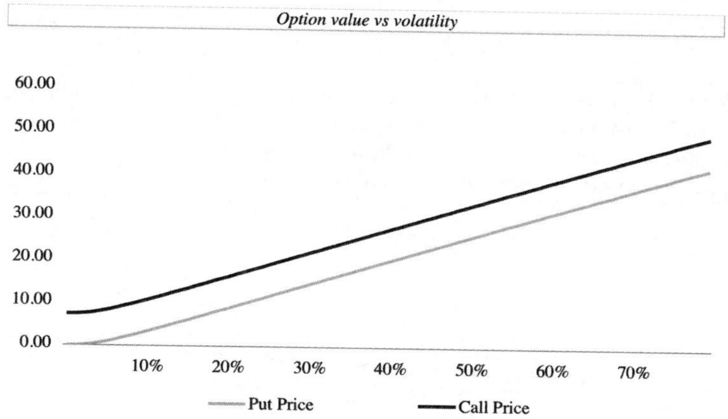

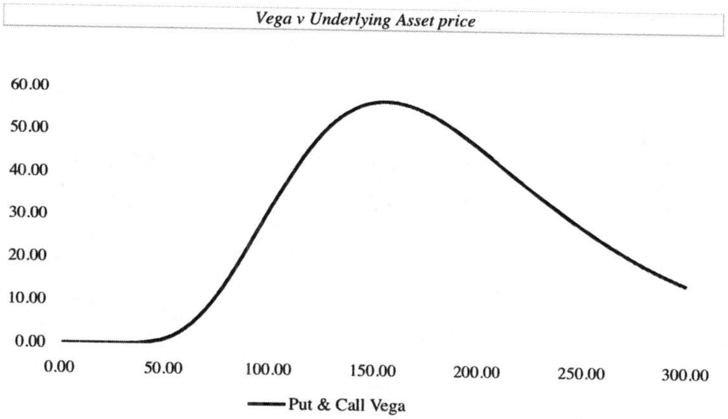

The volatility and time to expiry can be to show the combined effect on the price:

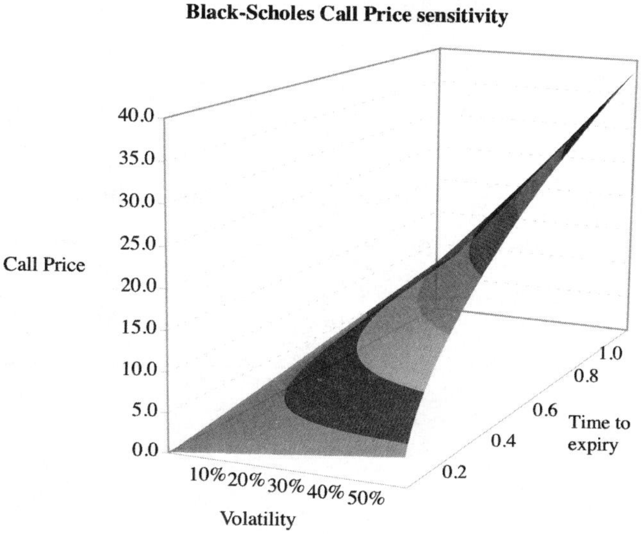

❒ *the risk free rate changes* ❸ *'Rho'*

The Rho is positive for Calls (the option price increases as rates increase) and negative for Puts (the option price decreases as rates increase. The value of rho
- is normally greatest for deep in-the-money options;
- decreases as the option becomes out-of-the-money

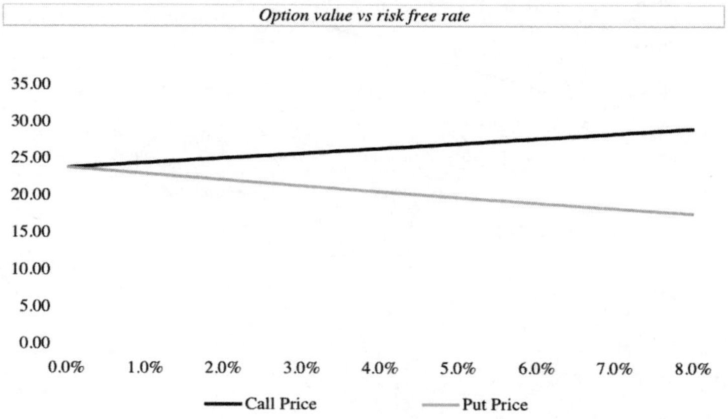

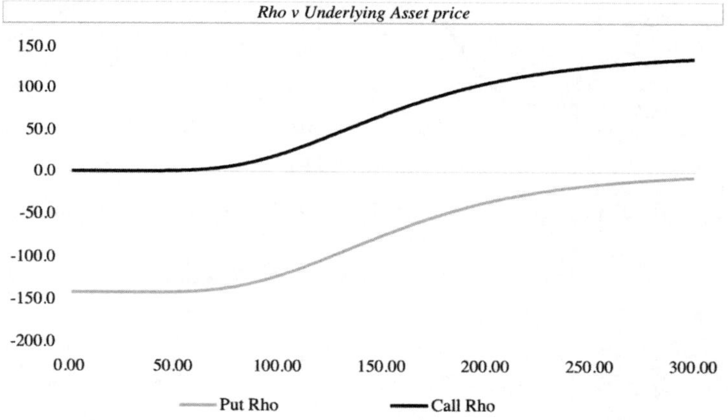

The 'gamma' shows how the delta changes as the underlying asset price changes:

The value of gamma:
- is normally greatest for at-the-money options, when time value is greatest;
- increases (at-the-money option) or decreases (deep in- or out-of-the-money option) as the expiry date approaches

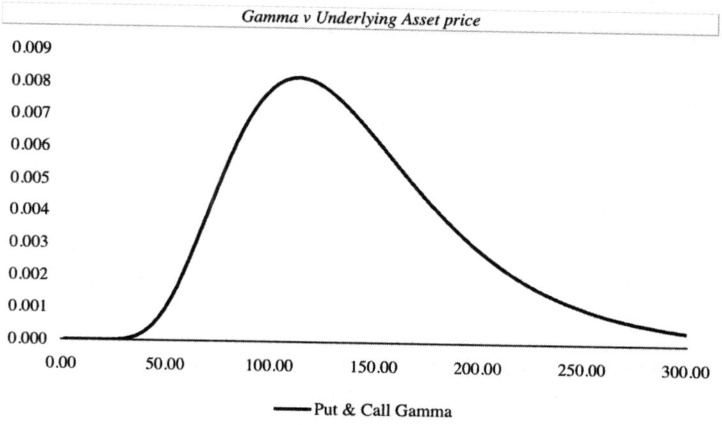

SENSITIVITIES

See **Example B4.11**

		Per what?	*What changes?*	*By what?*	Call (price 27.03)		Put (price 19.72)	
					Measure	Price change	Measure	Price change
Delta	$= e^{-qT} N(d1)$	£1	Share price	+ £1	0.6274	+ 0.6274		
	$= e^{-qT} (N(d1)-1)$			+ £1			-0.3726	- 0.3726
Theta	see below	365 days	Time	- 1 day	-14.7064	-0.0403		
				- 1 day			-7.5722	- 0.0207
Vega	$= S\sqrt{T}\, e^{-qT} N'(d1)$	£1	Volatility	+ 1%	56.7630	+ 0.5676		
	"						56.7630	+ 0.5676
Rho	$= XT\, e^{-rT} N(d2)$	£1	Risk free rate	+ 1%	67.0756	+ 0.6708		
	$= XT\, e^{-rT} N(-d2)$						-75.6088	- 0.7561
Gamma	$= e^{-qT} N'(d1)\ /\ S\sigma\sqrt{T}$	£1	Delta	gamma	0.0063	n/a		
	"						0.0063	n/a

Call theta $= -\{ S\, N'(d1)\, \sigma\, e^{-qT} \} / 2\sqrt{T} + qS\, N(d1)\, e^{-qT} - rX\, e^{-rT} N(d2)$

Put theta $= -\{ S\, N'(d1)\, \sigma\, e^{-qT} \} / 2\sqrt{T} - qS\, N(-d1)\, e^{-qT} + rX\, e^{-rT} N(-d2)$

where q - dividend yield

ADVANCED OPTION PRICING

The reader is advised to turn elsewhere for a discussion of the following specialised topics:

- Exotic options — Option structures and payoffs can be structured in a number of ways, other than a simple, or 'plain vanilla', Call or Put option with a fixed exercise price. Some examples are given below:

  - Forward start — For an American option, exercise can only take place after a specified period (i.e. the option life starts in the future). As normal, a European option can only be exercised at expiry.

- Compound — An option on another option.
- Chooser — The holder can choose, after a specified period, whether the option is to be a Call or Put.
- Barrier — An option can come into existence or terminate when the stock price reaches a specified level.
- Binary (Digital) — A fixed amount is received if the underlying asset price is in-the-money at the expiry date ('all-or-nothing') or at some time during the life of the option ('one-touch').
- Lookback — The payoff on exercise depends on the highest or lowest stock price during the option life.
- Asian — The payoff on exercise depends on the average stock price (geometric or arithmetic) during part or all of the option life

See Hull (2003), Haug (1998).

- Volatility
  - *Estimating volatility*: there are a number of 'Time-Series' models such as the Exponentially Weighted Moving Average Model ('EWMA'), and Generalised Autoregressive Conditional Heteroscedasticity ('GARCH') model.
  - *Implied volatility*: the volatility (standard deviation) of a given stock price can be inferred from the actual market quoted option price for that stock by adjusting the volatility input into an option pricing model so the resulting option price equals the quoted option price (in practice, using the Microsoft Excel™ 'goal seek' function). The volatility 'smile' shows the implied volatility as a function of the exercise price.

See Chriss (1997)

- Trees
  - *Trinomial Trees:* the asset or stock price has three possible values at each node, rather than just two as in the standard Binomial Tree. There will now be 2n+1 nodes at any time period n (compared to n+1 for the Binomial model).
  - *Implied Trees*: the Binomial or trinomial Tree for a given quoted option price can be constructed.

See Clewlow & Strickland (2000), Copeland and Antikarov (2001), Chriss (1997)

B5 OPTION PRICING APPLICATIONS

REAL OPTIONS

Introduction

An investor may have the right to expand, contract or abandon a new capital project for a given cost or salvage value at some future date (a Real Option). The value of the project at that date (Enterprise Value) may be increased if it is optimal to exercise the project's embedded option and change the scale of investment (to produce a positive payoff, as measured by a positive Net Present Value, NPV). Whether or not it is optimal depends on market conditions, uncertainties and other risk factors that determine the project's value at the exercise date. The option need not be exercised if conditions are not optimal.

A project's Enterprise Value at the date of the initial investment can be estimated using traditional Discounted Cash Flow (DCF) methods, and any embedded options can be valued using financial option pricing techniques. The combined value incorporates the investor's flexibility to change the scale of the investment.

This section focuses on the use of Binomial Trees to value simple expansion and contraction options. In practice, Real Options valuation would be more complicated, and may require 'decision tree' analysis, simulation techniques, many more time steps in the Tree, and, possibly, more than two scenarios at each time step (for example, a trinomial tree). (See Chapter 1 for a discussion on Real Options in general, Appendix B1 for DCF Valuation and Appendix B4 for basic option pricing models.)

Valuing Real Options with Binomial Trees

The value of a new capital project with an embedded option can be estimated using a Binomial Tree approach (the procedure shown below is based on the method used by Copeland and Antikarov (2001)).

❶ Estimate the DCF Enterprise Value without flexibility at the date of the initial investment (EV_0 at time 0) by discounting future expected Free Cash Flows (FCF) (cash flow scenarios, ignoring any options, weighted by their true probabilities) at a risk-adjusted discount rate (WACC): this is equivalent to the current stock price in an equity option model.

❷ For each chosen time period from time 0 until the last Real Option exercise date (i.e. option expiry date), t_0 - t_n, calculate the FCF 'distribution rate' (similar to the dividend yield used to value options when the underlying share pays dividends):

$$\text{Distribution rate} = \frac{FCF_{t_i}}{PV_{t_i}\left(FCF_{t_{i+1}} \rightarrow t_n\right) + FCF_{t_i}}$$

where PV_{t_i} - Present Value at time i
FCF_{t_i} - Free Cash Flows at time i
$FCF_{t_{i+1}} \rightarrow t_n$ - Free Cash Flows remaining after time i

❸ Estimate the volatility (standard deviation) of the project returns (the change in EV over a period) from either historic or implied volatility on comparable projects, or by simulating the EV based on given uncertainties that determine FCF (standard deviation of key value drivers), to produce the project return volatility over the first period (see Copeland and Antikarov (2001) for further discussion on this approach, and Mun (2002) for other estimation techniques).

❹ Construct a Binomial Tree using the volatility estimate and a given risk free rate (continuously compounded): the following are calculated at each node (working backwards from the final expiry date, except for EV):

- Enterprise Value without flexibility (EV) (similar to the ex-dividend stock price in an equity option model): EV_0 is assumed to increase and decrease each period by the Binomial up and down factors, after being reduced by the FCF distribution rate;
- Enterprise Value with flexibility (EV_F): EV at each node is adjusted by the change in value arising from an exercise of the option (this may be an increase or decrease in value);
- Intrinsic Value: the greater of the value with and without flexibility (max $\{EV, EV_F\}$), since the option will not be exercised if $EV_F<EV$;
- Continuing Value (CV): the PV of the expected option embedded value (EV_{OV}) at the next time period (the risk-neutral probability weighted EV_{OV} in the up and down states at the next time period, discounted at the risk free rate);
- Enterprise Value plus Option Value (EV_{OV}): the greater of the Intrinsic Value and the Continuing Value (max {CV, IV}) plus FCF for that date.

Example B5.1 Example – Real Options Valuation - Binomial Tree

A company is considering whether to invest £88m in a new project. Based on a 5 year Free Cash Flow (FCF) forecast, with year 5 cash flows growing 3.5% in perpetuity, the project value, using a risk-adjusted discount rate of 8.11% (the risk free rate is 5.13%, or 5.0% continuously compounded), is £84m. The investment will allow the company to make a one-off additional investment in the project at the end of any year from years 2 to 5 (at known costs of between £15m and £30m); this should generate incremental FCFs and increase the project value at those dates by 20% to 35% (this is similar to an American Call Option).

The DCF Enterprise Value without flexibility at time 0 (EV_0) and the FCF distribution rates are calculated as follows (EV at each date is also shown):

DISCOUNTED CASH FLOW HIGHLIGHTS

£m		0	Forecast Year 1	2	3	4	5	TV	Notes
Free Cash Flows ($FCFt_i$)	A		3.68	3.86	4.05	4.25	4.47	100.36	1
Disc Factor at 8.11%			*0.9250*	*0.8556*	*0.7915*	*0.7321*	*0.6772*	*0.6772*	
PV of cash flows at time 0		84.01	3.40	3.30	3.21	3.11	3.03	67.96	
Present Values at each year end									
Free Cash Flows ($FCFt_i$)			3.68	3.86	4.05	4.25	4.47		
Enterprise Value (ex-div)	B	*84.01*	*87.15*	*90.35*	*93.63*	*96.96*	*100.36*		2
Enterprise Value (cum-div)	C	84.01	90.82	94.21	97.68	101.22	104.82		
Distribution rate	***= A ÷ C***		***4.0%***	***4.1%***	***4.1%***	***4.2%***	***4.3%***		
Rate of return (discrete)(WACC)	$(C_{t+1} - B_t) / B_t$			8.11%	8.11%	8.11%	8.11%		
Rate of return (continuous)	$LN(C_{t+1} / B_t)$			7.80%	7.80%	7.80%	7.80%		

1. Terminal value = 4.47 x (1+ 3.50%) / (8.11% - 3.50%)
2. Year 5 PV = TV / (1 + WACC) + Year 5 Cash Flow
   Year 4 PV = Year 5 PV / (1 + WACC) + Year 4 Cash Flow etc

WACC	8.11%
Terminal growth	3.50%

The FCF forecast was estimated by calculating the expected FCFs each period, based on a range of FCFs and associated true probabilities (as shown to the right).

The volatility of the project returns is estimated to be 40% (standard deviation). The Binomial parameters are as follows:

£m	Forecast Year 1	2	3	4	5
Scenario 1	5.07	7.35	10.65	15.43	22.35
True probability	*0.5000*	*0.2500*	*0.1250*	*0.0625*	*0.0313*
Scenario 2	2.28	3.30	4.78	6.93	10.04
True probability	*0.5000*	*0.5000*	*0.3750*	*0.2500*	*0.1563*
Scenario 3		1.48	2.15	3.11	4.51
True probability		*0.2500*	*0.3750*	*0.3750*	*0.3125*
Scenario 4			0.97	1.40	2.03
True probability			*0.1250*	*0.2500*	*0.3125*
Scenario 5				0.63	0.91
True probability				*0.0625*	*0.1563*
Scenario 6					0.41
True probability					*0.0313*
Expected	**3.68**	**3.86**	**4.05**	**4.25**	**4.47**
Sum of probabilities	1.0000	1.0000	1.0000	1.0000	1.0000

Model assumptions	
EV today without flexibility	84.01
Risk Free interest rate	5.00%
Volatility	40.0%
Time step (fraction of year)	1.0000
Number of time periods	5

Parameters		
Up-move factor	1.4918	U = EXP(40.0%*SQRT(1.0000))
Down-move factor	0.6703	D = 1/1.4918
Risk-free return	1.0513	r = EXP(5.00%*1.0000)
Risk-neutral probability	0.4637	p* = (1.0513 - 0.6703)/(1.4918 - 0.6703)

The 5 period Binomial Tree is as follows:

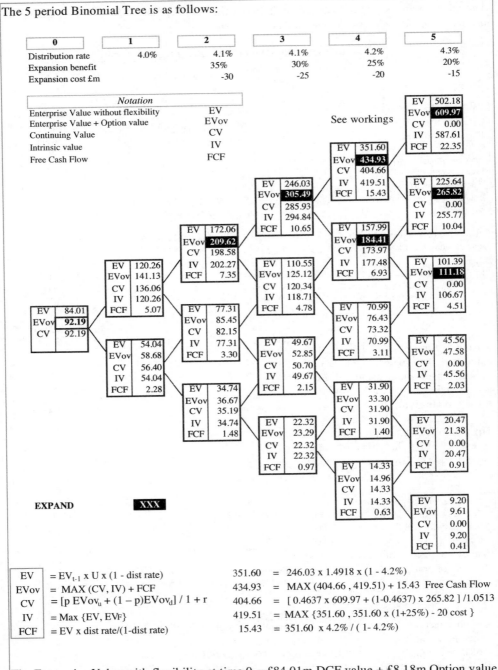

	0	1	2	3	4	5
Distribution rate		4.0%	4.1%	4.1%	4.2%	4.3%
Expansion benefit			35%	30%	25%	20%
Expansion cost £m			-30	-25	-20	-15

Notation	
Enterprise Value without flexibility	EV
Enterprise Value + Option value	EVov
Continuing Value	CV
Intrinsic value	IV
Free Cash Flow	FCF

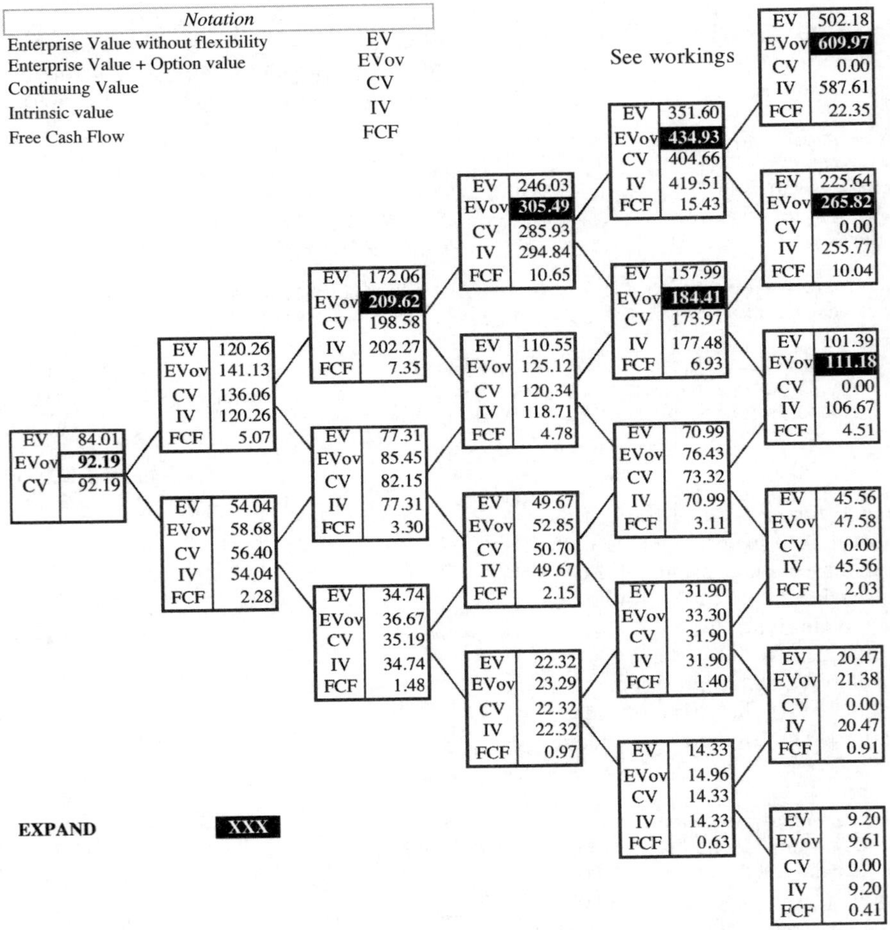

EV	$= EV_{t-1} \times U \times (1 - \text{dist rate})$
EVov	= MAX (CV, IV) + FCF
CV	$= [p\ EVov_u + (1 - p)EVov_d] / 1 + r$
IV	$= \text{Max}\ \{EV, EV_F\}$
FCF	= EV x dist rate/(1-dist rate)

351.60 = 246.03 x 1.4918 x (1 - 4.2%)
434.93 = MAX (404.66 , 419.51) + 15.43 Free Cash Flow
404.66 = [0.4637 x 609.97 + (1-0.4637) x 265.82] /1.0513
419.51 = MAX {351.60 , 351.60 x (1+25%) - 20 cost }
15.43 = 351.60 x 4.2% / (1- 4.2%)

The Enterprise Value with flexibility at time 0 = £84.01m DCF value + £8.18m Option value. The project would be acceptable since the option embedded value £92.19 exceeds the cost of investment £88m,

Free Cash Flows at each node are calculated by multiplying the EV (cum-div, grossed up by the distribution rate as above) at each node by the FCF distribution rate. The true probability (p) of the value of the project increasing from one node to the next is 0.500 (this can be implied from the risk-neutral probability equation, using the risk-adjusted rate of return: 0.500 = (1 + 8.11% - 0.6703)/(1.4918 - 0.6703)). The expected FCF at each time period, using true probabilities (FCF x p), gives the FCF used in the DCF valuation. The expected FCF, using the risk neutral probability (FCF x p*), are 'certainty equivalents' (see **Example B1.13** in Appendix B1), which can be discounted at the risk-free rate to give the same PV as when discounting the true probability weighted FCF by the WACC.

Expected cash flows using true probability p, discounting at the 8.11% risk-adjusted rate:

Period	Node	Routes	Prob	FCF
0	1	1	1.000	0.00
1	1	1	0.500	5.07
1	2	1	0.500	2.28
2	1	1	0.250	7.35
2	2	2	0.250	3.30
2	3	1	0.250	1.48
3	1	1	0.125	10.65
3	2	3	0.125	Exercise 4.78
3	3	3	0.125	2.15
3	4	1	0.125	0.97
4	1	1	0.063	15.43
4	2	4	0.063	6.93
4	3	6	0.063	3.11
4	4	4	0.063	1.40
4	5	1	0.062	0.63
5	1	1	0.031	22.35
5	2	5	0.031	10.04
5	3	10	0.031	4.51
5	4	10	0.031	2.03
5	5	5	0.031	0.91
5	6	1	0.031	0.41

The probability at each node is the probability times the number of routes to that node (see **B4.8** in Appendix B4); the sum at each time period = 1.0.

	1	2	3	4	5
Expected FCF	3.68	3.86	4.05	4.25	4.47
Discount Factor	0.9250	0.8556	0.7915	0.7321	0.6772
PV of Expected FCF	3.40	3.30	3.21	3.11	3.03

Expected cash flows using risk-neutral probability p*, discounting at the 5.13% risk free rate:

Period	Node	Routes	Prob	FCF
0	1	1	1.000	0.00
1	1	1	0.464	5.07
1	2	1	0.536	2.28
2	1	1	0.215	7.35
2	2	2	0.249	3.30
2	3	1	0.288	1.48
3	1	1	0.100	10.65
3	2	3	0.115	Exercise 4.78
3	3	3	0.133	2.15
3	4	1	0.154	0.97
4	1	1	0.046	15.43
4	2	4	0.053	6.93
4	3	6	0.062	3.11
4	4	4	0.072	1.40
4	5	1	0.083	0.63
5	1	1	0.021	22.35
5	2	5	0.025	10.04
5	3	10	0.029	4.51
5	4	10	0.033	2.03
5	5	5	0.038	0.91
5	6	1	0.044	0.41

	1	2	3	4	5
Expected FCF	3.57	3.65	3.73	3.80	3.88
Discount Factor	0.9512	0.9048	0.8607	0.8187	0.7788
PV of Expected FCF	3.40	3.30	3.21	3.11	3.03

The Enterprise Value (EV – ignoring options) at each node depends on the volatility of its returns. At each node, the up and down EV at the next period are calculated using the up and down factors 1.4918 and 0.6703, which were set using the assumed 40% volatility. At each node, this volatility (constant standard deviation) can be shown as (see **B4.7** in Appendix B4):

$$\text{Standard Deviation } \sigma = \ln\left(\frac{EV_{up}}{EV_{down}}\right) \times \sqrt{p\,(1-p)}$$

where p is the true probability (0.5 in this case) and ln the natural logarithm.

The expected EV at each time period, using true probabilities, gives the DCF Enterprise Values at each year-end, as shown below.

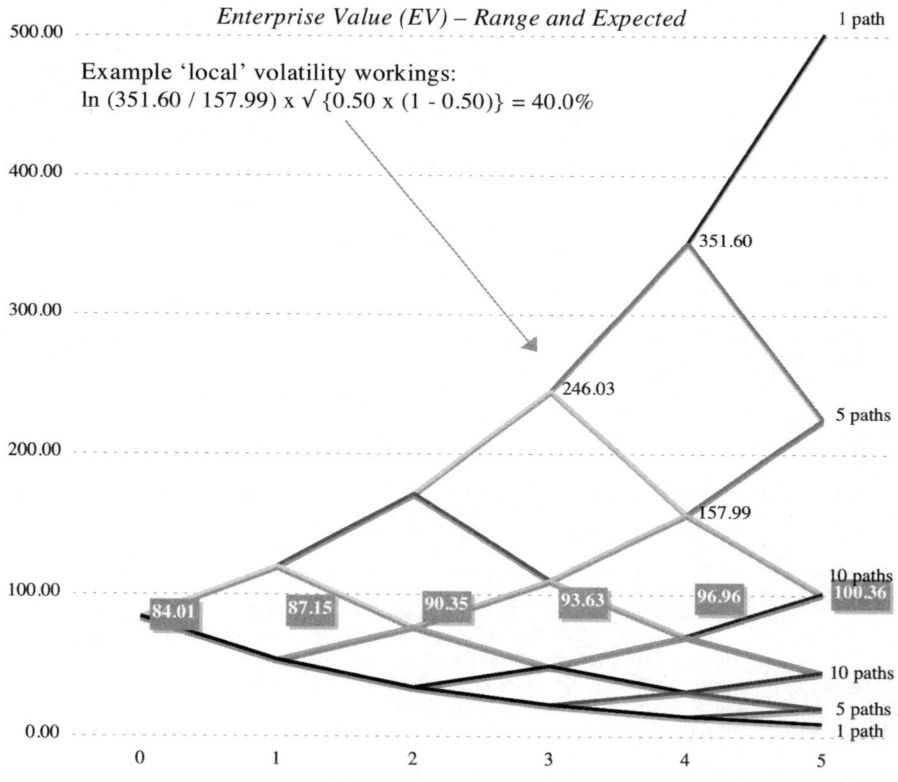

In order to incorporate the embedded expansion option into the DCF model, the incremental cash flows arising from the exercise of an option for each node in a time period (all possible states) would have to be probability weighted (using true probabilities) in order to obtain one expected incremental cash flow that would be added to the base case (DCF forecast ignoring options). However the single expected incremental cash flow would incorporate probability weighted incremental cash flows where it would not be optimal to exercise the option (i.e. expected negative FCF under some scenarios) – the binomial tree ignores such nodes (recognising that the option would not be exercised).

If it is assumed that the expansion option will be exercised at the end of year 5, the probability weighted NPV from exercising the option can be added in. This increases the EV from the base case £84.01m to £87.45m (difference = £3.44m option NPV at time 0). This is still below the £88m cost of investment and so would be rejected. This is because the expected incremental perpetuity cash flows from exercising the option at year 5 (£0.4111m) include probability weighted negative cash flows (perpetuity cash flows that give the negative NPVs in the bottom three nodes at time 5) that are ignored in the above options pricing tree. This increases the value of the option (the equivalent European option value is £89.5m).

FCF	Free Cash Flows
EV	Enterprise Value (ignoring options)
NPVo	NPV of option if exercised at year 5
EV_F	Enterprise Value (option exercised)
Prob.	Binomial True Probability

0

FCF	0.000
EV	84.011
NPVo	3.434
EV_F	87.445
Prob.	1.000

1

FCF	5.07	2.28
EV	120.26	54.04
NPVo	9.30	-1.87
EV_F	134.63	54.44
Prob.	0.5000	0.5000

2

FCF	7.35	3.30	1.48
EV	172.06	77.31	34.74
NPVo	18.38	1.72	-5.76
EV_F	197.78	82.33	30.46
Prob.	0.2500	0.5000	0.2500

3

FCF	10.65	4.78	2.15	0.97
EV	246.03	110.55	49.67	22.32
NPVo	32.29	7.44	-3.72	-8.74
EV_F	288.97	122.78	48.10	14.54
Prob.	0.1250	0.3750	0.3750	0.1250

4

FCF	15.43	* 6.93	3.11	1.40	0.63
EV	351.60	157.99	70.99	31.90	14.33
NPVo	53.45	16.38	-0.28	-7.77	-11.13
EV_F	420.48	181.29	73.82	25.53	3.83
Prob.	0.0625	0.2500	0.3750	0.2500	0.0625

5

FCF	22.35	10.04	4.51	2.03	0.91	0.41
EV	502.18	225.64	101.39	45.56	20.47	9.20
NPVo	85.44	30.13	5.28	-5.89	-10.91	-13.16
EV_F	609.97	265.82	111.18	41.70	10.48	-3.55
Prob.	0.0313	0.1563	0.3125	0.3125	0.1563	0.0313

*

6.93	See Real Option Binomial Tree
157.99	See Real Option Binomial Tree
16.38	={ 30.13 x 0.5000 + 5.28 x (1 - 0.5000) } / (1 + 8.11%)
181.29	=157.99 + 16.38
0.25	See Expected FCF Tree

Expected cash flows and EV (true probability weighted):

	0	1	2	3	4	5
FCF		3.68	3.86	4.05	4.25	4.47
EV	84.011	87.15	90.35	93.63	96.96	100.36
	84.011	90.82	94.21	97.68	101.22	104.82

	0	5
FCF		0.411
NPV	3.434	5.0711
	87.445	

Σ True probability weighted year 5 NPVo
Constant year 5 extra FCF received in perpetuity

The company can also reduce the scale of operations by 50% at the end of any year from years 2 to 5 (but only once), and save costs with a total PV of £20m (American Put Option). This increases the project value further to £94.24m.

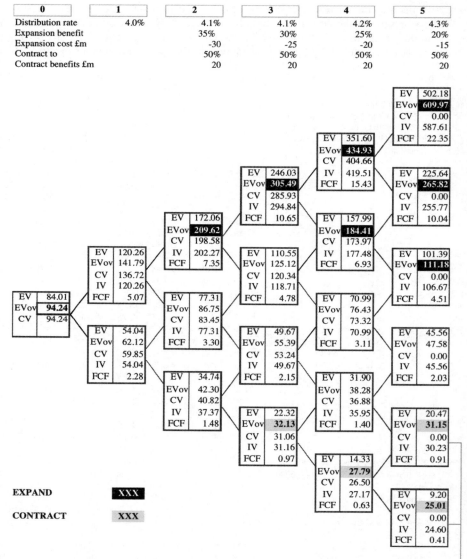

	0	1	2	3	4	5
Distribution rate		4.0%	4.1%	4.1%	4.2%	4.3%
Expansion benefit			35%	30%	25%	20%
Expansion cost £m			-30	-25	-20	-15
Contract to			50%	50%	50%	50%
Contract benefits £m			20	20	20	20

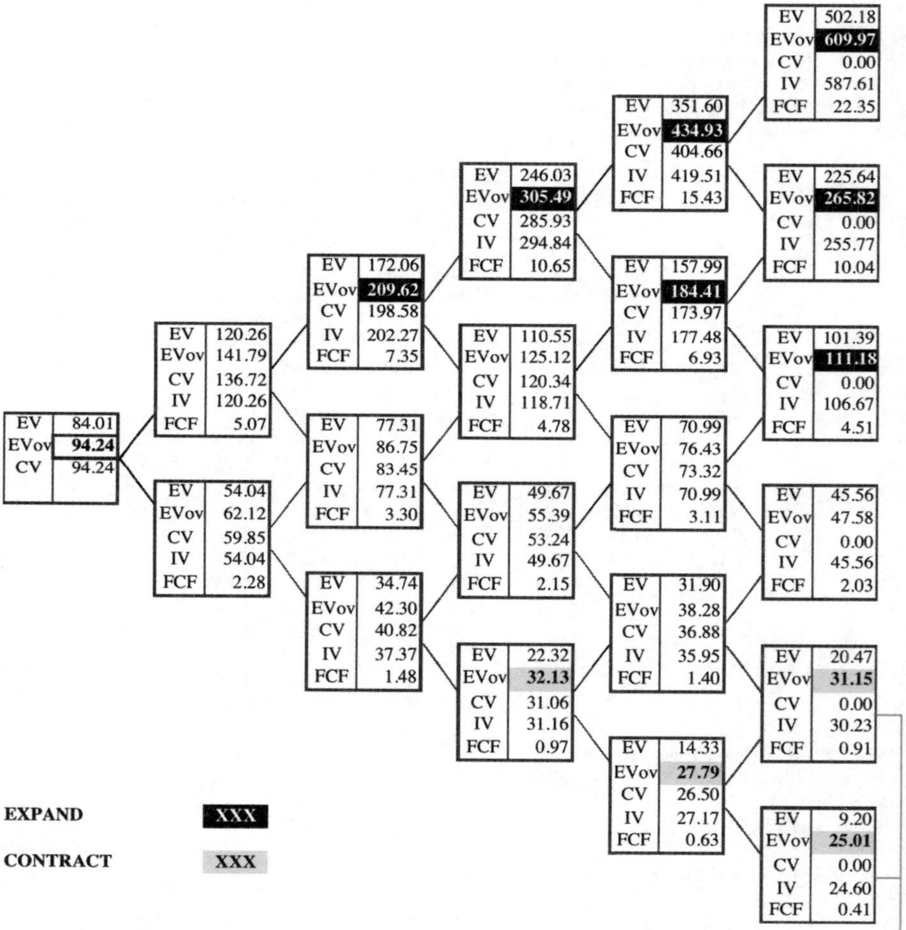

IV = 50% x EV + £20m NPV contraction benefit (savings) = 50% x £20.47m + £20m = £30.23m in the up state, and 50% x £9.20m + £20m = £24.60m in the down state. EVov = Max {IV, EV} plus FCF.

CONVERTIBLE BONDS

Introduction

A Convertible can be issued with a lower coupon rate than an otherwise identical option-free bond (both issued at par), due to the potential profit (payoff) available to the bondholder from exercising their right to convert into equity. A Convertible, therefore, can be priced as an option-free bond (see Appendix B2) plus an option, valued using option pricing models (see Chapter 2 for an introduction to Convertibles and Appendix B4 for option pricing).

Conversion Option

On conversion, the holder will, effectively, pay an exercise price, by surrendering the bond, and receive a certain number of shares for that bond (Conversion Ratio). The value of the shares received on conversion (Conversion Value or 'Parity' = Conversion Ratio x share price) should be greater than the value of the surrendered bond if held to maturity and not converted (Investment Value) - the difference is equivalent to an option's Intrinsic Value. However, it may be optimal to convert at a later date due to the extra Time Value of the conversion option, in which case the Convertible fair price would exceed the Conversion Value and would reflect the 'Continuing Value' of the Convertible.

Equity vs. Debt Value

When the Conversion Value is much greater than the Investment Value, the Convertible fair price will reflect the value of the underlying equity and its volatility, and the bond's value as straight debt will be less relevant (i.e. the impact of changes in market yields and interest rates will be less); conversely, when the Conversion Value is less than the Investment Value, the Convertible fair price will equal the Investment Value (the fair price should never fall below its value as straight debt).

Conversion Premium

A Convertible allows an investor to benefit from a rise in the share price, whilst giving protection if the Conversion Value falls below the Investment Value. Instead of purchasing shares immediately (equal in number to the Conversion Ratio, with the purchase price equal to the Conversion Value at that date), an investor should be prepared to purchase a Convertible at a premium over this Conversion Value, receive a higher income (the coupon yield, the coupon divided by the Convertible price, will usually exceed the dividend yield), and benefit from the Convertible's risk/return features. If the bond is held long enough, this initial Conversion premium (Convertible purchase price less Conversion Value at the purchase date) can be recovered from the income differential ('payback'):

B5.1

$$\text{Payback (years) ('break-even')} = \frac{\underset{\text{(at purchase date)}}{\text{Convertible price}} - \overbrace{\underset{\text{(at purchase date)}}{\text{Share price}} \times \text{Conversion Ratio}}^{\text{Conversion Value on purchase}}}{\text{Convertible coupon} - \text{Dividend per share} \times \text{Conversion Ratio}}$$

Callable Convertibles

Most issuers of bonds (straight or Convertible) are given the right to serve notice to bondholders of an intention to redeem, or 'Call', the bonds early at pre-agreed dates and prices (at a premium to the redemption price, so as to preserve the initial promised yield). This provides a benefit for an issuer, who may want to redeem the bonds in order to restructure its pool of debt, or, more likely, to refinance the bonds at a lower cost, following a fall in interest rates and the required yield on its debt. However, a callable bond increases risk for a bondholder, since the yield expected on purchase may not be realised: if interest rates fall and the bond is called, the holder may have to reinvest the call proceeds at, potentially, a lower rate of return. The fair price of a callable bond will be less than the fair price of an otherwise identical non-callable bond (similar coupon, maturity and risk), due to this extra risk (the difference being the value of the issuer's call option).

Under the terms of a callable bond, an issuer would normally be prevented from calling the bonds until a certain period after issue had expired ('Call protection'). The bonds are unlikely to be called if the call price exceeds the bond trading price (otherwise it would be cheaper to repurchase them on the market), unless there are clear economic benefits from refinancing the old bonds at that price (on an after-tax NPV basis, net of all repurchase costs). For a Convertible, the call provision can be conditional on certain events occurring ('Soft Call'), such as the underlying share price reaching specified levels, or unconditional ('Hard Call').

Although a straight bond may be called in order to refinance at a lower cost, a Convertible is likely to be called for another reason: if notice is given that the issuer intends to call the Convertible at a price below the current Conversion Value, bondholders are likely to convert to receive the higher value shares ('Forced Conversion')(where this occurs, any accrued interest on the bond would be foregone, since accrued interest would only be paid when the bond is repurchased). Forcing conversion allows the issuer to avoid a cash payout on redemption, and allows the Convertible to be seen as a form of deferred equity financing (but with less dilution than a straight upfront issue of shares due to the lower number of shares being issued, assuming share prices have risen). Hence, to force conversion, both the Convertible trading price (i.e. fair price) and the Conversion Value must exceed the Call price (the issuer is likely to wait until the Conversion Value comfortably exceeds the Call price); as is discussed below, when forced conversion is certain, the Convertible fair price will equal the Conversion Value.

Pricing methods

Black-Scholes Model ('BSM')

The fair price of a Convertible can be seen as the value of straight, option-free debt (Investment Value) plus the value of a conversion option:

$$\text{Convertible price} = \underset{\text{(Investment Value)}}{\text{Value as straight bond}} + \text{Value of conversion option}$$

The Investment Value is simply the fair price of the Convertible if held to maturity and not converted (i.e. the present value of all future coupons and the redemption amount, discounted at the yield required for a comparable straight bond with identical coupon, maturity and risk characteristics). This component varies over time as interest rates, the time to maturity and the issuer's credit risk change.

The conversion option, assuming conversion can only take place at expiry (i.e. a European option), can be calculated using the BSM (see Appendix B4, **B4.16** and **B4.17** for non-dividend paying and dividend paying stocks, respectively). This component varies over time as the risk free rate, the time to maturity, the share price and the volatility of equity returns (which may reflect a change in the issuer's credit risk) all change.

The share price and exercise price inputs to the model can be on a per share basis (the option value is then multiplied by the Conversion Ratio to show the 'embedded' option per bond) or on a per bond basis (no adjustment is needed to the option value). The option value per share would use the share price at the valuation date and the bond Conversion Price[1] (face value of the bond ÷ Conversion Ratio); the option value per bond would use the Conversion Value (share price at the valuation date x Conversion Ratio) and the face value of the bond.

The underlying share price may or may not incorporate an expectation that new shares will be issued for delivery on conversion, thereby diluting the equity value per share (if the company purchased the shares on the market, then the equity value should, in theory, fall by the purchase cost). The BSM calculated option value would need to be adjusted as follows:

$$\text{Diluted value} = \text{Call Option} \times \frac{1}{1 + \dfrac{\text{Shares issued}}{\text{Shares in issue before exercise}}} \qquad \textbf{B5.2}$$

1 This approach to estimating the Convertible's exercise price is suggested by Connolly (1998 p191). An alternative method is to use the bond's Investment Value (see Woodson (2002 p79)), which would change over time.

Binomial Model ('BM')

If conversion can take place over a period, the Convertible can be valued using the BM (which allows for American options).

❒ Non-callable / no dividends

At each coupon date until maturity, the Conversion Value and Investment Value are calculated using a Binomial Tree:

- the current Conversion Value (current share price x Conversion Ratio) is assumed to increase by a factor 'u' and decrease by 'd' at each time period, until the bond maturity date ($u = e^{\sigma\sqrt{\delta t}}$ and $d = 1/u$, using the 'CRR' approach discussed in Appendix B4 – see **B4.18**);
- the Investment Value will be the same for all nodes at any given date:
  - at maturity, it will equal the redemption value plus the final coupon;
  - at the previous date, it will be this maturity value discounted by a risk adjusted rate of return (risk free rate for this period plus a credit risk premium) plus the coupon received at this prior date;
  - this approach is carried out for all prior periods, working backwards until the valuation date.

The Convertible fair price at maturity (at each node) will be the greater of the Conversion Value and the Investment Value (Convertible holders will either convert to receive shares with a higher value, or take no action and receive the redemption amount and final coupon). The price at the previous coupon date (at each node) will be the greater of the Conversion Value, the Investment Value and the present value of the Convertible fair price if conversion occurred at some future date (the 'Continuing Value', 'V'), being the present value of the risk-neutral probability-weighted Convertible fair price ('C') at the next period:

$$\text{Continuing Value } V_j = \frac{p(C_{j+1u}) + (1-p)(C_{j+1d})}{1+r} + \text{coupon} \qquad \textbf{B5.3}$$

where $j+1_u$, $j+1_d$ up and down states at next node after node j
p risk-neutral probability
r discount rate

The Convertible fair price will reflect equity (Conversion Value), debt (Investment Value), or both. If the bond is not converted but redeemed, then a cash outlay is required, which introduces a risk of default; on conversion, since shares are issued, there is no cash payment. Hence, 1 the debt component in next period's Convertible fair price (C_{j+1u} and C_{j+1d}) should be discounted at a risk adjusted rate and the equity component discounted at the risk free rate, and the two added, or 2 the whole Convertible price should be discounted at a 'blended' rate. These two approaches are discussed below.

1 The Convertible fair price at each node for the next period is split into an equity and debt component, which are probability weighted and discounted at the relevant rate (equity at risk free rate, debt at risk adjusted rate):

- at maturity (t+1), the Convertible will be priced as 100% equity (Conversion Value) or 100% debt (Investment Value);
- at the previous time period t, the Continuing Value will be the sum of the discounted, probability weighted equity and debt components at the up and down nodes at the next time period (t+1) – this will also be the Convertible fair price at t, unless the price is set, again, by the Conversion Value (100% equity) or the Investment Value (100% debt);
- the equity and debt components at time t are then discounted to determine the prior period equity and debt components, and so on.

$$V_j = \frac{p(E_{j+1u}) + (1-p)(E_{j+1d})}{1+r} + \frac{p(D_{j+1u}) + (1-p)(D_{j+1d})}{1+r+CRP} \qquad \textbf{B5.4}$$

where

$j+1_u$, $j+1_d$	up and down states at next node after node j
p	risk-neutral probability
r	risk free rate
CRP	credit risk premium

(See Tsiveriotis and Fernandes (1998), Hull (2003 p.653).)

Example B5.2 Discounting debt and equity components at different rates

The fair price for a semi-annual coupon-paying Convertible at the coupon date immediately before maturity (5th node down at time 9), is calculated as follows

Bond face value	£100	
Redemption amount	£100	
Coupon (semi-annual)	3.00%	
Coupon per period	£1.50	
Maturity date	5 years	
Current share price	£10	
Conversion ratio	8	
Conversion value today	£80	
Equity volatility	40%	
Dividends per share	0	
Risk free (discrete)	5.127%	(2.53% a period)
Credit Risk Premium	2%	(1.03% a period)

Time 9 (5th node down)

CV	106.15	
IV	99.51	1.500
D	53.06	3.56%
E	65.10	2.53%
C	**118.17**	2.90%

Time 10 Maturity date (5th and 6th nodes down)

140.85	
101.50	1.500
0.00	
140.85	
140.85	

80.00	
101.50	1.500
101.50	
0.00	
101.50	

Workings for Time period 9

CV (Conversion Value) = £80 x up factor 1.3269^5 x down factor 0.7536^4 = 106.15
IV (Investment Value) = (£100 + £1.50)/1.0356 + £1.50 = £99.51
D (Debt) = [£0.00 x 0.4739 + £101.50 x (1 – 0.4739)] / 1.0356 + £1.50 = £53.06
E (Equity) = [£140.85 x 0.4739 + £0.00 x (1 – 0.4739)] / 1.0253 = £65.10
C (Convertible Price) = £53.06 + £65.10 = £118.17

2 Alternatively, the Convertible fair price at each node for the next period is discounted, using a 'blended' discount rate in the **B5.3** formula:

$$\text{Blended rate} = r\,(w) + (r + \text{CRP})(1 - w) = r + \text{CRP}\,(1 - w) \qquad \textbf{B5.5}$$

where
- r — risk free rate
- CRP — Credit Risk Premium
- w — a measure of the equity component embedded in the next period Convertible fair price, which can be estimated using the convertible's 'delta' or the probability of conversion:

A w = the Convertible's delta (sensitivity of price to change in share price):

$$\text{Delta} = \frac{C_u - C_d}{CV_u - CV_d}$$

(See Woodson (2002 p.106), Philips (1997 p.48).)

Example B5.3 Discounting at blended rate (delta)

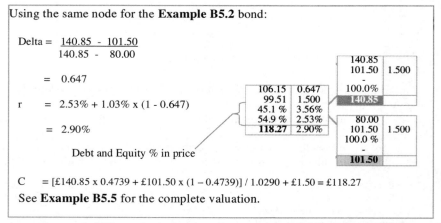

Using the same node for the **Example B5.2** bond:

$$\text{Delta} = \frac{140.85 - 101.50}{140.85 - 80.00}$$

$$= 0.647$$

$$r = 2.53\% + 1.03\% \times (1 - 0.647)$$

$$= 2.90\%$$

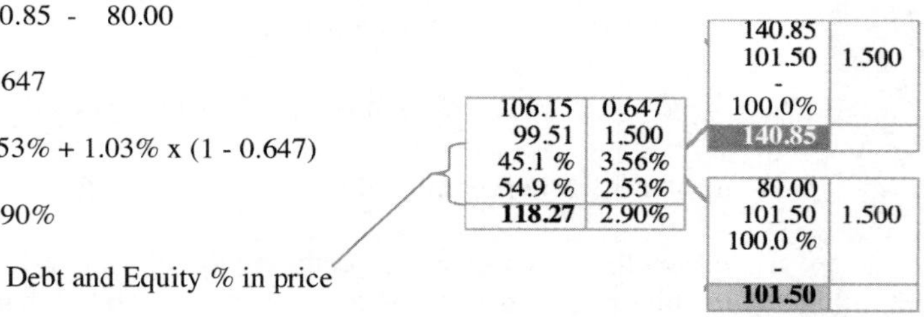

C = [£140.85 x 0.4739 + £101.50 x (1 – 0.4739)] / 1.0290 + £1.50 = £118.27

See **Example B5.5** for the complete valuation.

B w = the probability of converting into equity, which will either be 1.0 when conversion is certain (for example, when the Conversion Value exceeds the Investment Value at maturity) or 0.0 when the bond will be held to maturity (Investment Value exceeds Conversion Value at maturity):

$$\text{Probability of conversion} = P_u \times p + P_d \times (1 - p)$$

where
- P_u, P_d - probability of conversion at next period up and down states
- p - risk neutral probability

(See Goldman Sachs (1993).)

Example B5.4 Discounting at blended rate (conversion probability)

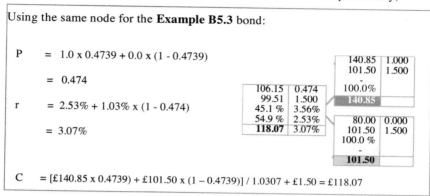

Using the same node for the **Example B5.3** bond:

$P = 1.0 \times 0.4739 + 0.0 \times (1 - 0.4739)$

$= 0.474$

$r = 2.53\% + 1.03\% \times (1 - 0.474)$

$= 3.07\%$

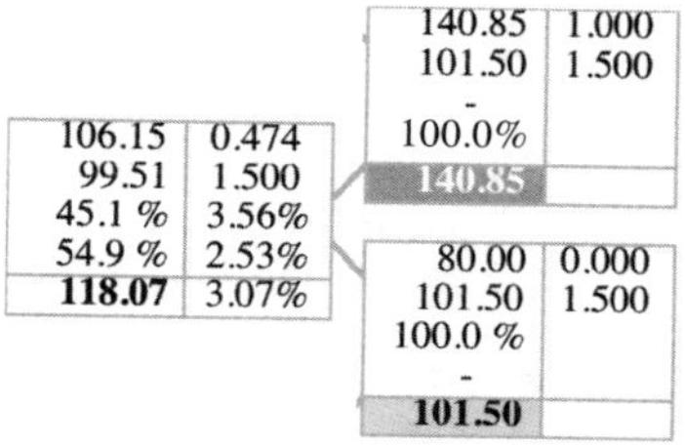

C = [£140.85 x 0.4739) + £101.50 x (1 – 0.4739)] / 1.0307 + £1.50 = £118.07

The risk free rate and credit spread can be assumed to change over time. Interest rate and credit risk models can be used to forecast rates, although neither of these will be covered here. In the examples that follow, a constant rate is assumed.

A Convertible pricing example using the delta blended rate 2 A is given below.

Example B5.5 Convertible pricing - blended rate using delta ratio

CONVERTIBLE ASSUMPTIONS		
Number of bonds		150,000
Convertible Face Value	£	100
Coupon - paid semi annually		3.00%
Call protection		5 yrs
Maturity date		5 yrs
Redemption price		100%
Bond credit spread		2%

UNDERLYING SHARE ASSUMPTIONS		
Share price at Convertible issue	£	10.00
Number of shares in issue		15,000,000
Dividend yield		0%
Market Value of shares		£150.00m

A 3% semi-annual coupon-paying Convertible is to be issued (there is no Call provision and the underlying share pays no dividends). Each bond can convert into 8 ordinary shares every 6 months over the bond's 5 year life.

BINOMIAL TREE ASSUMPTIONS	
Stock price	£10.00
Risk free rate (Continuous)	5.00%
Risk adjusted (Continuous)	7.00%
Volatility	40.0%
Time step	0.50
Time periods	10

CONVERSION ANALYSIS	
Conversion premium at issue	25%
Conversion Price = Share price at Convertible issue x (1 + Conversion Premium)	£12.50
Conversion Ratio = Convertible Face Value / Convertible Price	8.00 shares
Conversion Value = Share Price x Conversion Ratio	£80.00
Conversion Premium = (Convertible Fair Price - Conversion Value) / Conversion Value	40.92%
Market Conversion Price = Convertible Fair Price / Conversion Ratio	£14.09
Market Conversion Premium = (Market Conversion Price - Share Price)	£4.09
Income differential = (Coupon p.a. / Conversion Ratio) - Dividend p.a.	£0.38
Payback = Market Conversion Premium / Income differential	10.91yrs

BINOMIAL TREE PARAMETERS		
Up-move factor	1.3269	u = EXP(40.0%*SQRT(0.5000))
Down-move factor	0.7536	d = 1/1.3269
1 + risk-free return (discrete)	1.0253	1 + r = EXP (5.00% x 0.5000)
1 + risk-adjusted return (discrete)	1.0356	1 + r = EXP (7.00% x 0.5000)
Risk-neutral probability	0.4739	p = (1.0253 - 0.7536)/(1.3269 - 0.7536)

BOND INVESTMENT VALUE AT ISSUE

Fair Price of bond after issued date ('clean price' at start of interest period):

$$= \left\{ \text{Coupon} \times \frac{1}{r/m} \times \left[1 - \frac{1}{(1 + r/m)^{mn}} \right] \right\} + \frac{\text{Nominal value}}{(1 + r/m)^{mn}}$$

$$= \left\{ £1.50 \times \frac{1}{0.0356} \times \left[1 - \frac{1}{(1 + 0.0356)^{\wedge}10} \right] \right\} + \frac{£100.00}{(1 + 0.0356)^{\wedge}10}$$

$$= £12.44 + £70.48$$

$$= \mathbf{£82.92}$$

The fair price of the Convertible is £115.12 (pre-dilution) (£112.73 after the issue of new shares). See the following page.

❒ Callable / no dividends

If the cost of calling the bonds (the Call price plus accrued coupon) is less than the trading price of the bonds (Convertible fair price = max {Conversion Value, Investment Value, Continuing Value without a call }), the Convertible is likely to be called, although in practice this is only likely if the cost of calling the bonds is also less than the Conversion Value (Forced Conversion). Hence the Convertible fair price is as follows:

Max { Conversion Value, Min (Convertible fair price without a call, Call price + coupon) }.

See **Example B5.6**. This example is the same as **Example B5.5** but with a Call price of £110 and £105 at the end of years 3 and 4. The option price reduces to £111.19 (pre-dilution) (the difference of £3.93 being the value of the Call option for the issuer).

❒ Callable / dividends

Where dividends are paid on the underlying share, the effect of the share going ex-dividend (the price falls to strip out the accrued dividend no longer available to the purchaser) needs to be incorporated. The ex-dividend price is increased or decreased at the next node before a dividend is deducted, to arrive at that node's ex-dividend price which is then increased or decreased in the same manner at the next node. The dividend can be either a dividend per share or a dividend yield (percentage of the cum-dividend calculated share price at each node).

See **Example B5.7** (and Appendix B4 for equity options on dividend paying stocks). This example is the same as **Example B5.6** but with a constant 1% dividend yield paid per period. The option price reduces to £107.22 (pre-dilution).

Example B5.5 (cont.) - NON-CALLABLE / NO DIVIDENDS

CONVERTIBLE VALUATION

Embedded option	£32.22
Straight debt	£82.90
Value of Convertible - undiluted (no new shares issued)	**£115.12**
% of face value	115.1%
Embedded option x1/ (1 + dilution factor)	£29.83
Straight debt	£82.90
Value of Convertible - diluted (shares issued)	**£112.73**
% of face value	112.7%

CV	Conversion Value	Delta
IV	Investment Value	Coupon
D	Debt component %	Risk-adj rate
E	Equity component %	Risk free rate
C	Convertible Price	Blended rate

Period	CV	Delta	IV	Coupon	D	Risk-adj rate	E	Risk free rate	C	Blended rate
0	80.00	0.711	82.90	0.000	54.6 %	3.56%	45.4 %	2.53%	**115.12**	2.83%
1	106.15	0.795	85.86	1.500	41.2 %	3.56%	58.8 %	2.53%	**135.54**	2.74%
1	60.29	0.570	85.86	1.500	70.6 %	3.56%	29.4 %	2.53%	**102.92**	2.98%
2	140.85	0.870	87.36	1.500	27.5 %	3.56%	72.5 %	2.53%	**163.16**	2.67%
2	80.00	0.669	87.36	1.500	57.3 %	3.56%	42.7 %	2.53%	**114.79**	2.87%
2	45.44	0.398	87.36	1.500	84.1 %	3.56%	15.9 %	2.53%	**95.11**	3.15%
3	186.90	0.930	88.92	1.500	16.0 %	3.56%	84.0 %	2.53%	**202.92**	2.60%
3	106.15	0.769	88.92	1.500	41.8 %	3.56%	58.2 %	2.53%	**132.68**	2.77%
3	60.29	0.498	88.92	1.500	74.1 %	3.56%	25.9 %	2.53%	**102.02**	3.05%
3	34.24	0.220	88.92	1.500	93.7 %	3.56%	6.3 %	2.53%	**91.64**	3.34%
4	247.99	0.971	90.54	1.500	7.8 %	3.56%	92.2 %	2.53%	**259.09**	2.56%
4	140.85	0.861	90.54	1.500	26.4 %	3.56%	73.6 %	2.53%	**159.43**	2.67%
4	80.00	0.614	90.54	1.500	60.0 %	3.56%	40.0 %	2.53%	**112.64**	2.93%
4	45.44	0.298	90.54	1.500	88.2 %	3.56%	11.8 %	2.53%	**95.42**	3.25%
4	25.81	0.074	90.54	1.500	98.6 %	3.56%	1.4 %	2.53%	**91.10**	3.49%
5	329.06	0.993	92.21	1.500	3.2 %	3.56%	96.8 %	2.53%	**336.84**	2.54%
5	186.90	0.935	92.21	1.500	13.4 %	3.56%	86.6 %	2.53%	**198.74**	2.60%
5	106.15	0.738	92.21	1.500	42.6 %	3.56%	57.4 %	2.53%	**129.20**	2.80%
5	60.29	0.402	92.21	1.500	79.0 %	3.56%	21.0 %	2.53%	**101.06**	3.15%
5	34.24	0.110	92.21	1.500	96.9 %	3.56%	3.1 %	2.53%	**93.30**	3.45%
5	19.45	0.000	92.21	1.500	100.0 %	3.56%	-	2.53%	**92.21**	3.56%
6	436.63	1.000	93.94	1.500	1.3 %	3.56%	98.7 %	2.53%	**442.41**	2.53%
6	247.99	0.982	93.94	1.500	5.0 %	3.56%	95.0 %	2.53%	**255.06**	2.55%
6	140.85	0.857	93.94	1.500	24.3 %	3.56%	75.7 %	2.53%	**154.89**	2.68%
6	80.00	0.537	93.94	1.500	64.2 %	3.56%	35.8 %	2.53%	**110.01**	3.01%
6	45.44	0.168	93.94	1.500	93.5 %	3.56%	6.5 %	2.53%	**96.10**	3.39%
6	25.81	0.000	93.94	1.500	100.0 %	3.56%	-	2.53%	**93.94**	3.56%
6	14.66	0.000	93.94	1.500	100.0 %	3.56%	-	2.53%	**93.94**	3.56%
7	579.36	1.000	95.73	1.500	0.8 %	3.56%	99.2 %	2.53%	**583.75**	2.53%
7	329.06	1.000	95.73	1.500	1.3 %	3.56%	98.7 %	2.53%	**333.45**	2.53%
7	186.90	0.951	95.73	1.500	9.3 %	3.56%	90.7 %	2.53%	**193.89**	2.58%
7	106.15	0.698	95.73	1.500	43.6 %	3.56%	56.4 %	2.53%	**124.72**	2.84%
7	60.29	0.261	95.73	1.500	86.3 %	3.56%	13.7 %	2.53%	**100.11**	3.29%
7	34.24	0.000	95.73	1.500	100.0 %	3.56%	-	2.53%	**95.73**	3.56%
7	19.45	0.000	95.73	1.500	100.0 %	3.56%	-	2.53%	**95.73**	3.56%
7	11.05	0.000	95.73	1.500	100.0 %	3.56%	-	2.53%	**95.73**	3.56%
8	768.75	1.000	97.59	1.500	0.4 %	3.56%	99.6 %	2.53%	**771.71**	2.53%
8	436.63	1.000	97.59	1.500	0.7 %	3.56%	99.3 %	2.53%	**439.59**	2.53%
8	247.99	1.000	97.59	1.500	1.2 %	3.56%	98.8 %	2.53%	**250.96**	2.53%
8	140.85	0.869	97.59	1.500	19.8 %	3.56%	80.2 %	2.53%	**149.07**	2.67%
8	80.00	0.409	97.59	1.500	72.0 %	3.56%	28.0 %	2.53%	**106.60**	3.14%
8	45.44	0.000	97.59	1.500	100.0 %	3.56%	-	2.53%	**97.59**	3.56%
8	25.81	0.000	97.59	1.500	100.0 %	3.56%	-	2.53%	**97.59**	3.56%
8	14.66	0.000	97.59	1.500	100.0 %	3.56%	-	2.53%	**97.59**	3.56%
8	8.33	0.000	97.59	1.500	100.0 %	3.56%	-	2.53%	**97.59**	3.56%
9	1,020.05	1.000	99.51	1.500	0.1 %	3.56%	99.9 %	2.53%	**1,021.55**	2.53%
9	579.36	1.000	99.51	1.500	0.3 %	3.56%	99.7 %	2.53%	**580.86**	2.53%
9	329.06	1.000	99.51	1.500	0.5 %	3.56%	99.5 %	2.53%	**330.56**	2.53%
9	186.90	1.000	99.51	1.500	0.8 %	3.56%	99.2 %	2.53%	**188.40**	2.53%
9	106.15	0.647	99.51	1.500	45.1 %	3.56%	54.9 %	2.53%	**118.27**	2.90%
9	60.29	0.000	99.51	1.500	100.0 %	3.56%	-	2.53%	**99.51**	3.56%
9	34.24	0.000	99.51	1.500	100.0 %	3.56%	-	2.53%	**99.51**	3.56%
9	19.45	0.000	99.51	1.500	100.0 %	3.56%	-	2.53%	**99.51**	3.56%
9	11.05	0.000	99.51	1.500	100.0 %	3.56%	-	2.53%	**99.51**	3.56%
9	6.27	0.000	99.51	1.500	100.0 %	3.56%	-	2.53%	**99.51**	3.56%
10	1,353.51	1.000	101.50	1.500	-		100.0 %		**1,353.51**	
10	768.75	1.000	101.50	1.500	-		100.0 %		**768.75**	
10	436.63	1.000	101.50	1.500	-		100.0 %		**436.63**	
10	247.99	1.000	101.50	1.500	-		100.0 %		**247.99**	
10	140.85	1.000	101.50	1.500	-		100.0 %		**140.85**	
10	80.00	0.000	101.50	1.500	100.0 %		-		**101.50**	
10	45.44	0.000	101.50	1.500	100.0 %		-		**101.50**	
10	25.81	0.000	101.50	1.500	100.0 %		-		**101.50**	
10	14.66	0.000	101.50	1.500	100.0 %		-		**101.50**	
10	8.33	0.000	101.50	1.500	100.0 %		-		**101.50**	
10	4.73	0.000	101.50	1.500	100.0 %		-		**101.50**	

XXX CB price = 100% Debt

XXX CB price = 100% Equity

Conv. Price = MAX {Conversion Value, Investment Value, Continuing Value}

EXAMPLE WORKINGS FOR - cell U*

CV	=	(prior period value 186.90 x up factor 1.3269)
IV	=	next period value 92.21 / (1 + risk adjusted rate per period 3.56%) + coupon 1.50
C	=	{ Cu [336.84] x p [0.4739] + Cd [198.74] x (1-p) [0.5261] } / (1 + blended rate 2.56%) + coupon
delta	=	(Cu [336.84] - Cd [198.74) / (SVu [329.06] - SVd [186.90])
blended rate	=	delta x risk free rate + (1-delta) x risk adjusted rate = risk free rate + credit spread x (1-delta)

Example B5.6 - CALLABLE / NO DIVIDENDS

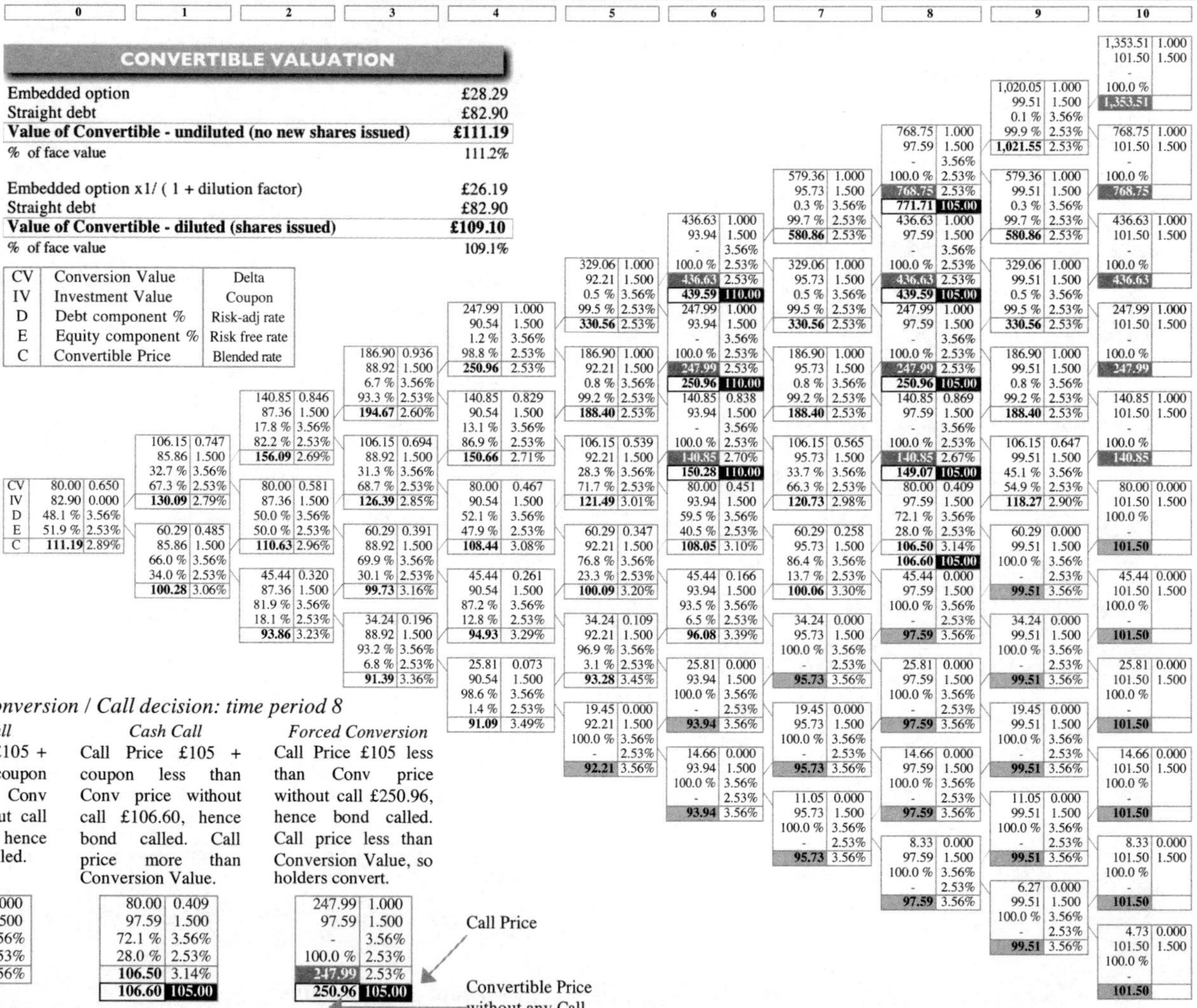

CONVERTIBLE VALUATION

Embedded option	£28.29
Straight debt	£82.90
Value of Convertible - undiluted (no new shares issued)	**£111.19**
% of face value	111.2%
Embedded option x1/ (1 + dilution factor)	£26.19
Straight debt	£82.90
Value of Convertible - diluted (shares issued)	**£109.10**
% of face value	109.1%

CV	Conversion Value	Delta
IV	Investment Value	Coupon
D	Debt component %	Risk-adj rate
E	Equity component %	Risk free rate
C	Convertible Price	Blended rate

Conversion / Call decision: time period 8

No Call

Call Price £105 + £1.5 coupon exceeds the Conv price without call £97.59, hence bond not called.

45.44	0.000
97.59	1.500
100.0 %	3.56%
-	2.53%
97.59	3.56%

Cash Call

Call Price £105 + coupon less than Conv price without call £106.60, hence bond called. Call price more than Conversion Value.

80.00	0.409
97.59	1.500
72.1 %	3.56%
28.0 %	2.53%
106.50	3.14%
106.60	105.00

Forced Conversion

Call Price £105 less than Conv price without call £250.96, hence bond called. Call price less than Conversion Value, so holders convert.

247.99	1.000
97.59	1.500
-	3.56%
100.0 %	2.53%
247.99	2.53%
250.96	105.00

Call Price

Convertible Price without any Call

Example B5.7 - CALLABLE + DIVIDEND (1% YIELD PER PERIOD)

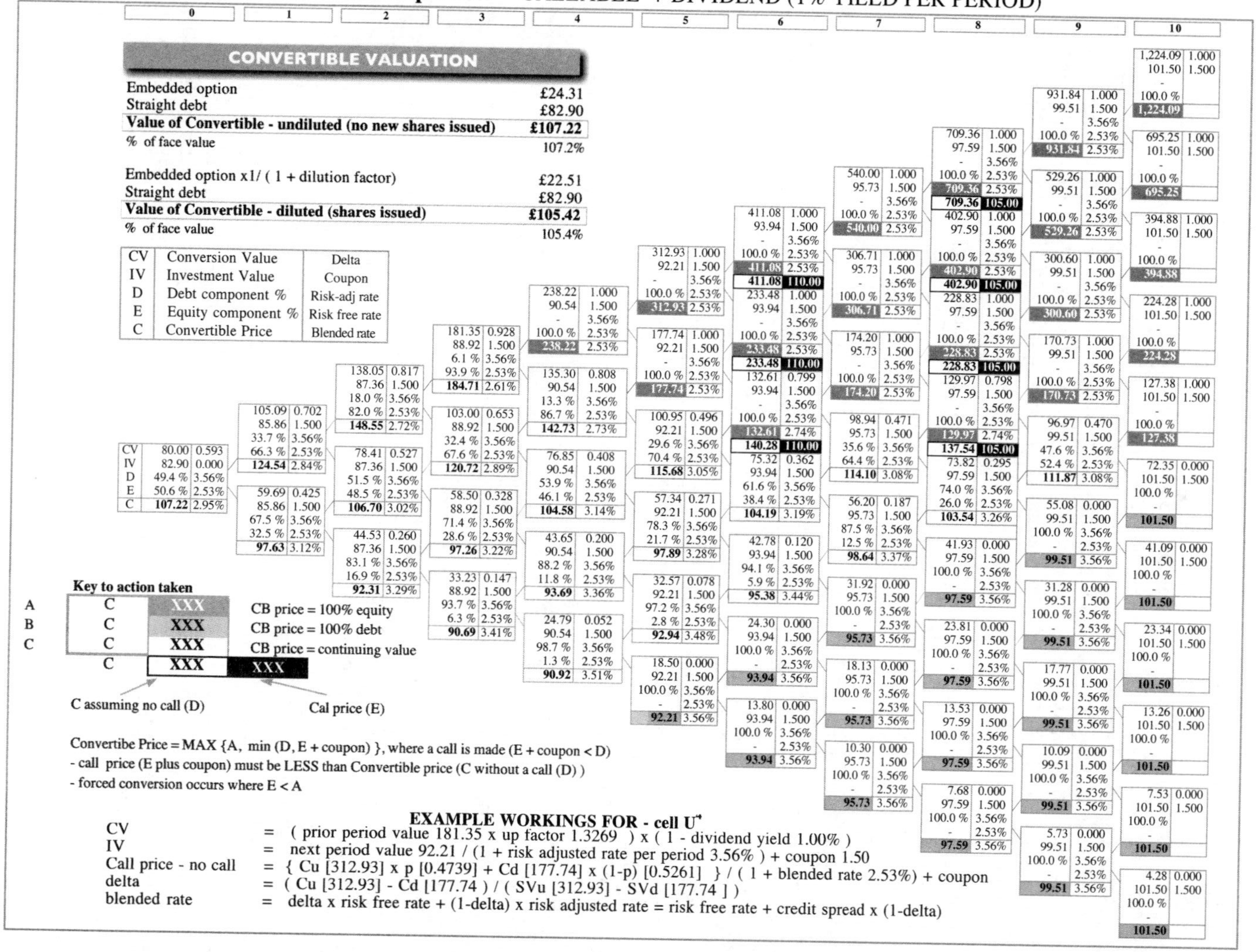

WARRANTS

This example should be read in conjunction with the section on Warrants in Chapter 2.

Example B5.8 Warrant valuation

Assume 16.67m warrants can be exercised at £2.70 in 2 year's time with each warrant being entitled to 1 share. The current share price is £2.20 and there are 100m shares in issue; the volatility of the equity returns is 30% and the risk free rate (continuously compounded) is 5.0%. No dividends are paid. The warrant can be calculated using the Black-Scholes ('BS') model for a call option:

$$\text{Warrant value } W = \frac{1}{1 + (16.67m / 100m)} \times \text{BS Call Value where } S = £2.20 + W, \quad X = £2.70$$

Current share price	S	2.20
Share price + warrant value (see below)		2.24
Shares in issue		100.0 m
Warrant exercise Price	X	2.70
Warrant shares issued		16.67 m
Ordinary shares per warrant		1
Volatility (%)(standard deviation) - shares plus warrants	σ	30.00%
Risk Free Rate (%) (continous)	r	5.00%
Time to Expiry (years)	T	2.0000
Dividend Yield (%)	q	0.00%
d1 = (LN(2.24 / 2.70) + (5.00% + 0.5 x 30.00%^2) x 2) / (30.00% x SQRT(2))		0.0108
d2 = (LN(2.24 / 2.70) + (5.00% - 0.5 x 30.00%^2) x 2) / (30.00% x SQRT(2)) = 0.0108 - 30.00% x SQRT(2)		-0.4134
N(d1) = NORMSDIST(0.0108)		0.5043
N(d2) = NORMSDIST(-0.4134)		0.3396
Equity value per share = 2.24 x N(d1)		1.13
PV of ex price = (2.70 x EXP(-5.00 x 2)) x N(d2)		0.83
Call Price		0.30
Dilution factor = 1 shares each / (1+(16.67m warrants x 1 shares each) / 100.0)		0.8571
Warrant price		0.26

	Number	*Price*	*Value*
Ordinary shares	100.0 m	£2.20	£220.00 m
Warrant entitlement		£0.26	£4.31 m
Equity Value	*100.00 m*	*£2.24*	*£224.3 m*

INTEREST RATE & CURRENCY OPTIONS

Interest Rate Futures Options

Futures on Options can be valued using an adjusted version of the Black-Scholes Model (Black (1976)):

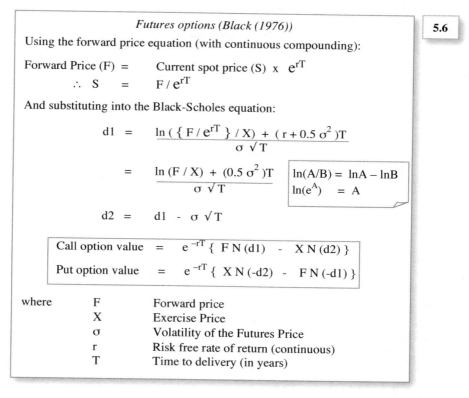

5.6

Futures options (Black (1976))

Using the forward price equation (with continuous compounding):

Forward Price (F) = Current spot price (S) x e^{rT}

$\therefore$ S = F / e^{rT}

And substituting into the Black-Scholes equation:

$$d1 = \frac{\ln(\{F / e^{rT}\} / X) + (r + 0.5\,\sigma^2)T}{\sigma\sqrt{T}}$$

$$= \frac{\ln(F / X) + (0.5\,\sigma^2)T}{\sigma\sqrt{T}}$$

$\ln(A/B) = \ln A - \ln B$
$\ln(e^A) = A$

$$d2 = d1 - \sigma\sqrt{T}$$

Call option value = $e^{-rT}\{F\,N(d1) - X\,N(d2)\}$

Put option value = $e^{-rT}\{X\,N(-d2) - F\,N(-d1)\}$

where

	F	Forward price
	X	Exercise Price
	σ	Volatility of the Futures Price
	r	Risk free rate of return (continuous)
	T	Time to delivery (in years)

Currency Options

Pricing basics

European Currency Options can be priced (in the domestic currency) using a Black-Scholes-Merton type formula for a dividend paying stock, where the continuous dividend yield q% is replaced with the continuous foreign currency risk free rate:

5.7

Currency Option (Garman and Kohlhagen (1983)

Call option value = $S\,e^{-r_f T}\,N(d1) \;-\; X\,e^{-rT}\,N(d2)$

Put option value = $X\,e^{-rT}\,N(-d2) \;-\; S\,e^{-r_f T}\,N(-d1)$

- S — Spot exchange rate (value, in domestic currency, of one unit of foreign currency if exchanged today)
- X — Exercise price (agreed value, in home currency, of one unit of foreign currency if exchanged on the Exercise Date)
- T — Time to maturity
- r — Risk free rate (continuously compounded) – domestic currency
- r_f — Risk free rate (continuously compounded) – foreign currency

$$d1 = \frac{\ln(S/X) + (r - r_f + 0.5\,\sigma^2)T}{\sigma\sqrt{T}} \qquad d2 = d1 - \sigma\sqrt{T}$$

where σ is the annual standard deviation of logarithmic daily returns of the spot exchange rate

N (x) is the cumulative probability function for a standardised normal variable.

Example 5.9 Currency Option pricing

A Call on Sterling against the US Dollar (equivalent to a put on the US Dollar against Sterling) exercisable at expiry in 3 months time at 1.65 would be valued at $0.02877 per £1 (or 2.88 cents), if the current exchange rate was £/$: 1.65, the 1 month continuously compounded risk free rates were 3.5% (£) and 1.5% ($), and the £/$ volatility was 10%:

Spot rate		S	£1 = US$1.6500
Exercise Price		X	1.6500
Volatility (%)(standard deviation)		σ	10.00%
Time to Expiry (years)	3 mths	T	0.2500
Risk free rate - domestic	US$	r	1.50%
Risk free rate - foreign	£	r_F	3.50%
d1 = (LN(1.65 / 1.65) + ([1.50% - 3.50%] + 0.5 x 10.00%^2) x 0.25) / (10.00% x SQRT(0.25))			-0.075000
d2 = (LN(1.65 / 1.65) + ([1.50% - 3.50%] - 0.5 x 10.00%^2) x 0) / (10.00% x SQRT(0)) = -0.0750 - 10.00% x SQRT(0.25 years)			-0.125000
N(d1) = NORMSDIST(-0.0750)			0.470107
N(d2) = NORMSDIST(-0.1250)			0.450262
3 month forward rate (= 1.65 x EXP (-3.50% x 0.25 years))			1.6356
Forward rate x N(d1)			0.76892
PV of ex price (= 1.65 x N(d2) x EXP(-1.50% x 0.25 years))			0.74015
Call Price			**$0.02877 per £1**

A European currency option can be shown in terms of Black's (1976) Futures Option model (see above), with a slight amendment (Hull (2003 p.277)):

Currency Option Price in terms of Forward Price

5.8

Forward Price (F) = Current spot price (S) x $e^{(r - r_f)T}$

$\therefore \; S = F / e^{(r - r_f)T}$

$$d_1 = \frac{\ln(\{F / e^{(r - r_f)T}\} / X) + (r - r_f + 0.5\sigma^2)T}{\sigma\sqrt{T}}$$

$$= \frac{\ln(F / X) + (0.5\sigma^2)T}{\sigma\sqrt{T}} \qquad d2 = d1 - \sigma\sqrt{T}$$

Call Option value = $e^{-rT}\{F\,N(d1) - X\,N(d2)\}$

Put Option value = $e^{-rT}\{X\,N(-d2) - F\,N(-d1)\}$

The Call Option value in **Example B5.9** would be calculated as follows: $e^{-1.50\% \times 0.25}$ x (F x 0.470107 – 1.65 x 0.450262) = 0.02877 where F = $1.65^{(1.50\% - 3.50\%) \times 0.25}$ = 1.6418.

American Currency Options, where early exercise is possible, can be priced using a Binomial Tree with the risk neutral probability being calculated using the interest rate differential.

Example B5.10 Currency Option pricing

If the European call option from **Example B5.9** was an American option, then, using the same information, and allowing for 6 time periods (over 0.25 years), the relevant Binomial Tree inputs would be:

Model assumptions		
Spot rate		1.65
ExercisePrice		1.65
Risk Free interest rate	Domestic	1.50%
Risk Free interest rate	Foreign	3.50%
Volatility		10.0%
Time step (fraction of year)		0.0417
Number of time periods		6

Parameters		
Up-move factor	1.0206	U = EXP(10.0%*SQRT(0.0417))
Down-move factor	0.9798	D = 1/1.0206
Domestic risk free factor	1.0006	r = EXP(2%*0.0417)
Differential risk free factor	0.9992	= EXP((1.50% - 3.50%) x 0.04 years)
Risk-neutral probability	0.4745	p* = (0.9992 - 0.9798)/(1.0206 - 0.9798)

The call option has a value of $0.02867 per £1 (the European equivalent is $0.02743 – this would converge to the above $0.02877 as the number of time steps increased):

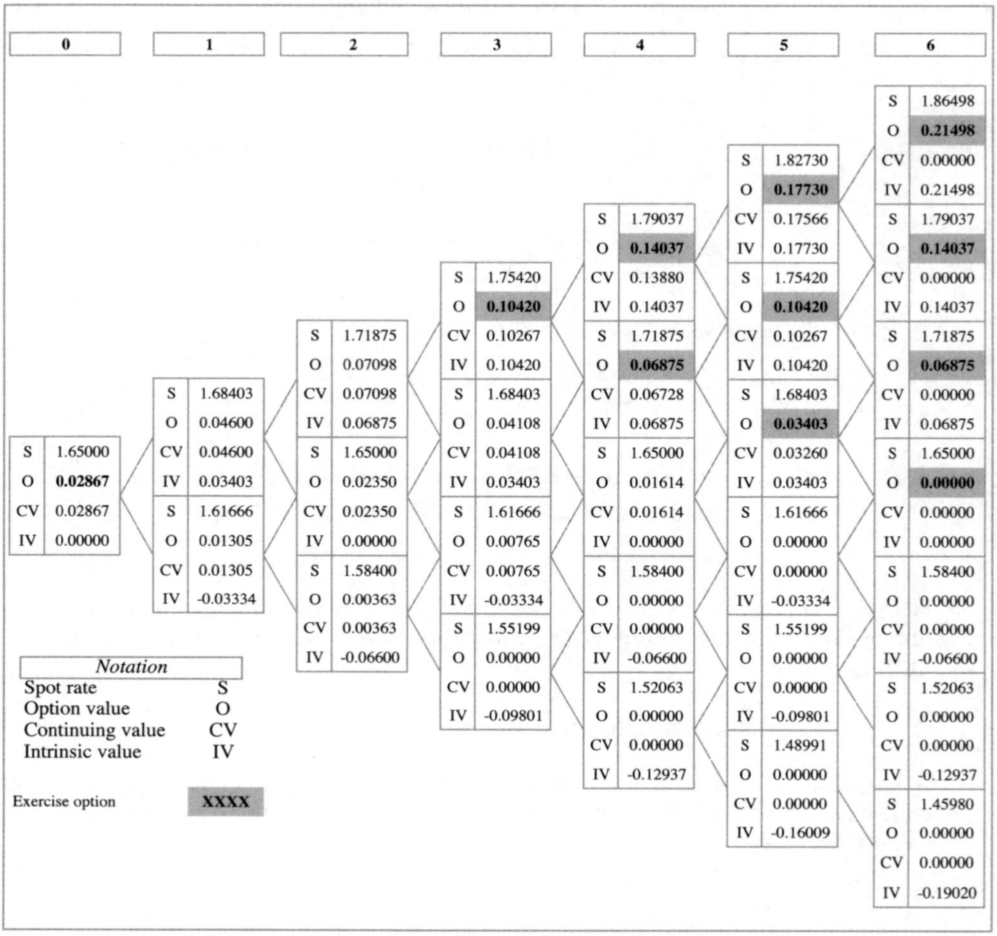
0
1
2
3
4
5
6
S 1.65000
O 0.02867
CV 0.02867
IV 0.00000
S 1.68403
O 0.04600
CV 0.04600
IV 0.03403
S 1.61666
O 0.01305
CV 0.01305
IV -0.03334
S 1.71875
O 0.07098
CV 0.07098
IV 0.06875
S 1.65000
O 0.02350
CV 0.02350
IV 0.00000
S 1.58400
O 0.00363
CV 0.00363
IV -0.06600
S 1.75420
O 0.10420
CV 0.10267
IV 0.10420
S 1.68403
O 0.04108
CV 0.04108
IV 0.03403
S 1.61666
O 0.00765
CV 0.00765
IV -0.03334
S 1.55199
O 0.00000
CV 0.00000
IV -0.09801
S 1.79037
O 0.14037
CV 0.13880
IV 0.14037
S 1.71875
O 0.06875
CV 0.06728
IV 0.06875
S 1.65000
O 0.01614
CV 0.01614
IV 0.00000
S 1.58400
O 0.00000
CV 0.00000
IV -0.06600
S 1.52063
O 0.00000
CV 0.00000
IV -0.12937
S 1.82730
O 0.17730
CV 0.17566
IV 0.17730
S 1.75420
O 0.10420
CV 0.10267
IV 0.10420
S 1.68403
O 0.03403
CV 0.03260
IV 0.03403
S 1.61666
O 0.00000
CV 0.00000
IV -0.03334
S 1.55199
O 0.00000
CV 0.00000
IV -0.09801
S 1.48991
O 0.00000
CV 0.00000
IV -0.16009
S 1.86498
O 0.21498
CV 0.00000
IV 0.21498
S 1.79037
O 0.14037
CV 0.00000
IV 0.14037
S 1.71875
O 0.06875
CV 0.00000
IV 0.06875
S 1.65000
O 0.00000
CV 0.00000
IV 0.00000
S 1.58400
O 0.00000
CV 0.00000
IV -0.06600
S 1.52063
O 0.00000
CV 0.00000
IV -0.12937
S 1.45980
O 0.00000
CV 0.00000
IV -0.19020
Notation
Spot rate S
Option value O
Continuing value CV
Intrinsic value IV
Exercise option XXXX

APPENDIX C

LEASING

C LEASING

NATURE AND CHARACTERISTICS

Lease Agreement

Under a lease agreement, one party (the 'lessor') grants another (the 'lessee') full use of an asset for a period ('primary lease term') in return for a rental, subject to certain terms and conditions. The lessor may have legal title to the asset, or lease it from its legal owner (the 'head lessor'); the lessee may be entitled to 'sub-lease' the asset to a 'sub-lessee'. There may, therefore, be more than one lease agreement relating to a single asset.

The lessee would normally return the asset to the lessor at the end of the primary lease term, having maintained it and restored it to the minimum condition stated in the lease agreement; however, it may be granted the right to extend the lease into a 'Secondary' term at a stipulated rent ('Renewal Option') or to purchase the asset ('Purchase option').

Lease Cash Flows

The lessor would have a 'Net Cash Investment' ('NCI') in the lease, initially equivalent to the cost incurred in making the asset available to the lessee (the asset purchase price, any related acquisition costs, any financing or holding costs from the purchase date to the date of the lease commencement, and any costs associated with arranging the lease agreement). During the lease, the lessor would receive from the lessee periodic rentals in advance or arrears, either fixed or structured in some way, reducing the NCI.

Tax payments (which increase the NCI) will arise on rental income less allowable deductions for expenditure incurred: (1) the purchase price and other allowable capitalised costs will normally be tax deductible over time, either on a straight line basis or weighted towards early years ('accelerated'); (2) ongoing operating and financing costs associated with maintaining the lease or asset will also be deductible.

At the end of the primary lease term, the lessor may have an unrecovered NCI. In order to achieve the required economic profit (indicated by the lease yielding an after-tax Internal Rate of Return in excess of the lessor's required rate), the lessor would need to realise additional value from the asset, either by selling or re-leasing it at a market rent. A significant risk for the lessor is the uncertainty associated with the value of the asset at the end of the lease term ('Residual Value'). The extent to which the lessor is able to recover its investment in the lease from contractual arrangements (rentals and any commitments to buy the asset, for example), is a key factor in determining the accounting treatment for both the lessor and lessee.

LEASE CLASSIFICATION

If the lessor can earn its required rate of return from cash flows that the lessee has contracted to pay or guarantee over a non-cancellable term ('Minimum Lease Payments', being rentals and any payments for a part of or all of the Residual Value), the lease would be termed a 'Full Payout' lease. The lessor has effectively sold its economic interest in the asset to the lessee, and its required return would be achieved whatever the Residual Value: any proceeds from the sale of the asset at the lease end could be returned to the lessee as a rebate of rentals (if the asset had a nil Residual Value, then the lease term would represent 100% of the asset's remaining economic life at the start of the lease).

The lease may provide for legal title to be transferred to the lessee at the end of the lease, either automatically ('Conditional Sale Agreement') or for a nominal purchase price ('Bargain Purchase Option'). Alternatively, the lessee may be able to extend the lease for a secondary term at a rental substantially below market rent ('Bargain Renewal Option'). Such arrangements (where, at the start of the lease, exercise of any purchase or renewal option was reasonably assured) would indicate that the lease was a Full Payout lease, and that the asset was likely to have negligible Residual Value or that the lessor was not exposed to any Residual Value.

In a Full Payout lease (as for any lease), the lessor will remain exposed to the credit risk that the lessee defaults on its lease obligations (in a non-Full Payout lease, the lessor would also face asset risk), putting the lessor, effectively, in the position of a lender: the lessee has acquired economic interest in the asset by 'borrowing' from the lessor and repaying the loan principal plus interest in the form of rentals. The lessee would normally have to record the asset on its balance sheet, financed with a loan repaid from the capital element of rental payments.

The lease may not be a Full Payout lease, but may still involve the lessor passing to the lessee the majority of the risks and rewards associated with the asset. If (1) the fair value of the asset at the start of the lease (the purchase price or some other arm's- length value) is substantially recovered from the present value of the lessee's Minimum Lease Payments (US and UK requirement), or (2) there is evidence to show that the lease term (including a secondary term under a Bargain Renewal Option) covers substantially the remaining useful economic life of the asset at the start of the lease (implying a low Residual Value)(US requirement), or (3) the lease contains a clause transferring legal title automatically or under a Bargain Purchase Option (US requirement), then the lease will be treated in the same manner as for a Full Payout lease. Such leases ('Finance Leases' in the UK, 'Capital Leases' in the US) would be recorded as an asset and liability on the lessee's balance sheet (with the finance charge element of the rental being allocated to the profit and loss account); all other 'Operating Leases' would not be recorded in the lessee's balance sheet – the rental payment would be charged to the profit and loss account. **Exhibit C1** discusses Lease Classification and accounting in more detail.

LEASE FINANCIAL EVALUATION

Introduction to Lease Cash Flow Analysis

An example will be used to illustrate how the Net Present Value (NPV) and Internal Rate of Return (IRR) measures discussed in Appendix B1 can be applied to leases.

Example C1 The Lessor's pre-tax NPV and IRR ('Implicit Rate') – Full Payout Lease

Assume a lessor purchases an asset for £1m and immediately leases it for 4 years, at the end of which it has nil value. The Lessor has a low pre-tax cost of capital of 8.0% and a target pre-tax profit margin on top of this of 0.60%. Annual rentals in arrears are set at £305,979 p.a. (for simplicity – in practice, monthly, quarterly or semi-annual rentals would be paid, and the analysis carried out on a daily basis).

Discounting the cash flows at the pre-tax hurdle rate of 8.0% results in a positive NPV of £13,441:

Year	Rental	Asset cost	Net Cash Flows	Disc Factor @ 8.00%	Present Value
0		(1,000,000)	(1,000,000)	1.0000	(1,000,000)
1	305,979		305,979	0.9259	283,314
2	305,979		305,979	0.8573	262,328
3	305,979		305,979	0.7938	242,896
4	305,979		305,979	0.7350	224,904
	1,223,915	**(1,000,000)**	**223,915**		**13,441**

This NPV can be shown using the loan balance method: cash flows are compounded forward to an end date (interest is charged on each period's opening Net Cash Investment in the lease), and the NPV is the sum extracted on day one that produces a zero end balance:

Year	Rental	Asset cost	NPV extracted	Interest 8.00%	Net Cash Flows	Net Cash Investment
0		(1,000,000)	**(13,441)**		(1,013,441)	(1,013,441)
1	305,979			(81,075)	224,904	(788,537)
2	305,979			(63,083)	242,896	(545,641)
3	305,979			(43,651)	262,328	(283,314)
4	305,979			(22,665)	283,314	**0**
	1,223,915	**(1,000,000)**	**(13,441)**	**(210,475)**	**0**	

For the NPV to be zero, a higher interest charge is required:

Year	Rental	Asset cost	Interest **IRR=8.60%**	Net Cash Flows	Net Cash Investment
0		(1,000,000)		(1,000,000)	(1,000,000)
1	305,979		(86,023)	219,955	(780,045)
2	305,979		(67,102)	238,877	(541,168)
3	305,979		(46,553)	259,426	(281,742)
4	305,979		(24,236)	281,742	**0**
	1,223,915	**(1,000,000)**	**(223,915)**	**0**	

Since the discount, or compound, rate which produces a zero NPV is the IRR, the 8.60% pre-tax IRR can be separated into the pre-tax cost of capital (8.0%) and the pre-tax profit margin (0.60%).

The Residual Value is the fair value of the asset at the end of the lease that the lessor expects to realise from a sale or re-lease (in present value terms at that date).

Example C2 Residual Values

Using **Example C1**, assume that at the end of the lease the asset has a value equivalent to just under 20% of its £1m current value (£185,348). The lessor could realise this by selling it to a third party when the lease terminates. Assuming the lessor's target IRR is still 8.60%, the rental would have to be reduced to £265,210:

Year	Rental	Asset cost / Residual Value	Interest IRR=8.60%	Net Cash Flows	Net Cash Investment
0		(1,000,000)		(1,000,000)	(1,000,000)
1	265,210		(86,023)	179,187	(820,813)
2	265,210		(70,609)	194,601	(626,212)
3	265,210		(53,869)	211,342	(414,870)
4	265,210	185,348	(35,689)	414,870	**0**
	1,060,842	**(814,652)**	**(246,190)**	**0**	

Rather than look to the lessee to achieve its target yield, the lessor now takes some Residual Value risk: unless the receipt of £185,348 at the lease end is certain or guaranteed, the lessor's target yield is exposed to asset risk (ignoring the Residual Value, the return would be about zero). This contrasts with the Full Payout lease example (**Example C1**), where the lessor obtained its target yield entirely from the annual rental and was not exposed to any fluctuations in the underlying value of the asset, or any other asset risks (the yield was achieved from fixed contracted cash flows and the only risk assumed was the risk of lessee default, similar to a lender in a loan agreement).

Lessee Evaluation

Finance Leases

A lessee should determine whether the after-tax cost of financing a new asset using a Finance Lease (where an economic interest is effectively purchased) is less than the after-tax cost of purchasing the asset (an economic and legal interest is purchased)('Lease vs. Purchase'). Leasing is preferred if the present value of the lease cash flows (rentals and tax relief thereon) is less than the present value of the purchase cash flows (financing cash flows and tax relief thereon, and tax relief on the asset).

The lessee should also include (1) the total Residual Value as a cash inflow in the purchase cash flows (representing the asset salvage value), net of tax, and (2) any part of this Residual Value that it is to guarantee as a cash outflow in the leasing cash flows, net of tax (the guaranteed portion could be payable as an agreed maximum extra end-of-lease rental, to cover any shortfall if the lessor is unable to realise the expected Residual Value).

If after-tax rentals are contractual and certain (other than the risk of a change in tax rates or legislation), then the leasing cash flows can be treated as debt cash flows and valued using the after-tax marginal cost of borrowing (based on a loan equal to the asset cost, with a similar maturity to the lease term, secured on the underlying asset). If tax relief on debt interest is immediate, the after-tax cost of debt is simply the pre-tax borrowing rate x (1 – tax rate). Any delay after payment of the interest before the tax relief is available (the cash flow impact) needs to be incorporated in the borrowing rate being used as the discount rate.

If all cash flows are discounted at the lessee's after-tax cost of debt, then one approach would be to compare the present value of the 'incremental' lease cash flows (all cash flows other than debt cash flows) to the asset cost (since this equals the present value of the after-tax debt cash flows). Leasing would be preferred if the present value of the incremental leasing cash flows was less than the cost of the asset (this could also be shown by the IRR of the incremental leasing cash flows being less than the after-tax cost of borrowing).

The Residual Value is an uncertain cash flow (so too, it could be argued, is the related tax cash flow), and hence should, strictly, be discounted at a separate risk-adjusted discount rate (such as the Cost of Capital). However, this would reduce the relative value of purchasing to leasing, so only needs to be considered if leasing is not preferred when discounting the Residual Value at the (lower) after-tax cost of debt.

Since a Finance Lease is similar to a loan, any benefit from leasing is likely to be due to tax reasons. As legal owner, the lessor may be able to obtain tax deductions for the asset that have a positive cash flow impact (by reducing tax on rental income) and a present value greater than would be available to the lessee if it owned the asset. This may be due to a difference in the tax treatment in the lessor and lessee's respective tax jurisdictions (in a 'Cross Border' lease) or a difference in tax rates, or because the lessee has insufficient taxable profits to absorb the available tax relief.

If tax benefits available to the owner of an asset (ignoring financing) have to be deferred to future periods due to a lack of taxable profits (perhaps due to accumulated tax losses), the after-tax cost of purchasing the asset (in present value terms) will be higher. It may be possible to recover some of this present value cost by leasing the asset from a Finance Lessor with sufficient taxable profits: the lessor's required rate of return could be achieved with rentals that had an after-tax cost to the lessee (in present value terms) below the after-tax cost of purchasing the asset.

Example C3 Finance Lease vs Purchase Decision

Using **Examples C2**, assume the lessee (1) has a *pre-tax* cost of debt for a £1m loan of 10.0% (effective rate), (2) has a *post-tax* cost of capital (adjusted for the Residual Value risk) of 9.0% (effective rate), (3) pays tax at 30%, due 9 months after the year end, and (4) is to guarantee £46,239 of the expected £185,348 Residual Value (as is discussed later in **Exhibit C1**, this lessee guarantee is required in order for the lease to be classified a Finance Lease).

The effective after-tax borrowing cost is 7.15% (or 6.97% nominal, compounded quarterly), calculated as follows (and not simply 10.0% x (1 – 30% tax rate)):

Year	Debt Principal	Interest Pre-tax Debt Cost *10.00%*	Tax @ 30.0%	Net Cash Flows	Disc. Factor Post-tax Debt Cost *7.15%*	Present Value
0.00	1,000,000			1,000,000	1.0000	1,000,000
1.00		(100,000)		(100,000)	0.9333	(93,326)
1.75			30,000	30,000	0.8861	26,584
2.00		(100,000)		(100,000)	0.8710	(87,097)
2.75			30,000	30,000	0.8270	24,810
3.00		(100,000)		(100,000)	0.8128	(81,284)
3.75			30,000	30,000	0.7718	23,154
4.00	(1,000,000)	(100,000)		(1,100,000)	0.7586	(834,449)
4.75			30,000	30,000	0.7203	21,609
		(400,002)	**120,001**	**(280,001)**		**0.00**

The time delay adjusted post-tax borrowing rate can be approximated using the following equation (PricewaterhouseCoopers (2002 p.77)):

$$r^* = r \times \left(1 - \frac{t}{(1 + r^{**})^d}\right) = 10.0\% \times \left(1 - \frac{0.30}{(1 + 10.0\% \times 0.7)^{0.75}}\right) = 7.15\%$$

where r^* = post tax cost of debt; r^{**} = $r(1 - t)$; r = the pre tax cost of debt; t = effective tax rate; d = time delay in years

Note: a second run can give a more accurate approximation (not needed in this case): the first approximation of r^*, 7.15% above, is used instead of r^{**}.

Two scenarios are shown: (1) available profits, (2) insufficient profits in years 1-3:

(1) The lessee has sufficient taxable profits to be able to claim tax relief as early as possible. If incremental leasing cash flows are discounted at the post-tax cost of debt, the lessee would be indifferent, since the present value equals the value of the loan / asset:

Incremental Leasing Cash Flows: Pure Lease Cash Flows plus Opportunity Cost of Purchase

Year	Rentals	Residual Value (RV) Guarantee	Tax ▣ @ 30.0%	**Lease**	Residual Value (RV)	Lost tax relief ▣ on Asset Allowances: Non-RV	Lost tax relief ▣ on Asset Allowances: RV	**Asset**
1.00	(265,210)			(265,210)				0
1.75			90,726	90,726		(75,000)		(75,000)
2.00	(265,210)			(265,210)				0
2.75			85,880	85,880		(56,250)		(56,250)
3.00	(265,210)			(265,210)				0
3.75			80,617	80,617		(42,188)		(42,188)
4.00	(265,210)	(46,239)		(311,449)	(185,348)			(185,348)
4.75			74,901	74,901		(31,641)	(39,317)	(70,958)
	(1,060,842)	**(46,239)**	**332,124**	**(774,956)**	**(185,348)**	**(205,078)**	**(39,317)**	**(429,744)**

Discounting incremental leasing cash flows (lease + asset/purchase cash flows) at the post-tax cost of debt should make the lessee indifferent between leasing and purchasing.

Year	**Incremental Lease Cash Flows**	Disc Factor Cost of Debt 7.15%	Present Value
1.00	(265,210)	0.9333	(247,510)
1.75	15,726	0.8861	13,936
2.00	(265,210)	0.8710	(230,991)
2.75	29,630	0.8270	24,504
3.00	(265,210)	0.8128	(215,574)
3.75	38,429	0.7718	29,660
4.00	(496,797)	0.7586	(376,866)
4.75	3,943	0.7203	2,840
	(1,204,700)		**(1,000,000)**

▣ Based on UK tax treatment: see **Exhibit C1** for comment and **Examples C8** and **C9** for tax workings.

The lessee's after-tax incremental leasing cash flows will have an implicit rate that can be calculated using the 'loan balance' method for IRRs (see **Examples B1.5** and **B1.6** in Appendix B1). The effective rate equals the pre-tax cost of debt, suggesting a zero NPV leasing advantage.

Year	Leasing Cash Flows	Interest @ 10.00% Effective	Tax on Interest 30%	Net Cash Investment
0.00				1,000,000
1.00	(265,210)	100,006		834,795
1.75	15,726	61,861	(30,002)	882,381
2.00	(265,210)	21,279		638,449
2.75	29,630	47,311	(24,942)	690,449
3.00	(265,210)	16,650		441,889
3.75	38,429	32,746	(19,188)	493,875
4.00	(496,797)	11,910		8,988
4.75	3,943	666	(13,596)	**(0)**
	(1,204,700)	**292,429**	**(87,729)**	

For completeness, the present values will be shown separately:

Pure lease cash flows

Year	Rental	Tax on rentals @ 30.0%	Residual Value (RV) Guarantee	Tax on RV rental @ 30.0%	Cash Flows	Disc Factor Post-tax Debt Cost 7.15%	Present Value
1.00	(265,210)				(265,210)	0.9333	(247,510)
1.75		90,726			90,726	0.8861	80,396
2.00	(265,210)				(265,210)	0.8710	(230,991)
2.75		85,880			85,880	0.8270	71,023
3.00	(265,210)				(265,210)	0.8128	(215,574)
3.75		80,617			80,617	0.7718	62,220
4.00	(265,210)		(46,239)		(311,449)	0.7586	(236,262)
4.75		61,029		13,872	74,901	0.7203	53,951
	(1,060,842)	**318,253**	**(46,239)**	**13,872**	**(774,956)**		**(662,746)**

Purchase cash flows

Year	Debt interest + principal Pre-tax 10.00%	Tax on interest @ 30.0%	Tax on Non-RV allowances @ 30.0%	Residual Value (RV)	Tax on RV allowances @ 30.0%	Cash Flows	Disc Factor Post-tax Debt Cost 7.15%	Present Value
1.00	(100,000)					(100,000)	0.9333	(93,326)
1.75		30,000	75,000			105,000	0.8861	93,045
2.00	(100,000)					(100,000)	0.8710	(87,097)
2.75		30,000	56,250			86,250	0.8270	71,329
3.00	(100,000)					(100,000)	0.8128	(81,284)
3.75		30,000	42,188			72,188	0.7718	55,715
4.00	(1,100,000)			185,348		(914,652)	0.7586	(693,846)
4.75		30,000	31,641		39,317	100,958	0.7203	72,719
	(1,400,002)	**120,001**	**205,078**	**185,348**	**39,317**	**(850,258)**		**(662,746)**

Discounting with the post-tax cost of debt does not result in any leasing advantage. However, as noted above, the Residual Value and related tax should be discounted at a higher rate to reflect the uncertainty of the amount of Residual Value and guarantee that the lessee will be called on for by way of the extra rental (which will determine the tax cash flow). This is discussed below, however first a second scenario is shown.

(2) The lessee has insufficient profits in years 2 and 3 (only enough to absorb the interest on the debt for a purchase, so as not to change the effective after-tax cost of debt), but can utilise all carried forward losses in year 4: leasing is now marginally preferred.

Pure lease cash flows

Year	Rental	Tax on rentals @ 30.0%	Residual Value (RV) Guarantee	Tax on RV rental @ 30.0%	Cash Flows	Disc Factor Post-tax Debt Cost 7.15%	Present Value
1.00	(265,210)				(265,210)	0.9333	(247,510)
1.75		30,000			30,000	0.8861	26,584
2.00	(265,210)				(265,210)	0.8710	(230,991)
2.75		30,000			30,000	0.8270	24,810
3.00	(265,210)				(265,210)	0.8128	(215,574)
3.75		30,000			30,000	0.7718	23,154
4.00	(265,210)		(46,239)		(311,449)	0.7586	(236,262)
4.75		228,252		13,872	242,124	0.7203	174,400
	(1,060,842)	**318,253**	**(46,239)**	**13,872**	**(774,956)**		**(681,388)**

Purchase cash flows

Year	Debt interest + principal Pre-tax 10.00%	Tax on interest @ 30.0%	Tax on Non-RV allowances @ 30.0%	Residual Value (RV)	Tax on RV allowances @ 30.0%	Cash Flows	Disc Factor Post-tax Debt Cost 7.15%	Present Value
1.00	(100,000)					(100,000)	0.9333	(93,326)
1.75		30,000	0			30,000	0.8861	26,584
2.00	(100,000)					(100,000)	0.8710	(87,097)
2.75		30,000	0			30,000	0.8270	24,810
3.00	(100,000)					(100,000)	0.8128	(81,284)
3.75		30,000	0			30,000	0.7718	23,154
4.00	(1,100,000)			185,348		(914,652)	0.7586	(693,846)
4.75		30,000	205,078		39,317	274,396	0.7203	197,645
	(1,400,002)	**120,001**	**205,078**	**185,348**	**39,317**	**(850,258)**		**(683,361)**

This small benefit (£1,973) increases to £15,020 when the Residual Value and related tax are discounted at the lessee's post-tax Cost of Capital (adjusted to reflect the uncertainty associated with the Residual Value estimate):

Pure lease cash flows

Year	Non-RV Cash Flows	RV Cash Flows	Total Cash Flows	Disc Factor Post-tax Debt Cost 7.15%	Disc Factor WACC 9.00%	Present Value
1.00	(265,210)	0	(265,210)	0.9333		(247,510)
1.75	30,000	0	30,000	0.8861		26,584
2.00	(265,210)	0	(265,210)	0.8710		(230,991)
2.75	30,000	0	30,000	0.8270		24,810
3.00	(265,210)	0	(265,210)	0.8128		(215,574)
3.75	30,000	0	30,000	0.7718		23,154
4.00	(265,210)	(46,239)	(311,449)	0.7586	0.7084	(233,943)
4.75	228,252	13,872	242,124	0.7203	0.6641	173,620
	(742,589)	**(32,367)**	**(774,956)**			**(679,848)**

Purchase cash flows

Year	Non-RV Cash Flows	RV Cash Flows	Total Cash Flows	Disc Factor Post-tax Debt Cost 7.15%	Disc Factor WACC 9.00%	Present Value
1.00	(100,000)	0	(100,000)	0.9333		(93,326)
1.75	30,000	0	30,000	0.8861		26,584
2.00	(100,000)	0	(100,000)	0.8710		(87,097)
2.75	30,000	0	30,000	0.8270		24,810
3.00	(100,000)	0	(100,000)	0.8128		(81,284)
3.75	30,000	0	30,000	0.7718		23,154
4.00	(1,100,000)	185,348	(914,652)	0.7586	0.7084	(703,144)
4.75	235,078	39,317	274,396	0.7203	0.6641	195,435
	(1,074,923)	**224,666**	**(850,258)**			**(694,868)**

In practice, a lessee would look for a larger leasing advantage than in this example. The above 1.5% benefit (£15,020 ÷ £1m asset cost) ignores lease arrangement costs and fees, and any ongoing incremental costs arising because of the lease, all of which would erode the benefit.

Operating Leases

A lessee may prefer to lease an asset for only part of its economic life, forcing the lessor to sell or re-lease the asset at the end of the Operating Lease term in order to achieve its target rate of return (for the precise tests used to determine the appropriate accounting treatment for a lease – Finance or Operating – see **Exhibit C1**). A lessee may prefer an Operating Lease due to:

- commercial reasons: the lessee may only need the asset for a short time, or it may not wish to be exposed to asset risk (for example, if the lessee believed it would need to replace the asset after a few years due to technological changes, it could avoid any Residual Value risk and simply hand the asset back to the Operating Lessor); or
- financial reasons: it may not wish to show an asset and liability, as under a Finance Lease, in order to preserve its financial ratios (analysts, including Rating Agencies, may well make an adjustment to capitalise Operating Leases, reducing any apparent benefit of this off-balance sheet treatment).

Lessor Evaluation

The Lessor's Rate of Return

Lessors are likely to focus on the rate of return, or yield, in a lease, rather than its Net Present Value (similar to a loan analysis). An example will be used to illustrate the main yield measure:

Example C4 Lease profit measures

Using the example from **Examples C2** and **C3,** the main return measures can be illustrated.

- Pre-tax Implicit Rate: This is the lessor's IRR based on the asset cost, Residual Value and rentals. In practice, the lessor would not inform the lessee what total Residual Value estimate it has made, in order to keep its target yield confidential. Using the loan balance method for calculating the IRR, where the rate calculated is pre-tax (since the tax effects of the interest have already been taken into account in the tax cash flows – see Examples **B1.5** and **1.6** in Appendix B1) produces an effective rate of 8.71%:

Year	Rental	Asset Cost / RV	Tax charge on rentals @ 30.0% ■	Tax rellief on asset @ 30.0%	Post-Tax Leasing Cash Flows	Interest 8.71%	Tax on on interest @ 30.0%	Net Cash Flows	Net Cash Investment
0.00		(1,000,000)			(1,000,000)			(1,000,000)	(1,000,000)
1.00	265,210				265,210	(87,120)		178,091	(821,909)
1.75			(79,563)	75,000	(4,563)	(53,139)	26,136	(31,566)	(853,476)
2.00	265,210				265,210	(18,011)		247,200	(606,276)
2.75			(79,563)	56,250	(23,313)	(39,198)	21,345	(41,166)	(647,441)
3.00	265,210				265,210	(13,663)		251,548	(395,894)
3.75			(79,563)	42,188	(37,376)	(25,596)	15,858	(47,113)	(443,007)
4.00	265,210	185,348			450,559	(9,349)		441,210	(1,797)
4.75			(79,563)	70,958	(8,605)	(116)	10,518	1,797	**(0)**
	1,060,842	**(814,652)**	**(318,253)**	**244,396**	**172,333**	**(246,190)**	**73,857**	**172,333**	

■ UK tax assumptions:(1) tax is paid at 30%, 9 months after the year end, (2) tax on rentals is based on the 'straight line' rental income, and (3) allowances are given on the asset based on UK Capital Allowance provisions – see **Exhibit C1** and **Example C9**. (It is also assumed that the asset is sold at its Residual Value and that the lessee RV guarantee is not called on.)

- Post-Tax Implicit Rate: This is the Pre-Tax Implicit Rate, ignoring tax on the interest (6.21%):

Year	Post-Tax Leasing Cash Flows	Interest 6.21%	Tax on on interest @ 30.0%	Net Cash Flows	Net Cash Investment
0.00	(1,000,000)			(1,000,000)	(1,000,000)
1.00	265,210	(62,139)		203,072	(796,928)
1.75	(4,563)	(36,859)	0	(41,422)	(838,350)
2.00	265,210	(12,731)		252,480	(585,871)
2.75	(23,313)	(27,097)	0	(50,410)	(636,281)
3.00	265,210	(9,662)		255,548	(380,733)
3.75	(37,376)	(17,609)	0	(54,985)	(435,718)
4.00	450,559	(6,617)		443,942	8,225
4.75	(8,605)	380	0	(8,225)	**(0)**
	172,333	**(172,333)**	**0**	**172,333**	

- **Pre-tax Actuarial margin** The implicit rate calculation is split into the cost of funds (with a lower reinvestment rate applicable to surplus cash balances) and a margin (zero for surplus cash balances), with tax being calculated on the cost of funds element only. Assuming the lessor's pre-tax cost of capital is 8.0% (effective rate) (charged to negative Net Cash Investment balances) and the reinvestment rate 5.0% (effective rate) (earned on positive Net Cash Investment balances – being a conservative estimate for income earned on surplus cash balances), then the extra pre-tax return of 0.70% (on negative NCI balances) represents a profit or margin:

Year	Post-Tax Leasing Cash Flows	Interest **8.00%** **5.00%** Pre-tax	Tax on interest @ 30.0%	Profit **0.70%** **0.00%** Pre-tax	Tax on margin @ 30.0%	Net Cash Flows	Net Cash Investment
0.00	(1,000,000)					(1,000,000)	(1,000,000)
1.00	265,210	(80,000)		(6,992)		178,218	(821,782)
1.75	(4,563)	(48,830)	24,000	(4,306)	2,098	(31,601)	(853,383)
2.00	265,210	(16,578)		(1,488)		247,144	(606,238)
2.75	(23,313)	(36,022)	19,622	(3,176)	1,738	(41,151)	(647,390)
3.00	265,210	(12,577)		(1,129)		251,505	(395,885)
3.75	(37,376)	(23,523)	14,580	(2,074)	1,292	(47,102)	(442,986)
4.00	450,559	(8,606)		(772)		441,181	(1,806)
4.75	(8,605)	(107)	9,671	(9)	857	1,806	**0**
	172,333	**(226,243)**	**67,873**	**(19,947)**	**5,984**	**0**	

- **Post-tax Actuarial margin** This is the calculated in the same way as the actuarial pre-tax margin, but tax on the margin is ignored:

Year	Post-Tax Leasing Cash Flows	Interest **8.00%** **5.00%** Pre-tax	Tax on interest @ 30.0%	Profit **0.50%** **0.00%** Post-tax	Tax on margin @ 30.0%	Net Cash Flows	Net Cash Investment
0.00	(1,000,000)					(1,000,000)	(1,000,000)
1.00	265,210	(80,000)		(5,000)		180,210	(819,790)
1.75	(4,563)	(48,711)	24,000	(3,072)	0	(32,347)	(852,136)
2.00	265,210	(16,554)		(1,063)		247,593	(604,543)
2.75	(23,313)	(35,921)	19,580	(2,266)	0	(41,921)	(646,464)
3.00	265,210	(12,559)		(807)		251,845	(394,618)
3.75	(37,376)	(23,448)	14,544	(1,479)	0	(47,758)	(442,377)
4.00	450,559	(8,594)		(552)		441,413	(964)
4.75	(8,605)	(57)	9,630	(4)	0	964	**(0)**
	172,333	**(225,844)**	**67,753**	**(14,242)**	**0**	**0**	

- **'External' return** This is simply the pre-tax cost of funds (8.0%) plus pre-tax margin (0.7%).

Rentals can be structured in any manner (constant or uneven) that ensures the lessor's required rate of return will be achieved (usually the post-tax actuarial margin), subject to the constraint that the lessee's after-tax lease rentals are minimised and low enough to make leasing attractive.

The present value of the rentals will depend on a number of factors, including:

- the costs to be recovered (including the asset cost);
- the lessor's cost of funds;
- the lessor's risks (these are discussed below);
- the lease term and Residual Value (both of which partly depend on the estimated economic life of the asset);
- any options given to the lessee, such as the right to renew the lease or purchase the asset, the right to replace the asset with another lessor asset ('Flex' option) or the right to terminate the lease early ('Walk Away' option).

The Lessor's Risks

The main risks for a lessor are as follows:

- **Default / Credit Risk** — If the lessee fails to pay a rental when due, there is less chance that the lessor will realise its target rate of return, unless some compensation is factored in. Any loss suffered would be relatively greater for a lessor under a Finance Lease, where the target yield is more dependent on the lessee's performance (in an Operating Lease, more of the yield comes from realisation of the asset at the end of the lease).

  A default would normally result in a termination of the lease; the lessor would seek to recover the asset as quickly as possible either as titleholder or, where the lessor is sub-leasing the asset, via exercising its rights under security arrangements (there may be additional risk if the lessee is subject to foreign insolvency laws that prevent quick repossession of the asset). Further protection could be given via:

  - a third party guaranteeing the lessee's rentals (credit risk would then relate to the guarantor);
  - requiring the lessee to prepay a proportion of rentals upfront ('Defeasance'), or to provide cash collateral.

- **Asset and Residual Value Risk** — If the lessor is taking greater Residual Value risk, it will need to ensure the asset value is preserved. The lease agreement will require the lessee to maintain the asset and return it in an acceptable state. Further protection may be obtained from insurance arrangements and third party Residual Value guarantees (where the end-of-lease realisable value is underwritten).

- Financial and Tax Risk — The lessor will want to ensure actual cash flows are no worse than assumed at the start of the lease, in order to safeguard the expected rate of return. Ignoring any deviations from the agreed rental schedule (discussed in Credit Risk above), changes will arise if the initial assumptions regarding tax rates, tax allowances, the cost of funds and the reinvestment rate become invalid.

  Any changes in the tax legislation or unforeseen taxes (such as the imposition of withholding taxes on cross border leasing transactions) need to be factored into the lease agreement. A Finance Lease agreement will typically contain full tax indemnities from the lessee, to ensure this risk is protected against.

  The interest rate risk associated with the asset finance would be managed using techniques discussed in Chapter 4, taking into consideration the rental structure. If rentals and debt finance are denominated in different currencies, then currency risk will also need to be managed.

- Sovereign risk — For cross border leasing, political risk would need to be considered (as for any cross border loan).

LEVERAGED LEASING

Leveraged Leases are Finance Leases where a substantial part of the asset cost is debt funded on a 'Non-Recourse' basis (equity investors are not liable to the debt providers if the lessee defaults on any rentals), allowing the lessor to obtain a disproportionate benefit by receiving all the tax benefits associated with the asset, even though its equity interest in the lease may be relatively small (often as low as 20%). The tax benefits can then be shared with the lessee via a reduced rental charge.

Leveraged leases involve additional factors to consider:

- Structure — The entity acting as lessor may well be a Special Purpose Vehicle, or Trust, funded by equity and debt investors, with debt provided on a non-recourse basis (debt providers would be given security over the asset being leased and future lease rentals).

  The equity investors' share of rental receipts (equity cash flows) will be after payment of debt interest / principal and tax (on rental income, after deductions for debt interest paid and any allowances given for asset ownership). The equity investors themselves may be partly debt financed, which will affect their cash flow needs.

- **Tax deferral** — The lessor will benefit from deferring the payment of tax for as long as possible. The interaction of tax allowances for the asset, tax relief for debt interest, and tax on rentals, will lead to timing differences. In the early years, deductible costs are likely to exceed taxable income, whereas later in the lease this will reverse and tax will become payable (but at a lower present value). Tax not paid in the early years can effectively be reinvested in a 'tax pool' that can grow and be used to pay tax in later years.

  In the early years, the lessor is likely to be able to recover its equity investment fairly quickly due to tax deferral. Equity surplus cash balances may arise during this period (the 'Disinvestment' phase), which effectively act as a 'Sinking Fund' to finance future tax payments. As tax is paid, so the lease reverts to an 'Investment' phase (negative cash balances) until the Residual Value is realised.

  A reinvestment, or deposit, rate will have to be assumed for the Disinvestment phase (in **Example C4**, a 5% rate was assumed when calculating the profit margins – this was not required, since cash balances remained negative - but in practice a lower rate, or a nil rate, may be assumed, to be prudent). Positive cash balances, therefore, will reduce the post-tax yield for the lessor, and need to be minimised. This can be achieved by structuring the debt cash flows.

- **Debt** — As the debt ratio (leverage) is increased, pre-tax equity cash flows (rentals less debt interest and principal repaid) reduce, but tax deferral increases due to higher deductible interest. This will increase the likelihood of positive cash balances arising. The debt ratio and repayment profile will need to be optimised to minimise the likelihood of such positive cash balances.

  See **Example C10** — During the Disinvestment phase pre-tax equity cash flows should be minimised whilst tax benefits (net tax repayments) are maximised, in order to reduce surplus cash balances. Later in the lease, when tax becomes payable, pre-tax equity cash flows need to be sufficient to pay the tax without having to rely on any sinking fund (i.e. tax is paid from cash flows arising in the period rather than accumulated from prior periods in the form of positive balances).

- **Rental structure** — The optimal rental profile will minimise the lessee's incremental leasing cash flows and achieve the lessor's target yield (usually stated as the post-tax actuarial margin). At the same time debt structuring will need to be optimised.

Rentals can be structured in any way (constant, increasing/decreasing, variable, prepaid, or deferred), providing the profile suits the lessee's requirements and achieves the lessor's objectives (the tax treatment of uneven rentals, however, may be damaging to the lessor).

'Defeasance' arises where the lessee places on deposit (usually a liquid investment, such as Zero Coupon bonds) an amount equal to the present value of future rentals that can be used to pay the periodic rentals (i.e. the deposit plus interest is just enough to pay off rentals over the lease term). Defeasance can be of the whole rent ('Fully Defeased'), the debt servicing element only ('Debt Defeasance') or the equity free cash flows only ('Equity Defeasance').

Fully Defeased leases are usually limited to 'Big Ticket' tax-based sale and leasebacks, where the lessee obtains an immediate NPV cash benefit equivalent to the asset sale price less the Defeasance amount (but no other form of financing). Debt providers would be given collateral over the Defeasance deposit, reducing credit risk and the lessor's cost of debt. The lessee will benefit from any difference between the implicit cost of the lease and the defeasance deposit rate, which will reduce the required amount of prepaid rent and increase the NPV (the lessor must not be taxed up-front on the defeasance as if it was pre-paid rent). These structures are often complicated, involving a number of back-to-back leases ('Lease-In Lease-Out') designed to maximise the combined tax benefits (usually involving a Cross Border lease).

- **Cross border leasing** — An owner of an asset may be able to claim allowances on that asset, depending on whether they have legal title or an effective economic ownership. Some tax jurisdictions give allowances to legal owners; others to 'economic owners'. A single asset may, therefore, provide allowances for a Finance Lessor (legal owner) *and* a Finance Lessee (economic owner), where they are based in certain jurisdictions. This would be termed a 'Cross Border Double Dip' lease (although tax harmonisation is reducing the opportunity to exploit such anomalies). There may be other non-tax benefits from cross border leasing (for example, an inadequate lessee domestic leasing market).

- **Ending the lease** — Lessees are usually given the right to terminate the lease early as at pre-determined dates and termination prices, calculated so as to achieve the equity investors' target yield (the termination sum is the present value of future cash flows if the lease continued, plus termination costs).

Exhibit C1 - UK Accounting and Tax for Leases

This section gives an overview of the main UK lease accounting and corporation tax provisions in force at the time of writing (December 2004), with a focus on Finance Lessees for new assets (sale and leasebacks are ignored). The accounting discussion will focus on the required treatment rather than disclosure or presentation issues; International and US Accounting Standards are referred to where there is a significant difference to the UK treatment. Taxation issues will be limited to the treatment of rentals and asset allowances (indirect taxes and other taxes, such as Stamp Duty, are not covered).

Leases are covered in the UK under Statement of Standard Accounting Practice ('SSAP') 21 ('Accounting for Leases and Hire Purchase Contracts') and Financial Reporting Standard ('FRS') 5 ('Reporting the Substance of Transactions'); lessors should also comply with the code of practice outlined in the Statement of Recommended Accounting Practice ('SORP') entitled 'Accounting Issues in the Asset Finance and Leasing Industry'. International Accounting Standard ('IAS') 17 ('Leases'), and Statement of Financial Accounting Standard ('FAS') 13 ('Accounting for Leases') are the relevant International and US Standards, respectively.

Finance Leases

Accounting

A lease will be classified a Finance Lease if the risks and rewards associated with ownership of the asset are substantially transferred to the lessee. If the present value (PV) of the lessee's 'Minimum Lease Payments'(MLP)[1] over the Lease Term[2], discounted at the lessor's Implicit Rate of Interest[3], is at least 90% of the Fair Value[4] of the asset, it will be assumed that this has occurred, unless, in exceptional circumstances, it can be clearly demonstrated otherwise (the '90% test').

1 All rentals and any part of the Residual Value (RV) that the lessee, or a party related to it, has guaranteed.

2 The agreed Primary term and any Secondary term that the lessee elects to add on under a Renewal Option, if, at the inception of the lease, it is reasonably certain that the lessee will exercise this option.

3 The pre-tax Internal Rate of Return (IRR) of all non-tax cash flows that the lessor is expecting to receive and retain over the Lease Term, being the lessee's MLP and the remaining part of the RV (which may or may not be guaranteed by a third party). If the lessee does not know the lessor's implicit rate (since it does not know what RV the lessor is assuming), it should estimate the rate based on what it would expect to pay for such a lease.

4 The sale price of the asset, based on an arm's length transaction, less any grants received, at the start of the lease (the date from which rentals start to accrue, or the date the asset is first used by the lessee, if earlier).

Example C5 The 90% test

The lessee needed to provide a guarantee for part of the RV in **Examples C2** and **C3** to obtain Finance Lease classification. From Example C2, the lessor's pre-tax implicit rate of interest is 8.60%, based on the lessee's rentals and the total expected RV (including the portion guaranteed by the lessee). Discounting the lessee's MLP (rentals plus the portion of the RV it has agreed to guarantee) at this rate, gives a PV of 90%:

Year	Rental	RV Guarantee	Net Cash Flows	Disc.Factor 8.60%	Present Value
0					
1	(265,210)		(265,210)	0.9208	(244,203)
2	(265,210)		(265,210)	0.8479	(224,860)
3	(265,210)		(265,210)	0.7807	(207,049)
4	(265,210)	(46,239)	(311,449)	0.7189	(223,888)
	(1,060,842)	**(46,239)**	**(1,107,081)**		**(900,000)**
				% cost	*90.0%*

The Implicit Rate is the lessor's IRR based on future expected cash flows arising over the economic life of the asset, being the lease term and thereafter. If the majority of this return is to be derived from lessee cash flows arising over the lease term, rather than from the asset's economic life after the lease term (i.e. the RV), then the lessee will have, effectively, acquired economic ownership of the asset.

The 90% test is reinforced by FRS 5's requirement for the accounting treatment of any transaction to reflect its commercial substance rather than legal form, taking into account the extent of each party's rights to future economic benefits and exposure to risks (and the likely sharing of these rewards and risks). FRS 5 would require an assessment of whether any options are likely to be exercised, based on the extent to which exercising would be in the commercial interests of the option holder (either to obtain a gain or to avoid a loss from not exercising).

If a lessee had a Bargain Purchase Option ('BPO') to acquire the asset at significantly below its market value, or a Bargain Renewal Option ('BRO') at substantially below market rent, then such options are likely to be exercised, unless there are features of the transaction or circumstances that suggest otherwise. In these cases, it would be in the lessee's interest to exercise, due to the significant resulting financial benefit; the BPO would result in Finance Lease classification (the lessor's original RV estimate would be replaced with the lessee's bargain purchase price), and the BRO may or may not result in such classification (the Secondary lease term rentals would be included as part of the lessee's MLP and the lessor's estimate of the RV would be as at the end of the Secondary, rather than Primary, lease term). Both of these cases indicate that the original RV estimate was inappropriate as to amount and timing (in the BRO case – this may indicate that the remaining economic life of the asset at the end of the Secondary lease term is insignificant). They also suggest that ownership will be transferred to the lessee, either legal ownership (in the case of the BPO) or economic ownership (in the case of the BRO).

At the start of the lease, the PV of the lessee's MLP would be shown under Fixed Assets and Liabilities in the lessee balance sheet, representing the economic interest in the asset fair value acquired by the lessee, effectively financed by a loan. If the asset's fair value is a "sufficiently close approximation" (para. 33 SSAP 21) to the PV of the MLP, then the fair value may be used instead.

The initial amount recorded under Fixed Assets (the lessee's effective cost of purchase) should be depreciated over the shorter of the lease term and the asset's useful life. If the lease grants the lessee an option to purchase the asset (at whatever price) once the lease obligations have been satisfied, the useful life should be used. A lease with a purchase option is termed a 'Hire Purchase Contract' in the UK (usually having a nominal purchase price); if these "are of a financing nature" (para. 31 SSAP 21), they should be treated as if a Finance Lease (which would require judgement as to whether the purchase option would be exercised, as discussed above), otherwise, like all leases not classified Finance Leases, it should be treated as an Operating Lease (discussed below).

The initial amount recorded under liabilities (the lessee's effective loan) is amortised each accounting period by an amount representing the principal component of the rental charge, being the gross rental less a deemed Finance Charge. Over the whole lease term, the total Finance Charge will represent total MLP (undiscounted) less the amount initially recorded under liabilities (the PV of the MLP or fair value, if this can be substituted, as noted above). Finance Charges are allocated to accounting periods so as to "produce a constant periodic rate of charge on the remaining balance of the obligation" (para. 35 SSAP 21), or a reasonable approximation. One method is to use the interest arising under the 'loan balance' method for calculating the implicit rate for the lessee (see **Example C1**).

Example C6 Lessee - Finance Lease – Accounting

The lessee's accounting impact in **Example C3** will be as follows:

Year	MLP	Finance Charge 8.60%	PV MLP
0			(900,000)
1	265,210	(77,421)	(712,211)
2	265,210	(61,267)	(508,267)
3	265,210	(43,723)	(286,779)
4	311,449	(24,670)	0

	PROFIT & LOSS			FIXED ASSETS			LIABILITIES			
Year	Depreciation	Finance Charge	P&L Charge (pre-tax)	'Cost'	Depreciation	Book Value	b/f	MLP	Finance Charge	c/f
0				900,000		900,000				(900,000)
1	(225,000)	(77,421)	(302,421)	900,000	(225,000)	675,000	(900,000)	265,210	(77,421)	(712,211)
2	(225,000)	(61,267)	(286,267)	900,000	(450,000)	450,000	(712,211)	265,210	(61,267)	(508,267)
3	(225,000)	(43,723)	(268,723)	900,000	(675,000)	225,000	(508,267)	265,210	(43,723)	(286,779)
4	(225,000)	(24,670)	(249,670)	900,000	(900,000)	0	(286,779)	311,449	(24,670)	0
	(900,000)	(207,081)	(1,107,081)					1,107,081	(207,081)	

The lessee's total MLP are allocated to the P&L based on a mix of straight line amortisation (depreciation) and a constant rate on a reducing balance (finance charge). The tax and cash impact are discussed below in **Example C8**.

A lessor will initially record a sale and a debtor / receivable from the lessee, to reflect the substance of a Finance lease. The initial debtor balance is the lessor's Net Investment in the lease, being the undiscounted amount of future expected cash flows (the lessee's MLP and the unguaranteed RV) less Gross Earnings allocated to future periods. Gross earnings are allocated to each accounting period so as to give a constant periodic rate of return to the lessor's Net Cash Investment, or using some other suitable method.

Example C7 Lessor - Finance Lease – Accounting

The lessor's receivables balance in **Example C3** will be as follows:

Workings							RECEIVABLES			
Year	Post-Tax Margin	Pre-Tax Margin	Pre-Tax Finance Cost	Gross Earnings	Capital	Rentals	Net Investment b/f	Rent (capital only)	Net Investment c/f	Net Cash Investment
0									1,000,000	1,000,000
1	5,000	7,143	80,000	87,143	178,068	265,210	1,000,000	(178,068)	821,932	819,790
2	4,135	5,908	65,265	71,173	194,037	265,210	821,932	(194,037)	627,895	604,543
3	3,072	4,389	48,480	52,869	212,342	265,210	627,895	(212,342)	415,553	394,618
4	2,034	2,906	32,099	35,005	230,205	265,210	415,553	(230,205)	185,348	964
	14,242	20,346	225,844	246,190	814,652	1,060,842				

The Post-Tax margin has been calculated using the Actuarial After Tax Method (see the Post-Tax Actuarial margin in **Example C4**), and grossed up at the 30% tax rate to arrive at the equivalent pre-tax margin (this is consistent with the leasing SORP). The balance of the pre-tax Gross Earnings represents the lessor's cost of funds. The related tax is shown in **Example C9**. The Net Cash Investment is zero at time 4.75, when the final tax is paid.

International and US Accounting Comparison (significant differences to SSAP 21)
(ignoring sale and leasebacks and specific assets, such as land and property)

- Finance Lease (IAS 17) and Capital Lease (FAS 13) classification:
  - ☞ (IAS 17) a lease that transfers "substantially all the risks and rewards incidental to ownership of the asset" [para. 4]: judgement should be used when analysing the substance of the transaction to assess the degree of risk / reward transfer between lessor and lessee (examples are given that indicate where this might arise, which include fairly similar cases as the four criteria listed under FAS 13 below, without any percentage requirements);
  - ☞ (FAS 13): a lease that (1) transfers legal ownership to the lessee by the end of the lease term, or (2) contains a Bargain Purchase Option, or (3) has a term equal to at least 75% of the asset's economic life, or (4) has MLP whose present value is at least 90% of the asset's fair value (the discount rate should be the lessor's Implicit Rate only if it is known and is less than the lessee's incremental borrowing rate, otherwise the latter should be used)((3) and (4) are ignored if the lease starts when the asset has 25% or less of its life left).
- Initial asset and liability in lessee's financial statements: both IAS 17 and FAS 13 require the initial amount to be the PV of the MLP (SSAP 21 permits fair value, where it is a reasonable approximation of this).
- Lessor income recognition: both IAS 17 and FAS 13 require lessor income to be based on the Net Investment in the lease (i.e. pre-tax), rather than the Net Cash Investment as under SSAP 21 (although FAS 13 does permit the latter for Leveraged Leases, meeting the definition criteria).

Taxation

As at December 2004 (see note below), a UK *lessee* would be granted tax relief on rental allocated to the profit and loss account in accordance with SSAP 21 (depreciation and finance charge) as shown above (this is consistent with the Inland Revenue Statement of Practice No. 3/91).

Example C8 Lessee - Finance Lease – Taxation

The tax on the lessee's rentals and RV guarantee (which would be payable as an extra rental) in **Example C3** is shown below (see **Example C6** for other items – Deferred Tax is ignored for simplicity):

	PROFIT & LOSS		**RESERVES**	FIXED ASSETS	CASH			TAX DEBTOR	LEASE LIABILITY	**NET ASSETS**
Year	P&L Charge (pre-tax)	Tax charge at 30%	Cumulative P&L		Tax	Rental	Cash Balance			
0										
1	(302,421)	90,726	(211,695)	675,000		(265,210)	(265,210)	90,726	(712,211)	(211,695)
1.75					90,726		(174,484)			
2	(286,267)	85,880	(412,082)	450,000		(265,210)	(439,695)	85,880	(508,267)	(412,082)
2.75					85,880		(353,815)			
3	(268,723)	80,617	(600,188)	225,000		(265,210)	(619,025)	80,617	(286,779)	(600,188)
3.75					80,617		(538,408)			
4	(249,670)	74,901	(774,956)	0		(311,449)	(849,857)	74,901	0	(774,956)
4.75					74,901					
	(1,107,081)	332,124			257,223	(1,107,081)				

If the lease is a Hire Purchase Contract with a Bargain Purchase Option (i.e. the lessee has the right to acquire legal title for a nominal sum), the lessee would be treated, for the purposes of determining rights to tax allowances on that asset, as owning the asset from the date it starts using the asset (usually the start of the lease) and selling the asset on the option exercise date if the option is not actually exercised (s.67 Capital Allowances Act 2001). This treatment will also arise if the option price is more than a nominal amount, depending on the amount of the option price (and if it incorporates a capital element – see Pricewaterhouse Coopers (2002 p.66) for further discussion).

As at December 2004 (see note below), a UK *lessor* would be taxed on accrued rentals, after deducting allowable operating and financing costs and tax allowances on the asset (uneven rentals that result in the Gross Earnings, as calculated above, exceeding the rental charged in the period will result in the Gross Earnings being taxed instead under Sch. 12 Finance Act 1997). As legal owner of the asset, the lessor would be able to claim Capital Allowances on allowable expenditure incurred on the asset, unless, as discussed above, the lease is a Hire Purchase Contract. **Example C9** shows allowances being given (1) on a reducing balance method based on 25% of the 'Tax Written Down Value' at the start of each period ('Writing Down Allowance'), and (2) by way of an adjustment on the sale of the asset (a 'Balancing Allowance' or 'Balancing Charge' is given to ensure the final Tax Written Down Value equals the sale price). A detailed discussion of the numerous Capital Allowance rules is beyond the scope of this book.

Example C9 Lessor - Finance Lease – Taxation

The lessor's tax in Examples C4 is calculated as follows:

Year	TAX COMPUTATION Rental	Capital Allowances	Finance	Taxable profits	Tax at 30%	TAX ALLOCATION Rental	Capital Allowances	Finance
0								
1	265,210	(250,000)	(80,000)	(87,143)	26,143	(79,563)	75,000	24,000
2	265,210	(187,500)	(65,265)	(71,173)	21,352	(79,563)	56,250	19,580
3	265,210	(140,625)	(48,480)	(52,869)	15,861	(79,563)	42,188	14,544
4	265,210	(236,527)	(32,099)	(35,005)	10,502	(79,563)	70,958	9,630
	1,060,842	(814,652)	(225,844)	246,190	73,857	(318,253)	244,396	67,753

Year	CAPITAL ALLOWANCES Tax Written Down Value b/f	Writing Down Allowances at 25%	Balancing Charge	Tax Written Down Value c/f
0				1,000,000
1	1,000,000	(250,000)		750,000
2	750,000	(187,500)		562,500
3	562,500	(140,625)		421,875
4	421,875	(105,469)	(131,058)	185,348
		(683,594)	(131,058)	

It is assumed that the lessor sells the asset for £185,348 (the Residual Value).

☞ The tax treatment of leasing in the UK is subject to change, following announcement in late 2004 by the Government of proposals to be included in the legislation for 2006 that, effectively, treat certain leases as loans (to be defined in statute and termed 'Funding Leases', which would include all Finance Leases). The lessee would be granted tax deductions in respect of the asset (capital allowances that are currently given to the legal owner / lessor) and financing costs (finance charge element of rental); the lessor would be charged tax on the finance income element only of the rentals (similar to loan interest income). Some leases may be exempted (short term leases, as shown above, for example).

All examples in this Appendix are based on current legislation and ignore the proposed changes.

Operating Leases

Accounting & Tax

The *lessee* would simply record the periodic rental as a charge to the profit and loss account on a straight-line basis over the lease term, and should be able to claim tax relief on the amount charged. A *lessor* will account for the asset in the normal manner, recording it as a fixed asset and depreciating it over its economic life. Lease rental will be accrued in the profit and loss account on a straight-line basis over the lease term, and tax will be payable on rental income less capital allowances on the asset (subject to the above new proposals).

Example C10 Leveraged Lease - Domestic

This example illustrates how a lessor and lessee might evaluate a Leveraged Lease, based on UK accounting and taxation provisions (2004). The lessor's objective is to maximise its post-tax actuarial margin, subject to certain constraints, such as minimising the post-tax present value of the lessee's incremental leasing cash flows and preserving the optimal tax treatment. In practice, the NPV benefit for the lessee would need to be larger than shown below, since arrangement costs (and any other incidental tax) have been ignored. The lessor would also use linear programming techniques to optimise the structure (particular the debt profile).

- To simplify matters, the lease starts on the first day of the accounting year of both parties.
- The lessor will finance the asset with 80% debt on a non-recourse basis.
- The Residual Value will be guaranteed by a third party, unrelated to the lessee (whose Minimum Lease Payments are rentals only).
- All yields shown are effective (borrowing costs are in nominal terms).
- Both parties pay tax at 30%, can claim Capital Allowances, and are tax paying in all years (1/4 of the annual tax charge is paid each quarter end starting 6 months after the start of the year).

The post-tax actuarial margin over the lessor's cost of funds (nil reinvestment rate) is 1.12%, which is acceptable to the lessor. The lessee benefits by £1.36m from leasing (0.53% cheaper than debt), mainly because of the lessor's relatively low cost of debt (in practice, the lessor / lessee cost of debt difference is unlikely to be so great, and the benefit would be due to the leasing creating extra tax benefits).

LEASE ASSUMPTIONS	
Lease start date	1 January 2004
Asset cost	£100.00 m
Financed by lessor	80.00% debt :20.00% equity
Primary lease term	5 years
Primary lease rental	£5.42m per quarter, in arrears
Residual Value	10.0% of cost (i.e. £10m)
Lessee Residual Value guarantee	None
Lessee renewal and purchase options	None

LESSOR / LESSEE ASSUMPTIONS	
Lessor	
Accounting and tax jurisdiction	UK
Accounting year end	31 December
Tax pay date	Quarterly - months 6, 9, 12, 15
Tax rate	30%
Upfront costs as a % of asset cost	0%
Cost of debt (pre-tax)	4.75%
Cost of debt (post-tax)	3.40%
Cost of equity	11.50%
Lessee	
Accounting and tax jurisdiction	UK
Accounting year end	31 December
Tax pay date	Quarterly - months 6, 9, 12, 15
Tax rate	30%
Upfront costs as a % of asset cost	0%
Cost of debt (pre-tax)	7.00%
Cost of debt (post-tax)	5.02%
Cost of equity	11.50%

RESULTS	
Lessor	
Pre-tax implicit rate	6.32%
Post-tax Return on Equity	9.24%
Post-tax profit take-out (margin)	1.12% over 11.5%
Reinvestment rate	0.00%
NPV of post-tax margin	£0.57 m
NPV / asset cost	0.57%
Lessee	
PV of Minimum Lease Payments	£92.64 m
As a % of asset cost	92.6%
Lease classification	Finance Lease
PV of incremental lease cash flows	£98.64 m
NPV of lease v purchase decision	£1.36 m
NPV / asset cost	1.36%
Leasing cost	4.49%
Leasing v Borrowing cost	0.53%

Example C10 (cont.) – Lessor Evaluation – Pre-Tax Implicit Rate + Post-Tax Return on Equity – *Constant Equity Ratio*

Period (yrs)	Date	Days	Cost / RV	Rentals	**Implicit Rate**	Net Investment	Debt Cash Flows		Equity Cash Flows	Tax thereon	Net Equity Cash Flows	**Equity Return**	Equity amortisation	Equity Investment	Debt Outstanding	Capital	Equity Ratio
					6.32%		Principal	Interest				**9.24%**					
0			(100,000)			100,000.00	80,000.00	-	(20,000.00)		(20,000.00)			20,000.00	80,000.00	100,000.00	20.00%
0.25	31 Mar 2004	91		5,420	1,540.23	96,120.23	(3,221.50)	(947.40)	1,251.10		1,251.10	445.72	805.38	19,194.62	76,778.50	95,973.12	20.00%
0.50	30 June 2004	91		5,420	1,480.48	92,180.71	(3,679.33)	(909.25)	831.42	516.19	1,347.61	427.77	919.83	18,274.79	73,099.16	91,373.95	20.00%
0.75	30 Sep 2004	92		5,420	1,435.52	88,196.23	(3,719.36)	(875.19)	825.45	516.19	1,341.64	411.80	929.84	17,344.95	69,379.80	86,724.75	20.00%
1.00	31 Dec 2004	92		5,420	1,373.47	84,149.70	(3,771.75)	(830.66)	817.60	516.19	1,333.78	390.85	942.94	16,402.01	65,608.06	82,010.07	20.00%
1.25	31 Mar 2005	90		5,420	1,281.75	80,011.45	(3,845.03)	(768.42)	806.55	516.19	1,322.73	361.48	961.26	15,440.76	61,763.03	77,203.79	20.00%
1.50	30 June 2005	91		5,420	1,232.36	75,823.82	(3,470.99)	(731.43)	1,217.59	(5.73)	1,211.86	344.11	867.75	14,573.01	58,292.04	72,865.05	20.00%
1.75	30 Sep 2005	92		5,420	1,180.80	71,584.61	(3,510.38)	(697.91)	1,211.71	(5.73)	1,205.98	328.39	877.60	13,695.41	54,781.66	68,477.07	20.00%
2.00	31 Dec 2005	92		5,420	1,114.78	67,279.39	(3,559.83)	(655.88)	1,204.29	(5.73)	1,198.57	308.61	889.96	12,805.46	51,221.83	64,027.29	20.00%
2.25	31 Mar 2006	90		5,420	1,024.79	62,884.18	(3,625.71)	(599.93)	1,194.37	(5.73)	1,188.64	282.21	906.43	11,899.03	47,596.13	59,495.16	20.00%
2.50	30 June 2006	91		5,420	968.56	58,432.74	(3,346.83)	(563.66)	1,509.51	(407.62)	1,101.89	265.18	836.71	11,062.32	44,249.29	55,311.62	20.00%
2.75	30 Sep 2006	92		5,420	909.97	53,922.71	(3,386.66)	(529.78)	1,503.56	(407.62)	1,095.94	249.28	846.67	10,215.66	40,862.63	51,078.29	20.00%
3.00	31 Dec 2006	92		5,420	839.73	49,342.44	(3,434.36)	(489.23)	1,496.41	(407.62)	1,088.79	230.20	858.59	9,357.07	37,428.27	46,785.34	20.00%
3.25	31 Mar 2007	90		5,420	751.57	44,674.02	(3,494.23)	(438.37)	1,487.39	(407.62)	1,079.77	206.22	873.56	8,483.51	33,934.03	42,417.54	20.00%
3.50	30 June 2007	91		5,420	688.08	39,942.10	(3,287.32)	(401.86)	1,730.81	(719.92)	1,010.90	189.06	821.83	7,661.68	30,646.71	38,308.39	20.00%
3.75	30 Sep 2007	92		5,420	622.01	35,144.11	(3,328.41)	(366.92)	1,724.67	(719.92)	1,004.75	172.65	832.10	6,829.57	27,318.30	34,147.87	20.00%
4.00	31 Dec 2007	92		5,420	547.30	30,271.41	(3,375.29)	(327.07)	1,717.64	(719.92)	997.72	153.90	843.82	5,985.75	23,943.00	29,928.76	20.00%
4.25	31 Mar 2008	91		5,420	466.25	25,317.66	(3,426.51)	(283.54)	1,709.94	(719.92)	990.03	133.40	856.63	5,129.12	20,516.49	25,645.62	20.00%
4.50	30 June 2008	91		5,420	389.95	20,287.61	(4,100.01)	(242.97)	1,077.02	62.29	1,139.31	114.31	1,025.00	4,104.12	16,416.48	20,520.60	20.00%
4.75	30 Sep 2008	92		5,420	315.94	15,183.55	(4,154.61)	(196.55)	1,068.85	62.29	1,131.13	92.48	1,038.65	3,065.47	12,261.88	15,327.35	20.00%
5.00	31 Dec 2008	92	10,000	5,420	236.45	(0.00)	(12,261.88)	(146.81)	3,011.32	62.29	3,073.60	69.08	3,004.53	60.94	-	60.94	100.00%
5.25	31 Mar 2009	90			-	(0.00)			-	62.29	62.29	1.34	60.94	0.00	-	0.00	100.00%
			(90,000)	108,400	18,400.00		-	(11,002.81)	7,397.19	(2,219.16)	5,178.03	5,178.03	20,000.00				

- The pre-tax implicit rate (6.32%) is used to determine whether the lessee must classify the lease as a Finance Lease (the 90% test).
- The lessor's post-tax Return on Equity is used to determine the Equity Investment (this is not the same as the Equity Net Cash Investment based on the post-tax actuarial margin – discussed on the following page).
- Debt has been structured so as to ensure there is a positive pre-tax equity cash flow in all years and a minimum 20% Equity Investment (although this is a UK lease, this illustrates the requirement under US IRS Procedure 2001-29).
- Debt interest is at 4.75% nominal, whilst the 6.32% implicit rate and 9.24% equity return are effective rates. All interest is charged on a daily basis.

Period (yrs)	Date	Rent	Asset Allowances (Tax depreciation)	Debt Interest	Taxable Income	**Tax**
1.00	31 Dec 2004	21,680.00	(25,000.00)	(3,562.49)	(6,882.49)	2,064.75
2.00	31 Dec 2005	21,680.00	(18,750.00)	(2,853.64)	76.36	(22.91)
3.00	31 Dec 2006	21,680.00	(14,062.50)	(2,182.59)	5,434.91	(1,630.47)
4.00	31 Dec 2007	21,680.00	(10,546.88)	(1,534.23)	9,598.90	(2,879.67)
5.00	31 Dec 2008	21,680.00	(21,640.63)	(869.86)	(830.49)	249.15
		108,400.00	(90,000.00)	(11,002.81)	7,397.19	(2,219.16)

- Tax is paid at 30% on a quarterly basis, with ¼ of the annual tax charge paid 6, 9, and 12 months after the start of the relevant year and 3 months after the year end.
- Asset Allowances are UK Capital Allowances (Tax Depreciation in the US). A Balancing Allowance arises when the Residual Value is realised, to ensure all allowances are given.

Example C10 (cont.) – Lessor Evaluation – Post-Tax Actuarial Profit Margin and Equity Net Cash Investment – *Constant Equity Ratio*

Period (yrs)	Date	Days	Net Equity Cash Flows	**Pre-tax Interest** **11.50% / 0.00%**	Tax thereon	Equity Net Cash Investment (pre-margin)	**Post-Tax Actuarial Profit Margin** **1.1238% / 0%**	Cumulative Profit Margin	Equity Net Cash Investment (post-margin)	Net Equity Investment b/f	New net Equity Investment	Allocated to Net Income	Net Equity Investment b/f
0			(20,000.00)			(20,000.00)		-	(20,000.00)	-	20,000.00	-	20,000.00
0.25	31 Mar 2004	91	1,251.10	(550.72)		(19,299.62)	(56.31)	(56.31)	(19,355.93)	20,000.00	(1,251.10)	607.03	19,355.93
0.50	30 June 2004	91	1,347.61	(532.99)	156.34	(18,328.66)	(54.50)	(110.81)	(18,439.47)	19,355.93	(1,347.61)	431.14	18,439.47
0.75	30 Sep 2004	92	1,341.64	(513.41)	156.34	(17,344.09)	(52.49)	(163.30)	(17,507.39)	18,439.47	(1,341.64)	409.56	17,507.39
1.00	31 Dec 2004	92	1,333.78	(487.46)	156.34	(16,341.42)	(49.84)	(213.14)	(16,554.56)	17,507.39	(1,333.78)	380.96	16,554.56
1.25	31 Mar 2005	90	1,322.73	(450.77)	156.34	(15,313.11)	(46.09)	(259.23)	(15,572.34)	16,554.56	(1,322.73)	340.51	15,572.34
1.50	30 June 2005	91	1,211.86	(428.80)	125.56	(14,404.50)	(43.84)	(303.07)	(14,707.57)	15,572.34	(1,211.86)	347.09	14,707.57
1.75	30 Sep 2005	92	1,205.98	(409.51)	125.56	(13,482.47)	(41.87)	(344.94)	(13,827.41)	14,707.57	(1,205.98)	325.82	13,827.41
2.00	31 Dec 2005	92	1,198.57	(385.00)	125.56	(12,543.35)	(39.36)	(384.30)	(12,927.65)	13,827.41	(1,198.57)	298.81	12,927.65
2.25	31 Mar 2006	90	1,188.64	(352.01)	125.56	(11,581.16)	(35.99)	(420.30)	(12,001.46)	12,927.65	(1,188.64)	262.45	12,001.46
2.50	30 June 2006	91	1,101.89	(330.47)	96.05	(10,713.69)	(33.79)	(454.09)	(11,167.77)	12,001.46	(1,101.89)	268.21	11,167.77
2.75	30 Sep 2006	92	1,095.94	(310.95)	96.05	(9,832.64)	(31.79)	(485.88)	(10,318.52)	11,167.77	(1,095.94)	246.68	10,318.52
3.00	31 Dec 2006	92	1,088.79	(287.30)	96.05	(8,935.09)	(29.37)	(515.25)	(9,450.35)	10,318.52	(1,088.79)	220.62	9,450.35
3.25	31 Mar 2007	90	1,079.77	(257.33)	96.05	(8,016.59)	(26.31)	(541.56)	(8,558.15)	9,450.35	(1,079.77)	187.58	8,558.15
3.50	30 June 2007	91	1,010.90	(235.66)	67.55	(7,173.80)	(24.10)	(565.66)	(7,739.46)	8,558.15	(1,010.90)	192.20	7,739.46
3.75	30 Sep 2007	92	1,004.75	(215.49)	67.55	(6,316.99)	(22.03)	(587.69)	(6,904.68)	7,739.46	(1,004.75)	169.97	6,904.68
4.00	31 Dec 2007	92	997.72	(192.25)	67.55	(5,443.96)	(19.66)	(607.35)	(6,051.31)	6,904.68	(997.72)	144.35	6,051.31
4.25	31 Mar 2008	91	990.03	(166.63)	67.55	(4,553.01)	(17.04)	(624.39)	(5,177.39)	6,051.31	(990.03)	116.11	5,177.39
4.50	30 June 2008	91	1,139.31	(142.57)	38.57	(3,517.69)	(14.58)	(638.96)	(4,156.65)	5,177.39	(1,139.31)	118.57	4,156.65
4.75	30 Sep 2008	92	1,131.13	(115.73)	38.57	(2,463.72)	(11.83)	(650.79)	(3,114.51)	4,156.65	(1,131.13)	88.99	3,114.51
5.00	31 Dec 2008	92	3,073.60	(86.72)	38.57	561.74	(8.87)	(659.66)	(97.92)	3,114.51	(3,073.60)	57.01	97.92
5.25	31 Mar 2009	90	62.29	(2.67)	38.57	659.93	(0.27)	(659.93)	(0.00)	97.92	(62.29)	(35.63)	0.00
			5,178.03	(6,454.43)	1,936.33		(659.93)				(5,178.03)	5,178.03	

Period (yrs)	Date	Equity Interest	**Tax**
1.00	31 Dec 2004	(2,084.59)	625.38
2.00	31 Dec 2005	(1,674.07)	502.22
3.00	31 Dec 2006	(1,280.73)	384.22
4.00	31 Dec 2007	(900.72)	270.22
5.00	31 Dec 2008	(514.31)	154.29
		(6,454.43)	1,936.33

- The lessor's pre-tax Cost of Capital is 11.50% effective (it is assumed the equity participants finance their investment entirely with equity, hence this represents the Cost of Equity).
- The Post-Tax Actuarial Profit margin is 1.1238% effective; a zero reinvestment rate for positive cash balances is assumed.
- The present value of the margin is equivalent to 0.572% of the asset cost (calculated by extracting this sum on day one – rather than allocating it over the lease term at the 1.1238% rate).

Example C10 (cont.) – Lessor Evaluation – Post Tax Actual Margin – *Zero Net Equity Cash Flows*

If debt is not structured so as to maintain sufficient leverage and maximise tax relief on interest, the Post-Tax Actuarial Margin will reduce. To illustrate this, debt servicing is set so that Net Equity Cash Flows are zero until debt is fully paid off. A loss is now incurred.

Period (yrs)	Date	Days	Cost / RV	Rentals	Debt Cash Flows		Equity Cash Flows	Tax thereon	**Net Equity Cash Flows**	Equity Ratio	**Pre-tax Interest**	Tax thereon	Equity Net Cash Investment	**Post-Tax Actuarial Profit Margin**	Cumulative Profit Margin	Equity Net Cash Investment
					Principal	Interest					**11.50% / 0.00%**		(pre-margin)	**-1.4443% / 0%**		(post-margin)
0			(100,000)		80,000.00	-	(20,000.00)		(20,000.00)	20.00%			(20,000.00)		-	(20,000.00)
0.25	31 Mar 2004	91		5,420	(4,472.60)	(947.40)	-			21.20%	(549.55)		(20,549.55)	73.07	73.07	(20,476.48)
0.50	30 June 2004	91		5,420	(5,034.74)	(894.43)	(509.17)	509.17		22.64%	(562.64)	170.76	(20,941.43)	74.81	147.89	(20,793.55)
0.75	30 Sep 2004	92		5,420	(5,085.19)	(843.98)	(509.17)	509.17		24.27%	(577.71)	170.76	(21,348.39)	76.81	224.70	(21,123.69)
1.00	31 Dec 2004	92		5,420	(5,146.07)	(783.10)	(509.17)	509.17		26.11%	(586.89)	170.76	(21,764.51)	78.03	302.73	(21,461.78)
1.25	31 Mar 2005	90		5,420	(5,223.37)	(705.80)	(509.17)	509.17		28.21%	(583.16)	170.76	(22,176.91)	77.54	380.28	(21,796.64)
1.50	30 June 2005	91		5,420	(4,736.32)	(651.79)	31.89	(31.89)		30.39%	(598.92)	181.63	(22,594.20)	79.64	459.91	(22,134.28)
1.75	30 Sep 2005	92		5,420	(4,785.87)	(602.24)	31.89	(31.89)		32.90%	(614.96)	181.63	(23,027.53)	81.77	541.68	(22,485.85)
2.00	31 Dec 2005	92		5,420	(4,843.16)	(544.94)	31.89	(31.89)		35.79%	(624.73)	181.63	(23,470.63)	83.06	624.74	(22,845.88)
2.25	31 Mar 2006	90		5,420	(4,911.74)	(476.37)	31.89	(31.89)		39.16%	(620.77)	181.63	(23,909.76)	82.55	707.29	(23,202.47)
2.50	30 June 2006	91		5,420	(4,544.62)	(423.50)	451.89	(451.89)		42.83%	(637.55)	193.35	(24,353.96)	84.77	792.06	(23,561.90)
2.75	30 Sep 2006	92		5,420	(4,594.37)	(373.74)	451.89	(451.89)		47.15%	(654.63)	193.35	(24,815.24)	87.04	879.10	(23,936.14)
3.00	31 Dec 2006	92		5,420	(4,649.38)	(318.73)	451.89	(451.89)		52.34%	(665.02)	193.35	(25,286.92)	88.42	967.52	(24,319.39)
3.25	31 Mar 2007	90		5,420	(4,710.76)	(257.35)	451.89	(451.89)		58.67%	(660.80)	193.35	(25,754.37)	87.87	1,055.39	(24,698.98)
3.50	30 June 2007	91		5,420	(4,434.24)	(204.42)	781.34	(781.34)		65.99%	(678.67)	205.82	(26,227.22)	90.24	1,145.64	(25,081.59)
3.75	30 Sep 2007	92		5,420	(4,485.08)	(153.58)	781.34	(781.34)		75.19%	(696.85)	205.82	(26,718.25)	92.65	1,238.29	(25,479.96)
4.00	31 Dec 2007	92		5,420	(4,538.78)	(99.88)	781.34	(781.34)		87.10%	(707.92)	205.82	(27,220.35)	94.13	1,332.41	(25,887.94)
4.25	31 Mar 2008	91		5,420	(3,803.73)	(45.05)	1,571.23	(781.34)	789.89	100.00%	(711.34)	205.82	(26,935.98)	94.58	1,427.00	(25,508.99)
4.50	30 June 2008	91		5,420	-	-	5,420.00	0.43	5,420.43	100.00%	(700.92)	181.14	(22,035.35)	93.20	1,520.20	(20,515.15)
4.75	30 Sep 2008	92		5,420	-	-	5,420.00	0.43	5,420.43	100.00%	(569.98)	181.14	(17,003.77)	75.78	1,595.98	(15,407.78)
5.00	31 Dec 2008	92	10,000	5,420	-	-	15,420.00	0.43	15,420.43	100.00%	(428.08)	181.14	(1,830.28)	56.92	1,652.90	(177.38)
5.25	31 Mar 2009	90					-	0.43	0.43	-	(4.82)	181.14	(1,653.54)	0.64	1,653.54	(0.00)
			(90,000)	108,400	-	(8,326.30)	10,073.70	(3,022.11)	7,051.59		(12,435.90)	3,730.77		1,653.54		

Example C10 (cont.) – Lessee Evaluation – 90% Test and Lease vs Purchase

Period (yrs)	Date	Days	Rentals	Discount Rate 6.32% lessor IRR	PV of Min. Lease Payments	Rentals	Tax on rentals	Cost + Residual foregone	Tax on allowances	Lease Cash Flows	Interest 4.4854%	Equivalent Loan Balance	PV Lease Cash Flows 5.02%
0								100,000.00		100,000.00		100,000.00	
0.25	31 Mar 2004	91	(5,420.00)	0.9848	(5,337.79)	(5,420.00)	-	-	-	(5,420.00)	1,099.93	95,679.93	(5,354.28)
0.50	30 June 2004	91	(5,420.00)	0.9699	(5,256.82)	(5,420.00)	1,791.88	-	(1,875.00)	(5,503.12)	1,052.41	91,229.22	(5,370.47)
0.75	30 Sep 2004	92	(5,420.00)	0.9550	(5,176.21)	(5,420.00)	1,791.88	-	(1,875.00)	(5,503.12)	1,014.55	86,740.65	(5,304.64)
1.00	31 Dec 2004	92	(5,420.00)	0.9404	(5,096.84)	(5,420.00)	1,791.88	-	(1,875.00)	(5,503.12)	964.63	82,202.15	(5,239.61)
1.25	31 Mar 2005	90	(5,420.00)	0.9263	(5,020.37)	(5,420.00)	1,791.88	-	(1,875.00)	(5,503.12)	894.18	77,593.21	(5,176.77)
1.50	30 June 2005	91	(5,420.00)	0.9122	(4,944.22)	(5,420.00)	1,713.26	-	(1,406.25)	(5,112.99)	853.47	73,333.69	(4,751.45)
1.75	30 Sep 2005	92	(5,420.00)	0.8982	(4,868.40)	(5,420.00)	1,713.26	-	(1,406.25)	(5,112.99)	815.53	69,036.24	(4,693.21)
2.00	31 Dec 2005	92	(5,420.00)	0.8845	(4,793.75)	(5,420.00)	1,713.26	-	(1,406.25)	(5,112.99)	767.74	64,691.00	(4,635.67)
2.25	31 Mar 2006	90	(5,420.00)	0.8712	(4,721.83)	(5,420.00)	1,713.26	-	(1,406.25)	(5,112.99)	703.69	60,281.71	(4,580.08)
2.50	30 June 2006	91	(5,420.00)	0.8580	(4,650.20)	(5,420.00)	1,630.92	-	(1,054.69)	(4,843.77)	663.06	56,101.00	(4,286.31)
2.75	30 Sep 2006	92	(5,420.00)	0.8448	(4,578.90)	(5,420.00)	1,630.92	-	(1,054.69)	(4,843.77)	623.89	51,881.12	(4,233.76)
3.00	31 Dec 2006	92	(5,420.00)	0.8319	(4,508.68)	(5,420.00)	1,630.92	-	(1,054.69)	(4,843.77)	576.96	47,614.32	(4,181.86)
3.25	31 Mar 2007	90	(5,420.00)	0.8194	(4,441.04)	(5,420.00)	1,630.92	-	(1,054.69)	(4,843.77)	517.94	43,288.49	(4,131.71)
3.50	30 June 2007	91	(5,420.00)	0.8070	(4,373.67)	(5,420.00)	1,543.37	-	(791.02)	(4,667.64)	476.14	39,096.98	(3,933.20)
3.75	30 Sep 2007	92	(5,420.00)	0.7946	(4,306.61)	(5,420.00)	1,543.37	-	(791.02)	(4,667.64)	434.79	34,864.13	(3,884.99)
4.00	31 Dec 2007	92	(5,420.00)	0.7824	(4,240.57)	(5,420.00)	1,543.37	-	(791.02)	(4,667.64)	387.72	30,584.20	(3,837.36)
4.25	31 Mar 2008	91	(5,420.00)	0.7705	(4,176.24)	(5,420.00)	1,543.37	-	(791.02)	(4,667.64)	336.40	26,252.96	(3,790.83)
4.50	30 June 2008	91	(5,420.00)	0.7588	(4,112.90)	(5,420.00)	1,450.56	-	(1,623.05)	(5,592.48)	288.76	20,949.25	(4,486.86)
4.75	30 Sep 2008	92	(5,420.00)	0.7472	(4,049.83)	(5,420.00)	1,450.56	-	(1,623.05)	(5,592.48)	232.97	15,589.74	(4,431.86)
5.00	31 Dec 2008	92	(5,420.00)	0.7357	(3,987.73)	(5,420.00)	1,450.56	(10,000.00)	(1,623.05)	(15,592.48)	173.37	170.63	(12,205.07)
5.25	31 Mar 2009	90	-	0.7247	-	-	1,450.56	-	(1,623.05)	(172.48)	1.86	(0.00)	(133.39)
			(108,400.00)	*92.6%*	(92,642.57)	(108,400.00)	32,520.00	(10,000.00)	(27,000.00)	(12,880.00)	12,880.00		(98,643.39)

- The present value of the lessee's Minimum Lease Payments, discounted at the lessor's pre-tax implicit rate (6.32%) is 92.6% of the fair value of the asset. One of the requirements for Finance Lease status has, therefore, been met (if the lessee's own 7.0% pre-tax cost of debt is used, the PV is 91.2%).
- The after-tax implicit cost of the incremental leasing cash flows is 4.49%, which is below the lessee's marginal post-tax cost of debt (5.02% (5.0151%)- see next page).
- The present value of the incremental leasing cash flows, discounted at the 5.02% marginal post-tax cost of debt is 98.6% of the asset's £100m cost.
- Leasing is, therefore, preferred to a purchase (even before discounting the Residual Value at a risk adjusted discount rate, which is technically preferred).

Example C10 (cont.) – Lessee Evaluation – Lessee post-tax cost of debt

The post-tax equivalent of the lessee's 7.0% pre-tax cost of debt is 5.02%:

Period (yrs)	Date	Days	Principal	Interest 7.0%	Tax on Interest	Debt Cash Flows	Disc. Factor 5.02%	Present Value
0			100,000.00			100,000.00	1.0000	100,000.00
0.25	31 Mar 2004	91		(1,745.21)		(1,745.21)	0.9879	(1,724.04)
0.50	30 June 2004	91		(1,764.38)	525.00	(1,239.38)	0.9759	(1,209.51)
0.75	30 Sep 2004	92		(1,764.38)	525.00	(1,239.38)	0.9639	(1,194.68)
1.00	31 Dec 2004	92		(1,726.03)	525.00	(1,201.03)	0.9521	(1,143.52)
1.25	31 Mar 2005	90		(1,745.21)	525.00	(1,220.21)	0.9407	(1,147.84)
1.50	30 June 2005	91		(1,764.38)	525.00	(1,239.38)	0.9293	(1,151.75)
1.75	30 Sep 2005	92		(1,764.38)	525.00	(1,239.38)	0.9179	(1,137.63)
2.00	31 Dec 2005	92		(1,726.03)	525.00	(1,201.03)	0.9066	(1,088.91)
2.25	31 Mar 2006	90		(1,745.21)	525.00	(1,220.21)	0.8958	(1,093.03)
2.50	30 June 2006	91		(1,764.38)	525.00	(1,239.38)	0.8849	(1,096.74)
2.75	30 Sep 2006	92		(1,764.38)	525.00	(1,239.38)	0.8741	(1,083.30)
3.00	31 Dec 2006	92		(1,726.03)	525.00	(1,201.03)	0.8633	(1,036.91)
3.25	31 Mar 2007	90		(1,745.21)	525.00	(1,220.21)	0.8530	(1,040.83)
3.50	30 June 2007	91		(1,764.38)	526.44	(1,237.95)	0.8427	(1,043.16)
3.75	30 Sep 2007	92		(1,764.38)	526.44	(1,237.95)	0.8323	(1,030.37)
4.00	31 Dec 2007	92		(1,745.21)	526.44	(1,218.77)	0.8221	(1,001.97)
4.25	31 Mar 2008	91		(1,745.21)	526.44	(1,218.77)	0.8122	(989.82)
4.50	30 June 2008	91		(1,764.38)	525.00	(1,239.38)	0.8023	(994.36)
4.75	30 Sep 2008	92		(1,764.38)	525.00	(1,239.38)	0.7925	(982.17)
5.00	31 Dec 2008	92	(100,000.00)	(1,726.03)	525.00	(101,201.03)	0.7828	(79,215.47)
5.25	31 Mar 2009	90			525.00	525.00	0.7734	406.02
			-	(35,019.18)	10,505.75	(24,513.42)		(0.00)

Example C10 (cont.) – Lessee Accounting – P&L vs Cash Impact

Period (yrs)	Date	Days	PROFIT & LOSS Depreciation charge	Finance Charge	Pre-tax Impact	Tax @ 30%	Post-tax Impact	Cumulative P&L	CASH Rental	Tax @ 30%	Post-Tax Rental	Cumulative Cash Flows
BY QUARTER												
0												
0.25	31 Mar 2004	91	(4,568.67)	(1,426.91)	(5,995.59)	1,798.68	(4,196.91)	(4,196.91)	(5,420.00)		(5,420.00)	(5,420.00)
0.50	30 June 2004	91	(4,619.44)	(1,365.41)	(5,984.85)	1,795.45	(4,189.39)	(8,386.30)	(5,420.00)	1,791.88	(3,628.12)	(9,048.12)
0.75	30 Sep 2004	92	(4,670.20)	(1,317.39)	(5,987.59)	1,796.28	(4,191.31)	(12,577.61)	(5,420.00)	1,791.88	(3,628.12)	(12,676.24)
1.00	31 Dec 2004	92	(4,670.20)	(1,253.50)	(5,923.70)	1,777.11	(4,146.59)	(16,724.20)	(5,420.00)	1,791.88	(3,628.12)	(16,304.36)
1.25	31 Mar 2005	90	(4,568.67)	(1,162.58)	(5,731.25)	1,719.38	(4,011.88)	(20,736.08)	(5,420.00)	1,791.88	(3,628.12)	(19,932.48)
1.50	30 June 2005	91	(4,619.44)	(1,110.02)	(5,729.46)	1,718.84	(4,010.62)	(24,746.70)	(5,420.00)	1,713.26	(3,706.74)	(23,639.22)
1.75	30 Sep 2005	92	(4,670.20)	(1,055.19)	(5,725.40)	1,717.62	(4,007.78)	(28,754.48)	(5,420.00)	1,713.26	(3,706.74)	(27,345.95)
2.00	31 Dec 2005	92	(4,670.20)	(987.22)	(5,657.42)	1,697.23	(3,960.20)	(32,714.67)	(5,420.00)	1,713.26	(3,706.74)	(31,052.69)
2.25	31 Mar 2006	90	(4,568.67)	(898.08)	(5,466.75)	1,640.03	(3,826.73)	(36,541.40)	(5,420.00)	1,713.26	(3,706.74)	(34,759.43)
2.50	30 June 2006	91	(4,619.44)	(838.49)	(5,457.92)	1,637.38	(3,820.55)	(40,361.95)	(5,420.00)	1,630.92	(3,789.08)	(38,548.50)
2.75	30 Sep 2006	92	(4,670.20)	(776.42)	(5,446.62)	1,633.99	(3,812.64)	(44,174.59)	(5,420.00)	1,630.92	(3,789.08)	(42,337.58)
3.00	31 Dec 2006	92	(4,670.20)	(704.11)	(5,374.31)	1,612.29	(3,762.02)	(47,936.60)	(5,420.00)	1,630.92	(3,789.08)	(46,126.66)
3.25	31 Mar 2007	90	(4,568.67)	(616.86)	(5,185.53)	1,555.66	(3,629.87)	(51,566.47)	(5,420.00)	1,630.92	(3,789.08)	(49,915.74)
3.50	30 June 2007	91	(4,619.44)	(549.78)	(5,169.22)	1,550.77	(3,618.45)	(55,184.93)	(5,420.00)	1,543.37	(3,876.63)	(53,792.37)
3.75	30 Sep 2007	92	(4,670.20)	(480.03)	(5,150.23)	1,545.07	(3,605.16)	(58,790.09)	(5,420.00)	1,543.37	(3,876.63)	(57,669.00)
4.00	31 Dec 2007	92	(4,670.20)	(403.10)	(5,073.30)	1,521.99	(3,551.31)	(62,341.40)	(5,420.00)	1,543.37	(3,876.63)	(61,545.63)
4.25	31 Mar 2008	91	(4,568.67)	(321.41)	(4,890.09)	1,467.03	(3,423.06)	(65,764.46)	(5,420.00)	1,543.37	(3,876.63)	(65,422.26)
4.50	30 June 2008	91	(4,619.44)	(242.88)	(4,862.32)	1,458.70	(3,403.62)	(69,168.08)	(5,420.00)	1,450.56	(3,969.44)	(69,391.69)
4.75	30 Sep 2008	92	(4,670.20)	(164.95)	(4,835.15)	1,450.54	(3,384.60)	(72,552.68)	(5,420.00)	1,450.56	(3,969.44)	(73,361.13)
5.00	31 Dec 2008	92	(4,670.20)	(83.11)	(4,753.31)	1,425.99	(3,327.32)	(75,880.00)	(5,420.00)	1,450.56	(3,969.44)	(77,330.56)
5.25	31 Mar 2009	90	-	-					-	1,450.56	1,450.56	(75,880.00)
			(92,642.57)	(15,757.43)	(108,400.00)	32,520.00	(75,880.00)		(108,400.00)	32,520.00	(75,880.00)	
BY YEAR												
31 Dec 2004			(18,528.51)	(5,363.21)	(23,891.72)	7,167.52	(16,724.20)	(16,724.20)	(21,680.00)	5,375.64	(16,304.36)	(16,304.36)
31 Dec 2005			(18,528.51)	(4,315.02)	(22,843.53)	6,853.06	(15,990.47)	(32,714.67)	(21,680.00)	6,931.67	(14,748.33)	(31,052.69)
31 Dec 2006			(18,528.51)	(3,217.10)	(21,745.61)	6,523.68	(15,221.93)	(47,936.60)	(21,680.00)	6,606.03	(15,073.97)	(46,126.66)
31 Dec 2007			(18,528.51)	(2,049.76)	(20,578.28)	6,173.48	(14,404.79)	(62,341.40)	(21,680.00)	6,261.03	(15,418.97)	(61,545.63)
31 Dec 2008			(18,528.51)	(812.35)	(19,340.86)	5,802.26	(13,538.60)	(75,880.00)	(21,680.00)	5,895.06	(15,784.94)	(77,330.56)
31 Dec 2009			-	-	-	-	-		-	1,450.56	1,450.56	
			(92,642.57)	(15,757.43)	(108,400.00)	32,520.00	(75,880.00)		(108,400.00)	32,520.00	(75,880.00)	

- Depreciation is the PV of the Minimum Lease Payments (MLP) amortised over the 5 year lease term on a straight-line basis.
- The Finance Charge represents interest on the deemed loan (the present value of the remaining MLP at any date) at the lessor's pre-tax implicit rate (see next page).
- Tax at 30% is relieved against the P&L charge, and the annual tax charge is paid quarterly starting 6 months after the start of the year.

Example C10 (cont.) – Lessee Accounting – Balance Sheet Impact

BY QUARTER			CASH	FIXED ASSETS			LEASE LIABILITY				TAX ASSET				NET ASSETS
Period (yrs)	Date	Days	Cumulative Cash Flows	PV of MLP at start	Accumulated Depreciation	Fixed Assets	'Loan' b/f	Principal (rentals)	Interest at Implicit Rate 6.32%	'Loan' c/f	Tax Debtor b/f	Tax relief arising P&L	Tax relief received Cash	Tax Debtor c/f	Fixed Assets + Cash + Tax Asset - Lease Liability
0	[illegible]	-		92,642.57		92,642.57	92,642.57	-		92,642.57	-	-	-	-	-
0.25	31 Mar 2004	91	(5,420.00)	92,642.57	(4,568.67)	88,073.89	92,642.57	(5,420.00)	1,426.91	88,649.48	-	1,798.68	-	1,798.68	(4,196.91)
0.50	30 June 2004	91	(9,048.12)	92,642.57	(9,188.11)	83,454.46	88,649.48	(5,420.00)	1,365.41	84,594.89	1,798.68	1,795.45	(1,791.88)	1,802.25	(8,386.30)
0.75	30 Sep 2004	92	(12,676.24)	92,642.57	(13,858.31)	78,784.26	84,594.89	(5,420.00)	1,317.39	80,492.28	1,802.25	1,796.28	(1,791.88)	1,806.65	(12,577.61)
1.00	31 Dec 2004	92	(16,304.36)	92,642.57	(18,528.51)	74,114.05	80,492.28	(5,420.00)	1,253.50	76,325.78	1,806.65	1,777.11	(1,791.88)	1,791.88	(16,724.20)
1.25	31 Mar 2005	90	(19,932.48)	92,642.57	(23,097.19)	69,545.38	76,325.78	(5,420.00)	1,162.58	72,068.35	1,791.88	1,719.38	(1,791.88)	1,719.38	(20,736.08)
1.50	30 June 2005	91	(23,639.22)	92,642.57	(27,716.63)	64,925.94	72,068.35	(5,420.00)	1,110.02	67,758.37	1,719.38	1,718.84	(1,713.26)	1,724.95	(24,746.70)
1.75	30 Sep 2005	92	(27,345.95)	92,642.57	(32,386.83)	60,255.74	67,758.37	(5,420.00)	1,055.19	63,393.57	1,724.95	1,717.62	(1,713.26)	1,729.30	(28,754.48)
2.00	31 Dec 2005	92	(31,052.69)	92,642.57	(37,057.03)	55,585.54	63,393.57	(5,420.00)	987.22	58,960.79	1,729.30	1,697.23	(1,713.26)	1,713.26	(32,714.67)
2.25	31 Mar 2006	90	(34,759.43)	92,642.57	(41,625.70)	51,016.87	58,960.79	(5,420.00)	898.08	54,438.87	1,713.26	1,640.03	(1,713.26)	1,640.03	(36,541.40)
2.50	30 June 2006	91	(38,548.50)	92,642.57	(46,245.14)	46,397.43	54,438.87	(5,420.00)	838.49	49,857.35	1,640.03	1,637.38	(1,630.92)	1,646.48	(40,361.95)
2.75	30 Sep 2006	92	(42,337.58)	92,642.57	(50,915.34)	41,727.23	49,857.35	(5,420.00)	776.42	45,213.78	1,646.48	1,633.99	(1,630.92)	1,649.55	(44,174.59)
3.00	31 Dec 2006	92	(46,126.66)	92,642.57	(55,585.54)	37,057.03	45,213.78	(5,420.00)	704.11	40,497.89	1,649.55	1,612.29	(1,630.92)	1,630.92	(47,936.60)
3.25	31 Mar 2007	90	(49,915.74)	92,642.57	(60,154.22)	32,488.35	40,497.89	(5,420.00)	616.86	35,694.74	1,630.92	1,555.66	(1,630.92)	1,555.66	(51,566.47)
3.50	30 June 2007	91	(53,792.37)	92,642.57	(64,773.65)	27,868.92	35,694.74	(5,420.00)	549.78	30,824.53	1,555.66	1,550.77	(1,543.37)	1,563.05	(55,184.93)
3.75	30 Sep 2007	92	(57,669.00)	92,642.57	(69,443.85)	23,198.71	30,824.53	(5,420.00)	480.03	25,884.55	1,563.05	1,545.07	(1,543.37)	1,564.75	(58,790.09)
4.00	31 Dec 2007	92	(61,545.63)	92,642.57	(74,114.05)	18,528.51	25,884.55	(5,420.00)	403.10	20,867.65	1,564.75	1,521.99	(1,543.37)	1,543.37	(62,341.40)
4.25	31 Mar 2008	91	(65,422.26)	92,642.57	(78,682.73)	13,959.84	20,867.65	(5,420.00)	321.41	15,769.06	1,543.37	1,467.03	(1,543.37)	1,467.03	(65,764.46)
4.50	30 June 2008	91	(69,391.69)	92,642.57	(83,302.17)	9,340.40	15,769.06	(5,420.00)	242.88	10,591.94	1,467.03	1,458.70	(1,450.56)	1,475.16	(69,168.08)
4.75	30 Sep 2008	92	(73,361.13)	92,642.57	(87,972.37)	4,670.20	10,591.94	(5,420.00)	164.95	5,336.89	1,475.16	1,450.54	(1,450.56)	1,475.14	(72,552.68)
5.00	31 Dec 2008	92	(77,330.56)	92,642.57	(92,642.57)	-	5,336.89	(5,420.00)	83.11	-	1,475.14	1,425.99	(1,450.56)	1,450.56	(75,880.00)
5.25	31 Mar 2009	90	(75,880.00)	92,642.57	(92,642.57)	-	-	-	-	-	1,450.56	-	(1,450.56)	-	(75,880.00)
								(108,400.00)	15,757.43						

BY YEAR	CASH	PV of MLP at start	Accumulated Depreciation	Fixed Assets	'Loan' b/f	Principal (rentals)	Interest	'Loan' c/f	Tax Debtor b/f	Tax relief arising P&L	Tax relief received Cash	Tax Debtor c/f	NET ASSETS
31 Dec 2004	(16,304.36)	92,642.57	(18,528.51)	74,114.05	92,642.57	(21,680.00)	5,363.21	76,325.78	-	7,167.52	(5,375.64)	1,791.88	(16,724.20)
31 Dec 2005	(31,052.69)	92,642.57	(37,057.03)	55,585.54	76,325.78	(21,680.00)	4,315.02	58,960.79	1,791.88	6,853.06	(6,931.67)	1,713.26	(32,714.67)
31 Dec 2006	(46,126.66)	92,642.57	(55,585.54)	37,057.03	58,960.79	(21,680.00)	3,217.10	40,497.89	1,713.26	6,523.68	(6,606.03)	1,630.92	(47,936.60)
31 Dec 2007	(61,545.63)	92,642.57	(74,114.05)	18,528.51	40,497.89	(21,680.00)	2,049.76	20,867.65	1,630.92	6,173.48	(6,261.03)	1,543.37	(62,341.40)
31 Dec 2008	(77,330.56)	92,642.57	(92,642.57)	-	20,867.65	(21,680.00)	812.35	-	1,543.37	5,802.26	(5,895.06)	1,450.56	(75,880.00)
						(108,400.00)	15,757.43						

APPENDIX D

RONONI ENTERPRISES – CASE STUDY

D1 MANAGEMENT BUYOUT

The directors of Rononi Enterprises ('Rononi') are preparing an offer to acquire the company. The parent company recently acquired Rononi, which has only been trading for less than two years, as part of a larger group acquisition, but now wants to sell the business for strategic reasons. The directors intend to offer £10m for the debt-free company (equivalent to 2x current revenues), but only have £2m of funds. Discussions are being held with potential co-investors.

A private equity investor, Omivon Capital ('Omivon'), having reviewed management's business plan and three year financial forecasts, is interested in pursuing the proposal further. It has prepared its own forecasts to cover its intended investment holding period, and is evaluating how best to structure the transaction to achieve its target pre-tax Internal Rate of Return (IRR) of 25% from an exit at the end of year 5. It is reasonably confident that the growth projections will enable Rononi to float at that date, however, to be prudent, it will assume that exit will be via a trade sale.

The management buyout is likely to be structured as follows:

- Management and Omivon will establish a new company ('NewCo'), by way of a subscription at par for £2.9m of 1p Ordinary shares in the ratio 70%:30% (cost of equity investment £2m and £0.9m, respectively);
- Omivon will provide the balance of the £10m purchase price (£7.1m) by subscribing for £1 Convertible Redeemable Preference Shares in Newco;
- Newco will acquire 100% of the share capital of Rononi from the vendor for £10m in cash (the business and net assets of Rononi will then be transferred to Newco by way of a 'hive-up', and Newco will be renamed Rononi).

Omivon's own 5 year financial forecast, partly based on management's 3 year forecast, suggests that some £28m of new funding will be required. If debt cannot be supported due to insufficient profits, cash flows or security, Omivon will make up the shortfall by subscribing for additional Convertible Preference shares, up to a maximum amount of £18m, above which management must contribute equity funding, in order to demonstrate its commitment and share the risk. It is believed that £10m of debt funding can be raised in the form of a medium term, revolving bank loan, which will need to be finalised by the start of year 2. Future funding by year is as follows

	NEW FUNDING				
	Management	Omivon		Bank	Total
	Equity	*Equity*	*Conv Pref*	*Debt*	*Total*
Start year 1			15.0		15.0
Start year 2			3.1	5.4	8.4
Start year 3				2.4	2.4
Start year 4				1.7	1.7
Start year 5				0.5	0.5
			18.0 (rounding difference)	**10.0**	**28.0**

The transaction summary is as follows:

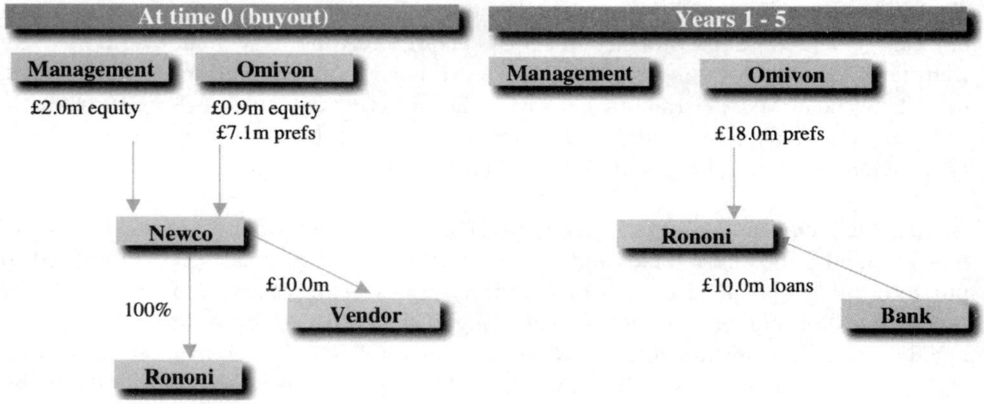

Based on an EBITDA multiple of 7.0 and a P/E multiple of 13.0 (for minority quoted shareholdings), and year 5 EBITDA and net profits of £27.6m and £12.0m, respectively, an exit Equity Value (based on an average of the two multiples) of £118.8m is estimated (this is after deducting a 25% discount for non-marketability, since the exit is assumed to be a private trade sale)(see ❼). Omivon will need to receive £65.3m for its total £26m investment (£0.9m equity, £25.1m non-equity) at the end of year 5 in order to achieve its total pre-tax IRR of 25.0% (see ❻). It will have to convert 15.1% of its Preference shares, at a conversion ratio of 0.739530 Ordinary shares for one Preference share, in order to receive the required equity proceeds. The conversion ratio is set at a level that prevents Omivon from obtaining more than 49% on full conversion, since management wishes to retain a 51% controlling interest. In the event of default, however, Omivon will be entitled to convert at a ratio of 1:1 in order to take over control of the company.

The estimated total Equity Value (after the part conversion) is £118.8m. Omivon would receive £40.1m from the sale of its Ordinary shares and £25.2m from the redemption of its remaining Preference shares. Omivon will also be paid outstanding dividends on its Preference shares. The redemption sum includes a redemption premium equivalent to 17.8% of the face value of the redeeming shares (it is assumed that Rononi will be permitted under company law provisions to redeem the shares).

Omivon's detailed evaluation is as follows:

❶ Determine the opening balance sheet position

Net Assets acquired	*Closing Balance Sheet £m*	*Acquisition Funding* £m	*Consolidated Newco* £m
Operating fixed assets			
At cost	10.0		10.0
Accumulated depreciation	(1.0)		(1.0)
	9.0		9.0
Operating working captal	0.5		0.5
Operating capital	**9.5**		**9.5**
Gross bank debt	0.0	0.0	0.0
less: cash	0.5		0.5
Net Debt	(0.5)		(0.5)
Convertible Preference Shares		7.1	7.1
Debt and Non-Equity	(0.5)		6.6
Ordinary shares £0.01 each	*50.0 m*		
Nominal value	0.5	0.5	0.5
Share premium	9.8	2.4	2.4
Reserves	(0.3)		
Equity	10.0		2.9
Financial capital	**9.5**	*10.0*	**9.5**

❷ Estimate future funding requirements

	Opening	Forecast 1 £m	2 £m	3 £m	4 £m	5 £m
Cashflow requirements						
Revenues		13.8	34.4	61.9	99.0	133.7
Operating profits (EBIT)		(0.1)	3.4	8.0	14.9	21.4
less: taxes paid on operating profits		0.0	(0.9)	(2.4)	(4.5)	(6.4)
Net Operating Profits After Taxes paid ('NOPAT')		(0.1)	2.5	5.6	10.4	15.0
Net capex (gross capex - depreciation)		(14.6)	(9.5)	(6.4)	(9.4)	(8.7)
Working capital investment		(0.7)	(1.2)	(1.3)	(2.2)	(2.1)
Free cash flows		(15.5)	(8.1)	(2.0)	(1.2)	4.2
Cumulative free cash flows		(15.5)	(23.6)	(25.6)	(26.8)	(22.6)
Balance Sheet & funding gap	*Opening*					
Fixed assets	9.0	23.6	33.1	39.5	48.9	57.5
Gross working capital	0.5	1.2	2.4	3.7	5.9	8.0
Operating capital	9.5	24.9	35.5	43.2	54.8	65.6
Gross debt - funding gap	0.0	15.0	23.1	25.1	26.3	22.1
less: cash	0.5	0.0	0.0	0.0	0.0	0.0
Net debt	(0.5)	15.0	23.1	25.1	26.3	22.1
Equity share capital	2.9	2.9	2.9	2.9	2.9	2.9
Preference share capital	7.1	7.1	7.1	7.1	7.1	7.1
Cumulative net operating profits (NOPAT)	0.0	(0.1)	2.4	8.1	18.5	33.4
Financial capital	9.5	24.9	35.5	43.2	54.8	65.6

	Total	1	2	3	4	5
		Forecast				
		£m	£m	£m	£m	£m
Funding allocation						
Funding drawdown / (repayments)		15.0	8.1	2.0	1.2	(4.2)
Post-tax financing costs of new funding		0.0	0.3	0.4	0.5	4.7
		15.0	8.4	2.4	1.7	0.5
being	*Total*					
Equity	0.0	0.0	0.0	0.0	0.0	0.0
Convertible pref	18.0	15.0	3.1	0.0	0.0	0.0
Bank debt	10.0	0.0	5.4	2.4	1.7	0.5
	28.0	15.0	8.4	2.4	1.7	0.5
Operating assumptions						
Revenue growth rate		175.0%	150.0%	80.0%	60.0%	35.0%
EBITDA margin		6.8%	17.5%	19.1%	19.8%	20.6%
EBIT margin		-0.5%	10.0%	13.0%	15.0%	16.0%
Working cap / revenues		9.0%	7.0%	6.0%	6.0%	6.0%
Revenues / fixed assets		x 0.6	x 1.0	x 1.6	x 2.0	x 2.3
Capex / revenues		113.8%	35.0%	16.4%	14.3%	11.1%
Capex / depreciation		15.6 x	4.7 x	2.7 x	3.0 x	2.4 x
Depreciation on cost b/f		10.0%	10.0%	10.0%	10.0%	10.0%
Effective tax rate on EBIT		0.0%	27.2%	30.0%	30.0%	30.0%

❸ Determine financial terms for debt and Preference shares

The above funding allocation, and the resulting post-tax cash financing costs, involves a circular calculation (funding determines the financing cost, which requires funding itself), and depends on (1) the capacity to support debt, (2) the maximum amount of Preference share capital Omivon is prepared to contribute, and (3) other financial terms (interest costs, Preference share coupon, etc.).

It is assumed that the capacity of Newco/Rononi to support debt is determined by minimum interest coverage (EBIT / gross interest) and maximum 'loan-to-liquidation value' ratios that a lender is expected to require. The debt will be a medium term, floating rate 'revolving' facility (principal can be drawn down and repaid at the borrower's discretion during the loan term), secured on Rononi's assets (the loan-to-liquidation value ratio giving some comfort as to recovery of principal).

Where debt cannot be supported, Omivon will contribute funding by way of £1 Convertible Redeemable Preference shares. These will be convertible into Rononi Ordinary shares to give a final maximum holding of 49% (if a default arises, no maximum limit will be imposed and the conversion ratio will be 1:1). Shares not converted but redeemed (at Omivon's option) will attract a redemption premium.

Preference shares will be paid an annual dividend based on the higher of a fixed rate (applied to the face value) and a percentage appropriation of post-tax profits ('participating rate'). A dividend will only be paid if Free Cash Flows are sufficient to cover it, otherwise it will be accrued for and be paid at the time of redemption and/or conversion.

On a liquidation, realised assets will be used to (1) pay off bank debt, (2) then settle normal trade creditors and other liabilities, before (3) any payments are made for the Preference shares (the redemption value plus accrued, unpaid dividends). Ordinary shareholders will be entitled to any surplus remaining.

The main terms of debt and Preference shares are as follows:

❹ Prepare the financial statements

		Forecast				
	Year	1	2	3	4	5
Debt						
Risk free rate		5.0%	5.0%	5.0%	5.0%	5.0%
Debt risk premium		3.0%	3.0%	2.5%	2.5%	2.0%
Forecast floating rate debt costs		8.0%	8.0%	7.5%	7.5%	7.0%
EBIT / gross interest	Min	x 8.00	x 8.00	x 6.00	x 5.00	x 5.00
Gross debt / recoverable assets	Max	30.0%	30.0%	40.0%	40.0%	40.0%
Maximum gross debt	Max	0.0	5.4	13.0	16.4	19.7
Preference Shares	£1.00 each					
Fixed rate coupon		10.0%	10.0%	10.0%	10.0%	10.0%
Participating dividend rate		15.0%	15.0%	15.0%	15.0%	15.0%
Fixed assets x	75.0% recoverable	17.7	24.8	29.6	36.6	43.2
Stock x	23.0% av recoverable	0.0	0.0	0.1	0.5	1.7
Trade debtors x	40.0% recoverable	0.9	1.8	2.7	4.0	4.3
Working capital		0.9	1.8	2.8	4.5	6.0
Cash x	100.0% recoverable	0.0	0.0	0.0	0.0	0.0
Current assets		0.9	1.8	2.8	4.5	6.0
Recoverable assets		*18.7*	*26.6*	*32.4*	*41.1*	*49.2*

	Actual	Forecast					
Year	-1	1	2	3	4	5	
		£m	£m	£m	£m	£m	*Note*
Profit & Loss							
Revenues	5.0	13.8	34.4	61.9	99.0	133.7	
EBITDA	0.8	0.9	6.0	11.8	19.6	27.6	
Depreciation	(1.0)	(1.0)	(2.6)	(3.8)	(4.8)	(6.2)	
EBIT	(0.3)	(0.1)	3.4	8.0	14.9	21.4	
Interest	0.0	0.0	(0.4)	(0.6)	(0.7)	(0.7)	1
Pre-tax profit	(0.3)	(0.1)	3.0	7.5	14.1	20.7	
Tax	0.0	0.0	(0.8)	(2.2)	(4.2)	(6.2)	2
Post-tax profits	(0.3)	(0.1)	2.2	5.2	9.9	14.5	
Preference share dividends		(2.2)	(2.5)	(2.5)	(2.5)	(2.5)	3
Retained profits	(0.3)	(2.3)	(0.3)	2.7	7.4	12.0	

	Forecast					
Year	1	2	3	4	5	
	£m	£m	£m	£m	£m	*Note*
Cash Flow						
EBITDA	0.9	6.0	11.8	19.6	27.6	
Capital expenditures	(15.6)	(12.0)	(10.1)	(14.2)	(14.9)	
Increase in working capital	(0.7)	(1.2)	(1.3)	(2.2)	(2.1)	
Tax on operating cash flows	0.0	(0.9)	(2.4)	(4.5)	(6.4)	2
Free Cash Flows	(15.5)	(8.1)	(2.0)	(1.2)	4.2	
Equity	0.0	0.0	0.0	0.0	0.0	
Preference share capital	15.0	3.1	0.0	0.0	0.0	4
Bank debt	0.0	5.4	2.4	1.7	0.5	4
Funding	15.0	8.4	2.4	1.7	0.5	
Post-tax debt interest costs	0.0	(0.3)	(0.4)	(0.5)	(0.5)	1
Preference share dividends	0.0	0.0	0.0	0.0	(4.2)	3
Funding costs	0.0	(0.3)	(0.4)	(0.5)	(4.7)	
Net cash flows	(0.5)	0.0	(0.0)	0.0	0.0	
Opening cash	0.5	0.0	0.0	0.0	0.0	
Closing cash	0.0	0.0	0.0	0.0	0.0	5
Balance Sheet						
Operating fixed assets						
At cost	25.6	37.7	47.8	62.0	76.9	
Accumulated depreciation	(2.0)	(4.6)	(8.3)	(13.1)	(19.3)	
	23.6	33.1	39.5	48.9	57.5	
Operating working captal	1.2	2.4	3.7	5.9	8.0	6
Operating capital	24.9	35.5	43.2	54.8	65.6	
Gross bank debt	0.0	5.4	7.8	9.5	10.0	
less: cash	0.0	0.0	0.0	0.0	0.0	
Net Debt	0.0	5.4	7.8	9.5	10.0	
Face value of convertible prefs	22.1	25.2	25.2	25.2	25.2	
Accrued preference share dividends	2.2	4.7	7.2	9.8	8.1	3
Conv Prefs	24.3	29.9	32.4	34.9	33.2	
Non-equity	24.3	35.3	40.2	44.4	43.3	
Ordinary shares # £0.01 each	*50.0 m*	*50.0 m*	*50.0 m*	*50.0 m*	*50.0 m*	
Nominal value	0.5	0.5	0.5	0.5	0.5	
Share premium	2.4	2.4	2.4	2.4	2.4	
Reserves	(2.3)	(2.6)	0.1	7.5	19.5	
Equity	0.6	0.3	3.0	10.3	22.3	
Financial capital	24.9	35.5	43.2	54.8	65.6	

Notes to accounts

1. Interest costs

Year		1	2	3	4	5
Gross debt - assumed funded at year start		0.0	5.4	7.8	9.5	10.0
Interest rate		8.0%	8.0%	7.5%	7.5%	7.0%
Interest		0.0	(0.4)	(0.6)	(0.7)	(0.7)
Tax on interest (see note 2)		0.0	0.1	0.2	0.2	0.2
Post-tax interest		0.0	(0.3)	(0.4)	(0.5)	(0.5)

2. Tax

Year		1	2	3	4	5
Pre-tax profits		(0.1)	3.0	7.5	14.1	20.7
Adjusted for brought forward losses		0.0	2.7	7.5	14.1	20.7
Tax rate		30%	30%	30%	30%	30%
Tax	A	0.0	(0.8)	(2.2)	(4.2)	(6.2)
EBIT		(0.1)	3.4	8.0	14.9	21.4
Adjusted for brought forward losses on EBIT		0.0	3.1	8.0	14.9	21.4
Tax rate		30%	30%	30%	30%	30%
Tax on operating cash flows	B	0.0	(0.9)	(2.4)	(4.5)	(6.4)
Tax relief on interest	A - B	0.0	0.1	0.2	0.2	0.2

Since the example attempts to show financial evaluation techniques, the tax assumptions have been simplified to avoid further complications. It has been assumed, therefore, that (1) capital expenditure qualifying for tax relief is the same as the depreciation charge, and (2) tax is paid on the last day of the relevant year.

3. Preference share dividends

Year		1	2	3	4	5
Preference shares - assumed funded at year start		22.1	25.2	25.2	25.2	25.2
Fixed rate coupon		10%	10%	10%	10%	10%
Fixed coupon	A	*2.2*	*2.5*	*2.5*	*2.5*	*2.5*
Post-tax profits		(0.1)	2.2	5.2	9.9	14.5
Participating dividend rate		15%	15%	15%	15%	15%
Dividend	B	*0.0*	*0.3*	*0.8*	*1.5*	*2.2*
Higher of A and B		2.2	2.5	2.5	2.5	2.5
Free Cash flows		(15.5)	(8.1)	(2.0)	(1.2)	4.2
Dividends accruing in year paid		0.0	0.0	0.0	0.0	(2.5)
Dividends unpaid in prior years paid		0.0	0.0	0.0	0.0	(1.7)
Cumulative unpaid dividends		2.2	4.7	7.2	9.8	8.1

4. Preference shares and bank debt

Bank debt is at levels that satisfy the lender's expected ratios. The facility will be a medium term revolving facility, to be negotiated at the end of year 1. If new non-debt funding is required after year 2 over and above that shown above, Omivon will require management to contribute a pro-rata share of new equity.

5. Cash

For simplicity, it is assumed that no surplus cash is held (this is unlikely in practice).

Notes to accounts (cont.)

6. Working capital

Year	1	2	3	4	5
Stock	0.4	1.0	1.9	3.0	4.0
Trade debtors	2.2	4.5	6.8	9.9	10.7
Trade creditors	(1.4)	(3.1)	(5.0)	(6.9)	(6.7)
Gross working capital	1.2	2.4	3.7	5.9	8.0

❺ Ensure debt ratios are not breached

		Forecast				
	Year	1	2	3	4	5
Debt risk ratios						
EBIT / gross interest	Min	x 8.00	x 8.00	x 6.00	x 5.00	x 5.00
	Actual	--	x 8.00	x 13.74	x 20.78	x 30.49
Gross debt / recoverable assets	Max	30.0%	30.0%	40.0%	40.0%	40.0%
	Actual	0.0%	20.2%	24.1%	23.2%	20.4%
Maximum gross debt	Max	0.0	5.4	13.0	16.4	19.7
	Actual	0.0	5.4	7.8	9.5	10.0
Financial information	EBIT	(0.1)	3.4	8.0	14.9	21.4
	Gross interest	0.0	(0.4)	(0.6)	(0.7)	(0.7)
	Recoverable assets	18.7	26.6	32.4	41.1	49.2

❻ Determine the required proceeds on exit for a stated pre-tax IRR

			Year	MBO date	1	2	3	4	5
				£m	£m	£m	£m	£m	£m
Equity				(0.9)	-	-	-	-	-
Convertible redeemable preference shares				(22.1)	(3.1)	-	-	-	-
Investment made at start of year				(23.0)	(3.1)	-	-	-	-
Dividends paid in year					-	-	-	-	4.2
Deferred dividends									8.1
Redemption of convertibles									25.2
Required equity value on exit									40.1
Minimum required proceeds on exit									**65.3**
Additional upside									-
Net cash flow	Actual IRR	25.0%		(23.0)	(3.1)	-	-	-	77.5
Interest income	Reinvestment rate	5.0%			-	-	-	-	-
Interest expense	Required IRR	25.0%			(5.7)	(7.9)	(9.9)	(12.4)	(15.5)
Net investment c/f				(23.0)	(31.8)	(39.7)	(49.6)	(62.0)	-

❼ Determine the exit Equity Value, based on assumed valuation multiples, and the final shareholding

The estimated Equity Value will be based on an average conservative multiple (EBITDA x7 and P/E x 13), using adjusted average multiples for comparable quoted companies. To be prudent, Omivon assumes that an exit will be achieved in year 5 by way of a trade sale, and hence a discount for lack of marketability (25%) is applied.

It is assumed that the Equity Value will be affected by the redemption and/or conversion of the Preference shares. Full redemption (assuming this does not breach company law provisions) will require financing, and hence the earnings figure used for the P/E multiple derived valuation must be reduced by the post-tax financing cost; on full conversion the face value of the Preference shares will no longer be deducted in arriving at the Equity Value derived using the EBITDA multiple. In both cases, Preference share dividends will no longer be deducted in calculating earnings.

The following analysis assumes the redemption premium is set at a level that ensures Omivon achieves its required IRR of 25%. The following needs to occur at the end of year 5:

- Investment cash flows over the holding period (funding and dividends) are as forecast;
- 15.1% of Preference shares convert at the fixed conversion ratio of 0.739530 Ordinary shares for each Convertible (adjusted for future dilution if new Ordinary shares are issued), increasing Omivon's holding from 30% to 33.7%;
- non-converting Preference shares are redeemed at a premium of 17.8% to their face value or 2.1% of the Enterprise Value less net debt and accrued Preference share dividends (ignoring the above 25% discount), giving total redemption proceeds of £25.2m (the £8.1m of accrued dividends will be paid at the same time);
- the Equity Value (adjusted for conversion and redemption – see below) is £118.8m, of which 33.7% accrues to Omivon (£40.1m).

The total proceeds (£65.3m) equals the target proceeds

Final value analysis

		Preference Shares		Conv. Ratio & premium	Ordinary Shares		Value	Total value
		No	£m		%	No	£m	£m
At end year 5 - pre conversion		25,160,384	25.2		30.0%	15,010,497	34.4	114.5
Conversion	15.1%	(3,802,036)	(3.8)	0.739530	3.7%	2,811,721	4.3	
Redeeming shares		21,358,348	21.4					
Redemption premium			3.8	17.8%				
Equity value adjustment							1.5	4.3
Final		**21,358,348**	**25.2**		**33.7%**	**17,822,218**	**40.1**	**118.8**

Final shareholdngs

	Management		Omivon		Total
	Shares '000s	Holding	Shares '000s	Holding	Shares '000s
On day 1	34,989.5	70.0%	15,010.5	30.0%	50,000.0
End year 5	34,989.5	70.0%	15,010.5	30.0%	50,000.0
Conversion			2,811.7	33.7%	2,811.7
Final holdings	**34,989.5**	**66.3%**	**17,822.2**	**33.7%**	**52,811.7**

Exit proceeds analysis

		Investment	Shares '000s	Equity entry price £	Equity exit price £	Equity exit value £m	Omivon proceeds £m
Redemption of conv. prefs (+ premium)		21.4		1.00	1.18		**25.2**
Pre-conversion shares		0.9	15,010.5	0.06	2.25	33.8	
Converted shares		3.8	2,811.7	1.35	2.25	6.3	
Omivon	25.0% IRR	26.0	17,822.2	1.46	2.25	40.1	**40.1**
Management		2.0	34,989.5	0.06	2.25	78.7	
		28.0	**52,811.7**	**0.13**	**2.25**	**118.8**	**65.3**

The year 5 Equity Values with no redemption or conversion, with full redemption and conversion, and for the final solution, are shown below:

		No redemption / conversion	*100% Redeeemed*	*100% Converted*	*15.1% converting 84.9% redeeming*
EBITDA		27.6			
Enterprise value	*EBITDA multiple of x 7*	193.1			
less: net debt		(10.0)			
less: redemption value of preference shares		(25.2)		25.2	3.8
less: redemption premium					(3.8)
less: accrued preference share dividends		(8.1)			
Equity value		149.8	149.8	175.0	149.8
Profit available for ordinary shareholders		12.0			
add back: preference share dividends			2.5	2.5	2.5
less: finance cost of redemption and dividends			(2.3)	(0.6)	(2.3)
add: tax relief thereon			0.7	0.2	0.7
Adjusted proforma net profits		12.0	12.8	14.1	12.8
Equity value	*P/E multiple of x 13*	155.5	167.0	183.1	167.0
Average equity value		152.7	158.4	179.0	158.4
Average equity value - after 25% discount		114.5	118.8	134.3	118.8
Value of pre-conversion shares			35.7	40.3	35.7
Value of converted shares				25.0	4.4
Value of equity			35.7	65.3	40.1
Value of preference shares			25.2	0.0	21.4
Redemption premium			0.0	(0.0)	3.8
Shortfall			4.4	0.0	0.0
Total proceeds required on exit			65.3	65.3	65.3

Note: the cost of financing the new debt required to redeem the Preference shares (with the premium) and pay the accrued dividends is based on the year 5 cost of debt (7.0%) (full conversion will only require financing the amount of accrued dividends).

	100% Redeeemed	*100% Converted*	*15.1% converting 84.9% redeeming*
Required holding calculation			
Pre- conversion shares	50.0m	50.0m	50.0m
New shares on conversion		18.6m	2.8m
Diluted shares	50.0m	68.6m	52.8m
Share price	2.38	1.96	2.25
Exit value	118.8	134.3	118.8
Required equity proceeds on exit	40.1	65.3	40.1
Required holding	33.7%	48.6%	33.7%
Maximum holding	49.0%	49.0%	49.0%
Pre-conversion holding	30.0%	30.0%	30.0%
Post-conversion holding	30.0%	49.0%	33.7%

The redemption premium / adjusted Enterprise Value ratio (2.1%) referred to above is calculated as follows:

Redemption premum ratio

	Enterprise Value	Net Debt	Accrued Dividends on Preference Shares	Equity Value + Pref. Share Value	Face Value of Pref. Shares	Redemption Premium	Equity Value (before discount)
EBITDA multiple value	193.1	(10.0)	(8.1)	175.0	(21.4)	(3.8)	149.8
P/E multiple value	210.3	(10.0)	(8.1)	192.2	(21.4)	(3.8)	167.0
Average: Base Case Values	**201.7**			**183.6**			**158.4**
			Premium % =	*2.1%*	*After 25.0% discount =*		*118.8*

In the analysis above, the redemption premium is the balancing figure required to achieve the target 25% IRR: conversion ensures equity proceeds of £40.1m are achieved (subject to the maximum 49% holding not being exceeded), and the redemption premium ensures non-equity proceeds of £25.2m are achieved. Payment of any redemption amount, however, would be subject to any relevant company law provisions (such as the requirement for Rononi to be solvent after the redemption payment).

If the Equity Value exceeds £118.8m, fewer Preference shares need to be converted in order to obtain the target 25% IRR: conversion will occur until the Equity Value is £133.6m (x 30% = £40.1m), above which Omivon achieves an IRR greater than 25% from a sale of its existing 30% shareholding and a redemption of 100% of its Preference shares at no premium (the £133.6m Equity Value is equivalent to a £221.5m Enterprise Value before the 25% non-marketability discount: £133.6m ÷ 75% + £10.1m net debt + £25.2m face value of Preference shares + £8.1m unpaid dividends).

If the Equity Value is less than £118.8m, a greater proportion of the Preference shares will need to be converted. Maximum conversion takes place when the Equity Value falls to £81.8m (x max 49% = £40.1m). However, a redemption premium would still be needed to achieve the £25.2m (this would have to apply to a single remaining Preference share).

❽ Consider downside risk (liquidation)

		Forecast				
	Year	1	2	3	4	5
		£m	£m	£m	£m	£m
Liquidation Value						
Fixed assets x	75.0% recoverable	17.7	24.8	29.6	36.6	43.2
Stock x	23.0% av recoverable	0.0	0.0	0.1	0.5	1.7
Trade debtors x	40.0% recoverable	0.9	1.8	2.7	4.0	4.3
Working capital		0.9	1.8	2.8	4.5	6.0
Cash x	100.0% recoverable	0.0	0.0	0.0	0.0	0.0
Current assets		0.9	1.8	2.8	4.5	6.0
Recoverable assets		*18.7*	*26.6*	*32.4*	*41.1*	*49.2*
Available for:						
Debt		0.0	5.4	7.8	9.5	10.0
Trade creditors		1.4	3.1	5.0	6.9	6.7
Convertible preference shares - face value		17.3	18.2	19.6	24.6	25.2
Convertible preference shares - accrued divi		0.0	0.0	0.0	0.0	7.3
Ordinary shareholders		0.0	0.0	0.0	0.0	0.0
		18.7	26.6	32.4	41.1	49.2
Exposure analysis						
Preference shares - face value		22.1	25.2	25.2	25.2	25.2
less: recovered on liquidation		(17.3)	(18.2)	(19.6)	(24.6)	(25.2)
Exposure for preference shares		4.8	7.0	5.5	0.5	0.0
Exposure for ordinary shares		0.9	0.9	0.9	0.9	0.9
Total exposure		5.7	7.8	6.4	1.4	0.9
% investment		24.7%	30.1%	24.6%	5.3%	3.3%
Probability of liquidation		30%	20%	10%	5%	5%
Probability weighted exposure		1.7	1.6	0.6	0.1	0.0
Downside risk: shortfall on liquidation						
Management		2.0	2.0	2.0	2.0	2.0
Omivon		5.7	7.8	6.4	1.4	0.9
Investment lost on liquidation		7.7	9.8	8.4	3.4	2.9
Omivon's share of risk		73.9%	79.7%	76.2%	40.8%	30.0%

(Liquidation costs have been deducted in arriving at the recoverable assets figure).

Omivon's maximum exposure is £7.8m (less than £2m after adjusting for the probability of default / liquidation).

❿ Consider overall risk / return analysis and establish final requirements

Omivon will achieve its target IRR of 25% if financial results and funding needs are the same as forecast above, and it can exit at the end of year 5 at the assumed Equity Value (£118.8m). This can be achieved if 15.1% of the Preference shares convert into Ordinary shares and the remainder are redeemed at face value plus a 17.8% redemption premium. If the year 5 Equity Value is between £81.8m and £133.6m, a minimum 25% pre-tax IRR can still be achieved if a redemption premium is given, based on an agreed schedule of redemption premium/Enterprise Value ratios. Omivon must also be given the right to convert any non-redeeming Preference shares into Ordinary shares up to the maximum 49%.

D2 BANK LENDING REVIEW

Rononi Enterprises arranged a medium term £10m revolving bank facility during year 1. The actual performance for year 1 was as expected as at the start of the year (from the 3 year business plan – see Appendix D1), however actual performance for year 2 was not as expected: revenue growth was 10% below expectations, the gross profit margin 0.5% below, and the EBIT margin 4% below. Further, investment in Fixed and Working capital, as a percentage of revenues, was 8% higher. Year 2 Free Cash Flows, therefore, were -£11.2m, some £3m below expectations.

The funding requirement for year 2 was expected to be £8.4m as at the date of the management buyout, being bank debt of £5.4m and Convertible Redeemable Preference shares of £3m (the start of year 1 – see the Cash Flow ❹ in Appendix D1). The actual requirement was £11.4m. Because margins reduced, the maximum debt, based on the bank's minimum / maximum debt servicing ratios (see ❸ in Appendix D1), reduced from £5.4m to £3.1m. Omivon had already stated at the time of the MBO that it would not provide additional Preference share funding above the £3.1m it was expecting to provide, and hence £5.2m of equity had to be raised at the start of year 2 (£11.4m funding requirement - £3.1m debt - £3.1m Preference shares). Management and Omivon shared the £5.2m equity funding pro-rata to their shareholdings (70%:30%), and new shares were issued at an agreed price of £2 each (2.6m £0.10 ordinary shares were issued).

Management have updated the financial forecasts for years 3 – 5 (see ❶ below). At the start of year 3, they hold discussions with the bank to increase the existing facility from £10m to £15m. It has become apparent that the seasonal sales pattern is more pronounced than expected, with over 70% of sales occurring in the second and third quarters. A monthly cash flow forecast for year 3 reveals a peak funding requirement of £12.5m in month 9 (reducing to £4.5m by the year end, due to net cash collections)(see ❸). Although this is within the maximum permitted year end level (£12.9m see ❹), the bank has expressed some concern, and carries out a financial review of Rononi.

Gross profit margins are expected to improve from 26.5% to 28% over years 3-5, as revenues increase £57.8m to £108.3. Over this period, EBIT margins are forecast to increase from 10% to 15%, and EBITDA margins from about 17% to 20%. With investment in Fixed and Working capital being fairly steady at an average £9m p.a. and £3m p.a., respectively, Free Cash Flow becomes positive in year 4, increasing to £4.9m in year 5.

The bank does not expect that the full £15m facility will be required in years 4 and 5, and is comfortable with the level of risk implied from the debt servicing ratios. It therefore agrees to increase the facility size to £15m to cover the peak funding requirement during year 3. However, the bank requests management to review its Working capital management policy, and make every effort to accelerate the collection from customers, so as to level out monthly funding needs.

❶ Financial Statements: years 1 – 2 (actual) and 3 – 5 (business plan at start year 3)

	Actual		Forecast		
	1	2	3	4	5
	£m	£m	£m	£m	£m
PROFIT & LOSS					
Revenues	13.8	33.0	57.8	86.6	108.3
Cost of Sales	(10.3)	(24.9)	(42.4)	(62.8)	(78.0)
Gross Profit	3.4	8.1	15.3	23.8	30.3
General and Administrative costs	(2.5)	(3.5)	(5.6)	(8.3)	(8.5)
Depreciation	(1.0)	(2.6)	(3.9)	(4.7)	(5.7)
Earnings Before Interest & Tax ('EBIT')	(0.1)	2.0	5.8	10.8	16.2
Interest expense	0.0	(0.3)	(0.6)	(0.6)	(0.6)
Profit Before Taxation	(0.1)	1.8	5.3	10.2	15.6
Taxation	0.0	(0.4)	(1.6)	(3.0)	(4.7)
Profit for the year	(0.1)	1.3	3.7	7.1	10.9
Preference share dividends	(2.2)	(2.5)	(2.5)	(2.5)	(2.5)
Retained profit	(2.3)	(1.2)	1.2	4.6	8.4
CASH FLOW					
EBITDA	0.9	4.6	9.7	15.5	21.8
Taxes on EBITDA	(0.3)	(1.4)	(2.9)	(4.6)	(6.6)
Net funds flow	0.7	3.2	6.8	10.8	15.3
(Increase) / decrease in working capital	(0.7)	(2.4)	(3.3)	(2.6)	(2.9)
Operating cash flows - pre capex	(0.1)	0.8	3.5	8.2	12.4
Capital expenditures	(15.6)	(12.9)	(8.7)	(9.5)	(9.2)
Taxes on capital expenditures	0.3	0.9	1.2	1.4	1.7
Net Operating Free Cash Flows	**(15.5)**	**(11.2)**	**(4.0)**	**0.1**	**4.9**
Debt interest paid	0.0	(0.3)	(0.6)	(0.6)	(0.6)
Increase / (decrease in short term debt)	0.0	3.1	4.4	0.4	0.4
Debt cash flows	0.0	2.9	3.9	(0.2)	(0.2)
Tax relief on interest expense	0.0	0.1	0.2	0.2	0.2
Post-tax debt cash flows	0.0	3.0	4.0	(0.0)	(0.0)
Conv. Redeemable Preference Shares	15.0	3.1	0.0	0.0	0.0
Preference Share dividends	0.0	0.0	0.0	(0.1)	(4.9)
Equity funding	0.0	5.2	0.0	0.0	0.0
Financing cash flows	**15.0**	**11.2**	**4.0**	**(0.1)**	**(4.9)**
BALANCE SHEET					
Fixed Assets - Net Book Value b/f	9.0	23.6	34.0	38.8	43.6
- Capex less depreciation	14.6	10.3	4.8	4.8	3.5
- Net Book Value c/f	23.6	34.0	38.8	43.6	47.1
Working capital - Stocks / inventories	0.4	1.0	1.7	2.6	3.2
- Trade debtors	2.2	5.6	9.8	13.0	14.6
- Trade creditors	(1.4)	(3.0)	(4.6)	(6.1)	(5.4)
	1.2	3.6	6.9	9.5	12.5
Operating Capital	**24.9**	**37.6**	**45.7**	**53.1**	**59.6**
Short term debt	0.0	3.1	7.6	8.0	8.4
less: cash	0.0	0.0	0.0	0.0	0.0
Net Debt	0.0	3.1	7.6	8.0	8.4
Ordinary Share Capital	2.9	8.0	8.0	8.0	8.0
Profit for year	(2.3)	(1.2)	1.2	4.6	8.4
Reserves	0.0	(2.3)	(3.5)	(2.3)	2.3
	0.6	4.6	5.7	10.3	18.7
Preference Share Capital	22.1	25.2	25.2	25.2	25.2
Deferred dividend on preference shares	2.2	4.7	7.2	9.6	7.3
	24.3	29.9	32.4	34.8	32.5
Financial Capital	**24.9**	**37.6**	**45.7**	**53.1**	**59.6**

❷ Comparison of 3 year Business Plans : years 1–3 (at start year 1) and 3–5 (at start year 3)

		Forecast at start year 1				
		Actual		Forecast at start year 3		
		1	2	3	4	5
Profitability and return						
Revenue Growth	*Change in revenues / last year revenues*	175.0% *+0.0%*	140.0% *-10.0%*	75.0% *-5.0%*	50.0%	25.0%
Pre-tax Return on Av Operating Capital	*EBIT / average Operating Capital*	-0.4% *+0.0%*	7.2% *-5.7%*	16.3% *-7.8%*	26.3%	33.8%
EBIT margin	*EBIT / revenues*	-0.5% *+0.0%*	6.1% *-3.9%*	10.1% *-2.9%*	12.4%	14.9%
Asset turnover	*Revenues / average Operating Capital*	x 0.9 *+ x 0.0*	x 1.2 *- x 0.1*	x 1.6 *- x 0.2*	x 2.1	x 2.3
Fixed Asset Turn	*Average fixed assets / revenues*	118.7% *+0.0%*	87.3% *+4.7%*	63.0% *+4.3%*	47.5%	41.9%
Working capital turnover	*Average gross working capital / revenues*	6.3% *+0.0%*	7.4% *+2.1%*	9.1% *+4.2%*	9.5%	10.2%
Stock turnover	*Average stock / revenues*	1.5% *-1.1%*	2.1% *+0.0%*	2.4% *+0.0%*	2.5%	2.7%
Days stock held	*Stock turnover x 365 days*	5 days *+ 0 days*	8 days *+ 0 days*	9 days *+ 0 days*	9 days	10 days
Debtors turnover	*Average trade debtors / revenues*	11.6% *+1.1%*	11.8% *+2.1%*	13.4% *+4.2%*	13.2%	12.8%
Average collection period	*Debtors turnover x 365 days*	42 days *+ 4 days*	43 days *+ 8 days*	49 days *+ 15 days*	48 days	47 days
Creditors turnover	*Average trade creditors / revenues*	6.8% *+0.0%*	6.6% *+0.1%*	6.6% *+0.1%*	6.2%	5.3%
Average payment period	*Creditors turnover x 365 days*	25 days *+ 0 days*	24 days *+ 0 days*	24 days *+ 0 days*	23 days	19 days
Cashflow						
EBITDA margin	*EBITDA / revenues*	6.8% *+0.0%*	13.8% *-3.6%*	16.7% *-2.3%*	17.9%	20.2%
Capex / Revenues		113.8% *+0.0%*	39.0% *+4.0%*	15.0% *-1.4%*	11.0%	8.5%
Change in working capital / Revenues		5.4% *+0.0%*	7.3% *+3.9%*	5.7% *+3.6%*	3.0%	2.7%

Free Cash Flows can be reconciled between those expected at the start of year 1 and the position at the start of year 3 as follows:

At start year 1	Forecast		
At start year 3	Actual		Forecast
	1	2	3
Revenues expected at start year 1	13.8	34.4	61.9
variance	0.0	(1.4)	(4.1)
at start year 3	13.8	33.0	57.8
EBITDA expected at start year 1	0.9	6.0	11.8
variance	0.0	**(1.4)**	**(2.1)**
at start year 3	*0.9*	*4.6*	*9.7*
-ve variance contribution	--	*41.1%*	*51.8%*
Capex expected at start year 1	(15.6)	(12.0)	(10.1)
variance	0.0	**(0.8)**	1.5
at start year 3	*(15.6)*	*(12.9)*	*(8.7)*
-ve variance contribution	--	*24.0%*	--
Working capital investment at start year 1	(0.7)	(1.2)	(1.3)
variance	0.0	**(1.2)**	**(2.0)**
at start year 3	*(0.7)*	*(2.4)*	*(3.3)*
-ve variance contribution	--	*35.0%*	*48.2%*
Tax at start year 3	0.0	(0.5)	(1.7)
Free cash flow	**(15.5)**	**(11.2)**	**(4.0)**

Three year revenues and EBIT margins expected at the start of year 1 and yr 3

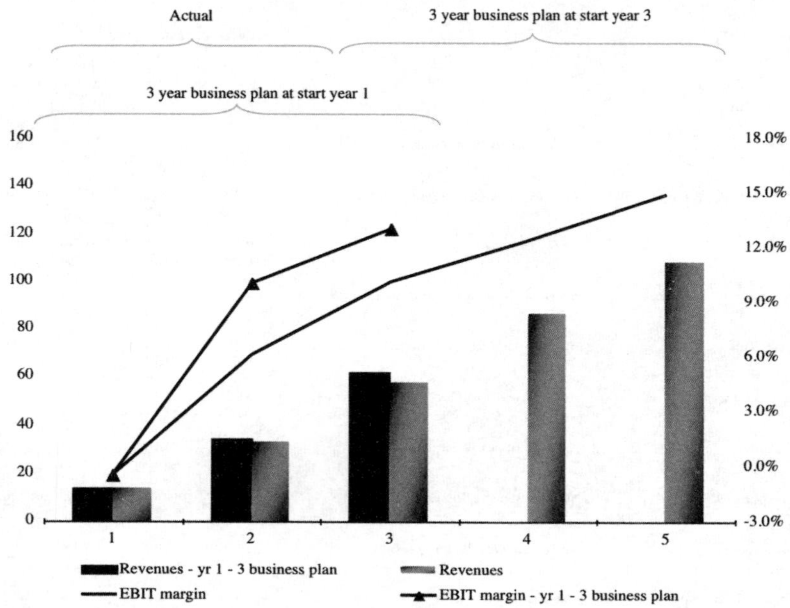

Three year Free Cash Flows – expected at the start of year 1 and 3

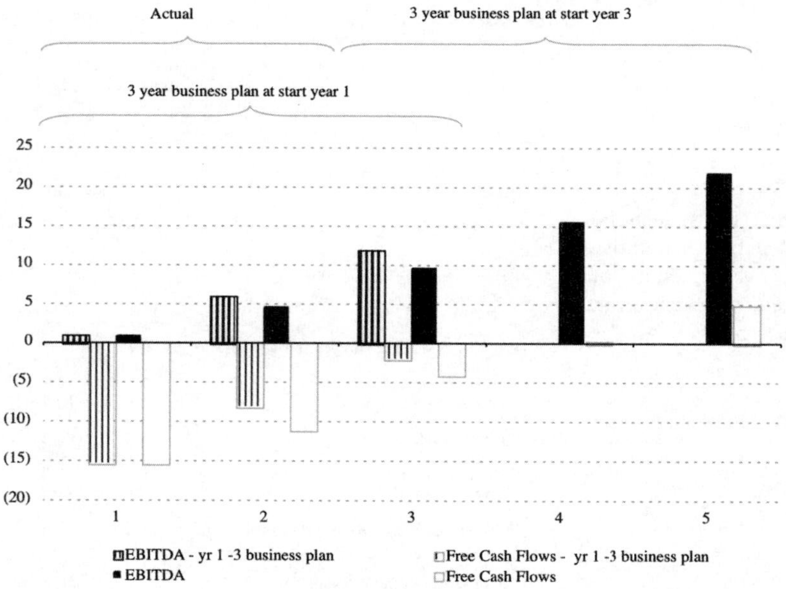

❸ Working capital review for year 3

Year 3 pre-tax operating cash flows, ignoring capital expenditures (i.e. £9.7m EBITDA less the £3.3m increase in Working capital), can be analysed as follows:

Forecast year 3

	Profit & Loss		Cash		Working Capital	
Sales	57.8		48.5			
Cost of sales	(42.4)		(38.6)			
Operating costs	(5.6)		(5.6)			
Profit	9.7	-	4.3	=	5.4	this year
Change in working capital	(3.3)		2.7		(2.7)	last year
Cash purchased stock, unsold at year end			(0.6)		0.6	next year
Operating cash flow	6.4		6.4		3.3	
Opening			0.0		3.6	
Closing			*6.4		6.9	

	*
EBITDA	9.7
Change in working capital	(3.3)
Operating cash flow	6.4
Capex	(8.7)
Tax on EBITDA	(2.9)
Tax relief on capex	1.2
Free Cash Flows	(4.0)
Actual cash balance	nil

Only 44% of EBITDA is realised in cash (£4.3m / £9.7m): 84% of sales are collected in the period, whereas 92% of direct costs and operating overheads are paid for in the year. Working capital can be analysed further:

Working Capital Investment

	Opening Balance Sheet	Stock purchases	Direct overheads	Operating costs	Stock sales (36% mark -up)	Settlement of opening balances	Closing Balance Sheet
Stock at cost	1.0	34.6	8.6		(42.4)		1.7
Trade debtors	5.6				9.3	(5.0)	9.8
Trade creditors	(3.0)	(4.0)	0.0	0.0		2.4	(4.6)
Gross working capital	3.6	30.5	8.6	0.0	(33.2)	(2.7)	6.9
Cash	0.0	(30.5)	(8.6)	(5.6)	48.5	2.7	6.4*
Net working capital	3.6	0.0	0.0	(5.6)	15.3	0.0	13.3

Note

- Cost of sales £42.4m = stock purchases less the increase in stock (£33.9m, 80%) plus direct overheads (£8.6m, 20%), both at a 36% mark-up (allowing for a rounding difference).
- Sales collected £48.5m = sales value of stocks (£57.8m = £42.4m x 1.36) x 84% collected.
- The net Working capital increase due to stock sales (£15.3m) represents gross profit. The net Working capital change over the period (£13.3m - £3.6m) represents EBITDA.
- It is assumed that direct and indirect overheads (operating costs, excluding depreciation) are paid for during the year (trade creditors relate to material purchases).

This analysis ignores the monthly pattern of sales and purchases during year 3, the resulting funding requirement and the related financing cost. Sales and purchases per quarter are as follows:

Seasonality

	Year 3 Quarter 1	2	3	4	Total
Sales	13%	29%	43%	16%	100%
Collected	5%	19%	27%	32%	84%
Purchases	16%	42%	28%	14%	100%
Paid	9%	24%	42%	13%	88%

MONTHS AFTER SALE	PAYMENT DELAY FROM DATE OF SALE				
	QUARTER				
	Opening	1	2	3	4
0 (i.e. in month)	30%	5%	10%	0%	0%
1	50%	40%	42%	0%	0%
2	10%	45%	43%	50%	31%
3	0%	10%	5%	25%	40%
4	0%	0%	0%	25%	29%
Total	*90%*	*100%*	*100%*	*100%*	*100%*

MONTHS AFTER PURCHASE	PAYMENT DELAY FROM DATE OF PURCHASE				
	QUARTER				
	Opening	1	2	3	4
0 (i.e. in month)	30%	10%	10%	0%	0%
1	50%	40%	40%	30%	0%
2	0%	50%	50%	70%	45%
3	0%	0%	0%	0%	55%
4	0%	0%	0%	0%	0%
Total	*80%*	*100%*	*100%*	*100%*	*100%*

A review of the monthly forecasts for year 3 reveals the following:

- A decision was taken to grant an extra month of credit to customers with effect from the start of quarter 3 (hence no sales in quarters 3 and 4 were collected until 2 months after the month of sale). The company could only obtain similar credit from its suppliers in quarter 4 (stock is purchased on average 1 month prior to a sale).

- The change in policy resulted in the difference in the monthly average debtors' days less creditors' days increasing from 3 in the first half to 22 in the second half. This increased the time delay from payments to supplies to receipts from customers, increasing the funding requirement.

- Working capital investment alone is enough to require a peak funding of £4.2m in month 6 (Working capital financing costs are assumed to be 7.5% p.a. and are £0.13m for the year). The deficit reduces after this month as more credit is taken from customers.

- Taking into account capital expenditures (paid quarterly), and the tax charge on operating cash flows (ignoring tax on financing), the peak funding increases to £12.5m in month 9 (increasing the above £0.13m financing cost to approximately £0.5m for the year).

MONTH	Opening	1	2	3	4	5	6	7	8	9	10	11	12	TOTAL
Profit & Loss														
Sales		1.7	2.9	2.9	3.5	4.3	8.7	11.6	8.7	4.3	3.5	2.9	2.9	57.8
Cost of sales		(1.3)	(2.1)	(2.1)	(2.5)	(3.2)	(6.4)	(8.5)	(6.4)	(3.2)	(2.5)	(2.1)	(2.1)	(42.4)
Gross profit		0.5	0.8	0.8	0.9	1.1	2.3	3.1	2.3	1.1	0.9	0.8	0.8	**15.3**
Operating costs		(0.2)	(0.3)	(0.3)	(0.3)	(0.4)	(0.8)	(1.1)	(0.8)	(0.4)	(0.3)	(0.3)	(0.3)	(5.6)
Depreciation		(0.1)	(0.2)	(0.2)	(0.2)	(0.3)	(0.6)	(0.8)	(0.6)	(0.3)	(0.2)	(0.2)	(0.2)	(3.9)
EBIT'		0.2	0.3	0.3	0.3	0.4	0.9	1.2	0.9	0.4	0.3	0.3	0.3	**5.8**
EBITDA		0.3	0.5	0.5	0.6	0.7	1.5	1.9	1.5	0.7	0.6	0.5	0.5	9.7
Change in working capital		(0.3)	0.0	(0.5)	(0.5)	(1.5)	(3.5)	(3.9)	(3.9)	0.2	3.5	4.6	2.4	(3.3)
Operating cash flow		0.0	0.5	0.0	0.1	(0.8)	(2.1)	(2.0)	(2.5)	0.9	4.1	5.1	2.9	**6.4**
Capital expenditure				(2.2)			(2.2)			(2.2)			(2.2)	(8.7)
Tax on operating cash flows													(1.7)	(1.7)
Free cash flows		0.0	0.5	(2.2)	0.1	(0.8)	(4.2)	(2.0)	(2.5)	(1.2)	4.1	5.1	(1.0)	**(4.0)**
Opening cash		0.0	0.0	0.5	0.6	0.6	(0.1)	(2.2)	(4.2)	(6.7)	(5.8)	(1.8)	3.3	
Operating cash flows		0.0	0.5	0.0	0.1	(0.8)	(2.1)	(2.0)	(2.5)	0.9	4.1	5.1	2.9	
Financing costs			0.00	0.00	0.00	0.00	(0.00)	(0.01)	(0.03)	(0.04)	(0.04)	(0.01)	0.00	(0.13)
Closing cash		0.0	0.5	0.6	0.6	(0.1)	(2.2)	(4.2)	(6.7)	(5.8)	(1.8)	3.3	6.2	
Capex / tax		0.0	0.0	(2.2)	0.0	0.0	(2.2)	0.0	0.0	(2.2)	0.0	0.0	(3.9)	
Additiona financing costs			0.00	0.00	(0.01)	(0.01)	(0.01)	(0.04)	(0.05)	(0.07)	(0.08)	(0.05)	(0.02)	(0.35)
Closing cash		0.0	0.5	(1.6)	(1.5)	(2.3)	(6.6)	(8.6)	(11.2)	(12.5)	(8.5)	(3.5)	(4.5)	
	Opening													
Stock	1.0	2.1	2.1	2.5	3.2	6.4	8.5	6.4	3.2	2.5	2.1	2.1	1.7	
Trade debtors	5.6	5.6	4.8	5.1	5.6	6.4	10.6	16.5	21.2	19.3	15.6	11.2	9.8	
Trade creditors	3.0	3.8	3.1	3.3	3.9	6.5	9.3	9.1	6.7	4.4	3.7	4.0	4.6	
Working capital	3.6	3.9	3.9	4.3	4.8	6.3	9.8	13.8	17.7	17.5	14.0	9.4	6.9	
as % of annual sales		6.7%	6.7%	7.5%	8.4%	11.0%	17.0%	23.8%	30.6%	30.2%	24.2%	16.2%	12.0%	**16.2%** av
Working Capital														
Opening debtors received		1.7	2.8	0.6	0.0	0.0	0.0	0.0	0.0	0.0	0.0	0.0	0.0	5.0
Opening creditors paid		(0.9)	(1.5)	0.0	0.0	0.0	0.0	0.0	0.0	0.0	0.0	0.0	0.0	(2.4)
Receipts from customers		0.1	0.8	2.1	3.0	3.5	4.5	5.7	3.9	6.2	7.2	7.2	4.3	48.5
Payments to creditors		(0.2)	(0.9)	(1.8)	(1.9)	(2.5)	(4.0)	(5.3)	(4.9)	(4.3)	(2.4)	(1.4)	(0.8)	(30.5)
Payment of operating costs		(0.2)	(0.3)	(0.3)	(0.3)	(0.4)	(0.8)	(1.1)	(0.8)	(0.4)	(0.3)	(0.3)	(0.3)	(5.6)
Payment of overheads		(0.5)	(0.4)	(0.5)	(0.6)	(1.3)	(1.7)	(1.3)	(0.6)	(0.5)	(0.4)	(0.4)	(0.3)	(8.6)
Net cash flow		0.0	0.5	0.0	0.1	(0.8)	(2.1)	(2.0)	(2.5)	0.9	4.1	5.1	2.9	**6.4**

FUNDING REQUIRED DURING YEAR 3

														Total
Operating cash flows	£m	0.0	0.5	0.0	0.1	(0.8)	(2.1)	(2.0)	(2.5)	0.9	4.1	5.1	2.9	6.4
														Av
Stock days	days	30	30	30	30	30	30	30	30	30	30	30	28	*30*
Debtor days	days	47	49	49	44	43	44	84	84	84	89	89	89	*66*
Creditor days	days	41	43	43	43	43	43	52	52	52	77	76	76	*53*
Cash cycle	days	36	37	36	31	31	31	62	62	62	43	43	41	*43*

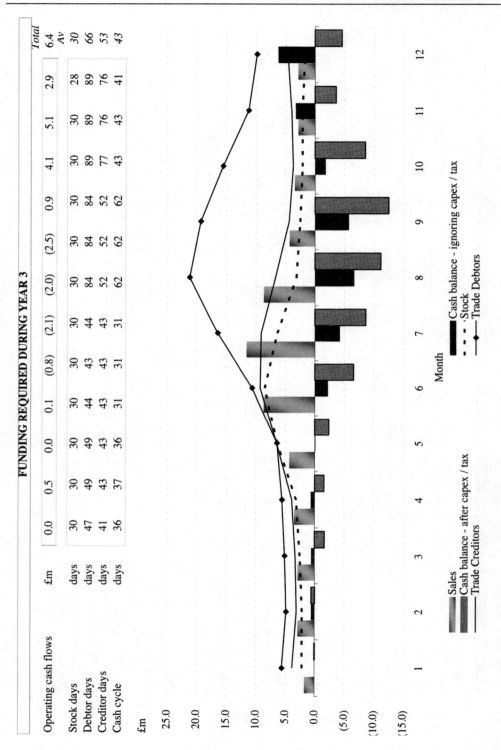

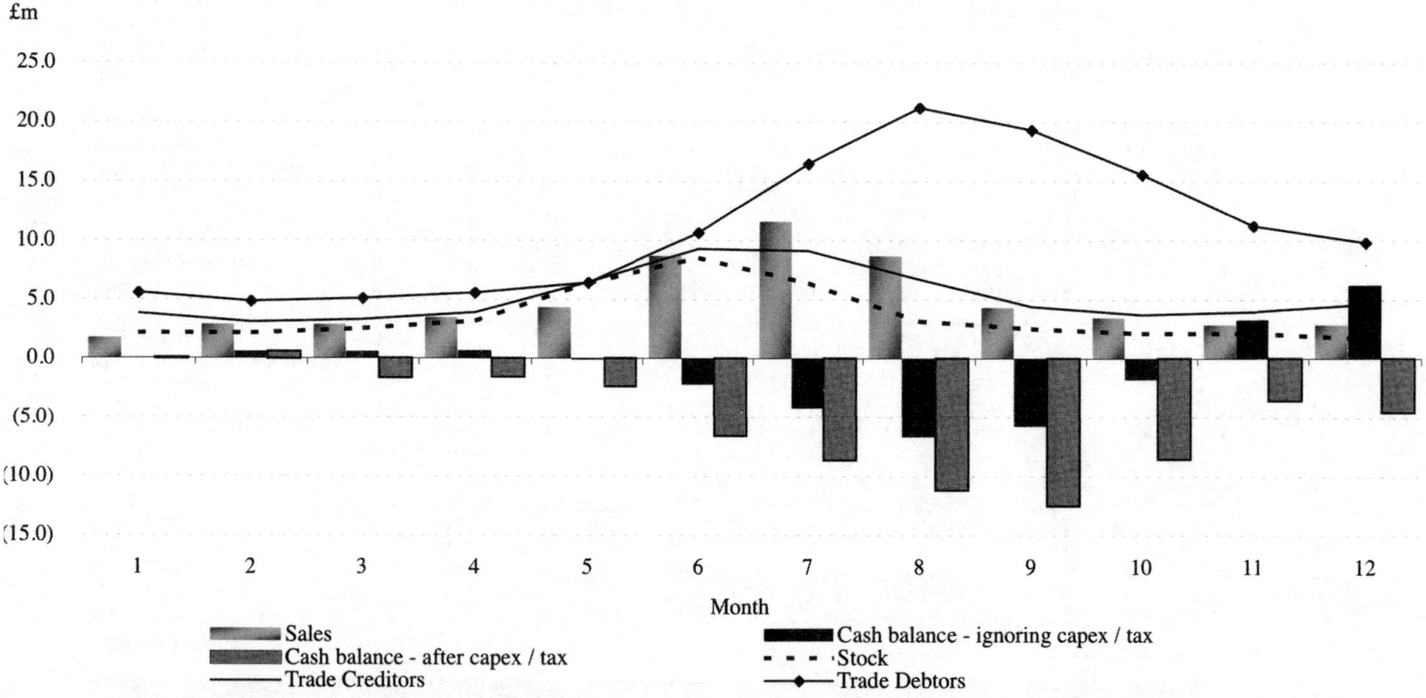

❹ Debt servicing review

The bank is satisfied that its loan will not exceed the maximum it will permit, according to its own measures of debt capacity and financial risk. The key measures are as follows:

		Actual		Forecast at start year 3		
		1	2	3	4	5
Debt capacity						
EBIT / debt interest		--	x 8.0	x 10.3	x 18.0	x 27.5
Minimum required		*8.0*	*8.0*	*6.0*	*5.0*	*5.0*
Gross debt / recoverable assets	Debt / liquidation value of assets	0.0%	11.1%	22.1%	20.0%	18.8%
Maximum permitted		*30.0%*	*30.0%*	*40.0%*	*40.0%*	*40.0%*
Actual debt		0.0	3.1	7.6	8.0	8.4
Maximum permitted		*0.0*	*3.1*	*12.9*	*15.9*	*17.9*
Debt service coverage						
EBIT / (debt + non-equity interest)	EBIT / (debt interest + pref divs paid)	--	x 8.0	x 10.3	x 15.0	x 3.0
EBITDA / debt servicing	EBITDA / (principal + interest payment)	--	x 18.3	x 17.1	x 25.9	x 37.2
EBITDA / debt interest	-	--	x 18.3	x 17.1	x 25.9	x 37.2
EBITDA / debt repayments	-	--	--	--	--	--
Free cash flow ('FCF") / gross debt	-	--	-x 3.6	-x 0.5	x 0.0	x 0.6
FCF / debt service	-	--	-x 44.8	-x 7.1	x 0.2	x 8.3
Funds flow / gross debt	-	--	x 1.0	x 0.9	x 1.4	x 1.8
Funds flow / debt service	-	--	x 12.8	x 11.9	x 18.1	x 26.0
Gross debt / EBITDA	-	x 0.0	x 0.7	x 0.8	x 0.5	x 0.4
Leverage + gearing						
Gross debt / Total assets	Gross debt / Total assets (incl. cash)	--	7.7%	15.0%	13.5%	12.9%
Gross leverage	Gross debt / (gross debt + equity/non-equity)	0.0%	9.5%	19.7%	18.4%	16.0%
Gross gearing	Gross debt / equity	0.0%	68.3%	131.8%	77.2%	44.8%
Liquidity measures						
Current Ratio	Current Assets / Current Liabilities	x 1.9	x 1.1	x 0.9	x 1.1	x 1.3
Quick Ratio	(Cash + Trade debtors) / current liabilities	x 1.6	x 0.9	x 0.8	x 0.9	x 1.1
Workings for definitions						
Recoverable assets		18.7	28.2	34.3	39.8	44.7
Gross new investment ('GNI')	Capex + Increase in working capital	16.4	15.3	12.0	12.1	12.1
Funds Flow	(EBITDA - taxes paid thereon)	0.7	3.2	6.8	10.8	15.3
Free Cash Flows ('FCF')	EBITDA - GNI - operating taxes paid	(15.5)	(11.2)	(4.0)	0.1	4.9
Operating taxes paid - pre capex	Tax on EBITDA only	(0.3)	(1.4)	(2.9)	(4.6)	(6.6)
Operating taxes paid - post capex	Tax on EBITDA - capital allowances	0.0	(0.5)	(1.7)	(3.2)	(4.8)
Effective tax rate on EBIT	Excludes tax on financing	0.0%	25.2%	30.0%	30.0%	30.0%

D3 INITIAL PUBLIC OFFERING

At the end of year 5, shareholders of Rononi Enterprises (management and Omivon, the financial investor) decide to offer 25% of the company, by way of an Initial Public Offering of new shares (Primary Offering), to institutional investors (via a bookbuilding process) and the general public (retail investors). Management wishes to retain a 51% holding post-float, and so, via its investment holding company, will subscribe for shares to avoid dilution. Omivon will not participate in the offering. Existing shareholders will not be permitted to sell any shares until the expiry of a six month 'lock-up' period (to maintain price stabilisation). The main features of the IPO are summarised below.

- The pre-float Equity Value of Rononi, based on a 10 year DCF valuation, is estimated to be £160m, or £2.61 per share, after Preference shares are part redeemed (see ❶). It is expected that this price will increase 10% on the first day of trading.

- Omivon will not need to convert any of its Convertible Redeemable Preference shares to achieve its target 25% IRR (based on the float price) (see ❷). However, it will convert to a final 40% holding (the maximum agreed with management) to allow for some upside. The above Equity Value assumes, therefore, that Omivon converts 45% of its Preference shares at a conversion ratio of 0.777902; the remaining Preference shares (£13.9m face value) will be redeemed at par, and the £3.2m of accrued Preference share dividends will be paid off at the same time (total £17.1m).

- Rononi wants to raise £70m for capital investment and 'general corporate purposes', after deducting IPO costs and fees (5% of float size) and the £17.1m due to Omivon. The float size will need to be £92m, therefore (see ❸).

- Management will subscribe for 35% of the total offer, with the remainder being allocated to institutional and retail investors in a 70:30 ratio. The price for institutions is £2.64 (bookbuild price), with retail investors being allowed a small discount (£2.54 retail price). The average price is £2.61 (also management's subscription price) (see ❹).

- The arranging bankers will over-allocate by short selling shares (up to 15% of the institutional / retail offer), and will be granted a 'Greenshoe' option to enable them to cover the short position at a guaranteed minimum price of £2.61.

	Shares				**Cash raised (£m)**			
	Management	Omivon	New Shareholders	Total	Management	Omivon	New Shareholders	Total
Pre-IPO	36.8	24.5		61.3				
Shareholding	*60.0%*	*40.0%* *post conversion*		*100.0%*				
IPO								
Main IPO	12.5	-	22.8	35.3	32.6	-	59.5	92.1
Redemption of prefs / divs						(17.1)		(17.1)
IPO - cash target (pre fees)	*12.5*	-	*22.8*	*35.3*	*32.6*	*(17.1)*	*59.5*	*75.0*
Greenshoe	3.6	-	3.4	7.0	9.3	-	8.9	18.2
Total IPO	*16.0*	-	*26.2*	*42.3*	*41.8*	*(17.1)*	*68.4*	*93.2*
Post-IPO	52.8	24.5	26.2	103.6				
Shareholding	*51.0%*	*23.7%*	*25.3%*	*100.0%*		See ❺		

❶ Equity Value at IPO

The financial statements for the last 5 years (since the MBO at time 0) are as follows:

	Actual 1	2	3	4	5
	£m	£m	£m	£m	£m
Profit & Loss					
Revenues	13.8	33.0	57.8	83.7	100.5
EBITDA	0.9	4.6	10.0	15.8	19.7
Depreciation	(1.0)	(2.6)	(3.9)	(4.7)	(5.6)
EBIT	(0.1)	2.0	6.1	11.1	14.1
Interest	0.0	(0.3)	(0.4)	(0.4)	(0.4)
Pre-tax profit	(0.1)	1.8	5.8	10.7	13.8
Tax	0.0	(0.4)	(1.7)	(3.2)	(4.1)
Post-tax profits	(0.1)	1.3	4.0	7.5	9.6
Preference share dividends	(2.2)	(2.5)	(2.5)	(2.5)	(2.5)
Retained profits	(2.3)	(1.2)	1.5	5.0	7.1
Cash Flow					
EBITDA	0.9	4.6	10.0	15.8	19.7
Capital expenditures	(15.6)	(12.9)	(8.7)	(8.4)	(8.0)
Increase in working capital	(0.7)	(2.4)	(1.0)	(1.2)	(1.2)
Tax on operating cash flows	0.0	(0.5)	(1.8)	(3.3)	(4.2)
Free Cash Flows	(15.5)	(11.2)	(1.5)	2.9	6.2
Equity	0.0	5.2	(0.0)	0.0	0.0
Preference share capital	15.0	3.1	0.0	0.0	0.0
Bank debt	0.0	3.1	1.8	0.3	0.3
Funding	15.0	11.4	1.8	0.3	0.3
Post-tax debt interest costs	0.0	(0.2)	(0.3)	(0.3)	(0.3)
Preference share dividends	0.0	0.0	0.0	(2.9)	(6.2)
Funding costs	0.0	(0.2)	(0.3)	(3.1)	(6.5)
Net cash flows	(0.5)	0.0	(0.0)	0.0	0.0
Opening cash	0.5	0.0	0.0	(0.0)	0.0
Closing cash	0.0	0.0	0.0	(0.0)	0.0
Balance Sheet					
Operating fixed assets					
At cost	25.6	38.5	47.2	55.6	63.6
Accumulated depreciation	(2.0)	(4.6)	(8.4)	(13.1)	(18.7)
	23.6	34.0	38.8	42.4	44.9
Operating working captal	1.2	3.6	4.6	5.9	7.0
Operating capital	24.9	37.6	43.4	48.3	51.9
Net Debt (nil cash)	(0.0)	3.1	4.9	5.2	5.4
Face value of conv. prefs	22.1	25.2	25.2	25.2	25.2
Accrued pref. share divs.	2.2	4.7	7.2	6.9	3.2
Conv Prefs	24.3	29.9	32.4	32.0	28.3
Non-equity	24.3	33.0	37.3	37.2	33.7
Ordinary shares # £0.01 each	*50.0 m*	*52.6 m*	*52.6 m*	*52.6 m*	*52.6 m*
Nominal value	0.50	0.53	0.53	0.53	0.53
Share premium	2.4	7.5	7.5	7.5	7.5
Reserves	(2.3)	(3.5)	(2.0)	3.0	10.1
Equity	0.6	4.6	6.1	11.1	18.2
Financial capital	24.9	37.6	43.4	48.3	51.9

Note: new equity was raised in year 2, as discussed in Appendix D2.

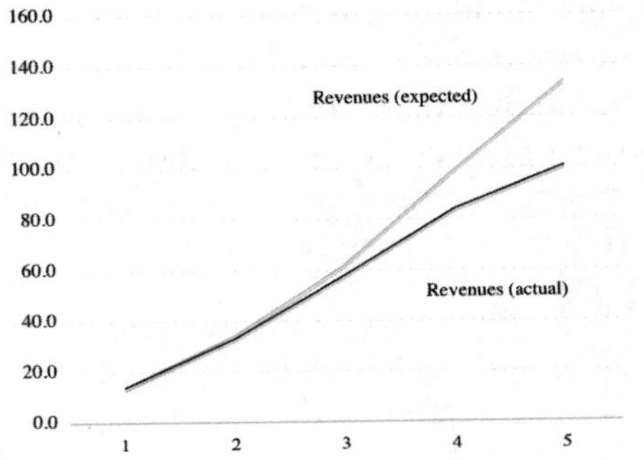

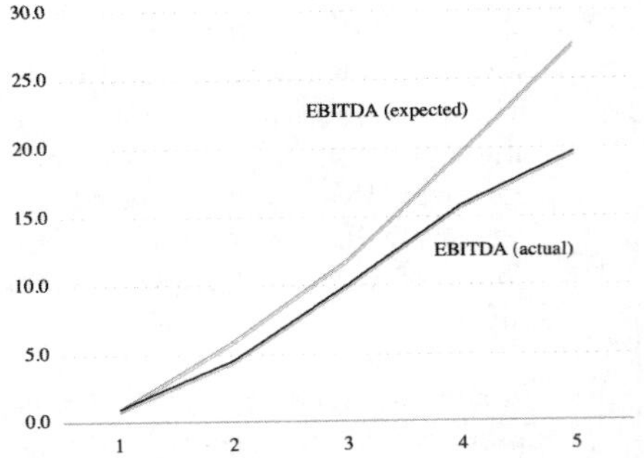

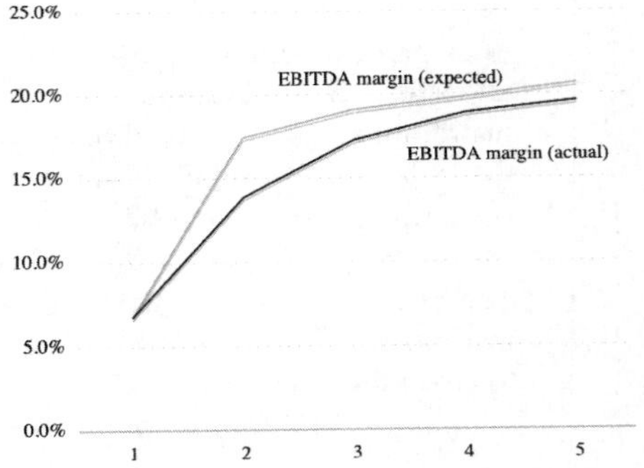

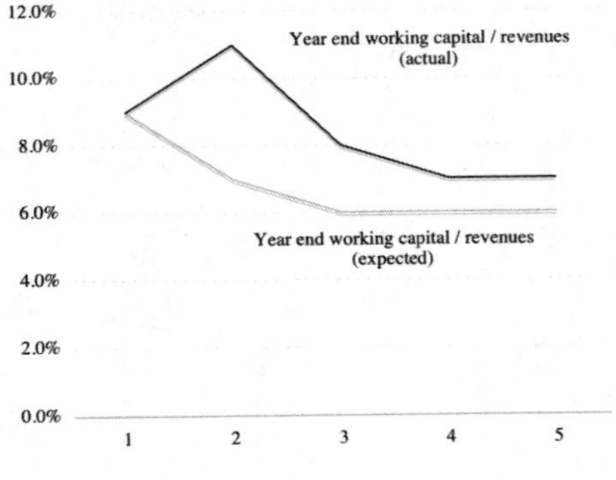

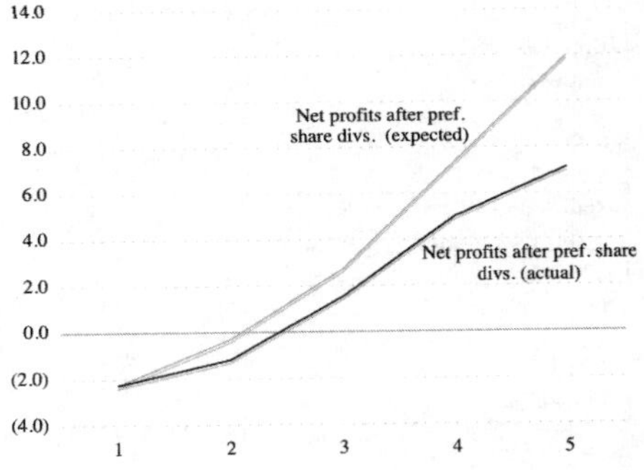

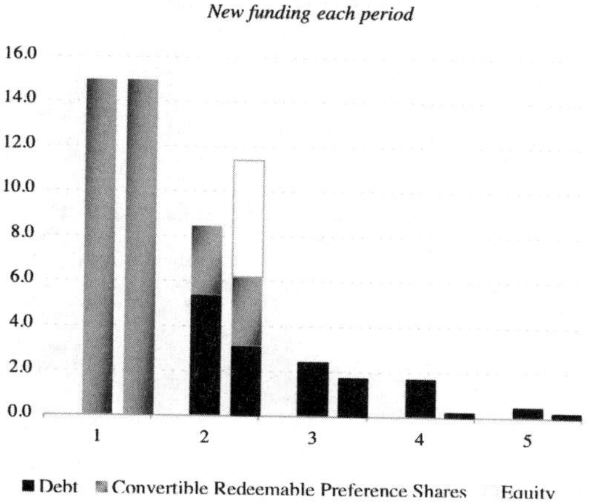

Expected : left hand column,
Actual : right hand column

Since additional non-debt funding was required in year 2, over that expected at time 0, as agreed, management and Omivon provided new equity funding, pro-rata to their shareholdings, at a price of £2 per share.

Maximum debt levels are below expected, due to poorer performance:

Max. debt (£m)	1	2	3	4	5
Expected	0.0	5.4	13.0	16.4	19.7
Actual	0.0	3.1	13.0	14.5	15.6

The Equity Value at IPO is estimated to be £160m (£153.6m per the following DCF valuation, rounded up to the nearest £10m):

	Actual	Forecast									
	Yr 5 +	1	2	3	4	5	6	7	8	9	10
		£m	£m	£m	£m	£m	£m	£m	£m	£m	£m
Free Cash Flows											
Revenues	100.5	115.6	132.9	148.8	163.7	180.1	198.1	217.9	239.7	263.7	276.9
Cost of Sales	(72.3)	(83.2)	(97.0)	(108.7)	(120.3)	(132.4)	(146.6)	(163.4)	(182.2)	(203.0)	(213.2)
Gross Profit	28.1	32.4	35.9	40.2	43.4	47.7	51.5	54.5	57.5	60.6	63.7
General and Administrative costs	(8.4)	(9.6)	(11.0)	(12.3)	(14.4)	(16.9)	(18.6)	(21.5)	(22.5)	(24.7)	(25.8)
Depreciation	(5.6)	(6.4)	(7.2)	(8.1)	(9.1)	(10.2)	(11.4)	(12.7)	(14.1)	(15.7)	(17.4)
EBIT	14.1	16.4	17.7	19.8	19.8	20.6	21.5	20.2	20.9	20.2	20.5
Add back: depreciation	5.6	6.4	7.2	8.1	9.1	10.2	11.4	12.7	14.1	15.7	17.4
EBITDA	19.7	22.7	24.9	27.9	28.9	30.8	32.9	33.0	35.1	35.9	37.9
Taxes on EBITDA	(5.9)	(6.8)	(7.5)	(8.4)	(8.7)	(9.3)	(9.9)	(9.9)	(10.5)	(10.8)	(11.4)
Net funds flow	13.8	15.9	17.4	19.5	20.3	21.6	23.1	23.1	24.5	25.1	26.5
Change in Working capital	(1.2)	(1.1)	(1.2)	(1.1)	(1.0)	(1.1)	(1.3)	(1.4)	(1.5)	(1.7)	(0.9)
Operating cash flows - pre capex	12.6	14.8	16.2	18.4	19.2	20.4	21.8	21.7	23.0	23.5	25.6
Capital expenditures	(8.0)	(8.1)	(9.3)	(10.4)	(11.1)	(11.7)	(12.9)	(14.2)	(15.6)	(17.1)	(16.6)
Taxes on capital expenditures	1.7	1.9	2.2	2.4	2.7	3.1	3.4	3.8	4.2	4.7	5.2
Free Cash Flows	6.2	8.7	9.0	10.4	10.9	11.8	12.3	11.3	11.7	11.0	14.2
Discount factor		0.9183	0.8432	0.7743	0.7110	0.6529	0.5996	0.5506	0.5056	0.4642	0.4263
PV of Free Cash Flows	**69.8**	8.0	7.6	8.1	7.8	7.7	7.4	6.2	5.9	5.1	6.1
Key performance indicators											
Revenue growth	20.0%	15.0%	15.0%	12.0%	10.0%	10.0%	10.0%	10.0%	10.0%	10.0%	5.0%
EBIT / revenues	14.1%	14.2%	13.3%	13.3%	12.1%	11.4%	10.9%	9.3%	8.7%	7.7%	7.4%
EBITDA / revenues	19.6%	19.7%	18.7%	18.7%	17.7%	17.1%	16.6%	15.1%	14.6%	13.6%	13.7%
Capex / Revenues	8.0%	7.0%	7.0%	7.0%	6.8%	6.5%	6.5%	6.5%	6.5%	6.5%	6.0%
Capex / Depreciation	1.4 x	1.3 x	1.3 x	1.3 x	1.2 x	1.1 x	1.1 x	1.1 x	1.1 x	1.1 x	1.0 x
Working Capital / Revenues	7.0%	7.0%	7.0%	7.0%	7.0%	7.0%	7.0%	7.0%	7.0%	7.0%	7.0%
Tax rate	30.0%	30.0%	30.0%	30.0%	30.0%	30.0%	30.0%	30.0%	30.0%	30.0%	30.0%
Pre-Tax ROIC	29.3%	31.5%	32.4%	34.1%	32.2%	31.9%	32.1%	29.0%	28.8%	26.8%	26.0%
Post-Tax ROIC	20.5%	22.0%	22.6%	23.9%	22.5%	22.4%	22.5%	20.3%	20.2%	18.7%	18.2%

WACC	PV 1-10yrs	PV of Terminal Value			Enterprise Value			Non-Equity	Equity Value		
		Perpetuity growth rate			*Perpetuity growth rate*				*Perpetuity growth rate*		
		1.5%	3.0%	4.5%	1.5%	3.0%	4.5%		1.5%	3.0%	4.5%
6.9%	76.9	137.1	192.6	317.5	214.0	269.5	394.4	22.5	191.5	247.0	371.9
7.9%	73.2	105.4	139.6	204.2	178.6	212.9	277.4	22.5	156.1	190.4	254.9
8.9%	69.8	83.1	105.8	143.9	152.9	175.6	213.7	22.5	130.4	153.1	191.2
9.9%	66.6	66.8	82.5	107.0	133.5	149.2	173.6	22.5	111.0	126.7	151.1
10.9%	63.7	54.5	65.8	82.5	118.2	129.5	146.1	22.5	95.7	107.0	123.6

IPO Equity Value = £160m (£153.1m rounded up), implying a £182.5 Enterprise Value.

Net debt	5.4
Preference Shares	25.2
less: converting at IPO	(11.2)
Preference shares not converting	13.9
Accrued dividends on preference shares	3.2
	22.5

Terminal Value (TV)

Year 10 cash flows	14.2
Growth rate	3.0%
Year 11 cash flows	14.6

$$TV = \frac{14.6}{(8.9\% - 3.0\%)}$$

PV x 0.4263

= 105.8

Cost of Capital

Risk Free Rate	Rf	4.75%
Equity Risk Premium	Rm - Rf	4.50%
Proxy Equity Ungeared Beta	Bu	1.0
Target D:E ratio (MV)	D:E	20%
Tax rate	t	30.0%
Equity Geared Beta	Bg = Bu x (1 + [D (1-t) / E])	1.1
Cost of equity	Keg = Rf + Bg (Rm-Rf)	9.9%
Cost of debt	Kd	7.0%
After tax cost of debt	Kdt = Kd x (1-t)	4.9%
Nominal WACC	Kdt x (D/D+E) + Keg x (E/D+E)	8.9%

❷ Preference shares to be redeemed

Omivon needs an Equity Value on exit of £43.2m. The following shows actual cash flows and the required proceeds for the target 25% IRR (the additional £9.6m results in an IRR of 27.9%):

		Year	MBO date	1	2	3	4	5
			£m	£m	£m	£m	£m	£m
Equity			(0.9)	(1.6)	-	-	-	
Convertible redeemable preference shares			(22.1)	(3.1)	-	-	-	
Investment made at start of year			(23.0)	(4.6)	-	-	-	-
Dividends paid in year				-	-	-	2.9	6.2
Deferred dividends								3.2
Redemption of convertibles								25.2
Required equity value on exit								43.2
Minimum required proceeds on exit								**68.3**
Additional upside								9.6
Net cash flow	Actual IRR	27.9%	(23.0)	(4.6)	-	-	2.9	87.3
Interest income	Reinvestment rate	5.0%		-	-	-	-	-
Interest expense	Required IRR	25.0%		(5.7)	(8.3)	(10.4)	(13.0)	(15.5)
Net investment c/f			(23.0)	(33.3)	(41.6)	(52.1)	(62.2)	9.6

The float Enterprise Value is £182.5m (see ❶). With full redemption of Preference shares, the final Equity Value would be £149.4m (see below), allowing Omivon to achieve its target £43.2m from its existing 30% shareholding. However, under the terms of the Preference shares, at this Enterprise Value level, Omivon can convert up to a maximum 40% shareholding. The final Equity Value (£160m) can be reconciled to the £158.4m expected at the date of the MBO (£118.8m with the 25% discount for non-marketability added back, since exit will be by way of a float and not, as originally expected, from a trade sale - see ❼ in Appendix D1):

		No redemption / conversion	100% Redeeemed	44.7% converting 55.3% redeeming
EBITDA		19.7		
Enterprise value	*EBITDA multiple of x 9*	182.5		
less: net debt		(5.4)		
less: redemption value of preference shares		(25.2)		11.2
less: redemption premium				0.0
less: accrued preference share dividends		(3.2)		
Equity value		148.8	148.8	160.0
Profit available for ordinary shareholders		7.1		
add back: preference share dividends			2.5	2.5
less: finance cost of redemption and dividends			(2.0)	(1.2)
add: tax relief thereon			0.6	0.4
Adjusted proforma net profits		7.1	8.2	8.8
Equity value	*P/E multiple of x 18*	129.4	150.0	160.0
Average equity value		139.1	149.4	160.0
Average equity value - after 0% discount		139.1	149.4	160.0
Value of pre-conversion shares			44.8	48.0
Value of converted shares				0.0
Value of equity			44.8	48.0
Value of preference shares			25.2	13.9
Redemption premium			0.0	6.4
Shortfall			(1.7)	0.0
Total proceeds required on exit			68.3	68.3

Required holding calculation			
Pre- conversion shares		52.6m	52.6m
New shares on conversion			8.7m
Diluted shares		52.6m	61.3m
Share price	£	2.84	2.61
Exit value	£m	149.4	160.0
Required equity proceeds on exit	£m	43.2	43.2
Required holding		30.0%	30.0%

	EBITDA x	*P/E x*	Enterprise Value	Net Debt	Pref. divs. unpaid	Equity Value + Pref. Shares	Pref Shares	Redemption Premium	Equity Value
At MBO			201.7	(10.0)	(8.1)	183.6	(21.4)	(3.8)	158.4
Rating adjustment	*x 7.0 ---> x 9.3*	*x 13.0 ---> x 18.2*	35.0			35.0			35.0
Results adjustment	*£27.6m ---> £19.7m*	*£12.0m ---> £7.1m*	(54.1)			(54.1)			(54.1)
Net debt / divs adjustment				4.6	4.9	9.5			9.5
Conv/ redemption adjustment							7.4	3.8	11.2
			182.5	(5.4)	(3.2)	173.9	(13.9)	0.0	160.0

Omivon's conversion and shareholding just before the IPO are as follows:

		Preference Shares		Conv. Ratio & premium	Ordinary Shares		Value	Total value
		No	£m		%	No	£m	£m
At end year 5 - pre conversion		25,160,384	25.2		30.0%	15,789,335	41.8	139.1
Conversion	44.7%	(11,244,756)	(11.2)	0.777902	10.0%	8,747,316	13.9	
Redeeming shares		13,915,629	13.9					
Redemption premium			0.0	0.0%				
Equity value adjustment							8.4	20.9
Final		**13,915,629**	**13.9**		**40.0%**	**24,536,651**	**64.0**	**160.0**

Final shareholdngs

	Management			Omivon			TOTAL
	Cost £m	Shares '000s	Holding	Cost £m	Shares '000s	Holding	Shares '000s
On day 1	2.0	34,989.5	70.0%	0.9	15,010.5	30.0%	50,000.0
End year 1	3.6	1,815.5	70.0%	1.6	778.8	30.0%	2,594.3
End year 5	5.6	36,805.0	70.0%	2.4	15,789.3	30.0%	52,594.3
Conversion				11.2	8,747.3	40.0%	8,747.3
Pre-IPO holdings	**5.6**	**36,805.0**	**60.0%**	**13.7**	**24,536.7**	**40.0%**	**61,341.6**

Exit proceeds analysis

		Cost	Shares '000s	Equity entry price £	Equity exit price £	Equity exit value £m	Omivon proceeds £m
Redemption of Prefs.		13.9		1.00	1.00		**13.9**
Pre-conversion shares		2.4	15,789.3	0.15	2.61	41.2	
Converted shares		11.2	8,747.3	1.29	2.61	22.8	
Omivon	27.9% IRR	27.6	24,536.7	1.12	2.61	64.0	**64.0**
Management		5.6	36,805.0	0.15	2.61	96.0	
		33.2	**61,341.6**	**0.31**	**2.61**	**160.0**	**77.9**

Both management and Omivon will be prevented, under the terms of the listing prospectus, from selling shares on the market during a 'lock-up' period, assumed, in this example, to be six months from the first share trading date. Omivon's final exit IRR will, therefore, depend on Rononi share performance during this period.

❸ Required cash to be raised

Rononi wants to raise net proceeds of approximately £70m for future capital investment opportunities. If £17m is immediately paid to Omivon (£13.9m non-converting Preference shares to be redeemed plus £3.2m accrued dividends), and fees and costs amount to 5%, then the float needs to be £92m (£70m = £92m x (1 – 5%) - £17m).

❹ Pricing

Management, via its investment holding company, wants to retain a 51% holding after the IPO, and so will need to subscribe for new shares to avoid dilution. A large part of the required £41.85m investment cost (£32.56m plus £9.29m if the Greenshoe option is exercised), will be funded by a new financial investor taking a stake in management's holding company. At a float price of £2.61 (£160m Equity Value / 61.34m shares), some 35.3m new shares will need to be issued to raise £92m.

1	Shares to be issued for required funding	Funding required			£92m
		Pre-IPO share price		see 4.	£2.61
		Shares to be issued		X	35,299,300
2	Management's required shares	Required share of float			35.4%
		x shares issued =		Y	12,481,800
3	Retail vs institutional allocation	Non-Management shares		X - Y	22,817,500
		Retail	30.0%		6,845,250
		Institutions	70.0%		15,972,250

4 Valuation	Latest EBITDA			£19.7m
	x multiple	x 9.3		£182.5m
	less: net debt + non-equity			(£22.5m)
	Equity value		A	£160.0m
	Cash from float			£92.1m
	Day 1 premium	10.0%		£25.2m
			C	£277.3m
	Current shares		B	61,341,628
	IPO shares (pre-greenshoe)			35,299,300
			D	96,640,928
	Average IPO price		A / B	£2.61
	Trading price (pre-greenshoe)		C / D	£2.87
5 Retail and bookbuild price	Discount to trading price			8%
	Bookbuild price			£2.64
	Discount to bookbuild price			£0.10
	Retail price			£2.54
	Retail IPO	£2.54		£17.4m
	Institutional IPO	£2.64		£42.1m
		£2.61		£59.5m
	Management IPO			£32.6m
				£92.1m

❺ Share allocations and final position

	IPO TO RAISE £92m BEFORE GREENSHOE					AFTER GREENSHOE			
Shareholder	Shares issued	Cash cost	Prefs redeemed		Shares	Shares issued	Cash cost		Shares
	#	£m	£m	%	#	#	£m	%	#
Management	12,481,800	(32.56)	-	51.0%	49,286,777	3,562,521	(9.29)	51.0%	52,849,298
Omivon			17.07	25.4%	24,536,651			23.7%	24,536,651
New investors	22,817,500	(59.52)		23.6%	22,817,500	3,422,625	(8.93)	25.3%	26,240,125
Total	35,299,300	(92.07)	17.07	100.0%	96,640,928	6,985,146	(18.22)	100.0%	103,626,075

GREENSHOE

Greenshoe size		
Required cash on IPO		92,072,680
less: Management share		(32,556,815)
IPO size for Greenshoe	£	59,515,865
Greenshoe at 15.0%	£	8,927,380
Shares issued at £2.61		3,422,625

Shares issued for Greenshoe		
Issued to Bankers	49.0%	3,422,625
Management subscription	51.0%	3,562,521
		6,985,146

The arranging bankers will be entitled to over-allocate shares (short selling using a stock lending agreement with an existing shareholder, in this case Omivon), which it will buy back (to cover its short position) during the 30 day period after the start of trading in Rononi shares, either in the market (if market demand needs to be stimulated to prevent a flagging price) or from Rononi at a fixed price under a Greenshoe option (when new shares will be issued). The Greenshoe is fixed at 15% of the cash raised from new investors (£59.5m), at the average price of £2.61.

FINAL SHARE ALLOCATIONS AND COST

	Price	Shares	£m
Management			
Subscription for main IPO at 35.4%	£ 2.61	12,481,800	32.56
Greenshoe	£ 2.61	3,562,521	9.29
		16,044,321	**41.85**
Other			
Public - Retail	£ 2.54	6,845,250	17.38
Public - Institutional	£ 2.64	15,972,250	42.14
Shares issued on main IPO	£ 2.61	22,817,500	59.52
Greenshoe	£ 2.61	3,422,625	8.93
		26,240,125	**68.44**

EQUITY VALUE / **VALUE SHARING**

		Price £	Shares	Value £m	Management	Omivon	Others
Value on IPO *		2.61	61,341,628	160.0	96.0	64.0	-
Main IPO		2.61	35,299,300	92.1			
Value after primary offering		2.61	96,640,928	252.1	128.6	64.0	59.5
Premium on day 1 of trading	10.0%	0.26		25.2			
Trading price		2.87	96,640,928	277.3	141.4	70.4	65.5
Greenshoe option		2.61	6,985,146	18.2			
		2.85	103,626,075	295.5	150.7	70.0	74.8

* = 9.3 x latest EBITDA (£19.7m) = £182.5m less net debt / prefs (£22.5m) = £160.0m

❻ Share Capital

	Pre-conversion	*Conversion*	*At IPO*	*IPO*	*Issue costs*	*Post IPO*
Number of shares	52,594,312	8,747,316	61,341,628	42,284,447		103,626,075
	£'000s	*£'000s*	*£'000s*	*£'000s*	*£'000s*	*£'000s*
Share Capital (£0.01 each)	525.9	87.5	613.4	422.8		1,036.3
Share premium	7,520.7	11,157.3	18,678.0	109,869.5	(5,514.6)	123,032.8
		11,244.8		110,292.3		
Redeeming		13,915.6		(13,915.6)		
Preference Shares		25,160.4				
Accrued dividends		3,157.1		(3,157.1)		
Cash retained				93,219.7 ***		
Costs at 5%				(5,514.6)		
Net				**87,705**		

	Shares	£m	
New shares issued pre-Greenshoe (=22.8m + 12.5m)	**35,299,300**	**92.07**	
less: redemption of pref shares + accrued divs		(17.07)	
	35,299,300	75.00	
Opening shares	61,341,628		
Pre-Greenshoe shares in issue	96,640,928	75.00	
Greenshoe	6,985,146	18.22	
Share + Retained cash (pre-costs / fees)	**103,626,075**	**93.22**	***

D4 VALUATION

Rononi Enterprises has identified an acquisition target, Tokan Ltd, and is preparing a valuation to determine the offer price for a majority holding of the unquoted shares. For its most recent financial year, Tokan's EBIT and EBITDA margins were 9% and 13%, respectively, on £55m of revenue. Net profits were £3.2m and net debt £26.1m.

The valuation will be based on a Discounted Cash Flow (DCF) approach, adjusted to take account of current market multiples. Rononi's estimate of Tokan's base case DCF Enterprise Value (stand-alone value for existing business, assuming marketable shares and no control) is £105.6m (85% in the Terminal Value), giving an Equity Value of £79.5m (see ❶). Scenario analysis suggests a likely Enterprise Value range of £47m (revenues 5% lower in each year than the base case, combined with administrative costs up to 1% higher in each year: Pessimistic A + Pessimistic C in ❺) to £150m (revenues 2-5% higher each year than in the base: Optimistic A in ❺).

The final Equity Value for a majority interest is estimated to be £72.8m (£7.28 per share), based on weighted DCF and multiple based valuations:

	Weighting	Equity Value
DCF Value	90%	£79.5 m
Trading multiples [1]	10%	£54.8 m
Value (weighted): minority quoted		*£77.0 m*
Illiquidity discount [2]		25%
Value: minority private		*£57.8 m*
Control Value (26.0%) [3]		£15.0 m
Value: majority private		*£72.8 m*
Shares in issue		10.0 m
Value per share (ignoring synergies)		**£7.28**

1. The multiple valuation is based on EBITDA and P/E multiples for comparable quoted companies (median of a sample of trading prices, reflecting minority holdings), applied to Tokan's most recent financial results.

	Tokan	Average Comparable Quoted Trading	
'Trailing' multiples	*Latest year £m*	*Multiple*	*Equity Value £m*
EBITDA	7.0	9.0 x	36.9
Profit After Tax	3.2	23.0 x	72.7
Median			**54.8**

The EBITDA multiple gives an Enterprise Value from which net debt of £26.1m is deducted.

2. The DCF valuation gives a fair value for a quoted holding (see Bruner (2004 p.457)), as the discount rate (when calculated using CAPM) is based on minority quoted prices (equity risk premium, betas). Since Tokan is private, an illiquidity discount for non-marketability is applied (to the DCF and multiples valuation).

3. The Control Value represents the estimated additional value that Rononi could create by exercising control over Tokan's existing investment and financing policies (extra DCF value arising due to management improvements and restructuring – rather than synergies).

❶ DCF VALUATION SUMMARY

The Discounted Cash Flow (DCF) Enterprise Value is estimated to be £105.6m, based on a 10 year Free Cash Flow forecast and a Terminal Value (85% of the Enterprise Value) that assumes year 10 cash flows grow 3% p.a. in perpetuity. This gives an Equity Value of £79.5m after net debt of £26.1m is deducted.

		£m
PV of yrs 1-10 Free Cash Flows, discounted at 9.36% - 10.69%	14.8%	15.6
PV of post yr 10 Free Cash Flows (Terminal Value)	85.2%	90.0
Today's DCF Enterprise Value	100.0%	105.6
less: gross debt (£26.1m) less surplus cash (£0.0m) - net debt		(26.1)
Today's DCF Equity Value		79.5

The discount rate is Tokan's Weighted Average Cost of Capital (WACC), which reduces over the 10 year forecast period until the target long term capital structure is reached (30% by year 9 – see ❸).

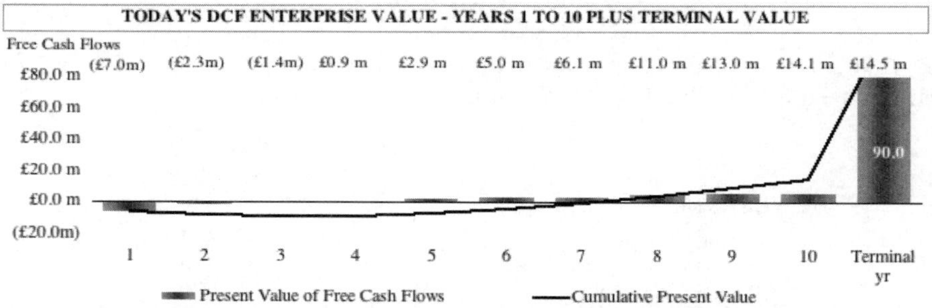

Extracts from the financial forecast are given below (see ❻ for more detail):

FORECAST YEAR	1	2	3	4	5	6	7	8	9	10
	£m	£m	£m	£m	£m	£m	£m	£m	£m	£m
Revenues	82.5	119.6	167.5	226.1	293.9	352.7	405.6	466.4	527.1	579.8
Pre-tax profits	(0.4)	2.7	5.9	10.8	16.8	21.1	24.2	28.5	32.6	35.6
Tangible fixed assets	47.3	51.9	57.3	63.5	70.9	79.4	89.3	97.2	106.4	117.1
Working capital	4.1	6.0	8.4	11.3	14.7	17.6	20.3	23.3	26.4	29.0
Operating Capital	51.4	57.9	65.6	74.8	85.5	97.0	109.6	120.5	132.7	146.0
Gross / Net debt (nil surplus cash)	35.3	39.8	43.5	45.1	45.4	48.5	51.5	64.4	66.5	68.5
Equity	16.1	18.0	22.2	29.7	40.2	48.6	58.1	56.1	66.2	77.5
Financial Capital	51.4	57.9	65.6	74.8	85.5	97.0	109.6	120.5	132.7	146.0
EBITDA	12.0	16.8	21.7	29.0	36.5	43.5	50.0	49.5	57.3	64.1
Capital investment	(18.1)	(17.2)	(20.3)	(23.8)	(27.8)	(31.4)	(35.8)	(29.2)	(33.5)	(38.2)
Taxes on operating cash flows	(0.8)	(1.8)	(2.7)	(4.3)	(5.8)	(7.1)	(8.0)	(9.4)	(10.8)	(11.8)
Free Cash Flows to the Firm	(7.0)	(2.3)	(1.4)	0.9	2.9	5.0	6.1	11.0	13.0	14.1
Debt funding	9.2	4.5	3.7	1.7	0.3	3.1	3.1	12.9	2.1	2.0
Net interest expenses (after tax)	(2.2)	(2.3)	(2.3)	(2.5)	(1.9)	(1.7)	(1.8)	(1.9)	(2.4)	(2.5)
Dividends paid	0.0	0.0	0.0	0.0	(1.3)	(6.4)	(7.4)	(21.9)	(12.7)	(13.6)
Net cash flows	0.0	0.0	0.0	0.0	(0.0)	(0.0)	0.0	0.0	0.0	0.0
Revenue growth rate	50.0%	45.0%	40.0%	35.0%	30.0%	20.0%	15.0%	15.0%	13.0%	10.0%
EBITDA / revenues	14.5%	14.0%	13.0%	12.8%	12.4%	12.3%	12.3%	10.6%	10.9%	11.1%
EBIT / revenues	3.4%	5.0%	5.5%	6.4%	6.6%	6.7%	6.6%	6.7%	6.8%	6.8%
Capex / revenues	20.0%	12.8%	10.7%	9.2%	8.3%	8.1%	8.2%	5.6%	5.8%	6.1%
Pre-tax return on opening capital	6.6%	11.7%	15.8%	21.9%	26.0%	27.5%	27.6%	28.5%	29.9%	29.5%
Pre-tax return on opening equity	-1.8%	11.3%	20.5%	29.1%	33.6%	33.4%	31.7%	34.9%	37.3%	34.7%
Debt / capital (book values)	68.6%	68.8%	66.2%	60.3%	53.1%	49.9%	47.0%	53.4%	50.1%	46.9%
Target debt / capital (market values)	10.0%	15.0%	20.0%	20.0%	25.0%	25.0%	30.0%	25.0%	30.0%	30.0%
Actual debt / capital (market values)	24.7%	28.5%	28.7%	28.3%	26.8%	25.0%	25.0%	25.0%	30.0%	30.0%
Cost of debt (pre-tax)	12.3%	9.3%	8.3%	8.3%	6.0%	5.4%	5.4%	5.4%	5.4%	5.4%
Cost of equity (geared)	11.4%	11.7%	11.7%	11.6%	11.5%	11.4%	11.4%	11.4%	11.8%	11.8%
Cost of capital (post-tax)(WACC)	10.7%	10.2%	10.0%	10.0%	9.6%	9.5%	9.5%	9.5%	9.4%	9.4%
Discount Factor	0.9034	0.8199	0.7455	0.6779	0.6187	0.5650	0.5160	0.4713	0.4309	0.3940

❷ DCF TERMINAL VALUE

The Terminal Value has been estimated assuming year 11 Free Cash Flows grow at 3.0% in perpetuity (formula **B1.28** in Appendix B1):

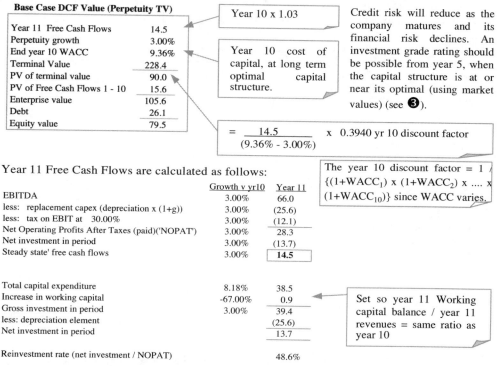

Base Case DCF Value (Perpetuity TV)

Year 11 Free Cash Flows	14.5
Perpetuity growth	3.00%
End year 10 WACC	9.36%
Terminal Value	228.4
PV of terminal value	90.0
PV of Free Cash Flows 1 - 10	15.6
Enterprise value	105.6
Debt	26.1
Equity value	79.5

Year 10 x 1.03

Year 10 cost of capital, at long term optimal capital structure.

$= \frac{14.5}{(9.36\% - 3.00\%)}$ x 0.3940 yr 10 discount factor

Credit risk will reduce as the company matures and its financial risk declines. An investment grade rating should be possible from year 5, when the capital structure is at or near its optimal (using market values) (see ❸).

The year 10 discount factor = 1 / $\{(1+WACC_1) \times (1+WACC_2) \times .... \times (1+WACC_{10})\}$ since WACC varies.

Year 11 Free Cash Flows are calculated as follows:

	Growth v yr10	Year 11
EBITDA	3.00%	66.0
less: replacement capex (depreciation x (1+g))	3.00%	(25.6)
less: tax on EBIT at 30.00%	3.00%	(12.1)
Net Operating Profits After Taxes (paid)('NOPAT')	3.00%	28.3
Net investment in period	3.00%	(13.7)
Steady state' free cash flows	3.00%	**14.5**

Total capital expenditure	8.18%	38.5
Increase in working capital	-67.00%	0.9
Gross investment in period	3.00%	39.4
less: depreciation element		(25.6)
Net investment in period		13.7
Reinvestment rate (net investment / NOPAT)		48.6%

Set so year 11 Working capital balance / year 11 revenues = same ratio as year 10

(Note: it is assumed that capital expenditure eligible for tax relief is equivalent to the annual depreciation charge, to simplify matters. Tax on EBIT is, therefore, at the assumed 30% statutory rate).

The following diagram shows that, whilst 85% of the £105.6m Enterprise Value derives from the terminal period (after year 10), most of this is concentrated in the earlier terminal period years (the present value of Free Cash Flows, including years 1 – 10, weighted by time period - the 'Duration' - is 25 years). Also shown is cumulative Enterprise Value in terms of the value of year 1 cash flows in perpetuity plus the value of the growth in Free Cash Flows in each period in perpetuity (71% of the Enterprise Value derives from cash flow growth over years 1 to 10, with the balance coming from the 3% growth from year 11 in perpetuity).

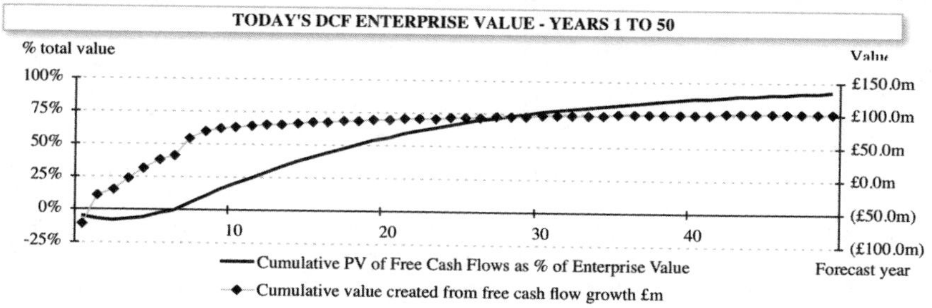

	1	2	3	4	5	6	7	8	9	10
Cash Flow	(7.0)	(2.3)	(1.4)	0.9	2.9	5.0	6.1	11.0	13.0	14.1
Change in free cash flow	(7.0)	4.7	0.9	2.2	2.1	2.1	1.1	4.8	2.0	1.1
Sum of discount factors in perpetuity	10.35	9.45	8.63	7.88	7.20	6.59	6.02	5.51	5.03	4.60
PV change in free cash flow in perpetuity	(72.1)	44.5	7.8	17.4	14.8	13.9	6.7	26.7	10.2	5.1
Cumulative	(72.1)	(27.6)	(19.8)	(2.4)	12.4	26.3	33.0	59.7	69.9	75.0
% of enterprise value	-68.2%	-26.1%	-18.8%	-2.2%	11.8%	24.9%	31.3%	56.5%	66.2%	71.0%

The Return On Invested Capital has the following profile over years 10 – 50 (i.e. the first 40 years of the Terminal Period)(see **B1.24** – **B1.26** in Appendix B1):

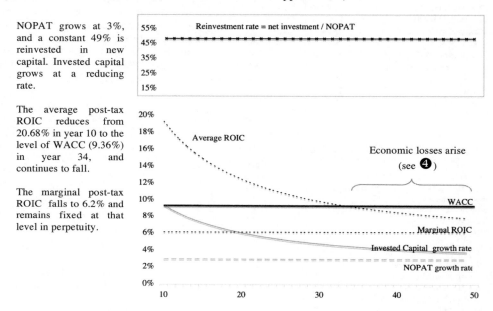

NOPAT grows at 3%, and a constant 49% is reinvested in new capital. Invested capital grows at a reducing rate.

The average post-tax ROIC reduces from 20.68% in year 10 to the level of WACC (9.36%) in year 34, and continues to fall.

The marginal post-tax ROIC falls to 6.2% and remains fixed at that level in perpetuity.

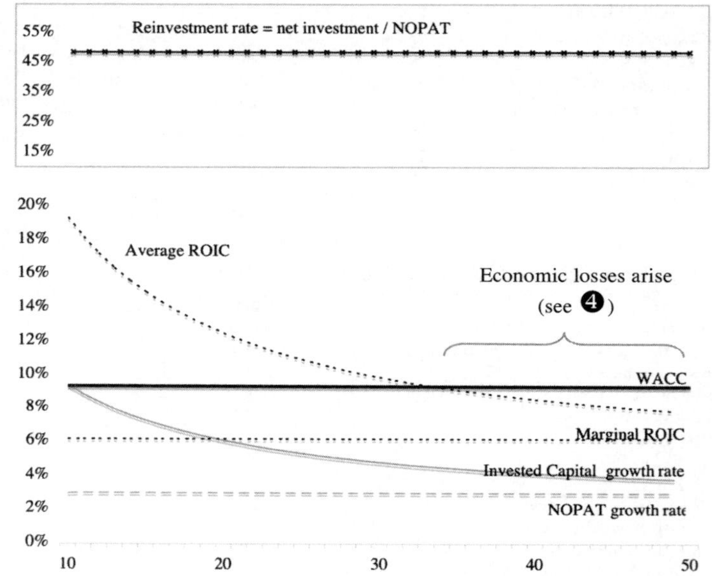

❸ CAPITAL STRUCTURE & COST OF CAPITAL

This example illustrates the effect of a changing capital structure on the Cost of Capital (WACC), as discussed in Appendix B1, partly based on the approach outlined by Damodaran (2001 Ch. 19) applied to each period. The rating ratios and debt premium figures are illustrative, and the initial Cost of Debt excessively high, in order to demonstrate the effect.

FORECAST YEAR			1	2	3	4	5	6	7	8	9	10
CALCULATING WACC												
Risk Free Rate			4.75%	4.75%	4.75%	4.75%	4.75%	4.75%	4.75%	4.75%	4.75%	4.75%
Equity Risk Premium			4.50%	4.50%	4.50%	4.50%	4.50%	4.50%	4.50%	4.50%	4.50%	4.50%
Asset (ungeared beta)			1.20	1.20	1.20	1.20	1.20	1.20	1.20	1.20	1.20	1.20
Ungeared cost of equity			10.15%	10.15%	10.15%	10.15%	10.15%	10.15%	10.15%	10.15%	10.15%	10.15%
Gearing - gross debt / equity ratio (market values)			32.8%	39.8%	40.3%	39.4%	36.6%	33.3%	33.3%	33.3%	42.9%	42.9%
Equity beta (zero debt beta)			1.48	1.53	1.54	1.53	1.51	1.48	1.48	1.48	1.56	1.56
Geared Cost of equity			*11.39%*	*11.66%*	*11.67%*	*11.64%*	*11.53%*	*11.41%*	*11.41%*	*11.41%*	*11.77%*	*11.77%*
Debt beta applicable to equity risk premium			1.67	1.00	0.78	0.78	0.28	0.13	0.13	0.13	0.13	0.13
Debt premium over risk free rate			7.50%	4.50%	3.50%	3.50%	1.25%	0.60%	0.60%	0.60%	0.60%	0.60%
Cost of debt (required return)			12.25%	9.25%	8.25%	8.25%	6.00%	5.35%	5.35%	5.35%	5.35%	5.35%
Tax rate			30.0%	30.0%	30.0%	30.0%	30.0%	30.0%	30.0%	30.0%	30.0%	30.0%
After tax cost of debt			*8.58%*	*6.48%*	*5.78%*	*5.78%*	*4.20%*	*3.75%*	*3.75%*	*3.75%*	*3.75%*	*3.75%*
Leverage - gearing / (1 + gearing)			24.7%	28.5%	28.7%	28.3%	26.8%	25.0%	25.0%	25.0%	30.0%	30.0%
WACC			**10.69%**	**10.18%**	**9.98%**	**9.98%**	**9.57%**	**9.49%**	**9.49%**	**9.49%**	**9.36%**	**9.36%**
Free Cash Flows	£m		(7.0)	(2.3)	(1.4)	0.9	2.9	5.0	6.1	11.0	13.0	14.1
Terminal value												228.4
Enterprise value	£m	105.6	123.8	138.7	153.9	168.4	181.6	193.8	206.1	214.6	221.7	228.4
Debt		26.1	35.3	39.8	43.5	45.1	45.4	48.5	51.5	64.4	66.5	68.5
Equity (DCF market value)	£m	79.5	88.5	98.9	110.4	123.3	136.2	145.4	154.5	150.3	155.2	159.9
Leverage ratio (market values) - start of year			**24.7%**	**28.5%**	**28.7%**	**28.3%**	**26.8%**	**25.0%**	**25.0%**	**25.0%**	**30.0%**	**30.0%**

A DCF Enterprise Value needs to be calculated as at each year end of the forecast period (the Terminal Value is based on the perpetuity method), in order to determine the leverage ratio using market values.

FORECAST YEAR	0	1	2	3	4	5	6	7	8	9	10
WACC		10.69%	10.18%	9.98%	9.98%	9.57%	9.49%	9.49%	9.49%	9.36%	9.36%
Free Cash Flows to the Firm		(7.0)	(2.3)	(1.4)	0.9	2.9	5.0	6.1	11.0	13.0	14.1
PV of future FCF at each year	15.6	24.2	28.9	33.2	35.6	36.1	34.5	31.7	23.7	12.9	0.0
PV of Terminal Value at each year	90.0	99.6	109.8	120.7	132.8	145.5	159.3	174.4	191.0	208.8	228.4
Enterprise Value	105.6	123.8	138.7	153.9	168.4	181.6	193.8	206.1	214.6	221.7	228.4
Net Debt	(26.1)	(35.3)	(39.8)	(43.5)	(45.1)	(45.4)	(48.5)	(51.5)	(64.4)	(66.5)	(68.5)
Equity Value	79.5	88.5	98.9	110.4	123.3	136.2	145.4	154.5	150.3	155.2	159.9

The target capital structure has been estimated as follows:

1. for a range of leverage ratios (market value debt / DCF Enterprise Value), interest, 'Funds Flow' and debt coverage ratios are calculated to derive a likely credit rating (based on the 'worst' ratio) and required debt premium as at each year for each level of capital structure, based on an assumed relationship between debt premium and the rating (the table to the right is illustrative – the ratios and debt premium for ratings below investment grade BBB are somewhat extreme in order to illustrate the 'migration' to investment grade status);

Rating	*Min EBIT / Interest*	*Min Funds Flow / Debt*	*Max Debt / EBITDA*	*Debt Premium*
AAA	20.00 x	215.0%	0.20 x	0.25%
AA	13.50 x	65.0%	1.00 x	0.40%
A+	8.00 x	50.0%	1.15 x	0.60%
A	6.50 x	45.0%	1.20 x	0.90%
A-	5.00 x	40.0%	1.30 x	1.25%
BBB	4.50 x	30.0%	1.45 x	2.00%
BB	2.25 x	20.0%	3.50 x	3.50%
B+	1.75 x	15.0%	4.45 x	4.50%
B	1.00 x	10.5%	5.40 x	6.00%
B-	0.75 x	5.0%	6.35 x	7.50%
CCC	0.50 x	3.5%	7.30 x	10.00%
CC	0.30 x	1.0%	8.30 x	11.50%
C	0.10 x	0.0%	9.30 x	12.00%
D	0.00 x	0.0%	10.30 x	14.00%

Funds Flow = EBITDA less operating taxes paid

2. the target leverage or capital ratio is that which gives the lowest WACC.

FORECAST YEAR	Debt ratio (mkt values) start of year	1	2	3	4	5	6	7	8	9	10
EBIT / gross interest	10.0%	3.20 x	9.07 x	12.35 x	18.13 x	22.44 x	25.20 x	26.82 x	29.44 x	32.56 x	34.33 x
	15.0%	1.64 x	3.92 x	7.80 x	11.64 x	14.96 x	16.80 x	17.88 x	19.63 x	21.71 x	22.89 x
	20.0%	1.23 x	2.94 x	4.00 x	8.73 x	10.80 x	12.13 x	12.91 x	14.72 x	16.28 x	17.17 x
	25.0%	0.72 x	2.10 x	3.20 x	5.53 x	8.18 x	9.70 x	10.33 x	11.34 x	12.54 x	13.22 x
	30.0%	0.60 x	1.51 x	2.67 x	3.77 x	5.71 x	7.21 x	8.15 x	8.42 x	10.45 x	11.02 x
	35.0%	0.46 x	1.29 x	2.04 x	3.23 x	4.00 x	4.49 x	5.85 x	5.25 x	7.10 x	8.42 x
	40.0%	0.41 x	0.99 x	1.54 x	2.83 x	3.50 x	3.93 x	4.19 x	4.59 x	5.08 x	6.55 x
	45.0%	0.36 x	0.73 x	1.37 x	2.24 x	3.11 x	3.50 x	3.72 x	4.08 x	4.52 x	4.76 x
	50.0%	0.32 x	0.66 x	1.23 x	1.74 x	2.80 x	3.15 x	3.35 x	3.68 x	4.07 x	4.29 x
Funds Flow From Operations / debt (EBITDA less operating taxes paid)	10.0%	105.7%	120.8%	136.7%	160.4%	182.2%	200.5%	216.6%	194.8%	216.8%	236.0%
	15.0%	70.5%	80.5%	91.1%	107.0%	121.5%	133.7%	144.4%	129.9%	144.5%	157.3%
	20.0%	52.9%	60.4%	68.3%	80.2%	91.1%	100.3%	108.3%	97.4%	108.4%	118.0%
	25.0%	42.3%	48.3%	54.7%	64.2%	72.9%	80.2%	86.6%	77.9%	86.7%	94.4%
	30.0%	35.2%	40.3%	45.6%	53.5%	60.7%	66.8%	72.2%	64.9%	72.3%	78.7%
	35.0%	30.2%	34.5%	39.0%	45.8%	52.1%	57.3%	61.9%	55.7%	61.9%	67.4%
	40.0%	26.4%	30.2%	34.2%	40.1%	45.6%	50.1%	54.1%	48.7%	54.2%	59.0%
	45.0%	23.5%	26.8%	30.4%	35.7%	40.5%	44.6%	48.1%	43.3%	48.2%	52.4%
	50.0%	21.1%	24.2%	27.3%	32.1%	36.4%	40.1%	43.3%	39.0%	43.4%	47.2%
Gross Debt / EBITDA	10.0%	0.88 x	0.74 x	0.64 x	0.53 x	0.46 x	0.42 x	0.39 x	0.42 x	0.37 x	0.35 x
	15.0%	1.32 x	1.11 x	0.96 x	0.80 x	0.69 x	0.63 x	0.58 x	0.62 x	0.56 x	0.52 x
	20.0%	1.76 x	1.48 x	1.28 x	1.06 x	0.92 x	0.84 x	0.78 x	0.83 x	0.75 x	0.69 x
	25.0%	2.20 x	1.85 x	1.60 x	1.33 x	1.15 x	1.04 x	0.97 x	1.04 x	0.94 x	0.86 x
	30.0%	2.64 x	2.22 x	1.92 x	1.59 x	1.38 x	1.25 x	1.16 x	1.25 x	1.12 x	1.04 x
	35.0%	3.08 x	2.59 x	2.24 x	1.86 x	1.61 x	1.46 x	1.36 x	1.46 x	1.31 x	1.21 x
	40.0%	3.52 x	2.96 x	2.56 x	2.12 x	1.84 x	1.67 x	1.55 x	1.66 x	1.50 x	1.38 x
	45.0%	3.96 x	3.33 x	2.88 x	2.39 x	2.07 x	1.88 x	1.74 x	1.87 x	1.68 x	1.56 x
	50.0%	4.40 x	3.69 x	3.20 x	2.65 x	2.31 x	2.09 x	1.94 x	2.08 x	1.87 x	1.73 x

FORECAST YEAR	Debt ratio (mkt values) start of year	1	2	3	4	5	6	7	8	9	10
Possible credit rating	10.0%	BB	**A+**	**A+**	**AA**	**AA**	**AA**	**AA**	**AA**	**AA**	**AA**
	15.0%	B	BB	**A**	**A+**	**AA**	**AA**	**AA**	**AA**	**AA**	**AA**
Shaded = Investment Grade	20.0%	B	BB	BB	**A+**	**A+**	**A+**	**A+**	**AA**	**AA**	**AA**
	25.0%	CCC	B+	BB	**BBB**	**A**	**A+**	**A+**	**A+**	**A+**	**A+**
	30.0%	CCC	B	BB	BB	**BBB**	**A-**	**A**	**A-**	**A+**	**A+**
	35.0%	CC	B	B+	BB	BB	BB	**BBB**	BB	**BBB**	**A-**
	40.0%	CC	B-	B	BB	BB	BB	BB	BB	BB	**BBB**
	45.0%	CC	CCC	B	B+	BB	BB	BB	BB	BB	BB
	50.0%	CC	CCC	B	B	BB	BB	BB	BB	BB	BB
Resulting debt premium	10.0%	3.50%	0.60%	0.60%	0.40%	0.40%	0.40%	0.40%	0.40%	0.40%	0.40%
	15.0%	6.00%	3.50%	0.90%	0.60%	0.40%	0.40%	0.40%	0.40%	0.40%	0.40%
	20.0%	6.00%	3.50%	3.50%	0.60%	0.60%	0.60%	0.60%	0.40%	0.40%	0.40%
	25.0%	10.00%	4.50%	3.50%	2.00%	0.90%	0.60%	0.60%	0.60%	0.60%	0.60%
	30.0%	10.00%	6.00%	3.50%	3.50%	2.00%	1.25%	0.90%	1.25%	0.60%	0.60%
	35.0%	11.50%	6.00%	4.50%	3.50%	3.50%	3.50%	2.00%	3.50%	2.00%	1.25%
	40.0%	11.50%	7.50%	6.00%	3.50%	3.50%	3.50%	3.50%	3.50%	3.50%	2.00%
	45.0%	11.50%	10.00%	6.00%	4.50%	3.50%	3.50%	3.50%	3.50%	3.50%	3.50%
	50.0%	11.50%	10.00%	6.00%	6.00%	3.50%	3.50%	3.50%	3.50%	3.50%	3.50%
Resulting WACC (showing min.)	10.0%	**10.09%**	**9.89%**	9.89%	9.87%	9.87%	9.87%	9.87%	9.87%	9.87%	9.87%
	15.0%	10.32%	10.06%	**9.79%**	9.76%	9.74%	9.74%	9.74%	9.74%	9.74%	9.74%
	20.0%	10.38%	10.03%	10.03%	**9.63%**	9.63%	9.63%	9.63%	9.60%	9.60%	9.60%
	25.0%	11.14%	10.18%	10.00%	9.74%	**9.55%**	**9.49%**	9.49%	**9.49%**	9.49%	9.49%
	30.0%	11.34%	10.50%	9.97%	9.97%	9.66%	9.50%	**9.43%**	9.50%	**9.36%**	**9.36%**
	35.0%	11.90%	10.55%	10.19%	9.94%	9.94%	9.94%	9.57%	9.94%	9.57%	9.39%
	40.0%	12.15%	11.03%	10.61%	9.91%	9.91%	9.91%	9.91%	9.91%	9.91%	9.49%
	45.0%	12.40%	11.93%	10.67%	10.20%	9.88%	9.88%	9.88%	9.88%	9.88%	9.88%
	50.0%	12.65%	12.13%	10.73%	10.73%	9.85%	9.85%	9.85%	9.85%	9.85%	9.85%
TARGET											
Leverage ratio (start of year)		10.00%	10.00%	15.00%	20.00%	25.00%	25.00%	30.00%	25.00%	30.00%	30.00%
Rating		**BB**	**A+**	**A**	**A+**	**A**	**A+**	**A**	**A+**	**A+**	**A+**
Target WACC (minimum)		**10.09%**	**9.89%**	**9.79%**	**9.63%**	**9.55%**	**9.49%**	**9.43%**	**9.49%**	**9.36%**	**9.36%**
ACTUAL											
Leverage ratio (start of year)		24.7%	28.5%	28.7%	28.3%	26.8%	25.0%	25.0%	25.0%	30.0%	30.0%
EBIT / gross interest		0.87 x	1.84 x	2.79 x	4.01 x	7.19 x	9.70 x	10.33 x	11.34 x	10.45 x	11.02 x
FFO / gross debt		42.8%	42.4%	47.6%	56.8%	68.0%	80.2%	86.6%	77.9%	72.3%	78.7%
Gross debt / EBITDA		2.17 x	2.11 x	1.83 x	1.50 x	1.24 x	1.04 x	0.97 x	1.04 x	1.12 x	1.04 x
Book debt ratio (start of year)		61.4%	68.6%	68.8%	66.2%	60.3%	53.1%	49.9%	47.0%	53.4%	50.1%
Rating		**B-**	**B+**	**BB**	**BB**	**A-**	**A+**	**A+**	**A+**	**A+**	**A+**
Actual WACC		**10.69%**	**10.18%**	**9.98%**	**9.98%**	**9.57%**	**9.49%**	**9.49%**	**9.49%**	**9.36%**	**9.36%**

Cost of Capital (WACC)

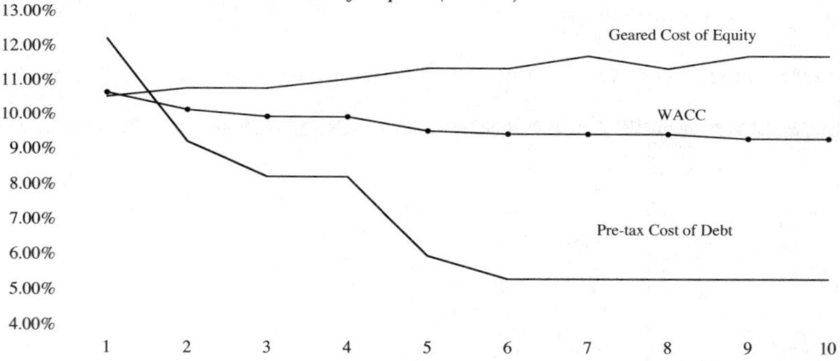

❹ ALTERNATIVE VALUATION APPROACHES

ENTERPRISE VALUE : ECONOMIC PROFITS (WACC)

The Enterprise Value is also equal to the book value of Invested Capital (and non-operating assets) plus the present value of future 'Economic Profits' (also known as 'Economic Value Added', or EVA^{TM} – see **B1.24** and Valuation Method **III** in Appendix B1):

		£m
Current Invested Capital (= book value of fixed assets and operating working capital)		42.5
Present Value of yrs 1-10 economic profit, discounted at 9.36% - 10.69%	see below	30.6
Present Value of year 11 economic profit in perpetuity discounted at 9.36%	see below	61.4
Present Value of terminal economic profit due to growth discounted at 9.36%		(29.0)
Enterprise value		**105.6**

Forecast period

Year	(ROIC -	WACC)	x Opening Invested Capital	= Economic Profit	PV discounting at WACC
1	4.59%	10.69%	42.5	(2.6)	(2.3)
2	8.18%	10.18%	51.4	(1.0)	(0.8)
3	11.08%	9.98%	57.9	0.6	0.5
4	15.33%	9.98%	65.6	3.5	2.4
5	18.20%	9.57%	74.8	6.5	4.0
6	19.28%	9.49%	85.5	8.4	4.7
7	19.31%	9.49%	97.0	9.5	4.9
8	19.95%	9.49%	109.6	11.5	5.4
9	20.91%	9.36%	120.5	13.9	6.0
10	20.68%	9.36%	132.7	15.0	5.9
Forecast period economic profit					**30.6**

Terminal Period

Year 11 NOPAT		28.3
Year 11 opening capital	÷	146.0
ROIC average	=	19.36%
less: WACC	–	9.36%
Economic profit %	=	9.99%
x Year 11 capitall = economic profit		14.6
Valued in perpetuity (= / 9.36%)		155.9
Year 10 discount factor	x	0.3940
PV of Year 11 Economic Profit (received in perpetuity)		**61.4**

Economic loses are generated in those years in the Terminal period when the average post-tax ROIC is less than WACC (see ❷). The PV of the Terminal period Economic Profits (32.40 = 61.4 – 29.0) can also be shown as follows:

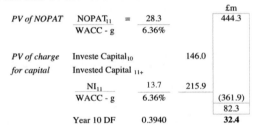

					£m
PV of NOPAT	$\frac{NOPAT_{11}}{WACC - g}$	=	$\frac{28.3}{6.36\%}$		444.3
PV of charge for capital	Investe Capital$_{10}$			146.0	
	Invested Capital $_{11+}$				
	$\frac{NI_{11}}{WACC - g}$		$\frac{13.7}{6.36\%}$	215.9	(361.9)
					82.3
	Year 10 DF		0.3940		**32.4**

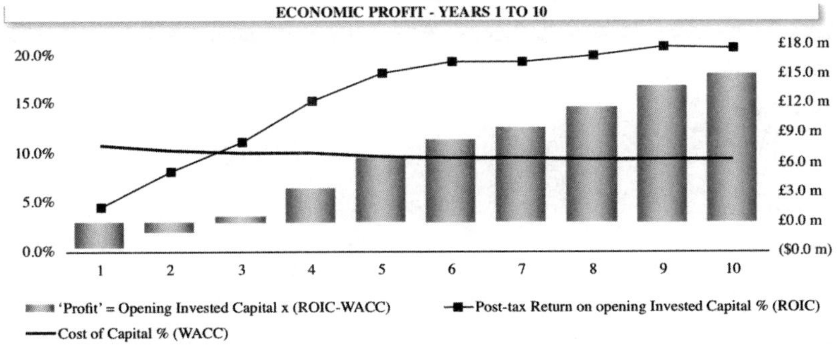

ENTERPRISE VALUE : TAX BENEFITS (UNGEARED COST OF EQUITY)

The DCF Enterprise Value (using WACC) can be broken down into a debt free component (Free Cash Flows discounted at the cost of capital if debt free, i.e. ungeared Cost of Equity) and a tax 'shield' component (value of tax relief on debt interest discounted at the ungeared Cost of Equity) (see Valuation Method **VI** in Appendix B1). Although shown slightly differently below, the tax component can be shown as:

Tax relief cash flow = Opening debt x (Ungeared Cost of Equity x t – p(1-t))
where t = tax rate on debt interest, p = Debt Risk Premium (pre-tax Cost of Debt – risk free rate)

FORECAST YEAR		1	2	3	4	5	6	7	8	9	10
Cost of Equity (ungeared)		10.15%	10.15%	10.15%	10.15%	10.15%	10.15%	10.15%	10.15%	10.15%	10.15%
Discount factor		0.9079	0.9079	0.9079	0.9079	0.9079	0.9079	0.9079	0.9079	0.9079	0.9079
FREE CASH FLOW COMPONENT											
Free Cash Flows		(7.0)	(2.3)	(1.4)	0.9	2.9	5.0	6.1	11.0	13.0	14.1
PV at ungeared cost of equity at time 0	**92.3**	(6.3)	(1.9)	(1.0)	0.6	1.8	2.8	3.1	5.1	5.4	5.4
PV at each year end	*92.3*	*108.6*	*121.9*	*135.6*	*148.5*	*160.7*	*172.0*	*183.3*	*190.9*	*197.3*	*203.2*
FREE CASH FLOW COMPONENT											
Enterprise Value at start of year		105.6	123.8	138.7	153.9	168.4	181.6	193.8	206.1	214.6	221.7
Debt / Enterprise Value at start of year		24.71%	28.49%	28.71%	28.25%	26.80%	25.00%	25.00%	25.00%	30.00%	30.00%
Debt premium (pre-tax cost of debt - risk free rate)		7.50%	4.50%	3.50%	3.50%	1.25%	0.60%	0.60%	0.60%	0.60%	0.60%
Rate of tax relief on debt		30.00%	30.00%	30.00%	30.00%	30.00%	30.00%	30.00%	30.00%	30.00%	30.00%
Enterprise Value x Ungeared Cost of Equity x tax rate		3.2	3.8	4.2	4.7	5.1	5.5	5.9	6.3	6.5	6.8
less: Enterprise Value x debt premium x (1-tax rate))		(5.5)	(3.9)	(3.4)	(3.8)	(1.5)	(0.8)	(0.8)	(0.9)	(0.9)	(0.9)
Debt reduction element		(2.3)	(0.1)	0.8	0.9	3.7	4.8	5.1	5.4	5.6	5.8
x opening debt ratio = tax shield on debt		(0.6)	(0.0)	0.2	0.3	1.0	1.2	1.3	1.4	1.7	1.7
PV of Tax Shield at ungeared cost of equity at time	**13.3**	(0.5)	(0.0)	0.2	0.2	0.6	0.7	0.6	0.6	0.7	0.7
PV at each year end	*13.3*	*15.2*	*16.8*	*18.3*	*19.8*	*20.9*	*21.8*	*22.7*	*23.7*	*24.4*	*25.2*
Enterprise value	**105.6**	**123.8**	**138.7**	**153.9**	**168.4**	**181.6**	**193.8**	**206.1**	**214.6**	**221.7**	**228.4**

(see ❸)

TERMINAL VALUES

		Year 10	*Year 11 on*	*Tax benefit*	*Free Cash Flow*
Enterprise Value	E	228.4	Grows 3% p.a.		
Ungeared Cost of Equity	K	10.15%	No change		
Debt premium	p	0.60%	No change		
Leverage	L	30.00%	No change		
Tax rate	t	30.00%	No change		
Year 11 tax shield component = EL [K t - p(1 - t)] = where EL is the value of debt				1.8	14.5
Growing in perpetuity at 3% p.a. discounted at 10.15% k =				**25.2**	**203.2**

EQUITY VALUE : EQUITY CASH FLOWS (GEARED COST OF EQUITY)

The Equity Value can be derived directly by discounting equity cash flows (in this example, they are paid out as dividends) at the geared Cost of Equity. The 'Residual Income', or 'Abnormal Earnings', is similar to Economic Profits but relates to equity returns rather than total returns to equity and debt holders. (See Methods **IV** and **V** in Appendix B1).

FORECAST YEAR		1	2	3	4	5	6	7	8	9	10
Cost of Equity (geared) (Ke)		11.39%	11.66%	11.67%	11.64%	11.53%	11.41%	11.41%	11.41%	11.77%	11.77%
Discount factor		0.8977	0.8040	0.7200	0.6449	0.5782	0.5190	0.4659	0.4181	0.3741	0.3347
EQUITY CASH FLOWS											
Free Cash Flows to Equity (dividends)		0.0	0.0	0.0	0.0	1.3	6.4	7.4	21.9	12.7	13.6
PV at geared cost of equity at time 0	79.5	0.0	0.0	0.0	0.0	0.7	3.3	3.4	9.2	4.8	4.6
PV at each year end	*79.5*	*88.5*	*98.9*	*110.4*	*123.3*	*136.2*	*145.4*	*154.5*	*150.3*	*155.2*	*159.9*
RESIDUAL INCOME / ABNORMAL EARNINGS											
Opening book value of equity (BVe)		16.4	16.1	18.0	22.2	29.7	40.2	48.6	58.1	56.1	66.2
Net profits	÷	(0.3)	1.9	4.1	7.5	11.7	14.8	16.9	19.9	22.8	25.0
Return on equity (ROE)	=	-1.74%	11.92%	22.80%	34.06%	39.46%	36.85%	34.84%	34.32%	40.61%	37.70%
Residual income (=BVe x (ROE - Ke)) at time 0		(2.2)	0.0	2.0	5.0	8.3	10.2	11.4	13.3	16.2	17.2
PV at each year end	63.1	72.4	80.8	88.2	93.5	96.0	96.8	96.4	94.1	89.0	82.3
Closing book value of equity	16.4	16.1	18.0	22.2	29.7	40.2	48.6	58.1	56.1	66.2	77.5
Equity Value at each year end	*79.5*	*88.5*	*98.9*	*110.4*	*123.3*	*136.2*	*145.4*	*154.5*	*150.3*	*155.2*	*159.9*

Year 10 dividends	13.6
Growth rate	3.00%
Year 11 dividends	14.0
Perpetuity growth rate	3.00%
Geared Cost of Equity	11.77%
Growing perpetuity value	159.9

❺ VALUATION SENSITIVITIES

The base case Enterprise Value ranges from £67.8m to £215.1m (-36% to +104% of the base case), if the equity risk premium component of WACC and the perpetuity growth rate for the Terminal Value are as shown to the right.

EQUITY RISK PREMIUM	TERMINAL PERPETUITY GROWTH RATE 1.0%	3.0%	5.0%
5.50%	67.8	83.5	110.6
4.50%	82.8	**105.6**	149.3
3.50%	103.0	137.8	215.1

Assuming WACC and the perpetuity growth rates are unchanged from the base case, the Enterprise Value ranges from £47m (pessimistic scenario A + C combined) to £231 (optimistic scenario A + B). The very optimistic scenario is shown for illustrative purposes.

Operating assumptions - varation (+ / -) around the Base Case

Base Case +/-	1	2	3	4	5	6	7	8
Revenue Growth rate A								
Very Optimistic	+ 10.0%	+ 10.0%	+ 10.0%	+ 10.0%	+ 5.0%	+ 5.0%	+ 5.0%	+ 5.0%
Optimistic	+ 5.0%	+ 5.0%	+ 5.0%	+ 5.0%	+ 2.0%	+ 2.0%	+ 2.0%	+ 2.0%
Prudent (=Base Case)	*50.0%*	*45.0%*	*40.0%*	*35.0%*	*30.0%*	*20.0%*	*15.0%*	*15.0%*
Pessimistic	- 5.0%	- 5.0%	- 5.0%	- 5.0%	- 5.0%	- 5.0%	- 5.0%	- 5.0%
Gross Profit Margin - B								
Very Optimistic	+ 4.0%	+ 4.1%	+ 3.5%	+ 4.2%	+ 4.1%	+ 4.3%	+ 1.3%	+ 3.0%
Optimistic	+ 2.0%	+ 2.1%	+ 1.5%	+ 2.2%	+ 2.1%	+ 2.3%	- 0.2%	+ 1.0%
Prudent (=Base Case)	*30.0%*	*29.9%*	*29.5%*	*28.8%*	*27.9%*	*27.7%*	*27.7%*	*26.0%*
Pessimistic	+ 0.0%	+ 0.0%	+ 0.0%	+ 0.0%	+ 0.0%	+ 0.0%	+ 0.0%	- 0.2%
Indirect Costs / Revs - C								
Very Optimistic	- 2.0%	- 2.0%	- 2.0%	- 1.6%	- 2.1%	- 2.0%	- 2.0%	- 2.2%
Optimistic	- 1.0%	- 1.0%	- 1.0%	- 0.6%	- 1.1%	- 1.0%	- 1.0%	- 1.2%
Prudent (=Base Case)	*10.0%*	*11.0%*	*12.0%*	*11.6%*	*11.1%*	*11.0%*	*11.0%*	*11.2%*
Pessimistic	+ 1.0%	+ 1.0%	+ 1.0%	+ 0.4%	+ 0.9%	+ 1.0%	+ 1.0%	+ 0.8%
Capex / Revenues - D								
Very Optimistic	- 10.0%	- 3.8%	- 1.7%	- 1.2%	- 0.8%	- 1.1%	- 1.7%	- 0.6%
Optimistic	- 10.0%	- 2.8%	- 1.7%	- 0.2%	- 0.3%	- 0.6%	- 1.2%	- 0.1%
Prudent (=Base Case)	*20.0%*	*12.8%*	*10.7%*	*9.2%*	*8.3%*	*8.1%*	*8.2%*	*5.6%*
Pessimistic	+ 0.0%	+ 0.2%	+ 0.3%	+ 0.3%	- 0.3%	- 0.1%	- 0.2%	+ 0.4%

Sensitivities for years 9 and 10 are the same as for year 8

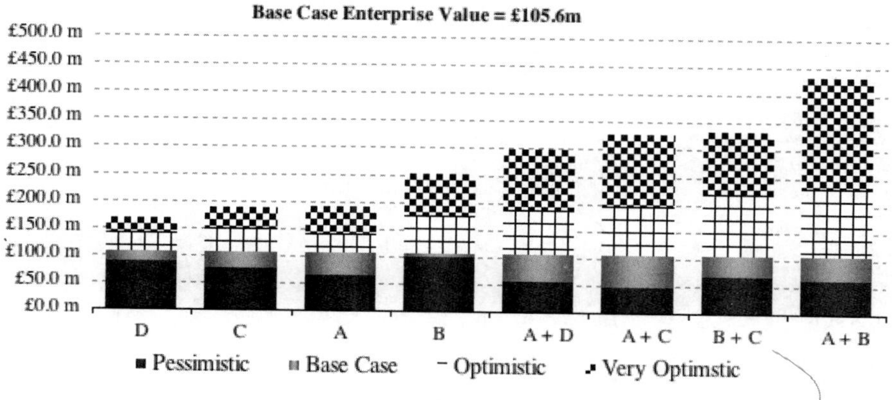

The impact on the EBITDA margin of B + C, for example, is as follows:

Base Case +/-	1	2	3	4	5	6	7	8
Very Optimistic	+ 6.0%	+ 6.1%	+ 5.5%	+ 5.8%	+ 6.2%	+ 6.3%	+ 3.3%	+ 5.2%
Optimistic	+ 3.0%	+ 3.1%	+ 2.5%	+ 2.8%	+ 3.2%	+ 3.3%	+ 0.8%	+ 2.2%
Prudent (=Base Case)	14.5%	14.0%	13.0%	12.8%	12.4%	12.3%	12.3%	10.6%
Pessimistic	- 1.0%	- 1.0%	- 1.0%	- 0.4%	- 0.9%	- 1.0%	- 1.0%	- 1.0%

❻ BASE CASE FINANCIAL FORECASTS

FORECAST YEAR	1	2	3	4	5	6	7	8	9	10
	£m	£m	£m	£m	£m	£m	£m	£m	£m	£m
PROFIT & LOSS ACCOUNT										
Revenues	82.5	119.6	167.5	226.1	293.9	352.7	405.6	466.4	527.1	579.8
Cost of sales	(57.8)	(83.9)	(118.1)	(161.0)	(211.9)	(255.0)	(293.3)	(345.2)	(390.0)	(429.0)
Gross Profit	24.8	35.8	49.4	65.1	82.0	97.7	112.4	121.3	137.0	150.7
General and administrative expenses	(12.8)	(19.0)	(27.7)	(36.1)	(45.5)	(54.2)	(62.4)	(71.8)	(79.7)	(86.7)
Depreciation	(9.2)	(10.7)	(12.5)	(14.6)	(17.1)	(19.9)	(23.2)	(18.3)	(21.3)	(24.9)
Operating profit (EBIT)	2.8	6.0	9.2	14.4	19.5	23.6	26.8	31.2	36.0	39.2
Interest Expense	(3.2)	(3.3)	(3.3)	(3.6)	(2.7)	(2.4)	(2.6)	(2.8)	(3.4)	(3.6)
Profit Before Tax	(0.4)	2.7	5.9	10.8	16.8	21.1	24.2	28.5	32.6	35.6
Corporation tax	0.1	(0.8)	(1.8)	(3.2)	(5.0)	(6.3)	(7.3)	(8.5)	(9.8)	(10.7)
Profit After Tax	(0.3)	1.9	4.1	7.5	11.7	14.8	16.9	19.9	22.8	25.0
Ordinary dividends	0.0	0.0	0.0	0.0	(1.3)	(6.4)	(7.4)	(21.9)	(12.7)	(13.6)
Retained profit	**(0.3)**	**1.9**	**4.1**	**7.5**	**10.4**	**8.4**	**9.5**	**(2.0)**	**10.1**	**11.3**
BALANCE SHEET										
Fixed assets at cost	71.5	86.9	104.8	125.7	150.0	178.5	211.7	237.8	268.3	303.9
Depreciation	(24.2)	(35.0)	(47.5)	(62.1)	(79.2)	(99.1)	(122.3)	(140.6)	(161.9)	(186.8)
Tangible Fixed Assets	47.3	51.9	57.3	63.5	70.9	79.4	89.3	97.2	106.4	117.1
Cash	0.0	(0.0)	(0.0)	0.0	0.0	(0.0)	0.0	0.0	0.0	(0.0)
Trade debtors	8.3	12.0	16.7	22.6	29.4	35.3	40.6	46.6	52.7	58.0
Stocks	4.1	6.0	8.4	11.3	14.7	17.6	20.3	23.3	26.4	29.0
Current Assets	12.4	17.9	25.1	33.9	44.1	52.9	60.8	70.0	79.1	87.0
Total Assets	59.7	69.8	82.4	97.5	114.9	132.3	150.2	167.2	185.4	204.0
Trade Creditors	8.3	12.0	16.7	22.6	29.4	35.3	40.6	46.6	52.7	58.0
Debt	35.3	39.8	43.5	45.1	45.4	48.5	51.5	64.4	66.5	68.5
Total Liabilities	43.5	51.8	60.2	67.7	74.8	83.7	92.1	111.0	119.2	126.5
Net Assets	**16.1**	**18.0**	**22.2**	**29.7**	**40.2**	**48.6**	**58.1**	**56.1**	**66.2**	**77.5**
Share Capital - £1 nominal value	10.0	10.0	10.0	10.0	10.0	10.0	10.0	10.0	10.0	10.0
Profit and Loss Account	6.1	8.0	12.2	19.7	30.2	38.6	48.1	46.1	56.2	67.5
Capital and Reserves	**16.1**	**18.0**	**22.2**	**29.7**	**40.2**	**48.6**	**58.1**	**56.1**	**66.2**	**77.5**

CASH FLOWS

	1	2	3	4	5	6	7	8	9	10
Operating profit (EBIT)	2.8	6.0	9.2	14.4	19.5	23.6	26.8	31.2	36.0	39.2
Depreciation and amounts provided	9.2	10.7	12.5	14.6	17.1	19.9	23.2	18.3	21.3	24.9
EBITDA	12.0	16.8	21.7	29.0	36.5	43.5	50.0	49.5	57.3	64.1
Increase in working capital	(1.6)	(1.9)	(2.4)	(2.9)	(3.4)	(2.9)	(2.6)	(3.0)	(3.0)	(2.6)
Net operating cash flows	10.4	14.9	19.3	26.1	33.1	40.5	47.4	46.5	54.3	61.5
less: tax paid on EBITDA	(3.6)	(5.0)	(6.5)	(8.7)	(11.0)	(13.0)	(15.0)	(14.9)	(17.2)	(19.2)
Capital expenditures	(16.5)	(15.4)	(17.9)	(20.9)	(24.4)	(28.4)	(33.2)	(26.1)	(30.5)	(35.6)
less: tax relief thereon	2.8	3.2	3.8	4.4	5.1	6.0	7.0	5.5	6.4	7.5
Free Cash Flows	**(7.0)**	**(2.3)**	**(1.4)**	**0.9**	**2.9**	**5.0**	**6.1**	**11.0**	**13.0**	**14.1**
Financing costs:										
Interest paid	(3.2)	(3.3)	(3.3)	(3.6)	(2.7)	(2.4)	(2.6)	(2.8)	(3.4)	(3.6)
add: tax relief thereon	1.0	1.0	1.0	1.1	0.8	0.7	0.8	0.8	1.0	1.1
Post-tax financing costs	(2.2)	(2.3)	(2.3)	(2.5)	(1.9)	(1.7)	(1.8)	(1.9)	(2.4)	(2.5)
Net cash flow before new funding	(9.2)	(4.5)	(3.7)	(1.7)	1.0	3.3	4.3	9.1	10.6	11.6
Funding: debt increase / (decrease)	9.2	4.5	3.7	1.7	0.3	3.1	3.1	12.9	2.1	2.0
Free Cash Flows to Equity	**0.0**	**0.0**	**0.0**	**0.0**	**1.3**	**6.4**	**7.4**	**21.9**	**12.7**	**13.6**
Equity dividends paid	0.0	0.0	0.0	0.0	(1.3)	(6.4)	(7.4)	(21.9)	(12.7)	(13.6)
Net cash inflow (outflow)	**0.0**	**0.0**	**0.0**	**0.0**	**0.0**	**0.0**	**0.0**	**0.0**	**0.0**	**0.0**
NOPAT' (EBIT less operating taxes)	*2.0*	*4.2*	*6.4*	*10.1*	*13.6*	*16.5*	*18.7*	*21.9*	*25.2*	*27.4*

FORECAST YEAR			1	2	3	4	5	6	7	8	9	10
Ratios												
Growth												
Revenue			50.0%	45.0%	40.0%	35.0%	30.0%	20.0%	15.0%	15.0%	13.0%	10.0%
Gross profit			54.7%	44.5%	38.1%	31.8%	25.9%	19.1%	15.0%	7.9%	13.0%	10.0%
EBIT			-44.2%	115.6%	52.4%	56.8%	35.4%	21.1%	13.6%	16.7%	15.2%	8.9%
Pre-tax profits			-112.9%	-773.0%	114.0%	83.5%	55.3%	26.2%	14.4%	17.8%	14.3%	9.5%
Invested Capital			21.0%	12.6%	13.4%	14.0%	14.3%	13.4%	13.0%	9.9%	10.1%	10.0%
Margins % of revenues												
Cost of sales			70.0%	70.1%	70.5%	71.2%	72.1%	72.3%	72.3%	74.0%	74.0%	74.0%
General and admin costs			15.5%	15.9%	16.5%	16.0%	15.5%	15.4%	15.4%	15.4%	15.1%	14.9%
Depreciation			11.2%	9.0%	7.5%	6.5%	5.8%	5.6%	5.7%	3.9%	4.0%	4.3%
EBIT			3.4%	5.0%	5.5%	6.4%	6.6%	6.7%	6.6%	6.7%	6.8%	6.8%
EBITDA			14.5%	14.0%	13.0%	12.8%	12.4%	12.3%	12.3%	10.6%	10.9%	11.1%
Economic profit			-3.2%	-0.9%	0.4%	1.5%	2.2%	2.4%	2.3%	2.5%	2.6%	2.6%
Capital investment												
Capex / Revenues			20.0%	12.8%	10.7%	9.2%	8.3%	8.1%	8.2%	5.6%	5.8%	6.1%
Capex / Depreciation			1.8 x	1.4 x	1.4 x	1.4 x	1.4 x	1.4 x	1.4 x	1.4 x	1.4 x	1.4 x
Change in Working Capital / Revenues			2.0%	1.6%	1.4%	1.3%	1.2%	0.8%	0.7%	0.7%	0.6%	0.5%
Tax and financing												
Effective Tax Rate			30.0%	30.0%	30.0%	30.0%	30.0%	30.0%	30.0%	30.0%	30.0%	30.0%
Pre-tax cost of debt			12.25%	9.25%	8.25%	8.25%	6.00%	5.35%	5.35%	5.35%	5.35%	5.35%
Asset turnover	*Balance Sheet measure*											
Tangible Fixed Assets / Revenues	Closing		57.3%	43.4%	34.2%	28.1%	24.1%	22.5%	22.0%	20.8%	20.2%	20.2%
	Average		52.9%	41.5%	32.6%	26.7%	22.9%	21.3%	20.8%	20.0%	19.3%	19.3%
Working Capital / Revenues	Closing		5.0%	5.0%	5.0%	5.0%	5.0%	5.0%	5.0%	5.0%	5.0%	5.0%
	Average		4.0%	4.2%	4.3%	4.4%	4.4%	4.6%	4.7%	4.7%	4.7%	4.8%
Revenues / Invested Capital	Closing		1.6 x	2.1 x	2.6 x	3.0 x	3.4 x	3.6 x	3.7 x	3.9 x	4.0 x	4.0 x
	Average		1.8 x	2.2 x	2.7 x	3.2 x	3.7 x	3.9 x	3.9 x	4.1 x	4.2 x	4.2 x
Return On Invested Capital												
Pre-Tax ROIC	Opening		6.6%	11.7%	15.8%	21.9%	26.0%	27.5%	27.6%	28.5%	29.9%	29.5%
	Average		5.9%	11.0%	14.8%	20.5%	24.3%	25.8%	25.9%	27.2%	28.4%	28.1%
After-Tax ROIC	Opening		4.6%	8.2%	11.1%	15.3%	18.2%	19.3%	19.3%	20.0%	20.9%	20.7%
	Average		4.2%	7.7%	10.4%	14.3%	17.0%	18.1%	18.1%	19.0%	19.9%	19.7%
Breakdown of Post-tax Return on Equity												
Post-tax Return On average Equity (ROE) *Net Income*			(286)	1,923	4,115	7,550	11,726	14,796	16,924	19,941	22,787	24,953
Average Stockholder's Equity			16,270	17,088	20,107	25,939	34,933	44,361	53,338	57,112	61,152	71,857
		=	-1.8%	11.3%	20.5%	29.1%	33.6%	33.4%	31.7%	34.9%	37.3%	34.7%
ROE = ROA + (L / E)(ROA - cost of liabilities)			-1.8%	11.3%	20.5%	29.1%	33.6%	33.4%	31.7%	34.9%	37.3%	34.7%
Post-tax Return On average Assets (ROA) *Net Income + Net Interest Expense*			1,951	4,208	6,415	10,060	13,621	16,497	18,739	21,871	25,199	27,444
Average Total Assets			53,331	64,750	76,113	89,920	106,195	123,615	141,237	158,669	176,287	194,721
		=	3.7%	6.5%	8.4%	11.2%	12.8%	13.3%	13.3%	13.8%	14.3%	14.1%
Liabilities / Equity (L / E) *Average Liabilities*			37,062	47,662	56,006	63,980	71,263	79,255	87,899	101,557	115,135	122,864
Average Equity			16,270	17,088	20,107	25,939	34,933	44,361	53,338	57,112	61,152	71,857
		=	227.8%	278.9%	278.5%	246.7%	204.0%	178.7%	164.8%	177.8%	188.3%	171.0%
"Cost of liabilities" [net interest / total liabs]			6.0%	4.8%	4.1%	3.9%	2.7%	2.1%	2.1%	1.9%	2.1%	2.0%
Financial Risk Measures												
EBIT / gross interest			0.9 x	1.8 x	2.8 x	4.0 x	7.2 x	9.7 x	10.3 x	11.3 x	10.4 x	11.0 x
EBITDA / gross interest			3.8 x	5.1 x	6.6 x	8.1 x	13.5 x	17.9 x	19.3 x	18.0 x	16.6 x	18.0 x
Funds Flow / Debt			0.3 x	0.4 x	0.5 x	0.6 x	0.7 x	0.8 x	0.8 x	0.6 x	0.7 x	0.8 x
Free operating cash flow / Debt			(0.2 x)	(0.1 x)	(0.1 x)	(0.0 x)	0.0 x	0.1 x	0.1 x	0.2 x	0.2 x	0.2 x
Pretax return on average Capital Employed			5.9%	11.0%	14.8%	20.5%	24.3%	25.8%	25.9%	27.2%	28.4%	28.1%
Debt / Capital			68.6%	68.8%	66.2%	60.3%	53.1%	49.9%	47.0%	53.4%	50.1%	46.9%
Debt / EBITDA			2.9 x	2.4 x	2.0 x	1.6 x	1.2 x	1.1 x	1.0 x	1.3 x	1.2 x	1.1 x
Debt / Market Value (DCF) Equity			39.8%	40.3%	39.4%	36.6%	33.3%	33.3%	33.3%	42.9%	42.9%	42.9%
Debt / Enterprise (DCF) Value			28.5%	28.7%	28.3%	26.8%	25.0%	25.0%	25.0%	30.0%	30.0%	30.0%

Definitions

Gross interest	Gross interest charge before deducting capitalised interest and interest income
Funds Flow	EBITDA less tax paid on operating profits (incl. relief for capital investment)
Debt	Long term debt + current maturities of long term debt + short term debt + Commercial paper + Capitalised leases
Free op. cash flow	EBITDA – cash taxes – other non-cash items – capex and working capital change
Capital Employed	Total Debt + Shareholders common equity + preferred stock + minority interest + non-current deferred taxes
Capital	Debt + Shareholders' equity + Preference Shares + Minority Interest
MV Equity	Year end DCF Equity Value

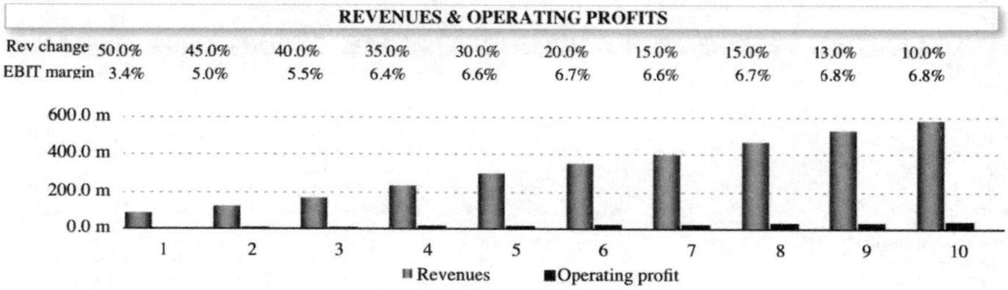
REVENUES & OPERATING PROFITS
Rev change 50.0% 45.0% 40.0% 35.0% 30.0% 20.0% 15.0% 15.0% 13.0% 10.0%
EBIT margin 3.4% 5.0% 5.5% 6.4% 6.6% 6.7% 6.6% 6.7% 6.8% 6.8%
600.0 m
400.0 m
200.0 m
0.0 m
1 2 3 4 5 6 7 8 9 10
Revenues
Operating profit

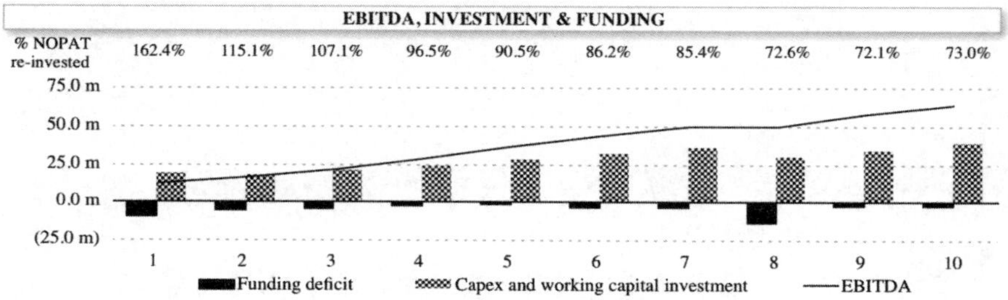
EBITDA, INVESTMENT & FUNDING
% NOPAT re-invested 162.4% 115.1% 107.1% 96.5% 90.5% 86.2% 85.4% 72.6% 72.1% 73.0%
75.0 m
50.0 m
25.0 m
0.0 m
(25.0 m)
1 2 3 4 5 6 7 8 9 10
Funding deficit
Capex and working capital investment
EBITDA

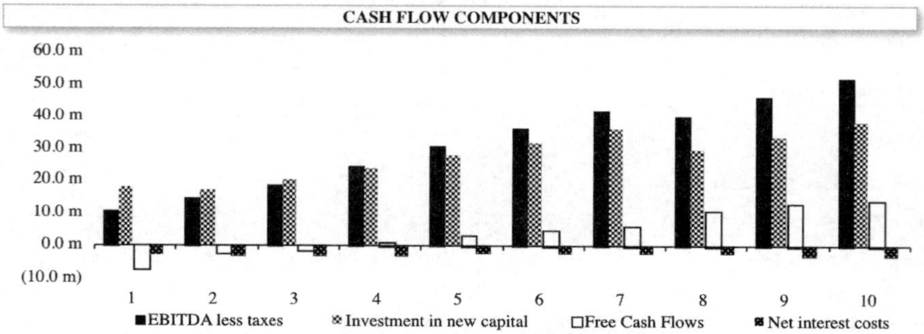
CASH FLOW COMPONENTS
60.0 m
50.0 m
40.0 m
30.0 m
20.0 m
10.0 m
0.0 m
(10.0 m)
1 2 3 4 5 6 7 8 9 10
EBITDA less taxes
Investment in new capital
Free Cash Flows
Net interest costs

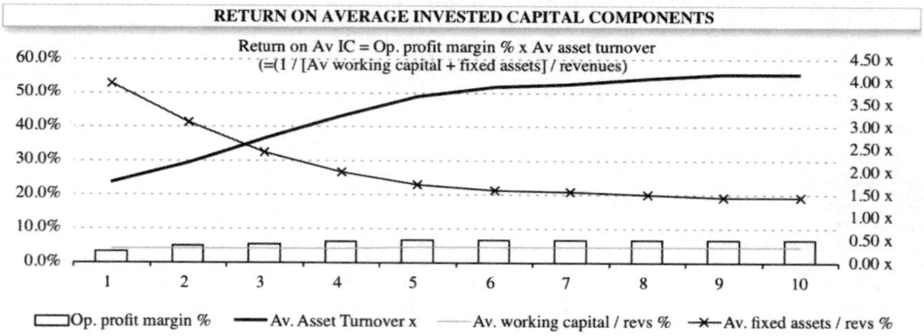
RETURN ON AVERAGE INVESTED CAPITAL COMPONENTS
Return on Av IC = Op. profit margin % x Av asset turnover
(=(1 / [Av working capital + fixed assets] / revenues)
60.0%
50.0%
40.0%
30.0%
20.0%
10.0%
0.0%
4.50 x
4.00 x
3.50 x
3.00 x
2.50 x
2.00 x
1.50 x
1.00 x
0.50 x
0.00 x
1 2 3 4 5 6 7 8 9 10
Op. profit margin %
Av. Asset Turnover x
Av. working capital / revs %
Av. fixed assets / revs %

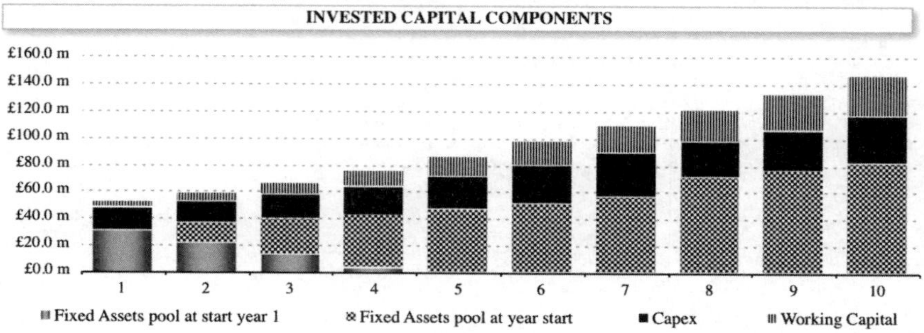
INVESTED CAPITAL COMPONENTS
£160.0 m
£140.0 m
£120.0 m
£100.0 m
£80.0 m
£60.0 m
£40.0 m
£20.0 m
£0.0 m
1 2 3 4 5 6 7 8 9 10
Fixed Assets pool at start year 1
Fixed Assets pool at year start
Capex
Working Capital

D5 ACQUISITION

Having carried out its valuation of Tokan Ltd (see Appendix D4), Rononi is preparing an offer for 80% (the remaining 20% shareholder does not wish to sell). It is considering how to structure the acquisition (purchase price and form of consideration), and is to evaluate the post-acquisition financial impact (economic and accounting).

The stand-alone value for 100% is £72.8m (which includes the value of control – see Appendix D4). Cost synergies from elimination of duplicate functions and operating efficiencies are expected to add £16.4m (or £13.1m for 80% - see ❹). The value for Rononi for 100%, therefore, is £89.2m or £71.4m for 80% (£8.92 per share for 8m shares to be acquired).

Rononi is to offer £6.60 per share (which is acceptable to the selling shareholder), approximately 14% above its estimate of a fair price for a private minority holding (£5.78 per share from Appendix D4 before the value of control), giving a total purchase price of £52.8m. Transaction costs are estimated at £1m (1.25% of the transaction size – the cost of purchase and value of debt being refinanced), giving a total acquisition cost of £53.8m and economic gain of £17.6m (£71.4m value to Rononi less £53.8m). The corresponding IRR is 12.7% (3.8% above Rononi's cost of capital), or 11.7% excluding synergies (see ❻).

The selling shareholder (Scodley Bott Ltd) would like to receive a mix of cash and Rononi shares. Rononi is prepared to offer a 25% shares : 75% cash mix, giving the vendor a 4.1% holding; it also offers the vendor all-share and all-cash alternatives (see ❼).

The purchase price can be funded from existing £87.7m cash balances (the balance retained from the very recent IPO – see Appendix D3), without a significant impact on Rononi's credit standing or its forecast EPS over years 1-3 (see ❽ and ❾). Tokan's existing £26.1m debt would be refinanced with new debt at a rate that reflects the post-acquisition group's likely rating (based on Rononi's superior credit quality).

The vendor accepts the 25% shares : 75% cash offer.

❶ CURRENT FINANCIAL INFORMATION

Rononi's current share price is £3.00, giving it a market capitalisation of £310.9m (based on its post-float 103.6m shares in issue – see ❺ Appendix D3). It has net surplus cash of £82.3m (net of debt) after its recent IPO (reflected in the market price). Recent results for Rononi and Tokan are as follows:

	Rononi	Tokan
Revenues	100.5	55.0
Cost of sales	(72.3)	(39.0)
Gross Profit	28.1	16.0
General and administrative expenses	(8.4)	(9.0)
Depreciation	(5.6)	(2.0)
Operating profit (EBIT)	14.1	5.0
Interest Expense	(0.4)	(1.8)
Profit Before Tax	13.8	3.2
Corporation tax	(4.1)	0.0
Profit After Tax	9.6	3.2

❷ SHAREHOLDERS

Post IPO in Appendix D3

	Rononi			Tokan		
	%	*Shares held*	*Mkt Value £m*	*%*	*Shares held*	*Mkt Value £m*
Management	51.0%	52.8m	158.5			
Omivon + other	49.0%	50.8m	152.3			
Scodley Bott Ltd				80.0%	8.0m	44.0
A. Mainwaring				20.0%	2.0m	11.0
	100.0%	103.6m	310.9	100.0%	10.0m	55.0

❸ FINANCIAL FORECAST EXTRACTS

	Rononi				£m	Tokan				£m
Forecast year	1	2	3	4	5	1	2	3	4	5
Revenues	115.6	132.9	148.8	163.7	180.1	82.5	119.6	167.5	226.1	293.9
EBITDA	22.7	24.9	27.9	28.9	30.8	12.0	16.8	21.7	29.0	36.5
Capex/workCap	(9.1)	(10.5)	(11.5)	(12.1)	(12.9)	(18.1)	(17.2)	(20.3)	(23.8)	(27.8)
Tax	(4.9)	(5.3)	(5.9)	(5.9)	(6.2)	(0.8)	(1.8)	(2.7)	(4.3)	(5.8)
Forecast Free Cash Flow	8.7	9.0	10.4	10.9	11.8	(7.0)	(2.3)	(1.4)	0.9	2.9
Revenue growth	15.0%	15.0%	12.0%	10.0%	10.0%	50.0%	45.0%	40.0%	35.0%	30.0%
EBIT margin	14.2%	13.3%	13.3%	12.1%	11.4%	3.4%	5.0%	5.5%	6.4%	6.6%
Capex / revenue	7.0%	7.0%	7.0%	6.8%	6.5%	20.0%	12.8%	10.7%	9.2%	8.3%
Capex / EBITDA	35.6%	37.4%	37.4%	38.2%	38.0%	20.0%	12.8%	10.7%	9.2%	8.3%

See ❶ Appendix D3 for Rononi and ❻ Appendix D4 for Tokan.

❹ SYNERGIES

The management of Rononi believes it can extract cost savings from combining the operations, and improving operating efficiencies in general. These should, in effect, increase Tokan's EBIT margin by 0.5% - 1.0% over the forecast period. Highlights of the combined operations over the first forecast 5 years are as follows:

£m	1	2	3	4	5
Rononi	115.6	132.9	148.8	163.7	180.1
Tokan	82.5	119.6	167.5	226.1	293.9
Synergies	0.0	0.0	0.0	0.0	0.0
Revenues	**198.1**	**252.5**	**316.3**	**389.8**	**474.0**
Rononi	22.7	24.9	27.9	28.9	30.8
Tokan	12.0	16.8	21.7	29.0	36.5
Synergies	0.9	1.1	1.2	1.4	1.5
EBITDA	**35.6**	**42.7**	**50.8**	**59.3**	**68.9**
Rononi	(8.1)	(9.3)	(10.4)	(11.1)	(11.7)
Tokan	(16.5)	(15.4)	(17.9)	(20.9)	(24.4)
Synergies	0.0	0.0	0.0	0.0	0.0
Capex	**(24.6)**	**(24.7)**	**(28.3)**	**(31.9)**	**(36.1)**
Rononi	(1.1)	(1.2)	(1.1)	(1.0)	(1.1)
Tokan	(1.6)	(1.9)	(2.4)	(2.9)	(3.4)
Synergies	0.0	0.0	0.0	0.0	0.0
Working Capital change	**(2.7)**	**(3.1)**	**(3.5)**	**(4.0)**	**(4.5)**
Rononi	(4.9)	(5.3)	(5.9)	(5.9)	(6.2)
Tokan	(0.8)	(1.8)	(2.7)	(4.3)	(5.8)
Synergies	(0.3)	(0.3)	(0.4)	(0.4)	(0.5)
Tax on operating items	**(6.0)**	**(7.4)**	**(9.1)**	**(10.7)**	**(12.5)**
Rononi	8.7	9.0	10.4	10.9	11.8
Tokan	(7.0)	(2.3)	(1.4)	0.9	2.9
Synergies	0.6	0.8	0.9	1.0	1.1
Free Cash Flow	**2.3**	**7.5**	**9.9**	**12.7**	**15.8**

	1	2	3	4	5
Revenue growth					
Rononi	15.0%	15.0%	12.0%	10.0%	10.0%
Tokan	50.0%	45.0%	40.0%	35.0%	30.0%
Combined	*27.4%*	*27.5%*	*25.3%*	*23.2%*	*21.6%*
EBITDA / Revenues					
Rononi	19.7%	18.7%	18.7%	17.7%	17.1%
Tokan	14.5%	14.0%	13.0%	12.8%	12.4%
Combined	*18.0%*	*16.9%*	*16.1%*	*15.2%*	*14.5%*
EBIT / Revenues					
Rononi	14.2%	13.3%	13.3%	12.1%	11.4%
Tokan	3.4%	5.0%	5.5%	6.4%	6.6%
Combined	*10.1%*	*9.8%*	*9.5%*	*9.1%*	*8.8%*
Capex / Revenues					
Rononi	7.0%	7.0%	7.0%	6.8%	6.5%
Tokan	20.0%	12.8%	10.7%	9.2%	8.3%
Combined	*12.4%*	*9.8%*	*9.0%*	*8.2%*	*7.6%*

Year 5 synergy Free Cash Flows increase 10% p.a. until year 10, after which they are expected to grow at 3% in perpetuity, giving a present value of £16.4m (80% = £13.1m), using a 9.9% discount rate (it is assumed that Tokan's post-acquisition cost of debt will reflect Rononi credit risk, and its target capital structure will be the same as Rononi's – hence a 7% pre-tax cost of debt and 20% capital structure have been assumed in the WACC calculation).

❺ PURCHASE PRICE

Rononi and the vendor, Scodley Bott Ltd, prepare their own price analysis. The vendor assesses its minimum required price based on an average of its own chosen EBITDA and P/E multiples, illiquidity discount and control premium. It estimates a fair price with control of £6.00 per share; Rononi's estimate is £7.28 per share (ignoring synergies), or £5.78 without control (see Appendix D4). Rounding this down to £5.50 and adding a 20% control premium gives an offer price of £6.60. (No information about how this offer price has been calculated will be given to the Vendor.)

Based on the valuation summary in Appendix D4, the purchase price can be shown as follows:

£m		*Equity Value*	*Per Share*
Minority quoted shareholding		77.0	£7.70
Illiquidity discount	25%	(19.3)	-£1.93
Minority private shareholding		*57.8*	*£5.78*
Rounded down		*55.0*	*£5.50*
Control premium	20%	11.0	£1.10
Offer price for 100%		66.0	£6.60
Offer for 80%		**52.8**	**£6.60**

❻ ECONOMIC GAINS

Based on its own valuation of Tokan, Rononi estimates the economic gains to be £17.6m or 33% of the purchase price (£1.2m ignoring synergies, 2% of the purchase price).

£m		*Equity Value 80%*	*Equity Value 100%*	*Per Share*
Rononi estimate of stand-alone intrinsic value (majority)		58.2	72.8	£7.28
add: present value of synergies		13.1	16.4	£1.64
Value		71.4	89.2	£8.92
Value acquired	80%	71.4		£8.92
less:	purchase price	(52.8)		-£6.60
	transaction costs (see below)	(1.0)		-£0.13
Economic gains		**17.6**		**£2.20**

				NPV / cost	**NPV**	**IRR**
Purchase price		52.8	Excl. synergies	*8.3%*	4.4	11.7%
Tokan debt refinanced by b		26.1	Synergies	*24.4%*	13.1	
Transaction size		*78.9*	*Incl. synergies*	*32.6%*	*17.6*	12.7%
Costs	1.25%	1.0	vs Rononi WACC			8.9%

❼ CONSIDERATION AND FINANCING

Rononi considers three options: 100% shares, 25% shares : 75% cash, and 100% cash. Rononi sets the Exchange Ratio equal to the offer price in shares divided by its existing share price (see **1.7** and **1.8** in Chapter 1 for discussion on Exchange Ratios).

For the all share offer, the Exchange Ratio (2.20 = £6.60 ÷ £3.00) is towards the low end of the acceptable range (14% up the 2.0824 minimum to 2.9317 maximum range). This would give the vendor a 14.5% shareholding in the combined group (valued at £55.3m, with a pro-rata £2.5m share of the NPV benefits). The post-acquisition Rononi share price would increase from the current £3.00 to £3.14.

The 25% shares : 75% cash offer would give the vendor a 4.1% shareholding and a £0.7m share of the NPV benefit (post-acquisition share price of £3.16).

All the NPV benefit accrues to the existing Rononi shareholders for a 100% cash offer (share price increases to £3.17). Rononi has £87.7m of cash, retained from its IPO (see Appendix D3), and can, therefore, pay the £52.8m purchase price in cash without significantly reducing its credit standing. Net debt would increase by the £52.8m acquisition cost in cash plus £1.0m transaction costs (Rononi will refinance all of Tokan's £26.1m debt with new debt on more favourable terms).

TRANSACTION ANALYSIS

£m unless stated otherwise

		% Consideration in Shares		
		100%	**25%**	**0%**
Existing Rononi cash balances		0.0	39.6	52.8
Debt funding		0.0	0.0	0.0
Cash consideration		0.0	39.6	52.8
Shares consideration		52.8	13.2	0.0
Acquisition of shares		**52.8**	**52.8**	**52.8**
Rononi cash balances		87.7	87.7	87.7
less: allocated to share purchase		0.0	(39.6)	(52.8)
less: cash not required for refinancing		(86.7)	(47.1)	(33.9)
Cash available for acquisition		1.0	1.0	1.0
New bank facilities		26.1	26.1	26.1
Refinancing debt and pay fees/costs		**27.1**	**27.1**	**27.1**
		79.9	**79.9**	**79.9**
Increase in net debt		1.0	40.6	53.8
Existing acquirer Shares		103.6 m	103.6 m	103.6 m
Existing acquirer share price	E	£ 3.00	£ 3.00	£ 3.00
Acquirer value	A	310.9	310.9	310.9
Target value (80%)		58.2	58.2	58.2
Synergies		13.1	13.1	13.1
Transaction costs		(1.0)	(1.0)	(1.0)
Purchase price in cash		0.0	(39.6)	(52.8)
Combined Value	B	381.2	341.6	328.4
Purchase cost in shares	C	52.8	13.2	0.0
Purchase price in shares	D	£ 6.60	£ 1.65	£ 0.00
NPV		17.6	17.6	17.6
Exchange Ratio	= D ÷ E	2.2000	0.5500	0.0000
Existing target shares acquired		8.0 m	8.0 m	8.0 m
New acquirer shares issued		17.6 m	4.4 m	0.0 m
Post-acquisition shares		121.2 m	108.0 m	103.6 m
Post-acquisition share price		£ 3.14	£ 3.16	£ 3.17
Target shareholders		14.52%	4.07%	0.00%
Acquirer shareholders		85.48%	95.93%	100.00%
Target shareholders		55.3	13.9	0.0
Acquirer shareholders		325.9	327.7	328.4
Combined Value		381.2	341.6	328.4
Target shareholders: cash plus shares value		55.3	53.5	52.8
Share of NPV benefits		2.5	0.7	0.0
Share		*14.52%*	*4.07%*	*0.00%*
Minimum shareholding	= C ÷ B	13.85%	3.86%	0.00%
Minimum Exchange Ratio	see **1.7**	2.0824	0.5206	0.0000
Maximum shareholding	= 1 - (A ÷ B)	18.46%	9.00%	5.35%
Maximum Exchange Ratio	see **1.8**	2.9317	1.2817	0.7317

❽ CLOSING BALANCE SHEET

	RONONI	TOKAN	100% SHARES – ACQUISITION ADJUSTMENTS			100% SHARES – RONONI	25% SHARES	25% SHARES – RONONI	0% SHARES	0% SHARES – RONONI
See ❶ in App.D3 (year 5)	At Acquisition	At Acquisitio-	*Acq'n costs*	*Consolid-ation*	*Goodwill / Minorities*	Post Acquisition				
Fixed Assets	44.9	40.0		40.0		84.9				
Working Capital	7.0	2.5		2.5		9.5	Same as 100% shares		Same as 100% shares	
Invested Capital	51.9	42.5				94.4				
Goodwill					40.7 [2]	40.7				
	51.9	**42.5**		***42.5***	***40.7***	**135.1**				
See ❻ in App.D3										
Cash	87.7	0.0	(1.0)	0.0		86.7	(40.6)	47.1	(53.8)	33.9
Debt	5.4	26.1		26.1		31.5 [1]		31.5		31.5
Net Debt	(82.3)	26.1	***1.0***	***26.1***		(55.2)	***40.6***	(15.6)	***53.8***	(2.4)
Ordinary share capital	1.0	10.0	18.1	Not consolidated: included in goodwill calculation		19.1	4.5	5.6	0.0	1.0
Share premium	123.0	0.0	34.7			157.7	8.7	131.7	0.0	123.0
Reserves	10.1	6.4				10.1		10.1		10.1
Equity	134.2	16.4	***52.8***			187.0	***13.2***	147.4	***0.0***	134.2
Minority interests	0.0	0.0			3.3	3.3		3.3		3.3
	51.9	**42.5**	***53.8***	***26.1***	***3.3***	**135.1**	***53.8***	**135.1**	***53.8***	**135.1**

Notes

1 Tokan's £26.1m consolidation debt is a new facility replacing the old facility, on more favourable terms (reflecting the post-acquisition Rononi Group credit risk).

2 Goodwill effectively represents the price paid for future Economic Profits, being the excess of the consideration over the fair value of net tangible assets acquired (after revaluation to fair value, where applicable – none is required in this example). Under UK accounting standards, Goodwill may be amortised; under International Standards, a charge to profit is incurred if Goodwill is impaired. This example assumes annual amortisation.

	£m	£m	
Cost of Tokan equity being acquired		52.8	
Transaction costs		1.0	
Net assets acquired	16.4	←	x 20% = £3.3m minority interest
Asset revaluations	0.0		
Other adjustments	0.0		
Fair value of net tangible assets	16.4		
	x 80.0% =	(13.1)	
Goodwill		**40.7**	
Amortisation period		over 10 yrs	
Annual amortisation charge		£4.1 m	

❾ ACCOUNTING IMPACT OF CONSIDERATION OPTIONS: YEARS 1 - 3

PROFIT & LOSS

£m	100% SHARES 1	2	3	25% SHARES 1	2	3	0% SHARES 1	2	3
Rononi	16.4	17.7	19.8						
Tokan	2.8	6.0	9.2						
Synergies	0.9	1.1	1.2						
EBIT	**20.0**	**24.8**	**30.2**	**20.0**	**24.8**	**30.2**	**20.0**	**24.8**	**30.2**
Rononi	3.5	3.7	4.2						
Tokan	0.0	0.0	0.0						
Synergies	0.0	0.0	0.1						
Acquisition / refinancing effects	(0.0)	(0.0)	(0.0)	(1.6)	(1.7)	(1.7)	(2.2)	(2.2)	(2.3)
Interest income	**3.5**	**3.7**	**4.2**	**1.9**	**2.1**	**2.5**	**1.4**	**1.5**	**2.0**
Rononi	(0.4)	0.0	0.0						
Tokan	(3.2)	(3.3)	(3.3)						
Synergies	0.0	0.0	0.0						
Acquisition / refinancing effects	1.4	1.0	1.0	1.4	1.0	1.0	1.4	1.0	1.0
Interest expense	**(2.2)**	**(3.3)**	**(3.3)**	**(2.2)**	**(3.3)**	**(3.3)**	**(2.2)**	**(3.3)**	**(3.3)**
Rononi	19.5	21.4	24.0						
Tokan	(0.4)	2.7	5.9						
Synergies	0.9	1.1	1.3						
Acquisition / refinancing effects	1.3	1.0	1.0	(0.3)	(0.6)	(0.7)	(0.8)	(1.2)	(1.3)
Profit Before Tax (pre Goodwill)	**21.3**	**25.3**	**31.2**	**19.7**	**25.3**	**31.2**	**19.2**	**25.3**	**31.2**
Rononi	(5.8)	(6.4)	(7.2)						
Tokan	0.1	(0.8)	(1.8)						
Synergies	(0.3)	(0.3)	(0.4)						
Acquisition / refinancing effects	(0.4)	(0.3)	(0.3)	0.1	0.2	0.2	0.2	0.4	0.4
Tax	**(6.4)**	**(7.9)**	**(9.6)**	**(5.9)**	**(7.4)**	**(9.1)**	**(5.8)**	**(7.2)**	**(9.0)**
Tokan	(0.3)	(0.7)	(1.1)						
Minority interests	**(0.3)**	**(0.7)**	**(1.1)**	**(0.3)**	**(0.7)**	**(1.1)**	**(0.3)**	**(0.7)**	**(1.1)**
Rononi	13.6	15.0	16.8						
Tokan	(0.5)	1.2	3.0						
Synergies	0.6	0.8	0.9						
Acquisition / refinancing effects	0.9	0.7	0.7	(0.2)	(0.4)	(0.5)	(0.5)	(0.8)	(0.9)
Profit After Tax & Minorities	**14.7**	**17.7**	**21.3**	**13.5**	**16.6**	**20.2**	**13.2**	**16.2**	**19.8**
Rononi	0.0	0.0	0.0						
Tokan	0.0	0.0	0.0						
On consolidation	(4.1)	(4.1)	(4.1)						
Goodwill	**(4.1)**	**(4.1)**	**(4.1)**	**(4.1)**	**(4.1)**	**(4.1)**	**(4.1)**	**(4.1)**	**(4.1)**
Rononi	13.6	15.0	16.8						
Tokan	(0.5)	1.2	3.0						
Synergies	0.6	0.8	0.9						
Acquisition / refinancing effects	(3.1)	(3.4)	(3.4)	(4.2)	(4.5)	(4.6)	(4.6)	(4.9)	(5.0)
Profit After Tax After Goodwill	**10.6**	**13.6**	**17.3**	**9.5**	**12.5**	**16.1**	**9.1**	**12.1**	**15.7**

		1	2	3
Interest income	- all	4.00%	4.00%	4.00%
Interest expense	- *Rononi / merged*	7.00%	6.50%	6.00%
	Tokan (old rate)	12.25%	9.25%	8.25%
Tax on Pre-tax profit at	- all	30%	30%	30%

Tokan's cost of debt has been set relatively high to show the beneficial impact of refinancing. Over a 10yr forecast, Tokan's cost of debt converges towards Rononi's, as its credit rating improves.

Capital expenditure eligible for tax relief is assumed to be equal to the depreciation charge for the period (for simplicity), hence tax is simply 30% x pre-tax profits (taxable profits equal accounting profits in this example).

Deferred tax has been ignored.

BALANCE SHEET

£m	100% SHARES 1	2	3	25% SHARES 1	2	3	0% SHARES 1	2	3
Rononi	46.6	48.8	51.1						
Tokan	47.3	51.9	57.3						
Synergies	0.0	0.0	0.0						
Fixed Assets	**93.9**	**100.7**	**108.4**	**93.9**	**100.7**	**108.4**	**93.9**	**100.7**	**108.4**
Rononi	8.1	9.3	10.4						
Tokan	4.1	6.0	8.4						
Synergies	0.0	0.0	0.0						
Net Operating Current Assets	**12.2**	**15.3**	**18.8**	**12.2**	**15.3**	**18.8**	**12.2**	**15.3**	**18.8**
Rononi	54.7	58.1	61.5						
Tokan	51.4	57.9	65.6						
Synergies	0.0	0.0	0.0						
Total Invested Capital	**106.1**	**115.9**	**127.1**	**106.1**	**115.9**	**127.1**	**106.1**	**115.9**	**127.1**
Rononi	0.0	0.0	0.0						
Tokan	0.0	0.0	0.0						
Synergies	0.0	0.0	0.0						
Acquisition / refinancing effects	36.6	32.5	28.5						
Goodwill	**36.6**	**32.5**	**28.5**	**36.6**	**32.5**	**28.5**	**36.6**	**32.5**	**28.5**
Rononi	54.7	58.1	61.5						
Tokan	51.4	57.9	65.6						
Synergies	0.0	0.0	0.0						
Acquisition / refinancing effects	36.6	32.5	28.5						
Invested Capital + Goodwill	**142.7**	**148.5**	**155.6**	**142.7**	**148.5**	**155.6**	**142.7**	**148.5**	**155.6**
Rononi	93.1	104.8	118.1						
Tokan	0.0	0.0	(0.0)						
Synergies	0.6	1.4	2.3						
Acquisition / refinancing effects	(1.0)	(1.1)	(1.1)	(41.7)	(42.9)	(44.1)	(55.3)	(56.9)	(58.4)
Cash	**92.7**	**105.1**	**119.4**	**52.0**	**63.3**	**76.3**	**38.5**	**49.3**	**62.0**
Rononi	0.0	0.0	0.0						
Tokan	35.3	39.8	43.5						
Synergies	0.0	0.0	0.0						
Acquisition / refinancing effects	(1.0)	(1.7)	(2.4)						
Debt	**34.3**	**38.1**	**41.1**	**34.3**	**38.1**	**41.1**	**34.3**	**38.1**	**41.1**
Rononi	(93.1)	(104.8)	(118.1)						
Tokan	35.3	39.8	43.5						
Synergies	(0.6)	(1.4)	(2.3)						
Acquisition / refinancing effects	0.1	(0.6)	(1.3)	40.8	41.2	41.7	54.3	55.2	56.1
Net Debt / (Cash)	**(58.4)**	**(67.0)**	**(78.3)**	**(17.7)**	**(25.1)**	**(35.2)**	**(4.1)**	**(11.2)**	**(20.9)**
Rononi	124.1	124.1	124.1						
Acquisition / refinancing effects	52.8	52.8	52.8	13.2	13.2	13.2	0.0	0.0	0.0
Ordinary Share Capital	**176.9**	**176.9**	**176.9**	**137.3**	**137.3**	**137.3**	**124.1**	**124.1**	**124.1**
Rononi	23.8	38.8	55.6						
Tokan	6.1	8.0	12.2						
Synergies	0.6	1.4	2.3						
Tokan pre-acquisition reserves	(6.4)	(6.4)	(6.4)						
Minority interest	(0.3)	(0.9)	(2.1)						
Post-tax financing impact	0.9	1.6	2.3	(0.2)	(0.6)	(1.1)	(0.5)	(1.4)	(2.3)
Goodwill impact	(4.1)	(8.1)	(12.2)						
Acquisition / refinancing effects	(9.8)	(13.9)	(18.4)	(10.9)	(16.1)	(21.8)	(11.3)	(16.9)	(23.0)
Reserves	**20.7**	**34.4**	**51.6**	**19.6**	**32.1**	**48.2**	**19.3**	**31.4**	**47.1**
Rononi	0.0	0.0	0.0						
Tokan	3.5	4.2	5.4						
Minority Interests	**3.5**	**4.2**	**5.4**	**3.5**	**4.2**	**5.4**	**3.5**	**4.2**	**5.4**
Rononi	54.7	58.1	61.5						
Tokan	45.0	52.1	61.0						
Synergies	0.0	0.0	0.0						
Acquisition / refinancing effects	43.1	38.3	33.1	43.1	38.3	33.1	43.1	38.3	33.1
Financial Capital & Minorities	**142.7**	**148.5**	**155.6**	**142.7**	**148.5**	**155.6**	**142.7**	**148.5**	**155.6**

RATIOS

	100% SHARES			25% SHARES			0% SHARES		
	1	2	3	1	2	3	1	2	3
After tax ROIC (pre-goodwill)									
Rononi	22.0%	22.6%	23.9%						
Tokan	4.6%	8.2%	11.1%						
Combined	*14.9%*	*16.4%*	*18.2%*	*14.9%*	*16.4%*	*18.2%*	*14.9%*	*16.4%*	*18.2%*
After tax ROIC (post-Goodwill)									
Rononi	22.0%	22.6%	23.9%						
Tokan	4.6%	8.2%	11.1%						
Combined	*10.4%*	*12.2%*	*14.2%*	*10.4%*	*12.2%*	*14.2%*	*10.4%*	*12.2%*	*14.2%*
EBIT / gross interest expense									
Rononi	x 43.0	--	--						
Tokan	x 0.9	x 1.8	x 2.8						
Combined	*x 9.1*	*x 11.1*	*x 13.2*	*x 9.1*	*x 11.1*	*x 13.2*	*x 9.1*	*x 11.1*	*x 13.2*
EBITDA / gross interest expense									
Rononi	x 59.7	--	--						
Tokan	x 3.8	x 5.1	x 6.6						
Combined	*x 16.1*	*x 19.1*	*x 22.2*	*x 16.1*	*x 19.1*	*x 22.2*	*x 16.1*	*x 19.1*	*x 22.2*
Gross debt / EBITDA									
Rononi	--	--	--						
Tokan	x 2.9	x 2.4	x 2.0						
Combined	*x 1.0*	*x 0.9*	*x 0.8*	*x 1.0*	*x 0.9*	*x 0.8*	*x 1.0*	*x 0.9*	*x 0.8*
Net debt / Net debt + BV equity									
Rononi	--	--	--						
Tokan	68.6%	68.8%	66.2%						
Combined	*-40.9%*	*-45.1%*	*-50.3%*	*-12.4%*	*-16.9%*	*-22.6%*	*-2.9%*	*-7.5%*	*-13.4%*
EPS									
Rononi	£0.13	£0.14	£0.16						
Tokan	-£0.03	£0.19	£0.41						
Combined (pre-Goodwill)	£0.12	£0.15	£0.18	£0.13	£0.15	£0.19	£0.13	£0.16	£0.19
Combined (post-Goodwill)	£0.09	£0.11	£0.14	£0.09	£0.12	£0.15	£0.09	£0.12	£0.15
Average ROE									
Rononi	9.7%	9.7%	9.8%						
Tokan	-1.8%	11.3%	20.5%						
Combined	*7.6%*	*8.7%*	*9.7%*	*8.9%*	*10.2%*	*11.4%*	*9.5%*	*10.8%*	*12.1%*
Average ROE (post-Goodwill)	*5.5%*	*6.7%*	*7.9%*	*6.2%*	*7.7%*	*9.1%*	*6.6%*	*8.1%*	*9.6%*

The Earnings Per Share impact for a purchase price with 0% - 100% cash is shown below (the balance of the purchase price being shares in Rononi). As the percentage of cash in the purchase price increases, so interest income decreases (debt is constant) and net financing costs (gross interest expense less interest income) increase. Profits After Tax (PAT) (used to calculated EPS), therefore, decrease. As the cash percentage increases, the number of shares in issue decreases. In this example, EPS increases (compared to Rononi alone) because the percentage decrease in PAT is less than the percentage decrease in the number of shares.

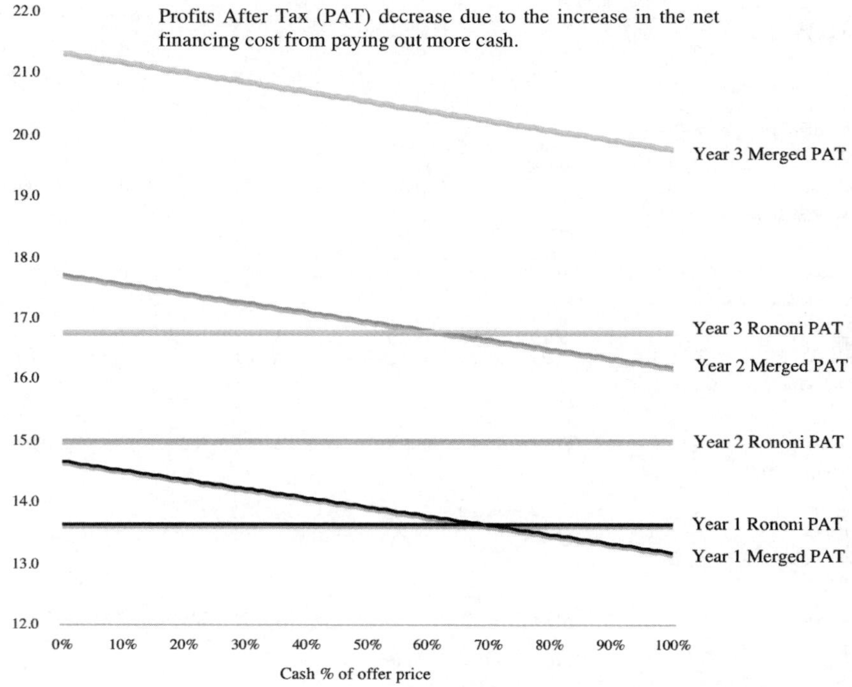

Profits After Tax (PAT) decrease due to the increase in the net financing cost from paying out more cash.
22.0
21.0
20.0
19.0
18.0
17.0
16.0
15.0
14.0
13.0
12.0
Year 3 Merged PAT
Year 3 Rononi PAT
Year 2 Merged PAT
Year 2 Rononi PAT
Year 1 Rononi PAT
Year 1 Merged PAT
0%
10%
20%
30%
40%
50%
60%
70%
80%
90%
100%
Cash % of offer price

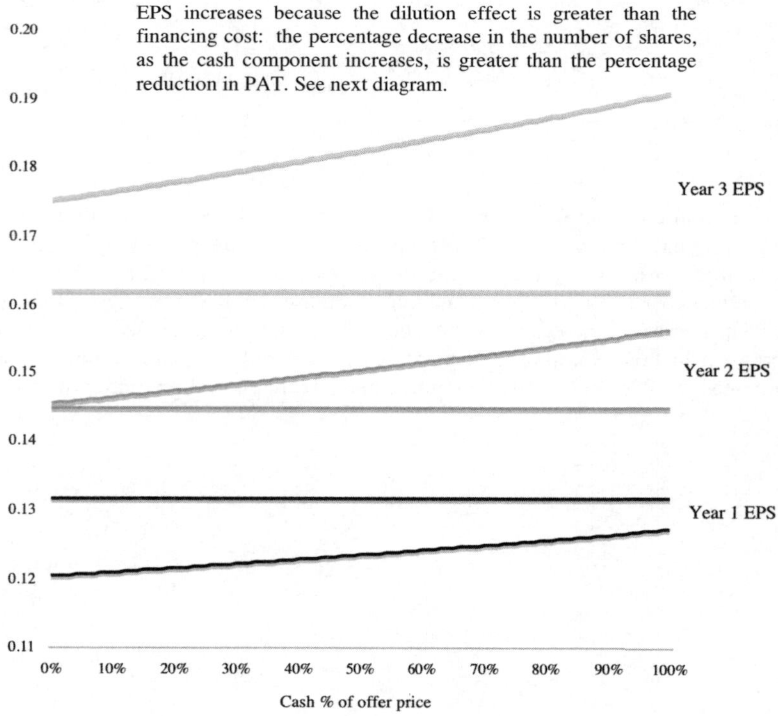

EPS increases because the dilution effect is greater than the financing cost: the percentage decrease in the number of shares, as the cash component increases, is greater than the percentage reduction in PAT. See next diagram.
0.20
0.19
0.18
0.17
0.16
0.15
0.14
0.13
0.12
0.11
Year 3 EPS
Year 2 EPS
Year 1 EPS
0%
10%
20%
30%
40%
50%
60%
70%
80%
90%
100%
Cash % of offer price

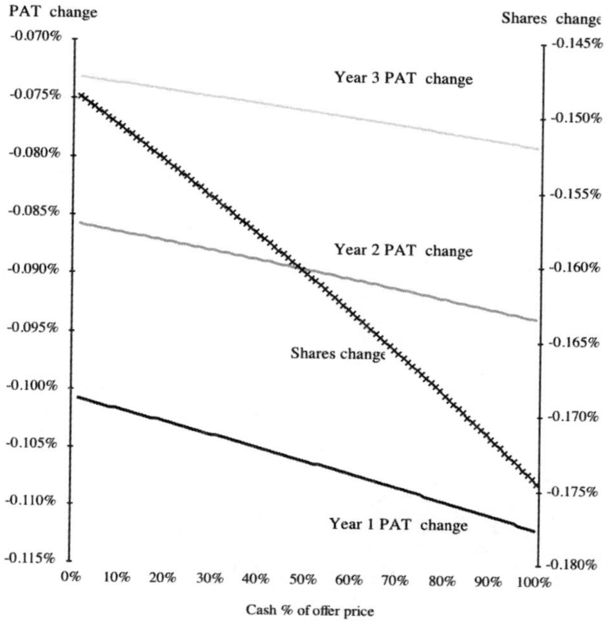

If Rononi did not have the £87.7m of cash from the IPO, then increasing the cash component would significantly affect its credit risk, as shown by leverage (debt / debt plus book value of equity) and interest coverage ratios:

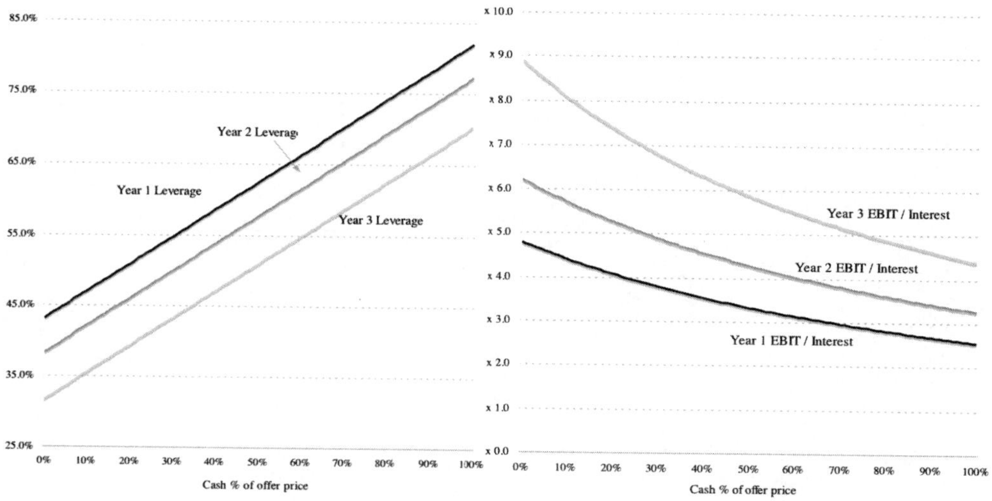

D6 INTEREST RATE FUTURES HEDGING

After the acquisition of Tokan, Rononi increased its borrowings further, refinancing its debt into a single £50m floating rate facility (3 month £ LIBOR). It is now 17 January, and Rononi's Treasurer is concerned that interest rates will increase (3 month LIBOR is 3.832% - see ❶), and so decides to hedge by selling Short Term Interest Rate Futures (see ❷) in order to lock into implied Forward Rates for the next 3 month interest period on the £50m loan, commencing on 15 May.

Futures prices (and implied rates) for the next delivery dates are (see ❸): 19 March: 96.00 (4.00%), 18 June: 95.75 (4.25%), and 17 September: 95.50 (4.50%). The yield curve is positively sloped, therefore (slope = daily increase in rates = 0.002747%). The 15 May to 15 August interest period (92 days) straddles the June delivery date, with 34 days falling in the March forward period and 58 days in the June forward period (see ❹ and ❺). Hence (1) there is a delivery date before the start of the interest period, and (2) the interest period falls into two futures periods.

Rononi's Treasurer expects to lock into an effective rate of 4.16% on 15 May, implied from linear interpolation (4.00% implied rate on 19 March + 0.25% increase over the next 91 day period to the implied rate on 18 June x 57 days to 15 May / 91). This is 33 basis points above 3 month LIBOR on 17 January. The borrower is to use an 'interpolative' hedge to lock into this 4.16% linearly interpolated rate.

The basic number of contracts for the 92 day period (= £100m loan size / £0.5m contract size = 100) will be adjusted to ensure the maturities are the same (= 100 x (92/365 year interest period) / 0.25 year futures period = 100.82 contracts). Contracts will be lifted at the start of the interest period, or a delivery date, if earlier. On 17 January, March contracts (37) and June contracts (62) will be sold, calculated by adjusting the 100.82 contracts for the proportion of the futures period being covered (x 34 / 91 and x 57 / 91, respectively) and 'tailing' the hedge to account for interest on the futures profit or loss from the date of lifting to the end of the interest period (see below for calculation). On 19 March, the March contracts (37) will be lifted (bought back), and, to maintain the full hedge, June contracts (37) will immediately be sold (see ❻). The borrower wants to protect against an adverse change in the yield curve on or just before the 15 May interest reference date, which will affect the June futures price. A 'straddle' hedge (selling 37 June contracts and buying 37 September contracts) is also to be traded on 19 March as a basis hedge.

It will be assumed that actual rates on 19 March and 15 May are 0.1% higher than the implied rates (linearly interpolated) on 17 January and 19 March, respectively, and that the yield curve slope does not change (Scenario 1) or it inverts on 15 May (Scenario 2)(see ❼). The straddle hedge will have a zero profit or loss in Scenario 1 (assuming a linear Forward rate curve), but, in Scenario 2, since the decrease in the expected rates for 17 September from 19 March to 15 May will be greater than the decrease in the expected rates for 18 June, a profit will be made, reducing the net financing rate.

The effective rates are: (1) 4.36% without hedging, (2) 4.16% under Scenarios 1 and 2 (using basis hedging – without it, the Scenario 2 rate would be 4.40%), being the expected rate on 17 January. If the curve steepens rather than inverts, Scenario 2 rates would be 4.15% (basis hedging) or 3.92% (no basis hedging).

❶

CASH MARKET PRICES AT VALUE DATE				
Value date	Fri	17 Jan		
LIBOR on 17 Jan	3 month	3.832%	17 Jan to Thurs 17 April	90 days
	6 month	3.950%	17 Jan to Thurs 17 July	181 days
Forward rate on 17 Jan	3 month	4.028% borrowing rate	17 Apr to Thurs 17 July	91 days
Implied futures prices on 17 Jan	96.17	17 Jan - 17 Apr		
	95.97	17 Apr - 17 Jul	Basis = +0.20	

❷

FUTURES TERMS		
Type	3 month Sterling Short Term Interest Rate Future	
Exchange	LIFFE	
Contract size	£500,000	
Min price change	0.01	
Tick size	£12.50	= £500,000 x 0.01 /100 x (90 / 360)
Delivery months	March, June, September, December	
Last trading day	3rd Wed in delivery month	
Delivery day	Next business day after last trading date	
Settlement price	100 minus 3 month LIBOR (BBA rate at 11.00am on last trading day)	

❸

FUTURES PRICES				
First forward period				
Last trading date	Wed	19 Mar	Settled	Thurs 20 Mar
Actual futures price on 17 Jan	**96.00**	**Forward rate = 4.00%**		
Second forward perod				
Last trading date	Wed	18 Jun	Settled	Thurs 19 Jun
Actual futures price on 17 Jan	**95.75**	**Forward rate = 4.25%**		
Third forward perod				
Last trading date	Wed	17 Sep	Settled	Thurs 18 Sep
Actual futures price on 17 Jan	**95.50**	**Forward rate = 4.50%**		

❹

UNDERLYING LOAN AND HEDGING PERIODS					
Next loan rollover date		Thurs	15 May		
Days to start of loan interest period		118 days	Fri 17 Jan - Thurs 15 May		
Loan interest period	3 mths to	Fri	15 Aug	Interest period	92 days
Interpolated rate from forward rates		4.16%	= 4.00% + (4.25% - 4.00%) x (57 / 91)		
Days to start of first forward period		61 days	Fri 17 Jan - Wed 19 Mar		
Days from start of first forward period to loan start		57 days	Wed 19 Mar - Thurs 15 May	}	91 days
Days in first forward period being hedged	34 days in Mar	34 days	Thurs 15 May - Wed 18 June	}	
Days in second forward period being hedged	58 days in June	58 days	Wed 18 June - Fri 15 August		
Total hedged period		92 days			

❺

TIMELINE

Position on 17 Jan

CASH AND FORWARD MARKETS	19 Mar	91 days	18 Jun	91 days	17 Sep
Current 3mth LIBOR	**3.83%** (circled)				
		Mar futures period		Jun futures period	
Rates expected on 17 Jan	**4.00%**	→	**4.25%**	→	**4.50%**
Futures prices on 17 Jan	96.00		95.75		95.50
Basis on 17 Jan	0.17		0.42		0.67

LOAN	19 Mar	15 May	18 Jun	15 Aug	17 Sep
		Loan interest period (15 May → 15 Aug)			
Linearly interpolated expected rates	57 days	**4.16%**	34 days 58 days	**4.41%**	33 days

4.16% = 4.00% + (4.25% - 4.00%) x (57 / 91)

4.41% = 4.25% + (4.50% - 4.25%) x (58 / 91)

Date	17 Jan	19 Mar	15 May	18 Jun	15 Aug	17 Sep
Event	Deal date	First delivery	Loan rollover - hedge lifted	Second delivery	Loan rollover	Third delivery
Days in prior period	0	61 days	57 days	34 days	58 days	33 days

Solid arrow: Forward period
Dashed arrow: Loan interest period
Ellipse: Actual 3mth rates

❻

CALCULATING THE NUMBER OF CONTRACTS

Face value of loan		£50m	
Basic number of contracts		100.00 contracts	= £50.0m / £0.5m
Hedge ratio 1 : maturity difference	x	1.0082	= (92 / 365) / 0.25 years
Contracts x hedge ratio 1	=	100.82 contracts	
Number of Mar contracts			
Contracts		100.82 contracts	
Hedge ratio 2: discounting for margin interest	x	0.9798	= 1 / [(1+4.000% x 57/365)(1+4.157% x 92/365)]
Contracts for first period		98.78 contracts	
Hedge ratio for first forward period		37.36%	34 days / 91days
Fractional contracts		*36.91 contracts*	
Number of June contracts			
Contracts		100.82 contracts	
Hedge ratio 2: discounting for margin interest	x	0.9896	= 1 / (1 + 4.157% x 92 / 365)
Contracts for first period		99.78 contracts	
Hedge ratio for second forward period		62.64%	57 days / 91days
Fractional contracts		*62.50 contracts*	

❼

SCENARIO ANALYSIS

It will be assumed that on 19 March 3 month LIBOR is 4.10% (vs 4.00% expected on 17 January) and the implied Forward Rates for 18 June and 17 September are 4.35% and 4.60%, respectively (increasing a similar 0.10% compared to the Forward Rates on 17 January). This parallel shift in the yield curve will increase the interpolated rate for 15 May by 0.10% to 4.26%:

Position on 19 Mar

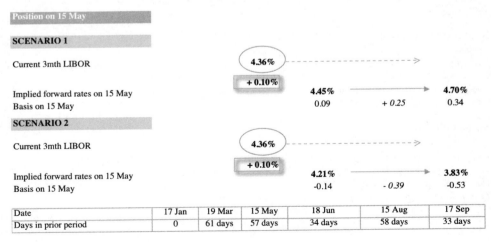

CASH AND FORWARD MARKETS	19 Mar	91 days	18 Jun	91 days	17 Sep
Current 3mth LIBOR	4.10%				
				Jun futures period	
Rates expected on 19 Mar	**4.10%**	→	**4.35%**	→	**4.60%**
Futures prices on 19 Mar	95.90		95.65		95.40
Basis on 19 Mar	0.00	*+ 0.25*	0.25	*+ 0.25*	0.50

LOAN	19 Mar		15 May		18 Jun		15 Aug		17 Sep
				Loan interest period					
Linearly interpolated expected rates		57 days	**4.26%**	34 days		58 days	**4.51%**	33 days	
			+ 0.10%						

4.26% = 4.10% + (4.35% - 4.10%) x (57 / 91)

4.51% = 4.35% + (4.60% - 4.35%) x (58 / 91)

Date	17 Jan	19 Mar	15 May	18 Jun	15 Aug	17 Sep
Event	Deal date	First delivery	Loan rollover - hedge lifted	Second delivery	Loan rollover	Third delivery
Days in prior period	0	61 days	57 days	34 days	58 days	33 days

→ Forward period

- - -> Loan interest period

○ Actual 3mth rates

Two scenarios will be used for the likely position on 15 May, when the hedge is lifted:

Position on 15 May

SCENARIO 1

	15 May	18 Jun		17 Sep
Current 3mth LIBOR	4.36% - - ->			
	+ 0.10%			
Implied forward rates on 15 May		**4.45%**	→	**4.70%**
Basis on 15 May		0.09	*+ 0.25*	0.34

SCENARIO 2

	15 May	18 Jun		17 Sep
Current 3mth LIBOR	4.36% - - ->			
	+ 0.10%			
Implied forward rates on 15 May		**4.21%**	→	**3.83%**
Basis on 15 May		-0.14	*- 0.39*	-0.53

Date	17 Jan	19 Mar	15 May	18 Jun	15 Aug	17 Sep
Days in prior period	0	61 days	57 days	34 days	58 days	33 days

SCENARIO 1

Actual rates on 19 March (March contracts expire) and 15 May (interest period starts) are 0.10% higher than the implied rates on 17 January and 19 March. The slope of the yield curve remains the same (parallel shift)

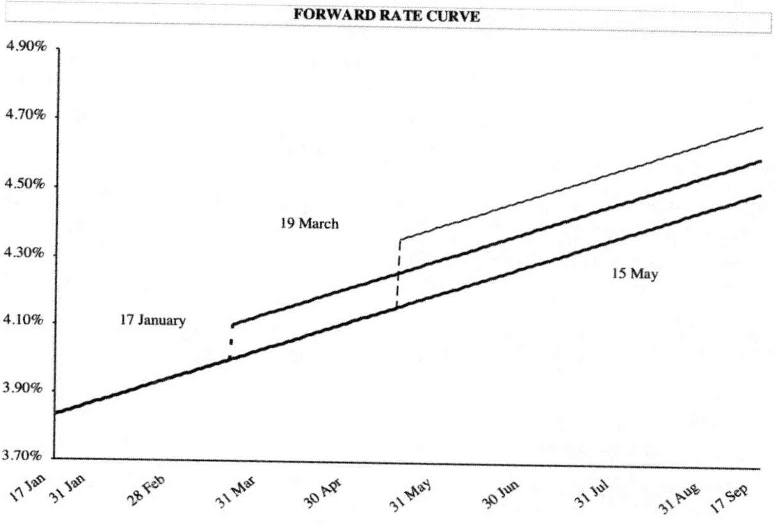

SCENARIO 2

As for Scenario 1 but the yield curve inverts on 15 May

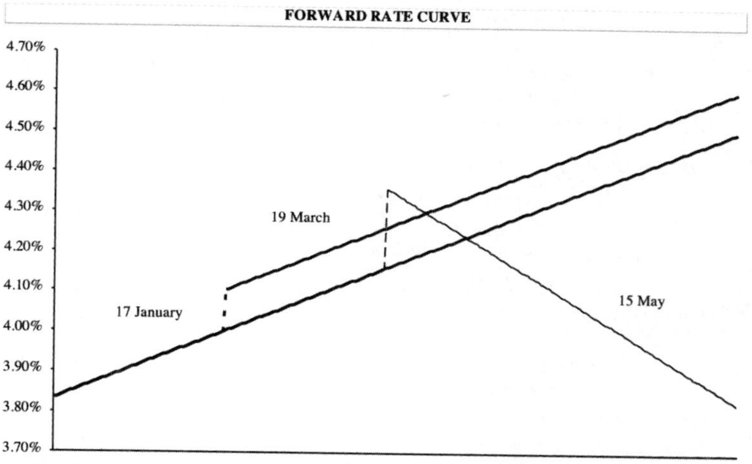

❼ ①

SCENARIO 1

PRICES, RATES AND FUTURES POSITIONS

	Actual 3mth LIBOR	Interest Period	March futures	June futures	Sept futures	Cumulative profit
Delivery dates		15 May	19 March	18 June	17 Sep	
Days in periods			61 days	91 days	91 days	
Relevant date (trade / closed out)	17 Jan		19 March	15 May		
Days in periods			61 days	57 days		
Price on 17 January			96.00	95.75	95.50	
Implied rate	**3.83%**	**4.16%**	**4.00%**	**4.25%**	**4.50%**	
Basis			0.17	0.42	0.67	
Difference with prior futures				0.25	0.25	
Slope of forward rate curve	01 Jan		0.002747%	0.002747%		
Price on 19 March			95.90	95.65	95.40	
Implied rate	**4.10%**	**4.26%**	4.10%	4.35%	4.60%	
Basis			0.00	0.25	0.50	
Difference with prior futures				0.25	0.25	
Basis change				**+ 0.00**	**+ 0.00**	
Compared to expected at 17 Jan			+ 0.10%	+ 0.10%	+ 0.10%	
Slope of forward rate curve			0.002747%	0.002747%		
Rate without basis change		4.26%		4.35%	4.60%	
Mark-to-market profit / (loss)			£4,625	£7,750		£12,375
			settled	*open*		
Prices on 15 May				95.55	95.30	
Implied rate	**4.36%**	**4.36%**		4.45%	4.70%	
Basis				0.09	0.34	
Difference with prior futures					0.25	
Basis change					**+ 0.00**	
Compared to expected at 17 Jan				+ 0.20%	+ 0.20%	
Compared to expected at 19 Mar				+ 0.10%	+ 0.10%	
Slope of forward rate curve				0.002747%		
Rate without basis change				4.45%	4.70%	
Profit / (loss) - non basis trade				£15,500		£20,125
Profit / (loss) - non basis trade				£4,625		£24,750
Profit / (loss) - basis trade				£4,625	(£4,625)	**£24,750**
						before interest

+ £299 interest = £25,049
(see next page)

TRADING					
Traded on 17 January	SELL	37	March contracts	36.91 contracts	(fractional)
	SELL	62	June contracts	62.50 contracts	(fractional)
Traded on 19 March	SELL	37	June contracts		
	SELL	37	June contracts	Straddle'	
	BUY	37	September contracts		

Delivery dates	15 May	19 March	18 June	17 Sep
Position on 19 March				
Traded on 17 January				
Tick change on trade		10 ticks		
Profit / (loss) = 37 contracts x £12.50 tick size x 10 ticks		£4,625		
Interest at 4.10% for 149 days from 19 Mar to 15 Aug		£77		
Total position		**£4,702**		
Position on 15 May				
Traded on 17 January				
Tick change on trade			20 ticks	
Profit / (loss) = 62 contracts x £12.50 tick size x 10 ticks			£15,500	
Interest at 4.36% for 92 days from 15 May to 15 Aug			£170	
Total position			**£15,670**	
Traded on 19 March				
Tick change on trade			10 ticks	
Profit / (loss) = 37 contracts x £12.50 tick size x 20 ticks			£4,625	
Interest at 4.36% for 92 days from 15 May to 15 Aug			£51	
Total position			**£4,676**	
		x 2 for straddle =	**£9,352**	
Tick change on trade				10 ticks
Profit / (loss) = 37 contracts x £12.50 tick size x 10 ticks				(£4,625)
Interest at 4.36% for 92 days from 15 May to 15 Aug				(£51)
Total position				**(£4,676)**

Traded on 17 January	**£20,373**	**£25,049**
Traded on 19 March	**£4,676**	

HEDGING RESULTS				
3mth LIBOR = 4.357% maturing Thurs	15 May 92 days			
Expected financing cost on 17 Jan	£50.0m x 4.157% x 92 / 365	=	Rate = 4.16%	**(£523,845)**
Expected financing cost on 19 Mar	£50.0m x 4.257% x 92 / 365	=	Rate = 4.26%	**(£536,447)**
Actual financing cost on 15 May	£50.0m x 4.357% x 92 / 365	=	Rate = 4.36%	(£549,050)
Profit on lifting of 37 March and 62 June traded on 17 Jan				£20,373
Net cost after 17 Jan trade			Rate = 4.19%	(£528,678)
Result on lifting 37 June traded on 19 Mar				£4,676
Result of 19 Mar basis hedge				£0
Final net cost			Rate = 4.16%	**(£524,002)**
Actual vs expected on 17 Jan expectation	£524,002 - £523,845 =		See ❽ ①	**(£157)**

	Expected 17 Jan	Expected 19 Mar	Actual 15 May	Rate	Futures position
On 17 Jan	(£523,845)	(£523,845)	(£523,845)	4.16%	
Rates increase at all maturities		(£12,603)	(£12,603)	0.10%	£20,125
Rates increase due to yield curve slope change		£0	£0	0.00%	
On 19 Mar		(£536,447)	(£536,447)	4.26%	
Rates increase at all maturities			(£12,603)	0.10%	£4,625
Rates increase due to yield curve slope change			£0		£0
Interest cost on 15 May			**(£549,050)**	**4.36%**	£24,750
Interest on futures margins					£298
Hedging result				-0.20%	**£25,048**
Net financing cost after hedging				**4.16%**	**(£524,002)**

❼②

SCENARIO 2

PRICES, RATES AND FUTURES POSITIONS

	Actual 3mth LIBOR	Interest Period	March futures	June futures	Sept futures	Cumulative profit
Delivery dates		15 May	19 March	18 June	17 Sep	
Days in periods			61 days	91 days	91 days	
Relevant date (trade / closed out)	17 Jan		19 March	15 May		
Days in periods			61 days	57 days		
Price on 17 January			96.00	95.75	95.50	
Implied rate	**3.83%**	**4.16%**	**4.00%**	**4.25%**	**4.50%**	
Basis			0.17	0.42	0.67	
Difference with prior futures				0.25	0.25	
Slope of forward rate curve	01 Jan		0.002747%	0.002747%		
Price on 19 March			95.90	95.65	95.40	
Implied rate	**4.10%**	**4.26%**	4.10%	4.35%	4.60%	
Basis			0.00	0.25	0.50	
Difference with prior futures				0.25	0.25	
Basis change				**+ 0.00**	**+ 0.00**	
Compared to expected at 17 Jan			+ 0.10%	+ 0.10%	+ 0.10%	
Slope of forward rate curve			0.002747%	0.002747%		
Rate without basis change		4.26%		4.35%	4.60%	
Mark-to-market profit / (loss)			£4,625	£7,750		£12,375
			settled	*open*		
Prices on 15 May				95.79	96.18	
Implied rate	**4.36%**	**4.36%**		4.21%	3.83%	
Basis				-0.14	-0.53	
Difference with prior futures					-0.39	
Basis change					**- 0.64**	
Compared to expected at 17 Jan				- 0.04%	- 0.68%	
Compared to expected at 19 Mar				- 0.14%	- 0.78%	
Slope of forward rate curve	*YIELD CURVE CHANGES SLOPE*			-0.004253%		
Rate without basis change				4.21%	4.46%	
Profit / (loss) - non basis trade				(£3,100)		£1,525
Profit / (loss) - non basis trade				(£6,475)		(£4,950)
Profit / (loss) - basis trade				(£6,475)	£36,075	**£24,650**
						before interest

+ £297 interest = £24,947
(see next page)

TRADING					
Traded on 17 January	SELL	37	March contracts	36.91 contracts	(fractional)
	SELL	62	June contracts	62.50 contracts	(fractional)
Traded on 19 March	SELL	37	June contracts		
	SELL	37	June contracts	Straddle'	
	BUY	37	September contracts		

Delivery dates	15 May	19 March	18 June	17 Sep
Position on 19 March				
Traded on 17 January				
Tick change on trade		10 ticks		
Profit / (loss) = 37 contracts x £12.50 tick size x 10 ticks		£4,625		
Interest at 4.10% for 149 days from 19 Mar to 15 Aug		£77		
Total position		**£4,702**		
Position on 15 May				
Traded on 17 January				
Tick change on trade			-4 ticks	
Profit / (loss) = 62 contracts x £12.50 tick size x 10 ticks			(£3,100)	
Interest at 4.36% for 92 days from 15 May to 15 Aug			(£34)	
Total position			**(£3,134)**	
Traded on 19 March				
Tick change on trade			-14 ticks	
Profit / (loss) = 37 contracts x £12.50 tick size x -4 ticks			(£6,475)	
Interest at 4.36% for 92 days from 15 May to 15 Aug			(£71)	
Total position			**(£6,546)**	
	x 2 for straddle =		**(£13,092)**	
Tick change on trade				-78 ticks
Profit / (loss) = 37 contracts x £12.50 tick size x -78 ticks				£36,075
Interest at 4.36% for 92 days from 15 May to 15 Aug				£396
Total position				**£36,471**

Traded on 17 January	**£1,568**	**£24,947**
Traded on 19 March	**£23,379**	

HEDGING RESULTS			
3mth LIBOR = 4.357% maturing	Thurs	15 May	92 days

Expected financing cost on 17 Jan	£50.0m x 4.157% x 92 / 365 =	Rate = 4.16%	**(£523,845)**
Expected financing cost on 19 Mar	£50.0m x 4.257% x 92 / 365 =	Rate = 4.26%	**(£536,447)**
Actual financing cost on 15 May	£50.0m x 4.357% x 92 / 365 =	Rate = 4.36%	(£549,050)
Profit on lifting of 37 March and 62 June traded on 17 Jan			£1,568
Net cost after 17 Jan trade		Rate = 4.34%	(£547,482)
Result on lifting 37 June traded on 19 Mar			(£6,546)
Result of 19 Mar basis hedge			£29,925
Final net cost		Rate = 4.16%	**(£524,103)**

Actual vs expected on 17 Jan expectation £524,103 - £523,845 = See ❽ ② **(£258)**

	Expected 17 Jan	Expected 19 Mar	Actual 15 May	Rate	Futures position
On 17 Jan	(£523,845)	(£523,845)	(£523,845)	4.16%	
Rates increase at all maturities		(£12,603)	(£12,603)	0.10%	£1,525
Rates increase due to yield curve slope change		£0	£0	0.00%	
On 19 Mar		(£536,447)	(£536,447)	4.26%	
Rates increase at all maturities			(£12,603)	0.10%	(£6,475)
Rates increase due to yield curve slope change			£0		£29,600
Interest cost on 15 May			**(£549,050)**	**4.36%**	£24,650
Interest on futures margins					£297
Hedging result				-0.20%	**£24,947**
Net financing cost after hedging				**4.16%**	**(£524,103)**

❽ ① SCENARIO 1

RECONCILIATION OF ACTUAL VS EXPECTED

	Expected	*Actual*
Traded on 17 January		
March lifted on 19 Mar: 36.91 contracts x £12.50 tick value x 10 ticks =	£4,613	£4,625
Interest = x (1 / 0.9798 hedge ratio - 1)	£95	£77
Total	*£4,709*	*£4,702*
June lifted on 15 May: 62.50 contracts x £12.50 tick value x 10 ticks as at 19 Mar	£7,812	£7,750
Interest = x (1 / 0.9896 hedge ratio - 1)	£82	£85
Total	*£7,894*	*£7,835*
	£12,603	*£12,538*
Difference		(£65)
Change in June lifted on 15 May since 19 Mar (= 10tick profit plus interest)		£7,835
Traded on 19 March		
June lifted on 15 May: 36.91 contracts x £12.50 tick value x 100,000 ticks = £4,625		
Interest = x (1 / 0.9896 hedge ratio - 1) = £51		
Total		*£4,676*
Impact on Position on 15 May		
15 May parallel yield curve shift = £50.0m x (4.36% - 4.26%) x (92 / 365)		(£12,603)
19 Mar non-parallel yield curve shift = £50.0m x (4.26% - 4.26%) x (92 / 365)		£0
Basis hedge on 19 Mar		£0
Variance with 17 Jan expectation	**£524,002 - £523,845 =**	**(£157)**

❽ ② SCENARIO 2

RECONCILIATION OF ACTUAL VS EXPECTED

	Expected	*Actual*
Traded on 17 January		
March lifted on 19 Mar: 36.91 contracts x £12.50 tick value x 10 ticks =	£4,613	£4,625
Interest = x (1 / 0.9798 hedge ratio - 1)	£95	£77
Total	*£4,709*	*£4,702*
June lifted on 15 May: 62.50 contracts x £12.50 tick value x 10 ticks as at 19 Mar	£7,812	£7,750
Interest = x (1 / 0.9896 hedge ratio - 1)	£82	£85
Total	*£7,894*	*£7,835*
	£12,603	*£12,538*
Difference		(£65)
Change in June lifted on 15 May since 19 Mar (= 14 tick loss plus interest)		(£10,969)
Traded on 19 March		
June lifted on 15 May: 36.91 contracts x £12.50 tick value x -140,000 ticks = £-6,475		
Interest = x (1 / 0.9896 hedge ratio - 1) = £-71		
Total		*(£6,546)*
Impact on Position on 15 May		
15 May parallel yield curve shift = £50.0m x (4.36% - 4.26%) x (92 / 365)		(£12,603)
19 Mar non-parallel yield curve shift = £50.0m x (4.26% - 4.26%) x (92 / 365)		£0
Basis hedge on 19 Mar		£29,925
Variance with 17 Jan expectation	**£524,103 - £523,845 =**	**(£258)**

BIBLIOGRAPHY

Books

Amembal, S. P. (1992), *Equipment Leasing: A Complete Handbook.* McGraw-Hill.
Amram, M., and N. Kulatilaka (1999), *Real Options: Managing Strategic Investment in an Uncertain World.* Boston: Harvard Business School Press.
Antczak, G., and K. Walton (2004), *Tolley's Corporation Tax 2004-05.* Tolley LexisNexis™.
Arzac, E.R. (2005), *Valuation: for Mergers, Buyouts, and Restructuring.* John Wiley & Sons, Inc.
Benninga, S. (2000), *Financial Modeling.* The MIT Press.
Brealey, R.A., and S.C. Myers (2003), *Principles of Corporate Finance* (7th edition.). McGraw-Hill Irwin.
Bruner, R.F. (2004), *Applied Mergers & Acquisitions.* John Wiley & Sons, Inc.
Buetow Jr., G.W., and F. J. Fabozzi (2001), *Valuation of Interest Swaps and Swaptions.* Pennsylvania: Frank J. Fabozzi Associates.
Buckley, A. (1995), International Capital Budgeting. Prentice Hall.
Calamos, J. (1998), *Convertible Securities.* McGraw-Hill.
Choudhry, M. (2001), *The Bond & Money Markets: Strategy, Trading, Analysis.* Butterworth-Heinemann.
Chriss, N.A. (1997), *Black-Scholes and Beyond: Option Pricing Models.* McGraw-Hill.
Clewlow, L., and C. Strickland (1998), *Implementing Derivative Models.* New York: John Wiley & Sons, Inc.
Collins, A.S., and J.T. Murphy (1997), *Negotiating International Business Acquisitions Agreements.* London: Sweet & Maxwell.
Connolly, K.B. (1998), *Pricing Convertible Bonds.* Chichester, W.Sussex: John Wiley & Sons Ltd.
Copeland, T., and V. Antikarov (2001), *Real Options: A Practitioner's Guide.* New York: Texere.
Copeland, T., and J.F. Weston (1992), *Financial Theory and Corporate Policy* (3rd edition). Reading, MA: Addison-Wesley.
Copeland, T., T. Koller, and J.Murrin (2000), *Valuation: Measuring and Managing the Value of Companies* (3rd edition). New York: John Wiley & Sons, Inc.
Cox, J. C., and M. Rubinstein (1985), *Option Markets.* New Jersey: Prentice Hall.
Cuthbertson, K., and D. Nitzsche (2001), *Financial Engineering: Derivatives and Risk Management.* Chichester, W.Sussex: John Wiley & Sons Ltd.
Damodaran, A. (2001), *Corporate Finance: Theory and Practice* (2nd edition.). John Wiley & Sons, Inc.
Damodaran, A. (2002), *Investment Valuation: Tools and Techniques for Determining the Value of Any Asset* (2nd edition.). John Wiley & Sons, Inc.
Das, S. (1994), *Swap & Derivative Financing: The Global Reference to Products, Pricing, Applications and Markets.* Chicago: Irwin

Das, S. (ed) (1997), *Risk Management and Financial Derivatives - A Guide to the Mathematics*. McGraw-Hill.

Dimson, E., P. Marsh, and M. Staunton (2002), *Triumph of the Optimists: 101 Years of Global Investment Returns*. Princeton, NJ: Princeton University Press.

Dubofsky, D.A., and T.W. Miller Jnr. (2003), *Derivatives: Valuation and Risk Management*. New York: Oxford University Press, Inc.

Fabozzi, F. (2000), *The Handbook of Fixed Income Securities* (6th Edition). McGraw-Hill.

Fabozzi, F.J., and S.V. Mann (2001), *Introduction to Fixed Income Analytics*. Pennsylvania: Frank J. Fabozzi Associates.

Fernàndez, P. (2002), *Valuation Methods and Shareholder Value Creation*. San Diego/London: Academic Press.

Fitzgerald, M.D. (1993), *Financial Futures* (2nd Edition). London: Euromoney Publications plc.

Flavell, R. (2002), *Swaps and Other Derivatives*. Chichester, W.Sussex: John Wiley & Sons Ltd.

Geddes, R. (2002), *IPOs & Equity Offerings*. Butterworth-Heinemann.

Haug, E. H. (1998), *The Complete Guide To Option Pricing Formulas*. McGraw-Hill.

Herbst, A.F. (2002), *Capital Asset Investment*. Chichester, W.Sussex: John Wiley & Sons, Ltd.

Hull, J.C. (2003), *Options, Futures, and Other Derivatives* (5th Edition). NewJersey: Prentice Hall.

Jackson, M., and M. Staunton (2001), *Advanced Modelling in Finance using Excel and VBA*. Chichester, W.Sussex: John Wiley & Sons Ltd.

James, P. (2003), *Option Theory*. Chichester, W.Sussex: John Wiley & Sons, Ltd.

Jarrow, R., and A. Rudd (1983), *Option Pricing*. Homewood, Il: Richard Irwin, Inc.

Kolb, R.W. (2003), *Futures, Options and Swaps*. Oxford: Blackwell.

Madden, B.L. (1998), *CFROI Cash Flow Return on Investment Valuation: A Total System Approach to Valuing a Firm*. New York: Butterworth-Heinemann.

Martin, J. (2001), *Applied Math for Derivatives: A Non-Quant Guide to the Valuation and Modeling of Financial Derivatives*. Singapore: John Wiley & Sons (Asia) Lte Ltd.

McDonald, R.L (2003), *Derivatives Markets*. Boston: Addison Wesley.

Mun, J. (2002), *Real Options Analysis: Tools and Techniques for Valuing Strategic Investments and Decisions*. New Jersey: John Wiley & Sons, Inc.

Nevitt, P.K., and F. Fabozzi (1995), *Project Financing (6th Edition)*. Euromoney Institutional Investors plc.

Ogier, T., J. Rugman, and L. Spicer (2004), *The Real Cost of Capital: a business field guide to better financial decisions*. FT Prentice Hall.

Penza, P., and V.K. Bansal (2001), *Measuring Market Risk with Value At Risk*. New York: John Wiley & Sons, Inc.

Pereiro, L.E. (2002), *Valuation of Companies in Emerging Markets*. John Wiley & Sons, Inc.

Philips, G.A. (1997), *Convertible Bond Markets*. London: Macmillan Press.

Pratt, S. P. (2001), *Business Valuation Discounts and Premiums.* New York: John Wiley & Sons, Inc.

Pricewaterhouse Coopers Leasing Team (2002), *Leasing in the UK* (4th Edition). Tolley LexisNexis™.

Rappaport, A. (1998), *Creating Shareholder Value.* New York: Free Press.

Rendleman Jr., R. J. (2002), *Applied Derivatives: Options, Futures, and Swaps.* Oxford: Blackwell Publishers Ltd.

Rubinstein, M. (1999), *Rubinstein on Derivatives: Futures, Options and Dynamic Strategies.* London: Risk Publications.

Saunders, A. and L. Allen (2002), *Credit Risk Measurement.* New York: John Wiley & Sons, Inc.

Sirower, M. (1997), *The Synergy Trap: How Companies Lose the Acquisition Game.* New York: Free Press.

Stafford Johnson, R. (2004), *Bond Evaluation, Selection, and Management.* Oxford: Blackwell Publishing Ltd.

Steiner, Bob (2002), *Foreign Exchange and Money Markets.* Butterworth-Heinemann.

Stern, J.M., and D.H.Chew, Jr. (eds.)(2003), *The Revolution in Corporate Finance* (4th Edition). Oxford: Blackwell Publishers Ltd.

Stewart, G.B. (1991), *The Quest for Value.* New York: Harper (1991)

Stulz, R.M. (2003a), *Risk Management & Derivatives.* Thompson - South-Western.

Tuckman, B. (2002), *Fixed Income Securities: Tools for Today's Markets.* New Jersey: John Wiley & Sons, Inc.

Walton, K., and A. Flint (2004), *Tolley's Capital Gains Tax 2004-05.* Tolley LexisNexis™.

Ward, K. (1993), *Corporate Financial Strategy.* Butterworth-Heinemann

Watsham, T.J., and K. Parramore (1997), *Quantitative Methods in Finance.* London: Thompson.

Wilmott, P. (2000), *Paul Wilmott on Quantitative Finance (2 vols).* Chichester, W.Sussex: John Wiley & Sons, Ltd.

Wilmott, P., S. Howison, and J.Dewynne (1995), *The Mathematics of Financial Derivatives: A Student Introduction.* Cambridge University Press.

Wilson, A., M. Davies, M. Curtis, and G. Wilkinson-Riddle (2001). *UK & International GAAP (7th Edition).* London: Butterworths Tolley.

Woodson, H, (2002), *Global Convertible Investing.* New York: John Wiley & Sons, Inc.

Papers

Black, F. (1976), "The Pricing of Commodity Contracts", *Journal of Financial Economics*, 3, 1976, 167-79.

Black, F., and M. Scholes (1973), "The Pricing of Options and Corporate Liabilities," *Journal of Political Economy*, 81(3), 1973, 637-659.

Cox, J., and S. Ross (1976), "The Valuation of Options for Alternative Stochastic Processes", *Journal of Financial Economics*, 3(1), 1976, 145-166.

Cox, J., S. Ross, and M.Rubinstein (1979), "Option Pricing: A Simplified Approach", *Journal of Financial Economics*, 7(3), 1979, 229-264.

Fama, E.F., and K.R. French (1992), "The Cross-Section of Expected Stock Returns", *Journal of Finance*, 47, 1992, 427-465.

Fama, E.F., and K.R. French (1997), "Industry Costs of Equity", *Journal of Financial Economics*, 43, 1997, 153-193.

Galai, D., and M. Schneller (1978), "Pricing Warrants and the Value of the Firm", *Journal of Finance*, 33, 1978, 1339-42.

Goldman Sachs (1993), "Valuing convertible bonds as derivatives", Quantitative Strategies Research Notes

Garman, M., and S. Kohlhagen (1983), "Foreign Currency Option Values", *Journal of International Money and Finance*, 2(3), 1983, 231-7.

Grullon, G., and D.L.Ikenberry (2003), "What Do We Know About Stock Repurchases?" in Stern and Chew (eds.)(2003).

Hamada, R.S. (1972), "The Effect of the Firm's Capital Structure on the Systematic Risk of Common Stock", *Journal of Finance*, 27, 1972, 435-452.

Harris, R.S., and J.J. Pringle (1985), "Risk-Adjusted Discount Rates: Extensions from the Average-Risk Case", Journal of Financial Research, 8, 1985, 237-244.

Jensen, M.C. (1986), "Agency Costs of Free Cash Flow, Corporate Finance, and Takeovers", *American Economic Review,* 76(2), 1986, 323-329.

Merton, R.C. (1973), "The Theory of Rational Option Pricing", *Bell Journal of Economics and Management Science*, 4(1), 1973, 141-183.

Miles, J., and R. Ezzell (1980), "The Weighted Average Cost of Capital, Perfect Capital Markets, and Project Life: A Clarification", *Journal of Financial and Quantitative Analysis,* 15, 1980, 719-730.

Modigliani, F., and M.H. Miller (1958), "The Cost of Capital, Corporate Finance, and the Theory of Investment", *American Economic Review*, 48, 1958, 261-297.

Modigliani, F., and M.H. Miller (1963), "Corporate Income Taxes and the Cost of Capital: A Correction", *American Economic Review*, 53, 1963, 433-443.

Myers, S.C. (1974), "Interactions of Corporate Financing and Investment Decisions - Implications for Capital Budgeting", *Journal of Finance*, 29, 1974, 1-25.

Myers, S.C. (1977), "Determinants of Corporate Borrowing", *Journal of Financial Economics,* 5, 1977, 147-175.

Myers, S.C. (2003), "Still Searching for Optimal Capital Structure" in Stern and Chew (eds.)(2003).

Ross, S. A. (1976), "The Arbitrage Theory of Capital Asset Pricing", *Journal of Economic Theory*, 13 (3), 1976, 341-360.

Ross, S. A. (1977), "The Determination of Financial Structure: The Incentive Signaling Approach", *Bell Journal of Economics*, 8, 1977, 23-40.

Stulz, R.M. (2003b), "Rethinking Risk Management" in Stern and Chew (eds.)(2003).

Tsiveriotis, K., and C. Fernandes (1998), "Valuing Convertible Bonds with Credit Risk", *Journal of Fixed Income*, 8(2), 1998, 95-102.

INDEX